Contents

The Pocket Oxford Classical Greek Dictionary

Edited by
James Morwood
John Taylor

OXFORD
UNIVERSITY PRESS

OXFORD
UNIVERSITY PRESS

Great Clarendon Street, Oxford OX2 6DP

Oxford University Press is a department of the University of Oxford. It furthers the University's objective of excellence in research, scholarship, and education by publishing worldwide in

Oxford New York

Auckland Cape Town Dar es Salaam Hong Kong Karachi Kuala Lumpur Madrid Melbourne Mexico City Nairobi New Delhi Shanghai Taipei Toronto

With offices in

Argentina Austria Brazil Chile Czech Republic France Greece Guatemala Hungary Italy Japan South Korea Poland Portugal Singapore Switzerland Thailand Turkey Ukraine Vietnam

Oxford is a registered trade mark of Oxford University Press in the UK and in certain other countries

Published in the United States by Oxford University Press Inc., New York

First published 2002

British Library Cataloguing in Publication Data

Data available

Library of Congress Cataloging in Publication Data

Data available

ISBN-13: 978-0-19-860512-6

19

Typeset in Monotype Arial, Nimrod, Greek 486 Polytonic and Times Greek SF by Alliance Phototypesetters, Pondicherry, India

Printed in Great Britain by Clays Lt[illegible]

Preface

It may be that the most incredible fact about the study of classical Greek in English-speaking countries is not that it survives, remarkable though that phenomenon is, but rather that there has not in recent memory existed a two-way Greek–English English–Greek dictionary. Can that be said of any other important language? With the publication of this dictionary, however, this is a fact no longer.

The Greek–English section of the dictionary is based on Karl Feyerabend's *Pocket Greek Dictionary* (*Classical Greek–English*), now more than 90 years old. We have tried to see this slim volume into the modern world, not only by eliminating archaic English and tempering, though, we hope, not obliterating the Germanic influence, but also by giving more information about a considerable number of words. We hope that what we have done will be largely self-explanatory.

The sections on Pronunciation, Numerals, and the 'Top 101 irregular verbs' have been reproduced from the *Oxford Grammar of Classical Greek* (Oxford, 2001). Irregular verbs from the last have been marked with a dagger in the text. If other verbs have irregular futures and aorists, these are given without comment. If the future but not the aorist is irregular, the future alone is given without a gloss. If the future is regular or non-existent, the aorist is given with a gloss. All compound verbs are given with a hyphen between the prefix and the verb, e.g. προ-βουλεύω. If the reader feels that the verb may be irregular, he or she should look up the uncompounded form.

The dictionary centres on Attic Greek (though the spelling σσ, not ττ, is used). However, its Feyerabend heritage should ensure that it is also a useful aid for Homeric and New Testament Greek.

The English–Greek section, which contains some 5,000 words, is aimed at the likely demands of today's classicist. For anyone writing Greek sentences or proses for public examinations in schools, or for university work, it should prove invaluable.

As in the companion Grammar, long α, ι, and υ are marked with a macron in headwords except where they carry the circumflex accent or iota subscript, while short vowels are never marked; for the details, see the section on pronunciation (pp. ix–xi). We have, however, not marked vowel length at all in the English–Greek section, since it can be checked by looking up the words found there in the Greek–English section. On the other hand, the list of proper names does include macra because these names are not in the Greek–English section. English names throughout are given in their Latinized spelling since this is how they normally appear in that language.

Acknowledgements

Though the creation of this book had for some time been a much-cherished ambition of its compilers, it was at a meeting of the Greek Committee of the Joint Association of Classical Teachers in spring 2001 that it all at once seemed feasible. That fact, and the fact that it now appears as soon as autumn 2002, are not only indicative of what we see as the paramount importance, in the parlous state of Greek studies today, of the speedy appearance of the dictionary. They also betoken a considerable debt to a number of individuals and institutions.

Gratitude is due first of all to the Oxford University Press for understanding the urgent need for a new dictionary of classical Greek, and especially the need for the English–Greek vocabulary. We hope that it will not appear supererogatory in an Oxford book to make the point, but the fact is that the Press of that university has shown an impressive sense of its commitment to classical scholarship in its endeavour to keep the subject alive in English-speaking countries. Everyone in our profession has good cause to be grateful to Vivian Marr (dictionaries and grammars), to Dick Capel Davies (school publications) and to Hilary O'Shea (academic publications). In the spring of 2001, showing a characteristically supportive spirit, Pat Easterling suggested that the Hellenic Society might be willing to back this project. Through the admirable brokering of Russell Shone and Brian Sparkes, this has indeed proved to be the case, and we are delighted to express our considerable gratitude for the funds awarded by the society's schools sub-committee and made available through the generosity of the Leventis Foundation. These have enabled us to commission the secretarial help without which the dictionary could not possibly have been produced in the time. Richard Ashdowne has not only keyed in the entire book but contributed much valuable editorial and typographical advice. We owe him a great deal. Nikoletta Kanavou, Myrto Hatzimichali, Luke Pitcher, and Andrew Hodgson have shown themselves admirably conscientious proof-readers as well as improving the dictionary by their helpful suggestions.

We are deeply indebted to colleagues from Leicester University – Graham Shipley, Eva Parisinou, and Colin Adams – who have strengthened the dictionary very considerably by suggesting the inclusion of words and translations which will make it more useful for ancient historians, as well as for students of classical civilization and Egyptology. John Penney has shown characteristic generosity in clarifying a number of philological points for the compilers. Della Thompson of the Oxford University Press has proved a most supportive editor.

In acknowledging the generous help we have received from others, we, of course, accept complete responsibility for any errors or misjudgements that appear in the following pages.

James Morwood
Grocyn Lecturer, Classics Faculty,
Wadham College,
Oxford

John Taylor
Head of Classics,
Tonbridge School

Proprietary terms

The Greek alphabet and its pronunciation

Greek letter	written as: small	capital	English equivalent	Recommended pronunciation[1] (standard southern British English)
alpha	α	Α	a	short: as in awake, Italian amare long: as in father, Italian amare
beta	β	Β	b	as English b
gamma	γ	Γ	g	as in go before κ, χ, ξ, γ: as in ink, lynx, finger
delta	δ	Δ	d	as French d (with tongue on teeth, not gums)
epsilon	ε	Ε	e	short, as in pet
zeta	ζ	Ζ	sd	as in wisdom
eta	η	Η	ē	long, as in air
theta	θ	Θ	th	as in top (emphatically pronounced); later, as in thin
iota	ι	Ι	i	short: as in lit, French vitesse long: as in bead
[short iota is often written under η, ω or long ᾱ, i.e. ῃ, ῳ, ᾳ (iota subscript) – see under Diphthongs, below]				
kappa	κ	Κ	c	hard c: as in skill; contrast khi
lambda	λ	Λ	l	as in leap
mu	μ	Μ	m	as in met
nu	ν	Ν	n	as in net
xi	ξ	Ξ	x	as in box
omicron	ο	Ο	o	short, as in pot, German Gott
pi	π	Π	p	as in spot; contrast phi
rho	ρ	Ρ	r	Scottish rolled r

[1] Where two recommendations are given for pronunciation, the first is a less accurate approximation than the second.

Greek letter	written as small	capital	English equivalent	Recommended pronunciation (standard southern British English)
sigma	σ, ς	Σ	s	as in sing, lesson

[ς is used at the end of a word, σ elswhere, e.g. ὅστις. Many Greek texts print a so-called lunate sigma, ϲ, capital Ϲ (in the shape of the crescent moon), which is used in all positions, e.g. ὅϲτιϲ.]

Greek letter	small	capital	English equivalent	Recommended pronunciation
tau	τ	Τ	t	as English t in stop (with tongue on teeth not gums); contrast theta
upsilon	υ	Υ	u, y	short: as in French lune, German Müller long: as in French ruse, German Mühle
phi	φ	Φ	ph	as in pot (emphatically pronounced); later, as in foot
khi	χ	Χ	ch	as in kill (emphatically pronounced); later, as in Scottish loch
psi	ψ	Ψ	ps	as in lapse
omega	ω	Ω	ō	as in saw

In this dictionary, where α, ι or υ are long, they are marked by a macron (i.e. ᾱ, ῑ, ῡ), unless they are already shown to be long either by an iota subscript beneath them (i.e. ᾳ) or by a circumflex above them (except that, when ι or υ forms part of a diphthong, a circumflex does not indicate that the ι or υ is long but that the diphthong as a whole is long). See also p. v.

Diphthongs

ᾳ (ᾱ with iota subscript)	as long ᾱ (more correctly with ι sounded at the end)
αι	as in high
αυ	as in how
ει	as in fiancée, German Beet
ευ	as in Cockney belt
ῃ (η with iota subscript)	as η (more correctly with ι sounded at the end)
ηυ	as ευ, but with the first part longer
οι	as in boy, coin
ου	as in pool, French rouge

Greek letter	written as small	capital	English equivalent	Recommended pronunciation (standard southern British English)
υι				close to French huit
ῳ (ω with iota subscript)				as ω (more correctly with ι sounded at the end)

Breathings and accents are written over the second letter of a diphthong, e.g. οἶδα (I know). Where one of the above combinations is pronounced as two separate vowels, breathings are written over the first letter, e.g. ἄϊδρις (ignorant), while the accent is written over the vowel to which it belongs. Note also the diaeresis (¨).

In many modern texts the iota subscript will not be found. The iota will be placed at the same level as the other letters (e.g. ωι, not ῳ). This was in fact the practice in classical times. The iota subscript was a later invention.

Double consonants

When double consonants are used, the sound is correspondingly lengthened, e.g.

νν unnamed (compare unaimed)
ππ hip-pocket
σσ disservice
ττ rat-trap

The exception is γγ which is pronounced as in linger, i.e. as if νγ. Similarly, γκ γχ are pronounced with an ‘n’ as in encore and anchor. Note also that in many words Attic has ττ where other dialects (including Ionic) have σσ: thus θάλαττα (the sea) is Attic, cf. θάλασσα.

Breathings

Words which begin with a vowel have a breathing mark over the first (in the case of a diphthong, over the second) letter. This will either be:

῾ the ‘rough’ breathing, denoting the sound ‘h’; or
᾿ the ‘smooth’ breathing, denoting the absence of the sound ‘h’

Note that all words beginning with ρ and υ take a rough breathing, e.g. ῥόδον (rose) and ὕδωρ (water), hence, e.g., ‘rheumatism’ and ‘hydraulics’. Some examples:

ἡ, αὕτη, αὐτή, ὁ ῥήτωρ (speaker)

Note the position of the breathing with capital letters: Ἡρόδοτος, Αἴσχυλος.

Abbreviations

acc	accusative
act	active
adj	adjective
adv	adverb
aor	aorist
comp	comparative
conj	conjunction
dat	dative
def	definite
Dor	Doric
fem	feminine
foll	following
fut	future
gen	genitive
Hebr	Hebrew
impers	impersonal
impf	imperfect
impv	imperative
infin	infinitive
int	interjection
intr	intransitive
mid	middle
nom	nominative
opt	optative
pass	passive
pf	perfect
pl	plural
plpf	pluperfect
pple	participle
prep	preposition
pres	present
pron	pronoun
refl	reflexive
sg	singular
subj	subjunctive
sup	superlative
tr	transitive
usu	usually
voc	vocative

* indicates a word that is *postpositive*, i.e. cannot appear as the first word of a clause.
† indicates a verb which appears in the table of irregular verbs on pp. 435–447.

Αα

α, Α (ἄλφα) first letter of the alphabet
■ **α′** *as a numeral* = 1

ἅ *Dor* ▸ ἡ

ἅ *Dor* ▸ ἥ

ἆ, ἀᾶ *int* ah, alas

ἀάατος ον invulnerable, unviolated; infallible

ἀᾱγής ές unbroken, not to be broken; strong

ἄαπτος ον untouched; unapproachable

ἀάσχετος ον ▸ **ἄσχετος**

ἀάω, ἀάζω *aor* ἄασα *or* ᾆσα hurt, derange

ἀβακέω say nothing

ἀβαρής ές without weight, not offensive

ἀβασάνιστος ον unexamined, untested

ἀβασίλευτος ον independent

ἄβατος ον impassible; inaccessible; consecrated

ἀβέβαιος ον unsure, unsteady, precarious

ἀβελτερίᾱ ᾱς ἡ silliness; stupidity

ἀβέλτερος (ᾱ) ον silly, stupid

ἀβίωτος ον not worth living, intolerable

ἀβλαβής ές harmless; unhurt

ἀβλής (*gen* ῆτος) not yet shot, unused

ἄβλητος ον unwounded

ἀβληχρός ᾱ όν weak, delicate; slow

ἀβουλέω be unwilling

ἀβούλητος ον involuntary; undesired

ἀβουλίᾱ ᾱς ἡ thoughtlessness; irresolution, indecision

ἄβουλος ον inconsiderate, ill-advised; careless

ἁβροδίαιτος ον living delicately

ἄβρομος ον roaring, noisy

ἁβρός ᾱ όν luxurious; delicate, weak; elegant

ἁβροσύνη ης ἡ **ἁβρότης** ητος ἡ luxury, elegance

ἀβροτάζω miss, fail

ἄβροτος (η) ον immortal; divine; holy

ἁβρῡ́νω treat delicately; spoil; adorn; *mid* pride oneself on + *dat*

ἄβυσσος ον unfathomable; abyss, bottomless pit

ἀγάζομαι ▸ **ἄγαμαι**

ἀγαθοεργίᾱ ᾱς ἡ deserving deed

ἀγαθοεργός οῦ ὁ benefactor

ἀγαθός ή όν good, proper; apt; useful; brave, strong; noble, well-born; wise; honest, righteous; patriotic
■ **τὸ ἀγαθόν** the good, good fortune; welfare; benefit, interest

ἀγαθωσύνη ης ἡ goodness, kindness

ἀγαίομαι ▸ **ἄγαμαι**

ἀγακλεής ές **ἀγακλειτός** ή όν **ἀγακλυτός** ή όν highly renowned, glorious, illustrious

ἀγαλλιάω *and mid* rejoice, shout

ἀγάλλω ἀγαλῶ ἤγηλα adorn, glorify; *pass* take delight in

ἄγαλμα ατος τό ornament; splendid work; statue

ἀγαλματοποιός οῦ ὁ sculptor

ἄγαμαι ἀγάσσομαι ἠγασάμην wonder, stare; admire, praise; be jealous; be indignant *or* angry

ἀγαμένως *adv* approvingly

ἄγαμος ον unmarried; ill-fated

ἄγᾱν *adv* much; too much

a

ἀγανακτέω be annoyed *or* discontented (with someone *or* something *dat*)

ἀγανακτητός ή όν irritating

ἀγάννιφος ον covered with snow

ἀγανοφροσύνη ης ἡ gentleness, meekness

ἀγανόφρων ον tender-hearted, meek

ἀγάομαι ▸ **ἄγαμαι**

ἀγαπάζω *and mid,* **ἀγαπάω** welcome; treat kindly; love, esteem; be contented, acquiesce

ἀγάπη ης ἡ love, charity

ἀγαπήνωρ (*gen* ορος) manly

ἀγαπητός ή όν beloved; amiable; welcome; sufficient
■ **ἀγαπητῶς** sufficiently; scarcely

ἀγάρροος ον (*also* ἀγάρρους ουν) gushing vigorously

ἀγάστονος ον much-groaning, rushing vehemently

ἀγαστός ή όν admirable

ἀγαυός ή όν illustrious; high, noble

ἀγαυρός ᾱ́ όν admirable, proud

ἀγγαρεύω send as a courier

ἀγγαρήιον ου τό Persian mail service

ἄγγαρος ου ὁ **ἀγγαρήιος** ου ὁ courier, riding postman

ἀγγεῖον ου τό container, receptacle, urn

ἀγγελίᾱ ᾱς ἡ message, news; order

ἀγγελιηφόρος ου ὁ message-bearer; Persian chamberlain

ἀγγέλλω† announce, report; tell, order

ἄγγελμα ατος τό ▸ **ἀγγελία**

ἄγγελος ου ὁ/ἡ messenger; envoy; angel

ἀγγήιον ου τό **ἄγγος** εος τό ▸ **ἀγγεῖον**

ἄγε, ἄγετε come on!

ἀγείρω *aor* ἤγειρα gather, collect; collect by begging

ἀγελαῖος α ον gregarious, forming a flock

ἀγελείη ης ἡ the forager (of Athena)

ἀγέλη ης ἡ herd, flock; troop, band

ἀγεληδόν *adv* in herds

ἀγενεᾱλόγητος ον of unrecorded descent

ἀγένειος ον beardless, boyish

ἀγεν(ν)ής ές unborn; not noble, common; unmanly

ἀγέν(ν)ητος ον unborn, uncreated; ignoble

ἀγέραστος ον without a gift of honour, disregarded

ἄγερσις εως ἡ collection, gathering

ἀγέρωχος ον valiant, gallant; impetuous

ἄγευστος ον untasted, tasteless

ἄγη ης ἡ astonishment, awe; envy

ἀγηλατέω banish

ἀγηνορίη ης ἡ manliness; haughtiness

ἀγήνωρ (*gen* ορος) manly, magnanimous; haughty

ἀγήραος ον **ἀγήρᾱτος** ον **ἀγήρως** ων not ageing, imperishable

ἀγητός ή όν ▸ **ἀγαστός**

ἁγιάζω, ἁγίζω consecrate

ἁγιασμός οῦ ὁ sanctification

ἀγῑνέω lead; carry, convey

ἅγιος ᾱ ον holy, sacred, venerable

ἁγιότης ητος ἡ **ἁγιωσύνη** ης ἡ holiness, sanctity

ἀγκάζομαι *mid* lift up in the arms

ἀγκαλέω ▸ **ἀνακαλέω**

ἀγκάλη ης ἡ **ἀγκαλίς** ίδος ἡ **ἀγκοίνη** ης ἡ bent arm

ἀγκάς *adv* in the arms

ἄγκιστρον ου τό fishing hook

ἀγκλῑ́νω ▸ **ἀνακλῑ́νω**

ἄγκος εος τό ravine, valley

ἀγκρεμάννῡμι ▸ **ἀνακρεμάννῡμι**

ἀγκύλη ης ἡ bend, loop, noose; thong

ἀγκυλομήτης ου ὁ/ἡ cunning, deceitful, artful

ἀγκύλος η ον crooked, curved

ἀγκυλότοξος ον with curved bow

ἀγκυλοχείλης (*gen* ου) with crooked beak

ἄγκῡρα ᾱς ἡ anchor; support

ἀγκών ῶνος ὁ curve, bend; elbow; projection

ἀγλαΐᾱ ᾱς ἡ splendour, pomp, magnificence; delight; pride

ἀγλαΐζω ἀγλαϊῶ ἠγλάϊσα make splendid, glorify

ἀγλάϊσμα ατος τό ornament

ἀγλαόκαρπος ον bearing splendid fruit

ἀγλαός ή όν splendid, shining; magnificent

ἀγλαώψ (*gen* ῶπος) bright, beaming; bright-eyed

ἄγλωσσος ον barbarous, foreign

ἄγναφος ον not carded

ἁγνείᾱ ᾱς ἡ purity, chastity

ἁγνεύω be pure *or* chaste;

ἁγνίζω ἁγνιῶ purify, expiate

ἁγνισμός οῦ ὁ purification, expiation

ἀγνοέω ignore, not to know; mistake; overlook; doubt; go wrong (by mistake)

ἀγνόημα ατος τό **ἄγνοια** ᾱς ἡ ignorance; mistake

ἁγνός ή όν pure, chaste; holy, sacred; purifying

ἁγνότης ητος ἡ purity

ἄγνῡμι ἄξω ἔαξα *or* ἧξα break (in pieces)

ἀγνωμονέω act thoughtlessly

ἀγνωμοσύνη ης ἡ lack of judgement, imprudence; misunderstanding; obstinacy; unfairness

ἀγνώμων ον imprudent; unfeeling, unfair; obstinate; not knowing, mistaking

ἀγνώς (*gen* ῶτος) unknown, strange; not knowing, ignorant

ἀγνωσίᾱ ᾱς ἡ ignorance, obscurity

ἄγνω(σ)τος ον unknown; unrecognisable, unintelligible

ἄγονος ον unborn; childless; barren

ἀγορᾱ́ ᾶς ἡ meeting, congregation, assembly; council; speech; eloquence; market-place, market; victuals; commerce, trade

ἀγοράζω be in a market-place frequently; buy *or* sell (in the market)

ἀγοραῖος ον belonging to a public assembly *or* a market; idler in the agora

ἀγορᾱνόμος ου ὁ regulator of the market-place

ἀγοράομαι speak in an assembly *or* publicly

ἀγοραστής οῦ ὁ buyer

ἀγορεύω ▸ **ἀγοράομαι**

ἀγορῆθεν *adv* from an assembly

ἀγορήνδε *adv* into an assembly

ἀγορητής οῦ ὁ public speaker, orator

ἀγορητύς ύος ἡ gift of speaking

ἀγός οῦ ὁ leader, captain

ἄγος ους τό abomination, blood-guiltiness; expiation

ἅγος ους τό reverence, awe

ἀγοστός οῦ ὁ palm of the hand

ἄγρᾱ ᾱς ἡ hunting; capture, game

ἀγράμματος ον unlettered

ἄγραπτος ον unwritten; not registered

ἀγραυλέω live in the open air

ἄγραυλος ον living in the fields, rural

ἄγραφος ον unwritten; not registered

ἀγρευτής οῦ ὁ hunter

ἀγρεύω, ἀγρέω hunt, catch
■ **ἄγρει, ἀγρεῖτε** come on!

ἀγριαίνω ἀγριανῶ ἠγρίᾱνα grow angry

ἀγριέλαιος ου ἡ wild olive, oleaster

ἄγριος ᾱ ον living in the fields; wild; brutal, cruel; malignant; furious, passionate

ἀγριότης ητος ἡ wildness, cruelty

ἀγριόφωνος ον with a harsh voice

ἀγριόω infuriate; *pass* grow angry *or* cruel

ἀγροβότης ου ὁ feeding in the fileds

ἀγρόθεν *adv* from the field *or* country

ἀγροικίᾱ ᾱς ἡ rusticity, boorishness

ἄγροικος ον (*or* ἀγροῖκος ον) rustic, boorish, churlish

ἀγροιώτης ▸ **ἀγρότης**

ἀγρόνδε *adv* to the country

ἀγρονόμος ον living in the country; overseer of public lands

ἀγρόνομος ον used for pasture

ἀγρός οῦ ὁ field, arable land; estate, farm; country (as opposed to town)

ἀγρότερος ᾱ ον wild; country-loving

ἀγρότης ου ὁ country-man, hunter

ἀγρυπνέω be sleepless *or* awake

ἀγρυπνίᾱ ᾱς ἡ sleeplessness

ἄγρυπνος ον sleepless, wakeful

ἀγρώσσω hunt, catch

ἄγρωστις ιδος ἡ field-grass, green provender

ἀγυιά ᾶς ἡ road, path, street

ἀγυιεύς έως ὁ protector of the roads (of Apollo)

ἀγύμναστος ον untrained, unskilled

ἄγυρις ιος ἡ congregation, meeting

ἀγυρτάζω beg, collect

ἀγύρτης ου ὁ beggar, tramp

ἀγχέμαχος ον fighting hand to hand

ἄγχι *adv and prep + gen* near, at hand, close by
■ **ἆσσον** (*also* ἀσσολτέρω) *comp*
■ **ἄγχιστος** *sup*

ἀγχίαλος ον near the sea; surrounded by sea

ἀγχιβαθής ές deep near the shore

ἀγχίθεος ον godlike, dwelling with the gods

ἀγχιμαχητής οῦ ▸ **ἀγχέμαχος**

ἀγχίμολον *adv* near, close to

ἀγχίνοια ᾱς ἡ presence of mind, ready wit

ἀγχίνοος ον quick-witted, ingenious

ἀγχίπτολις ὁ/ἡ neighbouring

ἀγχιστείᾱ ᾱς ἡ **ἀγχιστεῖα** ων τά near relationship; right of inheritance

ἀγχιστεύς έως ὁ next of kin; heir apparent

ἀγχιστήρ ῆρος ὁ accomplice

ἀγχιστῖνος η ον close together

ἀγχίστροφος ον quick-changing

ἀγχόθεν *adv* from near

ἀγχόθι *adv* ▸ **ἄγχι**

ἀγχόνη ης ἡ throttling, strangulation; hanging

ἀγχοῦ *adv* near
■ **ἀγχότερος** *comp adj*
■ **ἀγχότατα, ἀγχοτάτω** *sup adv* nearest

ἄγχω ἄγξω ἦγξα throttle, strangle

ἀγχώμαλος ον nearly equal, undecided

ἄγω† *act tr* lead away, off, on, towards; conduct, drive, bring, convey, fetch, take along; estimate; direct, command, rule, instruct, guide; keep [a festival], spend; *intr* march, move, pass; *mid* lead *or* take (on, along) with *or* for oneself

ἀγωγεύς έως ὁ conveyer; leash

ἀγωγή ῆς ἡ abduction, transport, leading away; departure, march; leading, direction; education, the Spartan public upbringing, discipline; manner of life

ἀγώγιμος ον transportable; liable to seizure
■ **τὰ ἀγώγιμα** cargo

ἀγωγός οῦ ὁ/ἡ leader, guide

ἀγών ῶνος ὁ assembly; meeting-place; place of combat, arena; prize-combat, contest; lawsuit; exertion, labour, struggle, danger

ἀγωνάρχης ου ὁ ▸ **ἀγωνοθέτης**

ἀγωνίᾱ ᾱς ἡ struggle, labour; fear, agony

ἀγωνιάω ἀγωνιᾱ́σω ἠγωνίᾱσα struggle, compete; be distressed *or* anxious

ἀγωνίζομαι ἀγωνιοῦμαι ἠγωνισάμην fight, struggle; carry on a lawsuit; speak publicly; exert oneself

ἀγώνιος ον belonging to a (prize-) combat

ἀγώνισις εως ἡ combat

ἀγώνισμα ατος τό contest; lawsuit; prize, splendid *or* showy thing; exploit, brave deed

ἀγωνισμός οῦ ὁ contention, competition

ἀγωνιστής οῦ ὁ prize-fighter, rival, champion; advocate, defender

ἀγωνοθετέω direct the games; (act as) umpire

ἀγωνοθέτης ου ὁ director of the games, umpire

ἀδαγμός οῦ ὁ itching, biting

ἀδαημονίη ης ἡ ignorance

ἀδαήμων ον **ἀδαής** ές ignorant

ἀδάκρῡτος ον tearless; unwept ■ **ἀδακρῡτί** *adv*

ἀδαμάντινος η ον of steel, steely

ἀδάμας αντος ὁ the hardest metal, steel; diamond

ἀδάμα(σ)τος ον untamed; invincible, inexorable; unwedded

ἀδάπανος ον without expense

ἄδαστος ον not yet distributed

ἀδδεής ▸ **ἀδεής**

ἀδδέω ▸ **ἀδέω**

ἄδδην ▸ **ἄδην**

ἀδεής ές fearless, undaunted; safe; with impunity

ἄδεια ας ἡ fearlessness, security; impunity, safe-conduct; permission, liberty; latitude

ἀδειής ▸ **ἀδεής**

ἀδείμαντος ον intrepid

ἄδειπνος ον without the evening meal, unfed

ἀδελφεοκτόνος ου ὁ the murderer of a brother or sister

ἀδελφή ῆς ἡ sister

ἀδελφιδέος (*also* ἀδελφιδοῦς) ου ὁ nephew

ἀδελφιδῆ ῆς ἡ niece

ἀδελφός οῦ ὁ brother

ἀδελφότης ητος ἡ brotherhood

ἄδερκτος ον not seeing

ἄδεσμος ον unfettered

ἀδευκής ές bitter, unkind; ignominious

ἀδέψητος ον untanned

ἁ̄δέω be sated with + *dat*

ἀδηλέω be uncertain *or* at a loss

ἄδηλος ον unseen, invisible, secret, obscure, dark; unknown; uncertain

ἀδηλότης ητος ἡ uncertainty

ἀδημονέω be uneasy, distressed *or* puzzled

ἄδην, ἅ̄δην (*also* ἅδδην) *adv* enough, sufficiently, abundantly, to the full

ἀδῇος ον uninfested

ἀδήρῑτος ον unfought, undisputed

Ἅιδης ου ὁ Hades; the underworld

ἀδηφάγος ον voracious, devouring

ἀδῄωτος ον not ravaged

ἀδιάβατος ον impassable

ἀδιάκριτος ον undecided

ἀδιάλειπτος ον incessant, continuous

ἀδιάλλακτος ον irreconcilable

ἀδιάλυτος ον indissoluble

ἀδιάφθαρτος ον **ἀδιάφθορος** ον incorruptible; unbribable; imperishable

ἀδιήγητος ον indescribable

ἀδικέω act unjustly *or* lawlessly; sin; be wrong; injure, wrong, maltreat; offend; *pass* be wronged

α

ἀδίκημα ατος τό **ἀδικίᾱ** ᾱς ἡ **ἀδίκιον** ου τό wrong, injury; offence

ἄδικος ον unjust, unlawful; dishonest; wrong; unmanageable

ἀδινός (*also* ἁδινός) ή όν loud; crowded, thronging

ἀδιόρθωτος ον not regulated

ἀδμής (*gen* ῆτος) (*also* ἄδμητος) untamed; unmarried

ἀδόκητος ον unexpected

ἀδοκίμαστος ον unproved, not approved; under age

ἀδόκιμος ον spurious; disreputable

ἀ̄δολεσχέω prattle

ἀ̄δολέσχης ου ὁ prattler, gossiper

ἀ̄δολεσχίᾱ ᾱς ἡ gossip

ἄδολος ον guileless; genuine, pure

ἀδόξαστος ον certain, unquestionable; unexpected

ἀδοξέω be held in no esteem

ἀδοξίᾱ ᾱς ἡ ill-repute, disrepute

ἄδοξος ον inglorious, disreputable

ἄδος τό (*also* ἅδος) satiety

ἄδρηστος ον not running away

ἁδρός ά όν grown up, in full growth, stout

ἁδροτής ῆτος ἡ full vigour, ripeness; rich gift

ἁδρῡ́νω ἁδρυνῶ make ripe

ἀδυναμίᾱ ᾱς ἡ **ἀδυνασίᾱ** ᾱς ἡ lack of power, weakness, poverty

ἀδυνατέω be unable

ἀδύνατος ον unable; inefficient; feeble, weak; frail; invalid, cripple; poor, needy; impossible

ἄδυτον ου τό holy place, sanctuary

ᾄδω ▸ **ἀείδω**

ἄδωρος ον without gifts; not giving; unbribed, incorruptible

ἀεθλ- ▸ **ἀθλ-**

ἀ̄εί, αἰεί *adv* always, for ever; every time

ἀ̄ειγενέτης ου ὁ **ἀ̄ειγενής** οῦ ὁ everlasting, immortal

ἀειδής ές shapeless; invisible

ἀείδω ᾄσομαι ἤεισα sing, sound; praise, announce

ἀεικείη ης ἡ ill-treatment

ἀεικέλιος (ᾱ) ον **ἀεικής** ές shameful, unseemly

ἀεικίζω ἀεικιῶ maltreat, dishonour; deface

ἀ̄είμνηστος ον not to be forgotten, memorable

ἀ̄είναος ▸ **ἀέναος**

ἀ̄είρυτος ον ever-flowing

ἀείρω ▸ **αἴρω**

ἄεισμα ▸ **ᾆσμα**

ἀ̄είφρουρος ον ever-watching, everlasting

ἀεκαζόμενος η ον unwilling

αἐκήλιος ▸ **ἀεικέλιος**

ἀέκητι *adv* against the will

ἀέκων ▸ **ἄκων**

ἀέλιος ▸ **ἥλιος**

ἄελλα ης ἡ storm, whirlwind, eddy

ἀελλαῖος α ον swift as a storm, stormy

ἀελλάς άδος ἡ storm

ἀελλής eddying

ἀελλόπος, ἀελλόπους (*gen* ποδος) ▸ **ἀελλαῖος**

ἀελπής ές ▸ **ἄελπτος**

ἀελπτέω have no hope

ἄελπτος ον unhoped for

ἀ̄έναος ον **ἀ̄ενάων** ουσα ον ever-flowing

ἀέξω ▸ **αὔξω**

ἀεργ- ▸ **ἀργ-**

ἄερκτος ον unfenced

ἀεροβατέω walk in the air

ἀερσίπους (*gen* ποδος) swift-trotting, high-stepping

ἄεσα (*also* ἆσα) *aor* sleep, rest at night

ἀεσιφροσύνη ης ἡ silliness

ἀεσίφρων ον silly, foolish

ἀετός οῦ ὁ eagle

ἀζαλέος ᾱ ον dry, parched

ἄζη ης ἡ mould, dirt

ἄζηλος ον unenvied; miserable, wretched

ἀζήλωτος ον unenviable

ἀζήμιος ον unpunished; blameless, harmless; not punishing

ἀζηχής ές unceasing, excessive

ἅζομαι stand in awe (of), dread, revere, worship

ἄζῡμος ον unleavened

ἄζυξ (*gen* υγος) unyoked, unmarried

ἅζω dry up; *pass* be parched

ἀηδής ές unpleasant

ἀηδίᾱ ᾱς ἡ displeasure, disgust; odiousness

ἀηδών όνος ἡ nightingale

ἀήθεια ᾱς ἡ unaccustomedness

ἀηθέσσω be unaccustomed

ἀήθης ες unusual; uncommon

ἄημα τό blast of wind, wind

ἄημι blow, breathe; *pass* be agitated

ἀήρ έρος ὁ/ἡ air; mist, cloud

ἀήσυλος ον ▸ **αἴσυλος**

ἀήτης ου ὁ blast, wind

ἄητος ον stormy, raging; panting

ἀήττητος ον unconquered, invincible

ἀθανασίᾱ ᾱς ἡ immortality

ἀθανατίζω make immortal; believe in immortality

ἀθάνατος ον immortal, everlasting

ἄθαπτος ον unburied

ἀθέᾱτος ον not seeing; unseen

ἀθεεί without god

ἀθέμι(σ)τος ον **ἀθεμίστιος** ον lawless, illegal; criminal; wicked; illicit

ἄθεος ον godless, atheist; abandoned by the gods

ἀθεράπευτος ον untended, neglected

ἀθερίζω *aor* ἀθέριξα despise, disdain

ἄθερμος ον without warmth

ἄθεσμος ον ▸ **ἀθέμιστος**

ἀθέσφατος ον unspeakably huge, enormous

ἀθετέω do away with, reject

ἀθέτησις εως ἡ abolition, removal

ἀθηρηλοιγός οῦ ὁ winnowing-fan

ἄθηρος ον without wild beasts *or* game

ἄθικτος ον untouched

ἀθλεύω (*also* ἀθλέω) contend (for a prize); struggle; suffer

ἄθλησις εως ἡ combat

ἀθλητήρ ῆρος ὁ **ἀθλητής** οῦ ὁ prize-fighter, pugilist, athlete; champion

ἄθλιος ᾱ ον miserable, wretched

ἀθλιότης ητος ἡ wretchedness, drudgery

ἀθλοθέτης ου ὁ the judge in the games, umpire

ἆθλον[1] ου τό prize

ἆθλον[2] ου τό **ἆθλος** ου ὁ contest, combat; labour, toil

ἀθλοφόρος ον prize-bearing

ἀθρέω look at, observe, view; consider

ἀθροίζω (*also* ἁθροίζω) *tr* gather, collect, assemble

ἄθροισις εως ἡ **ἄθροισμα** ατος τό collection, compiling, amassing

ἀθρόος η ον (*also* ἁθρόος) gathered, crowded, in one body, all at once

ἀθῡμέω be disheartened *or* discouraged

ἀθῡμίᾱ ᾱς ἡ dejection

ἄθῡμος ον faint-hearted, downcast

ἄθυρμα ατος τό toy, plaything

ἀθυρμάτιον ου τό little toy

ἀθυροστομέω speak freely, babble

ἀθυρόστομος ον garrulous, talkative

ἀθῡ́ρω play, amuse oneself

ἄθυτος ον unsacrificed; not having sacrificed

α

ἄθῳος ον unpunished; unhurt, spared; innocent, without fault

ἀθωράκιστος ον without breastplate

αἰ, αἴ *conj* if, if only

αἶ, αἰαῖ *int* woe! alas!

αἶα ᾱς ἡ earth, land

αἰάζω αἰάξω αἴαξα cry αἰαῖ, wail

αἰᾱνής ές everlasting; painful; dismal, gloomy

αἰγανέη ἡ javelin

αἴγε(ι)ος ᾱ ον of goats

αἴγειρος ου ἡ black poplar

αἰγιαλός οῦ ὁ beach, shore

αἰγίβοτος ον grazed by goats

αἰγίλιψ (*gen* ιπος) steep, precipitous

αἰγίοχος ον aegis-bearing

αἰγίπους πουν (*gen* ποδος) goat-footed

αἰγίς ίδος ἡ aegis, goatskin breastplate of Zeus *or* Athena; hurricane

αἴγλη ης ἡ brightness, lustre

αἰγλήεις εσσα εν bright, brilliant

αἰγοπρόσωπος ον goat-faced

αἰγυπιός οῦ ὁ vulture

αἰδέομαι αἰδέσομαι ᾐδεσάμην *mid and pass* be ashamed (of); fear; revere, respect

ἀΐδηλος ον destroying; invisible, obscure

αἰδήμων ον ▸ **αἰδοῖος**

Ἀΐδης αο *or* εω ὁ Hades; the underworld

ἀΐδιος ον everlasting

αἰδοῖον ου τό genitals

αἰδοῖος ᾱ ον shame-faced, bashful; modest; chaste; venerable, respectable

αἴδομαι ▸ **αἰδέομαι**

αἰδόφρων ον merciful

ἀϊδρείη ης ἡ ignorance, silliness

αἰδώς οῦς ἡ shame; modesty; decency; respect, awe; reverence, veneration; ignominy, disgrace

αἰεί ▸ **ἀεί**

αἰειγενέτης ου ▸ **ἀειγενέτης**

αἰέλουρος ου ὁ/ἡ cat

αἰέν ▸ **ἀεί**

αἰενάων ▸ **ἀέναος**

αἰένυπνος ον lulling in eternal sleep

αἴητος ▸ **ἄητος**

αἰθαλόεις εσσα εν sooty; smoky, burning

αἴθε *int* if only!

αἰθέριος (ᾱ) ον high in the air

αἰθήρ έρος ὁ/ἡ the upper air, clear sky

αἴθουσα ης ἡ colonnade

αἶθοψ (*gen* οπος) sparkling, shining; fiery, keen

αἴθρη ης ἡ **αἰθρίᾱ** ᾱς ἡ brightness of the sky; bright, clear sky

αἰθρηγενέτης ου **αἰθρηγενής** ές born in ether

αἶθρος ου ὁ the cold clear air of morning

αἴθυια ᾱς ἡ diver, water-hen

αἴθω *act tr* kindle, burn; *act intr and pass* burn, blaze

αἴθων ον burning; sparkling, ruddy, shining; tawny; fiery, hot

αἴκ', αἴκε ▸ **εἰ ἄν, ἐάν**

αἰκάλλω flatter

ᾱ̓ΐκή ῆς ἡ rush, impetus

αἰκής ▸ **ἀεικής**

αἰκίᾱ ᾱς ἡ bad treatment, outrage

αἰκίζω ▸ **ἀεικίζω**

αἴκισμα ατος τό **αἰκισμός** οῦ ὁ ▸ **αἰκία**

ᾱ̓ϊκῶς ▸ **ἀεικῶς** shamefully

αἴλινος ὁ a plaintive song, lament

αἴλουρος ου ὁ/ἡ cat

αἷμα ατος τό blood; bloodshed, murder; life, vigour, strength; relative, blood-relationship

αἱμάς άδος ἡ effusion of blood

αἱμασιᾱ́ ᾶς ἡ wall of dry stones; thornbush

αἱμάσσω make bloody; sprinkle *or* stain with blood

αἱματεκχυσίᾱ ᾱς ἡ bloodshed

αἱματηρός ᾱ́ όν **αἱματόεις** εσσα εν bloody, bleeding; blood-red

αἱματόω ▸ **αἱμάσσω**

αἱματώδης ες looking like blood, blood-red

αἱμοβαφής ές bathed in blood

αἱμορροέω discharge blood

αἱμοφόρυκτος ον bloody, raw

αἱμύλιος ον **αἱμύλος** η ον flattering, charming; wily

αἵμων (*gen* ονος) knowing, expert

αἰναρέτης ου ὁ terribly brave

αἴνεσις εως ἡ ▸ **αἴνη**

αἰνέω† praise; approve, recommend, agree (to); promise

αἴνη ης ἡ praise, renown

αἴνιγμα ατος τό riddle

αἰνίζομαι *mid* ▸ **αἰνέω**

αἰνίσσομαι *mid* speak in riddles, hint

αἰνόθεν: ∼ αἰνῶς *adv phrase* from horror to horror, most horribly

αἰνόμορος ον ill-fated

αἰνοπαθής ές suffering terribly

αἶνος ου ὁ saying, story, proverb; praise, encomium

αἰνός ή όν horrible, dreadful

αἴνυμαι *mid* take; take hold of, seize

αἰνῶς *adv* dreadfully

αἴξ (*or* αἶξ) αἰγός ὁ/ἡ goat

αἰόλλω move quickly to and fro

αἰολοθώρηξ (*gen* ηκος) with a shining breast-plate

αἰόλος η ον swift, quick-moving; wriggling; flitting; shining, glittering, bright; shifting, shifty

αἰολόστομος ον ambiguous in speech

αἰπεινός ή όν **αἰπήεις** εσσα εν ▸ **αἰπύς**

αἰπόλιον ου τό herd of goats

αἰπόλος ου ὁ goatherd

αἰπός ή όν **αἰπύς** εῖα ύ high, steep, precipitous; sheer, utter; arduous

αἵρεσις εως ἡ taking, capture; option, choice; election; inclination; cast of mind; sect, party; heresy

αἱρετίζω αἱρετιῶ choose

αἱρετικός ή όν heretical

αἱρετός ή όν takable, conquerable, superable; intelligible, comprehensible; chosen; eligible, acceptable; desirable

αἱρέω† *act* take, seize; overtake, catch, join; take away; capture, conquer, subdue; kill; convict; understand; *mid* take *or* seize for oneself; get, win, receive, enjoy; choose, prefer; wish

αἴρω† *act tr* raise, lift, elevate, erect; render prominent, extol, enhance, heighten, praise; take away, remove, carry away; take, seize, fetch, get; show, manifest; *act intr* set out, put to sea, set sail; *pass* rise, mount, soar; set out; grow, increase; grow excited; *mid* lift up, carry away, seize; get, win, gain, obtain; take in hand, undertake, undergo

αἶσα ης ἡ fate, destiny, lot; dispensation (of a god); share

αἰσθάνομαι† *mid* feel, perceive; notice, observe; know, understand

αἴσθησις εως ἡ sensation, perception, feeling; sense; knowledge, consciousness

αἰσθητήριον ου τό organ of sense

αἰσθητός (ή) όν perceptible

αἴσθομαι ▸ **αἰσθάνομαι**

ἀΐσθω breathe out

αἴσιμος (η) ον fatal; due, fit, just, convenient

αἴσιος (ᾱ) ον auspicious, lucky

ᾄσσω ᾄξω ᾖξα *intr* move quickly; run, rush, dash, dart; fly away, hurry up; rise, soar up; pounce; *tr* put in motion

α

ἄϊστος ον unseen, invisible

ἀϊστόω destroy, annihilate

αἴσυλος ον evil, godless

αἰσυμνητήρ ῆρος ὁ **αἰσυμνήτης** ου ὁ judge, umpire; ruler

αἶσχος εος τό disgrace, shame, ignominy; ugliness, deformity

αἰσχροκέρδεια (*or* -κερδίᾱ) ᾱς ἡ love of profit, greediness

αἰσχροκερδής ές greedy for profit, covetous

αἰσχρολογίᾱ ᾱς ἡ foul talk

αἰσχρός ᾱ́ όν ugly; shameful, base, ignominious; abusive

αἰσχρότης ητος ἡ ugliness; infamy

αἰσχῡ́νη ης ἡ shame, disgrace; violation; sense of shame, reverence

αἰσχυντηρός ᾱ́ όν bashful

αἰσχῡ́νω† *tr* disfigure, deform, shame; disgrace; *pass* be *or* get ashamed

αἰτέω ask, ask for; beg for; *mid* ask for oneself

αἴτημα ατος τό **αἴτησις** εως ἡ demand, request, entreaty

αἰτητός ή όν asked for, wanted

αἰτίᾱ ᾱς ἡ cause, reason, motive, inducement; guilt, imputation, charge, reproach

■ **αἰτίᾱν ἔχω** have a cause *or* reason; be at fault; be charged with

αἰτίᾱμα ατος τό imputation, charge

αἰτιάομαι αἰτιᾱ́σομαι ᾐτιᾱσάμην *mid* accuse; blame; impute, allege

αἰτίζω ask, beg for

αἴτιος ᾱ ον causing, responsible (for), guilty (of)

■ **ὁ αἴτιος** doer, author; culprit

■ **τὸ αἴτιον** ▸ **αἰτία**

αἰτίωμα ατος τό ▸ **αἰτίαμα**

αἰφνίδιος ον sudden

αἰχμάζω αἰχμάσω throw a lance

αἰχμαλωσίᾱ ᾱς ἡ captivity

αἰχμαλωτεύω, αἰχμαλωτίζω take prisoner

αἰχμαλωτίς ίδος ἡ female captive, slave

αἰχμάλωτος ον prisoner of war, captive; captured; slave

αἰχμή ῆς ἡ point, edge; lance; war, battle

αἰχμητής οῦ ὁ spearman, warrior

αἰχμοφόρος ου ὁ spear-carrier

αἶψα *adv* quickly, suddenly

αἰψηρός ᾱ́ όν quick, swift, sudden

ἀΐω perceive, observe, see, hear, feel; know

αἰών ῶνος ὁ/ἡ space of time, duration, period; age, lifetime; eternity; one's destiny

αἰώνιος (ᾱ) ον eternal

αἰώρᾱ ᾱς ἡ swing, hammock; see-saw movement

αἰωρέω lift up, swing; *pass* be suspended, hover, hang, soar (aloft), float; be anxious *or* in suspense; rise

ἀκαθαρσίᾱ ᾱς ἡ impurity

ἀκάθαρτος ον uncleaned, uncleansed; unatoned; unclean

ἀκαιρέομαι find no opportunity

ἀκαιρίᾱ ᾱς ἡ wrong time; lack of opportunity

ἄκαιρος ον unseasonable, inopportune, importunate

ἀκάκητα guileless (of Hermes)

ἄκακος ον harmless, innocent; ingenuous

ἀκαλαρρείτης ου soft-flowing

ἀκάλυπτος ον uncovered

ἀκάμᾱς (*gen* αντος) **ἀκάματος** (η) ον untired, indefatigable

ἄκαμπτος ον rigid, unbending

ἄκανθα ης ἡ thorn(-bush), thistle; acacia; spine, backbone

ἀκανθώδης ες thorny

ἀκαρπίᾱ ᾱς ἡ barrenness, unfruitfulness

ἄκαρπος ον without fruit, barren

ἀκάρπωτος ον without fruit, fruitless, unfulfilled

ἀκατάγνωστος ον blameless

ἀκατακάλυπτος ον unveiled, uncovered

ἀκατάκριτος ον uncondemned

ἀκατάλῡτος ον imperishable

ἀκατάπαστος ον insatiable

ἀκατάπαυστος ον restless, incessant

ἀκαταστασίᾱ ᾱς ἡ unrest, confusion

ἀκατάστατος ον unstable, unsteady

ἀκατάσχετος ον indomitable, unruly

ἀκατάψευστος ον not fictitious

ἄκατος ου ἡ **ἀκάτιον** ου τό light boat *or* ship

ἄκαυστος ον unburnt

ἀκαχίζω trouble, grieve

ἀκαχμένος η ον sharpened, pointed

ἀκείομαι ▸ **ἀκέομαι**

ἀκέλευστος ον unbidden

ἀκέομαι ἀκοῦμαι ἠκεσάμην *mid* heal, cure; repair; make amends for

ἀκέραιος ον unmixed, pure; uninjured, entire, untouched, fresh

ἀκερδής ές without gain, unprofitable; bad

ἀκερσεκόμης ου with unshorn hair

ἄκεσις εως ἡ cure, healing

ἄκεσμα ατος τό remedy, medicine

ἀκεστήρ ῆρος ὁ healer

ἀκεστός ή όν curable; easily revived

ἀκέφαλος ον without a head

ἀκέων ουσα ον silent

ἀκήδεστος ον **ἀκηδής** ές uncared for, neglected; unburied; reckless; unfeeling

ἀκηδέω + *gen* neglect

ἀκήλητος ον inflexible, not enchanted

ἀκήν *adv* silently

ἀκηράσιος ον **ἀκήρατος** ον **ἀκήριος**[1] ον ▸ **ἀκέραιος**

ἀκήριος[2] ον lifeless; cowardly, without spirit

ἀκήρυκτος ον unannounced, unknown; without mediation

ἀκίβδηλος ον unadulterated, sincere

ἀκιδνός η ον tiny, weak

ἄκῑκυς (*gen* υος) powerless, feeble

ἀκῑνάκης ου ὁ a short straight Persian sword

ἀκίνδῡνος ον without danger, safe; unfailing

ἀκῑ́νητος ον unmoved; immovable, firm, steady; inflexible; not to be touched

ἀκίχητος ον unattainable

ἀκκίζομαι ἀκκιοῦμαι pretend to be indifferent

ἄκλαυ(σ)τος ον unwept; tearless; unpunished

ἀκλε(ι)ής ές without fame, obscure

ἄκλειστος ον **ἄκλῃστος** ον not shut, unlocked

ἄκληρος ον without a share; needy

ἀκληρωτί *adv* without drawing lots

ἄκλητος ον uncalled

ἀκλινής ές unswerving

ἀκμάζω ἀκμάσω flourish, be in vigour *or* in the prime of life; abound in

ἀκμαῖος ᾱ ον full-grown, ripe; vigorous, at the prime; in time

ἄκματος ον ▸ **ἀκάματος**

ἀκμή ῆς ἡ point, edge; highest point; prime, bloom; climax; pitch; vigour, maturity

ἀκμήν *adv* just yet, still

ἀκμηνός ή όν full-grown

ἀκμής (*gen* ῆτος) untiring, unwearied

ἀκμόθετον ου τό anvil block

ἄκμων ονος ὁ anvil

ἄκνηστις ιος ἡ spine, backbone

ἀκοή ῆς ἡ sense of hearing; listening; ear; hearsay, news, rumour; sermon, preaching

α

ἀκοινώνητος ον unsocial

ἄκοιτις ιος ἡ wife

ἀκολάκευτος ον not flattered

ἀκολασίᾱ ᾱς ἡ licentiousness, debauchery

ἀκολασταίνω ἀκολαστανῶ be unrestrained

ἀκόλαστος ον unrestrained

ἄκολος ου ἡ bit, morsel

ἀκολουθέω + *dat* follow, attend; join; obey

ἀκόλουθος ον following, attending; follower, attendant; convenient, agreeing

ἀκομιστίη ης ἡ want of care *or* nursing

ἀκονάω sharpen

ἀκόνη ης ἡ whetstone

ἀκονῑτί *adv* without the dust of the arena; without effort

ἀκοντίζω ἀκοντιῶ ἠκόντισα throw (a spear); hit, pierce

ἀκόντιον ου τό javelin, spear

ἀκόντισις εως ἡ **ἀκόντισμα** ατος τό the throwing of a spear

ἀκοντιστής οῦ ὁ spearman, darter

ἄκοπος ον unwearied, not wearying

ἀκόρεστος ον **ἀκόρητος** ον insatiable; greedy; insolent

ἄκος εος τό remedy; healing

ἀκοσμέω be disorderly

ἀκόσμητος ον without order, disorderly, confused; unprovided

ἀκοσμίᾱ ᾱς ἡ disorder, confusion; unruliness

ἄκοσμος ον disorderly; refractory

ἀκουάζομαι listen to + *gen*; be invited

ἀκουή ▸ **ἀκοή**

ἄκουρος ον without a son *or* heir; unshaven

ᾱ̓κούσιος ον ▸ **ἄκων**

ἄκουσμα ατος τό anything heard; report; treat *or* feast for the ears; instruction

ἀκουστός ή όν audible

ἀκούω† + *acc of the sound* + *gen of the person who makes it* hear, know; listen to; obey; be called *or* reputed

ἄκρᾱ ᾱς ἡ end, point, top, height; citadel; headland

ἀκρᾱής ές blowing strongly

ἀκραιφνής ές pure, fresh, vigorous

ἄκραντος ον unfulfilled, unfinished; vain

ἀκρασίᾱ ᾱς ἡ **ἀκράτεια** ᾱς ἡ incontinence, intemperance

ἀκρατής ές powerless; immoderate, intemperate

ἀκρᾱτοποσίᾱ ᾱς ἡ drinking of unmixed wine

ἀκρᾱτοπότης ου ὁ drinker of unmixed wine

ἄκρᾱτος ον unmixed, pure; purified; strong, vigorous; perfect

ἀκράτωρ (*gen* ορος) ▸ **ἀκρατής**

ἀκρητο- *see* **ἀκρατο-**

ἀκρῑ́βεια ας ἡ accuracy, exactness, precision; strictness, severity, discipline; parsimony; perfection

ἀκρῑβής ές exact, accurate, careful; severe; proper; tight(ly fitting); parsimonious, frugal, scanty; perfect

ἀκρῑβολογέομαι *mid* be precise in language

ἀκρῑβόω know *or* examine thoroughly

ἄκρις ιος ἡ ▸ **ἄκρα**

ἀκρίς ίδος ἡ locust

ἀκρισίᾱ ᾱς ἡ disorder

ἀκριτόμῡθος ον talking immoderately

ἄκριτος ον without judgement, arbitrary; continuous, confused; untried, unjudged; undecided; countless

ἀκριτόφυλλος ον with dense foliage

ἀκρόᾱμα ατος τό anything heard; treat *or* feast for the ears

ἀκροάομαι ἀκροᾱ́σομαι ἠκροᾱσάμην *mid* + *acc of the sound*

+ *gen of the person who makes it* hear; listen; obey

ἀκρόᾱσις εως ἡ a hearing; obedience

ἀκροατήριον ου τό audience; lecture-room, place of audience

ἀκροᾱτής οῦ ὁ hearer, listener

ἀκροβολίζομαι *aor* ἠκροβολισάμην *mid* skirmish

ἀκροβόλισις εως ἡ **ἀκροβολισμός** οῦ ὁ skirmish(ing)

ἀκροβολιστής οῦ ὁ skirmisher

ἀκροβυστίᾱ ᾱς ἡ foreskin; the gentiles

ἀκρογωνιαῖος ᾱ ον: **ὁ ~ος λίθος** cornerstone

ἀκρόδρυον ου τό fruit-tree

ἀκροθῑ́νιον ου τό the best part of a heap; *in pl* first fruits, votive gift; booty

ἀκροκελαινιάω grow black on the surface

ἀκρόκομος ον with head shaven except on the crown

ἀκρομανής ές on the verge of madness

ἀκρόπολις εως ἡ acropolis; upper city, citadel

ἀκροπόλος ον high, lofty

ἀκροπόρος ον piercing through

ἄκρος ᾱ ον extreme, upper, topmost; outstanding, excellent

■ **τὸ ἄκρον** height, top, summit, extremity, border, surface

ἀκροσφαλής ές tottering; inclined

ἀκροτελεύτιον ου τό the last bit (of a verse)

ἀκροφῡ́σιον ου τό spout of a pair of bellows

ἀκρύσταλλος ον clear of ice

ἀκρωνυχίᾱ ᾱς ἡ tip of the nail; ridge of a mountain

ἀκρώρεια ᾱς ἡ top of a mountain

ἀκρωτηριάζω *and mid* take off the fore part *or* extremities; mutilate

ἀκρωτήριον ου τό point, height, top, peak; projection; promontory; beak (of ship); gable; extremity

ἀκτένιστος ον uncombed

ἀκτέριστος ον unburied; unconsecrated

ἀκτή¹ ῆς ἡ coast, shore, beach

ἀκτή² ῆς ἡ corn, meal

ἀκτήμων ον without property, poor

ἀκτῑ́ς ῖνος ἡ ray, beam; light, splendour; heat

ἄκυλος ἡ acorn

ἄκῡρος ον without authority, annulled; invalid, powerless

ἀκῡρόω abolish, cancel

ἀκωκή ῆς ἡ point, edge

ἀκώλῡτος ον unhindered

ἄκων οντος ὁ javelin

ἄ̄κων ουσα ον against one's will, involuntary, unwilling; acting against one's will

ἅλα τό ► **ἅλς**

ἀλάβαστρος ου ὁ **ἀλάβαστρον** ου τό onyx, alabaster; an alabaster vase for holding perfumes

ἅλαδε *adv* to the sea, seaward(s)

ἀλᾱζονείᾱ ᾱς ἡ boasting, swaggering, humbug

ἀλᾱζονεύομαι boast, brag, swagger

ἀλᾱζονικός ή όν **ἀλᾱζών** όνος ὁ/ἡ fraud, braggart, impostor; vagrant

ἀλαλᾱ́ ᾶς ἡ **ἀλαλαγμός** οῦ ὁ **ἀλαλητός** οῦ ὁ war-cry; shout

ἀλαλάζω ἀλαλάξομαι ἠλάλαξα *and mid* raise the war-cry

ἀλάλητος ον unspeakable

ἄλαλος ον speechless, dumb

ἀλαλύκτημαι *pf of* **ἀλυκτέω** be afraid *or* in anguish

ἀλάμπετος ον **ἀλαμπής** ές lustreless, darksome, without light

ἀλάομαι wander, stray, be banished, ramble about; doubt

ἀλαός ον blind; blinding

ἀλαοσκοπιή ῆς ἡ vain watch

ἀλαόω make blind

ἀλαπαδνός ή όν exhausted, feeble

a

ἀλαπάζω ἀλαπάξω empty, exhaust; overwhelm, destroy, kill

ἅλας ατος τό ▸ **ἅλς**

ἀλαστέω be angry, hate, resent

ἀλάστορος ον **ἀλάστωρ** ορος ὁ avenging demon, tormenter; accursed wretch; fiend

ἄλαστος ον unbearable; unceasing, lasting; memorable; wicked, hateful

ἀλᾱ́τᾱς ▸ **ἀλήτης**

ἀλαωτύς ύος ἡ act of blinding

ἀλγεινός ή όν painful, grievous; evil; unpleasant; vehement; difficult; suffering

ἀλγέω feel pain, suffer; be troubled *or* sad; grieve

ἀλγηδών όνος ἡ **ἄλγημα** ατος τό **ἄλγησις** εως ἡ **ἄλγος** εος τό pain, grief, sorrow

ἀλγῡ́νω grieve, cause pain; *pass* ▸ **ἀλγέω**

ἀλδαίνω strengthen, invigorate

ἀλδήσκω grow, thrive

ἀλέᾱ[1] ᾱς ἡ heat (of the sun)

ἀλέᾱ[2] ᾱς ἡ avoidance, escape

ἀλεγεινός ▸ **ἀλγεινός**

ἀλέγω, ἀλεγίζω, ἀλεγῡ́νω care for, attend (to), pay attention to

ἀλεεινός ή όν warm, warming

ἀλεείνω ▸ **ἀλέομαι**

ἀλεής ές in the midday heat

ἀλείατα τά *from* **ἄλειαρ** ▸ **ἄλευρον**

ἄλειμμα ατος τό ointment, fat, anointing-oil

ἄλεισον ου τό cup, bowl

ἀλείτης ου ὁ offender, sinner

ἄλειφαρ ατος τό anointing-oil

ἀλείφω ἀλείψω ἤλειψα anoint with oil; plaster, block up

ἄλειψις εως ἡ unction, anointing

ἀλεκτοροφωνίᾱ ᾱς ἡ cockcrow

ἄλεκτρος ον unwedded; extra-marital

ἀλεκτρυών όνος ὁ **ἀλέκτωρ** ορος ὁ cock

ἀλέκω ▸ **ἀλέξω**

ἀλεξάνεμος ον keeping off the wind

ἀλέξησις εως ἡ a keeping off, defence

ἀλεξητήρ ῆρος ὁ **ἀλεξήτωρ** ορος ὁ protector, guardian, helper

ἀλεξίκακος ον keeping off evil

ἀλεξίμορος ον defending from death

ἀλεξιφάρμακον ου τό antidote

ἀλέξω ἀλεξήσω keep off + *acc*; guard, protect, defend, help + *dat*; *mid* defend oneself; recompense, requite

ἀλέομαι *mid* turn aside; avoid, shun, escape

ἀλέτης ου ὁ **ἀλετρίς** ίδος ἡ grinder (of corn)

ἀλετρεύω ▸ **ἀλέω**

ἀλεύομαι ▸ **ἀλέομαι**

ἄλευρον ου τό meal, flour

ἀλέω *aor* ἤλεσα grind, pound

ἀλεωρή ῆς ἡ escape; protection

ἄλη ης ἡ ceaseless wandering; madness

ἀλήθεια ᾱς ἡ truth; veracity, uprightness; reality; propriety

ἀληθεύω speak the truth

ἀληθής ές true; sincere, frank; real, genuine, proper; actual

▪ **ἀληθῶς, ἀληθές** *adv* truly, really, indeed

ἀληθίζομαι *mid* ▸ **ἀληθεύω**

ἀληθινός ή όν ▸ **ἀληθής**

ἀλήθω ▸ **ἀλέω**

ἀλήιος ον not wealthy

ἄλημα ατος τό **ἀλήμων** ον wily trickster; vagrant, fugitive

ἄληπτος ον unattainable; inconceivable

ἀλής ές crowded, in a mass; all together

ἀλητεύω ▸ **ἀλάομαι**

ἀλήτης ου ὁ ▸ **ἄλημα**

ἄλθομαι *pass* be healed

ἁ̄λίᾱ ᾱς ἡ assembly

ἁλιάης ου ὁ ▸ **ἁλιεύς**

ἁλιᾱής ές blowing seaward
ἀλίαστος ον unyielding; incessant
ἀλίγκιος ον like, equal
ἁλιεύς έως ὁ fisherman; sailor
ἁλιευτικός ή όν appropriate to fishermen
ἁλιεύω fish
ᾱ̔λίζω *aor* ἥλισα *tr* assemble, gather together
ἁλίζω salt
ἄλιθος ον without stones
ἁλίκλυστος ον sea-washed
ἁλίκτυπος ον sea-beaten
ἀλίμενος ον harbourless; inhospitable
ἀλιμενότης ητος ἡ harbourlessness
ἁλιμῡρήεις εσσα εν flowing into the sea
ἅλινος η ον (made) of salt
ᾱ̔́λιος ▸ ἥλιος
ᾱ̔́λιος[1] ᾱ́ όν unprofitable, in vain
ᾱ̔́λιος[2] ᾱ́ όν belonging to the sea
ἁλιοτρεφής ές sea-nurtured
ἁλιόω frustrate, make fruitless
ἀλῑπαρής ές not fit for a suppliant
ἁλίπλᾱκτος ον sea-beaten; sea-roaming
ἁλίπλοος ον floating in the sea
ἁλιπόρφυρος ον of sea-purple, purple-dyed
ἁλίρροθος ον in the roaring sea; sea-beaten
ἅλις *adv* in crowds, in plenty; enough
ἀλίσγημα ατος τό pollution
ἁλίσκομαι† be taken, caught, captured *or* conquered; be found (out), apprehended *or* convicted
ἀλιταίνω *and mid* sin *or* offend against; transgress
ἀλιτήμων ον **ἀλιτήριος** ον **ἀλιτ(η)ρός** όν offending *or* sinning against; sinful; guilty
ἀλιτρίᾱ ᾱς ἡ wickedness
ἄλκαρ τό defence, protection
ἀλκή ῆς ἡ defensive power, force, prowess; guard, defence; battle, fight
ἄλκιμος (η) ον fit for battle, warlike, martial; valiant
ἀλκτήρ ῆρος ὁ defender, protector
ἀλκυών όνος ἡ kingfisher
ἀλλά *conj* but, yet, however; notwithstanding; at least; but, except; why, well, certainly, well then
ἀλλαγή ῆς ἡ change, alteration
ἀλλάσσω ἀλλάξω ἤλλαξα change, alter, transmute; requite; *mid* take in exchange
ἀλλαχῇ, ἀλλαχόθι, ἀλλαχοῦ *adv* elsewhere; to another place
ἀλλαχόθεν *adv* from another place
ἀλλαχόσε *adv* to another place
ἀλλέγω ▸ ἀναλέγω
ἄλλῃ *adv* ▸ ἀλλαχῇ; otherwise
ἀλληγορέω speak metaphorically, allegorize
ἀλλήλους *acc pron* ων one another, each other
ἀλληλοφαγίᾱ ᾱς ἡ eating of one another
ἀλληλοφθορίᾱ ᾱς ἡ mutual destruction
ἄλλην *adv* to another place
ἀλλογενής ές alien, foreign
ἀλλόγλωσσος ον using a foreign language, foreign
ἀλλογνοέω mistake (someone) for someone else, not know
ἀλλόγνωτος ον strange, unknown
ἀλλοδαπός ή όν strange, foreign, outlandish
ἀλλοειδής ές looking differently, of strange appearance
ἄλλοθεν *adv* from another place
ἄλλοθι *adv* elsewhere; far from + *gen*; in other ways
ἀλλόθροος ον speaking another language; foreign

ἀλλοῖος ᾱ ον different, heterogeneous; changed

ἀλλοιόω change, alter

ἀλλοίωσις εως ἡ change, permutation

ἀλλόκοτος ον different; uncommon, strange; unnatural

ἅλλομαι ἁλοῦμαι ἡλάμην *or* ἡλόμην *mid* spring, jump, leap; fly, run

ἀλλοπρόσαλλος ὁ changeable, fickle

ἄλλος η ο another, the other; different, strange, foreign; inconvenient; false
- **ἄλλως** *adv* otherwise (better *or* worse); in vain; at random; merely, simply; besides, already
- **ἄλλως τε καί** especially, above all

ἄλλοσε *adv* to another place

ἄλλοτε *adv* at another time

ἀλλοτριοεπίσκοπος ου ὁ busy-body

ἀλλότριος ᾱ ον belonging to others; foreign, alien, not related; hostile, adverse; changed, strange; inconvenient

ἀλλοτριότης ητος ἡ estrangement

ἀλλοτριόω estrange X *acc* from Y *gen*

ἀλλοτρίωσις εως ἡ estrangement

ἄλλοφος ον without a crest

ἀλλοφρονέω think otherwise *or* wrongly; be in a frenzy; have other views

ἀλλόφῡλος ον of another tribe, foreign

ἄλλυδις *adv* to somewhere else

ἀλλύεσκε *see* **ἀναλύω**

ἄλλως *see* **ἄλλος**

ἅλμα ατος τό jump, leap, bound

ἅλμη ης ἡ sea-water, sea; brine; saltiness

ἁλμυρός ᾱ όν salt, bitter, of the sea

ἀλοάω thresh; cudgel

ἄλοβος ον (of the liver) without lobe

ἀλογέω take no notice of, neglect; be out of one's senses

ἀλογίᾱ ᾱς ἡ disregard

ἀλόγιστος ον unreasonable, absurd; unfathomable

ἄλογος ον without reason, silly; unexpected; speechless

ἀλόη ἡ bitter aloes

ἁλόθεν *adv* from the sea

ἀλοιάω ▸ **ἀλοάω**

ἀλοιφή ῆς ἡ fat, grease; anything used for anointing

ἄλοξ οκος ἡ furrow; cornland

ἁλοσύδνη ἡ sea-born

ἁλουργής ές dyed with sea-purple

ἀλουσίᾱ ᾱς ἡ unwashedness, dirt

ἄλουτος ον unwashed, dirty

ἄλοχος ου ἡ wife

ἅλς ἁλός ὁ salt

ἅλς ἁλος ἡ salt water, sea

ἄλσος εος τό (sacred) grove, forest

ἁλυκός όν salt, brackish

ἀλυκτάζω ▸ **ἀλύω**

ἄλῡπος ον **ἀλῡ́πητος** ον without pain *or* grief; not grieving

ἄλυρος ον without a lyre; sad

ἅλυσις εως ἡ chain

ἀλῡσιτελής ές useless, unprofitable; injurious

ἀλύσκω, ἀλυσκάζω, ἀλυσκάνω avoid, escape

ἀλύσσω ▸ **ἀλύω**

ἄλυτος ον inseparable, indissoluble; continuous, ceaseless

ἀλύω be distressed, beside oneself, troubled *or* excited

ἄλφα τό first letter of the alphabet

ἀλφάνω *aor* ἦλφον earn, gain, acquire

ἀλφεσίβοιος ᾱ ον bringing in cattle; much-wooed

ἀλφηστής οῦ ὁ working for one's daily bread; laborious, industrious

ἄλφιτον ου τό barley-meal; bread

ἀλφιτοποιΐᾱ ᾱς ἡ the making of barley-meal

ἀλωή ῆς ἡ threshing floor

ἅλων ωνος ἡ ▸ **ἅλως**

ἀλωπεκῆ ἡ **ἀλωπεκίς** ίδος ἡ fox skin

ἀλώπηξ εκος ἡ fox

ἅλως ω *or* ωος ἡ threshing floor, corn on the floor; disk (of the sun or moon)

ἁλώσιμος ον **ἁλωτός** ή όν easily won *or* conquered *or* understood

ἅλωσις εως ἡ a taking, capture; conquest

ἀμ ▸ **ἀνά**

ἅμα *adv and prep* together, at the same time, at once, together with + *dat*

ἀμαθής ές ignorant, unlearned, unlettered; inexperienced; incalculable

ἀμαθίᾱ ᾱς ἡ ignorance; inexperience

ἄμαθος ἡ sand

ἀμαθῡ́νω reduce to sand, destroy utterly

ἀμαιμάκετος (η) ον irresistible; strong, stubborn

ἀμαλδῡ́νω destroy

ἀμαλλοδετήρ ῆρος ὁ binder of sheaves

ἀμαλός ή όν soft, feeble, delicate

ἅμαξα ης ἡ **ἄμαξα** ης ἡ waggon

ἁμαξεύω drive [a waggon]; *pass* be crossed by waggons

ἁμαξιαῖος ᾱ ον filling a waggon

ἁμαξίς ίδος ἡ little waggon

ἁμαξιτός όν practicable for waggons

ἆμαρ ▸ **ἦμαρ**

ἀμάραντος ον **ἀμαράντινος** ον unfading

ἀμάρη ης ἡ trench, ditch

ἁμαρτάνω† miss the centre of the target, err, fail, make a mistake, lose; offend, sin

ἁμαρτάς άδος ἡ **ἁμάρτημα** ατος τό **ἁμαρτίᾱ** ᾱς ἡ transgression, sin, offence, error

ἁμαρτέω ▸ **ὁμαρτέω**

ἁμαρτῆ *adv* at the same time, at once

ἁμαρτοεπής ές telling lies *or* speaking at random

ἀμάρτυρος ον unattested

ἁμαρτωλός όν sinful; sinner

ἁματροχάω run along with

ἁματροχίη ης ἡ collision of waggons

ἀμαυρός ᾱ́ όν dark, dim; blind; feeble; gloomy; indifferent

ἀμαυρόω darken, weaken

ἀμάχητος ον **ἄμαχος** ον without fighting; peaceful; unconquerable
■ **ἀμαχεί, ἀμαχητί** *adv* without resistance

ἀμάω mow, reap; gather

ἄμβασις ▸ **ἀνάβασις**

ἀμβατός όν ▸ **ἀναβατός**

ἀμβλήδην *adv* with sudden bursts; bubbling up

ἀμβλῡ́νω ἀμβλυνῶ ἤμβλῡνα blunt, dull; lessen, discourage

ἀμβλύς εῖα ύ blunt, dull; slack, feeble, weak

ἀμβλυώττω be dim-sighted

ἀμβολάδην ▸ **ἀμβλήδην**

ἀμβροσίᾱ ᾱς ἡ ambrosia (food of the gods)

ἀμβρόσιος ᾱ ον **ἄμβροτος** ον immortal, divine

ἀμβώσας *see* **ἀναβοάω**

ἀμέγαρτος ον unenvied; unhappy, miserable

ἀμέθυστος[1] ου ἡ amethyst

ἀμέθυστος[2] ον not drunken

ἀμείβω change, alter; exchange; pass, cross; *mid* reply, answer; requite

ἀμείβων οντος ὁ rafter (of a roof)

ἀμείλικτος ον **ἀμείλιχος** ον harsh, severe; relentless

α

ἀμείνων ον *comp from* **ἀγαθός** better, abler, nobler; stronger, more valiant

ἀμειξίᾱ ᾱς ἡ ▸ **ἀμιξία**

ἀμέλγω milk, drain; drink

ἀμέλει *adv* never mind; of course

ἀμέλεια ᾱς ἡ carelessness, negligence

ἀμελέτητος ον unpractised, unskilled

ἀμελέω be careless, heedless; neglect, overlook, omit

ἀμελής ές careless, negligent; neglected

ἄμεμπτος ον blameless; contented

ἆμεναι ▸ **ἀέμεναι,** *see* **ἄω**

ἀμενηνός όν feeble, weak, powerless

ἀμενηνόω make weak

ἁμέρᾱ ᾱς ἡ ▸ **ἡμέρα**

ἀμέρδω *aor* ἥμερσα rob, deprive (of something *gen*); become blind; *pass* get *or* become deprived of + *gen*

ἀμερής ές indivisible

ἀμέριμνος ον free from care; neglected

ἁμέριος ▸ **ἡμέριος**

ἀμέριστος ον indivisible

ἀμετάθετος ον unalterable

ἀμετακῑ́νητος ον immovable

ἀμεταμέλητος ον **ἀμετανόητος** ον unrepentant

ἁμέτερος ▸ **ἡμέτερος**

ἀμέτρητος ον **ἄμετρος** ον unmeasured, immense; boundless; innumerable, countless

ἀμετρίᾱ ᾱς ἡ want of measure *or* moderation

ἀμετροεπής ές knowing no limits in speech

ἁμῇ (*also* ἀμῇ) *adv* somehow, anyhow

ἀμήνῑτος ον not angry

ἀμητήρ ῆρος ὁ reaper

ἄμητος ου ὁ reaping, harvest, crop

ἀμήτωρ (*gen* ορος) motherless; unmotherly

ἀμηχανέω be at a loss, be helpless *or* embarrassed; lack (something *gen*)

ἀμήχανος ον helpless, embarrassed, puzzled; impossible, unattainable; incredible; indescribable; unconquerable; inflexible; irreversible, inevitable

ἀμίαντος ον undefiled

ἀμιγής ές **ἄμῑκτος** ον unmixed; unsociable; incompatible

ἅμιλλα ης ἡ rivalry, contest; combat; striving, desire

ἁμιλλάομαι *mid and pass* contend, rival, strive

ἁμίλλημα ατος τό ▸ **ἅμιλλα**

ἁμιλλητήρ ῆρος ὁ competitor, rival

ἀμῑξίᾱ ᾱς ἡ lack of communication; unsociability; purity

ἄμιππος ον swift as a horse; companion of a horse-soldier

ἄμισθος ον unpaid

ἀμιτροχίτων (*gen* ωνος) wearing nothing round the waist under the coat of mail

ἀμιχθαλόεις εσσα εν inaccessible, inhospitable

ἅμμα ατος τό knot, noose, band, girdle

ἄμμε ▸ **ἡμᾶς**

ἄμμες ▸ **ἡμεῖς**

ἄμμιγα ▸ **ἀναμίξ**

ἀμμῑ́γνῡμι ▸ **ἀναμίγνυμι**

ἀμμορίη ης ἡ having no share; misfortune

ἄμμορος ον without a share in + *gen*; unfortunate

ἄμμος ου ἡ sand; race course

ἀμνᾱστέω ▸ **ἀμνηστέω**

ἀμνημονέω + *gen* be forgetful of; make no mention of

ἀμνήμων ον forgetful, unmindful; forgotten

ἀμνηστέω ▸ **ἀμνημονέω**; *pass* fall into oblivion

ἀμνίον ου τό offering-bowl

ἀμνός οῦ ὁ/ἡ lamb

ἀμογητί *adv* without effort *or* trouble

ἁμοθεί *adv* unanimously

ἁμόθεν (*also* ἀμόθεν) *adv* from anywhere

ἀμοιβαῖος (ᾱ) ον **ἀμοιβάς** (*gen* άδος) alternate

ἀμοιβή ῆς ἡ change, exchange; reply, answer; recompense, return

ἀμοιβηδίς *adv* alternately

ἀμοιβός όν substitute, equivalent

ἄμοιρος ον without a share in + *gen*; free from; unfortunate

ἀμολγός οῦ ὁ dead (of night); twilight

ἄμορος ▸ **ἄμμορος**

ἄμορφος ον deformed, ugly

ἁμός ή όν (*also* ἀμός) our, ours; my, mine

ἄμοτον *adv* incessantly

ἁμοῦ *adv* anywhere, somewhere

ἄμουσος ον without the Muses; unrefined, boorish

ἄμοχθος ον without pains *or* trouble; lazy

ἀμπαυ- ▸ **ἀναπαυ-**

ἀμπείρω ▸ **ἀναπείρω**

ἀμπέλινος η ον of the vine

ἀμπελόεις εσσα εν rich in vines

ἄμπελος ου ἡ vine

ἀμπελουργός οῦ ὁ vine-dresser

ἀμπελών ῶνος ὁ vineyard

ἀμπεπαλών *see* **ἀναπάλλω**

ἀμπερές ▸ **διαμπερές**

ἀμπεχόνη ης ἡ clothing, upper garment

ἀμπ-έχω ἀμφέξω ἤμπισχον enclose, surround; clothe; *pass* be clothed

ἀμπηδάω ▸ **ἀναπηδάω**

ἀμπίσχω ▸ **ἀμπέχω**

ἀμπλάκημα ατος τό offence

ἀμπλακίσκω do wrong; come short of + *gen*

ἀμπν- ▸ **ἀναπν-**

ἀμπνέω ▸ **ἀναπνέω**

ἀμπνοή ῆς ἡ breath

ἀμπυκτήριον ου τό bridle

ἄμπυξ υκος ὁ/ἡ wheel; a woman's headband; diadem

ἄμπωτις εως ἡ ebb, low tide

ἀμυγδάλινος η ον of almonds

ἄμυγμα ατος τό a tearing, scratching

ἄμυδις *adv* together, at once

ἀμυδρός ᾱ́ όν dim, indistinct

ἀμύητος ον uninitiated; leaky

ἀμῡ́θητος ον unspeakable

ἀμῡ́μων ον blameless, noble, excellent

ἀμῡνάθω ▸ **ἀμύνω**

ἀμύντωρ ορος ὁ defender; avenger

ἀμῡ́νω ἀμυνῶ ἤμῡνα keep off, ward off X *acc* from Y *dat*; defend + *dat*; aid; requite; *mid* defend oneself; resist; requite

ἀμύσσω ἀμύξω ἤμυξα scratch, lacerate

ἀμφ-αγαπάζω treat kindly, greet warmly

ἀμφ-αγείρομαι *mid* assemble around one

ἀμφάδιος ᾱ ον public, known
▪ **ἀμφαδά, ἀμφαδόν, ἀμφαδίην** *adv*

ἀμφ-αΐσσομαι *mid* rush on *or* charge from all sides

ἀμφᾱ́κης ▸ **ἀμφήκης**

ἀμφ-αλείφω anoint all over

ἀμφ-αραβέω clink *or* rattle about

ἀμφασίη ης ἡ speechlessness

ἀμφ-αϋτέω sound all round

ἀμφ-αφάω *and mid* touch all round; handle

ἀμφ-έπω ▸ **ἀμφιέπω**

ἀμφ-έρχομαι *aor* ἀμφήλυθον surround

ἀμφ-ηγερέθομαι ▸ **ἀμφαγείρομαι**

ἀμφήκης ες double-edged

ἄμφ-ημαι sit round

ἀμφηρεφής ές covered all round, close-covered

ἀμφηρικός ή όν rowed on both sides, propelled by sculls

ἀμφί *adv* on both *or* all sides, around; about; *prep with acc* round, about, along, at, near; concerning; during; *with gen* near, round, about; concerning, for; *with dat* at, about, round; because of; by means of

ἀμφίαλος ον surrounded by the sea; between two seas

ἀμφ-ιάχω fly shrieking about

ἀμφι-βαίνω walk around, encompass; bestride; protect

ἀμφι-βάλλω throw *or* put round; embrace; ensnare; doubt, be uncertain; *mid* put on

ἀμφίβασις εως ἡ protection

ἀμφίβληστρον ου τό fishing-net

ἀμφιβολίᾱ ᾱς ἡ doubt

ἀμφίβολος ον shot at from all sides; ambiguous, doubtful; undecided, helpless

ἀμφίβροτος η ον covering the whole man

ἀμφι-γνοέω *aor* ἠμφεγνόησα be uncertain *or* doubtful about (something *acc*)

ἀμφιγυήεις lame in both feet (of Hephaestus)

ἀμφίγυος ον double-pointed

ἀμφι-δαίω *intr* burn around

ἀμφίδασυς εια υ tasselled all round

ἀμφιδέαι αἱ ligatures, clasps, bracelets

ἀμφιδέξιος ον skilled with both hands, very dextrous; ambiguous

ἀμφιδήρῑτος ον disputed, doubtful

ἀμφι-δῑνέω *tr* roll all round

ἀμφίδρομος ον running both ways, enclosing

ἀμφιδρυφής ές **ἀμφίδρυφος** ον having torn both cheeks; scratched on all sides

ἀμφίδυμος ον double

ἀμφι-δῠ́ομαι *mid* put on oneself

ἀμφι-έζω, ἀμφι-έννῡμι ἀμφιέσω ἠμφίεσα *and mid* put on, dress oneself in

ἀμφιέλισσα ης ἡ (of a ship) curved at both ends *or* handy *or* swaying to and fro, wheeling

ἀμφι-έπω be busy over; take care of; protect

ἀμφίεσμα ατος τό dress, clothes

ἀμφι-εύω singe all round

ἀμφ-ιζᾰ́νω sit, settle on + *dat*

ἀμφιθαλής ές with both parents living

ἀμφίθετος ον double-handled

ἀμφι-θέω -θεύσομαι run around + *acc*

ἀμφίθηκτος ον double-edged

ἀμφίθρεπτος ον congealed around

ἀμφίθυρος ον with double doors

ἀμφι-καλύπτω cover, wrap; veil, hide; enclose, envelop, shelter

ἀμφι-κεάζω cleave in two

ἀμφί-κειμαι lie around, embrace, come soon after

ἀμφικῑ́ων ον with pillars all round

ἀμφίκλυστος ον washed all around by waves

ἀμφίκομος ον with hair all round; with dense foliage

ἀμφικτίονες ων οἱ those who live around, neighbours

ἀμφικύπελλος ον double-handled *or* with double cup

ἀμφιλαφής ές wide, large, huge; copious

ἀμφι-λαχαίνω dig *or* hoe round

ἀμφι-λέγω + *acc* dispute about; dispute, question

ἀμφίλογος ον disputed, doubtful; altercating

ἀμφίλοφος ον surrounding the neck

ἀμφιλύκη ης ἡ dawn, twilight

ἀμφι-μάομαι wipe all round

ἀμφι-μάχομαι fight round

ἀμφιμέλᾱς αινα αν wrapped in darkness

ἀμφι-μῡκάομαι bellow, echo *or* low around

ἀμφινεικής ές **ἀμφινείκητος** ον contested on all sides; eagerly wooed

ἀμφι-νέμομαι dwell around + *acc*

ἀμφι-νοέω ▸ **ἀμφιγνοέω**

ἀμφι-ξέω smooth all round

ἀμφι-πέλομαι surround, hover around

ἀμφι-πένομαι ▸ **ἀμφιέπω**

ἀμφιπερι-στέφω surround on all sides

ἀμφιπερι-στρωφάω keep turning [a horse] in every direction

ἀμφι-πίπτω fall upon, embrace

ἀμφίπλεκτος ον entwined, entangled

ἀμφίπληκτος ον beaten on both sides; surging around

ἀμφιπλήξ (*gen* ῆγος) double-edged

ἀμφι-πολεύω ▸ **ἀμφιέπω**

ἀμφι-πολέω attend to, watch, guard

ἀμφίπολος ον attending, serving; servant

ἀμφι-πονέομαι *mid* ▸ **ἀμφιέπω**

ἀμφι-ποτάομαι *mid* flit around

ἀμφίπυρος ον surrounded by a blaze

ἀμφίρρυτος surrounded by sea

ἀμφίς *adv* on both sides, round about, on all sides; asunder, apart; far, remote; in two, twofold, differently; *prep with acc and dat* round about; *with gen* around; apart from, far from

ἀμφισβασίη ης ἡ ▸ **ἀμφισβήτησις**

ἀμφισ-βητέω (*also* -βατέω) ἀμφισβητήσω ἠμφεσβήτησα altercate; contradict, dispute, doubt; assert, claim

ἀμφισβητήσιμος ον **ἀμφισβήτητος** ον disputed, doubtful

ἀμφισβήτησις εως ἡ controversy, dispute, doubt

ἀμφ-ίσταμαι *mid* stand around, enclose

ἀμφίστομος ον (of a tunnel) double-mouthed; double

ἀμφι-στρατάομαι *mid* besiege, beleaguer

ἀμφιστρεφής ές turning *or* twisting to all sides

ἀμφι-τάμνω cut off all round

ἀμφι-τίθημι put round *or* on

ἀμφι-τρέμω tremble all over

ἀμφιτρής ῆτος with two openings *or* outlets

ἀμφι-τρομέω tremble for + *gen*

ἀμφίφαλος ον with double crest

ἀμφι-φοβέομαι *pass* tremble all round, flee on all parts *or* sides

ἀμφιφορεύς έως ὁ two-handled pitcher

ἀμφι-φράζομαι *mid* consider carefully

ἀμφι-χάσκω -έχανον gape round; gape for

ἀμφι-χέω pour *or* spread around *or* over; *pass* flow out; surround, embrace

ἀμφίχυτος ον poured around, thrown up around

ἀμφόδιον ου τό **ἄμφοδον** ου τό street; quarter (of town)

ἀμφορεύς έως ὁ ▸ **ἀμφιφορεύς**

ἀμφότερος ᾱ ον both, either

ἀμφοτέρωθεν *adv* from *or* on both sides

ἀμφοτέρως *adv* in either way

ἀμφοτέρωσε *adv* to both sides

ἀμφουδίς *adv* up from the ground

ἄμφω ἀμφοῖν *dual pron* both

ἄμφωτος ον two-eared, two-handled

ἀμώμητος ον **ἄμωμος** ον blameless

ἄμωμον ου τό amomum

ἀμῶς (*also* ἀμῶς) *adv* anyhow, nevertheless

ἄν *particle* denoting indefiniteness and possibility

ἄν ▸ ἐάν

ἀνά *adv* upwards, above, on high, on the top, thereon; *prep with acc* up, upwards; through, throughout, along, about; during; up to, according to, with; *with dat* on, upon

ἄνα (*for* ἀνάστηθι) up! get up!

ἀναβαθμός οῦ ὁ step, stairs

ἀνα-βαίνω *intr* go up, mount, ascend; go up the country; embark; set off; land; mount a horse; enter, appear; increase to; pass, end; *tr* go up, mount; step through, bestride; bring up; cause to ascend

ἀνα-βάλλω throw up; put back, defer, delay; *mid* put on; take upon oneself, undergo, incur; begin; lift up one's voice

ἀνάβασις εως ἡ a going up, ascent; inland expedition; ascending steps, stairs; cavalry

ἀναβάτης ου ὁ horseman

ἀναβατικός ή όν mounting swiftly

ἀνα-βιβάζω cause to go up *or* ascend; lead up; produce; *mid* cause to appear in court; take up

ἀνα-βιόω, ἀνα-βιώσκομαι *mid* return to life; call back to life

ἀνα-βλαστάνω shoot *or* blossom up again

ἀνα-βλέπω look up *or* back (upon); regain sight

ἀνάβλεψις εως ἡ looking up; recovery of sight

ἀνάβλησις εως ἡ delay

ἀνα-βοάω cry out, shout, scream, call

ἀναβολή ῆς ἡ mound; cloak; delay

ἀνα-βρῡχάομαι *mid* roar loudly

ἀνάγαιον ου τό upper apartment

ἀν-αγγέλλω report, give information (about)

ἀνα-γεννάομαι be born anew

ἀνα-γιγνώσκω know again, recognize; understand thoroughly; read, recite; persuade

ἀναγκάζω compel, force, urge, ask; persuade

ἀναγκαίη ης ἡ ▸ ἀνάγκη

ἀναγκαῖος (ᾱ) ον necessary, requisite, wanted, indispensable; inevitable, urgent, violent, compulsory; scanty; related, friendly, allied; forced

ἀναγκαστός ή όν compelled, forced

ἀνάγκη ης ἡ necessity, constraint, compulsion; fate, law of nature; means of coercion, violence, torture, confinement; need, distress

ἀνα-γνάμπτω bend back *or* round

ἄναγνος ον unclean, unholy

ἀνα-γνωρίζω recognize, acknowledge

ἀναγνώρισις εως ἡ recognition

ἀναγνωρισμός οῦ ὁ recognition; reading

ἀνάγνωσις εως ἡ reading

ἀναγόρευσις εως ἡ public proclamation

ἀν-αγορεύω proclaim publicly

ἀνάγραπτος ον written down

ἀναγραφεύς έως ὁ secretary

ἀναγραφή ῆς ἡ record, document

ἀνα-γράφω write down, record, enter; inscribe

ἀν-άγω lead *or* bring up [e.g. to a higher place, to the high sea]; lift up, raise, exalt; lead *or* bring back; *intr* set sail; retire; *mid and pass* put to sea, depart; set about a thing

ἀναγωγή ῆς ἡ departure, putting to sea

ἀνάγωγος ον uneducated, untrained

ἀναγώνιστος ον without conflict, without competing

ἀνα-δαίω light up

ἀναδασμός οῦ ὁ distribution, redistribution

ἀνα-δατέομαι divide again, redistribute

ἀνα-δείκνῡμι (*also* -ύω) reveal, make public; appoint

ἀνάδειξις εως ἡ publication; appointment

ἀνα-δέκομαι ▸ ἀναδέχομαι

ἀνάδελφος ον without brother *or* sister

ἀνα-δέρκομαι look up

ἀναδέσμη ης ἡ headband

ἀνα-δέχομαι *mid* take up, snatch up; undergo, bear, endure; promise; accept, receive

ἀνα-δέω fasten; tie round; *mid* take [a ship] in tow

ἀνα-διδάσκω teach better *or* thoroughly

ἀνα-δίδωμι produce, yield; deliver, distribute; *intr* burst out, bubble up

ἀνα-διπλόω make double

ἀνάδοτος ον given back

ἀναδῡ́ομαι rise, emerge; retire, recede, retreat; hesitate; shun, avoid doing

ἀνάεδνος ον without bridal gifts

ἀν-αείρω lift up, draw up; carry off, obtain

ἀνα-ζάω revive, return to life

ἀνα-ζεύγνῡμι harness again; start

ἀνα-ζέω boil up

ἀνα-ζητέω search; inquire after

ἀνα-ζώννῡμι gird up

ἀνα-ζωπυρέω rekindle, refresh, revive

ἀνα-θάλλω cause to sprout, renew

ἀνα-θαρρέω regain one's courage

ἀνα-θαρρῡ́νω encourage anew

ἀνάθεμα ατος τό accursed thing; curse

ἀναθεματίζω bind by a curse; swear

ἀνάθεσις εως ἡ dedication

ἀνα-θεωρέω view closely

ἀνα-θηλέω become green again

ἀνάθημα ατος τό consecrated gift, monument; delight, ornament

ἀνα-θορυβέω make a noise, applaud

ἀν-αθρέω observe closely, examine

ἀνα-θρῴσκω spring *or* jump up

ἀναίδεια ᾱς ἡ shamelessness

ἀναιδής ές shameless, reckless, impudent

ἀναίμων ον bloodless

ἀναιμωτί *adv* without bloodshed

ἀν-αίνομαι ἀνηνάμην *mid* refuse, decline; deny

ἀναίρεσις εως ἡ a lifting up, gathering; burial; destruction, murder

ἀν-αιρέω take *or* lift up; bury; give an oracle, prophesy; take away, abrogate, abolish, remove; destroy, kill; *mid* lift up for oneself; bury; accept, receive, obtain, take away; undergo, undertake

ἀναισθησίᾱ ᾱς ἡ insensibility, lack of perception

ἀν-αισθητέω lack perception

ἀναίσθητος ον unfeeling, senseless, stupid; imperceptible; painless

ἀν-αισιμόω consume, use

ἀναισίμωμα ατος τό expenditure for maintenance

ἀν-ᾱΐσσω jump up, gush forth

ἀναισχυντέω be shameless *or* impudent

ἀναισχυντίᾱ ᾱς ἡ impudence

ἀναίσχυντος ον impudent, shameless

ἀναίτιος ον guiltless, innocent

ἀνα-καθίζω *and mid* sit upright

ἀνα-καινίζω, ἀνα-καινόω renew, restore

ἀνακαίνωσις εως ἡ renewal

ἀνα-καίω kindle

ἀνα-καλέω call up, summon; call back; cry; *mid* call to assistance; summon; sound the retreat

ἀνα-καλύπτω uncover, unveil

ἀνα-κάμπτω *intr* bend back; return

ἀνάκανθος ον boneless

ἀνα-κάπτω snap up, swallow

a

ἀνά-κειμαι *mid* be offered *or* dedicated; be set up; depend on

ἀνακεῖον ου τό upper storey, upper apartment

ἀνάκειον ου τό prison

ἀνα-κεράννῡμι mix up

ἀνα-κεφαλαιόω sum up the argument

ἀνα-κηκίω spout up, gush forth

ἀνακηρύσσω proclaim

ἀνα-κινδῡνεύω rush into danger again

ἀνα-κῑνέω move *or* swing to and fro; stir up, awaken

ἀνακῑ́νησις εως ἡ excitement, commotion

ἀνα-κλαίω weep aloud, burst into tears

ἀνα-κλάω bend *or* break back

ἀνάκλησις εως ἡ invocation

ἀνα-κλῑ́νω *act tr* lean against; open; cause to recline; *pass* lie *or* lean back

ἀνα-κογχυλιάζω open and forge a seal

ἀνα-κοινόω communicate, impart; consult, take counsel (with)

ἀνακομιδή ῆς ἡ restitution

ἀνα-κομίζω carry up *or* back; bring back; *mid* carry up for oneself; recover

ἀν-ακοντίζω *intr* shoot up

ἀνα-κόπτω stop, push back

ἀνα-κουφίζω lift up; relieve

ἀνακούφισις εως ἡ + *gen* relief from

ἀνα-κρᾱ́ζω cry out, shout

ἀνα-κρεμάννῡμι hang up

ἀνα-κρῑ́νω question, examine; judge; *mid* litigate

ἀνάκρισις εως ἡ questioning, examination; preparation

ἀνάκρουσις εως ἡ a pushing back

ἀνα-κρούω thrust back; *mid* row back slowly

ἀνα-κτάομαι *mid* acquire *or* obtain again, regain

ἀνακτόριος ᾱ ον belonging to a lord *or* king

ἀνάκτορον ου τό sanctuary, temple; palace

ἀνα-κυκλέω revolve

ἀνα-κυμβαλιάζω (of chariots) fall over rattling

ἀνα-κύπτω rise out of, emerge

ἀνα-κωκῡ́ω wail aloud

ἀνακῶς *adv* carefully

ἀνακωχεύω hold back, stop, check; anchor on the high sea; preserve, retain; keep quiet

ἀνακωχή ῆς ἡ cessation, truce

ἀν-αλαλάζω raise the war-cry, cry aloud

ἀνα-λαμβάνω take *or* lift up; seize; take along with *or* upon one *or* into one's service; undergo, take in hand; take again, regain; restore, encourage; retrieve, retract; *mid* undergo, incur

ἀνα-λάμπω flame up

ἀναλγησίᾱ ᾱς ἡ lack of feeling

ἀνάλγητος ον unfeeling; painless

ἀνα-λέγω pick up, gather, collect; recount; *mid* pick up for oneself; read

ἀνα-λείχω lick up

ἀνάληψις εως ἡ a taking up, regaining, repairing; ascension

ἀνᾱλίσκω† spend, consume, use up, waste; kill

ἀνάλκεια ᾱς ἡ lack of strength, feebleness

ἄναλκις (*gen* ιδος) weak, cowardly

ἀναλογίᾱ ᾱς ἡ proportion; correspondence, analogy

ἀνα-λογίζομαι count up, calculate; consider

ἀναλογισμός οῦ ὁ reconsideration, deliberation, reasoning; ▸ **ἀναλογία**

ἀνάλογος ον answering, analogous

ἄναλος ον unsalted

ἀν-ᾱλόω ▸ **ἀναλίσκω**

ἄναλτος ον insatiable

ἀνάλυσις εως ἡ dissolution, end; retirement, death

ἀνα-λύω dissolve, detach, unloose; deliver; set out; return; die; *mid* compensate

ἀνᾱ́λωμα ατος τό **ἀνᾱ́λωσις** εως ἡ expense, cost

ἀνᾱ́λωτος ον unconquerable

ἀνα-μαιμάω rage through

ἀνα-μανθάνω inquire closely

ἀναμάξευτος ον impassable for waggons

ἀναμάρτητος ον faultless, unfailing

ἀνα-μάσσω wipe off on

ἀνα-μάχομαι renew battle; begin anew

ἀνα-μένω await; wait, stay; delay; endure

ἀνάμεσος ον in the interior

ἀνα-μετρέω measure back; measure out

ἀνάμῑγδα *adv* ▸ **ἀναμίξ**

ἀνα-μῑ́γνῡμι mix up together, intermix

ἀνα-μιμνῄσκω remind; mention; *pass* remember

ἀνα-μίμνω ▸ **ἀναμένω**

ἀναμίξ *adv* mixed up

ἀνα-μίσγω ▸ **ἀναμίνγυμι**

ἀνάμνησις εως ἡ remembrance

ἀνα-μορμῡ́ρω rush *or* foam up, roar loudly

ἀναμπλάκητος ον inevitable, unerring; without crime

ἀναμφίλογος ον **ἀναμφισβήτητος** ον undisputed, indisputable

ἀνανδρίᾱ ᾱς ἡ unmanliness, cowardice

ἄνανδρος ον unmanly, cowardly; without men

ἀνα-νέμομαι count up

ἀνα-νέομαι *mid* rise again, mount up

ἀνα-νεόω *and mid* renew

ἀνα-νεύω deny, refuse

ἀνα-νήφω become sober again

ἄναντα *adv* uphill

ἀνανταγώνιστος ον without a rival, without a struggle

ἀνάντης ες uphill, steep; difficult

ἀναντίρρητος ον indisputable

ἄναξ ἄνακτος ὁ lord, nobleman, king, prince, ruler, master

ἀνα-ξηραίνω dry up

ἀνάξιος (ᾱ) ον unworthy, not deserving; undeserved; worthless, contemptible

ἀνα-ξῡνόω ▸ **ἀνακοινόω**

ἀναξῡρίδες ων αἱ eastern trousers

ἀνα-οίγω ▸ **ἀνοίγω**

ἀνάπαλιν *adv* back again, over again in reverse

ἀνα-πάλλω swing up; *pass* spring up

ἀνάπαυλα ης ἡ **ἀνάπαυσις** εως ἡ inn; rest (from), pause

ἀναπαυ(σ)τήριος ον suitable for resting

ἀνα-παύω cause to cease *or* leave off, stop, finish; bring to rest; *mid* leave off, cease, repose; come to rest

ἀνα-πείθω persuade, seduce

ἀνα-πειράομαι *mid* try; (of soldiers) exercise, train

ἀναπείρω fix on a spit, kebab; impale

ἀνα-πεμπάζομαι *mid* think over

ἀνα-πέμπω send up *or* back

ἀνα-πετάννῡμι spread out, open

ἀνα-πέτομαι fly up *or* away

ἀνα-πηδάω jump up *or* forth

ἀνάπηρος ον maimed, crippled

ἀνα-πίμπλημι fill up, fulfil, perform; suffer; infect

ἀνα-πῑ́πτω fall back, recede, retire; lose heart; recline at table

ἀναπλάκητος ▸ **ἀναμπλάκητος**

ἀνα-πλάσσω shape, reshape, restore

ἀνα-πλέω sail up *or* back

ἀνάπλεως ων filled up, full; infected

ἀνα-πληρόω fill up, complete

ἀνάπλοος ου ὁ (*also* ἀνάπλους) a sailing upstream; landing-place

ἀνα-πλώω ▸ **ἀναπλέω**

ἀνάπνευσις εως ἡ respite (from), recovery of breath

ἀνα-πνέω breathe again, take breath; recover

ἀναπνοή ῆς ἡ breathing, recovery, rest

ἀνα-ποδίζω call *or* bring back, cross-examine

ἀνάποινος ον without ransom, gratis

ἀνα-πολέω repeat

ἀναπολόγητος ον inexcusable

ἀνα-πρᾱ́σσω exact, levy

ἀνα-πρήθω let *or* allow to burst forth

ἀνα-πτερόω set on the wing; incite, excite

ἀνα-πτύσσω unfold, develop; disclose, unveil

ἀνα-πτύω spit *or* spout up

ἀν-άπτω hang up, fasten, attach; kindle

ἀνα-πυνθάνομαι *mid* inquire, search, learn

ἀνάπυστος ον known, notorious

ἄναρθρος ον enfeebled; inarticulate

ἀναρίθμητος ον **ἀνάριθμος** ον numberless, countless; immense

ἀνᾱ́ριστος ον without breakfast

ἄναρκτος ον ungoverned, independent

ἀναρμοστέω be in disharmony

ἀναρμοστίᾱ ᾱς ἡ discord

ἀναρμοστός ή όν discordant, absurd; unprepared

ἀν-αρπάζω snatch up, draw up *or* out; sweep away, take by force; steal, destroy

ἀναρπαστός ή όν snatched *or* torn away

ἀνα-ρρήγνῡμι rend, break, tear open; tear in pieces; break forth

ἀνάρρησις εως ἡ publication

ἀνα-ρρῑπτέω, ἀναρρῑ́πτω whirl up; risk [danger], stake

ἀνα-ρροιβδέω swallow back

ἀνα-ρρώννῡμι strengthen *or* encourage again

ἀνάρσιος (ᾱ) ον incongruous; hostile; strange, monstrous

ἀν-αρτάω hang up; suspend; make dependent upon; delay; *mid* be prepared [to do]

ἀνάρτιος ον uneven, odd

ἀναρχίᾱ ᾱς ἡ anarchy

ἄναρχος ον without a leader

ἀνα-σείω shake up; stir to rebellion

ἀνα-σεύομαι *mid* spout forth

ἀνα-σκέπτομαι ▸ **ἀνασκοπέω**

ἀνα-σκευάζω pack up; transport, convey, clear away, dismantle; demolish [an argument]

ἀνα-σκολοπίζω ▸ **ἀνασταυρόω**

ἀνα-σκοπέω consider exactly

ἀνάσπαστος ον (*or* ἀνασπαστός όν) (of a door) opened; dragged along, exiled

ἀνα-σπάω draw up *or* back, tear up, open; drag away

■ **∼ λόγους** boast

ἄνασσα ης ἡ queen, lady, mistress

ἀνάσσω *and mid* rule, reign; be lord *or* master of *+ gen*

ἀν-ᾴσσω ▸ **ἀναΐσσω**

ἀνασταδόν *adv* upright, standing

ἀνάστασις εως ἡ a setting up; expulsion, evacuation, ruin; getting up; departure; resurrection

ἀνάστατος ον expelled, exiled; destroyed; rebelling

ἀνα-στατόω unsettle, upset

ἀνα-σταυρόω impale, crucify (afresh)

ἀνα-στέλλω drive *or* keep back

ἀνα-στενάζω, ἀνα-στεναχίζω, ἀνα-στενάχω, ἀνα-στένω groan aloud (over)

ἀνα-στρέφω *act tr* turn over, up *or* back; upset, throw down; lead back; *act intr* return; *mid and pass* return; wander, rove; dwell, stay; behave; rally

ἀναστροφή ῆς ἡ a turning back, return; a dwelling in; mode of life

ἀνα-στρωφάω turn to and fro

ἀνα-σῡ́ρομαι pull up one's clothes

ἀνασχετός όν tolerable

ἀνα-σχίζω rip up, slit

ἀνα-σῴζω *and mid* save; recover, restore; recall to memory

ἀνα-ταράσσω stir up, disturb

ἀνα-τάσσομαι arrange again; rehearse

ἀνᾱτεί *adv see* **ἄνατος**

ἀνα-τείνω *act tr* stretch *or* hold up, raise; extend, spread; *act intr and mid* stretch out *or* up, expand

ἀνα-τειχίζω rebuild [a wall]

ἀνατειχισμός οῦ ὁ a rebuilding

ἀνα-τέλλω *tr* raise, bring forth, produce; *intr* rise, grow, issue

ἀνα-τέμνω cut up, dissect

ἀνᾱτί *adv see* **ἄνατος**

ἀνα-τίθημι set up, consecrate, dedicate; put *or* lay on, load with; ascribe, impute, charge; put back, remove; *mid* shift, transpose, alter; retract

ἀνα-τῑμάω raise in price

ἀνα-τλῆναι *aor infin* bear, suffer

ἀνατολή ῆς ἡ sunrise, east

ἄνᾱτος ον unhurt, uninjured

ἀνα-τρέπω upset, overthrow, destroy, ruin; stir up; *mid and pass* fall down backwards; perish

ἀνα-τρέφω bring up, nourish; feed again

ἀνα-τρέχω run up *or* back, ascend, rise; sprout, shoot up

ἀνα-τρῖβω rub well

ἀνατροπή ῆς ἡ overthrow

ἄναυδος ον **ἀναύδητος** ον speechless; unutterable, unheard of

ἀνα-φαίνω cause to shine *or* flash up; show, make appear, reveal; *pass* appear, become conspicuous

ἀνα-φανδά, ἀναφανδόν *adv* openly, visibly

ἀνα-φέρω *act tr* carry, convey, bring up; offer; lift up, raise, heave; carry *or* bring back; refer to, ascribe, propose; bear, suffer; *act intr* rise, recover; give an account; *mid and pass* come to oneself, draw a long breath

ἀνα-φεύγω flee up *or* back, escape; disappear gradually

ἀνα-φλύω bubble up

ἀναφορᾱ́ ᾶς ἡ rising, ascent; way of retreat; means of repairing; repetition

ἀνα-φορέω ▸ ἀναφέρω

ἀνα-φράζομαι *mid* recognize

ἀνα-φρονέω recover one's senses

ἀνα-φῡ́ρω mix up; soil

ἀνα-φῡσάω blow out, puff up

ἀνα-φύω *act tr* let grow, bring forth; *act intr and mid* grow; sprout (again)

ἀνα-φωνέω proclaim, recite

ἀνα-χάζω *and mid* retire, recede

ἀνα-χαιτίζω throw off; upset; hold back

ἀνα-χέω pour upon; *pass* flow out, empty oneself

ἀνάχυσις εως ἡ excess, wantonness

ἀνα-χωρέω retire, retreat, withdraw; return

ἀναχώρησις εως ἡ a going back, retreat, departure; retirement, refuge, means of retreat

ἀνα-χωρίζω lead back

ἀνα-ψηφίζω cause to vote again

ἀναψῡχή ῆς ἡ a refreshing, recovery (from)

ἀνα-ψῡ́χω cool, refresh; *pass* recover

α

ἁνδάνω ἁδήσω ἕαδον + *dat* please; satisfy

ἄνδιχα *adv* asunder, in two

ἀνδραγαθίᾱ ᾱς ἡ manliness, valour, honesty

ἀνδραγαθίζομαι act bravely, behave decently

ἀνδράγρια ων τά spoil, booty

ἀνδρακάς *adv* man by man, one by one

ἀνδραποδίζω kidnap, enslave

ἀνδραποδισμός οῦ ὁ kidnapping, enslavement

ἀνδραποδιστής οῦ ὁ kidnapper, enslaver

ἀνδράποδον ου τό slave

ἀνδραποδώδης ες slavish; servile, base

ἀνδραχθής ές weighing a man down, as much as a man can carry

ἀνδρείᾱ ᾱς ἡ manliness, valour, courage

ἀνδρεῖος ᾱ ον of a man; manly, valiant, brave

ἀνδρειότης ητος ἡ ▸ **ἀνδρεία**

ἀνδρεϊφόντης ου ὁ man-slaying

ἀνδρεών ῶνος ὁ ▸ **ἀνδρών**

ἀνδρηΐη ης ἡ ▸ **ἀνδρεία**

ἀνδρήιος ᾱ ον ▸ **ἀνδρεῖος**

ἀνδρηλατέω exile, banish

ἀνδριαντο-ποιέω make statues

ἀνδριαντοποιός οῦ ὁ sculptor

ἀνδριᾱ́ς άντος ὁ statue

ἀνδρίζομαι behave like a man

ἀνδρικός ή όν ▸ **ἀνδρεῖος**

ἀνδρόγυνος ου ὁ man-woman, hermaphrodite, eunuch, effeminate man

ἀνδρόκμητος ον made by man, artefact

ἀνδροκτασίᾱ ᾱς ἡ slaughter of men

ἀνδροκτόνος ον man-slaying, husband-slaying

ἀνδρόμεος ᾱ ον human

ἀνδρομήκης ες of a man's height

ἀνδρόομαι *pass* become a man

ἀνδρόσφιγξ ιγγος ὁ a man-sphinx

ἀνδροτής ῆτος ἡ ▸ **ἀνδρεία**

ἀνδροφάγος ον eating men

ἀνδροφθόρος ον man-destroying

ἀνδρόφθορος ον of a slain man

ἀνδροφόνος ον man-killing

ἀνδρώδης ες ▸ **ἀνδρεῖος**

ἀνδρών ῶνος ὁ the men's quarters in a house

ἀνδύομαι ▸ **ἀναδύομαι**

ἀν-εγείρω awake, rouse; *pass* be roused; wake up

ἀνέγκλητος ον free from reproach

ἀνέδην *adv* let loose; freely; simply, without more ado; sluggishly

ἀνέεδνος ▸ **ἀνάεδνος**

ἀνεθέλητος ον unwished for

ἀν-ειλέω, ἀν-είλω roll up together

ἀν-ειμένος η ον let loose, uncontrolled, without restraint

ἄν-ειμι go up, rise; return

ἀνείμων ον without clothing

ἀν-ειπεῖν aor infin proclaim, announce

ἀν-είργω keep back

ἀν-είρομαι inquire from *or* about, ask

ἀν-ειρύω ▸ **ἀνερύω**

ἀν-είρω fasten *or* tie to

ἀν-ειρωτάω ▸ **ἀνερωτάω**

ἀνέκαθεν *adv* from above; (of time) from the first

ἀνέκβατος ον without outlet

ἀνεκδιήγητος ον indescribable

ἀνέκδοτος ον unmarried; unpublished

ἀνεκλάλητος ον unspeakable

ἀνέκλειπτος ον inexhaustible

ἀνεκ-πίμπλημι fill up *or* again

ἀνέκπληκτος ον intrepid, undaunted

ἀνεκτός όν **ἀνεκτέος** ᾱ ον bearable

ἀνέλεγκτος ον not examined; irrefutable

ἀνελεήμων ον **ἀνέλεος** ον merciless, without pity

ἀνελευθερίᾱ ᾱς ἡ slavish mind, meanness, stinginess

ἀνελεύθερος ον ignoble, servile, stingy

ἀν-ελίσσω unroll, open

ἀν-έλκω, ἀν-ελκύω draw up, back *or* out

ἀνέλπιστος ον unhoped for; hopeless, despairing

ἀνεμέσητος ον blameless, free from reproach

ἀνεμίζω drive with the wind

ἀνεμόεις εσσα εν windy; swift as the wind

ἄνεμος ου ὁ wind, storm

ἀνεμοσκεπής ές sheltering from the wind

ἀνεμοτρεφής ές fed by the wind

ἀνεμώλιος ον windy; good-for-nothing

ἀνένδεκτος ον inadmissible

ἀνεξέλεγκτος ον ▸ **ἀνέλεγκτος**

ἀνεξερεύνητος ον inscrutable

ἀνεξέταστος ον not examined; not scrutinized; uninquiring

ἀνεξεύρετος ον not to be found out, indiscoverable

ἀνεξίκακος ον forbearing; long-suffering

ἀνεξιχνίαστος ον untraceable, inscrutable

ἀνεπαίσχυντος ον having no cause for shame

ἀνεπαχθής ές not giving trouble, without constraint

ἀνεπιβούλευτον ου τό the absence of plots *or* intrigues, harmlessness

ἀνεπιδεής ές not needy

ἀνεπιεικής ές unreasonable, unfair

ἀνεπίκλητος ον ▸ **ἀνέγκλητος**

ἀνεπίληπτος ον unattacked, not open to attack; blameless

ἀνεπίσκεπτος ον unnoticed, not examined; inconsiderate

ἀνεπιστημοσύνη ης ἡ ignorance

ἀνεπιστήμων ον ignorant, unskilled

ἀνεπίτακτος ον not subject to control

ἀνεπιτήδειος ον unfit; harmful; unfriendly; adverse

ἀνεπιτῑ́μητος ον not to be criticised

ἀνεπίφθονος ον free from reproach

ἀν-έραμαι *pass* fall in love again with + *gen*

ἀν-ερεθίζω excite, provoke; *pass* be in a state of excitement

ἀν-ερείπομαι *mid* snatch up and carry off

ἀν-ερευνάω examine closely, investigate

ἀν-έρομαι ▸ **ἀνείρομαι**

ἀν-ερύω (of sails *and* ships) haul up

ἀν-έρχομαι go up, rise; come; come back, return, come home

ἀν-ερωτάω question, ask about

ἄνεσις εως ἡ remission; relaxation

ἀνέστιος ον homeless

ἀν-ετάζω search, inquire thoroughly (into)

ἄνευ *prep with gen* without; away from , far from; besides

ἄνευθεν *adv* far away, distant; ▸ **ἄνευ**

ἀνεύθετος ον inconvenient

ἀνεύθῡνος ον not responsible; guiltless

ἀν-ευρίσκω discover

ἀν-ευφημέω cry aloud with joy

ἀνέφελος ον cloudless; uncovered

ἀνεχέγγυος ον not giving surety

ἀν-έχω *act tr* hold *or* lift up; support, exalt, honour; restrain, stop; *act intr* project, reach; emerge, come up; stop, stay, persist; *mid* hold up; rise; stand upright; keep one's ground; hold out; bear, admit; keep one's temper

ἀνεψιᾱ́ ᾶς ἡ female cousin

ἀνεψιός ου ὁ male cousin

ἄνεω, ἄνεῳ *adv* in silence

ἀν-ηβάω grow young again

ἀν-ηγέομαι *mid* relate

ἄνηθον ου τό anise, dill

ἀνήκεστος ον incurable, irreparable; inexorable; immoderate

ἀνήκοος ον not hearing; not knowing

ἀνηκουστέω + *gen* not listen to, disobey

ἀν-ήκω have come; reach to; rest *or* depend on; be fit and proper; belong, appertain

ἀνήλιος ον sunless

ἀνήμελκτος ον unmilked

ἀνήμερος ον untamed, wild

ἀνήνεμος ον without wind, calm

ἀνήνοθα *pf used like an aor* gushed forth, mounted up

ἀνήνυ(σ)τος ον unfeasible; unsuccessful, endless

ἀνήνωρ ορ unmanly

ἀνήρ ἀνδρός ὁ man, male; husband; warrior, hero; man (as opposed to gods and beasts)

ἀνήριθμος ον ▸ **ἀνάριθμος**

ἀνήροτος ον unploughed, untilled

ἄνησον ▸ **ἄνηθον**

ἀνθ-αιρέομαι *mid* choose something *acc* instead of something *gen*

ἀνθ-αμιλλάομαι *pass* contend, rival

ἀνθ-άπτομαι + *gen* take hold of, seize in turns; grapple with, engage in; reach

ἀνθ-έλκω draw to the other side

ἀνθέμιον ου τό flower

ἀνθεμόεις (εσσα) εν flowery

ἀνθερεών ῶνος ὁ chin

ἀνθέριξ ικος ὁ ear of corn; stalk of the asphodel

ἀνθέω bloom, blossom, flourish; shine

ἀνθήλιος ον ▸ **ἀντήλιος**

ἀνθηρός ᾱ́ όν blooming, fresh; brightly-coloured; in full force

ἀνθ-ησσάομαι + *dat* give way in turn to

ἀνθίζω cover with flowers

ἄνθινος η ον flowery, fresh; brightly-coloured

ἀνθ-ίστημι *act tr* set against, oppose; *act intr and pass* oppose oneself to + *dat*, resist

ἀνθ-ομολογέομαι *mid* make a mutual agreement; confess freely and openly; return thanks

ἀνθ-οπλίζομαι + *dat* arm oneself against

ἀνθ-ορμέω + *dat* lie at anchor opposite

ἄνθος ους τό flower, blossom

ἀνθοσμίᾱς ου sweet-scented; (of wine) with a fine 'bouquet'

ἀνθρακιᾱ́ ᾶς ἡ burning charcoal

ἄνθραξ ακος ὁ coal

ἀνθρωπάρεσκος ον man-pleaser, time-serving

ἀνθρώπειος ᾱ ον **ἀνθρώπινος** η ον human

ἀνθρώπιον ου τό manikin; low fellow

ἀνθρωποειδής ές in the shape of a man

ἀνθρωποκτόνος ον man-slaying

ἄνθρωπος ου ὁ human being, man (as opposed to gods and beasts); anyone; husband; inhabitant; slave

■ ἡ **ἄνθρωπος** woman, concubine, female slave

ἀνθρωπο-φαγέω eat men

ἀνθρωποφυής ές of human species

ἀνθυπ-άγω accuse in turn

ἀνθυπατεύω be proconsul

ἀνθύπατος ου ὁ proconsul

ἀνθυπ-οπτεύομαι *pass* be suspected in turn

ἀνῑ́ᾱ ᾱς ἡ trouble, annoyance; pain, grief

ἀνῑάζω *aor* ἠνῑ́ασα annoy, tease; be distressed

ἀνῑάομαι *mid* heal again

ἀνιᾱρός ᾱ́ όν (*also* ἀνῑᾱρός) distressing, annoying, painful; distressed

ἀνίᾱτος ον incurable

ἀνιάω (*also* ἀνῑάω) distress, grieve; molest, annoy

ἀνῑ́δρῡτος ον restless, unsteady

ἀνῑδρωτῑ́ *adv* without sweat, lazily

ἀνίερος ον unholy, wicked

ἀν-ῑ́ημι *act tr* send up; raise, produce; let loose, relax, dismiss, detach, neglect, omit; incite; admit, permit, remit; *act intr* slacken, cease; *pass* be uncontrolled; be exposed, sacrificed *or* abandoned

ἀνῑηρός ᾱ́ όν ▸ **ἀνιαρός**

ἀνῑ́κητος ον unconquered; invincible

ἀνῑ́λεως ων unmerciful

ἀν-ιμάω pull up

ἄνιππος ον unmounted; unsuited to horses

ἀνιπτόπους (*gen* ποδος) with unwashed feet

ἄνιπτος ον unwashed

ἄνισος ον (*also* ἄνῑσος) unequal

ἀνισότης ητος ἡ inequality

ἀν-ισόω make equal, equalize

ἀν-ίστημι *act tr* set up, erect, build; raise, rouse, stir up; drive away, dislodge; raise from the dead; excite; *act intr and pass* be driven away; rise, get up; come forth, appear; start; recover oneself

ἀν-ιστορέω ask (about), investigate

ἀν-ίσχω ▸ **ἀνέχω**

ἀνίσωσις εως ἡ equalization; (in mathematics) inequality

ἀν-ιχνεύω trace back

ἀν-νέομαι ▸ **ἀνανέομαι**

ἀννώνη ης ἡ corn supply

ἄνοδος[1] ου ἡ way up; march up

ἄνοδος[2] ον impassable

ἀνοήμων ον unwise

ἀνόητος ον foolish, silly; inconceivable

ἄνοια ᾱς ἡ folly, lack of understanding

ἀν-οίγνῡμι, ἀν-οίγω open, uncover, disclose

ἀν-οιδέω swell up

ἀν-οικίζομαι settle up-country, migrate inland, lie inland

ἀν-οικοδομέω rebuild, build

ἄνοικος ον houseless, homeless

ἄνοικτος ον pitiless; unpitied

ἀνοιμωκτί *adv* without wailing, with impunity

ἄνοιξις εως ἡ an opening

ἀνοιστέος ᾱ ον to be reported

ἀνοιστός ή όν reported; pending

ἀνοκωχεύω, ἀνοκωχή *see* **ἀνακ-**

ἀνόλβιος ον **ἄνολβος** ον unfortunate, miserable

ἀνόλεθρος ον unhurt

ἀνολκή ῆς ἡ a drawing up

ἀν-ολολύζω cry out, scream, shout

ἀν-ολοφῡ́ρομαι *mid* break into loud wailing

ἄνομβρος ον without rain

ἀνομέω act contrary to the law

ἀνομίᾱ ᾱς ἡ lawlessness

ἀνόμματος ον eyeless, sightless

ἀνόμοιος ον unequal, unlike

ἀνομοιότης ητος ἡ inequality, dissimilarity

ἀν-ομολογέω *and mid* agree (again)

ἀνομολογούμενος η ον inconsistent, contradictory

ἄνομος ον lawless, wicked; pagan

ἀνόνητος ον useless

ἄνοος ον (*also contracted* ἄνους ουν) foolish

ἀνοπαῖα *adv* through the smoke vent, up into the air, unnoticed

ἄνοπλος ον unarmed

a

ἀν-ορθόω set up, set right; rebuild, restore

ἄνορμος ον harbourless

ἀν-όρνυμαι *mid* rise

ἀν-ορούω jump, go swiftly up

ἀνόσιος ον unholy, wicked

ἀνοσιότης ητος ἡ unholiness, profaneness

ἄνοσος ον free from disease

ἀνόστιμος ον **ἄνοστος** ον not returning

ἀνούτατος ον unwounded
■ ἀνουτητί *adv*

ἀνοχή ῆς ἡ armistice, truce; forebearance

ἄντα *adv and prep with gen* opposite, over against; face to face; straight on; against, before

ἀντ-αγοράζω buy in return

ἀντ-αγωνίζομαι *mid* + *dat* fight *or* struggle against; contend with

ἀνταγωνιστής οῦ ὁ adversary, rival

ἀντ-αδικέω wrong in return

ἀνταῖος ᾱ ον opposed; in front

ἀντ-αίρω (*also* ἀντ-αείρω) *and mid* lift in defence; withstand

ἀντ-αιτέω ask in return

ἀντακαῖος ου ὁ sturgeon

ἀντ-ακούω hear in turn

ἀντ-αλλάσσω exchange; give *or* take in exchange

ἀντ-αμείβομαι *mid* answer, reply; ▸ **ἀνταλλάσσω**

ἀντ-αμῡ́νομαι *mid* defend *or* revenge oneself, resist, pay back

ἀντανα-βιβάζω bring up *or* cause to go up against

ἀνταν-άγω *act tr* lead up against, take up to the high sea; *act int, mid and pass* sail to meet

ἀνταν-αιρέω neutralize, cancel

ἀντανα-μένω wait in turn

ἀντανα-πίμπλημι, ἀντανα-πληρόω fill *or* complete in turn

ἀντάν-ειμι + *dat* go up against

ἀνταν-ίσταμαι *mid* + *dat* rise up against

ἀντάξιος ᾱ ον worth just as much as + *gen*; equivalent

ἀντ-αξιόω claim in return

ἀνταπ-αιτέω demand in return

ἀνταπο-δίδωμι give back, pay back; correspond

ἀνταπόδοσις εως ἡ **ἀνταπόδομα** ατος τό a giving back in turn, requital

ἀνταπο-κρῑ́νομαι *mid* litigate; argue against

ἀνταπο-κτείνω kill in return

ἀνταπ-όλλῡμι destroy in return

ἀνταπο-φαίνω adduce as counter-evidence

ἀντ-αρκέω + *dat* be a match for; hold out (against)

ἀντ-ασπάζομαι *mid* welcome in return; receive kindly

ἀντ-ατῑμάζω defame in return

ἀντ-αυδάω speak against; answer

ἀντάω ▸ **ἀντιάω**

ἀντ-ειπεῖν *see* **ἀντιλέγω**

ἀντ-είρομαι ▸ **ἀντέρομαι**

ἀντεισ-άγω import in return

ἀντεκ-πέμπω send out in return

ἀντεκ-πλέω + *dat* sail out against

ἀντεκ-τρέχω sally out against

ἀντ-ελπίζω hope in return

ἀντεμ-βάλλω *intr* make an inroad in turn, attack in turn

ἀντεμ-βιβάζω change the crew

ἀντεμ-πίπλημι fill in turn

ἀντεμ-πίπρημι set on fire in revenge

ἀντέξ-ειμι, ἀντεξ-έρχομαι march out against

ἀντεξόρμησις εως ἡ a sailing against

ἀντεπ-άγω lead to attack in return; advance against

ἀντεπαν-άγομαι sail out against

ἀντέπ-ειμι, ἀντεπέξ-ειμι, ἀντεπεξ-ελαύνω, ἀντεπεξ-έρχομαι ▸ ἀντέξειμι

ἀντεπεξ-άγω go out against; extend the line of battle in the same way

ἀντεπι-βουλεύω think of countermeasures

ἀντεπι-θῡμέω desire (something *gen*) in return

ἀντεπι-κουρέω + *dat* help in return

ἀντεπι-μελέομαι *pass* make counter-preparations

ἀντεπι-τάσσω + *dat* order in turn

ἀντεπι-τειχίζομαι *mid* fortify in retaliation

ἀντεπι-τίθημι entrust [a letter] in answer

ἀντεραστής οῦ ὁ rival in love

ἀντ-ερείδω stand firm, resist pressure; place something *acc* firmly against *dat*

ἀντ-ερεῖν *see* ἀντιλέγω

ἀντ-έρομαι ask in return

ἀντέρως ωτος ὁ requited love

ἀντ-ευεργετέω, ἀντευ-ποιέω return a kindness

ἀντ-έχω hold against; keep off; bear, sustain; suffice; keep one's ground; *mid* object in defence; cling to; aim at; be attached to; take care of; resist

ἄντη ης ἡ supplication

ἀντήλιος ον facing the sun; eastern

ἄντην *adv* opposite, over against, face to face; in front, openly

ἀντήρης ες opposite, adverse

ἀντηρίς ίδος ἡ supporting beam

ἄντηστις εως ἡ a meeting

ἀντί *prep with gen* opposite, over against, before; in return for, for the sake of, instead of, for

ἀντιάζω ▸ ἀντιάω

ἀντιάνειρα ας ἡ a match for men

ἀντιάω go *or* advance to meet; approach, meet; attack; accept, partake of; experience; entreat; *mid* partake of

ἀντι-βαίνω + *dat* go against, resist; set one's foot against

ἀντι-βάλλω throw in turn; exchange; compare

ἀντίβιος ᾱ ον hostile, using force ■ **ἀντιβίην** *adv* with force, in battle

ἀντι-βλέπω + *dat* look straight at

ἀντι-βοηθέω + *dat* assist in turn; assist the adversary

ἀντι-βολέω go to meet, approach, meet + *dat*; partake of, share in + *gen*; entreat + *acc*

ἀντιβόλησις εως ἡ **ἀντιβολίᾱ** ᾱς ἡ entreaty

ἀντι-γενεηλογέω rival in ancestry

ἀντιγραφή ῆς ἡ counter-writ, accusatory libel, protest, reply in writing; transcribing, transcript

ἀντίγραφον ου τό copy

ἀντι-γράφω write in answer; remonstrate, protest

ἀντι-δάκνω bite in return

ἀντι-δέομαι *pass* beg in turn

ἀντιδια-τίθεμαι offer resistance

ἀντι-δίδωμι give in return, give back, repay, requite; atone for; offer exchange of property

ἀντι-δικέω be at law, litigate

ἀντίδικος ου ὁ opponent, adversary

ἀντίδοσις εως ἡ exchange of property; (at Athens) exchange of property as the result of a dispute about a liturgy

ἀντι-δράω requite

ἀντι-δωρέομαι *mid* present with in return

ἀντίθεος η ον godlike

ἀντι-θεραπεύω honour in return

ἀντίθεσις εως ἡ opposition, the contrary

ἀντι-θέω run against; compete in a race

ἀντίθυρον ου τό vestibule, floor

ἀντικάθ-ημαι sit over against

ἀντικαθ-ίζομαι be seated over against

α

ἀντικαθ-ίστημι *act tr* oppose, place in lieu of; encourage; *act intr and pass* resist, be opposed; be placed in lieu of

ἀντι-κακουργέω injure in turn

ἀντι-καλέω invite in turn

ἀντικατ-αλλάσσομαι *mid* exchange for

ἀντί-κειμαι be opposed

ἀντι-κελεύω command in turn

ἀντι-κλαίω weep in turn

ἀντικνήμιον ου τό shin

ἀντι-κόπτω, ἀντι-κρούω resist, struggle against

ἀντικρῡ́, ἄντικρυς *adv* over against, against, face to face; straight on; outright, thoroughly, downright

ἀντι-κῡ́ρω + *dat* meet, fall in with

ἀντιλαβή ῆς ἡ handle; weak part

ἀντι-λαμβάνω take *or* receive in turn *or* in return; *mid* take hold of, lay claim to, seize, take care of; take part with; hold fast

ἀντι-λέγω speak against, deny, dispute; resist; reply

ἀντίλεκτος ον disputed, controverted

ἀντίληψις εως ἡ a receiving in return; claim; objection; falling sick, infection; defence

ἀντι-λογέω ▸ ἀντιλέγω

ἀντιλογίᾱ ᾱς ἡ contradiction, controversy; lawsuit; contention, enmity

ἀντι-λογίζομαι *mid* count up *or* calculate on the other hand

ἀντιλογικός ή όν controversial, sophistical

ἀντι-λοιδορέω abuse in turn

ἀντίλυρος ον lyre-like

ἀντίλυτρον ου τό ransom

ἀντι-μάχομαι *mid* fight against

ἀντι-μέλλω await in turn

ἀντι-μέμφομαι *mid* blame in turn

ἀντι-μετρέω measure out again

ἀντιμέτωπος ον front to front

ἀντι-μηχανάομαι *mid* devise counter-measures

ἀντι-μῑ́μησις εως ἡ close imitation of

ἀντι-μισθίᾱ ᾱς ἡ requital, recompense

ἀντι-ναυπηγέω build ships against; take preventive measures in shipbuilding

ἀντίξοος ον hostile, opposed

ἀντιόομαι *pass* + *dat* resist

ἀντίος ᾱ ον opposite, confronting; opposed, contrary

ἀντιο-στατέω (of a wind) be opposed

ἀντιόω ▸ ἀντιάω

ἀντίπαλος ον wrestling against; rival, contrary, adversary; counterpoising, equivalent, counter-balanced

ἀντιπαρα-βάλλω compare, confront

ἀντιπαρ-αγγέλλω command in turn

ἀντιπαρα-θέω outflank

ἀντιπαρα-καλέω summon in turn; encourage in turn

ἀντιπαρα-κελεύομαι *mid* encourage in turn

ἀντιπαρα-λῡπέω annoy in turn

ἀντιπαρα-πλέω sail along on the other side

ἀντιπαρα-σκευάζομαι *mid* make counter-preparations

ἀντιπαρασκευή ῆς ἡ counter-preparation

ἀντιπαρα-τάσσω draw out in array against

ἀντιπαρα-τίθημι oppose, compare

ἀντιπάρ-ειμι march so as to meet

ἀντιπαρεξ-άγω lead to battle against

ἀντιπαρ-έρχομαι ▸ ἀντιπάρειμι

ἀντιπαρ-έχω offer in turn

ἀντι-πάσχω suffer in turn

ἀντι-παταγέω outclatter

ἀντι-πέμπω send against, in return, back *or* in supply

ἀντιπέραια ων τά the opposite coast

ἀντιπέρᾱν, ἀντιπέρᾱς *adv + gen* over against, opposite

ἀντίπετρος ον hard as stone, rocky

ἀντι-πῑ́πτω happen differently; be adverse; resist + *dat*

ἀντι-πλέω sail against

ἀντιπλήξ (*gen* ῆγος) wave-beaten

ἀντι-πληρόω man against *or* in turn; fill up with new members

ἀντι-ποθέω long for in turn

ἀντι-ποιέω do in return; retaliate; *mid* claim; rival; contend

ἀντίποινος ον paying back for, atoning for

ἀντι-πολεμέω + *dat* make war against

ἀντιπόλεμος ου ὁ enemy

ἀντι-πολιορκέω besiege in turn

ἀντι-πορεύομαι *pass* march against

ἀντίπορος ον on the opposite coast; opposite to

ἀντι-πρᾱ́σσω (*also* ἀντιπρήσσω) counteract

ἀντι-πρεσβεύομαι *mid* send ambassadors in turn

ἀντιπρό-ειμι, ἀντιπρόσ-ειμι advance against

ἀντιπροσ-ερρήθην *from* **ἀντιπροσαγορεύω** greet in turn

ἀντιπρόσωπος ον face to face

ἀντιπρο-τείνω stretch out in turn

ἀντίπρωρος prow to prow; face to face

ἀντίπυλος ον with opposite doors

ἀντίρροπος ον counterpoising, compensating for

ἀντισήκωσις εως ἡ equilibrium

ἀντι-ισόομαι *pass* be on an equal footing

ἀντίσπαστος ον spasmodic

ἀντίσταθμος ον equal in weight

ἀντι-στασιάζω form an adverse party

ἀντιστασιώτης ου ὁ political adversary

ἀντι-στατέω + *dat* resist

ἀντι-στοιχέω stand opposite in rows *or* pairs

ἀντι-στρατεύομαι *mid* + *dat* make war against

ἀντιστράτηγος ου ὁ general of the enemy

ἀντι-στρατοπεδεύομαι *mid* + *dat* encamp over against

ἀντίστροφος ον corresponding

ἀντ-ισχῡρίζομαι *mid* affirm in turn

ἀντ-ίσχω ▸ **ἀντέχω**

ἀντίταξις εως ἡ opposite line of battle

ἀντι-τάσσω draw up in battle against

ἀντι-τείνω resist, oppose

ἀντιτείχισμα ατος τό counter-fortification

ἀντι-τεχνάομαι *mid* form a counter-scheme

ἀντιτέχνησις εως ἡ counter-manoeuvring

ἀντι-τίθημι set against, oppose, compare; compensate, give for

ἀντι-τῑμάω honour in return; *mid* make a counterproposal of a fine

ἀντι-τῑμωρέομαι *mid* revenge oneself in turn

ἀντι-τίνω atone for, suffer punishment for

ἀντι-τολμάω act boldly in turn

ἀντι-τοξεύω shoot arrows in return

ἀντι-τορέω + *gen* bore through

ἄντιτος ον paid back, avenged

ἀντι-τυγχάνω + *gen* get in return

ἀντίτυπος ον repelled; echoing; repellent; stubborn

▪ **τὸ ἀντίτυπον** exact representation, antitype

ἀντι-τύπτω beat in turn

ἀντι-φερίζω + *dat* think oneself equal to

ἀντι-φέρω set against, oppose; *mid* resist, cope with

ἀντί-φημι contradict

ἀντι-φιλέω love in return

ἀντίφονος ον murdering in return

ἀντιφυλακή ῆς ἡ mutual caution

ἀντι-φυλάττομαι *mid* be on one's guard against

ἀντι-φωνέω reply, gainsay

ἀντι-χαίρω be glad in turn

ἀντι-χαρίζομαι *mid* + *dat* show kindness in turn

ἀντι-χειροτονέω vote against

ἀντι-χράω be sufficient

ἀντίχριστος ου ὁ Antichrist

ἀντλέω draw water; empty

ἄντλημα ατος τό bucket

ἀντλίᾱ ᾱς ἡ **ἄντλος** ου ὁ bilge-water; bottom of a ship

ἀντ-οικτίζω pity in turn

ἀντολή ▸ **ἀνατολή**

ἀντ-όμνῡμι swear in turn

ἀντ-ονομάζω name instead; call by a new name

ἀντ-ορύσσω dig a countermine

ἀντ-οφθαλμέω + *dat* meet face to face

ἀν-τρέπω ▸ **ἀνατρέπω**

ἄντρον ου τό cave, cavern

ἀντρώδης ες full of caves

ἄντυξ υγος ὁ circle, rim, edge; rail of a chariot

ἀντυπο-κρῖνομαι *mid* answer in return

ἀντυπ-ουργέω return kindness

ἀντωμοσίᾱ ᾱς ἡ plaintiff's oath; bill of indictment

ἀντ-ωνέομαι *mid* buy instead; outbid

ἀντ-ωφελέω help in return

ἀνυδρίᾱ ᾱς ἡ want of water, drought

ἄνυδρος ον without water, dry
■ **ἡ ἄνυδρος** desert

ἀνυμέναιος ον without the wedding song, unmarried

ἄνῡμι ▸ **ἀνύω**

ἀνύμφευτος ον **ἄνυμφος** ον unmarried; from an ill-starred marriage

ἀνυπέρβλητος ον insurpassable, insuperable

ἀνυπόδητος ον unshod, barefoot

ἀνυπόκριτος ον without pretence

ἀνύποπτος ον unsuspected

ἀνυπόστατος ον irresistible; without sure foundation

ἀνυπότακτος ον not subjected; disobedient, unruly

ἄνυσις εως ἡ achievement, success

ἀνυστός ή όν needing *or* able to be accomplished; feasible

ἀνύτω (*also* ἁνύτω) ▸ **ἀνύω**

ἀνυφ-αίνω weave anew

ἀνύω (*also* ἁνύω) accomplish, complete, achieve, perform, effect; travel over, advance; consume, finish

ἄνω[1] ▸ **ἀνύω**

ἄνω[2] *adv* up, upwards, on high, above,; up country, northwards; beyond
■ **ἀνωτέρω** *comp* higher up
■ **ἀνωτάτω** *sup* highest up

ἄνωγα *pf with pres sense* (*also* ἀνώγω) *pres* command, order, advise

ἀνώγαιον ου τό **ἀνώγεων** ω τό upper storey *or* apartment; granary; dining room

ἀνώδυνος ον free from pain, painless; easing pain

ἄνωθεν *adv* from on high, from above; above; downward; from the beginning; anew

ἀν-ωθέω push up *or* back; *mid* repel, repulse

ἀνώϊστος ον unexpected
■ **ἀνωϊστί** *adv*

ἀνώλεθρος ον indestructible

ἀνωμαλίᾱ ᾱς ἡ unevenness, inequality

ἀνώμαλος ον uneven, unequal

ἀνωμοτί *adv* without oath

ἀνωρίᾱ ᾱς ἡ wrong *or* unseasonable time

ἄνωρος ον untimely

ἀνωτερικός ή όν situated higher up, inland

ἀνωφελής ές **ἀνωφέλητος** ον useless, hurtful

ἄξενος ον inhospitable

ἄξεστος ον unpolished

ἀξίᾱ ᾱς ἡ worth, value, price; dignity, honour; merit, desert; someone's due

ἀξιαφήγητος ον worth relating

ἀξιέπαινος ον praiseworthy

ἀξῑ́νη ης ἡ axe, hatchet

ἀξιοβίωτος ον worth living

ἀξιοθαύμαστος ον admirable

ἀξιοθέᾱτος ον worth seeing

ἀξιόλογος ον worth naming; important

ἀξιόμαχος a match for (someone else) in battle

ἀξιομνημόνευτος ον memorable, worth mentioning

ἀξιόνῑκος ον deserving victory

ἀξιόπιστος ον trustworthy

ἄξιος ᾱ ον worth, equivalent, compensating; worthy, precious; due, deserved; right and proper

ἀξιόσκεπτος ον worthy of notice

ἀξιοστράτηγος ον worthy of being general

ἀξιοτέκμαρτος ον credible

ἀξιόχρεως ων considerable; sufficient; authentic; proper, convenient, worthy

ἀξιόω estimate; think worthy, esteem; request, claim; suppose, take for true

ἀξίωμα ατος τό **ἀξίωσις** εως ἡ valuation, estimation; dignity, rank, credit; consideration; importance; request, will; opinion

ἄξυλος ον not cleared of wood; scantily wooded

ἄξων ονος ὁ axle
■ **οἱ ἄξονες** the wooden tablets on which Solon's laws were written

ἀοιδή ῆς ἡ song, myth, legend

ἀοιδάω sing

ἀοίδιμος ον celebrated in song

ἀοιδός οῦ ὁ/ἡ singer, poet; enchanter

ἀοίκητος ον uninhabited

ἄοικος ον homeless, poor; uninhabitable

ἄοινος ον without wine, drinking no wine

ἄοκνος ον unhesitating; eager, willing

ἀολλής ές all together, in crowds

ἀολλίζω assemble

ἄοπλος ον unarmed, without heavy armour

ἄορ ἄορος τό sword

ἀόρᾱτος ον unseen, invisible; not having seen

ἀόριστος ον undefined

ἀορτήρ ῆρος ὁ baldrick (strap hanging from a sword-belt), shoulder-belt

ἀοσσητήρ ῆρος ὁ helper, protector

ἄουτος ον unwounded

ἀοχλησίᾱ ᾱς ἡ calm

ἀπαγγελίᾱ ᾱς ἡ report, narrative, recital

ἀπαγγέλλω report, announce, relate, declare; praise

ἀπαγής ές not firm *or* stiff

ἀπαγῑνέω carry off; pay

ἀπ-αγορεύω forbid, deny, dissuade; fail, fall short; be worn out; bid farewell to + *dat*

ἀπ-αγριόομαι *mid* become wild *or* savage

ἀπ-άγχω strangle; *mid* hang oneself

ἀπ-άγω lead *or* carry on *or* away; remove; march off, go away; lead up, back *or* home; *mid* take with one

ἀπαγωγή ῆς ἡ a leading off, taking home; payment; arrest and bringing before the magistrates of a person caught in the act

ἀπ-αδεῖν *see* **ἀφανδάνω**

ἀπ-ᾴδω sing out of tune

ἀπᾱείρω ▸ **ἀπαίρω**

ἀπ-αθανατίζω make immortal

ἀπαθής ές without pain, not suffering; uninjured; unfeeling; unaccustomed

ἀπαιδευσίᾱ ᾱς ἡ want of education, boorishness

ἀπαίδευτος ον uneducated, boorish

ἀπαιδίᾱ ᾱς ἡ childlessness

ἀπ-αίνυμαι take from, withdraw

ἀπ-αίρω *act tr* lift away, take *or* snatch away; cause to set out; *act intr* start, march *or* sail away; *mid* go away

ἄπαις (*gen* ἄπαιδος) childless

ἀπ-αΐσσω ▸ **ἀπᾴσσω**

ἀπ-αισχῡ́νομαι refuse through shame

ἀπ-αιτέω, ἀπ-αιτίζω demand back, reclaim

ἀπαίτησις εως ἡ reclamation

ἀπ-ακρῑβόω work exactly

ἀπάλαμνος ον awkward, wavering, inactive, helpless

ἀπ-αλγέω feel no more pain at; forget

ἀπ-αλείφω wipe off, expunge

ἀπ-αλέξω keep off; defend from; *mid* defend oneself

ἀπ-άλθομαι be thoroughly cured

ἀπαλλαγή ῆς ἡ separation; retreat; deliverance

ἀπαλλαξείω wish for deliverance

ἀπάλλαξις εως ἡ ▸ **ἀπαλλαγή**

ἀπ-αλλάσσω *act tr* set free, release, dismiss, remove, separate; *act intr* get off, get clear; *pass* go away, depart; be released

ἀπ-αλλοτριόω estrange, alienate

ἀπ-αλοιάω thresh out; crush

ἁπαλός ή όν soft, tender, delicate

ἁπαλότης ητος ἡ softness, tenderness; effeminacy

ἁπαλοτρεφής ές well-fed

ἀπ-αμάω cut off, mow

ἀπ-αμβλῡ́νω blunt, weaken

ἀπ-αμβροτεῖν *see* **ἀφαμαρτάνω**

ἀπ-αμείβομαι answer

ἀπ-αμελέω neglect utterly *or* altogether

ἀπ-αμῡ́νω keep off; *mid* repel; defend oneself

ἀπαν-αίνομαι *mid* deny; refuse

ἀπαν-αισχυντέω do with the utmost shamelessness

ἀπαν-ᾱλίσκω use up completely, waste; kill

ἀπάνευθεν *adv* from afar, far off; aside, apart; *prep with gen* without

ἀπαν-ίστημι *act tr* cause to rise *or* depart; *act intr and mid* rise, depart, emigrate

ἀπ-αντάω + *dat* come *or* go to meet, meet; advance against; come to pass, happen

ἁπάντῃ *adv* everywhere

ἀπάντησις εως ἡ meeting; reply

ἀπαντῑκρύ, ἀπαντίον *adv* right over against, right opposite

ἀπ-ανύω finish entirely

ἅπαξ *adv* once; at once, once and for all; for the first time

ἀπ-αξιόω think unworthy; detest, reject

ἀπαράβατος ον not passing away, unchangeable

ἀπ-αραιρῆσθαι *see* **ἀφαιρέω**

ἀπαραίτητος ον not to be moved by prayer, inexorable; inevitable

ἀπαράκλητος ον uncalled for

ἀπαρασκεύαστος ον
ἀπαράσκευος ον unprepared, unarmed

ἀπ-αράσσω dash down, strike *or* cut off; sweep off (the deck of a ship)

ἀπ-αρέσκω + *dat* displease; *mid* show displeasure

ἀπ-αριθμέω count over

ἀπαρίθμησις εως ἡ counting over, recounting

ἀπ-αρκέω be sufficient

ἀπ-αρνέομαι *pass and mid* deny; disown, refuse

ἄπαρνος ον denying utterly

ἀπ-αρτάω hang (up), attach; put away, remove

ἀπαρτί *adv* exactly, precisely

ἀπάρτι *adv* just now, at once; from this time

ἀπαρτιλογίᾱ ᾱς ἡ full amount; even number

ἀπαρτισμός οῦ ὁ consummation, completion

ἀπ-ᾱρύω skim off

ἀπ-αρχή ῆς ἡ beginning of a sacrifice, first offering, first-fruits

ἀπ-άρχομαι begin a sacred act

ἅπᾱς ἅπᾱσα ἅπαν all, all together; whole, entire; each, every

ἀπ-ᾴσσω leap down; rush away; digress

ἄπαστος ον not having tasted + *gen*

ἀπατάω cheat, deceive, beguile

ἀπάτερθεν *adv* apart; *prep with gen* far from

ἀπατεών ῶνος ὁ cheat

ἀπάτη ης ἡ cheating, deceit, fraud

ἀπατήλιος ον **ἀπατηλός** (ᾰ) όν deceitful

ἀπ-ατῑμάω despise thoroughly

ἀπάτωρ (*gen* ορος) fatherless

ἀπαύγασμα ατος τό reflection, image; efflux of light, effulgence

ἀπ-αυδάω forbid

ἀπαυθᾱδίζομαι, ἀπαυθᾱδιάζομαι *mid* speak *or* act boldly

ἀπ-αυράω take *or* snatch away from, rob (someone *acc*) of (something *acc*)

ἄπαυστος ον incessant

ἀπ-αυτομολέω desert, go of one's own accord

ἀπαφίσκω cheat, beguile

ἄπεδος ον even, flat, level

ἀπείθεια ᾱς ἡ disobedience

ἀπειθέω disobey + *dat*; be an unbeliever

ἀπειθής ές disobedient; unbelieving

ἀπ-εικάζω copy, portray; describe; compare

ἀπεικότως *adv* unjustly

ἀπ-ειλέω[1] force back

ἀπειλέω[2] threaten, menace; boast; promise

ἀπειλή ῆς ἡ **ἀπείλημα** ατος τό menace, threat; boast

ἀπειλητήρ ῆρος ὁ braggart

ἀπειλητήριος ᾱ ον **ἀπειλητικός** ή όν threatening

ἄπ-ειμι[1] be away *or* absent; be wanting

ἄπ-ειμι[2] go away, leave; return

ἀπεῖπον *aor act tr* tell plainly, pronounce; forbid, deny, refuse; renounce, resign; *act intr* fail, fall short; *mid* fail; refuse; renounce

ἀπείραστος ον **ἀπείρᾱτος** ον **ἀπείρητος** ον untried, unattempted; not having tried; inexperienced

ἀπ-είργω keep away, separate, define; remove; encompass; confine

ἀπειρέσιος η ον ▸ **ἄπειρος**

ἀπειρίᾱ ᾱς ἡ inexperience, ignorance

ἀπειρόκακος ον without bad experience, unused to evil

ἀπειρόκαλος ον ignorant of the beautiful, without taste, vulgar

ἄπειρος ον **ἀπείρων** ον unlimited, boundless, innumerable; inexperienced, ignorant

ἀπεκ-δέχομαι await; expect anxiously

ἀπεκ-δύομαι take off one's clothes

ἀπεκ-λανθάνομαι *mid* + *gen* forget entirely

ἀπελαύνω, ἀπελάω *act tr* drive away, expel; exclude; *act intr* march *or* ride off

ἀπελεγμός οῦ ὁ ill repute

ἀπέλεθρος ον immense

ἀπελεύθερος ον freedman

ἀπ-ελπίζω despair; hope to receive back

ἀπ-εμέω spit out, sick up

ἀπεμ-πολάω sell, smuggle out of

ἀπέναντι, ἀπεναντίον *adv + gen* over against, opposite

ἀπ-εναρίζω strip (someone *acc*) of arms *acc*

ἀπ-ενιαυτίζω go into exile for a year

ἀπ-εννέπω forbid

ἀπ-έοικα *perf* be unlike
■ **ἀπεικώς** υῖα ός unlikely, unnatural; unfair

ἅπερ just as

ἀπέραντος ον infinite, endless; impassable

ἀπ-εργάζομαι *mid* finish off, turn out complete; contrive, construct, finish

ἀπεργασίᾱ ᾱς ἡ a finish(ing), completing, causing

ἀπ-έργω ▸ **ἀπείργω**

ἀπ-έρδω complete

ἁπερεί just as, like

ἀπ-ερείδομαι *mid* support oneself upon, lean on; turn to; insist upon

ἀπερείσιος ον ▸ **ἀπειρέσιος**

ἀπερίοπτος ον reckless

ἀπερίσκεπτος ον inconsiderate

ἀπερίσπαστος ον undistracted, unmoved

ἀπερίτμητος ον uncircumcised

ἀπερίτροπος ον unconcerned

ἀπ-ερῡ́κω keep off *or* away; *mid* abstain

ἀπ-έρχομαι go away, depart; go over; return

ἀπερωεύς έως ὁ destroyer, one who thwarts

ἀπεσσούᾱ ▸ **ἀπεσσύη** he is gone (i.e. is dead)

ἀπ-εστώ οῦς ἡ absence

ἀπευθής ές inscrutable

ἀπ-ευθῡ́νω straighten; direct; judge; bind back

ἀπ-ευνάζω lull to sleep

ἀπ-εύχομαι *mid* wish (a thing) away, wish it may not appear; avert by praying; reject, despise

ἄπεφθος ον boiled down, refined

ἀπ-εχθαίρω hate, detest; make completely hateful

ἀπ-εχθάνομαι *mid* be *or* become hated

ἀπέχθεια ᾱς ἡ enmity, hatred

ἀπεχθής ές hateful; hostile

ἀπ-έχω hold off; prohibit; receive in full; be distant *or* far from + *gen*; *mid* abstain, desist
■ **ἀπέχει** it is enough

ἀπηλεγέως *adv* bluntly, without caring about the consequences

ἀπῆλιξ (*gen* ικος) elderly

ἀπηλιώτης ου ὁ east wind

ἀπήμαντος ον unhurt; without pain; harmless; wholesome

ἀπήνη ης ἡ waggon, chariot

ἀπηνής ές unfriendly, harsh

ἄπηρος ον unmaimed

ἀπήωρος ον high in the air

ἀπ-ιάλλω send away

ἀπίθανος ον incredible, unlikely; unconvincing, untrustworthy

ἀπιθέω ▸ **ἀπειθέω**

ἀπινύσσω be unconscious *or* senseless

ἄπιος η ον far away, distant

ἀπ-ῑπόω squeeze out

ἀπ-ισόω make equal

ἀπιστέω not believe; doubt; mistrust; disbelieve, disobey + *dat*

ἀπιστίᾱ ᾱς ἡ disbelief, doubt; mistrust; treachery

ἄπιστος ον unreliable, treacherous; incredible; doubtful; unbelieving, distrustful; disobedient

ἀπ-ισχῡρίζομαι *mid* oppose strongly, give a flat denial

ἀπ-ίσχω ▸ **ἀπέχω**

ἄπλᾱτος ον unapproachable

ἄπλετος ον immense, boundless

ἀπληστίᾱ ᾱς ἡ insatiability, greediness

ἄπληστος ον not to be filled, greedy; infinite

ἄπλοια ᾱς ἡ no sailing, detention in port

ἁπλοΐς ίδος ἡ a single garment

ἁπλόος η ον (*also* ἁπλοῦς ῆ οῦν) onefold, single; simple, plain; sincere, honest; sound
■ **ἁπλῶς** plainly, simply; decidedly, without ceremony, in a word

ἄπλοος ον (*also* ἄπλους ουν) unnavigable; unfit for sea, unseaworthy

ἁπλότης ητος ἡ simplicity; honesty

ἄπνευστος ον breathless

ἀπό *adv* off, away; back; *prep with gen* from, away from; from above; far from; apart from; since, immediately after; on the part of, by means of, because of, with; after

ἀποβάθρᾱ ᾱς ἡ gangway; ladder

ἀπο-βαίνω *intr* step off, alight, dismount, descend, land; turn out, end, come to pass, happen, succeed; prove, become; *tr* disembark

ἀπο-βάλλω throw off, drop; get clear of the shore; drive away, lose

ἀπο-βάπτω dip entirely

ἀπόβασις εως ἡ a landing, disembarkation

ἀποβάτης ου ὁ a man who leaps from one horse to another

ἀπο-βιβάζω *tr* disembark

ἀπο-βλάπτω injure, ruin utterly; *pass* be robbed of

ἀπο-βλαστάνω sprout forth

ἀποβλάστημα ατος τό descendant

ἀπο-βλέπω look at, regard

ἀπόβλητος ον rejectable

ἀπο-βλύζω spurt out

ἀποβολή ῆς ἡ a casting away; loss

ἀπο-βρίζω go soundly to sleep

ἀπο-γεισόω provide with a sheltering roof

ἀπο-γεύομαι *mid* + *gen* taste; try

ἀπο-γεφῡρόω dam up by dykes

ἀπο-γίγνομαι *mid* + *gen* be absent *or* away; get lost; depart this life

ἀπο-γιγνώσκω give up, resign; despair of + *gen*; reject the charge against, acquit + *gen*

ἀπόγνοια ᾱς ἡ + *gen* despair of

ἀπόγονος ον descendant

ἀπογραφή ῆς ἡ list, catalogue, register; census; indictment of fraud in taxpaying

ἀπο-γράφω write down, register, enlist; give evidence; bring an action against; *mid* get enlisted *or* registered; sign; note down; cause to be recorded; bring in a law-suit

ἀπο-γυιόω lame, enfeeble

ἀπο-γυμνόω strip bare, strip of [clothes]

ἀπο-δαίομαι *mid* assign; portion off, single out

ἀποδάσμιος ον parted from

ἀπο-δειδίσσομαι frighten from

ἀπο-δείκνῡμι, ἀπο-δεικνύω exhibit, set out; show, produce; prove, demonstrate; appoint, designate

ἀπο-δειλιάω lose courage

ἀπόδειξις εως ἡ a showing forth, publication, proof

ἀπο-δειροτομέω behead; butcher

ἀπο-δείρω ▸ **ἀποδέρω**

ἀπο-δεκατόω tithe, pay *or* take tithes of

ἀπόδεκτος ον welcome, acceptable

ἀπόδερμα ατος τό stripped off skin

ἀπο-δέρω flay, skin (off)

ἀπο-δέχομαι *mid* accept, receive; perceive, understand; approve of, acknowledge, believe

ἀπο-δέω[1] tie tightly

ἀπο-δέω[2] + *gen* lack, be in want of; be behind

ἀπο-δημέω be absent *or* abroad; depart, emigrate

ἀποδημητής οῦ ὁ someone inclined to *or* fond of travelling

ἀποδημίᾱ ᾱς ἡ absence from home, travel abroad

ἀπόδημος ον abroad, travelling

ἀπο-διδράσκω run away; shun, avoid; be lost to view

ἀπο-δίδωμι give away *or* back; return, requite, pay off; perform, accomplish; surrender, deliver; concede; abandon; *mid* sell, let out

ἀπο-δίεμαι frighten away

ἀπο-δικέω defend oneself in court

ἀπο-δῑνέω thresh [corn]

ἀποδιο-πομπέομαι *mid* expiate, avert threatened evils by offerings to Zeus

ἀποδι-ορίζω distinguish, separate

ἀπο-διώκω chase away

ἀπο-δοκιμάζω reject on scrutiny, disapprove of; turn out; ostracize

ἀπόδοσις εως ἡ return payment, restitution

ἀποδοχή ῆς ἡ a receiving back; approval

ἀπο-δοχμόω bend sideways

ἀπόδρασις εως ἡ escape, flight

ἀπο-δρύφω tear off the skin, lacerate

ἀπο-δῡ́νω undress, strip off

ἀπ-οδῡ́ρομαι lament bitterly

ἀποδυτήριον ου τό undressing room

ἀπο-δύω *tr* undress, strip off, take off [clothes]; *mid intr* get undressed

ἀπο-είκω + *gen* withdraw from

ἀπο-εργάθον, ἀπο-έργω ▸ **ἀπείργω**

ἀπο-ζάω eke out existence; earn a scanty livelihood

ἀπ-όζω smell of + *gen*

ἀπο-θαρρέω, ἀπο-θαρσέω gain courage, have full confidence

ἀπο-θαυμάζω wonder at, marvel

ἄποθεν ▸ **ἄπωθεν**

ἀπόθεσις εως ἡ a laying aside, keeping; storing away

ἀπόθεστος ον despised

ἀπόθετος ον hidden; precious

ἀπο-θέω run away

ἀποθήκη ης ἡ granary, receptacle, magazine

ἀπο-θησαυρίζω store up, hoard

ἀπο-θλί̄βω press hard

ἀπο-θνῄσκω -θανοῦμαι -ἔθανον die; be killed

ἀπο-θρῴσκω leap up *or* down

ἀποθῡ́μιος ον disagreeable

ἀπο-θύω sacrifice

ἀπ-οικέω dwell far (off); emigrate

ἀποικίᾱ ᾱς ἡ colony, settlement

ἀπ-οικίζω transplant; send away; colonize

ἀποικίς ίδος ἡ ▸ **ἀποικία**

ἀπ-οικοδομέω wall up, block up

ἄποικος ον emigrant, colonist, settler ■ **ἡ ἄποικος** colony

ἀπ-οικτίζομαι *mid* lament

ἀπ-οιμώζω bewail loudly

ἄποινα ων τά ransom, fine for homicide; compensation

ἀπ-οίχομαι *mid* + *gen* be gone *or* absent; be far from; go away

ἀποκαθ-αίρω wipe off, clean(se)

ἀποκάθαρσις εως ἡ lustration, expiation, purging off

ἀποκάθ-ημαι sit apart

ἀποκαθ-ίστημι, ἀποκαθ-ιστάνω *act tr* restore, re-establish; *act intr and pass* be restored

ἀπο-καίνυμαι surpass, conquer

ἀποκαίριος ον ▸ **ἄκαιρος**

ἀπο-καίω burn off *or* out; cause to freeze

ἀπο-καλέω call away, aside *or* back; name, give names

ἀπο-καλύπτω unveil, uncover

ἀποκάλυψις εως ἡ revelation, the Apocalypse

ἀπο-κάμνω grow tired; abandon from exhaustion

ἀπο-καπύω breathe out

ἀποκαρᾱδοκίᾱ ᾱς ἡ a yearning, earnest expectation

ἀποκατ-αλλάσσω reconcile anew

ἀποκατάστασις εως ἡ restoration

ἀπο-καυλίζω break off by the stalk

ἀπο-κᾴω ▸ **ἀποκαίω**

ἀπό-κειμαι lie apart *or* in store

ἀπο-κείρω cut off [hair]; shear off; cut in pieces

ἀπο-κεφαλίζω behead

ἀπο-κηδεύω cease to mourn for

ἀπο-κηδέω be careless

ἀποκινδῡ́νευσις εως ἡ risk, dangerous attempt

ἀπο-κινδῡνεύω make a bold attempt, try hopelessly

ἀπο-κῑνέω remove; drive away from + *gen*

ἀπο-κλαίω burst into tears; cease to weep

ἀπόκλεισις εως ἡ a shutting out, exclusion

ἀπο-κλείω shut *or* lock up, in *or* out; exclude, refrain; cut off, intercept

ἀπο-κληρόω choose *or* elect by lot

ἀπόκλησις εως ἡ ▸ **ἀπόκλεισις**

ἀπο-κλῑ́νω *act tr* turn aside, divert; *act intr and pass* deviate; stoop, fall; incline to

ἀπο-κλύζω wash away

ἀπο-κναίω rub off, wear out; worry to death

ἀπ-οκνέω hesitate; give up from fear

ἀπόκνησις εως ἡ + *gen* a shrinking from

ἀπο-κοιμάομαι *pass* sleep away from home; get a little sleep

ἀπο-κοιτέω sleep away from (one's post)

ἀπο-κολυμβάω escape by swimming

ἀποκομιδή ῆς ἡ retreat, getting away; carrying away

ἀπο-κομίζω carry away *or* back; *mid* fetch back; *pass* depart

ἀποκοπή ῆς ἡ cutting off; abolition

ἀπο-κόπτω cut off

ἀπο-κορυφόω answer concisely *or* briefly

ἀπο-κοσμέω clear away

ἀπο-κοτταβίζω fling the last drops of wine from the cup

ἀπο-κρατέω surpass all others

ἀπο-κρεμάννῡμι let hang down; hang up

ἀπόκρημνος ον sloping, precipitous; full of difficulties

ἀπόκριμα ατος τό answer; judicial sentence

ἀπο-κρῑ́νω separate; select; vary, distinguish; *pass and mid* part, separate (oneself); *mid* answer

ἀπόκρισις εως ἡ answer

ἀπόκροτος ον hard

ἀπο-κρούω beat off

ἀπο-κρύπτω hide from; conceal; lose from sight; *mid* hide oneself; conceal

ἀπόκρυφος ον hidden, secret

a

ἀπο-κτείνω -κτενῶ ἀπέκτεινα **ἀπο-κτιννύω, ἀπο-κτίννῡμι** kill

ἀπο-κυέω, ἀπο-κύω bring forth, give birth

ἀπο-κυλΐω roll away

ἀπο-κωλύω hinder, prevent

ἀπο-λαγχάνω get by lot

ἀπο-λαμβάνω take away *or* apart; separate; cut off; hinder; accept, receive; regain

ἀπο-λαμπρῡ́νομαι *pass* become famous

ἀπο-λάμπω shine from; reflect [light]

ἀπόλαυσις εως ἡ enjoyment, advantage

ἀπο-λαύω + *gen* enjoy, profit from

ἀπο-λέγω pick out, select

ἀπο-λείβομαι *pass* drip down

ἀπο-λείπω leave, lose, relinquish; leave behind; leave a distance; omit; go away, leave off; fail, fall short, be wanting; *pass* remain, be left, remain behind; miss; stay away; be parted

ἀπο-λείχω lick clean

ἀπόλειψις εως ἡ a leaving, retreat, depart; desertion

ἀπόλεκτος ον chosen out, choice

ἀπόλεμος ον unwarlike

ἀπο-λέπω peel *or* cut off

ἀπο-λήγω + *gen* leave off, end, cease (from)

ἀπόληψις εως ἡ an intercepting, a cutting off

ἄπολις ι (*gen* ιδος *or* εως) townless; homeless

ἀπ-ολισθάνω glide off, slip away (from)

ἀπο-λιχμάω lick off

ἀπ-όλλῡμι, ἀπολλύω ruin, destroy; kill; lose; *mid and pass* be ruined, undone, destroyed *or* lost; perish, die

ἀπο-λογέομαι *mid* defend *or* justify oneself; defend

ἀπολογίᾱ ᾱς ἡ defence

ἀπο-λογίζομαι *mid* give an account (of); discuss; calculate, enumerate

ἀπόλογος ου ὁ tale; fable

ἀπο-λούω wash off

ἀπ-ολοφῡ́ρομαι *mid* stop wailing

ἀπο-λῡμαίνομαι *mid* clean(se) oneself

ἀπολῡμαντήρ ῆρος ὁ destroyer, kill-joy; glutton, guzzler

ἀπόλυσις εως ἡ release, absolution

ἀπολυτικός ή όν disposed to release

ἀπολύτρωσις εως ἡ a ransoming, redemption

ἀπο-λύω loosen, set free, deliver; dismiss, acquit; absolve; *mid* free *or* justify oneself; *mid and pass* depart

ἀπο-λωβάω insult

ἀπο-μανθάνω unlearn

ἀπο-μαραίνομαι *pass* wither, dry up

ἀπο-μάσσω scrape *or* wipe off

ἀπο-μαστῑγόω scourge

ἀπο-ματαΐζω behave indecently

ἀπο-μάχομαι *mid* fight from; keep off; repudiate

ἀπόμαχος ον unfit for battle

ἀπο-μετρέω measure out

ἀπο-μηκῡ́νω lengthen *or* draw out

ἀπο-μηνίω stay angry

ἀπο-μῑμέομαι *mid* copy, counterfeit

ἀπο-μιμνήσκομαι *pass* remember, bear in mind

ἀπόμισθος ον without pay; paid off

ἀπο-μισθόω let out for hire

ἀπομνημονεύματα ων τά memoirs, memorable things

ἀπο-μνημονεύω keep in memory; recount

ἀπο-μνησικακέω + *dat* bear a grudge against

ἀπ-όμνῡμι swear; deny on oath

ἀπο-μονόω leave alone; exclude

ἀπ-ομόργνῡμι wipe off *or* clean

ἀπο-μῡθέομαι *mid* dissuade (from)

ἀπο-ναίω transplant; send home; *mid* emigrate

ἀπο-νέμω allot, assign

ἀπο-νέομαι go away; return

ἀπόνητος ον without pains, easy; unpunished

■ ἀπονητί *adv*

ἀπο-νίζω wash off; bathe

ἀπ-ονίναμαι *mid* + *gen* enjoy

ἀπο-νίπτω ▸ ἀπονίζω

ἀπο-νοέομαι *pass* be desperate

ἀπόνοια ᾱς ἡ folly; despair; foolhardiness

ἄπονος ον inactive, lazy; easy

ἀπο-νοστέω return home

ἀπονόσφιν *adv* + *gen* apart; far from

ἀπο-νοσφίζω separate from; deprive; flee from

ἀπόξενος ον inhospitable

ἀπο-ξενόω banish; *pass* live abroad

ἀπο-ξέω smooth, polish; cut off

ἀπο-ξηραίνω dry up

ἀπ-οξῡ́νω sharpen

ἀπο-ξυρέω shear off

ἀπο-ξῡ́ω shave clean; scrape off

ἀπο-παπταίνω look about timidly

ἀπο-παύω cause to leave off, cause to stop; *mid* leave off, cease

ἀπόπειρα ᾱς ἡ proof, trial, experiment

ἀπο-πειράω *and pass* try, prove

ἀπο-πέμπω send away *or* back; dismiss; *mid* get rid of

ἀπόπεμψις εως ἡ dismissal

ἀπο-πέτομαι *mid* fly away *or* back

ἀπο-πήγνῡμι cause to freeze; *pass* congeal, curdle

ἀπο-πηδάω leap off *or* away; desert

ἀπο-πίμπλημι fill up, complete; supply; satisfy

ἀπο-πίνω drink off

ἀπο-πῑ́πτω fall down

ἀπο-πλάζω, ἀπο-πλανάω lead astray; *pass* go astray

ἀπο-πλέω sail off *or* home

ἀπόπληκτος ον disabled by a stroke; astounded

ἀπο-πληρόω ▸ ἀποπίμπλημι

ἀπο-πλήσσομαι *pass* lose one's senses

ἀπόπλοος ου ὁ (*also* ἀπόπλους) a sailing away

ἀπο-πλῡ́νω rinse off

ἀπο-πλώω ▸ ἀποπλέω

ἀπο-πνέω (*also* ἀπο-πνείω) breathe forth, exhale; blow from

ἀπο-πνῑ́γω choke, strangle

ἀπόπολις ι (*gen* ιδος *or* εως) banished

ἀπο-πορεύομαι *pass* depart, go away

ἀπο-πρίω saw off

ἀποπρό *adv* from far away; far from + *gen*

ἀποπρο-αιρέω take away from before

ἀπόπροθεν *adv* from far away

ἀπόπροθι *adv* far off

ἀποπρο-ῑ́ημι send far (away); shoot; let drop

ἀπόπτολις ▸ ἀπόπολις

ἄποπτος ον seen from afar; invisible

ἀπόπτυστος ον detested

ἀποπτύω spit out

ἀπο-πυνθάνομαι question, inquire after

ἀπορέω be embarrassed, at a loss *or* helpless; be distressed *or* needy

ἀπόρθητος ον not sacked; indestructible

ἀπ-ορθόω make straight; direct

ἀπορίᾱ ᾱς ἡ embarrassment, helplessness, aporia; doubt; need; difficulty, *impasse*

ἀπ-όρνυμαι *mid* start, depart

ἄπορος ον impassable; difficult; impossible; extravagant; helpless; needy, poor; unable

ἀπ-ορούω leap off, rebound

ἀπο-ρραθῡμέω give up from timidity *or* laziness

ἀπο-ρραίνω spurt out, shed about

ἀπο-ρραίω tear from

ἀπο-ρράπτω sew up

ἀπο-ρρέω flow off *or* down; vanish

ἀπο-ρρήγνῡμι break off, sever

ἀπόρρητα ων τά illegal exports, contraband

ἀπόρρητος ον forbidden; unspeakable; secret; abominable

ἀπο-ρρῑγέω shrink from, recoil

ἀπο-ρρῑ́πτω, ἀπο-ρρῑπτέω throw away, reject; despise

ἀπορροή ῆς ἡ **ἀπόρροια** ᾱς ἡ a flowing off *or* out

ἀπο-ρροιβδέω shriek out

ἀπορρώξ ῶγος ὁ/ἡ *noun* a flowing out; distillation; *used as adj* steep, abrupt

ἀπ-ορφανίζομαι *pass* become an orphan

ἀπ-ορχέομαι *mid* lose by dancing

ἀπο-σαλεύω anchor in the open sea

ἀπο-σαφέω explain, illustrate

ἀπο-σβέννῡμι *act tr* extinguish; *act intr and pass* go out, be extinguished, expire

ἀπο-σείω shake off

ἀπο-σεύομαι *mid and pass* run away

ἀπο-σημαίνω announce by signs, signal; *mid* perceive; seal; confiscate

ἀπο-σήπομαι *pass* rot off; freeze off

ἀπο-σῑμόω turn aside; make snub-nosed

ἀπο-σιωπάω grow speechless

ἀπο-σκάπτω keep (off) by trenches

ἀπο-σκεδάννῡμι scatter, chase; remove, dismiss

ἀπο-σκευάζω clear away; *mid* pack up

ἀπο-σκηνέω, ἀπο-σκηνόω be encamped away from + *gen*

ἀπο-σκήπτω *tr* fling on; *intr* burst forth; end

ἀποσκίασμα ατος τό the casting of a shadow, trace

ἀπο-σκίδνημι ▸ **ἀποσκεδάννῡμι**

ἀπο-σκοπέω look at away from; regard

ἀπο-σκυδμαίνω be angry

ἀπο-σκώπτω tease, jeer

ἀπόσπασμα ατος τό morsel; rag, shred

ἀπο-σπάω *act tr* tear *or* pull off; *act intr and pass* go away, be separated

ἀπο-σπένδω pour out [a libation]

ἀπο-σπεύδω dissuade; prevent

ἀποσταδά, ἀποσταδόν *adv* from a distance

ἀπο-στάζω let drip; fall in drops

ἀποστασίᾱ ᾱς ἡ **ἀπόστασις** εως ἡ a standing away from; rebellion, apostasy; departure from

ἀποστάσιον ου τό written notice of divorce; the relinquishing of a claim

ἀπο-στατέω + *gen* stand apart (from); differ

ἀπο-σταυρόω fence with a palisade

ἀπο-στεγάζω take off a roof

ἀπο-στείχω step away, back; go away

ἀπο-στέλλω send away *or* out; forward; send back

ἀπο-στερέω rob, deprive (of); withhold, take away

ἀποστέρησις εως ἡ deprivation

ἀπο-στερίσκω ▸ **ἀποστερέω**

ἀπο-στίλβω shine

ἀποστολεύς έως ὁ Athenian magistrate who had to equip a naval squadron

ἀποστολή ῆς ἡ a sending, expedition; apostleship

ἀπόστολος ου ὁ messenger; traveller; apostle; naval expedition

ἀπο-στοματίζω recite, dictate; question

ἀπο-στρατοπεδεύομαι *mid* encamp at a distance

ἀπο-στρέφω *act tr* turn away *or* back; twist back; bring back; cause to return; drive away *or* back; turn to; *act intr and pass* turn away *or* round; return; abhor

ἀποστροφή ῆς ἡ turning away, averting; flight, escape; refuge

ἀπόστροφος ον turned away

ἀπο-στυγέω detest, loathe

ἀπο-στυφελίζω push back from

ἀπο-σῡλάω rob, strip off spoils from

ἀποσυνάγωγος ον ejected from the synagogue

ἀπο-σῡ́ρω tear off

ἀπο-σφακελίζω have one's limbs frost-bitten; fall into convulsions

ἀπο-σφάλλω mislead; frustrate; *pass* miss, fail

ἀπο-σφάζω, ἀπο-σφάττω cut the throat of, slaughter

ἀπο-σχίζω split off; sever

ἀπο-σῴζω save, shelter

ἀπότακτος ον set apart for special use; appropriated

ἀπο-τάμνω ▸ **ἀποτέμνω**

ἀπο-τάσσω set apart; assign specially; *mid* depart from

ἀπο-ταφρεύω fortify with a ditch

ἀπο-τείνω stretch out, lengthen; reach to; aim at; *pass* be extended

ἀπο-τειχίζω separate *or* surround by a wall; wall round *or* in; fortify

ἀπο-τείχισις εως ἡ **ἀπο-τείχισμα** ατος τό a blockading; circumvallation

ἀπο-τελευτάω *intr* end

ἀπο-τελέω finish, achieve, satisfy, effect, pay, fulfil

ἀπο-τέμνω cut off; tear off; separate; make one's own

ἀπο-τήκομαι melt away

ἀποτηλοῦ *adv* far

ἀποτίβατος ▸ **ἀπρόσβατος**

ἀπο-τίθημι put away, aside *or* down; *mid* put away, remove; omit; defer

ἀπο-τίλλω pluck out

ἀπο-τῑμάω value, tax; borrow money on a mortgage; *mid* get payment; fix a price, evaluate

ἀπο-τινάσσω shake off

ἀπο-τίνω, ἀπο-τίνῡμι pay back, repay, pay for; *mid* exact [a penalty *or* justice], punish; avenge

ἀπο-τμήγω ▸ **ἀποτέμνω**

ἄποτμος ον unhappy, ill-starred

ἀπο-τολμάω venture, dare; tell freely

ἀποτομή ῆς ἡ a cutting off

ἀποτομίᾱ ᾱς ἡ steepness

ἀπότομος ον steep, precipitous; severe

ἄποτος ον not drinking; undrinkable

ἀπο-τρέπω *act tr* turn away *or* back; restrain, dissuade; prevent; *pass and mid intr* turn away *or* back; return, fly; cease from

ἀπο-τρέχω run away

ἀπο-τρῑ́βω rub *or* scour off; *mid* efface

ἀποτρόπαιος ον averting

ἀποτροπή ῆς ἡ an averting, deterring, prevention; desertion

ἀπότροπος ον averted, banished; averting, horrible

ἀπότροφος ον brought up abroad

ἀπο-τρῡ́ω rub away, wear out

ἀπο-τρωπάω ▸ **ἀποτρέπω**

ἀπο-τυγχάνω miss, lose, fail; be unlucky

ἀπο-τυμπανίζω beat to death

ἀπο-τύπτομαι *mid* cease mourning

ἀπούρας *see* **ἀπαυράω**

ἀπ-ουρίζω alter boundary-stones; lessen

α

ἄπουρος ον distant
ἄπους ἄπουν (*gen* ἄποδος) footless; lame
ἀπουσίᾱ ᾱς ἡ absence
ἀπο-φαίνω display, point out, bring to light; prove, explain; describe; appoint; *pass* appear
ἀπο-φάσκω ▸ ἀπόφημι
ἀπο-φέρω carry off *or* away; carry, lead, take, bring back *or* up; pay back; transmit; indicate
ἀπο-φεύγω flee from, escape; avoid; be acquitted
ἀπό-φημι speak out, declare; deny; refuse
ἀπο-φθέγγομαι *mid* speak plainly
ἀπόφθεγμα ατος τό a saying, sentence; maxim
ἀπο-φθείρω destroy, ruin
ἀπο-φθινύθω perish; lose
ἀπο-φθί(ν)ω destroy; perish
ἀπο-φλαυρίζω despise, slight
ἀπο-φοιτάω go away
ἀποφορᾱ́ ᾶς ἡ tribute, tax
ἀπο-φορτίζομαι *mid* unburden oneself
ἀπο-φράγνῡμι bar, block up, stop
ἀπόφραξις εως ἡ a blocking up
ἀποφυγή ῆς ἡ escape, flight; refuge
ἀποφώλιος ον void, useless
ἀπο-χάζομαι *mid* withdraw
ἀποχειροβίωτος ον living by manual labour
ἀπο-χετεύω drain
ἀπο-χέω pour out; throw down
ἀπο-χόω dam up
ἀπο-χράω be enough; *pass* be contented; *mid* kill; + *dat* use to the full; misuse
ἀπόχρησις εως ἡ misuse; consumption
ἀποχρώντως *adv* sufficiently
ἀπο-χωλόω make lame
ἀπο-χώννῡμι ▸ ἀποχόω
ἀπο-χωρέω go away; retreat
ἀποχώρησις εως ἡ return, retreat
ἀπο-χωρίζω part, separate; *pass* part from
ἀπο-ψάω wipe off
ἀπο-ψηφίζομαι *mid* vote against, reject; acquit; *pass* be rejected
ἀπο-ψῑλόω make bald; deprive
ἄποψις εως ἡ view, prospect
ἀπο-ψῡ́χω breathe' out; swoon; cool, refresh; dry up
ἀπρᾱγμοσύνη ης ἡ inactivity; love of a quiet life; non-intervention
ἀπρᾱ́γμων ον inactive; peace-loving; without pains, easy
ἄπρᾱκτος ον (*also* ἄπρηκτος) effecting nothing, useless; inactive; not done, untried; impossible; unconquerable, incurable
ἀπρᾱξίᾱ ᾱς ἡ inaction
ἀπρεπής ές unbecoming, unseemly
ἀπρίατος (η) ον unbought, for nothing
■ **ἀπριάτην** *adv*
ἀπρίξ *adv* with closed teeth; holding tight; incessantly
ἀπρόθῡμος ον disinclined, not eager
ἄπροικος ον without a dowry
ἀπρομήθεια ᾱς ἡ lack of forethought
ἀπρονόητος ον unpremeditated, improvident
ἀπρόσβατος ον inaccessible
ἀπροσδόκητος ον unexpected; not expecting
ἀπροσήγορος ον not to be accosted; unkind
ἀπρόσιτος ον inaccessible
ἀπρόσκοπος ον innocent; blameless
ἀπρόσμαχος ον invincible
ἀπρόσμῑκτος ον having no communication with + *dat*
ἀπροσόμῑλος ον unsociable
ἀπροσωπολήπτως *adv* without respect of persons

ἀπροτίμαστος ον untouched, undefiled

ἀπροφάσιστος ον unevasive, unhesitating; unreserved, honest

ἀπροφύλακτος ον not guarded against, unforeseen

ἄπταιστος ον without stumbling

ἄπτερος ον **ἀπτήν** (*gen* ῆνος) unwinged; not flying away

ἀπτοεπής ές bold in speaking

ἀπτόλεμος ον ▸ **ἀπόλεμος**

ἅπτω ἅψω ἧψα fasten, attach, fix; kindle; *mid* touch, grasp, seize, lay hold of + *gen*; try; perceive; mention; undertake; *pass* catch fire, be kindled

ἀπύλωτος ον not shut off by a gate

ἀπύργωτος ον not fortified (by towers)

ἄπυρος ον **ἀπύρωτος** ον not touched by fire, uncooked, new

ἄπυστος ον not remembered *or* known; inaudible; not knowing

ἀπύω ▸ ἠπύω

ἄπωθεν *adv from afar*; *far from + gen*

ἀπ-ωθέω drive away; *mid* drive away *or* back; keep off, repel; despise

ἀπώλεια ᾱς ἡ destruction, ruin, loss

ἀπώμοτος ον abjured; declared impossible on oath; under oath not to do something

ἄπωσις εως ἡ a driving away

ἀπωστός ή όν expelled, driven away

ἀπωτάτω *sup adv* farthest off

ἀπωτέρω *comp adv* farther off

ἆρ *see* **αἴρω**

ἄρα *particle* then (logical); so then, after all (of realization)

ἆρα *particle* (denoting interrogation) is it (the case that ...)?

- **ἆρ' οὐ** surely ... ?
- **ἆρα μή** surely ... not?

ἀρᾱ́ ᾶς ἡ prayer; curse; destruction, revenge

ἀραβέω rattle, clatter

ἄραβος ου ὁ **ἀραγμός** οῦ ὁ a rattling, crashing

ἀραιός ᾱ́ όν thin, narrow, slender; weak

ἀραῖος (ᾱ) ον cursing; accursed; prayed to

ἀραίρηκα *alternative pf of* **αἱρέω**

ἀράομαι ἀρᾱ́σομαι ἠρησάμην *mid* pray, implore; wish; curse

ἀραρίσκω *aor* ἦρσα *or* ἤραρον join, put together, fit with; fix; build, fit out; *intr* be joined, fastened *or* fitted; suit; be equipped; please

ἀράσσω ἀράξω ἤραξα strike, knock, hammer, dash

ἀρᾱτός ή όν prayed for; accursed

ἀράχνη ης ἡ spider

ἀράχνιον ου τό spider's web, cobweb

ἀργαλέος ᾱ ον painful, troublesome, grievous

ἀργεϊφόντης ου ὁ swift messenger *or* killer of Argus (of Hermes)

ἀργεννός ή όν ▸ **ἀργής**

ἀργεστής (*gen* οῦ) clearing, brightening (of wind); white

ἀργέω be unemployed *or* inactive; lie fallow

ἀργής (*gen* ῆτος *or* έτος) white, shining, bright

ἀργίᾱ ᾱς ἡ laziness, leisure

ἀργικέραυνος ον with bright flashes of lightning

ἀργῑλώδης ες like clay, clayey

ἀργινόεις εσσα εν ▸ **ἀργής**

ἀργιόδους (*gen* όδοντος) with white teeth, white-toothed

ἀργίπους (*gen* ποδος) with white feet *or* swift-footed

ἄργμα ατος τό the firstlings (at a sacrifice)

ἀργολίζω ἀργολιῶ side with the Argives

ἀργός[1] ή όν bright, white; swift

ἀργός[2] όν lazy, idle; useless; not done; untilled, fallow

ἀργύρε(ι)ος ᾱ ον of silver

ἀργύριον ου τό silver; silver coin; money

ἀργυροδΐνης (*gen* ου) eddying like silver

ἀργυρόηλος ον with silver studs

ἀργυροκόπος ου ὁ silversmith

ἀργυρολογέω levy money

ἀργυρολογίᾱ ᾱς ἡ the levying of money

ἀργυρολόγος ον levying money

ἀργυρόπεζα ης ἡ **ἀργυρόπους** πουν (*gen* ποδος) silver-footed

ἄργυρος ου ὁ silver; money

ἀργυρότοξος ον with silver bow

ἀργυρώνητος ον bought with money

ἀργύφεος ᾱ ον **ἄργυφος** ον silver-shining, silver-white

ἄρδην *adv* on high, upwards; from on high; utterly, entirely

ἄρδις ιος ἡ point of arrow

ἀρδμός οῦ ὁ watering-place

ἄρδω *aor* ἦρσα water, irrigate

ἀρειή ῆς ἡ ▸ **ἀρά**

ἀρείων ον better; braver

ἄρεκτος ον unfinished

ἀρέομαι ▸ **ἀράομαι**

ἀρέσκεια ᾱς ἡ pleasing character; obsequiousness

ἀρέσκω ἀρέσω ἤρεσα *and mid* make good, make amends; conciliate, satisfy; + *dat* please; *pass* be agreeable *or* pleasant; be pleased *or* satisfied

ἀρεστός ή όν agreeable, acceptable

ἀρετάω be fit *or* proper, prosper

ἀρετή ῆς ἡ goodness, excellence, perfection, merit, fitness; bravery, valour; virtue

ἀρήγω ἀρήξω + *dat* help, aid

ἀρηγών όνος ὁ/ἡ helper

ἀρηίθοος ον swift in war

ἀρηικτάμενος η ον **ἀρηίφατος** ον killed in battle

ἀρηίφιλος ον loved by Ares

ἀρημένος η ον damaged, overwhelmed

ἀρήν ἀρνός ὁ/ἡ lamb, sheep

ἄρηξις εως ἡ help, defence

ᾱ̓ρητήρ ῆρος ὁ someone who prays, priest

ἄρητος ον unspeakable; prayed for

ᾱ̓ρητός ▸ **ἀρατός**

ἀρθμέω be joined together

ἄρθμιος ᾱ ον united, joined; friendly; concordant

ἄρθρον ου τό joint; limb

ἀρθρόω articulate

ἀρίγνωτος (η) ον easy to be known; well-known

ἀριδείκετος ον excellent

ἀρίδηλος ον **ἀρίζηλος** (η) ον most distinct, conspicuous, clear, excellent

ἀριθμέω number, count up; class

ἀριθμητικός ή όν arithmetical

ἀριθμός οῦ ὁ number; amount, quantity; a counting, muster

ἀριπρεπής ές eminent, splendid

ἀριστάω have breakfast

ἀριστείᾱ ᾱς ἡ heroism; sequence of great deeds from a hero

ἀριστεῖον ου τό victor's reward, prize

ἀριστερός ᾱ́ όν left, to the left; sinister, ominous; clumsy

■ **ἡ ἀριστερᾱ́** the left hand

ἀριστεύς έως ὁ the best *or* noblest man; prince, hero

ἀριστεύω be the best (one), excel

ἀριστίνδην *adv* according to noble birth

ἀριστο-κρατέομαι *pass* live ruled by an aristocracy

ἀριστοκρατίᾱ ᾱς ἡ aristocracy

ἀριστοκρατικός ή όν aristocratic

ἀριστόμαντις εως ὁ the best of the prophets

ἀριστο-ποιέομαι *mid* (get one's) breakfast

ἄριστος η ον *sup adj* best, bravest, noblest; aristocrat

ἀριστόχειρ (*gen* ειρος) with the bravest hand

ἀρισφαλής ές very slippery *or* treacherous

ἀριφραδής ές easily known; very thoughtful

ἄρκεσις εως ἡ help, service

ἀρκετός ή όν sufficient

ἀρκέω ἀρκέσω ἤρκεσα keep *or* ward off; help, assist, defend + *dat*; be enough for + *dat*; be able; *pass* be contented *or* satisfied

ἄρκιος ᾱ ον sufficient, sure

ἄρκος εος τό defence; solace

ἀρκούντως *adv* sufficiently, enough

ἀρκτέον *gerund of* **ἄρχομαι** to be started, to be ruled

ἄρκτος ου ὁ/ἡ bear

ἀρκτοῦρος ου ὁ bearherd

ἄρκυς υος ἡ net, snare

ἀρκύστατος (η) ον ensnared

ἅρμα ατος τό waggon, team

ἁρμάμαξα ης ἡ covered carriage

ἁρμάτειος ᾱ ον belonging to a waggon

ἁρματηλατέω drive a waggon

ἁρματηλάτης ου ὁ charioteer

ἁρματοπηγός οῦ ὁ cartwright, chariot-maker

ἁρμόδιος ᾱ ον fitting

ἁρμόζω ▸ **ἁρμόττω**

ἁρμονίᾱ ᾱς ἡ joint, union; cramp, clasp; treaty, decree; harmony, proportion

ἁρμός οῦ ὁ joint; groove; slit; peg

ἁρμοστήρ ῆρος ὁ **ἁρμοστής** οῦ ὁ harmost (Spartan governor)

ἁρμόττω ἁρμόσω ἥρμοσα *act tr* fit together, join, adjust; betroth, marry; *act intr* fit, suit, become, be convenient; *mid* be betrothed, married

ἄρνειος ᾱ ον of a lamb *or* sheep

ἀρνειός οῦ ὁ ram

ἀρνέομαι deny, disown, refuse; despise

ἀρνευτήρ ῆρος ὁ diver; tumbler

ἀρνήσιμος ον to be denied

ἄρνησις εως ἡ denial

ἀρνίον ου τό young lamb

ἀρνός *see* **ἀρήν**

ἄρνυμαι ἀροῦμαι ἀρόμην gain, earn, obtain, carry off

ἄροσις εως ἡ arable land

ἀροτήρ ῆρος ὁ ploughman

ἄροτος ου ὁ ploughing, husbandry; engendering; produce of the fields

ἀροτριάω ▸ **ἀρόω**

ἄροτρον ου τό plough

ἄρουρα ᾱς ἡ plough land, field, soil; acre

ἀρουραῖος ᾱ ον rustic

ἀρόω ἀρόσω ἤροσα plough; sow; beget

ἁρπαγή ῆς ἡ **ἁρπαγμός** οῦ ὁ robbing, plundering; spoil, plunder; kidnapping, rape

ἁρπάζω ἁρπάσω ἥρπασα snatch, seize, rob, plunder; do in haste

ἁρπακτήρ ῆρος ὁ robber

ἁρπαλέος ᾱ ον greedy; pleasant

ἅρπαξ (*gen* αγος) rapacious, robbing

ἁρπεδόνη ης ἡ cord, rope, bowstring

ἅρπη ης ἡ falcon, kite; sickle

ἅρπυια ᾱς ἡ whirlwind; harpy

ἀρραβών ῶνος ὁ pledge, deposit

ἄρραφος ον unsewed, without a seam

ἄρρηκτος ον unbreakable, not to be broken *or* tired

ἄρρην ▸ **ἄρσην**

ἄρρητος ον unsaid; unknown; unspeakable, secret, holy; abominable

ἄρρυθμος ον without rhythm *or* proportion

ἀρρωδέω ▸ **ὀρρωδέω**

ἀρρώξ (*gen* ῶγος) untorn

ἀρρωστέω be weak *or* sick

ἀρρώστημα ατος τό **ἀρρωστίᾱ** ᾱς ἡ weakness, sickness, depression

ἄρρωστος ον weak, sickly, languid

ἀρσενοκοίτης ου ὁ someone who goes to bed with men

ἄρσην εν (*gen* ενος) male; manly, vigorous, strong

ἀρτάνη ης ἡ rope, noose, sling

ἀρτάω, ἀρτέω fasten, fix; hang up; *pass* depend on; *mid* prepare

ἀρτεμής ές safe and sound, fresh

ἀρτέμων ονος *or* ωνος ὁ top-sail

ἄρτημα ατος τό earring

ἀρτηρίᾱ ᾱς ἡ windpipe; artery, vein

ἄρτι *adv* just now; lately, the other day

ἀρτιγέννητος ον newborn

ἀρτιεπής ές glib, ready of speech

ἀρτίκολλος ον close-glued

ἄρτιος ᾱ ον fit; ready; proper, perfect; (of numbers) even

■ ἀρτίως ▶ ἄρτι

ἀρτίπο(υ)ς (*gen* ποδος) sound *or* swift of foot

ἄρτισις εως ἡ equipment

ἀρτίφρων ον sensible, intelligent

ἀρτίχρῑστος ον newly spread

ἀρτοκόπος ου ὁ baker

ἀρτοποιίᾱ ᾱς ἡ bread-baking

ἀρτοπώλης ου ὁ baker

ἄρτος ου ὁ bread

ἀρτῡ́νας ου ὁ magistrate (at Argos and Epidauros)

ἀρτῡ́νω, ἀρτῡ́ω ἀρτυνῶ ἤρτῡνα join; arrange, prepare; devise

ἀρυστήρ ῆρος ὁ cup *or* ladle

ἀρύ(τ)ω, ἀρύσσω *aor* ἤρυσα draw [water]

ἀρχάγγελος ου ὁ archangel

ἀρχαιόγονος ον ancient, primeval

ἀρχαιολογέω tell old stories

ἀρχαῖος ᾱ ον ancient, primeval, old, time-honoured, antiquated; former, bygone

ἀρχαιότροπος ον old-fashioned

ἀρχαιρεσίᾱ ᾱς ἡ election of magistrates

ἀρχεῖον ου τό senate house, town hall

ἀρχέκακος ον mischief-making

ἀρχέλᾱος ον leading the people

ἀρχέπλουτος ον rich from long ago, with inherited wealth

ἀρχεύω lead, rule

ἀρχή ῆς ἡ beginning, origin; cause, motive, principle, element; leadership, power, rule, magistrate, magistracy, government; territory, empire; end, corner (of bandage, rope, sheet etc.)

ἀρχηγετέω, ἀρχηγετεύω begin with; rule

ἀρχηγέτης ου ὁ **ἀρχηγός** οῦ ὁ ruler, leader, head; author, founder

ἀρχῆθεν *adv* of old, originally

ἀρχίδιον ου τό minor office; minor officer

ἀρχιερατικός ή όν of the high priest

ἀρχιερεύς έως ὁ **ἀρχιέρεως** ω ὁ high priest, pontifex maximus (at Rome)

ἀρχικός ή όν commanding, authoritative

ἀρχιποιμήν ένος ὁ chief shepherd

ἀρχισυνάγωγος ου ὁ head of the synagogue

ἀρχιτέκτων ονος ὁ builder, architect, engineer

ἀρχιτελώνης ου ὁ chief tax-collector

ἀρχιτρίκλῑνος ου ὁ president of the banquet

ἀρχός οῦ ὁ leader

ἄρχω† + *gen* be the first, lead on, guide; begin; cause; be at the head (of), lead, rule, govern; be archon; *pass* be ruled, governed, subject; obey; *mid* begin, try

ἄρχων οντος ὁ leader, ruler, chief; archon, magistrate

ἆρῶ *fut from* **αἴρω**

ἀρωγή ῆς ἡ protection, help

ἀρωγός όν helping, aiding; helper

ἄρωμα[1] ατος τό spice

ἄρωμα[2] ατος τό arable land

ἀρώσιμος ον to be sown

ἀσάλευτος ον unshaken

ἀσάμινθος ου ἡ bathing tub

ἀσάομαι *pass* be disgusted

ἀσάφεια ᾱς ἡ indistinctness

ἀσαφής ές indistinct, uncertain, dubious

ἄσβεστος ον unquenchable; endless

ἀσέβεια ᾱς ἡ **ἀσέβημα** ατος τό impiety, wickedness

ἀσεβέω be impious, sin against the gods

ἀσεβής ές impious, sinful

ἀσελγαίνω ἀσελγανῶ behave uncontrollably *or* outrageously

ἀσέλγεια ᾱς ἡ outrageous behaviour

ἀσέληνος ον moonless

ἀσεπτέω ▸ **ἀσεβέω**

ἄση ης ἡ surfeit, distress

ἀσήμαντος ον without leader *or* shepherd

ἄσημος ον **ἀσήμων** ον without mark *or* sign; uncoined; indistinct, unintelligible; obscure

ἀσθένεια ᾱς ἡ **ἀσθένημα** ατος τό weakness; illness; neediness

ἀσθενής ές weak, feeble; sick; poor, insignificant

ἄσθμα ατος τό shortness of breath

ἀσθμαίνω gasp, pant

ἀσινής ές unhurt; innocuous, harmless

ἄσις εως ἡ mud, slime

ἀσῑτέω fast, abstain from food

ἀσῑτίᾱ ᾱς ἡ hunger, fast

ἄσῑτος ον without food, hungry

ἀσκελής ές weak; incessant

ἀσκέπαρνος ον unhewn

ἄσκεπτος ον not considered, not examined; inconsiderate

ἀσκευής ές **ἄσκευος** ον unprepared; unprotected

ἀσκέω fashion with skill; adorn; practise, exercise, train, drill; endeavour, strive

ἀσκηθής ές unhurt, undamaged

ἄσκησις εως ἡ practice, training; trade, profession

ἀσκητής οῦ ὁ athlete; hermit, monk

ἀσκητός ή όν curiously *or* artificially wrought; needing practice; trained

ἄσκοπος ον inconsiderate; unseen, invisible; unmeasurable; unexpected

ἀσκός οῦ ὁ hide; leather bag, wine-skin

ᾆσμα ατος τό song

ἄσμενος η ον willing, ready, glad

ἄσοφος ον unwise, foolish

ἀσπάζομαι *mid* welcome, greet, salute, hail; take leave; hug, caress, love

ἀσπαίρω jerk, struggle, kick

ἄσπαρτος ον unsown

ἀσπάσιος ᾱ ον **ἀσπαστός** ή όν welcome, longed for; delighted, glad, willing

ἀσπασμός οῦ ὁ greeting, embrace

ἄσπερμος ον without issue

ἀσπερχές *adv* eagerly, zealously; incessantly

ἄσπετος ον unspeakable, incessant, immense

ἀσπιδιώτης ου ὁ shield-bearing, warrior

ἀσπιδοπηγεῖον ου τό shield-factory

ἄσπῑλος ον unstained, spotless

ἀσπίς ίδος ἡ shield; hoplite; asp

ἀσπιστήρ ῆρος ὁ **ἀσπιστής** οῦ ὁ shield-bearer, warrior

ἄσπλαγχνος ον heartless; cowardly

ἄσπονδος ον without treaty *or* truce; implacable

ἄσπορος ον unsown

a

ἀσπουδί *adv* without commitment *or* struggle

ἅσσα ▸ **ἅτινα** *see* **ὅστις**

ἄσσα ▸ **τινά** *see* **τις**

ἀσσάριον ου τό small coin

ᾄσσω ▸ **ἀΐσσω**

ἀστάθμητος ον unsteady, unstable; unmeasurable

ἄστακτος ον gushing freely
■ **ἀστακτί** *adv*

ἀστασίαστος ον not disturbed by factions

ἀστατέω be unstable

ἀσταφίς ίδος ἡ raisins

ἄσταχυς υος ὁ ear of corn

ἀστέγαστος ον without shelter

ἀστεῖος ᾱ ον of a town; polite, accomplished

ἄστειπτος ον untrodden

ἀστεμφής ές firm, steady

ἀστένακτος ον without a sigh

ἀστεργής ές unkind, without love

ἀστερόεις εσσα εν starry, starred; sparkling

ἀστεροπή ῆς ἡ lightning

ἀστεροπητής οῦ ὁ wielder of lightning (of Zeus)

ἀστεφάνωτος ον not wreathed

ἀστή ῆς ἡ townswoman, female citizen

ἀστήρ έρος ὁ star; flame, fire

ἀστήρικτος ον unsupported, weak

ἀστιβής ές untrodden; inaccessible

ἀστικός ή όν of a town
■ **ὁ ἀστικός** townsman

ἄστικτος ον not tattooed

ἄστομος ον hard-mouthed; unable to hold with the teeth

ἄστοργος ον unkind

ἀστός οῦ ὁ townsman, citizen

ἀστοχέω miss, fail

ἀστόω ▸ **ἀϊστόω**

ἀστράβη ης ἡ pack-saddle; saddled mule

ἀστραγαλίζω play with dice

ἀστράγαλος ου ὁ joint of the spine; ankle-bone; die, dice

ἀστραπή ▸ **ἀστεροπή**

ἀστράπτω *aor* ἤστραψα flash, hurl lightning, shine

ἀστράτευτος ον exempt from service

ἀστρολογίᾱ ᾱς ἡ astronomy

ἀστρολόγος ου ὁ astronomer; astrologer

ἄστρον ου τό star, constellation

ἀστρονομίᾱ ᾱς ἡ astronomy

ἄστροφος ον not turning *or* looking back

ἄστρωτος ον without covering, uncovered

ἄστυ εως *or* εος τό city, capital; town (as opposed to country)

ἀστυβοώτης (*gen* ου) crying through the city (of a herald)

ἀστυγείτων ον neighbouring

ἀστυνόμος ον town-protecting, town-ruling; Athenian magistrate in charge of police, streets and public buildings

ἀσυγκρότητος ον untrained

ἀσύμβατος ον irreconcilable

ἀσύμβλητος ον incomprehensible

ἀσυμμετρίᾱ ᾱς ἡ disproportion, deformity

ἀσύμμετρος ον disproportionate

ἀσύμφορος ον inexpedient; useless; unfit

ἀσύμφωνος ον discordant

ἀσυνεσίᾱ ᾱς ἡ stupidity

ἀσύνετος ον stupid

ἀσύνθετος ον faithless, breaking treaties

ἀσύντακτος ον not arranged

ἀσύφηλος ον foolish, disgraceful, mortifying

ἇσυχαῖος ▸ **ἡσυχαῖος**

ἀσφάδαστος ον without convulsions, untrembling

ἀσφάλεια ᾱς ἡ safety, security, certainty, truth; safe-conduct; care

ἀσφαλής ές steadfast, incessant; safe, certain, true; careful

ἀσφαλίζομαι ἀσφαλιοῦμαι secure

ἄσφαλτος ου ἡ mineral pitch, asphaltum

ἀσφάραγος ου ὁ throat, gullet, windpipe

ἀσφόδελος ου ὁ asphodel (a plant of the lily kind)

ἀσχαλάω, ἀσχάλλω be grieved *or* indignant

ἄσχετος ον unable to be held back, incontrollable

ἀσχημονέω behave in a disgraceful fashion

ἀσχημοσύνη ης ἡ lack of decorum; indecency; deformity

ἀσχήμων ον indecent; ugly

ἀσχολίᾱ ας ἡ lack of leisure

ἄσχολος ον without leisure, busy

ἀσώματος ον incorporeal

ἀσωτίᾱ ᾱς ἡ wastefulness, gluttony

ἄσωτος ον debauched, profligate

ἀτακτέω be disorderly *or* undisciplined

ἄτακτος ον disorderly, undisciplined, dissolute

ἀταλαίπωρος ον without pains *or* patience; indifferent

ἀτάλαντος ον equal in weight; equivalent (to)

ἀταλάφρων ον harmless, childlike

ἀταξίᾱ ᾱς ἡ lack of discipline, disorder; licentiousness

ἀτάομαι *pass* be in terrible distress

ἀτάρ *conj* but, yet, however

ἀτάρακτος ον intrepid

ἀταρβής ές **ἀτάρβητος** ον fearless, dauntless

ἀταρπιτός οῦ ἡ **ἀταρπός** οῦ ἡ ▸ **ἀτραπιτός**

ἀταρτηρός ά όν mischievous, uncivil

ἀτασθαλίᾱ ᾱς ἡ recklessness, arrogance

ἀτασθάλλω act arrogantly

ἀτάσθαλος ον reckless, haughty

ἄταφος ον unburied

ἅτε *particle + pple* just as, as if; because, as

ἄτεγκτος ον unwetted

ἀτειρής ές not to be worn away, indestructible; unyielding, stubborn

ἀτείχιστος ον unfortified; not blockaded

ἀτέκμαρτος ον ambiguous, vague, uncertain

ἄτεκνος ον childless

ἀτέλεια ᾱς ἡ immunity; exemption from public responsibilities (usually financial); incompleteness

ἀτέλεστος[1] ον ▸ **ἀτελής**

ἀτέλεστος[2] ον not to be fulfilled; uninitiated

ἀτελεύτητος ον unfinished; inexorable

ἀτελής ές unfinished; not fulfilled; endless; imperfect; unsuccessful; invalid; free from taxes

ἀτέμβω hurt, injure; cheat; *pass* forfeit *+ gen*

ἀτενής ές strained, tight, intense; firm, persevering, inflexible, steady

ἀτενίζω look intently

ἄτερ *prep with gen* far from; without, besides; in spite of

ἀτέραμνος ον hard, inexorable

ἄτερθεν ▸ **ἄτερ**

ἀτερπής ές **ἄτερπος** ον unpleasing, sad

ἀτεχνίᾱ ᾱς ἡ lack of skill

ἄτεχνος ον without skill

■ **ἀτέχνως** *adv* plainly, simply; without art, empirically

α

ἀτεχνῶς *adv* really, of course; quite, utterly

ἀ̄τέω be foolhardy

ἄ̄τη ης ἡ delusion, reckless impulse; guilt, wickedness; punishment; evil, woe

ἄτηκτος ον unmelted

ἀτημέλητος ον not cared for; heedless

ἀ̄τηρίᾱ ᾱς ἡ evil, ruin

ἀ̄τηρός ᾱ́ όν **ἀ̄τήσιμος** ον ruinous; wicked

ἀτίζω not honour

ἀτῑμά(ζ)ω hold in low esteem, despise; disgrace, insult

ἀτῑ́μητος ον despised; not valued

ἀτῑμίᾱ ᾱς ἡ dishonour, disgrace; infamy, loss of civil rights

ἄτῑμος ον unhonoured, despised; deprived of civil rights; not considered worthy, unworthy; dishonouring, shameful, despicable; unestimated

ἀτῑ́μόω ▸ **ἀτιμάζω**

ἀτῑμώρητος ον unpunished; helpless

ἀτιτάλλω *aor* ἀτίτηλα bring up

ἄτῑτος ον unavenged; unpaid

ἄτλᾱτος ▸ **ἄτλητος**

ἀτλητέω think unbearable; be indignant

ἄτλητος ον unbearable

ἀτμίζω steam, smoke

ἀτμίς ίδος ἡ **ἀτμός** οῦ ὁ steam, vapour, smoke

ἄτοκος ον barren

ἀτολμίᾱ ᾱς ἡ lack of daring, cowardice

ἄτολμος ον cowardly

ἄτομος ον uncut, unmown; indivisible

ἀτοπίᾱ ᾱς ἡ unusualness, strangeness, absurdity

ἆτος ον insatiable

ἄτρακτος ου ὁ spindle

ἀτραπιτός οῦ ἡ **ἀτραπῑ̆τός** οῦ ἡ **ἀτραπός** οῦ ἡ path, road, (foot)way

ἀτρέκεια ᾱς ἡ full truth

ἀτρεκής ές sure, exact, strict, true

ἀτρέμας *adv* without trembling; quietly, silently

ἀτρεμέω keep quiet

ἀτρεμίζω ἀτρεμιῶ ▸ **ἀτρεμέω**

ἄτρεστος ον intrepid

ἀτριβής ές **ἄτριπτος** ον unhurt; untrodden; unhardened

ἄτρομος ον ▸ **ἀτρεμής**

ἄτροφος ον underfed

ἀτρύγετος ον unfruitful, desert; ever-fluctuating

ἄτρῡτος ον incessant, unabating

ἀτρῡτώνη ης ἡ the unwearied one (of Athena)

ἄτρωτος ον unwounded; invulnerable

ἄττα[1] ου ὁ father *in greetings*

ἄττα[2] ▸ **τινά** *see* **τις**

ἅττα ▸ **ἅτινα** *see* **ὅστις**

ἀτταταῖ *int* woe! alas!

ἀττέλεβος ου ὁ unwinged locust

ἀττικίζω side with the Athenians

ἀττικισμός οῦ ὁ siding with Athens

ἀτύζω alarm, harass; *pass* be frightened *or* benumbed; flee

ἀτυράννευτος ον not ruled by a tyrant

ἀτυχέω not obtain, fail; be unlucky *or* unfortunate

ἀτύχημα ατος τό **ἀτυχίᾱ** ᾱς ἡ misfortune

ἀτυχής ές unfortunate, unhappy

αὖ* *adv* back; again, once more; for another time; on the other hand; further

αὐαίνω, αὑαίνω αὐανῶ ηὔηνα dry up, scorch; *pass* become dry, wither

αὐγάζω view in the clearest light; shine on; perceive; *mid* discern, perceive

αὐγή ῆς ἡ brilliance; ray, beam; eye, glance

αὐδάζομαι *mid* **αὐδάω** *and mid* speak, utter, talk, cry, call; order, advise

αὐδή ῆς ἡ voice, speech; report, rumour

αὐδήεις εσσα εν gifted with speech

αὐερύω draw *or* bend back

αὖθε̄ ▸ **αὖθι** *or* **αὖτε**

αὐθᾰ́δεια ᾱς ἡ **αὐθᾱδίᾱ** ᾱς ἡ complacency; arrogance; obstinacy

αὐθᾰ́δης ες self-willed; arrogant; capricious; arbitrary

αὐθᾱδίζομαι *mid* be self-willed *or* arrogant

αὔθαιμος ον **αὐθαίμων** ον ▸ **αὐθόμαιμος**

αὐθαίρετος ον self-chosen

αὐθέντης ου ὁ doer; murderer; executioner

αὐθήμερον (*or* αὐθημερόν) *adv* on the same day; on the spot

αὖθι *adv* there, on the spot; straight away

αὐθιγενής ές home-born, native, indigenous

αὖθις ▸ **αὖ**

αὐθόμαιμος ον allied by blood; brother, sister

αὐῐ́αχος ον shouting together

αὖλαξ ακος ἡ furrow

αὔλειος ον belonging to the courtyard

αὐλέω play on the flute; *mid* be entertained by flute-playing

αὐλή ῆς ἡ yard for cattle; farmyard; courtyard; dwelling; palace, residence

αὔλημα ατος τό **αὔλησις** εως ἡ flute-playing

αὐλητής οῦ ὁ flute-player

αὐλητικός ή όν concerning flute-playing

αὐλητρίς ίδος ἡ flute-girl

αὐλίζομαι *aor* ηὐλισάμην *mid and pass* be fenced in; camp (in the open air); pass the night

αὔλιον ου τό hurdle; farmyard; grotto

αὖλις ιδος ἡ night-quarters; stable, place for roosting

αὐλός οῦ ὁ pipe, tube; nozzle, shank; flash of blood; flute

αὐλών ῶνος ἡ hollow way, ravine, defile; strait; canal; ditch

αὐλῶπις (*gen* ιδος) with a tube

αὐξάνω, αὔξω αὐξήσω ηὔξησα increase, augment, enlarge, let grow; praise; *pass* grow, improve, thrive

αὔξη ης ἡ **αὔξησις** εως ἡ growth, increase, thriving

ἄυπνος ον sleepless

αὔρᾱ ᾱς ἡ air, breath, breeze, draught

αὔριον *adv* tomorrow

αὐσταλέος ᾱ ον dry; bristly; dirty

αὐστηρίᾱ ᾱς ἡ **αὐστηρότης** ητος ἡ harshness, severity

αὐστηρός ᾱ́ όν harsh, sour, austere

αὐτάγγελος ον one's own messenger

αὐτάγρετος ον ▸ **αὐθαίρετος**

αὐτάδελφος ον full brother *or* sister

αὐτάρ *conj* but, yet, however; further

αὐτάρκεια ᾱς ἡ self-sufficiency, independence

αὐτάρκης ες self-sufficient, independent; secure; contented

αὖτε ▸ **αὖ**

αὐτεπάγγελτος ον of one's own accord

αὐτερέτης ου ὁ both rower and soldier

ἀϋτέω cry, shout; roar, ring

ἀϋτή ῆς ἡ cry; war-cry; battle

αὐτήκοος ον ear-witness

αὐτίκα *adv* straight away, instantly, directly; for instance

ἀϋτμή ῆς ἡ **ἀϋτμήν** ένος ὁ breath, blast, wind; odour; blaze

α

αὐτοβοεί *adv* at the first war-cry

αὐτογέν(ν)ητος ον self-engendered

αὐτο-γνωμονέω act of one's own volition; act on one's own judgement

αὐτόγνωτος ον self-resolved

αὐτοδαής ές self-taught

αὐτόδεκα just ten

αὐτοδίδακτος ον self-taught

αὐτόδικος ον with one's own jurisdiction

αὐτόδιον *adv* at once

αὐτοέντης ου ὁ ▸ **αὐθέντης**

αὐτοετές *adv* in the same year

αὐτόθεν *adv* from the spot, thence, from here; on the spot, at once; from the beginning; therefore; without ceremony

αὐτόθι *adv* on the spot, there, here

αὐτοκασιγνήτη ης ἡ full sister

αὐτοκασίγνητος ου ὁ full brother

αὐτοκατάκριτος ον self-condemned

αὐτοκέλευστος ον **αὐτοκελής** ές **αὐτόκλητος** ον of one's own accord, unbidden

αὐτοκρατής ές **αὐτοκράτωρ** ορ sovereign, independent; authorized; complete master

αὐτο-κτονέω commit suicide

αὐτόματος (η) ον self-moved; of one's own will, voluntary; accidental

αὐτο-μολέω desert, go over to the other side

αὐτομολίᾱ ᾱς ἡ desertion

αὐτόμολος ον deserter

αὐτο-νομέομαι govern oneself

αὐτονομίᾱ ᾱς ἡ independence

αὐτόνομος ον independent

αὐτονυχί *adv* in the same night

αὐτόξυλος ον of mere wood

αὐτόπαις παιδος ὁ genuine child

αὐτόπετρος ον of natural stone

αὐτοποιός όν self-grown

αὐτόπολις εως ἡ free state

αὐτοπολίτης ου ὁ citizen of a free state

αὐτόπρεμνος ον with the root; root and branch

αὐτόπτης ου ὁ eye-witness

αὐτός ή ό self, oneself, personal; by oneself, alone; *with ordinal adj* together with, oneself with; *in acc, gen and dat only* him, her, it

■ **ὁ αὐτός** ἡ αὐτή τὸ αὐτό the same

αὐτόσε *adv* to there, to the very place

αὐτοσταδίη ης ἡ a stand-up fight

αὐτοσφαγής ές killed by oneself *or* one's relatives

αὐτο-σχεδιάζω improvise; act unadvisedly; judge superficially

αὐτοσχεδίη ▸ **αὐτοσταδίη**

αὐτοσχεδόν *adv* nearby, hand to hand; in close fight

αὐτοτελής ές taxing oneself; arbitrary; complete in oneself

αὐτοῦ *adv* in the same place; there, here; at once

αὐτουργός ον self-working; poor farmer

αὐτοφυής ές natural

αὐτόφωρος ον caught in the very act; convicted by the facts

αὐτόχειρ (*gen* ρος) acting with one's own hand; doer; murderer

αὐτοχειρίᾱ ᾱς ἡ one's own deed; murder

αὐτόχθων ον (*gen* ονος) sprung from the land itself

αὐτοχόωνος ον solid, massive

αὔτως *adv* just so, quite so; still, only, solely; without ceremony, downright; in vain, uselessly; without reason

αὐχενίζω αὐχενιῶ cut one's neck

αὐχένιος ᾱ ον of the neck

αὐχέω boast, brag

αὔχημα ατος τό pride; boast; ornament

αὐχήν ένος ὁ neck, throat; neck of land; strait; defile; forking

αὔχησις εως ἡ ▸ **αὔχημα**

αὐχμέω be dry, squalid *or* rugged

αὐχμηρός ά όν dry, parched; squalid, wild; dark

αὐχμός οῦ ὁ drought; dirt

αὐχμώδης ▸ **αὐχμηρός**

αὔω[1] **αὔω** kindle, singe

αὔω[2] **ἀΰω** shout, call aloud, roar, sound

ἀφ-αγνίζομαι *mid* purify, offer atonement

ἀφαίρεσις εως ἡ a taking away

ἀφ-αιρέω take off, away *or* from; remove; rob, deprive; free from, diminish; subtract; *mid* take for oneself, obtain, deprive, rob; make an end of; prevent

ἄφαλος ον (of a helmet) without a boss in which the plume was fixed

ἀφ-αμαρτάνω + *gen* miss, lose

ἀφαμαρτοεπής ές failing in speech

ἀφ-ανδάνω displease

ἀφάνεια ᾱς ἡ obscurity, insignificance

ἀφανής ές unseen, invisible; hidden, secret; vanished; uncertain, unknown; insignificant, obscure

ἀφανίζω ἀφανιῶ make unseen, cause to vanish, hide, remove; destroy, annihilate; disfigure, deface; *pass* vanish, disappear, cease

ἀφάνισις εως ἡ **ἀφανισμός** οῦ ὁ a vanishing

ἄφαντος ον ▸ **ἀφανής**

ἀφ-άπτω fasten, tie to, hang on; *pass* hang, be hung on

ἄφαρ *adv* quickly, forthwith, presently

ἄφαρκτος ον ▸ **ἄφρακτος**

ἀφ-αρπάζω snatch away; rob

ἀφάρτερος ᾱ ον quicker

ἀφάσσω ▸ **ἀφάω**

ἄφατος ον unutterable, extraordinary; horrible, huge

ἀφαυρός ά όν weak, feeble

ἀφάω touch, feel

ἀφεγγής ές dark, gloomy; terrible

ἀφεδρών ῶνος ὁ a WC

ἀφειδέω be unsparing of; overlook, neglect

ἀφειδής ές unsparing; unmerciful, cruel; plentiful

ἀφειδίᾱ ᾱς ἡ profuseness; harshness

ἀφελής ές simple, plain, naive

ἀφ-έλκω draw *or* drag away

ἀφελότης ητος ἡ simplicity

ἄφενος εος τό wealth, stores

ἀφ-έρπω creep away

ἄφεσις εως ἡ a sending away; setting free, starting; dimission; remission

ἄφετος ον let loose *or* free

ἁφή ῆς ἡ a lighting, kindling; a touching, touch; sense of touch; joint

ἀφ-ηγέομαι *mid* lead the way, lead on *or* off; tell, relate

ἀφήγημα ατος τό **ἀφήγησις** εως ἡ tale, narration

ἄφ-ημαι sit far off

ἀφ-ημερεύω be absent at day

ἀφήτωρ ορος ὁ archer

ἀφθαρσίᾱ ᾱς ἡ immortality, incorruptibility

ἄφθαρτος ον incorruptible, immortal

ἄφθεγκτος ον speechless, mute; unspeakable

ἄφθιτος ον ▸ **ἄφθαρτος**

ἄφθογγος ον voiceless, speechless

ἀφθονίᾱ ᾱς ἡ freedom from envy, readiness; abundance, plenty

ἄφθονος ον free from envy; liberal; fertile; abundant, plentiful

ἀφ-ΐημι *act tr* send off *or* away; throw, shoot; let loose, set free, acquit; dissolve, break up; pronounce, utter; shed; give up, neglect; remit, forgive; *act intr* start; cease; *mid* free oneself; escape; start

ἀφ-ικάνω ▸ **ἀφικνέομαι**

ἀφικνέομαι† *mid* arrive at, come to; return; befall

ἀφιλάγαθος ον averse to good men

ἀφιλάργυρος ον not loving money

ἀφίλητος ον unloved

ἄφιλος ον friendless; unfriendly, unkind; ungrateful; disagreeable

ἄφιξις εως ἡ arrival; return; departure

ἀφ-ιππεύω ride off *or* back

ἄφιππος ον unskilled in riding; not fit for riding

ἀφ-ίπταμαι ▸ **ἀποπέτομαι**

ἀφ-ίστημι *act tr* put away, remove, depose; make fall off *or* revolt; *act intr and pass* go away; stand aloof; revolt; desist, abstain, omit; *mid* get weighed out, be paid

ἄφλαστον ου τό the curved stern of a ship with its ornaments

ἀφλοισμός οῦ ὁ foam

ἀφνειός ά όν rich, wealthy

ἄφνω *adv* suddenly

ἀφόβητος ον **ἄφοβος** ον fearless

ἄφοδος ου ἡ departure, retreat; expedient

ἀφ-ομοιόω make like, portray

ἀφ-οπλίζομαι *mid* take off one's armour; strip of arms

ἀφ-οράω *and mid* look away from; look from afar; behold

ἀφόρητος ον unbearable

ἀφορίζω divide by a boundary-line; select; define

ἀφ-ορμάω start, rush away

ἀφορμή ῆς ἡ starting point; support, means, resources, capital; cause, occasion, chance

ἄφορμος ον hastening away

ἄφορος ον barren

ἀφ-οσιόω purify; expiate; *mid* expiate one's sins, perform religious duties

ἀφραδέω be foolish

ἀφραδής ές foolish, silly, thoughtless, senseless

ἀφραδίᾱ ᾱς ἡ thoughtlessness

ἀφραίνω ▸ **ἀφραδέω**

ἄφρακτος ον unfenced; unguarded; unarmed

ἄφραστος ον unspeakable; unperceived, secret; inconceivable; unexpected

ἀφρέω cover with foam

ἀφρήτωρ (*gen* ορος) without family

ἀφρίζω ▸ **ἀφρέω**

ἀφροδῑσιάζω indulge in lust

ἀφροδῑσιος (ᾱ) ον indulging in love; belonging to Aphrodite

ἀφρονέω be foolish

ἀφροντιστέω be careless (about something)

ἀφρόντιστος ον thoughtless, careless; unthought of, unexpected

ἀφρός οῦ ὁ foam

ἀφροσύνη ης ἡ thoughtlessness

ἄφρων ον thoughtless, foolish, senseless

ἀφύη ης ἡ anchovy

ἀφυής ές ungifted, unfit

ἄφυκτος ον inevitable

ἀφυλακτέω not be on one's guard

ἀφύλακτος ον unguarded; careless, heedless

ἄφυλλος ον leafless

ἀφ-υπνόω fall asleep; wake up from sleep

ἀφυσγετός οῦ ὁ mud, mire, rubbish

ἀφύσσω ἀφύξω *or* ἀφύσω draw [water]; pour in; heap up

ἀφ-υστερέω come too late; withhold

ἀφώνητος ον ▸ **ἄφωνος**

ἀφωνίᾱ ᾱς ἡ speechlessness

ἄφωνος ον speechless; unspeakable

ἀχάλῑνος ον unbridled, unrestrained

ἄχαλκος ον without bronze arms

ἄχαρις ιν (*gen* ιτος) without grace *or* charm, displeasing; ungrateful; unrewarded

ἀχαριστέω be ungrateful

ἀχαριστίᾱ ᾱς ἡ ingratitude, want of charm

ἀχάρι(σ)τος ον ▸ **ἄχαρις**

ἀχειροποίητος ον not made by (human) hand

ἄχειρ (*gen* ρος) without hands ▪ **τὰ ἄχειρα** back

ἀχείρωτος ον unconquered

ἄχερδος ου ἡ wild pear tree

ἀχερωΐς ΐδος ἡ white poplar

ἀχεύω, ἀχέω be sad, mourn

ἀ̄χέω ▸ **ἠχέω**

ἀχθεινός ή όν burdensome, oppressive; cumbersome; angry

ἀχθηδών όνος ἡ grief

ἄχθομαι *pass* be burdened *or* annoyed; be sad, angry *or* unwilling

ἄχθος ους τό burden, load; sorrow, grief

ἀχθοφόρος ον carrying burdens

ἀχίτων ον (*gen* ωνος) without tunic

ἀχλυόεις εσσα εν dark, gloomy; grieving

ἀχλῦς ύος ἡ mist, gloom, darkness

ἀχλῡ́ω *aor* ἤχλῡσα grow dark

ἄχνη ης ἡ chaff; foam; dew

ἄχνυμαι be sad, mourn; be annoyed

ἄχολος ον allaying anger

ἄχομαι ▸ **ἄχνυμαι**

ἀχόρευτος ον **ἄχορος** ον without a dance; joyless

ἄχος εος τό pain, sorrow, grief

ἀχρεῖος (ᾱ) ον useless, weak

ἀχρηματίᾱ ᾱς ἡ lack of money

ἀχρήματος ον without money, poor

ἀχρημοσύνη ης ἡ ▸ **ἀχρηματία**

ἄχρηστος ον useless, unprofitable; foolish, bad, unfit; not yet employed

ἄχρι(ς) *adv* wholly, utterly; *prep with gen* until, as far as; *conj* until, as far as

ἀχυρμιή ῆς ἡ heap of chaff

ἄχυρον ου τό chaff

ἀ̄χώ οῦς ἡ ▸ **ἠχώ**

ἄψ *adv* back; again

ἄψαυστος ον untouched; without touching

ἀψεγής ές unblamed, blameless

ἀψευδέω not to lie

ἀψευδής ές truthful, trustworthy; genuine, true

ἀψίνθιον ου τό **ἄψινθος** ου ἡ wormwood

ἁψίς ῖδος ἡ arch, vault

ἀψόρροος ον flowing backwards

ἄψορρος ον going back

ἅψος εος τό joint, limb

ἀψόφητος ον **ἄψοφος** ον noiseless

ἄψυκτος ον that cannot be cooled

ἄψῡχος ον without soul, lifeless; spiritless

ἆω satiate; *mid* be satisfied

ἄωρος¹ ον untimely; unripe; ill-shaped

ἄωρος² ον invisible; pending

ἀωτέω sleep well

ἄωτος ου ὁ fine wool; fleece

Ββ

β, Β (βῆτα) second letter of the alphabet ■ **β´** *as a numeral* = 2

βαβαί *int* (exclamation of surprise) bless me!

βάδην *adv* step by step, slowly

βαδίζω βαδιοῦμαι ἐβάδισα step, pace, march

βάδισμα ατος τό a marching, pace

βάζω talk, say

βαθμός οῦ ὁ step, stair, degree

βάθος ους τό depth; height, extension; deep water

βάθρον ου τό step, stair; threshold; ladder; bench; seat; base, pedestal; soil; foundation

βαθύγαιος ον with deep soil

βαθυδῑνήεις εσσα εν **βαθυδί̄νης** ες deep-eddying

βαθύζωνος ον deep-girded

βαθύκολπος ον deep-bosomed

βαθύλειμος ον with high grass

βαθυλήιος ον with deep corn *or* crops

βαθῡ́νω deepen

βαθυρρείτης (*gen* ου) deep-flowing

βαθύρριζος ον deep-rooted

βαθύς εῖα ύ deep; high; wide; vehement

βαθυσκαφής ές deep-dug

βαθύσχοινος ον with deep rushes

βαίνω† *intr* take strides; walk, go, step; mount; arrive, go away; depart, die; *pf* stand fast, be settled; *tr* cause to go, bring; cause to descend

βάϊον ου τό palm-branch

βαιός ά́ όν little, small, short; humble

βαίτη ης ἡ coat of skin

βακτηρίᾱ ᾱς ἡ stick, staff

βακχεῖος (*or* βάκχειος) ᾱ ον Bacchic, in ecstasy

βακχεύω celebrate the rites of Bacchus; be frantic, be in ecstasy

βάκχη ης ἡ **βακχί̄ς** ίδος ἡ bacchante

βάκχιος ᾱ ον **βακχιώτης** (*gen* ου) ▸ **βακχεῖος**

βάκχος ου ὁ Bacchus (god of wine and the liberated spirit), wine; devotee of Bacchus, enthusiast

βαλανάγρᾱ ᾱς ἡ key

βαλανεῖον ου τό bath; bathing house

βαλανηφάγος η ον acorn-eating

βαλανηφόρος ον bearing acorns or dates

βάλανος ου ἡ acorn; date; chestnut; peg; door-bolt

βαλάντιον ου τό purse

βαλαντιοτομέω cut purses

βαλαντιότομος ου ὁ cutpurse, pickpocket

βαλβί̄ς ῖδος ἡ the rope drawn across the race course; starting-point; battlements

βαλιός ά́ όν dappled

βάλλω† *act tr* throw, cast, hurl, shoot; hit, wound, strike; push; let fall; put on; meet, catch; put; *act intr* fall; discharge; rush; *mid* throw oneself around; take to heart, bear in mind; deliberate

βαμβαίνω chatter with the teeth, stammer

βαναυσίᾱ ᾱς ἡ being a mere artisan; vulgar trade

βάναυσος ον of a craftsman *or* artisan; vulgar

βάξις εως ἡ speech, saying; oracle; report, talk

βαπτίζω βαπτιῶ dip, wash; baptize

βάπτισμα ατος τό **βαπτισμός** οῦ ὁ baptism

βαπτιστής οῦ ὁ dyer; baptizer

βάπτω βάψω ἔβαψα dip, wet; dye; temper, harden

βάραθρον ου τό pit (for criminals); ruin

βαρβαρίζω βαρβαριῶ behave *or* act like a barbarian; side with the Persians

βαρβαρικός ή όν **βάρβαρος** ον barbarous, not Greek; foreign; uncivilised, cruel

βαρβαρόφωνος ον speaking a foreign language

βαρβαρόω make barbarous; *pass* become barbarous

βάρδιστος *sup see* **βραδύς**

βαρέω ▸ **βαρύνω**

βᾶρις ιος *or* ιδος ἡ a flat-bottomed boat

βάρος ους τό weight, burden, load; grief, sorrow; plenty; dignity

βαρυάλγητος ον grieving sorely

βαρυᾱχής ές groaning heavily

βαρυβρεμέτης (*gen* ου) loud-thundering

βαρυβρώς (*gen* ῶτος) greedily eating

βαρύθω be weighed down *or* heavy

βαρῡ́νω βαρυνῶ ἐβάρῡνα weigh down, load; oppress, distress; *pass* be oppressed *or* tormented; be annoyed *or* angry

βαρύποτμος ον ill-fated, unhappy

βαρύς εῖα ύ heavy, burdensome, oppressive; weighty; [of the voice] deep, hollow, loud; troublesome, painful; unwholesome; hard, cruel; strong, mighty

βαρύστονος ον groaning heavily, painful

βαρυσύμφορος ον oppressed by misfortune

βαρύτης ητος ἡ heaviness; load, oppression; bass voice; harshness, pride

βαρύτῑμος ον very precious *or* costly

βαρύψῡχος ον low-spirited, dejected

βασανίζω βασανιῶ ἐβασάνισα test, try, examine; (put to the) torture

βασανισμός οῦ ὁ a torturing, torture

βασανιστής οῦ ὁ torturer, jailer

βάσανος ου ἡ touchstone; test, proof, trial; inquiry; inquiry by torture; torture

βασίλεια ᾱς ἡ queen, princess

βασιλείᾱ ᾱς ἡ kingdom, monarchy; hereditary monarchy

βασίλειος (ᾱ) ον kingly, royal, princely

■ **τὸ βασίλειον** royal palace, court; treasury

βασιλεύς έως ὁ a hereditary king, prince, ruler; emperor; *without def art* the king of Persia; lord, nobleman

βασιλεύω be (a hereditary) king, rule

βασιληΐς ίδος ἡ royal

βασιλικός ή όν kingly, royal, princely

βασιλίς ίδος ἡ **βασίλισσα** ης ἡ ▸ **βασίλεια**

βάσιμος ον passable

βάσις εως ἡ step, pace; foot; basis, foundation, pedestal

βασκαίνω βασκανῶ ἐβάσκηνα slander; fascinate, bewitch

βασκανίᾱ ᾱς ἡ slander; spell

βάσκανος ον slanderous, malignant; envious

βάσκω go, come

βασσάριον ου τό Libyan fox

βαστάζω βαστάσω ἐβάστασα touch; lift up; bear, hold up; carry away

βατός ή όν passable, accessible

βάτος[1] ου ἡ thorn-bush, bramble-bush, wild raspberry

βάτος[2] ου ὁ a liquid measure

βάτραχος ου ὁ frog

βάτταλος ου ὁ weakling

βαττο-λογέω prattle; speak stammeringly; say the same thing over and over again

βαφεύς έως ὁ dyer

βαφή ῆς ἡ a dipping, dyeing

βδέλλα ης ἡ leech

βδέλυγμα ατος τό abomination; idol

βδελυγμίᾱ ᾱς ἡ loathing, disgust, nausea

βδελυκτός ή όν abominable

βδελυρίᾱ ᾱς ἡ shamelessness

βδελυρός ᾱ́ όν disgusting; shameless

βδελύσσομαι βδελύξομαι ἐβδελύχθην *pass* abhor, detest, fear

βέβαιος (ᾱ) ον firm, steady; trusty; sure; certain

βεβαιότης ητος ἡ firmness, steadiness, safety, certainty

βεβαιόω make firm, confirm, assert; fulfil; *mid* secure for oneself; feel confirmed

βεβαίωσις εως ἡ confirmation

βέβηλος ον profane; unholy, unclean

βεβηλόω profane

βεβρώθω devour

βείομαι ▸ **βέομαι**

βέκος ους τό *a Phrygian word* bread

βέλεμνον ου τό missile

βελόνη ης ἡ point of an arrow; needle

βέλος ους τό missile, dart, javelin; terror

βέλτερος ᾱ ον ▸ **βελτίων**

βέλτιστος η ον *sup* the best, noblest *or* bravest

βελτῑ́ων ον *comp* better, braver, nobler

βένθος ους τό depth

βέομαι I shall live

βέρεθρον ου τό ▸ **βάραθρον**

βηλός οῦ ὁ threshold

βῆμα ατος τό step, stair; raised step, stage; speaker's platform; throne

βήξ βηχός ὁ/ἡ cough

βην *see* **βαίνω**

βήρυλλος ου ἡ beryl

βησ *see* **βαίνω**

βῆσσα ης ἡ glen, wooded valley

βήσσω cough

βητάρμων ονος ὁ dancer

βίᾱ ᾱς ἡ strength, force; violence

βιάζω force; use violence; overpower; maltreat, oppress, constrain; defy

βίαιος (ᾱ) ον forcible, violent; strong, oppressive; forced

βιαστής οῦ ὁ one using force, a violent man

βιάω ▸ **βιάζω**

βιβάζω βιβῶ ἐβίβασα cause to go; bring; lift up

βιβάσθω, βιβάω, βίβημι stride, step

βιβλαρίδιον ου τό **βιβλιάριον** ου τό **βιβλίδιον** ου τό little book *or* scroll

βιβλιοθήκη ης ἡ library

βιβλίον ου τό **βίβλος** ου ἡ bark of the papyrus; paper; book; letter

βιβλιοφύλαξ ακος ὁ keeper of archives

βιβρώσκω βρώσομαι ἔβρωσα eat up, consume

βῖκος (*or* βίκος) ου ὁ vessel, jug, flagon

βινέω fuck

βιόδωρος ον life-giving

βίος ου ὁ life; mode of life; livelihood; means

βιός οῦ ὁ bow

βιοστερής ές bereft of one's livelihood

βιοτεύω live

βιοτή ῆς ἡ **βίοτος** ου ὁ ▸ **βίος**

βιόω† live; *mid* maintain one's life; preserve life

βιώσιμος ον worth living; endurable

βιωτικός ή όν belonging to life, earthly

βλαβερός ά όν harmful, hurtful

βλάβη ης ἡ **βλάβος** ους τό damage; hurt; loss

βλάβω ▸ **βλάπτω**

βλᾱκείᾱ ᾱς ἡ sloth; stupidity

βλᾱκεύω be lazy *or* indolent

βλάξ βλᾱκός ὁ lazy, indolent, careless; stupid

βλάπτω βλάψω ἔβλαψα hinder, stop; weaken; damage, hurt; deceive, confound

βλαστάνω βλαστήσω ἔβλαστον sprout, bud, germinate; grow up; be descended from; *tr* bring forth

βλάστη ης ἡ **βλάστημα** ατος τό **βλαστός** οῦ ὁ sprout, bud; growth; descendant; origin

βλασφημέω blaspheme; slander

βλασφημίᾱ ᾱς ἡ blasphemy, slander

βλάσφημος ον blaspheming, slandering

βλεμεαίνω look fiercely; exult in

βλέμμα ατος τό look, glance

βλεπτός ή όν worth seeing

βλέπω look at *or* on; see, regard, observe; have sight; beware of

βλεφαρίς ίδος *or* ῖδος ἡ eyelash

βλέφαρον ου τό eyelid; eye

βλῆμα ατος τό shot; wound

βλῆτρον ου τό ring, hoop

βληχή ῆς ἡ a bleating

βλίττω cut out honeycombs, take honey

βλοσυρός ά όν grim, terrible

βλοσυρῶπις ιδος ἡ one who is grim-looking

βλωθρός ά όν tall, high grown

βλώσκω μολοῦμαι ἔμολον go; come

βοάγριον ου τό leather shield

βοάω cry, shout, roar, howl; call to; praise; *pass* be known *or* famous

βοεικός ή όν **βόειος** ᾱ ον of *or* for oxen; *in fem* [shield] of oxhide

βοεύς έως ὁ thong of ox-leather

βοή[1] ῆς ἡ cry, shout; war-cry; call; sound; loud speech *or* voice; prayer

βοή[2] ῆς ἡ oxhide

βοηδρομιών ῶνος ὁ name of a month (September to October)

βοήθεια ᾱς ἡ help, aid, rescue, succour; protection; auxiliary force

βοηθέω + *dat* come to the rescue (of); aid, help, assist

βοηθόος ον hastening to the battle-shout

βοηθός όν helping; assistant

βοηλασίᾱ ᾱς ἡ theft of cattle, rustling

βοηλάτης ου ὁ driver

βοητύς ύος ἡ a crying, shouting

βόθρος ου ὁ **βόθῡνος** ου ὁ hole, pit

βοιωτ-αρχέω be a magistrate of the Boeotians

βοιωτάρχης ου ὁ **βοιώταρχος** ου ὁ magistrate in Boeotia

βοιωτιάζω speak Boeotian; side with the Boeotians

βολή ῆς ἡ throw, shot; glance; ray

βολίζω throw the sounding lead

βολίς ίδος ἡ missile; plummet

βόλομαι ▸ **βούλομαι**

βόλος[1] ου ὁ ▸ **βολή**

βόλος[2] ου ὁ fishing net

βομβέω boom, hum, buzz, ring, make a hollow sound

βόμβος ου ὁ hollow sound

βορᾱ́ ᾶς ἡ food, meat

βόρβορος ου ὁ mud, mire, dirt

βορβορώδης ες muddy

βορέᾱς ου ὁ north wind; north

βόρειος ον **βορήιος** η ον northern

βορρᾶς ᾶ ὁ ▸ **βορέας**

βόρυς υος ὁ gazelle

βόσις εως ἡ food

β

βόσκημα ατος τό cattle, herd; pasture
βόσκω βοσκήσω feed, nourish; *pass and mid* be fed *or* maintained; graze
βόστρυχος ου ὁ lock of hair
βοτάνη ης ἡ fodder, pasture; herb
βοτήρ ῆρος ὁ shepherd
βοτόν οῦ τό *usu pl* grazing cattle
βοτρῡδόν *adv* in the shape of grapes
βότρυς υος ὁ grape
βούβαλις ιος ἡ antelope
βούβοτος ου ἡ pasture for cattle
βούβρωστις εως ἡ intense greediness; grinding poverty *or* misery
βουβών ῶνος ὁ groin; abdomen
βουγᾱΐος ου ὁ a great bully, braggart
βουθερής ές feeder of cattle
βουθυτέω sacrifice cattle
βούθυτος ον belonging to a sacrifice of cattle
βούκερως ων horned like an ox
βουκολέω feed cattle; *pass and mid* be fed, graze
βουκολίη ης ἡ **βουκόλιον** ου τό herd of cattle
βουκόλος ου ὁ cowherd, herdsman
βουλείᾱ ᾱς ἡ office of counsellor
βούλευμα ατος τό resolution; decree, plan; wish, opinion; counsel
βουλευτήριον ου τό council-house, council
βουλευτής οῦ ὁ counsellor
βουλευτικός ή όν belonging to counsellors
βουλεύω be a counsellor; *act and mid* take counsel; plan, devise; consider; determine, resolve; give counsel
βουλή ῆς ἡ will, determination; counsel, advice; project; council
βούλημα ατος τό **βούλησις** εως ἡ will, determination; purpose
βουληφόρος ον counselling
βουλῑμιάω suffer from ravenous hunger
βούλομαι† will, wish, want, like; be willing *or* resolved; prefer, choose
■ **ὁ βουλόμενος** the first to volunteer
βουλῡτός οῦ ὁ evening, time of unyoking oxen
βουνόμος ον cattle-feeding
βουνός οῦ ὁ hill, mount
βουπλήξ ῆγος ἡ goad
βουπόρος ον piercing through an ox
βούπρῳρος ον with the head of an ox
βοῦς βοός ὁ/ἡ cow, ox, bull; cattle; oxhide, shield of oxhide
βουφονέω kill oxen
βουφορβός οῦ ὁ cowherd
βοῶπις ιδος ἡ ox-eyed (of Hera)
βραβεῖον ου τό prize in a contest
βραβεύς έως ὁ **βραβευτής** οῦ ὁ judge, umpire
βραβεύω be a judge, (be) umpire; rule
βράγχος ου ὁ hoarseness, sore throat
βραδῡ́νω βραδυνῶ ἐβράδῡνα delay; loiter
βραδυπλοέω sail slowly
βραδύς εῖα ύ slow, heavy; lazy
βραδυτής ῆτος ἡ slowness, tardiness
βράσσων ον ▸ **βραδύτερος**
βραχεῖν *aor infin* to rattle, ring, roar
βράχιστος η ον ▸ **βραχύτατος**
βραχῑ́ων ονος ὁ arm, shoulder
βράχος εος τό *in pl* shallows
βραχυλογίᾱ ᾱς ἡ brevity in speech
βραχυλόγος ον short in speech
βραχύς εῖα ύ short, little, not far off; shallow
βραχύτης ητος ἡ shortness
βρέμω *and mid* roar, sound, clash
βρέφος εος τό unborn child; newborn child; young person, colt
βρεχμός οῦ ὁ forehead

βρέχω wet, sprinkle; send rain; *pass* get wet

βριαρός ᾱ́ όν weighty, strong

βρίζω *aor* ἔβριξα sleep, slumber

βριήπυος ον loud-shouting (of Ares)

βρῑθοσύνη ης ἡ weight, heaviness

βρῑθύς εῖα ύ weighty, heavy

βρῑ́θω βρίσω ἔβρῑσα *and mid* be weighty *or* loaded; be bent down; abound; outweigh, prevail

βρομέω hum, buzz

βρόμος ου ὁ noise, buzzing, roar

βροντάω thunder

βροντή ῆς ἡ thunder; stupefaction

βρότειος (ᾱ) ον *adj from* **βροτός** mortal, human

βροτόεις εσσα εν bloody

βροτολοιγός όν man-slaying (of Ares)

βρότος ου ὁ gore

βροτός ου ὁ/ἡ mortal; man

βροτόω stain with blood

βροχή ῆς ἡ rain

βρόχος ου ὁ rope, noose

βρυγμός οῦ ὁ a gnashing

βρῡ́κω bite; devour, eat greedily

βρῡχάομαι *mid and pass* roar, shout aloud

βρῡ́χω gnash the teeth

βρύω sprout, bud, swell with + *dat*; be full of + *gen*; send forth

βρῶμα ατος τό **βρώμη** ης ἡ **βρῶσις** εως ἡ **βρωτῡ́ς** ύος ἡ food, meat; an eating

βύβλινος η ον made of papyrus

βύβλος ου ἡ papyrus plant; papyrus roll, book; bark of papyrus

βύζην *adv* closely, thickly

βυθίζω let sink; sink

βῡθός οῦ ὁ depth, abyss

βύκτης (*gen* ου) howling (of wind)

βῡνέω ▸ **βύω**

βύρσα ης ἡ skin, hide

βυρσεύς έως ὁ **βυρσοδέψης** ου ὁ tanner

βύσσινος η ον of fine linen

βυσσοδομεύω build in the deep; ponder deeply

βυσσόθεν *adv* from the depths

βυσσός οῦ ὁ ▸ **βυθός**

βύσσος ου ἡ fine linen

βῡ́ω cram, stuff full

βωθέω ▸ **βοηθέω**

βῶλος ου ἡ clod of earth

βώμιος ᾱ ον belonging to an altar

βωμίς ίδος ἡ step, stair

βωμός οῦ ὁ raised place, step, stand, pedestal, altar

βωστρέω call to

βωτιάνειρα ᾱς ἡ man-feeding

βώτωρ ορος ὁ herdsman

Γγ

γ, Γ (γάμμα) third letter of the alphabet ■ **γ′** *as a numeral* = 3

γάγγραινα ης ἡ gangrene, cancer

γάζα ης ἡ **γαζοφυλάκιον** ου τό treasury

γαῖα ᾱς ἡ ▸ **γῆ**

γαιᾱ́οχος ▸ **γαιήοχος**

γαιήιος ᾱ ον sprung from Gaia, the Earth goddess

γαιήοχος ον earth-compassing; land-protecting

γαίω + *dat* exult in

γ

γάλα ακτος τό milk

γαλαθηνός ή όν milk-sucking

γαλακτοπότης ου ὁ milk-drinker

γαλέη ης ἡ **γαλῆ** ῆς ἡ weasel; cat

γαλήνη ης ἡ calm, stillness of wind; tranquility

γάλοως ω ἡ sister-in-law

γαμβρός οῦ ὁ son-in-law

γαμετή ῆς ἡ wife, married woman

γαμέτης ου ὁ husband

γαμέω† *male subject* marry; *mid female subject* marry, be given in marriage to + *dat*

γαμηλιών ῶνος ὁ month in the Attic calendar (January to February)

γαμίζω give in marriage; *pass* get married

γαμικός ή όν bridal

γαμίσκω ▸ **γαμίζω**

γᾱμόρος ▸ **γεωμόρος**

γάμος ου ὁ a wedding, marriage, wedding-feast

γαμφηλή ῆς ἡ *almost always in pl* jaw, beak

γαμψῶνυξ (*gen* υχος) with curved talons

γανάω shine, be bright

γάνυμαι *mid* be delighted

γάρ* *conj* for; since, as; why, what; if only!

γαργαλισμός οῦ ὁ a tickling

γαστήρ γαστρός ἡ belly; womb; sausage

γάστρᾱ ᾱς ἡ belly

γαστριμαργίᾱ ᾱς ἡ gluttony

γαυλι(τι)κός ή όν belonging to a merchant ship

γαῦλος ου ὁ milk-pail, bucket; merchant vessel

γαυριάω pride oneself

γδουπέω ▸ **δουπέω**

γε* *enclitic conj* at least, at any rate, even, just, of course, indeed

γέγωνα *perf* make oneself heard; cry, shout; proclaim

γέεννα ης ἡ the valley of Hinnom (the place of future punishment)

γείνομαι *mid* be begotten *or* born; beget

γειτνιάω be a neighbour

γείτων ονος ὁ/ἡ neighbouring; neighbour

γελασείω be inclined to laugh

γελαστής οῦ ὁ one who laughs, scoffer

γελαστός ή όν laughable

γελάω†, **γελοιάω** laugh, smile, shine; sneer at

γελοῖος (*also* γέλοιος) ᾱ ον laughable; facetious, jesting

γέλως ωτος ὁ **γέλος** ου ὁ laughter, laughing; joke, mocking

γελωτο-ποιέω cause laughter

γελωτοποιός οῦ ὁ jester, buffoon

γεμίζω γεμιῶ fill, load

γέμω be full (of + *gen*)

γεν *likely to be from* **γίγνομαι**

γενεᾱ́ ᾶς ἡ birth, descent; race, family, tribe; home; generation

γενεᾱ-λογέω trace a pedigree; *pass* derive one's pedigree

γενεᾱλογίᾱ ᾱς ἡ genealogy; pedigree

γενέθλη ης ἡ ▸ **γενεά**

γενέθλιος ον belonging to one's birth; belonging to a family

■ **τὰ γενέθλια** birthday feast

γένεθλον ου τό descendant; descent

γενειάς άδος ἡ beard; chin; cheek

γενειά(σκ)ω get a beard

γένειον ου τό chin; beard

γενέσιος ον ▸ **γενέθλιος**

γένεσις εως ἡ origin, birth, engendering; a being, creature; race

γενετή ῆς ἡ birth

γενέτης ου ὁ **γενέτωρ** ορος ὁ father; ancestor; son

γενηΐς ίδος ἡ axe; shovel

γεννάδᾱς (*gen* ου) noble

γενναῖος ᾱ ον innate; high-born, noble, generous, high-minded; genuine, sincere

γενναιότης ητος ἡ nobleness, magnanimity

γεννάω engender, beget, bring forth

γέννημα ατος τό product, fruit; child

γέννησις εως ἡ a begetting

γεννητής οῦ ὁ begetter, parent

γεννητός ή όν begotten, born

γεννήτωρ ορος ὁ ▸ **γεννητής**

γένος ους τό birth, descent; race, family, kindred; descendant, child; sex, gender; one's own country; kind, species; generation; a tribe (subdivision of a phratry)

γέντο he seized *or* grasped

γένυς υος ἡ chin; jaw; axe; *in pl* mouth

γεραιός ᾱ́ όν old, aged; old man ▪ **οἱ γεραίτεροι** the elders

γεραίρω γεραρῶ ἐγέρηρα honour, reward

γέρανος ου ἡ crane

γεραός ᾱ́ όν ▸ **γεραιός**

γεραρός ᾱ́ όν reverend; stately, majestic

γέρας αος *or* ως τό gift of honour; honour; privilege; gift, reward

γεροντ-αγωγέω guide an old man

γερόντιον ου τό old man

γερουσίᾱ ᾱς ἡ council of elders (especially at Sparta)

γερούσιος ᾱ ον belonging to the elders

γέρρον ου τό wicker-work; wicker shield; wickerwork booths in the Athenian agora

γερροφόρος ου ὁ bearer of a wicker shield

γέρων οντος ὁ old; old man; *in pl* elders, councillors

γεῦμα ατος τό taste, sample

γεύω give to taste; *mid* + *gen* taste, eat of; try

γέφῡρα ᾱς ἡ mound; bridge; battle-field

γεφῡρόω bridge over

γεωγράφος ου ὁ geographer

γεώδης ες earthy

γεωμέτρης ου ὁ surveyor, geometer

γεωμετρίᾱ ᾱς ἡ land-surveying; geometry

γεωμετρικός ή όν geometric

γεωμόρος ου ὁ land-owner

γεωπέδιον ου τό **γεώπεδον** ου τό piece of land

γεωπείνης (*gen* ου) poor in land

γεωργέω till, cultivate

γεωργίᾱ ᾱς ἡ agriculture; arable land

γεωργικός ή όν belonging to agriculture; farmer, skilled in farming

γεωργός όν tilling the ground; husbandman; farmer

γεωρυχέω dig mines

γῆ γῆς ἡ earth, land; soil, ground, field; home ▪ **γῆς ἔγκτησις** tenure of land granted to a foreigner

γηγενής ές earth-born

γῆθεν *adv* from the earth

γηθέω be glad, rejoice

γηθοσύνη ης ἡ joy, delight

γηθόσυνος ον joyful, glad

γήινος η ον of earth

γήλοφος ου ὁ hill

γημ *aor stem from* **γαμέω**

γη-οχέω possess land

γηραιός ᾱ́ όν old, aged

γῆρας αος *or* ως τό old age

γηράσκω, γηράω γηράσω ἐγήρασα become old; ripen

γηροβοσκός όν feeding one's old parent

γηρο-τροφέω feed in old age

γ

γηροτρόφος ον ▸ **γηροβοσκός**

γῆρυς υος ἡ voice; sound; speech

γῄτης ου ὁ husbandsman, farmer

γίγᾱς αντος ὁ giant

γίγνομαι† become, grow; be born, come into being; [of revenue] come in; result, amount to; happen, occur

γιγνώσκω† perceive, gain knowledge (of); know, learn, understand; judge, determine, decide; think; resolve

γῑ́νομαι ▸ **γίγνομαι**

γῑνώσκω ▸ **γιγνώσκω**

γλάγος εος τό milk

γλακτοφάγος ον living on milk

γλαυκιόων ουσα ον with sparkling eyes

γλαυκόμματος ον bright-eyed; owl-eyed; grey-eyed

γλαυκός ή όν clear, bright, gleaming; bluish

γλαῦξ (*or* γλαύξ) κός ἡ owl

γλαυκῶπις ιδος ἡ the bright-eyed *or* owl-eyed *or* grey-eyed one (of Athena)

γλαφυρός ᾱ́ όν hollow, convex; smoothed

γλεῦκος ους τό sweet wine

γλήνη ης ἡ eyeball; puppet, doll

γλῆνος εος τό ornament

γλίσχρος α ον slippery; scant, scarce, petty

γλίχομαι *mid* + *gen* be fond of, strive to gain

γλοιός οῦ ὁ resin, gum

γλουτός οῦ ὁ buttock

γλυκερός ᾱ́ όν ▸ **γλυκύς**

γλυκύθῡμος ον sweet-minded

γλυκύς εῖα ύ sweet; delightful, lovely; kind

γλυκύτης ητος ἡ sweetness

γλυφίς ίδος ἡ notch of an arrow

γλύφω γλύψω ἔγλυψα carve, engrave

γλῶσσα ης ἡ (*also* γλῶττα ης ἡ) tongue; mouth; speech; dialect

γλωσσόκομον ου τό case for money; case, casket

γλωχίς ῖνος ἡ point of a nail *or* arrow

γναθμός οῦ ὁ **γνάθος** ου ἡ jaw, mouth

γναμπτός ή όν curved, bent; flexible

γνάμπτω γνάμψω ἔγναμψα curve, bend

γναφεῖον ου τό **γναφεύς** έως ὁ ▸ **κναφεῖον, κναφεύς**

γνήσιος ᾱ ον legitimate; genuine, true

γνόφος ου ὁ darkness

γνύξ *adv* with bent knees

γνυφή ῆς ἡ hollow, cave

γνω *likely to be from* **γιγνώσκω**

γνῶμα ατος τό mark, token; knowledge

γνώμη ης ἡ mind, understanding, reason, judgement; opinion, persuasion; discretion; resolution, purpose; wish, intention; sentence, truism; advice, proposal

γνώμων ονος ὁ one who knows, judge, umpire, arbiter; overseer; sundial

γνωρίζω γνωριῶ perceive, make out, discover; know, become acquainted with; declare

γνώριμος ον known, familiar; perceptible, knowable; noble, aristocrat

γνωσι-μαχέω alter one's mind

γνῶσις εως ἡ knowledge, wisdom, understanding; judicial sentence

γνώστης ου ὁ one who knows

γνωστός ή όν ▸ **γνώριμος**

γνωτός ή όν known; knowable; kinsman, brother, sister

γοάω *and mid* wail, groan; bewail

γογγύζω γογγύσω murmur, mutter

γογγυστής οῦ ὁ mutterer

γοή ῆς ἡ ▸ **γόος**

γόης ητος ὁ enchanter, wizard; juggler, cheat

γοητείᾱ ᾱς ἡ sorcery, witchcraft, delusion

γοητεύω bewitch, cheat, delude

γόμος ου ὁ cargo, freight

γομφίος ου ὁ cheek-tooth, molar

γόμφος ου ὁ peg, nail

γονεύς έως ὁ parent, ancestor

γονή ῆς ἡ a begetting; birth, origin; descendant, offspring; seed

γόνιμος ον vigorous, productive

γόνυ γόνατος τό knee

γονυ-πετέω fall *or* go down on one's knees

γόος ου ὁ a weeping, lament, dirge; incantation

γοργός ή όν terrible, wild, fierce

γοργύρη ης ἡ (*also* γόργυρα ᾱς ἡ) underground dungeon

γοργῶπις (*gen* ιδος) fierce-looking (of Athena)

γοῦν* (γε οὖν) *particle* at least, at any rate; of course; for instance; yet, indeed

γουνάζομαι, γουνόομαι γουνάσομαι *mid* be prostrate, entreat, supplicate

γουνός οῦ ὁ high ground

γράδιον ου τό **γρᾱΐδιον** ου τό old woman, old hag

γραῖα ᾱς ἡ old woman; *adj* old, knowing

γράμμα ατος τό letter of the alphabet; writing, writ; notebook, letter, document, catalogue; inscription; picture; *in pl* letters, learning

γραμματεῖον ου τό tablet, notebook; document; account book

γραμματεύς έως ὁ scribe, writer, secretary

γραμματεύω be secretary

γραμματικός ή όν knowing how to read and write; belonging to grammar; a grammarian well-grounded in the rudiments

γραμματιστής οῦ ὁ secretary; schoolmaster

γραμμή ῆς ἡ stroke, line in writing

γραπτός ή όν written

γραπτύς ύος ἡ a scratching, wound

γραῦς γρᾱός ἡ old woman

γραφεύς έως ὁ writer; painter

γραφή ῆς ἡ picture, drawing; writing, document; bill of indictment, public prosecution

■ **γραφὴ παρανόμων** an indictment for proposing an illegal measure

γραφικός ή όν belonging to writing *or* painting

γραφίς ίδος ἡ writing style; stylus for writing

γράφω scratch, engrave; write, draw, paint; write down, register; describe; inscribe; *mid* write for oneself; note down; have something painted; indict

γρᾱώδης ες like an old woman

γρηγορέω be awake; live

γρηῦς, γρηΰς ▸ **γραῦς**

γρύζω grunt, mutter

γρῦψ γρῡπός ὁ griffin

γύαλον ου τό a hollow, curvature, bow; armour-plate; cave, grotto, den

γύης ου ὁ a measure of land; plough-land; corn-field

γυῖον ου τό joint, limb; knee, leg, arm

γυμνάζω train, exercise, accustom

γυμνασίᾱ ᾱς ἡ training, exercise

γυμνασίαρχος ου ὁ the manager of the gymnasium

γυμνάσιον ου τό exercise; place of exercise, training school, gymnasium

γυμναστής οῦ ὁ trainer of professional athletes

γυμναστικός ή όν fond of *or* skilled in athletic exercises, gymnastic

γυμνής ῆτος ὁ **γυμνήτης** ου ὁ light-armed foot-soldier

γυμνητείᾱ ᾱς ἡ light infantry

γυμνητεύω be naked *or* light-armed

γυμνητικός ή όν belonging to a light-armed foot-soldier

γυμνικός ή όν ▸ **γυμναστικός**

γυμνοπαιδίαι ῶν αἱ gymnastic festival

γυμνός ή όν naked; unarmed, lightly clad *or* armed; bare, destitute

γυμνότης ητος ἡ **γύμνωσις** εως ἡ nakedness, stripping

γυμνόω bare, denude

γυναικάριον ου τό ▸ **γύναιον**

γυναικεῖος ᾱ ον womanly, feminine

γυναικονόμος ου ὁ a magistrate with responsibility for women

γυναικωνῖτις ιδος ἡ women's apartment

γυναιμανής ές crazy about women

γύναιον ου τό (a term of endearment) little woman; darling; *used contemptuously* weak woman

γύναιος η ον ▸ **γυναικεῖος**

γυνή γυναικός ἡ woman, lady; wife; mistress; widow; servant

γῡρός ᾱ́ όν round, curved

γῡ́ψ γῡπός ὁ vulture

γύψος ου ἡ chalk, gypsum

γυψόω rub with chalk; smear with gypsum

γῶν ▸ **γοῦν**

γωνίᾱ ᾱς ἡ angle, corner; joiner's square; corner-stone

γωνιώδης ες angular

γωρῡτός οῦ ὁ bow-case, quiver

Δδ

δ, Δ (δέλτα) fourth letter of the alphabet
■ **δ'** *as a numeral* = 4

δᾳδοῦχος ου ὁ torch-bearer (at the Eleusinian mysteries)

δαήμων ον knowing, experienced

δαῆναι *aor infin* teach; learn; know

δᾱήρ έρος ὁ brother-in-law

δαί* *particle* then
■ **τί δαί;** what then?
■ **πῶς δαί;** how then?

δαιδάλεος ᾱ ον cunningly *or* curiously wrought

δαιδάλλω work *or* adorn curiously

δαΐζω δαΐξω ἐδάϊξα divide, tear, pierce; kill

δαϊκτάμενος η ον killed in battle

δαιμονάω, δαιμονίζομαι *pass* be mad *or* raving

δαιμόνιος ᾱ ον divine, godlike; possessed by a demon, unfortunate; supernatural, wonderful; poor, odd
■ **τὸ δαιμόνιον** divine being, lesser deity, evil spirit, demon, devil; guardian spirit; divine operation, fate; *in connexion with Socrates* genius

δαιμονιώδης ες devilish

δαίμων ονος ὁ/ἡ divine being, (lesser) deity, guardian spirit; evil spirit, demon, devil, spectre; fate, evil, death

δαίνῡμι δαίσω ἔδαισα give a feast; *mid* eat, feast

δάϊος ᾱ ον burning, hot; pernicious, hostile; unhappy

δαΐς ΐδος ἡ pine-wood; torch

δάϊς ϊος battle

δαίς δαιτός ἡ banquet, feast; food

δαίτη ης ἡ meal, feast

δαιτρεύω share out; carve

δαιτρόν οῦ τό share of a meal

δαιτρός οῦ ὁ the person who carves meat

δαιτροσύνη ης ἡ art of carving

δαιτυμών όνος ὁ guest, dinner-companion

δαιτύς ύος ἡ meal

δαΐφρων ον intelligent; warlike

δαίω[1] kindle, set on fire; *pass* burn, blaze

δαίω[2] *and mid* divide, distribute, share out; tear

δακ *aor stem from* **δάκνω**

δακέθῡμος ον gnawing at the heart

δάκνω[†] bite, sting; hurt, distress

δάκρυ υος τό **δάκρῡμα** ατος τό **δάκρυον** ου τό tear

δακρυόεις εσσα εν tearful; weeping

δακρυπλώω (of a drunkard) be bathed in tears

δακρυ-ρροέω shed tears

δακρῡ́ω weep; shed tears; weep for

δακτύλιος ου ὁ a ring, seal-ring

δάκτυλος ου ὁ finger; toe; finger's breadth; the metrical foot – ◡◡; short space

δᾱλός οῦ ὁ firebrand; piece of wood

δαμάζω ▸ **δαμάω**

δάμαλις εως ἡ young cow, calf

δάμᾱρ δάμαρτος ἡ wife

δαμάω δαμάσω ἐδάμασα tame, break in; subdue, overpower; kill; give in marriage

δανείζω lend, lend with interest; *mid* borrow

δάνειον ου τό **δάνεισμα** ατος τό loan

δανεισμός οῦ ὁ money-lending, usury

δαν(ε)ιστής οῦ ὁ money-lender, usurer

δᾱνός ή όν dry, parched

δάος εος τό torch

δαπανάω spend; spend on; consume, waste

δαπάνη ης ἡ **δαπάνημα** ατος τό spending, expense, cost; extravagance; tribute

δαπανηρός ά́ όν **δάπανος** ον expensive; extravagant

δάπεδον ου τό soil, flat country; floor

δάπτω δάψω tear in pieces; devour

δαρδάπτω tear in pieces; devour

δαρεικός οῦ ὁ Persian gold coin

δαρθάνω *aor* ἔδραθον sleep

δᾱρός ά́ όν ▸ **δηρός**

δᾴς δᾳδός ἡ ▸ **δαΐς**

δάσκιος ον thick-shaded, bushy

δάσμευσις εως ἡ distribution

δασμο-λογέω collect tribute (from)

δασμός οῦ ὁ division; tax, tribute

δασμοφόρος ον paying tribute

δασπλῆτις εως ἡ hard-striking, frightful

δασύμαλλος ον thickly fleeced, woolly

δασύς εῖα ύ hairy; bushy, densely-wooded; rough

δασύστερνος ον with shaggy breast

δατέομαι δάσομαι ἐδασάμην *mid* divide, share out; carve; crush

δάφνη ης ἡ laurel

δαφνηφόρος ον laurel-bearing

δαφοινός όν blood-red

δαψιλής ές liberal; plentiful, abundant

δέ* *particle* but; but on the other hand; further; thus; then

δέαται he seems

■ **δέατο** he seemed

δεδίσκομαι δεδίξομαι ἐδε(ι)διξάμην greet, welcome

δεδίσσομαι *mid* frighten, alarm; get frightened

δέδοικα fear *see* **δείδω**

δεδοκημένος η ον lying in wait

δ

δέελος η ον ▸ **δῆλος**

δέησις εως ἡ prayer, entreating

δεῖ† *impers + acc of person* one must, one ought

■ **τὸ δέον, τὰ δέοντα** what is needed; the necessary *or* proper thing; the thing required

■ **δεῖ** + *gen* there is need of

δεῖγμα ατος τό proof, sample, specimen; show, bazaar

δειγματίζω expose to shame; make a show of

δειδήμων ον fearful, timorous, cowardly

δείδια ▸ **δείδω**

δειδίσκομαι ▸ **δεδίσκομαι**

δειδίσσομαι ▸ **δεδίσσομαι**

δείδω δείσομαι ἔδεισα *pf (with pres meaning)* δέδοικα be afraid, fear, be alarmed

δειελιάω take an evening meal; wait till evening

δείελος ον belonging to the evening; evening

δεικανάομαι welcome, greet

δείκηλον ου τό representation, exhibition

δείκνῡμι†, **δεικνύω** show, point out, exhibit, display; prove, demonstrate, explain; tell; teach; *mid* welcome, drink to (someone); show, prove

δείλη ης ἡ afternoon; evening

δειλίᾱ ᾱς ἡ cowardice

δειλιάω be afraid

δείλομαι *mid* (of the sun) set (as evening approaches)

δειλός ή όν timid, cowardly; vile, contemptible, worthless; unhappy, luckless

δεῖμα ατος τό fear, terror, horror

δειμαίνω δειμανῶ fear, be afraid *or* alarmed

δειματόω frighten

δεῖνα ὁ/ἡ/τό a certain person, Mr X (one whom one cannot or will not name)

δεινο-λογέομαι *mid* complain passionately *or* loudly

δεινόπους (*gen* ποδος) striding fearsomely *or* terrifyingly

δεινός ή όν venerable; fearful, terrible, frightful, formidable, dangerous; extraordinary; mighty, powerful; clever, skilful; unheard of, shocking, strange, wonderful, marvellous

■ **τὸ δεινόν** danger, terror, distress

δεινότης ητος ἡ harshness, terrible nature, sternness; power, ability

δεινόω exaggerate

δεινώψ (*gen* ῶπος) horrible-looking

δεῖος ους τό ▸ **δέος**

δειπνέω take the main meal; dine

δείπνηστος ου ὁ meal-time

δειπνίζω δειπνιῶ ἐδείπνισα entertain at table

δεῖπνον ου τό meal, main meal of the day, dinner; banquet; food

δειπνο-ποιέομαι *mid* prepare a meal; dine

δειράς άδος ἡ ridge of a hill; rock

δειρή ῆς ἡ neck, throat

δειρο-τομέω cut the throat (of a person); behead

δείρω ▸ **δέρω**

δεισιδαιμονίᾱ ᾱς ἡ fear of the gods; religion; superstition

δεισιδαίμων ον godfearing; superstitious

δέκα ten

δεκαδαρχίᾱ ᾱς ἡ government by ten men

δεκάδαρχος ου ὁ **δεκαδάρχης** ου ὁ commander of ten men

δεκαδύο twelve

δεκαετής ές ten years old, lasting for ten years

δεκάκις *adv* ten times

δεκάμηνος ον ten months old

δεκαπέντε fifteen

δεκάπηχυς υ ten cubits long *or* high (a cubit is the distance between the elbow and the tip of the forefinger)

δεκαπλάσιος ᾱ ον tenfold

δεκάπλεθρος ον a thousand feet long

δεκάπρωτοι ων οἱ the chief municipal authorities of a city

δεκάρχης ου ὁ ▸ **δεκάδαρχος**

δεκαρχίᾱ ᾱς ἡ ▸ **δεκαδαρχία**

δεκάς άδος ἡ the number ten; a body of ten

δεκαταῖος ᾱ ον for ten days; ten days old

δεκατέσσαρες α fourteen

δεκατευτήριον ου τό customs house

δεκατεύω give *or* take a tenth, tithe; consecrate

δέκατος η ον tenth

δεκατόω take a tenth; *pass* give a tenth

δεκάφῡλος ον divided into ten tribes

δεκάχῑλοι αι α ten thousand

δεκέτης ες lasting ten years; ten years old

δέκνῡμι ▸ **δείκνυμι**

δέκομαι ▸ **δέχομαι**

δέκτης ου ὁ receiver, beggar

δεκτός ή όν acceptable

δελεάζω entice (by a bait), bait

δέλεαρ ατος τό bait

δέλτα τό delta

δελτίον ου τό **δέλτος** ου ἡ writing tablet

δέλφαξ ακος ἡ full-grown pig

δελφῑνοφόρος ον bearing a dolphin

δελφῑ́ς ῖνος ὁ dolphin

δέμας ατος τό body, figure, frame, stature; *adv* in the form *or* shape of

δέμνιον ου τό bed; bedstead, mattress

δέμω *aor* ἔδειμα build

δενδίλλω glance quickly

δένδρεον ου τό ▸ **δένδρον**

δενδρήεις εσσα εν rich in trees

δενδρο-κοπέω cut trees *or* vines; lay waste to

δένδρον ου τό **δένδρος** εος τό tree

δενδρο-τομέω ▸ **δενδροκοπέω**

δεννάζω abuse

δέννος ου ὁ abuse, reproach

δεξαμενή ῆς ἡ cistern, tank, reservoir

δεξιοβόλος ου ὁ javelin-man

δεξιολάβος ου ὁ spearman; guard

δεξιόομαι *mid* give the right hand to; greet

δεξιός ᾱ́ όν on the right hand side; prosperous, fortunate; dexterous, ready

■ **ἡ δεξιᾱ́** the right hand; promise, agreement

δεξιόσειρος ον right-hand (horse); vigorous, impetuous

δεξιότης ητος ἡ dexterity, readiness

δεξιόφιν *adv* to the right

δεξιτερός ᾱ́ ον ▸ **δεξιός**

δεξίωμα ατος τό offering of the right hand, pledge of friendship; acceptable thing

δέομαι *see* **δέω**

δέος ους τό fear, awe, reverence; danger

δέρκομαι *aor* ἔδρακον *pf (with pres sense)* δέδορκα *pass* look, see; look at

δέρμα ατος τό hide, skin; leather; bag

δερμάτινος η ον of leather

δέρρις εως ἡ hide, skin

δέρτρον ου τό the membrane which contains the bowels

δέρω δερῶ ἔδειρα skin, flay; cudgel

δέσμα ατος τό ▸ **δεσμός**

δεσμεύω, δεσμέω put in chains, throw into prison

δέσμη ης ἡ (*also* δεσμή ῆς ἡ) bundle

δέσμιος ον in chains, captive

δεσμός οῦ ὁ *but in pl both* οἱ δεσμοί *and* τὰ δεσμά fetter, bond, string, thong; cable; imprisonment

δ

δεσμοφύλαξ ακος ὁ jailer
δέσμωμα ατος τό fetter, bond
δεσμωτήριον ου τό prison
δεσμώτης ου ὁ **δεσμῶτις** ιδος ἡ prisoner
δεσπόζω be *or* become master, ruler
δέσποινα ης ἡ mistress, lady
δεσποσύνη ης ἡ absolute power
δεσπότης ου ὁ lord, master, owner
δεσποτικός ή όν imperious, despotic
δεσπότις ιδος ἡ ▶ **δέσποινα**
δετή ῆς ἡ sticks tied together; torch
δεύομαι ▶ **δέομαι**
δεῦρο, δευρί *adv* to here; come here!; till now, hitherto
δεύτατος η ον last
δεῦτε *pl of* **δεῦρο**
δευτεραῖος ᾱ ον on the second *or* following day
δευτερεῖα ων τά second prize
δευτερόπρωτος ον next to the first
δεύτερος ᾱ ον second, next; inferior
δεύω¹ wet, drench
δεύω² ▶ **δέω²**
δεχήμερος ον for ten days
δέχομαι *mid* take, accept, receive; approve; choose; suffer patiently; take for; receive kindly, treat; make head against, stand one's ground; lie in wait
δέψω *aor* ἐδέψησα soften, mould, knead; tan
δέω¹ bind, tie up, fasten, fetter, imprison
δέω² + *gen* want, lack, (be in) need (of); *mid* **δέομαι**; (be in) need (of); ask for, beg for, want
δή¹ *adv* ▶ **ἤδη**
δή²* *particle* now, already, just now; at once; then; of course, indeed, clearly; even; yet; only; therefore; as said before
δῆγμα ατος τό bite, sting
δηθά *adv* for a long time
δῆθεν* *particle* really, clearly (ironic); of course, really
δηθῦνω delay, loiter
δήϊος ᾱ ον ▶ **δάϊος**
δηϊότης ητος ἡ enmity; battle
δηιόω ▶ **δῃόω**
δηλαδή *adv* plainly, of course
δηλαυγῶς *adv* quite plainly
δηλέομαι *mid* hurt, damage, destroy
δήλημα ατος τό hurt, ruin, destruction
δηλήμων ον harmful, destructive
δήλησις εως ἡ a hurting, ruin
δηλονότι *adv* plainly, clearly, of course
δῆλος η ον visible, evident, plain, clear
δηλόω manifest, show, signify; explain, prove
■ **δηλοῖ** it is clear
δήλωσις εως ἡ a pointing out, manifestation; advertisement, order, proof
δημ-αγωγέω be a popular leader *or* demagogue
δημαγωγός οῦ ὁ popular leader, demagogue
δήμαρχος ου ὁ chief of a district; governor of the people
δήμευσις εως ἡ confiscation
δημεύω confiscate; make known, make public
δημ-ηγορέω be a public orator, address the people; make popular speeches
δημηγορίᾱ ᾱς ἡ public speech
δημηγορικός ή όν qualified for public speaking
δημηγόρος ου ὁ public orator
δημιοεργός ▶ **δημιουργός**
δήμιος ον belonging to the whole people, public; public executioner
δημιουργέω practise a trade; work; create

δημιουργίᾱ ᾱς ἡ trade; handicraft, work, creation

δημιουργικός ή όν belonging to craftsmen

δημιουργός οῦ ὁ one working for the common good; craftsman, workman, artist, master; maker, creator; magistrate

δημοβόρος ον devouring the people's goods

δημογέρων οντος ὁ elder of the people

δημόθεν *adv* at public expense

δημο-κρατέομαι *pass* live in a democracy

δημοκρατίᾱ ᾱς ἡ democracy

δημοκρατικός ή όν democratic

δημόλευστος ον stoned by the people

δῆμος ου ὁ land, country, district; common people, community; popular assembly; democracy

δημός οῦ ὁ fat

δημοσιεύω be in the service of the public; confiscate

δημόσιος ᾱ ον public, of *or* for the state; public officer *or* slave

■ **τὸ δημόσιον** the commons, state, state affairs; state treasury; state prison

■ **δημοσίᾳ** *adv* publicly, in the name of the state

δημοσιόω confiscate

δημοτελής ές public, at public expense

δημοτεύομαι *mid* belong to a demos, be a member of a deme

δημότης ου ὁ man of the people, private man; fellow citizen

δημοτικός ή όν belonging to the people, common, public, civilian

δημοῦχος ον tutelary, protector of the country

δημώδης ες popular; common

δήν *adv* for a long time; long ago

δηναιός ή όν long-living

δηνάριον ου τό denarius (a Roman coin)

δῆνος τό *only as pl (δήνεα)* counsel, project

δήξομαι *see* **δάκνω**

δῇος η ον ▸ **δάϊος**

δῃόω treat as an enemy, kill, fight; cut up, tear; destroy, waste

δήποτε *adv* ever, once, at some time

δήπου* δή που* δήπουθεν* *adv* indeed, certainly; perhaps

δηριάομαι *mid* **δηρίομαι** *mid* fight

δῆρις ιος ἡ fight, contest

δηρός ᾱ́ όν long

δῆτα* *adv* certainly, indeed, of course, plainly; therefore, then

δήω I shall find

διά *adv* asunder; through, throughout; *prep with acc* through; during; on account of, because of, by reason of; with a view to; *with gen* through, right through, through between; during; since; by means of, arising from

δια-βαδίζω go over

δια-βαίνω stride; cross, go over, step across

δια-βάλλω throw over, carry across; disunite; slander, accuse falsely, abuse; cheat

διάβασις εως ἡ a crossing, passage, bridge, ford, pass

διαβατήρια ων τά offering for a happy crossing

διαβατός ή όν passable, fordable

δια-βεβαιόομαι *mid* assert, confirm

δια-βιβάζω lead, bring *or* carry over

δια-βιόω live through; pass one's life

δια-βλέπω look through; look straight on *or* round; consider

δια-βοάω shout loudly; cry out, proclaim

διαβολή ῆς ἡ slander, calumny, false accusation, reproach; infamy; suspicion; hatred

δ

διάβολος ον slanderous
■ **ὁ διάβολος** slanderer, fiend, devil

διαβόρος ον eating through, consuming

διάβορος ον eaten through

δια-βουλεύομαι *mid* discuss pro and con, discuss thoroughly

διάβροχος ον wet; soaked; leaky

δια-βῡνέω thrust *or* push through

δι-αγγέλλω notify, announce, send message, proclaim; *mid* inform one another, pass the word of command

διάγγελος ου ὁ negotiator, go-between

δια-γελάω laugh at

δια-γίγνομαι *mid* continue, live on, survive, remain, continue in + *pple*; be between, elapse

δια-γιγνώσκω discern, distinguish; perceive exactly; resolve, determine, decide

δι-αγκυλίζομαι, δι-αγκυλόομαι *mid* hold the javelin in readiness

δια-γλάφω hollow out

διαγνώμη ης ἡ distinction; resolution, decree, judgement, sentence

δια-γνωρίζω make known

διάγνωσις εως ἡ ▸ **διαγνώμη**

δια-γογγύζω murmur among themselves

δι-αγορεύω state precisely

διάγραμμα ατος τό a drawing, figure; register; decree

δια-γράφω delineate; cross out; strike out, reject

δια-γρηγορέω remain awake

δι-άγω lead through, over, across *or* up; pass, live, spend; delay; continue, keep + *pple*

διαγωγή ῆς ἡ a leading across; course of life

δι-αγωνίζομαι *mid* fight against; carry on a lawsuit; fight to the end

δια-δαίομαι *mid* divide; destroy

δια-δάπτω tear apart, lacerate

δια-δατέομαι *mid* distribute

δια-δείκνῡμι point out exactly, explain, show

διαδέξιος ον quite auspicious

δια-δέρκομαι see *or* perceive through

δια-δέχομαι *mid* receive in turn; take up, succeed to; relieve

δια-δέω fasten *or* bind to; fetter

δια-δηλέομαι tear in *or* to pieces

διάδηλος ον quite distinct, manifest

διάδημα ατος τό diadem, headband

δια-διδράσκω run away, escape

δια-δίδωμι pass on, hand over; distribute

δια-δικάζω carry on a lawsuit; pass sentence

δια-δικαιόω plead; regard (something) as right

διαδικασίᾱ ᾱς ἡ decision; action for precedence, a suit brought to decide who was entitled to any right or privilege

διαδοχή ῆς ἡ a taking up; succession; relief

διάδοχος ον taking up, alternating; successor

δια-δρηστεύω run away

δια-δύομαι pass *or* slip though; escape

δια-είδομαι show clearly; appear clearly

δια-ζάω survive, maintain life

δια-ζεύγνῡμι disjoin, separate

διάζευξις εως ἡ a disjoining, parting

διάζωμα ατος τό girdle; apron

δια-ζώννῡμι put round oneself; encompass

δια-ζώω ▸ **διαζάω**

δι-άημι blow through

δια-θεάομαι *mid* view closely

δια-θειόω fumigate thoroughly

διάθεσις εως ἡ arrangement, disposition, condition; constitution; mind

διαθέτης ου ὁ arranger

δια-θέω run through *or* about; spread; run in contest

διαθήκη ης ἡ arrangement; will; treaty, covenant

δια-θορυβέω trouble profoundly

δια-θροέω spread a report

δια-θρῡλέω spread abroad; *pass* be commonly reported

δια-θρύπτω break in *or* to pieces; spoil, weaken; make vain

διαί ▶ **διά**

διαίνω διανῶ ἐδίηνα wet, moisten

διαίρεσις εως ἡ division; distribution; distinction

διαιρετός ή όν divided

δι-αιρέω divide, sever, cut in two; pull down, demolish, destroy; distribute; explain, interpret; define; decide

δι-αϊστόω kill, murder

δίαιτα ης ἡ life; mode of life; diet; food; dwelling, room

διαιτάω be umpire; *pass* lead a life, live, dwell

διαίτημα ατος τό ▶ **δίαιτα**

διαιτητής οῦ ὁ arbiter, umpire

δια-καθαρίζω clean(se) thoroughly

δια-καίω burn through

δια-καλύπτω cover completely

δια-καρτερέω last out, persevere

διακατ-ελέγχομαι confute utterly

δια-κεάζω split in two

διά-κειμαι be in a certain condition *or* state; be disposed; be settled

δια-κείρω frustrate

δια-κελεύομαι *mid* exhort, encourage, impel

διάκενος ον quite empty, hollow

δια-κηρῡκεύομαι *mid* negotiate through a herald

δια-κινδῡνεύω run a desperate risk, gamble everything

δια-κῑνέω shake thoroughly; throw into disorder

δια-κλάω break in two

δια-κλέπτω steal, remove by stealth; betray

δια-κληρόω assign by lot; let draw lots

διακομιδή ῆς ἡ a carrying over

δια-κομίζω carry over *or* across

διᾱκονέω *and mid* render service; + *dat* wait on, serve, attend to

διᾱκονίᾱ ᾱς ἡ service, attendance, business; office of deacon

διᾱκονικός ή όν serviceable; servile

διᾱ́κονος ου ὁ servant, attendant; deacon

δι-ακοντίζομαι *mid* compete at spear throwing

δια-κόπτω cut *or* break through; beat to pieces; interrupt

διάκορος ον satiated, glutted

διᾱκόσιοι αι α two hundred

δια-κοσμέω set in order, arrange

διακόσμησις εως ἡ **διάκοσμος** ου ὁ arrangement, battle-order

δι-ακούω hear out; listen to

δι-ακρῑβόω *and mid* do accurately; examine thoroughly; know exactly

διακριδόν *adv* outstandingly, above all

δια-κρῑ́νω distinguish, separate, divide; choose; decide, judge; *pass and mid* be divided; dispute with one another; be reconciled; doubt

διάκρισις εως ἡ separation; distinction; decision

διάκρουσις εως ἡ delay

δια-κρούω hinder, interrupt; *mid* push away from oneself; deceive, elude; delay

δ

διάκτορος ου ὁ guide, messenger of the gods

δια-κυκάω mix together

δια-κύπτω peep through

διακωλῡτής οῦ ὁ hinderer

δια-κωλῡ́ω hinder, prevent, check; forbid

δια-κωμῳδέω ridicule

διακωχή ῆς ἡ ▸ **διοκωχή**

δια-λαγχάνω assign by lot

δια-λαλέω talk over, talk of a great deal

δια-λαμβάνω separate, take apart; distinguish; divide, distribute; pause; grasp, seize, hold fast; deliberate

δια-λάμπω shine *or* flash through

δια-λανθάνω be hidden, escape notice

δια-λέγω pick out, choose; *pass* consider; talk (with), converse, negotiate; recite; speak [a dialect]

διάλειμμα ατος τό interval, gap

δια-λείπω leave an interval *or* gap; let pass; leave off, desist; lie between

διαλεκτικός ή όν skilled in discourse; belonging to dialectics

διάλεκτος ου ἡ conversation; speech; dialect

διαλλαγή ῆς ἡ change; reconciliation, agreement

διαλλακτής οῦ ὁ mediator

δι-αλλάσσω interchange, change; reconcile; differ; *pass and mid* exchange between one another; be reconciled; be different

δια-λογίζομαι *mid* consider, reflect; examine together

διαλογισμός οῦ ὁ consideration, thought; doubt

διάλογος ου ὁ conversation, dialogue

δια-λοιδορέομαι + *dat pass* fling gross insults at

δια-λῡμαίνομαι *mid* maltreat

διάλυσις εως ἡ a loosing, separation, ending; a paying off, settling of accounts; reconciliation, peace

διαλύτης ου ὁ destroyer

διαλυτός ή όν dissoluble, capable of being dissolved

δια-λύω dissolve, divide, separate; destroy; end, break off; reconcile; pay

δι-αμαρτάνω miss *or* fail entirely; not obtain; go wrong; make a mistake

διαμαρτίᾱ ᾱς ἡ mistake, failure, error

δια-μαρτυρέω refute by witnesses

δια-μαρτῡ́ρομαι *mid* give solemn evidence (of); beg earnestly; protest solemnly

δια-μαστῑγόω whip severely

δια-μάχομαι *mid* fight through; struggle, fight; endeavour

δι-αμάω *and mid* cut through; scrape away

δι-αμείβω exchange; change, alter; *mid* exchange for oneself; change one's mind

διαμέλλησις εως ἡ being on the point of (doing something), delay

δια-μέλλω delay continually

δια-μέμφομαι *mid* blame severely

δια-μένω remain, continue, persevere

δια-μερίζω divide; *pass and mid* be at variance

διαμερισμός οῦ ὁ dissension

δια-μετρέω measure out *or* off; sell; *mid* have measured out to one; share out among themselves

διαμετρητός όν measured out

δια-μηχανάομαι *mid* contrive, devise

δι-αμιλλάομαι *pass* contend, rival

δια-μιμνῄσκομαι remember continually

δια-μιστύλλω cut in little pieces

δια-μνημονεύω remember well; mention

δια-μοιράω share out, distribute; divide, tear apart

διαμπάξ *adv* right through, through and through

διαμπερές *adv* right through, through and through; continually; throughout; altogether

διαμῡθο-λογέω converse

δι-αναγκάζω force, compel

διανα-παύω give rest for a moment; *mid* rest for a while

δια-ναυμαχέω fight at sea

διάνδιχα *adv* two ways; in either way

δια-νέμω distribute, portion out; *mid* divide between themselves

δια-νεύω nod *or* beckon to

δια-νέω swim through

διαν-ίσταμαι *mid* + *gen* depart from, stand aloof from

δια-νοέομαι *pass* consider, reflect; think, intend

διανόημα ατος τό thought; purpose

διάνοια ᾱς ἡ thought, intellect, mind; opinion; intention

διαν-οίγω open; explain

διανομή ῆς ἡ distribution

δια-νυκτερεύω pass the night

δι-ανύ(τ)ω finish, accomplish

δια-παιδεύω educate thoroughly

διαπαντός *adv* throughout

διαπαρατριβή ῆς ἡ altercation, violent dispute

δια-παρθενεύω deflower [a virgin]

δια-πασσαλεύω fasten with nails; stretch out for tanning

δια-πάσσω sprinkle

δια-παύομαι *pass* cease; *mid* pause

δι-απειλέω threaten violently

διάπειρα ᾱς ἡ experiment, trial

δια-πειράομαι *pass* test, make trial (of); know by experience

δια-πείρω pierce *or* bore through

δια-πέμπω send over; send to; send in different directions

δια-περαίνω *and mid* finish, bring to an end

δια-περάω go over *or* across, pass; endure, get through

δια-πέρθω destroy totally

δια-πέτομαι *mid* fly through *or* away

δια-πίμπλημι fill up (completely)

δια-πῑ́νω compete with one another in drinking

δια-πῑ́πτω fall *or* go to pieces; escape

δια-πιστεύω entrust (something *acc*) to + *dat*

δια-πλέκω interweave; weave to the end

δια-πλέω sail through *or* across

δια-πλήσσω dash to pieces

διάπλους ου ὁ a sailing across, passage

δια-πνέω blow through; revive

δια-ποικίλλω variegate, adorn

δια-πολεμέω end the war; carry on the war

διαπολέμησις εως ἡ the ending of a war

δια-πολιορκέω besiege continually, blockade

διαπομπή ῆς ἡ legacy; message

δια-πονέω work out with labour, elaborate; train, make hardy; *mid* endeavour; get practised; be very distressed

διαπόντιος ον beyond the sea

δια-πορεύω carry over *or* through; *pass* go *or* march through

δι-απορέω *and mid* be at a loss, be undecided

δια-πορθέω ▸ **διαπέρθω**

δια-πορθμεύω carry over, across; carry a message

δια-πρᾱγματεύομαι *mid* examine closely; do a thing with care

δια-πρᾱ́σσω *and mid* finish, accomplish, bring about; procure, get; make an appointment; kill

διαπρεπής ές conspicuous, excellent

δια-πρέπω be prominent *or* conspicuous; adorn

δια-πρεσβεύομαι *mid* send embassies

δια-πρήσσω ▸ διαπράσσω

δια-πρηστεύω betray

δια-πρῑ́ω saw through; *pass* grow furious

διαπρό *adv* right through, thoroughly

διαπρύσιος (ᾱ) ον piercing; stretching far

δια-πτο(ι)έω frighten *or* scare away

δια-πτύσσω disclose, unfold

διάπυρος ον glowing, fiery

δια-πωλέω sell

δι-αράσσω strike *or* knock through

δι-αρθρόω articulate; form; dissect

δι-αριθμέω count up; *mid* count and classify

δι-αρκέω be sufficient; endure, last

διαρκής ές enduring; sufficient

διαρπαγή ῆς ἡ plundering

δι-αρπάζω tear to pieces; rob, plunder

δια-ρραίνω sprinkle, shed

δια-ρραίω tear *or* dash to pieces; destroy

δια-ρρέω flow through; vanish; melt away

δια-ρρήγνῡμι break through; break to *or* in pieces; destroy; rend; pierce; *pass* burst

διαρρήδην *adv* expressly, distinctly

δια-ρρῑπτέω, δια-ρρῑ́πτω throw through; fling about, distribute

διάρρῑψις εως ἡ flinging about, scattering

διάρροια ᾱς ἡ diarrhoea

δια-ρροιζέω whizz through

δια-σαφέω, δια-σαφηνίζω make quite clear, show plainly, explain; report

δια-σείω shake *or* stir violently; extort

δια-σεύομαι *mid* rush, run *or* dart through

δια-σημαίνω point out, mark out

διάσημος ον quite perceptible

δια-σιωπάω remain silent

δια-σκάπτω dig through

δια-σκαρῑφάομαι *mid* scrape up

δια-σκεδάννῡμι scatter about; disband; destroy

δια-σκέπτομαι ▸ διασκοπέω

δια-σκευάζομαι *mid* prepare for battle

δια-σκηνέω, δια-σκηνόω encamp in different quarters; rise from the table

δια-σκίδνημι ▸ διασκεδάννυμι

δια-σκοπέω *and mid* view closely, examine, consider; look round

δια-σκοπιάομαι *mid* spy out

δια-σκορπίζω scatter about; winnow; waste

δια-σμάω, δια-σμέω wipe out, rinse out

δια-σπάω tear apart, tear to pieces; sever; scatter; split

δια-σπείρω scatter about; waste

διασπορά ᾶς ἡ dispersion

δια-σπουδάζω *and mid* endeavour, do earnestly

δι-ᾴσσω rush through

διάστασις εως ἡ distance; interval; dissension, discord, enmity

δια-σταυρόομαι *mid* fortify with a palisade

δια-στέλλω *and mid* separate; distinguish; command

διάστημα ατος τό interval, distance

δια-στοιβάζω stuff in between

διαστολή ῆς ἡ distinction, difference

δια-στρέφω turn aside, pervert; distort; incite (to rebellion), stir up

διάστροφος ον distorted, crippled; perverted

δια-σῡ́ρω mock

διασφάξ ἄγος ἡ cleft, ravine

δια-σφενδονάω fling about from a sling; *pass* burst

δια-σχίζω cleave in two, tear asunder

δια-σῴζω save through; preserve; keep in memory

διαταγή ῆς ἡ **διάταγμα** ατος τό arrangement, order

δια-τάμνω ▸ **διατέμνω**

διάταξις εως ἡ arrangement (of troops), order of battle

δια-ταράσσω throw into great confusion

δια-τάσσω arrange well; draw up for battle; arrange separately; command

δια-τείνω stretch out; *act and mid* stretch oneself; exert oneself; affirm; get ready for shooting

διατείχισμα ατος τό fortification

δια-τελευτάω finish completely

δια-τελέω finish, complete; come to; continue *or* keep doing + *pple*

διατελής ές permanent

δια-τέμνω cut through; divide

δια-τετραίνω make a hole in; perforate

δια-τήκω melt

δια-τηρέω keep, preserve; watch; beware (of)

δια-τίθημι put asunder; arrange, manage, treat; influence; *pass* be inclined; *mid* dispose of; make a testament; sell off; settle; make use of

δια-τινάσσω shake to and fro

δια-τμήγω cut through; sever; scatter; distinguish; *pass* be dispersed

διάτορος ον pierced, piercing

δια-τρέφω keep (someone) nourished; breed, support

δια-τρέχω run *or* sail through

δια-τρέω flee in every direction

διατριβή ῆς ἡ a waste of time; delay, stay; pastime, employment, study, conversation

δια-τρῑ́βω rub away; waste, consume; prevent; delay; stay, live; busy *or* occupy oneself (with)

διατροφή ῆς ἡ sustenance, support

δια-τρῠ́γιος ον bearing grapes in succession

δι-αυγάζω shine through

διαυγής ές transparent

δίαυλος ου ὁ double pipe; a double course (in the stadium)

δια-φαίνω cause to shine through; *mid* shine through, become visible

διαφάνεια ᾱς ἡ transparency

διαφανής ές transparent; manifest, evident

διαφερόντως *adv* differently; eminently, especially

δια-φέρω carry across; bring to an end; live; bear; carry different ways, throw about; differ, be different; excel; *pass* be at variance

■ **διαφέρει** it makes a difference, it is of importance

■ **τὸ διαφέρον** interest, point of dispute

δια-φεύγω flee through; escape, avoid

διάφευξις εως ἡ escape

δια-φημίζω make known, divulge, spread abroad

δια-φθείρω destroy, ruin, corrupt, spoil, waste; bribe; *pass* be destroyed *or* lost; perish

διαφθορᾱ́ ᾶς ἡ destruction, ruin; corruption; seduction

διαφθορεύς έως ὁ destroyer; seducer

διαφ-ῑ́ημι dismiss

δια-φοιβάζω drive mad

δια-φοιτάω rove about

διαφορᾱ́ ᾶς ἡ difference

δια-φορέω carry over; carry across from one place to another; disperse; plunder; tear to pieces

δ

διάφορος ον different; at variance; excellent
■ **τὸ διάφορον** difference; disagreement, dispute, object of controversy; sum of money

διάφραγμα ατος τό partition wall; diaphragm

δια-φράζω show *or* tell clearly

δια-φρέω let through, let pass

δια-φυγγάνω ▸ **διαφεύγω**

διαφυγή ῆς ἡ an escaping

διαφυή ῆς ἡ growth between; joint, knot, partition

δια-φυλάσσω watch carefully, preserve

δια-φύομαι *mid* grow between, be connected with; intervene, elapse

δια-φῡσάω blow away

δι-αφύσσω draw out; drink up; tear out; rend

δια-φωνέω make a discordant noise; disagree + *dat*

δια-φώσκω dawn, show light through

δια-χάζω *and mid* retreat separated; withdraw

δια-χειμάζω pass the winter

δια-χειρίζω manage; *mid* slay

διαχείρισις εως ἡ management; direction

δια-χειροτονέω decide by vote

δια-χειροτονίᾱ ᾱς ἡ voting

δια-χέω pour out; melt, disperse; break up, frustrate; clear up; *pass* be melted; fall to pieces

δια-χόω heap up a mound

δια-χράομαι *mid* use, employ, have + *dat*; kill, destroy + *acc*

δια-χωρέω (of diarrhoea) go through

δια-χωρίζω separate

δια-ψεύδω *and mid* lie; deceive; *pass* be mistaken

δια-ψηφίζομαι *mid* decide by a vote

διαψήφισις εως ἡ **διαψηφισμός** οῦ ὁ voting by ballot

δια-ψῡ́χω cool; make dry

δίγλωσσος ον speaking two languages

διδακτικός ή όν skilled at teaching

διδακτός ή όν that can be taught; taught, instructed

διδασκαλεῖον ου τό school

διδασκαλίᾱ ᾱς ἡ teaching, instruction; rehearsing

διδασκαλικός ή όν suitable for teaching ▸ **διδακτικός**

διδασκάλιον ου τό science

διδάσκαλος ου ὁ teacher, master

διδάσκω† teach, instruct, train; show, prove; get a play ready; *pass* learn; *mid* contrive; have (someone) taught

διδαχή ῆς ἡ teaching, doctrine

δίδημι ▸ **δέω¹**

διδρᾱ́σκω -δρᾱ́σομαι -ἔδρᾱν run

δίδραχμος ον of two drachmas

διδυμᾱ́ων ονος ὁ twin brother

δίδυμος η ον double, twofold, twin

δίδωμι† give, present, grant; afford, pay; consecrate, devote; concede, permit, give over; pardon, release; allow

δι-εγγυάω give bail for; release on bail

δι-εγείρω wake up, arouse; raise

δί-ειμι¹ go *or* march through; discuss

δί-ειμι² be continually

δι-εῖπον *aor* explain, tell exactly; converse

δι-είργω separate, keep separate

δι-είρομαι question closely

δι-ειρύω draw across

δι-είρω put across

διέκ, διέξ *prep with gen* through and out of

διεκ-περάω go *or* sail through

διεκ-πλέω sail out through

διέκπλοος ου ὁ (*also* διέκπλους ου ὁ) a sailing through, a breaking of the enemy's lines (in a sea-fight)

διεκ-πλώω ▸ **διεκπλέω**

διέκροος ου ὁ (*also* διέκρους ου ὁ) passage for the stream to escape

δι-ελαύνω drive through, pierce through; ride *or* march through

δι-ελέγχω refute utterly *or* examine thoroughly

δι-έλκω, δι-ελκύω pull *or* tear apart

δίεμαι *mid* chase, frighten away; flee in awe

διεμ-πολάω sell; betray

διεν-θῡμέομαι *pass* think intently

δι-ενιαυτίζω live out the year

διεξ-ειλίσσω sift, separate

διέξ-ειμι *see* **διεξέρχομαι**

διεξ-ελαύνω drive, ride *or* march through

διεξ-ερέομαι question

διεξ-έρχομαι go out through, pass through, elapse; come to; go through, explain, recount

διεξ-ηγέομαι *mid* explain, recount

διεξ-ῑ́ημι let out through; empty oneself

διέξοδος ου ἡ passage, way out, issue, event; cross-road; detailed account, recital, statement

δι-εορτάζω keep a feast to the end

δι-έπω manage, take care of, attend to; arrange; pass through

δι-εργάζομαι *mid* ruin, kill

δι-έργω ▸ **διείργω**

δι-ερέσσω row through; row well

δι-ερευνάω *and mid* search, examine closely

διερμηνευτής οῦ ὁ interpreter

δι-ερμηνεύω interpret, translate

διερός[1] ᾱ́ όν quick

διερός[2] ᾱ́ όν active, alive; nimble; wet, liquid

δι-έρπω creep through, step through

δι-έρχομαι go, walk, drive *or* pass through; arrive at; narrate, explain; consider; (of time) pass

δι-ερωτάω question continually

δι-εσθίω eat *or* bite thoroughly

διετής ές of two years, lasting two years

διετήσιμος ον lasting the whole year

διετίᾱ ᾱς ἡ space of two years

δι-ευλαβέομαι take good care to; be on one's guard against

δι-ευτυχέω have continuous good fortune

δι-έχω keep separate; reach through; extend; stand apart, be distant
■ **τὸ διέχον** interval

δίζημαι διζήσομαι *mid* seek out, aspire to; examine

δίζυξ (*gen* υγος) doubly-yoked

δίζω doubt

δι-ηγέομαι *mid* explain, describe, narrate

διήγησις εως ἡ discussion, narration

δι-ηθέω sift, strain through; cleanse; filter through

δι-ηκονέω ▸ **διᾱκονέω**

δι-ήκω come through, pervade

δι-ημερεύω spend the whole day

διηνεκής ές uninterrupted, continual; far-reaching; exact, full

διήνεμος ον windy

διθάλασσος ον between two seas, where two seas meet

δῑθύραμβος ου ὁ dithyramb (a kind of lyric poetry)

δι-ῑ́ημι send, thrust *or* shoot through; let pass through; dismiss

δι-ικνέομαι *mid* go through; reach, meet; recount

διϊπετής ές fallen from heaven, heaven-sent

δι-ίστημι *act tr* separate, divide; place separately, set at variance; *act intr and mid* stand apart *or* at intervals; part; differ; be open; remove; quarrel

δι-ισχῡρίζομαι *mid* affirm confidently; rely on + *dat*

δ

διΐφιλος ον loved by Zeus

δικάζω judge, administer justice; decide, determine; *mid* plead, speak in court

δικαιοκρισίᾱ ᾱς ἡ just judgement

δίκαιος ᾱ ον just; righteous, honest; legal, lawful, right, proper; useful, fit, convenient; regular; entitled to, worthy of, bound to

▪ **τὸ δίκαιον, τὰ δίκαια** right, justice, privilege, legal question, argument, judicial proceeding(s)

δικαιοσύνη ης ἡ **δικαιότης** ητος ἡ justice; administration of justice

δικαιόω think right, justify; judge, condemn; claim, desire

δικαίωμα ατος τό right, argument, justification; legal claim; judgement; legal act

δικαίωσις εως ἡ summons; condemnation; legal claim; judgement, will and pleasure; justification

δικᾱνικός ή όν skilled in law, belonging to trials, judicial; lawyer; lawyer-like, arrogant, tedious

δικασπόλος ου ὁ judge

δικαστήριον ου τό lawcourt

δικαστής οῦ ὁ judge, juryman

δικαστικός ή όν judicial, of a judge; skilled in law

δίκελλα ης ἡ mattock, pickaxe, two-pronged hoe

δίκη ης ἡ custom, usage; right, law, order, justice; judgement, sentence; judicature, lawsuit, legal action, trial; fine, penalty, satisfaction

▪ **δίκην** *prep with gen* after the manner of, in the way of

▪ **δίκην δίδωμι** pay the penalty

δικλίς ίδος ἡ double-folding (door)

δικρατής ές doubly powerful

δίκροτος ον with two banks of oars; wide enough for two chariots

δικτυόκλωστος ον woven in meshes

δίκτυον ου τό fishing-net

δίλογος ον double-tongued, doubtful

δίλοφος ον with two peaks

δίμνεως ον worth two minae

διμοιρίᾱ ᾱς ἡ double amount

δῑνεύω, δῑνέω *tr and intr* whirl *or* spin around, eddy

δῑνη ης ἡ whirlpool, eddy

δῑνήεις εσσα εν eddying

δῑνωτός ή όν turned on a lathe, rounded; covered all round

διξός ή όν ▸ **δισσός**

διό (δι' ὅ) *adv and conj* for that reason; therefore

διόβολος ον hurled by Zeus

διογενής ές born from Zeus

δι-οδεύω, δι-οδοιπορέω travel through

δίοδος ου ἡ passage, thoroughfare; mountain pass; way

δι-οίγω open

δί-οιδα know exactly

δι-οικέω administer, manage; direct; treat

διοίκησις εως ἡ housekeeping; management, government; assize-district, group of provinces

διοικητής οῦ ὁ administrator, governor; (in Egypt) chief financial officer

δι-οικίζω let live apart; scatter; *mid* settle apart; change place

διοίκισις εως ἡ removal, change of living place

δι-οικοδομέω shut off by a wall

δι-οϊστέω shoot an arrow through *or* across

δι-οίχομαι pass away, be gone

διοκωχή ῆς ἡ a ceasing, an abating

δίολκος ου ὁ a slipway for dragging ships across the isthmus of Corinth

δι-όλλῡμι destroy *or* ruin completely; forget; *pass* perish completely

δι-όμνῡμι *and pass* swear, take an oath; affirm solemnly

δι-ομολογέω *and mid* agree (to), grant, accord

διόπερ ▸ διό

διοπετής ▸ διϊπετής

δι-οπτεύω spy about; look into

διοπτήρ ῆρος ὁ spy, scout

δι-οράω see through

διόργυιος ον two fathoms long

δι-ορθόω *and mid* set right, amend

διόρθωμα ατος τό **διόρθωσις** εως ἡ correction, amendment

δι-ορίζω divide; distinguish; define; ordain; banish

διόρυγμα ατος τό ditch, trench, canal

δι-ορύσσω dig through; rake up; undermine; block up

δῖος ᾱ ον shining, brilliant; excellent, noble; divine

διότι *conj* because, since; that

διοτρεφής ές cherished by Zeus

δι-ουρίζω ▸ διορίζω

δίπαλτος ον brandished with both hands

δίπηχυς υ two cubits long

διπλάζω double; *pass* be doubled

δίπλαξ ακος ἡ double-folded garment, cloak

διπλασιάζω double

διπλάσιος ᾱ ον double, twice as much

διπλασιόω double

δίπλεθρος ον two plethra *or* 200 feet long *or* wide

διπλόος η ον (*also* διπλοῦς ῆ οῦν) double, twofold; both; double-minded

διπλόω double

δίπους (*gen* ποδος) two-footed

δίπτυξ (*gen* υχος) **δίπτυχος** ον double-folded, folding; twofold

δίπυλος ον with two gates

δίς *adv* twice, double

δισθανής ές twice dying

δισκεύω, δισκέω throw the discus

δίσκος ου ὁ discus

δίσκουρα ων τά the distance a discus is thrown

δισμῡριάς άδος ἡ the number 20, 000

δισμῡ́ριοι αι α twenty thousand

δισσάρχης (*gen* ου) ruling jointly

δισσός ή όν double, twofold; ambiguous, doubtful

διστάζω doubt

δίστολος ον in pairs, together

δίστομος ον double-mouthed, with two entrances; two-edged

δισχίλιοι αι α two thousand

διτάλαντος ον weighing two talents

δι-ῡλίζω filter, strain off

διφάσιος ᾱ ον double, twofold

δῑφάω seek, search for, dive after

διφθέρᾱ ᾱς ἡ skin, hide, leather; anything made of leather; writing material, parchment; coat; bag; coverlet

διφθέρινος η ον of leather

διφρευτής οῦ ὁ charioteer

διφρ-ηλατέω drive in a chariot

διφρηλάτης ου ὁ ▸ **διφρευτής**

δίφρος ου ὁ chariot; chair, stool; chariot-board (on which the warrior and driver stood)

διφρο-φορέομαι *pass* be carried in a chair *or* litter

διφυής ές of double form

δίχα *adv* in two, at two, twofold, apart; at variance, different; *prep with gen* far from; without

διχάζω divide in two; make disagree, disunite

διχῇ *adv* ▸ **δίχα**

διχθά *adv* in two

διχθάδιος ᾱ ον double, twofold

διχο-γνωμονέω differ in opinion

διχόθεν *adv* from two sides

δ

διχοστασίᾱ ᾱς ἡ dissension, quarrel

διχο-στατέω disagree

διχο-τομέω split in two

διχοῦ ▸ **δίχα**

δίψα ης ἡ thirst

διψάω be thirsty, parched; thirst after

δίψιος ᾱ ον thirsty, parched

δίψῡχος ον double-minded, doubtful

δίω fear, flee; *mid* **δίεμαι**

διωβελίᾱ ᾱς ἡ payment of two obols (at Athens, a daily allowance paid to needy citizens)

διωγμός οῦ ὁ ▸ **δίωξις**

διώδυνος ον very painful

δι-ωθέω push *or* tear apart; pierce *or* break through; *mid* push away from oneself, repulse; refuse; break through

διωκάθω ▸ **διώκω**

διώκτης ου ὁ pursuer

διώκω pursue, chase, drive, hunt; expel, banish; run after, follow, catch; strive to win; be attached to; prosecute, accuse; drive a chariot; hasten; *mid* chase, drive before oneself

διώμοτος ον bound by oath

δίωξις εως ἡ chase, pursuit; persecution; pursuit (of an object)

διῶρυξ υχος ἡ ditch, trench, canal; underground passage

δμῆσις εως ἡ taming, breaking in

δμήτειρα ᾱς ἡ tamer

δμωή (*also* δμῳή) ῆς ἡ female slave, servant

δμώς ωός ὁ slave

δνοπαλίζω δνοπαλίξω shake, push about

δνοφερός ᾱ́ όν dark, dusky

δοάσσατο it seemed

δόγμα ατος τό opinion; decree, resolution; doctrine

δογματίζομαι *pass* be subject to statutes

δοιή ῆς ἡ doubt

δοιοί αί ά two, both

δοκάζω, δοκάω, δοκεύω expect; watch, lie in wait

δοκέω† think, suppose; resolve; seem, appear; appear to be something

■ **δοκῶ μοι** I seem to myself, I am determined

■ **δοκεῖ** it seems; it seems good; it is decreed; *with dat* it is decided by

■ **ἔδοξε** it was decreed *or* resolved

δόκησις εως ἡ opinion; suspicion; appearance

δοκιμάζω prove, test, examine; approve, declare good; examine and admit boys to the class of ephebe *or* to the rights of manhood

δοκιμασίᾱ ᾱς ἡ examination, a proving; a mustering; examination of ephebes before their admission to the rights of manhood

δοκιμαστής οῦ ὁ examiner, scrutineer

δοκιμή ῆς ἡ **δοκίμιον** ου τό examination, proof, test

δόκιμος ον tried, approved; esteemed; considerable

δοκός οῦ ἡ wooden beam

δολερός ᾱ́ όν cunning, deceitful

δολιόμῡθος ον crafty in speech

δολιόπους (*gen* ποδος) stealthy of foot, dodging

δόλιος ᾱ ον ▸ **δολερός**

δολιόω betray, cheat

δολίχαυλος ον with a long pipe

δολιχεγχής ές with a long spear

δολιχήρετμος ον with long oars

δολιχοδρόμος ον running the long course; prize-runner

δολιχός ή όν long, far

δόλιχος ου ὁ long course; stadium

δολιχόσκιος ον casting a long shadow

δολόεις εσσα εν ▸ **δολερός**

δολομήτης (*gen* ου) **δολόμητις** (*gen* ιος) wily, crafty

δολοποιός όν ▸ **δολερός**

δόλος ου ὁ bait, inducement; cunning, deceit, treachery; trick, stratagem

δολο-φρονέω plan treachery

δολοφροσύνη ης ἡ deceit, cunning, intrigue

δολόω cheat, entice, beguile; disguise

δόμα ατος τό gift

δόμος ου ὁ house, building; dwelling, apartment, room, hall; layer; home; family; household

δονακεύς έως ὁ thicket of canes *or* reeds

δονακόχλοος ον green with reeds

δόναξ ακος ὁ cane, reed; arrow; shepherd's pipe

δονέω shake, stir, drive about; *pass* be agitated; be in commotion

δόξα ης ἡ opinion, notion; expectation; false opinion, delusion, fancy; decree, project; judgement; reputation, report, honour; glory, splendour

δοξάζω think, believe, suppose, presume; extol

δοξόομαι *pass* have a reputation

δορᾱ́ ᾶς ἡ hide, skin

δοράτιον ου τό javelin; pole

δοριάλωτος ον **δορίκτητος** ον **δορίληπτος** ον taken in war, captive

δορίμαργος ον eager for combat

δορκάς άδος ἡ roe, gazelle

δορός οῦ ὁ leather bag

δορπέω have supper

δορπηστός οῦ ὁ supper-time, evening

δορπίᾱ ᾶς ἡ eve of a festival

δόρπον ου τό supper

δόρυ δόρατος τό wood, beam, timber; ship; pole; shaft of a spear; spear; battle, war; spear-bearer, warrior; army; booty

■ **ἐπὶ δόρυ** to the right hand

δορυάλωτος ον ▸ **δοριάλωτος**

δορυδρέπανον ου τό handle of a sickle; grappling-hook

δορύξενος ου ὁ companion in arms; comrade

δορυσσόητος ον **δορυσσόος** ον brandishing a spear, warlike

δορυ-φορέω be a bodyguard, attend as a guard

δορυφόρος ου ὁ spear-bearer; bodyguard

δοσίδικος ον ▸ **δωσίδικος**

δόσις εως ἡ act of giving; gift, present; portion

δοτήρ ῆρος ὁ **δότης** ου ὁ giver, dispenser

δουλ-αγωγέω make a slave; lead into slavery

δουλείᾱ ᾱς ἡ slavery, bondage, servility; slaves

δούλειος ον slavish, servile

δούλευμα ατος τό slavery; slave

δουλεύω be a slave, serve

δούλη ης ἡ female slave

δουλίᾱ ᾱς ἡ ▸ **δουλεία**

δουλικός ή όν **δούλιος** ᾱ ον ▸ **δούλειος**

δουλιχόδειρος ον long-necked

δουλοπρεπής ές befitting a slave

δοῦλος η ον slavish, servile; enslaved, subject

■ **ὁ δοῦλος, ἡ δούλη** slave

δουλοσύνη ης ἡ ▸ **δουλεία**

δουλόω enslave, subdue; discourage

δούλωσις εως ἡ enslaving, subjugation

δουπέω sound hollow; roar

δοῦπος ου ὁ hollow sound, thud, roaring, noise

δουράτεος ᾱ ον wooden

δουρηνεκές *adv* a spear's throw away

δουριάλωτος ον ▸ **δοριάλωτος**

δουρικλειτός όν **δουρικλυτός** όν famous as a spearman

δ

δουρίληπτος ον ▸ **δορίληπτος**

δουροδόκη ης ἡ case *or* stand for spears

δοχή ῆς ἡ receptacle; banquet

δόχμιος ᾱ ον **δοχμός** ή όν slanting, sideways

δράγμα (*or* δρᾶγμα) ατος τό handful, sheaf

δραγμεύω collect the corn into sheaves

δραίνω be about to do

δράκαινα ης ἡ she-dragon

δράκων οντος ὁ dragon; serpent

δραμ *likely to be from* **τρέχω**

δρᾶμα ατος τό action, deed; play

δράμημα ατος τό ▸ **δρόμος**

δρᾱπετεύω run away, escape

δρᾱπέτης ου ὁ runaway, runaway slave; falling to pieces

δρᾱσείω be willing to do

δρᾱσμός οῦ ὁ escape, flight

δράσσομαι δράξομαι ἐδραξάμην *mid* grasp, seize

δραστήριος ον active, busy, enterprising

δρατός ή όν flayed

δραχμή ῆς ἡ drachma

δράω δράσω ἔδρᾱσα be active; do, perform, accomplish

δρεπάνη ης ἡ ▸ **δρέπανον**

δρεπανηφόρος ον bearing a sickle

δρεπανοειδής ές sickle-shaped

δρέπανον ου τό sickle, scythe; curved sword, scimitar

δρέπ(τ)ω pluck

δρησμός οῦ ὁ ▸ **δρασμός**

δρήστειρα ᾱς ἡ **δρηστήρ** ῆρος ὁ worker, servant

δρηστοσύνη ης ἡ service

δρῑμύς εῖα ύ piercing, biting; violent, sharp, bitter; shrewd

δρίος ους τό thicket, brushwood

δρομαῖος ᾱ ον **δρομάς** (*gen* άδος) running, swift

δρομεύς έως ὁ runner

δρομικός ή όν good at running; swift

■ **τὰ δρομικά** foot race

δρόμος ου ὁ running, course, race; place for running, race-course, stadium

■ **δρόμῳ** at a run

δροσερός ᾱ́ όν dewy

δρόσος ου ἡ dew, dewdrop; water

δρύϊνος η ον made of oak

δρῡμός οῦ ὁ oak-coppice; wood

δρύοχος ου ὁ rib of ship

δρύπτω δρύψω ἔδρυψα peel off, scratch, tear; snatch away

δρῦς υός ἡ oak; tree; wood

δρυτόμος ον wood-cutting

δρύφακτον ου τό **δρύφακτος** ου ὁ fence, railing

δρύφω ▸ **δρύπτω**

δυάς άδος ἡ the number two, a pair

δύη ης ἡ misery, woe, pain

δύναμαι† *pass* be able (to), be strong enough (to); be strong, mighty *or* powerful; be worth; signify

δύναμις εως ἡ ability; might, power, strength; military force, army; talent, faculty; power of speech; miracle; influence; worth, value; meaning, signification

δυναμόω strengthen

δύνασις εως ἡ ▸ **δύναμις**

δυναστείᾱ ᾱς ἡ sovereignty, rule

δυναστεύω have power

δυνάστης ου ὁ lord, ruler, master; nobleman

δυνατέω be powerful

δυνατός ή όν able; strong, mighty, powerful; fit, apt; noble; possible

δῡ́νω ▸ **δύομαι**, *see* **δύω**

δύο two, both

δυοκαίδεκα ▸ **δώδεκα**

δυοκαιδεκάμηνος ον of twelve months
δῡ́ρομαι ▸ **ὀδῡ́ρομαι**
δυσᾱής ές stormy, ill-blowing
δυσάθλιος ον most miserable
δυσαίων (*gen* ωνος) living miserably
δυσάλγητος ον unfeeling
δυσάλωτος ον hard to catch
δυσάμμορος ον most unhappy
δυσανα-σχετέω find unbearable; be beside oneself, be extremely distressed
δυσάνεκτος ον unbearable
δυσᾱ́νεμος ον wind-beaten, stormy
δυσαπάλλακτος ον hard to ward off, stubborn
δυσαπότρεπτος ον hard to turn away
δυσάρεστος ον hard to please, morose
δυσαριστοτόκεια ᾱς ἡ unhappy mother of a hero
δύσαυλος ον inhospitable
δυσβάστακτος ον hard to bear
δύσβατος ον impassable, inaccessible; trodden in sorrow
δυσβουλίᾱ ᾱς ἡ bad counsel, folly
δυσγένεια ᾱς ἡ low birth
δύσγνωστος ον hard to understand
δυσγοήτευτος ον difficult to win over by enchantments
δυσδαιμονίᾱ ᾱς ἡ misery
δυσδιάβατος ον hard to cross
δυσειδής ές misshapen, ugly
δυσέμβατος ον hard to walk on, difficult of access
δυσέμβολος ον impregnable, inaccessible
δυσεντερίᾱ ᾱς ἡ dysentery
δυσεξαπάτητος ον hard to deceive
δυσεξέλεγκτος ον hard to refute
δύσερις (*gen* ιδος) quarrelsome, captious
δυσέριστος ον involving unholy strife
δυσερμήνευτος ον hard to interpret
δύσερως (*gen* ωτος) crossed in love; passionately loving
δυσέσβολος ον ▸ **δυσέμβολος**
δυσεύρετος ον hard to find
δύσζηλος ον irascible, exceedingly jealous
δυσηλεγής ές painful
δυσηχής ές ill-sounding, raging
δυσθαλπής ές chilly
δυσ-θανατέω die a difficult death
δυσθέᾱτος ον horrible, dismal
δύσθεος ον hated by the gods
δυσθεράπευτος ον hard to cure
δυσ-θετέομαι *pass* be extremely annoyed
δυσθρήνητος ον lamentable
δυσ-θῡμέω be disheartened
δυσθῡμίᾱ ᾱς ἡ ill humour; despondency
δύσθῡμος ον despondent; ill-humoured
δυσῑ́ᾱτος ον hard to heal; incurable
δύσιππος ον unfit for cavalry
δύσις εως ἡ sunset; west
δυσκάθαρτος ον difficult to expiate
δυσκάθεκτος ον hard to check
δυσκατέργαστος ον hard to bring about by hard work
δυσκέλαδος ον ill-sounding, harsh
δυσκηδής ές sad, sorry
δυσκλεής ές inglorious, infamous
δύσκλεια ᾱς ἡ infamy, shame
δυσκοινώνητος ον unsociable
δυσ-κολαίνω δυσκολανῶ be discontented, show displeasure
δυσκολίᾱ ᾱς ἡ discontent; difficulty
δύσκολος ον peevish, discontented, fretful; difficult, perplexing

δ

δυσκόμιστος ον unbearable

δύσκριτος ον hard to interpret *or* decide

δυσλόγιστος ον inconceivable

δυσμαθής ές difficult to learn; slow at learning

δυσ-μαχέω fight in vain

δύσμαχος ον hard to fight with; unconquerable

δυσ-μεναίνω be hostile, bear ill will

δυσμένεια ᾱς ἡ ill-will, enmity

δυσμενέων, δυσμενής ές hostile, malevolent

δυσμεταχείριστος ον hard to fight with

δυσμή ῆς ἡ ▸ **δύσις**

δυσμήτηρ τερος ἡ not a (true) mother

δύσμοιρος ον **δύσμορος** ον unhappy, miserable

δυσμορφίᾱ ᾱς ἡ ugliness

δύσνιπτος ον not to be washed off

δυσνόητος ον difficult to understand

δύσνοια ᾱς ἡ dislike, ill-will

δύσνοος ον (*also* δύσνους ουν) hostile, malign; ill-disposed

δύσνυμφος ον ill-wedded, ill-betrothed

δυσξύμβολος ον unsociable; driving a hard bargain

δυσξύνετος ον unintelligble, obscure

δύσοδμος ον ill-smelling

δύσοδος ον scarcely passable

δύσοιστος ον unbearable, hard to bear

δύσομβρος ον stormy, wintry

δύσοργος ον irascible

δυσοσμίᾱ ᾱς ἡ bad smell

δυσούριστος ον driven on by bad winds

δυσπάλαιστος ον unconquerable, hard to wrestle with

δυσπάρευνος ον ill-mated

δυσπαραμῡθητος ον inconsolable

Δύσπαρις ιδος ὁ unlucky Paris

δυσπάριτος ον hard to pass

δυσπειθής ές disobedient

δύσπειστος ον hard to persuade

δυσπέμφελος ον stormy

δυσπέρᾱτος ον hard to get through

δυσπετής ές difficult

δυσπινής ές very dirty, squalid

δύσπνοος ον (*also* δύσπνους ουν) breathless; [of winds] contrary

δυσπολέμητος ον hard to make war upon

δυσπολιόρκητος ον hard to take by siege

δυσπονής ές **δυσπόνητος** ον **δύσπονος** ον wearisome, laborious; hard-earned

δυσπόρευτος ον **δύσπορος** ον scarcely passable

δυσπορίᾱ ᾱς ἡ difficult crossing

δύσποτμος ον ill-fated

δυσπρᾱξίᾱ ας ἡ misfortune

δυσπρόσβατος ον **δυσπρόσοδος** ον hardly accessible, hard to get at; antisocial

δυσπρόσοιστος ον unfriendly, gloomy

δυσπρόσοπτος ον **δυσπρόσωπος** ον horrible to look at

δύσρῑγος ον sensible to cold

δυσσέβεια ᾱς ἡ impiety

δυσσεβέω be impious; act impiously

δυσσεβής ές impious, godless

δυστάλᾱς αινα αν most unhappy

δυστέκμαρτος ον hard to make out; hard to trace, inexplicable

δύστεκνος ον unhappy as a mother; unfortunate in children

δύστηνος ον unhappy; wretched, abominable

δυσ-τομέω speak ill of, bad-mouth

δυστράπελος ον **δύστροπος** ον stubborn

δυσ-τυχέω be unlucky; *pass* fail

δυστύχημα ατος τό ▸ **δυστυχία**

δυστυχής ές unlucky, unhappy, miserable

δυστυχίᾱ ᾱς ἡ bad luck, misfortune, mishap; defeat

δυσ-φημέω speak words of ill omen; speak ill of

δυσφημίᾱ ᾱς ἡ words of ill omen; abuse; infamy

δυσφιλής ές hateful; ugly

δυσ-φορέω bear with resentment; do unwillingly

δύσφορος ον hard to bear, heavy, oppressive; misleading

δύσφραστος ον inexplicable

δύσφρων ον sorrowful, melancholy; hostile, ill-disposed; senseless

δυσχείμερος ον wintry, stormy

δυσχείρωμα ατος τό hard work

δυσχείρωτος ον hard to overcome

δυσχεραίνω δυσχερανῶ ἐδυσχέρᾱνα be *or* become discontented *or* angry; disapprove, reject; make difficulties; rouse indignation

δυσχέρεια ᾱς ἡ annoyance, disgust; ill temper

δυσχερής ές hard to manage, difficult; annoying, unpleasant; peevish, unfriendly

δύσχρηστος ον hard to use; useless

δυσχωρίᾱ ᾱς ἡ disadvantageous ground

δυσώδης ες ill-smelling

δυσώνυμος ον bearing an ill-omened name; ominous; of bad repute

δυσ-ωπέομαι *pass* be shy *or* timid

δυσ-ωρέομαι keep a painful watch

δύτης ου ὁ diver

δύω[1] *and mid intr* dive, sink; enter; perish; *tr* put on

δύω[2] ▸ **δύο**

δύωδεκα ▸ **δώδεκα**

δυωδεκάβοιος ον worth twelve oxen

δυωδεκάπολις (*gen* ιος) belonging to a confederation of twelve cities

δυωδέκατος η ον ▸ **δωδέκατος**

δυωκαιεικοσίμετρος ον holding 22 measures

δυωκαιεικοσίπηχυς υ 22 cubits long

δῶ τό ▸ **δῶμα**

δώδεκα twelve

δωδεκάσκῡτος ον composed of twelve pieces of leather

δωδέκατος η ον twelfth

δωδεκάφῡλον ου τό the twelve tribes

δῶμα ατος τό dwelling, house; palace, temple; chamber, hall; roof; family, household

δωμάτιον ου τό room, bedchamber

δωρεᾱ́ ᾱς ἡ gift, present; gift of honour; benefit

■ **δωρεάν** *adv* as a free gift, gratis

δωρέω *and mid* give, present

δώρημα ατος τό ▸ **δωρεά**

δωρητός ή όν given; open to gifts

δωριστί *adv* in Dorian manner, dialect *or* tune

δωροδοκέω accept presents; be bribed; corrupt by bribes

δωροδόκημα ατος τό **δωροδοκίᾱ** ᾱς ἡ taking a bribe; corruption

δωροδόκος ον taking bribes

δῶρον ου τό gift, present

δωροφορίᾱ ᾱς ἡ the bringing of presents

δωσίδικος ον submitting to justice

δωτήρ ῆρος ὁ giver

δωτῑνάζω collect gifts

δωτί̄νη ης ἡ ▸ **δῶρον**

δώτωρ ορος ὁ ▸ **δωτήρ**

Εε

ε, Ε (ἒ ψιλόν) fifth letter of the alphabet
■ ε′ *as a numeral* = 5

ἕ (*more often* ἓ ἕ) *int* woe!

ἑ *enclitic* himself, herself, itself

ἔᾱ *int* (denoting wonder) ha! ah!

ἑάλων *aor from* **ἁλίσκομαι**

ἐᾱ́ν *conj* if; if it is the case that; as often as, whenever; if, whether

ἑᾱνός ή όν wrapping up; smooth, pliant; fine and white

ἑανός οῦ ὁ a woman's robe

ἔαρ ἔαρος τό spring, prime

ἐαρίζω ἐαριῶ pass the spring

ἐαρινός ή όν belonging to spring

ἑαυτόν ήν ό *pron acc* himself, herself, itself; oneself; *pl* themselves

ἑάφθη ▸ **ἥφθη**, *see* **ἅπτω**

ἐάω† let, permit, allow, suffer; let *or* leave alone *or* unnoticed; omit, give up

ἑβδομαῖος ᾱ ον on the seventh day; seven days old

ἑβδόματος η ον ▸ **ἕβδομος**

ἑβδομήκοντα seventy

ἑβδομηκοντάκις seventy times

ἕβδομος η ον seventh

ἔβενος ου ἡ ebony-tree, ebony

ἐγ-γείνομαι breed in

ἔγγειος ον within the boundaries of the country; in the earth

ἐγ-γελάω laugh at, mock

ἐγγενής ές blood-related; native; inborn

ἐγ-γηράσκω grow old at a place

ἐγ-γίγνομαι *mid* be born in; happen in, take place in, arise in; be innate *or* infused; intervene, pass; be possible

ἐγγίζω approach, draw near

ἔγγιον *comp* **ἔγγιστα** *sup from* **ἐγγύς**

ἐγ-γλύσσω have a sweetish taste

ἐγ-γλύφω engrave, carve, cut in

ἐγ-γνάμπτω bend in

ἔγγονος ου ὁ/ἡ relation; descendant

ἐγγραφή ῆς ἡ registration

ἐγ-γράφω engrave; write, draw *or* paint in; write down

ἐγ-γυαλίζω ἐγγυαλίξω hand over; grant

ἐγγυάω *and mid* stand security, guarantee; betroth, engage, promise; be betrothed

ἐγγύη ης ἡ security, bail, pledge

ἐγγυητής οῦ ὁ **ἔγγυος** ου ὁ someone who gives security

ἐγγύς *adv* near, in the neighbourhood, neighbouring; coming near; like, nearly; soon; at last
■ **ἐγγίων, ἐγγύτερος** *comp*
■ **ἔγγιστος, ἐγγύτατος** *sup*

ἐγγώνιος ον forming a (right) angle

ἐγείρω† awaken, rouse; stir, excite; raise

ἔγερσις εως ἡ a rousing, raising; awaking

ἐγερτί *adv* in an exciting way; eagerly, busily

ἐγκαθ-έζομαι *mid* sit down in, encamp in

ἐγκάθετος ον suborned; watcher

ἐγκαθ-ιδρύω set up in

ἐγκαθ-ίζω set in *or* upon; set oneself on; *mid* sit on; take one's seat

ἐγκαθ-ίστημι place, put *or* set in; establish, arrange; *intr* be established

ἐγκαθ-ορμίζομαι *mid* sail into harbour, come to anchor

ἐγκαίνια ων τά feast of the dedication of the temple

ἐγ-καινίζω renew, renovate

ἐγ-κακέω grow weary, relax; put off (with bad consequences)

ἐγ-καλέω call in; accuse, reproach, blame, bring a charge of something *acc* against someone *dat*; claim [a debt]

ἐγκαλλώπισμα ατος τό ornament

ἐγ-καλύπτω veil in, wrap up, hide

ἔγκαρπος ον fruitful

ἐγκάρσιος (ᾱ) ον oblique, transverse

ἐγ-καρτερέω persevere, persist (in); control oneself

ἔγκατα ων τά bowels, entrails

ἐγκατα-δέω bind fast in

ἐγκατα-ζεύγνῡμι join with, unite

ἐγκατα-κοιμάομαι *pass* sleep in

ἐγκατα-λαμβάνω catch in a place, seize, take, arrest; cut off

ἐγκατα-λέγω gather in; enlist

ἐγκατα-λείπω leave behind in (a place) *or* with (a person); *pass* be left behind

ἐγκατάληψις εως ἡ a catching, capture

ἐγκατα-μ(ε)ίγνῡμι mix up in; place between

ἐγκατα-πήγνῡμι thrust into, fix in

ἐγκατα-σκήπτω fling down into; fall upon; break out

ἐγκατα-τέμνω cut into pieces

ἐγκατα-τίθεμαι *mid* lay in *or* hide for oneself

ἐγκατ-οικέω live in *or* among

ἐγκατ-οικοδομέω build on a spot; build in, immure

ἐγ-καυχάομαι boast

ἔγ-κειμαι + *dat* lie in *or* on, be placed in; press on, urge, importune, attack; be intent upon

ἐγκέλευστος ον bidden, ordered; suborned

ἐγ-κεντρίζω ingraft

ἐγ-κεράννῡμι, ἐγ-κεράω mix in; *mid* suborn; contrive

ἐγκέφαλος ου ὁ brain; marrow

ἐγ-κλείω shut in, confine; shut

ἔγκλημα ατος τό accusation, charge, reproach, complaint, controversy; fault, guilt

ἔγκληρος ον sharing, partaking; heir, heiress; destined by lot

ἐγ-κλῄω, ἐγ-κληΐω ▸ ἐγκλείω

ἐγ-κλῑ́νω *act tr* bend *or* incline towards; *act intr and pass* be bent; lean on; yield; turn to flight

ἐγ-κοιλαίνω hollow out

ἔγκοιλος ον hollowed out

ἐγ-κολάπτω cut in, engrave

ἐγ-κομβόομαι make one's own; gird oneself

ἐγ-κονέω hasten; be busy

ἐγκοπή ῆς ἡ hindrance; incision, fracture

ἐγ-κόπτω hinder, trouble; delay

ἐγ-κοσμέω arrange within

ἔγκοτος ου ὁ resentment, hatred

ἐγ-κράζω shriek at

ἐγκράτεια ᾱς ἡ self-control, temperance; mastery over

ἐγ-κρατεύομαι *mid* be frugal *or* abstemious

ἐγκρατής ές strong; having mastery over; self-disciplined, sober

ἐγ-κρῑ́νω choose among; admit, accept, approve, adopt; reckon among

ἐγ-κροτέω strike against, beat time with the feet; *mid* strike one another

ἐγ-κρύπτω hide in

ἐγ-κτάομαι *mid* acquire possessions in a place

ἔγκτησις εως ἡ landed property in a place; tenure of land in a country *or* district (by a person not belonging to it), the right of holding such property (frequently as a privilege for foreigners)

ἐγ-κυκάω mix up in

ἐγ-κυκλόω move about in a circle

ε

ἐγ-κυλίομαι *pass* wallow in, be given to

ἔγκυος ον pregnant, with child

ἐγ-κύπτω stoop; peep, cast a side-glance

ἐγ-κυρέω, ἐγ-κῦρω + *dat* meet with; fall into

ἐγ-κωμιάζω praise, extol

ἐγκώμιον ου τό song of praise; eulogy

ἐγρεμάχης ες rousing the fight

ἐγρηγοράω be awake

ἐγρηγορτί *adv* awake

ἐγρήσσω be awake

ἐγ-χαλῑνόω bridle

ἐγ-χειρέω take in hand, undertake, try; attack + *dat*; put one's hand to

ἐγχείρημα ατος τό **ἐγχείρησις** εως ἡ an undertaking, execution

ἐγχειρητικός ή όν enterprising

ἐγχειρίδιον ου τό dagger, knife

ἐγ-χειρίζω hand over, deliver, entrust; *mid* take upon oneself

ἐγχειρίθετος ον handed over, delivered

ἔγχελυς υος *or* εως ἡ eel

ἐγχεσίμωρος ον fighting with the spear

ἐγχέσπαλος ον brandishing the spear

ἐγ-χέω pour in

ἔγχος ους τό spear, lance; weapon, sword

ἐγ-χραύω dash *or* push into

ἐγ-χρίμπτω cause to strike against (something *dat*); dash *or* drive against; bring near; approach, come to land; *pass* touch, verge, reach to + *dat*

ἐγ-χρῑ́ω anoint

ἐγ-χρονίζω delay; *pass* become habitual

ἐγ-χωρέω give way *or* room, allow
■ ἐγχωρεῖ + *dat* it is possible

ἐγχώριος (ᾱ) ον **ἔγχωρος** ον native, indigenous; inhabitant; rustic

ἐγώ *pron* I, myself
■ ἔγωγε I for my part, for myself

ἑδανός ή όν lovely, delicious

ἐδαφίζω ἐδαφιῶ level with the earth, dash to the ground

ἔδαφος ους τό ground, soil, floor, bottom

ἔδεσμα ατος τό food, meat, dish

ἐδεστής οῦ ὁ eater

ἐδεστός ή όν eatable; eaten, consumed

ἐδητύς ύος ἡ food

ἕδνα ων τά nuptial gifts; dowry

ἔδοξε *see* **δοκέω**

ἕδος ους τό **ἕδρα** ᾱς ἡ seat, chair, bench, row; sitting-part; abode, dwelling; temple, altar, statue; foundation; base, station, stand; act of sitting, a sitting still; session

ἑδραῖος ᾱ ον sitting still, sedentary, unmoved

ἑδραίωμα ατος τό foundation

ἕδρανον ου τό ▸ **ἕδρα**

ἑδριάομαι *mid* sit down

ἔδω ἔδομαι ἔφαγον eat, consume

ἐδωδή ῆς ἡ food, fodder; bait

ἐδώδιμος ον edible

ἑδώλιον ου τό seat, residence; rowing bench

ἕε ▸ **ἕ**

ἔεδνα ων τά ▸ **ἕδνα**

ἐεδνόομαι *mid* betroth

ἐεδνωτής οῦ ὁ father of a bride

ἐεικοσάβοιος ον worth twenty oxen

ἐείκοσι ▸ **εἴκοσι**

ἐέλδομαι ▸ **ἔλδομαι**

ἐέλδωρ τό ▸ **ἔλδωρ**

ἐέλπομαι ▸ **ἔλπομαι**

ἐεργάθω ▸ **ἐργάθω**

ἐέρση ▸ **ἔρση**

ἕζω set, place, settle; *mid* sit down; sit; settle (down)

ἐθάς (*gen* ἀδος) customary, accustomed to + *gen*

ἔθειρα ᾱς ἡ hair; mane; horse-tail; plume of a helmet

ἐθείρω till, cultivate

ἐθελοθρησκείᾱ ᾱς ἡ arbitrary worship

ἐθελο-κακέω be bad *or* cowardly on purpose

ἐθελοντηδόν, ἐθελοντήν, ἐθελοντί *adv* on purpose, willingly

ἐθελοντήρ (*gen* ῆρος) **ἐθελοντής** (*gen* οῦ) voluntary, willing

ἐθελόπονος ον willing to work

ἐθελοπρόξενος ου ὁ someone who voluntarily takes on the office of πρόξενος (the person who looks after the citizens of a certain foreign nationality in a city)

ἐθελούσιος (ᾱ) ον ▸ **ἐθελοντής**

ἐθέλω† be willing, wish, want, desire; be resolved *or* inclined; be able; have power; be accustomed; mean, purport

ἔθεν ▸ **ἕο, οὗ**

ἐθίζω ἐθιῶ εἴθισα accustom; *pass* be accustomed

ἐθνάρχης ου ὁ governor, prefect

ἐθνικός ή όν national; gentile

ἔθνος ους τό company, band; people, nation, tribe; class of men; gentiles

ἔθος ους τό custom, manner

ἔθω be accustomed

■ **εἰωθώς υῖα ός** *pf pple* accustomed, usual

εἰ *conj* if, whether

εἶα *int* come! well then

εἴᾱ *3 sg impf of* **ἐάω**

εἱαμενή ῆς ἡ riverside pasture, meadow

εἱανός οῦ ὁ ▸ **ἑανός**

εἶαρ ατος τό ▸ **ἔαρ**

εἰαρινός ή όν ▸ **ἐαρινός**

εἴβω *and mid* drop, trickle

εἰδάλιμος η ον shapely, comely

εἶδαρ ατος τό food, fodder; bait

εἶδον *aor from* **ὁράω**

εἶδος ους τό act of seeing; appearance, shape, form; beauty; notion, idea; kind, species; description; nature

εἴδω *but* ὁράω *is used in the pres aor* εἶδον *aor infin* ἰδεῖν *and mid* see, behold, perceive, know; have an appearance, look, seem; resemble; pretend *pf with pres sense* **οἶδα** *infin* εἰδέναι know, be knowing, skilled *or* cunning

εἰδωλεῖον ου τό idol's temple

εἰδωλόθυτος ον offered to idols

εἰδωλολατρείᾱ ᾱς ἡ idolatry

εἰδωλολάτρης ου ὁ idolater

εἴδωλον ου τό image, shape, phantom; vision, idol

εἶεν *adv* (*also* εἶέν) well then

εἶθαρ *adv* at once, immediately

εἴθε *int* if only!

εἰκάζω make like to; portray; compare; guess, conjecture; examine; *pass* resemble, be like

εἰκάθω ▸ **εἴκω**

εἰκασίᾱ ᾱς ἡ image

εἰκαστής οῦ ὁ guesser

εἴκελος η ον + *dat* like, resembling

εἰκῇ (*also* εἰκῆ) *adv* at random, heedlessly, in vain

εἰκός ότος τό probable, likely, natural, fair, reasonable; *as noun* likelihood, probability

εἰκοσαέτης ες twenty years old

εἰκοσάκις *adv* twenty times

εἴκοσι twenty

εἰκοσινήριτος ον multiplied by twenty, twentyfold

εἰκοσίπηχυς υ twenty cubits long

εἰκόσορος ον with twenty oars

εἰκοστός ή όν the twentieth

εἰκότως *adv* probably, naturally, of course, fairly, reasonably

εἴκω yield, give way, retire; submit to + *dat*; resign, grant, allow

ε

εἰκών όνος ἡ likeness, image, picture, painting; simile; phantom, notion

εἰκώς υῖα ός ▸ **ἐοικώς**

εἰλαπινάζω feast, dine in a large gathering

εἰλαπιναστής οῦ ὁ dinner-companion

εἰλαπίνη ης ἡ feast, banquet

εἶλαρ τό protection, shelter

εἰλάτινος η ον ▸ **ἐλάτινος**

εἰλέω, εἴλλω force together; strike; check, hem in; drive; *pass* be shut up *or* pressed together; be crowded, assembled *or* drawn together; go *or* turn about

εἴλησις εως ἡ heat of the sun

εἰλικρίνεια ᾱς ἡ purity

εἰλικρινής ές manifest, simple; pure, uncorrupted, genuine

εἰλίπους (*gen* ποδος) trailing the feet

εἵλκυσα *aor from* **ἕλκω**

εἴλλω *see* **εἰλέω**

εἷλον *aor from* **αἱρέω**

εἴλῡμα ατος τό cover, clothing

εἰλῡφάζω, εἰλυφάω roll along

εἰλύω roll, whirl; involve, enfold; *pass* roll on; crawl, creep, wind along; cling to; crouch

εἴλω ▸ **εἰλέω**

εἵλως ωτος ὁ **εἱλώτης** ου ὁ Helot, Spartan serf

εἷμα ατος τό garment, cover

εἱμαρμένη ης ἡ destiny

εἵμαρται *see* **μείρομαι**

εἰμι† *enclitic* be; exist, live, continue; take place, come to pass; dwell; be in a certain state; behave; be real; mean, signify; be descended; belong to

εἶμι† *pres with fut meaning in indicative* go, come, wander, travel, drive, sail, fly; march, progress, advance; go away; retire; arrive

εἰν ▸ **ἐν**

εἰναετής ές of nine years, nine years old

■ **εἰνάετες** *adv* nine years long

εἰνάκις ▸ **ἐνάκις**

εἰνακόσιοι αι α ▸ **ἐνακόσιοι**

εἰνάλιος ᾱ ον ▸ **ἐνάλιος**

εἰνάνυχες *adv* nine nights long

εἰνατέρες ων αἱ sisters-in-law

εἴνατος η ον ▸ **ἔνατος**

εἵνεκα ▸ **ἕνεκα**

εἰνί ▸ **ἐν**

εἰνόδιος ᾱ ον ▸ **ἐνόδιος**

εἰνοσίγαιος ου ὁ ▸ **ἐννοσίγαιος**

εἰνοσίφυλλος ον shaking the leaves

εἴξασι *see* **ἔοικα**

εἷος ▸ **ἕως**

εἶπον *aor from* **λέγω, ἀγορεύω**

εἰργάθω ▸ **εἴργω**

εἱργμός οῦ ὁ prison

εἱργμοφύλαξ ακος ὁ jailer

εἴργω, εἵργω, εἵργνῡμι press, enclose, shut in, confine, include, arrest; shut out, exclude, separate; prohibit, hinder, prevent; *mid* abstain from

εἵρερος ου ὁ slavery

εἰρεσίᾱ ᾱς ἡ rowing; the rowers, oarsmen

εἴρη ης ἡ place of assembly

εἰρήν ένος ὁ ▸ **ἰρήν**

εἰρηναῖος ᾱ ον peaceful

εἰρηνεύω keep peace, live in peace

εἰρήνη ης ἡ peace; peace-making; time of peace, rest

εἰρηνικός ή όν peaceful

εἰρηνο-ποιέω make peace

εἰρηνοποιός όν making peace; peace-maker

εἰρίνεος ον woollen

εἴριον ου τό wool

εἱρκτή ῆς ἡ enclosure; prison

εἰροκόμος ον working in wool

εἴρομαι *mid* ask; *see* **ἐρέω**

εἰροπόκος ον wool-fleeced

εἶρος ους τό wool

εἰρύω ▸ **ἐρύω**

εἴρω[1] say, speak, tell; report, order ■ **εἴρομαι** ▸ **ἐρέω**

εἴρω[2] *aor* εἶρα *or* ἔρσα string together, join

εἴρων ωνος ὁ dissembler, someone who is economical with the truth

εἰρωνείᾱ ᾱς ἡ dissimulation, disguise; mockery; evasion, pretext; irony

εἰρωνεύομαι *mid* pretend, dissemble, feign ignorance

εἰρωνικός ή όν ironical

εἰρωτάω ▸ **ἐρωτάω**

εἰς, ἐς *adv and prep with acc* into, towards, in; against; until; for; for the purpose of; up to; about

εἷς μία ἕν one, one alone, a single one; the same; each one, any one

εἶσα *see* **ἕζω**

εἰσαγγελεύς έως ὁ announcer, usher

εἰσαγγελίᾱ ᾱς ἡ announcement; state prosecution, impeachment

εἰσ-αγγέλλω announce, report; denounce, impeach

εἰσ-αγείρω gather into a place

εἰσ-άγω lead into; lead up; import; produce; admit, introduce; bring before an assembly, summon before a court; *mid* bring into one's house, marry

εἰσαεί *adv* for ever

εἰσ-αθρέω look at, discern

εἰσ-ακοντίζω throw spears into *or* against

εἰσ-ακούω listen to; obey, follow

εἰσ-άλλομαι *mid* leap into *or* upon, attack

εἰσάμην *see* **ἕζω**

εἰσανα-βαίνω go up into

εἰσαν-άγω lead up into

εἰσάν-ειμι go up into

εἰσάντα *adv* right opposite; in the face

εἰσάπαξ *adv* at once; for once

εἰσ-αράσσω drive into *or* back

εἰσαῦθις *adv* for another time, afterwards

εἰσαφ-ικᾱ́νω, εἰσαφ-ικνέομαι come *or* go into, arrive at

εἰσ-βαίνω go *or* come into

εἰσ-βάλλω *act tr* throw into; drive into; *act intr* throw oneself into; fall into; invade, make an inroad, enter; *mid* put on board

εἴσβασις εως ἡ embarkation

εἰσβατός ή όν accessible

εἰσ-βιβάζω put on board a ship, cause to embark

εἰσ-βλέπω look at

εἰσβολή ῆς ἡ inroad, attack; entrance; pass; river mouth

εἰσ-γράφω inscribe; *mid* write down for oneself; inscribe oneself

εἰσ-δέρκομαι look at, behold

εἰσ-δέχομαι *mid* receive, admit

εἰσδρομή ῆς ἡ attack, onslaught

εἰσ-δύνω, εἰσ-δύομαι enter, slip into; come over, seize

εἴσ-ειμι come *or* go into, enter; visit; make one's appearance; come before the court; come into one's mind, seize

εἰσ-ελαύνω, εἰσ-ελάω drive into; enter, invade

εἰσέπειτα *adv* in future, for the future

εἰσ-έργνῡμι shut up into

εἰσ-ερύω draw into

εἰσ-έρχομαι ▸ **εἴσειμι**

εἰσ-έχω stretch into, reach; shine into

ἐΐση *see* **ἴσος**

εἰσ-ηγέομαι *mid* lead into; introduce, propose, advise; instruct

εἰσήγησις εως ἡ proposing, contriving

εἰσηγητής οῦ ὁ proposer; contriver

εἰσ-ηθέω inject, syringe

εἰσ-θρῴσκω leap into

εἰσ-ιδρύω build in

εἰσ-ίζομαι *mid* sit down in

εἰσ-ῑ́ημι send into; put into; *mid* resort to, enter

εἰσίθμη ης ἡ entrance

εἰσ-ικνέομαι *mid* come into, arrive at

εἰσ-καλέω *and mid* call into; summon; invite

εἰσκατα-βαίνω go down into

εἴσ-κειμαι lie in; be put on board a ship

εἰσ-κηρύσσω call in; proclaim

εἰσκομιδή ῆς ἡ import(ation), supply

εἰσ-κομίζω bring into, import, procure; *mid* lay in provisions; *pass* take shelter in a place

εἴσκω ▸ **ἴσκω**

εἰσ-λεύσσω look into, behold

εἰσ-μαίομαι *mid* put in (the hand) to feel; touch to the quick

εἰσ-νέω swim over to

εἰσ-νοέω perceive, remark

εἴσοδος ου ἡ entrance; vestibule; admission

εἰσ-οικειόω introduce as a friend

εἰσοίκησις εως ἡ dwelling, home

εἰσ-οικίζομαι *pass* settle oneself in

εἰσ-οικοδομέω build into

εἰσ-οιχνέω step into, enter

εἰσόκεν *adv* until; as long as

εἴσομαι *fut from* **οἶδα**

εἰσοπίσω *adv* in future

εἴσοπτος ον visible

εἰσ-οράω look into, on *or* at; view, behold; perceive; consider

εἰσ-ορμάω *and pass* force one's way into

ἔισος, ἐΐσος ▸ **ἴσος**

εἰσ-παίω burst *or* rush in

εἰσ-πέμπω send *or* bring in

εἰσ-πέτομαι *mid* fly into; arrive at

εἰσ-πηδάω jump into

εἰσ-πῑ́πτω fall into, rush into; invade, attack, fall upon; be thrown into

εἰσ-πλέω sail into

εἴσπλους ου ὁ a sailing in; entrance of a harbour

εἰσ-ποιέω put in; add; give to be adopted

εἰσ-πορεύομαι *pass* go into, enter

εἴσπρᾱξις εως ἡ exaction of money

εἰσ-πρᾱ́σσω *and mid* exact, collect

εἰσ-ρέω flow into

εἰσ-τίθημι put *or* place into *or* on

εἰσ-τοξεύω shoot into

εἰσ-τρέχω run into

εἰσ-φέρω carry *or* bring into; bring in; contribute; pay [income tax]; bring forward, propose; *pass* get into

εἰσφορᾱ́ ᾶς ἡ contribution; income tax, property tax (levied for the purpose of war)

εἰσ-φορέω ▸ **εἰσφέρω**

εἰσ-φρέω let in, admit

εἰσ-χειρίζω hand over to

εἰσ-χέω pour into

εἴσω, ἔσω *adv* in(to a place), inward(s); within; between; within the reach of

εἰσ-ωθέομαι *mid* force one's way into

εἰσωπός όν between; visible; facing

εἶτα *adv* then; after, further; and then, and yet; therefore

εἴτε ... εἴτε *conj* either ... or; whether ... or

εἶχον *impf from* **ἔχω**

εἴωθα *pf (with pres sense) from* **ἔθω**

εἰωθότως *adv* in the customary way

εἵως ▸ **ἕως**

ἐκ, ἐξ *prep with gen* out of, from, from among, without, far from; since, immediately after; on the part of, because of, in consequence of

ἑκᾱ́εργος ον working from afar, shooting from afar (of Apollo)

ἕκαθεν *adv* from afar; far off

ἑκάς *adv* far off; *prep with gen* far from

ἑκασταχόθεν *adv* from every side

ἑκασταχόθι, ἑκασταχοῦ, ἑκάστοθι *adv* everywhere

ἑκασταχόσε *adv* to all sides

ἕκαστος η ον every, every one, each
■ **εἷς ἕκαστος** each one, every single one

ἑκάστοτε *adv* every time

ἑκατεράκις *adv* (at) both times

ἑκάτερθεν ▸ **ἑκατέρωθεν**

ἑκάτερος ᾱ ον each of (the) two, either; *pl* both, both parties

ἑκατέρωθεν *adv* from each side

ἑκατέρωσε *adv* to each side, each way, both ways

ἑκατηβελέτης ου ὁ the far shooter (of Apollo)

ἑκατηβόλος ον far-shooting (of Apollo)

ἕκᾱτι ▸ **ἕκητι**

ἑκατόγχειρος ον with a hundred hands (of Briareus)

ἑκατόζῡγος ον with a hundred rowing benches

ἑκατόμβη ης ἡ hecatomb (a sacrifice of a hundred oxen)

ἑκατόμβοιος ον worth a hundred oxen

ἑκατόμπεδος ον **ἑκατόμποδος** ον a hundred feet long

ἑκατόμπολις ι with a hundred cities

ἑκατόμπους (*gen* ποδος) with a hundred feet

ἑκατόμπυλος ον with a hundred gates

ἑκατόν οἱ αἱ τά a hundred

ἑκατονταέτης ες a hundred years old

ἑκατονταπλασίων ον hundredfold, a hundred times as much *or* many

ἑκατοντάρχης ου ὁ **ἑκατόνταρχος** ου ὁ centurion

ἑκατοντάς άδος ἡ the number one hundred

ἕκατος ου ὁ ▸ **ἑκηβόλος**

ἑκατοστός ή όν hundredth

ἑκατοστύς ύος ἡ ▸ **ἑκατοντάς**

ἐκ-βαίνω come *or* step out, disembark, leave; depart from; turn out, happen; digress; *tr* put on shore; transgress

ἐκ-βακχεύω make frantic, rouse to Bacchic frenzy

ἐκ-βάλλω throw *or* cast out; expel, banish; cast away; strike out; let fall, drop; lose; reject; recant

ἔκβασις εως ἡ disembarking, landing; way out; mountain pass; ascent

ἐκ-βάω ▸ **ἐκβαίνω**

ἐκ-βιάζομαι *pass* be wrested from

ἐκ-βλαστάνω sprout out

ἐκ-βοάω cry out, shout

ἐκβοήθεια ᾱς ἡ marching out to help; sally, sortie

ἐκ-βοηθέω march out to aid; sally forth

ἐκβολή ῆς ἡ a throwing out, expulsion, banishment; outlet; mountain pass; digression; loss; what is cast out; a shooting forth; origin

ἔκβολος ον cast out of (a place); outcast
■ **ὁ ἔκβολος** promontory, beach

ἐκ-βράσσω throw up on shore, cast ashore

ἐκ-βρῡχάομαι *mid* roar out

ἔκβρωμα ατος τό what is eaten

ἐκ-γαμίζω give away in marriage

ἐκ-γαμίσκομαι *pass* be given in marriage

ἐκ-γελάω laugh loudly

ἐκγενής ές without family

ἐκ-γί(γ)νομαι be born (of), be descended from; have gone by *or* elapsed; be permitted

ἔκγονος ον descended; descendant, offspring, relation; *pl* posterity

ἐκ-δακρῡ́ω burst into tears

ε

ἐκ-δαπανάω exhaust
ἔκδεια ᾱς ἡ falling short; being in arrears
ἐκ-δείκνῡμι show openly
ἐκ-δέκομαι ▸ **ἐκδέχομαι**
ἔκδεξις εως ἡ succession
ἐκ-δέρκομαι look out from
ἐκ-δέρω strip off the skin from
ἐκ-δέχομαι *mid* take *or* receive from; take upon oneself; acquire, learn; succeed, follow; wait, expect
ἐκ-δέω fasten *or* bind to; shut in; *mid* put on
ἔκδηλος ον quite plain, conspicuous; excellent
ἐκ-δημέω go *or* be abroad, travel away from home
ἔκδημος ον abroad, (away) from home
ἐκδια-βαίνω step completely through
ἐκ-διαιτάομαι depart from one's way of life
ἐκ-διδάσκω teach thoroughly
ἐκ-διδράσκω run away, escape
ἐκ-δίδωμι surrender, give up; give away in marriage; lend out (on hire); *intr* run out (into)
ἐκδι-ηγέομαι *mid* tell to the end
ἐκ-δικέω avenge, punish; exact vengeance for; defend, vindicate
ἐκδίκησις εως ἡ punishment, revenge
ἔκδικος ον lawless, unjust; avenging
ἐκ-διώκω expel
ἔκδοσις εως ἡ surrendering; giving in marriage
ἔκδοτος ον surrendered
ἐκδοχή ῆς ἡ expectation; succession
ἐκδρομή ῆς ἡ sally, raid; band of skirmishers
ἔκδρομος ου ὁ skirmisher
ἐκ-δύνω ▸ **ἐκδύομαι**
ἔκδυσις εως ἡ slipping out, escape; final event
ἐκ-δύω *act tr* strip off; *act intr and mid* get out of; escape
ἐκ-δωριόομαι *pass* become thoroughly Dorian
ἐκεῖ *adv* there; to there; then; in that case
ἐκεῖθεν *adv* from there; from that time; therefore
ἐκεῖθι, ἐκείνῃ ▸ **ἐκεῖ**
ἐκεῖνος η ο that
ἐκεῖσε *adv* to there; then
ἐκεχειρίᾱ ᾱς ἡ armistice, truce
ἐκ-ζέω boil over; break out; swarm with
ἐκ-ζητέω search eagerly; avenge
ἐκζήτησις εως ἡ matter of dispute
ἐκηβολίᾱ ᾱς ἡ shooting from afar; skill in archery
ἐκηβόλος ον shooter, archer (of Apollo)
ἕκηλος ον quiet, at one's ease; untroubled
ἕκητι *adv* by means of, through the help of; for the sake of
ἐκ-θαμβέομαι *pass* be amazed
ἔκθαμβος ον amazed, astounded
ἐκ-θαυμάζω wonder, be astonished
ἐκ-θεάομαι *mid* see to the end
ἔκθεσις εως ἡ exposure (of a child)
ἔκθετος ον exposed
ἐκ-θέω run out; make a sally
ἐκ-θηρεύω hunt down, catch
ἐκ-θλῖβω squeeze with great pressure; distress greatly
ἐκ-θνῄσκω be dying
ἐκ-θρῴσκω + *gen* leap out of *or* down
ἔκθῡμος ον courageous; passionate
ἐκ-θύω offer as atonement; *mid* atone for
ἐκ-καθαίρω cleanse, purify; clear away
ἐκ-καθεύδω sleep out of doors
ἐκκαίδεκα sixteen
ἐκκαιδεκάδωρος sixteen palms long

ἐκκαιδεκάπηχυς υ sixteen cubits long

ἐκ-καίω burn out; kindle, inflame

ἐκ-κακέω get tired, grow weary; be faint-hearted

ἐκ-καλέω call out, summon forth; elicit, exhort, excite

ἐκ-καλύπτω uncover

ἐκ-κάμνω get tired, grow weary; fall short

ἐκ-καρπόομαι *mid* enjoy the fruit of; derive advantage

ἐκκαταπ-άλλομαι leap down

ἔκ-κειμαι be exposed; be pasted up; be left bare of *+gen*

ἐκ-κενόω empty; unpeople, depopulate

ἐκ-κεντέω pierce

ἐκ-κηρύσσω proclaim through a herald; banish by proclamation

ἐκ-κῑνέω move out; stir, excite; expel

ἐκ-κίω go out

ἐκ-κλάω break in *or* to pieces

ἐκ-κλείω shut out; hinder, oppress

ἐκ-κλέπτω remove by stealth; abduct; deceive

ἐκκλησίᾱ ᾱς ἡ assembly of citizens *or* soldiers; the Jewish congregation; the Christian church

ἐκκλησιάζω hold an assembly; be a member of the assembly

ἐκκλησιαστής οῦ ὁ someone taking part in an assembly

ἐκκλησιαστικόν οῦ τό pay received for sitting in the assembly

ἔκκλητος ον called forth; member of an assembly

ἐκ-κλῑ́νω bend aside; avoid; *intr* turn away; give way; withdraw

ἐκ-κνάω rub off

ἐκ-κολάπτω chisel off, obliterate; *mid* come out of the egg (of birds)

ἐκ-κολυμβάω *+gen* swim out of

ἐκκομιδή ῆς ἡ bringing out; burial

ἐκ-κομίζω carry *or* bring out; save; bury; endure to the end

ἐκ-κομπάζω boast

ἐκκοπή ῆς ἡ hindrance; cutting out (of an arrow point from the body)

ἐκ-κόπτω knock out; cut off *or* down, fell; demolish; chase; destroy

ἐκ-κρέμαμαι *mid +gen* hang from *or* onto; depend on

ἐκ-κρεμάννυμαι hang from, cling to

ἐκ-κρῑ́νω single out; choose, select

ἔκκριτος ον chosen

ἐκ-κρούω beat out; expel, drive away; frustrate, thwart

ἐκ-κυβιστάω *+gen* tumble headlong out of; do a somersault (over)

ἐκ-κυλίνδω, ἐκ-κυλίω roll out; *pass* be rolled out; tumble out of

ἐκ-κῡμαίνω undulate; make the front-line uneven

ἐκ-κωφόω make deaf, deafen

ἐκ-λαγχάνω obtain (by lot *or* destiny)

ἐκ-λαλέω speak out, let slip, divulge

ἐκ-λαμβάνω take out of; choose; receive; perceive, undertstand

ἐκ-λάμπω shine forth

ἐκ-λανθάνω escape notice completely; cause to forget utterly; *mid + gen* forget utterly

ἐκ-λέγω pick out, choose; collect; exact

ἐκ-λείπω leave out, omit; forsake, abandon; be unmindful (of), neglect; *intr* cease, disappear; run short; die; be eclipsed

ἔκλειψις εως ἡ forsaking; disappearing; loss; eclipse

ἐκλεκτός ή όν selected

ἐκ-λέπω hatch

ἐκ-λήγω cease

ἔκλησις εως ἡ forgetfulness

ἐκλιπής ές failing, deficient; eclipsed; overlooked

ε

ἐκ-λογίζομαι *mid* calculate, consider

ἔκλυσις εως ἡ release; weakness

ἐκλυτήριος ον releasing

ἐκ-λύω loose, set free, release, redeem; dissolve, weaken, exhaust; put an end to; *pass* be exhausted *or* worn out, give up hope

ἐκ-λωβάομαι *mid* treat shamefully

ἐκ-λωπίζω uncover

ἐκ-μαίνω drive mad, enrage; *pass* rave, be frantic, be furious

ἐκ-μανθάνω learn thoroughly; learn by heart; examine closely

ἐκ-μάσσω wipe away; mould *or* model (in wax or plaster)

ἐκ-μείρομαι partake of

ἐκ-μετρέω measure out
■ **ἐκμετρέω τόν βίον** die

ἔκμηνος ον of six months

ἐκ-μηρύομαι *mid* wind out like a ball of thread; (of an army) file off

ἐκ-μῑμέομαι *mid* imitate closely

ἐκ-μισθόω let out for hire, farm out

ἐκ-μολεῖν *infin* go out

ἐκ-μυζάω suck out

ἐκ-μυκτηρίζω mock at

ἐκ-νέμω *and mid* go forth

ἐκ-νευρίζω cut the sinews

ἐκ-νεύω avoid; *intr* turn aside; fall headlong

ἐκ-νέω swim out of *or* away; escape

ἐκ-νήφω sleep off a drunken fit; become sober again

ἐκ-νίζω wash off; expiate

ἐκ-νῑκάω become victorious; prevail, be in use

ἐκ-νοστέω return again

ἑκούσιος (ᾱ) ον ▸ **ἑκών**

ἐκ-παγλέομαι be highly amazed, wonder at

ἔκπαγλος ον astonishing, frightful, terrible

ἐκ-παιδεύω educate thoroughly

ἐκ-παιφάσσω rush madly to the fray

ἔκπαλαι *adv* long ago, in time gone by

ἐκ-πάλλομαι *mid + gen* spurt out from

ἐκ-πατάσσω knock out; strike, afflict

ἐκ-παύομαι *mid* cease entirely

ἐκ-πείθω persuade

ἐκ-πειράομαι ἐκ-πειράζω try, test

ἐκ-πέλει ▸ **ἔξεστι** it is allowed

ἐκ-πέμπω send out *or* away; export; convey; chase, banish; dismiss; send for

ἔκπεμψις εως ἡ sending away

ἐκπεπταμένως *adv* extravagantly

ἐκ-περαίνω bring to an end, achieve

ἐκ-περάω go *or* pass through *or* along

ἐκ-πέρθω destroy utterly

ἐκ-πετάννῡμι spread out

ἐκ-πηδάω leap out *or* up; make a sally

ἐκ-πίμπλημι fill up; satiate, satisfy; atone for

ἐκ-πῑ́νω drink off, drain; drink

ἐκ-πιπράσκω sell off, sell out

ἐκ-πῑ́πτω fall out of *or* down; fall from, depart from; be hissed off; stop short; turn out, result; lose; cease; be banished *or* driven out of; be wrecked *or* cast on shore; come *or* sally forth; escape; empty itself

ἐκ-πλέω sail out, leave port; swim out; outsail

ἔκπλεως ων filled up, full; complete, abundant

ἐκ-πλήγνῡμι ▸ **ἐκπλήσσω**

ἐκπληκτικός ή όν terrifying

ἔκπληξις εως ἡ fright, terror, consternation; awe

ἐκ-πληρόω ▸ **ἐκπίμπλημι**

ἐκπλήρωσις εως ἡ filling up, completion

ἐκ-πλήσσω strike out, drive away; frighten, astound; *pass* be out of one's senses; be amazed, frightened *or* panic-struck

ἔκπλοος ου ὁ (*also* ἔκπλους ου ὁ) a sailing out; port of departure

ἐκ-πλῡ́νω wash out

ἐκ-πλώω ▸ **ἐκπλέω**

ἐκ-πνέω breathe out, forth *or* away; *intr* expire, be killed; (of winds) blow outwards

ἐκποδών *adv* out of the way, away

ἐκ-ποιέω complete, finish; build up

ἐκποίησις εως ἡ putting forth; emission of sperm

ἐκ-πολεμέω make war; rouse to war

ἐκ-πολιορκέω take by siege *or* assault, overpower

ἐκπομπή ῆς ἡ a sending out

ἐκ-πονέω work out, finish, execute; (of food) digest; bring to perfection; train; be eager

ἐκ-πορεύομαι *pass* march *or* go out

ἐκ-πορθέω devastate, plunder

ἐκ-πορίζω invert; contrive; provide

ἐκ-πορνεύω commit fornication

ἐκ-ποτέομαι fly down *or* out from

ἐκ-πρᾱ́ττω finish, achieve, effect, kill; exact punishment; avenge; *mid* avenge

ἐκ-πρεπής ές prominent, excellent, extraordinary

ἐκ-πρίασθαι *aor infin from* **ἐξωνέομαι**

ἐκ-πρῑ́ω saw off *or* out

ἐκπρο-καλέομαι *mid* summon out to oneself

ἐκπρο-λείπω forsake, abandon

ἐκπρο-τῑμάω honour above all others

ἐκ-πτύω spit out; detest

ἐκ-πυνθάνομαι *mid* search out, hear of

ἐκ-πυρόω set on fire

ἔκπυστος ον known, notorious

ἔκπωμα ατος τό drinking cup

ἐκ-ραίνω make to fall in drops from

ἐκ-ρέω flow out; vanish

ἐκ-ρήγνῡμι *act tr* break out *or* off, tear in *or* to pieces; *act intr and pass* sally forth, burst out; become known

ἐκ-ριζόω root out

ἐκ-ρίπτω throw out

ἐκροή ῆς ἡ **ἔκροος** ου ὁ (*also* ἔκρους ου ὁ) outflow

ἐκ-σαόω ▸ **ἐκσῴζω**

ἐκ-σείω shake out

ἐκ-σεύομαι *pass* rush out, hasten away

ἐκ-σημαίνω signify

ἐκ-σμάω wipe out *or* off

ἐκ-σπάω draw out

ἔκσπονδος ον excluded from a treaty

ἔκστασις εως ἡ astonishment, trance

ἐκ-στέλλω equip; send out

ἐκ-στέφω adorn with garlands

ἐκ-στρατεύω *and mid* march out to war; end war

ἐκ-στρατοπεδεύομαι *mid* encamp outside

ἐκ-στρέφω turn *or* pull out; turn inside out; change, make worse

ἐκ-σῴζω save

ἐκτάδιος (ᾱ) ον far off

ἐκταῖος ᾱ ον on the sixth day

ἐκ-τανύω ▸ **ἐκτείνω**

ἐκ-ταράσσω trouble greatly, agitate

ἐκ-τάσσω arrange, line up in battle order

ἐκ-τείνω stretch out, extend; draw out; strain; prostrate

ἐκ-τειχῑ́ζω build *or* fortify completely

ἐκ-τελέω finish, bring to an end, achieve, satisfy; spend [time]

ἐκ-τέμνω cut out from, cut off; castrate

ἐκτένεια ᾱς ἡ zeal, earnestness

ἐκτενής ές zealous, earnest, assiduous

ἐκ-τεχνάομαι *mid* contrive, devise

ἐκ-τίθημι put out *or* outside; explain

ἐκ-τῑμάω honour highly

ἔκτῑμος ον not honouring

ε

ἐκ-τινάσσω strike *or* shake out *or* off

ἐκ-τίνω pay off, requite, make amends (for); *mid* punish

ἐκ-τιτρώσκω miscarry

ἔκτοθεν ▸ **ἔκτοσθεν**

ἔκτοθι *adv outside*

ἐκ-τομίᾱς ου ὁ eunuch

ἐκ-τοξεύω shoot arrows out of; use up in shooting

ἐκτόπιος (ᾱ) ον **ἔκτοπος** ον away from a place, distant; strange, extraordinary

ἕκτος η ον sixth

ἐκτός *adv + gen* without, outside; out of, far from; except

ἔκτοσε *adv* outwards; out of *+ gen*

ἔκτοσθε(ν) *adv* (from) outside; *with gen* out of, far from

ἐκ-τραχηλίζω (of a horse) throw (the rider) over the head, throw down

ἐκ-τρέπω turn away *or* aside, divert; drive away; sprain; dissuade from; lead to; *pass and mid* turn (oneself) aside from; deviate; avoid

ἐκ-τρέφω feed, rear, bring up

ἐκ-τρέχω run out; sally forth

ἐκ-τρῑ́βω rub out; destroy by rubbing, destroy root and branch

ἐκτροπή ῆς ἡ turning off *or* aside, escape; resting-place; digression

ἐκ-τρῡχόω wear out

ἔκτρωμα ατος τό a child prematurely born, an abortion

ἐκ-τυφλόω make blind

ἐκτύφλωσις εως ἡ making blind

ἑκυρᾱ́ ᾶς ἡ mother-in-law

ἑκυρός οῦ ὁ father-in-law

ἐκ-φαίνω show forth, bring to light, reveal, betray; *pass* appear, come to light

ἐκφανής ές manifest, showing itself

ἔκφασις εως ἡ a saying, declaration

ἐκ-φαυλίζω make bad, depreciate

ἐκ-φέρω carry out of *or* away; bury; carry off [a prize]; steal; lead out *or* away; speak out, tell; produce; bring to light; proclaim, publish; put to sea; run ahead; *pass* come forth; come to; be agitated

ἐκ-φεύγω flee away, escape

ἔκ-φημι speak out

ἐκ-φθίνω consume, destroy

ἐκ-φοβέω frighten, frighten away

ἔκφοβος ον frightened

ἐκ-φοιτάω go out *or* away

ἐκφορᾱ́ ᾶς ἡ burial

ἐκ-φορέω ▸ **ἐκφέρω**

ἐκφόριον ου τό produce, crop; rent

ἐκ-φορτίζομαι be sold for exportation; be kidnapped, betrayed

ἐκ-φροντίζω devise; deliberate

ἔκφρων ον out of one's mind, mad

ἐκ-φυλάσσω watch carefully

ἐκ-φύω *act tr* cause to grow out of; produce, beget; *act intr and mid* grow from; be born from

ἐκ-χέω pour out, shed, spill; squander, spoil; *pass* stream out; indulge in

ἐκ-χράω[1] be enough

ἐκ-χράω[2] declare; give an oracle

ἐκ-χρηματίζομαι *mid* extort money

ἐκ-χώννῡμι heap up earth; fill with mud

ἐκ-χωρέω go away, depart; make way, cede, allow

ἐκ-ψῡ́χω breathe one's last

ἑκών οῦσα όν voluntary, willing; on purpose

ἐλᾱ́α ᾱς ἡ **ἐλαίᾱ** ᾱς ἡ olive-tree; olive

ἐλᾱίνεος ᾱ ον **ἐλᾱ́ινος** η ον of olive-wood

ἔλαιον ου τό olive-oil

ἔλαιος ου ὁ wild olive-tree

ἐλαιών ῶνος ὁ olive garden

ἔλασις εως ἡ driving, chasing; riding, march, expedition; attack

ἐλασσόω make less, damage; *pass* become smaller, decrease; be a loser; come short of

ἐλᾱ́σσων ον *comp from* ἐλαχύς

ἐλαστρέω drive, row

ἐλάτη ης ἡ pine, fir; oar; ship

ἐλατήρ ῆρος ὁ driver, charioteer

ἐλάτινος η ον of pine-wood

ἐλᾱττονέω be *or* have less

ἐλᾱ́ττωμα ατος τό loss, want

ἐλαύνω† drive, drive on, lead; chase, expel; harass, press; strike, beat, hit, hurt, wound; beat out [metal]; draw out; build; produce; *intr* drive, ride, row, march, advance

ἐλάφειος ον of deer

ἐλαφηβολίᾱ ᾱς ἡ deer hunt

ἐλαφηβολιών ῶνος ὁ ninth month of the Athenian calendar (March–April)

ἐλαφηβόλος ον shooting deer

ἔλαφος ου ὁ/ἡ deer, stag, hind

ἐλαφρίᾱ ᾱς ἡ levity

ἐλαφρός ᾱ́ όν light, swift, nimble; active; light-armed; easy, without trouble

ἐλαχίστερος ᾱ ον smaller, the smallest

ἐλαχύς ἐλάχεια (*not* εῖα) ἐλαχύ little, small

■ **ἐλᾱ́σσων** ον *comp* smaller, less, worse, inferior

■ **ἐλάχιστος** η ον *sup* smallest, least, shortest

ἐλάω ▸ ἐλαύνω

ἔλδομαι, ἐέλδομαι wish, long for; *pass* be wished for

ἐλεαίρω, ἐλεάω ▸ ἐλεέω

ἐλεγεῖον ου τό two lines of verse (the first a hexameter, the second a pentameter)

ἐλεγμός οῦ ὁ **ἔλεγξις** εως ἡ refuting; blaming; conviction

ἐλεγχείη ης ἡ ▸ ἔλεγχος[1]

ἐλεγχής ές shameful; cowardly; wretched

ἔλεγχος[1] ους τό reproach, disgrace; coward

ἔλεγχος[2] ου ὁ means of proving, proof, trial; conviction, refutation, reproach; test, examination; account; sentence, judgement

ἐλέγχω censure, reproach; put to shame, treat with contempt; despise, reject; convince; refute; prove, show; examine, search, question, cross-examine

ἐλεεινός όν pitiable, pitied, miserable; pitiful

ἐλεέω have pity (upon), pity

ἐλεημοσύνη ης ἡ charity, mercy; alms

ἐλεήμων ον pitiful; merciful

ἐλεητύς ύος ἡ pity, mercy

ἐλεινός ή όν ▸ **ἐλεεινός**

ἔλειος ον living in marshes

ἐλελίζω[1] *aor* ἠλέλιξα raise the war cry

ἐλελίζω[2] *aor* ἐλέλιξα cause to shake *or* tremble; whirl round, turn round quickly; *pass* tremble, shake; turn oneself quickly; *mid* coil

ἐλελίχθων ον earth-shaking

ἐλεόθρεπτος ον marsh-bred

ἐλεός οῦ ὁ kitchen-table; carving board

ἔλεος ου ὁ (*also* ους τό) pity, mercy

ἑλετός ή όν that can be taken *or* caught

ἐλευθερίᾱ ᾱς ἡ freedom, liberty; generosity

ἐλευθέριος ᾱ ον like a free man, noble-minded, frank, liberal, noble; freeing, delivering; releaser

ἐλεύθερος ᾱ ον free, freeborn, independent; free from, freed; liberal, free-spirited; noble, honest

ἐλευθερόω set free, release, acquit

ἐλευθέρωσις εως ἡ a setting free, release

ἔλευσις εως ἡ a coming, arrival

ἐλεφαίρομαι *mid* deceive, cheat with empty hopes

ε

ἐλεφάντινος η ον of ivory

ἐλέφᾱς αντος ὁ ivory; elephant

ἕλιγμα ατος τό what is rolled; medley; curl, lock of hair

ἑλιγμός οῦ ὁ a winding; a rolling

ἑλικτήρ ῆρος ὁ earring

ἑλικτός ή όν curved, rolled, wreathed; tortuous

ἑλίκωψ (*gen* ωπος) **ἑλικῶπις** (*gen* ιδος) with bright eyes

ἐλῑνύω rest, repose, keep quiet

ἕλιξ (*gen* ικος) twisted; with twisted horns

■ **ἡ ἕλιξ** a winding, coil, curl; circle; spiral line; bracelet, earring

ἑλίσσω ἑλίξω εἵλιξα turn round; roll *or* whirl round; swing; wind *or* wrap round; revolve, reflect; *pass and mid* turn round, coil oneself; move quickly, spin round

ἑλκεσίπεπλος ον **ἑλκεχίτων** (*gen* ωνος) with trailing robe

ἑλκέω ▸ ἕλκω

ἑλκηθμός οῦ ὁ dragging away

ἕλκος ους τό wound; ulcer; evil

ἑλκόω wound; *pass* ulcerate

ἑλκυστάζω drag along

ἑλκύω, ἕλκω† draw, drag, pull, tear; maltreat; bend *or* draw [a bow *or* sail]; draw up *or* down; weigh; tear off [the hair]; draw out, stretch

ἕλκωσις εως ἡ ulceration

ἐλ-λάμπομαι *mid* shine forth

ἐλλέβορος ου ὁ sneezewort, hellebore (a plant used to treat madness)

ἐλλεδανός οῦ ὁ straw-rope

ἔλλειμμα ατος τό a short-coming

ἐλ-λείπω *act* leave behind; leave out, omit, neglect; *act intr and pass* be left, remain; be inferior, lack, come short of; be needed

ἔλλειψις εως ἡ deficiency

ἔλλεσχος ον commonly talked of

ἑλληνίζω speak Greek; make Greek

ἑλληνικῶς, ἑλληνιστί *adv* in Greek fashion; in Greek

ἐλλιπής ές lacking, defective; inferior

ἐλ-λογάω, ἐλ-λογέω impute

ἐλ-λόγιμος ον notable, excellent

ἐλλός[1] οῦ ὁ young deer, fawn

ἐλλός[2] ή όν mute

ἐλ-λοχάω lie in wait (for)

ἐλλύχνιον ου τό wick of a lamp

ἕλος ους τό marsh, swamp; meadow

ἐλπίζω ἐλπιῶ ἤλπισα hope, expect; think; fear

ἐλπίς ίδος ἡ hope, expectation; fear

ἔλπω cause to hope; *mid* ▸ **ἐλπίζω**

ἐλπωρή ῆς ἡ ▸ **ἐλπίς**

ἔλυτρον ου τό cover, case; cistern, reservoir

ἐλύω ▸ **εἰλύω**

ἐλῶ *fut from* **ἐλαύνω**

ἐλωΐ, ἐλωεί *Hebr* my God!

ἕλωρ ωρος τό **ἑλώριον** ου τό booty, prey, spoil; penalty for killing

ἐμαυτόν ήν όν *acc* myself

ἐμ-βαδόν *adv* on foot, by land

ἐμ-βαίνω step in *or* into, enter; go on board, embark; mount; tread upon; be fixed upon; step on; intervene; *tr* bring into

ἐμ-βάλλω throw, put *or* lay in; throw upon; inject, cause; *intr* make an invasion; attack; take in hand; encounter, rush against; run out into

ἔμβαμμα ατος τό sauce, soup

ἐμ-βάπτω dip in

ἐμ-βάς άδος ἡ shoe, slipper

ἐμ-βασιλεύω + *dat* be king among

ἐμ-βατεύω step along, in *or* upon; come into possession (of); persist in

ἐμβάφιον ου τό bowl, vessel

ἐμ-βιβάζω bring in; put on board

ἐμ-βλέπω look at, look in the face

ἐμ-βοάω shout aloud, call to + *dat*

ἐμβολή ῆς ἡ attack, assault; a throwing in, shot; charge made by one ship against another; leak; head of a battering ram; entrance, pass; mouth of a river

ἐμ-βόλιμος ον inserted, intercalated

ἔμβολον ου τό **ἔμβολος** ου ὁ wedge; tongue of land between two rivers; wedge-shaped order of battle; beak *or* ram of a ship

ἔμβραχυ *adv* in short

ἐμ-βρέμομαι *mid* roar in

ἐμβρῑθής ές weighty, heavy; firm; grave

ἐμ-βρῑμάομαι be indignant, be deeply moved; criticize severely + *dat*

ἐμ-βροντάω thunder at; stun

ἐμβρόντητος ον thunderstruck; frightened, stupid

ἔμβρυον ου τό little lamb; embryo

ἔμετος ου ὁ a vomiting

ἐμέω ἐμῶ ἤμεσα vomit; spit out

ἐμ-μαίνομαι *pass* + *dat* be mad at

ἐμμανής ές raving, mad

ἐμμαπέως *adv* at once, quickly

ἐμ-μάχομαι *mid* fight a battle in

ἐμμέλεια ᾱς ἡ harmony; tune; dance

ἐμμελής ές harmonious, in tune; correct, regular, fit, agreeable; elegant, witty

ἐμμεμαώς υῖα ός eager, hasty, ardent, impetuous

ἐμ-μέμονα *pf* be agitated; be lost in passion

ἐμμενής ές steady, unceasing

ἐμ-μένω stay in [a place]; remain steadfast, keep to; continue

ἔμμετρος ον in measure, moderate; metrical

ἔμμηνος ον happening every month

ἐμ-μῑ́γνῡμι mix in; involve in; *intr* encounter + *dat*

ἔμμισθος ον paid, hired; earning money

ἐμμονή ῆς ἡ staying in; continuance

ἔμμονος ον staying in, steadfast

ἔμμορος ον + *gen* sharing in, endued with

ἐμός ή όν my, mine

ἐμ-πάζομαι + *gen* care for

ἐμπαιγμονή ῆς ἡ **ἐμπαιγμός** οῦ ὁ jesting, mocking

ἐμ-παίζω mock, jest, trifle with; deceive

ἐμπαίκτης ου ὁ mocker

ἔμπαιος ον + *gen* skilled, practised (in)

ἐμ-παίω strike in, stamp; entangle

ἔμπαλιν, τό ἔμπαλιν *adv* backwards, back; contrary to, in the reverse order; on the other side *or* hand

ἐμπαρ-έχω offer, hand over; abandon

ἔμπᾱς *adv* altogether, at all events; on the whole, throughout; yet, in spite of; although

ἐμ-πάσσω embroider

ἐμ-πεδάω bind with fetters, check

ἐμπεδ-ορκέω abide by one's oath

ἔμπεδος ον steadfast, unmoved, firm; certain; continuous

ἐμ-πεδόω make firm and fast, establish

ἐμπειρίᾱ ᾱς ἡ experience, knowledge, skill, practice

ἔμπειρος ον experienced, skilful; proved by experience

ἐμπερι-πατέω walk about (in)

ἐμ-πήγνῡμι + *dat* fix in, thrust in

ἔμπηρος ον crippled

ἔμπης ▸ ἔμπας

ἐμ-πικραίνομαι *pass* be embittered

ἐμ-πί(μ)πλημι fill full *or* up; satiate; *pass and mid* fill oneself; be satisfied *or* satiated; get tired of

ἐμ-πῑ́νω drink in, drink greedily

ἐμ-πίπτω + *dat* fall in *or* upon; rush into, throw oneself into; attack, assault, invade, burst in; fall in with; come over, seize

ἐμπίς ίδος ἡ gnat, mosquito

ἐμ-πίτνω ▸ **ἐμπίπτω**

ἐμ-πλάσσω plaster up

ἔμπλειος ᾱ ον ▸ **ἔμπλεος**

ἐμ-πλέκω plait in; entangle

ἔμπλεος ον full, filled up

ἐμ-πλέω sail in *or* on

ἐμπλήγδην *adv* rashly, at random

ἔμπληκτος ον stunned, stupefied; rash; fickle

ἔμπλην *adv + gen* close by

ἐμ-πλήσσω fall into

ἐμπλοκή ῆς ἡ a plaiting in

ἐμ-πνέω breathe in *or* on; breathe, live; inspire; *pass* recover oneself

ἔμπνοος ον (*also* ἔμπνους ουν) breathing, alive

ἐμ-ποδίζω bind, fetter; be in the way of, hinder; make doubtful; cause to fall

ἐμπόδιος ον impeding

ἐμπόδισμα ατος τό hindrance

ἐμποδών *adv + dat* before the feet, in the way, as a ; hindrance
▪ **τὸ ἐμποδών** what comes in one's way

ἐμ-ποιέω make *or* put in, inset; cause, inspire, suggest

ἐμ-πολάω buy, purchase; earn, gain by selling; *mid* acquire by trade; bribe

ἐμπολέμιος ον taking place in war

ἐμπολή ῆς ἡ traffic; merchandise

ἐμπολητός ή όν bought and sold

ἔμπολις εως ὁ fellow citizen

ἐμ-πολῑτεύω be a citizen, have civil rights

ἐμ-πορεύομαι *pass* travel to; *mid* trade, traffic; overreach

ἐμπορίᾱ ᾱς ἡ traffic, trade; commerce, business

ἐμπορικός ή όν commercial

ἐμπόριον ου τό trading place

ἔμπορος ου ὁ passenger (on a ship); traveller; merchant, trader

ἐμ-πορπάομαι *mid* fix on with a brooch

ἐμ-πρέπω excel, be conspicuous

ἐμ-πρήθω set on fire

ἔμπρησις εως ἡ setting on fire, conflagration

ἔμπροσθεν *adv* before, in front of, anterior, earlier

ἐμ-πτύω spit upon *or* at

ἐμπυριβήτης (*gen* ου) standing over the fire

ἔμπυρος ον in *or* on the fire
▪ **τὰ ἔμπῡρα** burnt sacrifices

ἐμ-φαγεῖν *aor infin* eat up, swallow

ἐμ-φαίνω show, make visible *or* conspicuous; *pass* show oneself, appear

ἐμφανής ές conspicuous, visible; manifest, clear; known, public

ἐμ-φανίζω ▸ **ἐμφαίνω**

ἔμφασις εως ἡ reflection (in mirror etc.)

ἐμφερής ές + *dat* equivalent to, similar to

ἐμ-φέρω bring on; hold up to; object to

ἔμφοβος ον fearful; frightened

ἐμ-φορέω bear in; *pass* be borne about; enjoy fully; do to excess

ἐμ-φράσσω stop *or* block up

ἐμ-φρουρέω keep guard in [a place]

ἔμφρουρος ον on guard in [a place]; garrisoned

ἔμφρων ον sensible; prudent

ἐμφῦλιος ον **ἔμφῡλος** ον of the same tribe, kindred; native

ἐμ-φῡσάω breathe upon

ἐμ-φυτεύω (im)plant

ἔμφυτος ον inborn, innate, implanted

ἐμ-φύω *act tr* implant; *act intr and mid* grow into; be rooted in; cling to; be inborn *or* innate; be in

ἔμψῡχος ον having a soul in one, alive

ἐν *adv* within; besides; *prep with dat* in, at, on; between, among; during, within; by means of, with, through; upon, by dint of

ἐναγής ές guilty, polluted; bound by an oath

ἐν-αγίζω sacrifice to the dead

ἐν-αγκαλίζομαι *mid* take in one's arms

ἐν-αγκυλάω put a thong on [a javelin] (to help with throwing it)

ἔναγχος *adv* just now, lately, the other day

ἐν-άγω lead in, on *or* to; bring into court, accuse; urge, incite, promote

ἐν-αγωνίζομαι *mid* contend in, on *or* among; be one of the prize-fighters

ἔναιμος ον filled with blood

ἐν-αίρω *and mid* kill; destroy

ἐναίσιμος ον **ἐναίσιος** ον foreboding, auspicious, sent by fate; seemly, proper, fit; favourable

ἐνάκις nine times

ἐνακισχίλιοι αι α nine thousand

ἐν-ακούω listen to

ἐνακόσιοι αι α nine hundred

ἐν-αλείφω anoint; whitewash

ἐναλίγκιος ον + *dat* resembling, like

ἐνάλιος (ᾱ) ον in *or* of the sea

ἐναλλάξ *adv* alternately

ἐν-αλλάσσω exchange; change, alter; *pass* deal with

ἐν-άλλομαι *mid* + *dat* leap on, rush upon

ἐν-αμέλγω milk into

ἐνάμιλλος ον + *dat* a match for, equal to

ἔναντα, ἔναντι *adv* opposite, face to face; in the presence of

ἐναντίβιον *adv* against

ἐναντίος ᾱ ον opposite, facing; opposing, contrary, reverse, discordant, contradictory; hostile, adverse; enemy

ἐναντιόω place opposite; *pass* oppose oneself (to), withstand, be adverse to; contradict; forbid

ἐναντίωμα ατος τό hindrance

ἐναντίωσις εως ἡ opposition

ἐναπο-δεικνῡμαι *mid* distinguish oneself

ἐναπο-θνῄσκω die in [a place]

ἐναπο-κλάω break off short in [a shield]

ἐναπ-όλλυμαι perish in [a place]

ἐναπο-νίζομαι wash oneself in

ἐν-άπτω fasten *or* bind to; kindle, set on fire; *mid* clothe oneself

ἔναρα ων τά armour; spoil

ἐνάργεια ᾱς ἡ distinctness, clearness

ἐναργής ές visible; distinct, bright, manifest

ἐναρηρώς υῖα ός fastened in

ἐναρίζω *aor* ἠνάριξα strip of arms; slay

ἐν-αριθμέω reckon among

ἐναρίθμιος ον **ἐνάριθμος** ον counted among; esteemed

ἐν-άρχομαι *mid* begin [the offering]

ἐναταῖος ᾱ ον on the ninth day

ἔνατος η ον ninth

ἐν-αυλίζω *and mid and pass* pass the night in [a place]; stop for the night

ἔναυλος[1] ου ὁ torrent; water channel

ἔναυλος[2] ον ringing in one's ears

ἔναυλος[3] ον dwelling in

ἐν-αύω kindle

ἐναφ-ῑ́ημι put in

ἐν-δατέομαι *mid* distribute; abuse; celebrate; *pass* be portioned out

ἐνδεής ές needy, wanting, lacking; deficient, incomplete; inferior, worse, less

ἔνδεια ᾱς ἡ want, need

ἔνδειγμα ατος τό proof

ἐν-δείκνῡμι mark out; denounce; *mid* display, make known, prove; declare oneself; show, hold out a prospect of

ἔνδειξις εως ἡ a marking out, proof

ἑνδεκάπηχυς υ eleven cubits long

ἑνδέκατος η ον eleventh

ἐν-δέκομαι ▸ **ἐνδέχομαι**

ἐνδελεχής ές continual

ἐν-δέμω build in

ἐνδέξιος ᾱ ον on *or* to the right hand; propitious, favourable

ἐν-δέχομαι *mid* take upon oneself; believe; approve of, admit ■ **ἐνδέχεται** it is possible *or* allowed

ἐν-δέω¹ bind *or* tie in, on *or* to

ἐν-δέω² + *gen* be in want (of); be wanting; *mid* be in want *or* need of ■ **ἐνδεῖ μοι** + *gen* I need *or* lack

ἔνδηλος ον ▸ **δῆλος**

ἐν-δημέω be at home

ἔνδημος ον at home, native; intestine

ἐν-διαιτάομαι *pass* live *or* dwell in

ἐνδια-τάσσω arrange in

ἐνδια-τρίβω pass *or* spend time in; continue

ἐν-διδύσκω put on

ἐν-δίδωμι surrender, give up; betray; offer; exhibit, show, prove; cause; give way (to); admit; *intr* surrender oneself; yield; empty oneself

ἐν-δίημι chase

ἔνδικος ον legal, right, just

ἔνδῑνα ων τά entrails

ἔνδῑος ον at midday

ἐνδίφριος ου ὁ companion *or* neighbour at table

ἔνδοθεν *adv* + *gen* from within; within

ἔνδοθι *adv* ▸ **ἔνδον**

ἐν-δοιάζω waver, hesitate; *pass* be thought possible; be a matter of doubt

ἐνδόμησις εως ἡ building, structure

ἐνδόμυχος ον hidden in the inmost part

ἔνδον *adv and prep* with gen within, at home, at heart

ἐνδοξάζω glorify

ἔνδοξος ον glorious, renowned; honoured

ἐν-δουπέω fall with a hollow sound

ἐνδυκέως *adv* carefully, thoughtfully, earnestly

ἔνδυμα ατος τό garment

ἐν-δυναμόω strengthen

ἐν-δυναστεύω rule in; prevail (upon) by authority

ἐν-δῡνω, ἐν-δῡνέω ▸ **ἐνδύομαι** *see* **ἐνδύω**

ἐν-δύω *act tr* put on; clothe; *act intr and mid* put on; wear; enter, go in; undergo, engage (oneself) in

ἐνέδρᾱ ᾱς ἡ lying in wait; ambush

ἐν-εδρεύω *and mid* lie in wait *or* ambush

ἔνεδρος ον inhabitant ■ **τὸ ἔνεδρον** ▸ **ἐνέδρα**

ἐν-ειλέω press in; wrap in

ἐν-ειλίσσω ▸ **ἐνελίσσω**

ἐν-είλλω ▸ **ἐνειλέω**

ἔν-ειμι be within, in, on *or* at; dwell in; be present, extant ■ **ἔνεστι** (*or* ἔνι) + *dat* it is possible for

ἐν-είρω file on a string; entwine; join

ἕνεκα, ἕνεκεν *prep* with gen on account of, for the sake of; with respect to, by force of

ἐν-ελίσσω wrap up in

ἐν-εμέω vomit in

ἐνενήκοντα ninety

ἐνενηκοστός ή όν ninetieth

ἐνεός ά όν deaf and dumb; speechless

ἐνέπω speak, tell, relate; address, accost

ἐν-εργάζομαι *mid* pursue one's trade at home; make in; create; inject

ἐνέργεια ᾱς ἡ activity, efficacy, effect

ἐν-εργέω be active, work

ἐνέργημα ατος τό ▸ **ἐνέργεια**

ἐνεργής ές **ἐνεργός** όν active, busy, working; fertile; effective, energetic

ἐν-ερείδω thrust in, fix upon

ἔνερθεν *adv* from below; below, in the nether world; *prep with gen* beneath

ἔνεροι ων οἱ the dead, those below the earth

■ **ἐνέρτερος** ᾱ ον *comp* lower

ἔνερσις εως ἡ a fitting in, a fastening

ἐνετή ῆς ἡ pin, brooch

ἐνετός ή όν inverted; suborned

ἐν-ευδαιμονέω be happy in (one's life)

ἐν-ευδοκιμέω make the most of (another's bad fortune) for one's glory

ἐν-εύδω + *dat* sleep in *or* on

ἐνεύναιον ου τό bed-clothes, bed

ἐνέχυρον ου τό pledge

ἐν-έχω keep within, entertain, cherish; be angry; *mid and pass* be held fast, be caught; be affected with

ἐν-ζεύγνῡμι bind together, fasten

ἐνηβητήριον ου τό place of amusement

ἐνηείη ης ἡ kindness

ἐνηής ές kind, friendly

ἔν-ημαι sit in

ἐνήνοθα *pf* grew on, was on

ἐνήνοχα *pf of* **φέρω**

ἔνθα *adv* there; to there; where; then; when

ἐνθάδε *adv* to there; there, here; now

ἐν-θᾱκέω + *dat* sit on *or* in

ἐνθᾱ́κησις εως ἡ a sitting on *or* in; seat

ἔνθαπερ *adv* just where

ἐνθαῦτα ▸ **ἐνταῦθα**

ἐν-θεάζω be inspired

ἔνθεν *adv* from there; from where; after that, since, thereupon

ἐνθένδε *adv* from here, henceforth

ἔνθενπερ *adv* just from where

ἔνθεος ον inspired

ἐν-θερμαίνω heat thoroughly

ἐνθεῦτεν ▸ **ἐντεῦθεν**

ἔνθηρος ον savage, wild

ἐν-θνῄσκω die in [a place]; die of

ἐν-θουσιάζω be inspired

ἐνθουσιασμός οῦ ὁ inspiration, ecstasy

ἐν-θρῴσκω + *dat* leap into *or* upon

ἐν-θῡμέομαι *pass* take to heart; consider, ponder, deliberate; devise

ἐνθῡ́μημα ατος τό argument, rhetorical syllogism

ἐνθῡ́μησις εως ἡ **ἐνθῡμίᾱ** ᾱς ἡ thought, consideration; device; advice, warning

ἐνθῡ́μιος ον perceived; taken to heart, causing scruple *or* care

ἐνθῡμιστός ή όν ▸ **ἐνθύμιος**

ἐν-θωρᾱκίζω arm with a coat of armour

ἔνι ▸ **ἔνεστι**

ἐνί ▸ **ἐν**

ἐνιαύσιος (ᾱ) ον one year old; for a year; year by year, yearly

ἐνιαυτός οῦ ὁ year

ἐν-ιαύω + *dat* sleep among (others)

ἐνιαχῇ, ἐνιαχοῦ *adv* in several places; sometimes

ἐν-ιδρύω set up in

ἐν-ίζω, ἐν-ιζάνω sit down in *or* on

ἐν-ῑ́ημι send, drive *or* let into; incite, cause; inspire

ἐνι-κλάω break off, frustrate

ἔνιοι αι α some, several

ἐνίοτε *adv* sometimes

ἐνῑπή ῆς ἡ scolding, abuse, reproach, threat

ἐνι-πίμπλημι ▸ **ἐμπίμπλημι**

ἐνίπλειος ον ▸ **ἔμπλειος**

ἐνι-πλήσσω ▸ **ἐμπλήσσω**

ἐν-ιππεύω ride in *or* on

ἐνι-πρήθω ▸ **ἐμπρήθω**

ἐνίπτω rebuke, reprove, blame; tell

ἐνι-σκίμπτω stick in; lower down

ἐνίσπω ▸ **ἐνέπω**

ἐνίσσω ▸ ἐνίπτω

ἐν-ίστημι *act tr* put *or* place in *or* on; *act intr and mid* undertake, begin; stand in; enter; be present *or* extant; be opposed (to), resist

ἐν-ισχύω strengthen

ἐν-ίσχω ▸ ἐνέχω

ἐνι-χρίμπτω ▸ ἐγχρίμπτω

ἐννάετες ▸ εἰνάετες

ἐν-ναίω + *dat* dwell in [a place]

ἐννάκις ▸ ἐνάκις

ἐν-ναυπηγέω build ships in [a place]

ἐννέα nine

ἐννεάβοιος ον worth nine oxen

ἐννεακαίδεκα nineteen

ἐννεάκρουνος ον with nine springs *or* water-pipes

ἐννεάμηνος ον of nine months

ἐννεάπηχυς υ nine cubits long

ἐννεάχῑλοι nine thousand

ἐννεόργυιος ον nine fathoms long

ἐννέπω ▸ ἐνέπω

ἐν-νεύω nod to, beckon

ἐννέωρος ον nine years old

ἐννήκοντα ▸ ἐνενήκοντα

ἐννῆμαρ *adv* for nine days

ἐν-νοέω *and mid and pass* have in mind, consider, think of; contrive, devise; plan, intend; think, believe; fear; perceive, observe; understand

ἔννοια ᾱς ἡ thought, consideration; notion; intent, mind

ἔννομος ον legal, lawful; just, right

ἐννοσίγαιος ου ὁ earth-shaker (of Poseidon)

ἔννους ουν sensible, prudent

ἕννῡμι ἕσω ἕσσα put on; *pass and mid* clothe oneself; *pf* be dressed

ἐν-νυχεύω pass the night in [a place], lurk in secret

ἐννύχιος (ᾱ) ον **ἔννυχος** ον at night, nightly

ἐνόδιος (ᾱ) ον by the road, on the road

ἐν-οικέω dwell in, inhabit

ἐνοίκησις εως ἡ dwelling in

ἐν-οικίζω settle in a place; *mid and pass* be settled, dwell in

ἐν-οικοδομέω build in *or* on; *mid* build for oneself

ἔνοικος ου ὁ inhabitant

ἐν-οινοχοέω pour in wine

ἐνοπή ῆς ἡ sound, voice; battle-cry; woeful cry

ἐνόπλιος ον **ἔνοπλος** ον in arms, armed

ἐν-οράω look at, see, observe; understand

ἔνορκος ον bound by oath; included in a treaty; sworn

ἐν-όρνῡμι arouse in; *mid* arise

ἐν-ορούω + *dat* leap upon

ἐνόρχης (*gen* ου) **ἔνορχις** (*gen* ιδος) **ἔνορχος** (*gen* ου) uncastrated

ἕνος η ον (*also* ἔνος) last year's, one year old

ἐνοσίχθων ονος ὁ earth-shaker (of Poseidon)

ἑνότης ητος ἡ unity; concord

ἐν-ουρέω urinate in

ἐν-οχλέω molest, trouble, be in one's way

ἔνοχος ον *usu* + *dat* held in, liable to, subject to

ἐν-ράπτω sew in

ἐν-σείω shake, drive *or* hurl into

ἐν-σημαίνω show *or* make known in, at *or* through; *mid* make oneself known

ἐν-σκευάζω equip, prepare, adorn

ἐν-σκήπτω hurl into; fall in

ἔνσπονδος ον allied; ally

ἐν-στάζω instil

ἐνστάτης ου ὁ adversary

ἐν-στέλλω clothe, dress

ἐν-στηρίζομαι *pass* be fixed in

ἐν-στρατοπεδεύω *and mid* encamp in

ἐν-στρέφομαι *pass* turn in

ἔνταλμα ατος τό ▸ **ἐντολή**

ἐν-τάμνω ▸ **ἐντέμνω**

ἐν-τανύω ▸ **ἐντείνω**

ἐν-τάσσω enrol; place *or* post in

ἐνταῦθα *adv* there; here; to there; to here; then; now; thereupon, in that case

ἐνταυθοῖ *adv* to here; to there; here

ἐν-ταφιάζω embalm; prepare for burial

ἐνταφιασμός οῦ ὁ embalming, burial

ἐντάφιος ον of *or* used in a burial

ἔντεα εων τά arms, armour; tools, appliances

ἐν-τείνω stretch *or* strain in; bend; versify; set to music; plait over; strain, exert; extend, stretch out

ἐν-τειχίζω fortify; build in; *mid* wall in

ἐν-τελευτάω die in [a place]

ἐντελής ές complete; perfect, spotless

ἐν-τέλλομαι *mid* command

ἐν-τέμνω cut in, engrave; kill, sacrifice

ἔντερον ου τό gut
■ **τὰ ἔντερα** entrails

ἐντεσιεργός όν working in harness

ἐντεταμένως *adv* vehemently, vigorously

ἐντεῦθεν *adv* from there; from here; henceforth; then, thereupon; therefore

ἔντευξις εως ἡ encounter, meeting, visit; conversation; prayer, petition

ἔντεχνος ον artistic, ingenious

ἐν-τήκω *act tr* melt in; impress; *act intr and pass* be impressed; be molten

ἐν-τίθημι put in; inspire; put *or* lay over *or* on

ἐν-τίκτω bear *or* produce in

ἔντῑμος ον honoured, noble, esteemed; costly, precious; honest

ἐντολή ῆς ἡ commandment, injunction

ἔντομος ον cut up
■ **τὰ ἔντομα** sacrifices, victims; insects

ἔντονος ον strained; earnest, vehement

ἐντόπιος ον **ἔντοπος** ον native; in *or* of a place

ἐντός *adv and prep* with *gen* within, inside

ἔντοσθεν ▸ **ἐντός**

ἐν-τρέπω turn round *or* over; put to shame; *pass* turn oneself round *or* towards; pay attention (to), notice; revere; feel shame *or* be ashamed (of); hesitate

ἐν-τρέφω feed *or* bring in [a place]

ἐν-τρέχω run in

ἐντριβής ές skilled, active

ἔντριψις εως ἡ rubbing in

ἔντρομος ον trembling

ἐν-τροπαλίζομαι *mid* turn oneself round repeatedly

ἐντροπή ῆς ἡ respect, regard; shame

ἔντροφος ον + *dat* brought up in; concerned with

ἐν-τρυφάω + *dat* revel in; be delicate; mock

ἐν-τυγχάνω + *dat* encounter, fall in with; incur; get; meet; visit; converse; entreat, accost
■ **ὁ ἐντυχών** the first person one meets, the man in the street

ἐν-τυλίσσω wrap up

ἐντῡ́νω prepare, equip, make ready; adorn

ἐντυπάς *adv* wrapped up tightly

ἐν-τυπόω stamp in, engrave

ἐντύω ▸ **ἐντύνω**

ἐνῡάλιος ον warlike (of Ares)

ἐν-υβρίζω insult (one) in (a thing)

ἔνυδρις εως ἡ otter

ἔνυδρος ον living in water; watery

ἐν-υπνιάζω *and mid* dream

ἐνύπνιον ου τό dream, vision

ἐνύπνιος ον in (one's) sleep, sleeping, in dreams

ἐνυφ-αίνω weave in

ἐνωμοτάρχης ου ὁ leader of an enomotia

ἐνωμοτίᾱ ᾱς ἡ enomotia (a division of Spartan soldiers (25 or 30 men))

ἐνώμοτος ον sworn, bound by oath

ἐνωπαδίως *adv* to one's face

ἐνωπή ῆς ἡ face
■ **ἐνωπῇ** openly

ἐνώπιος ον to the face, face to face
■ **τά ἐνώπια** inner *or* side walls

ἐν-ωτίζομαι hear

ἐξ ▸ **ἐκ**

ἕξ six

ἐξ-αγγέλλω *and mid* publish, tell, report, send word; blab out; promise

ἐξάγγελος ου ὁ messenger; (in drama) the messenger who relates what has happened inside the house or palace

ἐνάγγελτος ον told out, announced

ἐξ-αγῑνέω ▸ **ἐξάγω**

ἐξάγιστος ον most holy; abominable

ἐξ-άγνῡμι break away

ἐξ-αγοράζω *and mid* buy off; redeem

ἐξ-αγορεύω speak out, publish; betray

ἐξ-αγριαίνω, ἐξ-αγριόω make wild; exasperate

ἐξ-άγω lead out *or* away, carry out, export; lead to death; expel; bring forth; lead on, excite, seduce; *intr* march out, go on

ἐξαγωγή ῆς ἡ leading, carrying, drawing out; expulsion; way out

ἐξαγώγιμα ων τά exports

ἐξ-ᾴδω begin a song; sing one's last song

ἐξ-αείρω ▸ **ἐξαίρω**

ἑξάετες *adv* for six years

ἐξ-αιμάσσω make bloody

ἐξ-αίνυμαι take away; rob

ἐξαίρεσις εως ἡ a taking out, a way of taking out; disembowelling

ἐξαίρετος ον taken out; picked out; chosen, excellent

ἐξαιρετός όν that can be taken out

ἐξ-αιρέω take out; disembowel; disembark; pick out, choose; dedicate; except; take away, remove; capture; destroy; confound; drive away; *mid* take out for oneself; unload; rob; set free

ἐξ-αίρω lift up; extol, exalt, praise; excite; encourage; make angry; lead away, carry off, remove; *mid* carry off for oneself, win

ἐξαίσιος (ᾱ) ον undue; immoderate, extraordinary; lawless, violent

ἐξ-αΐσσω *and pass* rush out

ἐξ-αιτέω demand from, demand one's surrender; *mid* beg for oneself

ἔξαιτος ον chosen, much asked for

ἐξαίφνης *adv* suddenly

ἐξ-ακέομαι *mid* heal thoroughly; make up for; appease

ἑξάκις *adv* six times

ἑξακισμῡ́ριοι αι α sixty thousand

ἐξ-ακολουθέω follow

ἐξ-ακοντίζω throw a spear; shoot

ἑξακόσιοι αι α six hundred

ἐξ-ακούω hear, listen to

ἐξ-ακρῑβόω do exactly; make a precise statement

ἐξ-αλαπάζω sack; unpeople, destroy

ἐξ-αλείφω wipe out *or* off; destroy; besmear

ἐξ-αλέομαι, ἐξ-αλεύομαι *mid* avoid, shun; escape

ἐξ-αλλάσσω exchange; alter; turn away *or* aside

ἐξ-άλλομαι *mid* leap out of; spring down *or* away; (of horses) rear up

ἐξ-αλύσκω ▸ **ἐξαλέομαι**

ἐξ-αμαρτάνω make a mistake; miss one's aim; transgress, sin

ἐξαμαρτίᾱ ᾱς ἡ mistake, error

ἐξ-αμάω finish mowing *or* reaping; destroy

ἐξ-αμελέω + *gen* neglect completely

ἑξάμετρος ον of a hexameter, of six feet

ἑξάμηνος ον lasting six months

ἐξ-αναγκάζω drive away by force; compel

ἐξαν-άγομαι *mid and pass* put to sea, set sail

ἐξανα-δύομαι *mid* rise out of, emerge from

ἐξαν-ακρούομαι *mid* (of ships) retreat by backing water

ἐξαν-αλίσκω spend entirely; destroy utterly

ἐξανα-λύω set free, save

ἐξανα-σπάω draw out, tear away from

ἐξανάστασις εως ἡ resurrection

ἐξανα-τέλλω rise from

ἐξαναφανδόν *adv* openly

ἐξανα-χωρέω retreat, withdraw

ἐξ-ανδραποδίζω *and mid* reduce to slavery

ἐξ-ανδρόομαι *pass* grow up to be a man

ἐξαν-ευρίσκω find out, invent

ἐξαν-έχομαι *mid* take upon oneself, bear

ἐξ-ανθέω bloom forth; burst forth; fade

ἐξαν-ῑ́ημι send out, dismiss; *intr* slacken, relax

ἐξαν-ίστημι *act tr* make get up from; remove, expel; unpeople, destroy; lead out; *act intr and mid* rise; depart, start, emigrate; be driven out

ἐξ-αντλέω bale out

ἐξ-ανύ(τ)ω accomplish, fulfil, perform, manage; kill; finish one's journey, arrive

ἑξαπάλαιστος ον of six hand-breadths

ἐξαπ-αλλάσσω make completely free; *pass* come off

ἐξ-απατάω deceive utterly, cheat

ἐξαπάτη ης ἡ deception

ἐξ-απαφίσκω *and mid* ▸ **ἐξαπατάω**

ἑξάπεδος η ον six feet long

ἐξαπ-εῖδον *aor* see from afar

ἑξάπηχυς υ six cubits long

ἐξαπιναῖος (ᾱ) ον sudden

ἑξάπλεθρος ον six plethra long

ἑξαπλήσιος ον (*also* ἑξαπλάσιος) + *gen* six times as large as

ἐξαπο-βαίνω step out of

ἐξαπο-δίεμαι chase away

ἐξαπο-δῡ́νω put *or* take off

ἐξαπ-όλλῡμι *act tr* kill, destroy utterly; *act intr and mid* perish

ἐξαπο-νέομαι return

ἐξαπο-νίζω wash off

ἐξ-απορέω *and pass* be in great doubt *or* difficulty, despair

ἐξαπο-στέλλω send out *or* away

ἐξαπο-τῑ́νω satisfy in full, atone fully

ἐξαπο-φθείρω destroy utterly

ἐξ-άπτω fasten to, attach to; kindle; *mid* hang from, cling to; attach

ἐξ-αραίρημαι *see* **ἐξαιρέω**

ἐξ-αράομαι *mid* curse

ἐξ-αράσσω knock out of

ἐξ-αργέω do carelessly

ἐξ-αργυρίζω, ἐξ-αργυρόω turn into money

ἐξ-αριθμέω count; number, reckon

ἐξ-αρκέω suffice, be enough; satisfy; be able

ἐξαρκής ές sufficient, enough; in good order

ἐξαρκούντως *adv* enough

ἐξ-αρνέομαι *pass* deny; refuse

ἔξαρνος ον denying

ἐξ-αρπάζω snatch away; rob; rescue

ἐξ-αρτάω hang on, attach (to); make depend; *pass* be fastened *or* attached to, be hung upon

ἐξ-αρτίζω finish

ἐξ-αρτύω prepare, equip, fit out; *mid* fit out for oneself; get ready

ἔξαρχος ον beginning; leader of the chorus

ἐξ-άρχω *and mid* begin [a song]; take the lead

ἐξ-ασκέω adorn; train *or* teach thoroughly

ἐξ-ατῑμάζω dishonour completely; not to care for

ἐξ-αυαίνω dry *or* parch up

ἐξ-αυδάω speak out

ἐξ-αυλίζομαι *pass* go out of a camp

ἐξαυτῆς *adv* at once

ἐξαῦτις *adv* over again; back

ἐξ-αυχέω boast; believe firmly

ἐξ-αΰω cry aloud

ἐξαφ-αιρέομαι *mid* take out; rob

ἐξαφ-ίημι set free

ἐξαφ-ίσταμαι *mid* step aside; withdraw, depart

ἐξαφ-οράω see from a distance

ἐξ-αφύω, ἐξ-αφύσσω draw [water] out of

ἐξ-εγγυάω set free on bail; bail out

ἐξ-εγείρω arouse, awake

ἔξεδρος ον away from home

ἐξείης ▸ **ἑξῆς**

ἐξ-εικάζω make like, copy

ἔξ-ειμι¹ go out, away *or* forward; march out; come to an end

ἔξ-ειμι² originate from
■ **ἔξεστι** it is allowed *or* possible
■ **ἐξόν** it being possible

ἐξ-εῖπον *aor* speak out

ἐξ-είργω shut out, exclude, keep off; chase, expel; hinder, prevent; press, urge, compel

ἐξ-είρω¹ speak out (openly), publish, tell

ἐξ-είρω² thrust out

ἐξέλασις εως ἡ expulsion; departure; expedition

ἐξ-ελαύνω, ἐξ-ελάω drive out, expel, chase, banish; beat out, hammer out; *intr* set out, march out *or* on; ride out *or* up

ἐξ-ελέγχω test, examine, search out; convict, confute; prove; *pass* be wrong

ἐξ-ελευθεροστομέω speak out freely

ἐξ-ελίσσω unfold, develop, draw out

ἐξ-έλκω, ἐξ-ελκύω draw out; drag away; entice

ἐξ-εμέω vomit

ἐξεμ-πολάω, ἐξεμ-πολέω sell off; gain by trade; betray

ἐξ-εναρίζω strip of arms; slay

ἐξεπ-ᾴδω charm away, heal by incantation

ἐξεπ-εύχομαι *mid* boast loudly

ἐξ-επίσταμαι *pass* know thoroughly, understand fully

ἐξεπίτηδες *adv* on purpose

ἐξέρᾱμα ατος τό vomit

ἐξ-εργάζομαι *mid* make completely, execute, finish, accomplish, do; cause; cultivate; undo, destroy

ἐξεργαστικός ή όν skilled in work

ἐξ-έργω ▸ **ἐξείργω**

ἐξ-ερεείνω *and mid* ▸ **ἐξερέω¹**

ἐξ-ερείπω fall out of, tumble down

ἐξ-ερεύγω *pass* (of rivers) empty oneself

ἐξ-ερευνάω search out, inquire after

ἐξ-ερέω¹ *and mid* search out; examine; question

ἐξ-ερέω² *fut from* **ἐξείρω**

ἐξ-ερημόω make empty *or* desolate

ἐξ-έρομαι ▸ **ἐξερέω¹ ἐξείρομαι**

ἐξ-έρπω creep out of; come out

ἐξ-ερῡ́κω tear out

ἐξ-έρχομαι go *or* come out *or* away; march out; sally out; come to one's turn; come to an end, elapse, expire;

come to pass, come true; turn out, become

ἐξ-ερωέω shy, bolt; swerve from the course

ἐξεσίᾱ ᾱς ἡ sending out, mission

ἔξεσις εως ἡ dismissal, divorce

ἐξ-ετάζω search out; examine, test, question; review, muster

ἐξέτασις εως ἡ examination, scrutiny, searching out; review, inspection

ἐξεταστικός ή όν skilled in examining

ἐξέτης ες six years old

ἐξέτι *prep with gen* ever since, from

ἐξ-ευλαβέομαι *pass* be very cautious

ἐξεύρεσις εως ἡ **ἐξεύρημα** ατος τό invention

ἐξ-ευρίσκω find, discover, decipher; devise, invent; make possible, cause

ἐξεφ-ίεμαι *mid* command

ἐξ-έψω boil thoroughly

ἐξ-ηγέομαι *mid* lead; be leader, lead the way; direct, govern, guide, teach; explain, interpret; describe, tell, narrate

ἐξήγησις εως ἡ interpretation

ἐξηγητής οῦ ὁ teacher, adviser, guide; interpreter

ἐξήκοντα sixty

ἐξηκοστός ή όν sixtieth

ἐξ-ήκω have come; have arrived; have expired *or* elapsed; come true; come to pass

ἐξήλατος ον (of metal) beaten out

ἐξήλυσις εως ἡ going out, way out

ἐξῆμαρ *adv* for six days

ἐξ-ημερόω tame, cultivate, civilize

ἐξημοιβός όν for change

ἑξῆς *adv* in order, one after the other, successively; next; next to; further

ἐξ-ηχέω publish

ἐξ-ιᾱ́ομαι heal thoroughly

ἐξ-ιδιόομαι make completely one's own

ἐξ-ιδρῡ́ω make sit down

ἐξ-ῑ́ημι send out, away *or* forth; empty oneself; *mid* send from oneself

ἐξ-ῑθῡ́νω make quite straight

ἐξ-ικετεύω entreat earnestly

ἐξ-ικνέομαι come to, arrive at, reach; meet; obtain, attain; be sufficient, suffice

ἐξ-ῑλάσκομαι *mid* propitiate

ἕξις εως ἡ condition, state; behaviour, habit, way of life; faculty, skill

ἐξ-ισόω *act tr* make equal *or* even; *act intr and pass* be equal, resemble

ἐξ-ίστημι *act tr* put out of its place *or* away; change, alter; *act intr and mid + gen* step *or* stand aside from, retire *or* remove from; be far from; be beside oneself, lose one's senses; give up, abandon, leave; lose, forget; be changed; degenerate, go off

ἐξ-ιστορέω inquire into

ἐξ-ισχῡ́ω be quite able

ἐξ-ίσχω put forth

ἐξίτηλος ον destroyed, extinct, obsolete

ἐξιχνοσκοπέω *and mid* track, trace out

ἐξ-ογκόω make swell up; *pass* be overfull, be puffed (up)

ἐξοδίᾱ ᾱς ἡ marching out, expedition

ἐξοδοιπορέω + *gen* go out of

ἔξοδος ου ἡ way out; gate; mouth; going *or* marching out, start, sortie, expedition; procession; end, close

ἔξ-οιδα know well

ἐξοικήσιμος ον habitable

ἐξ-οικίζω drive from home; banish; *mid* go from home, emigrate

ἐξ-οικοδομέω build up

ἐξ-οιμώζω lament, wail

ἐξ-οιχνέω go out

ἐξ-οίχομαι have gone out *or* away

ἐξ-οκέλλω run aground; drift into

ἐξ-ολισθαίνω slip off

ἐξ-όλλῡμι *act tr* destroy wholly; *act intr and mid* perish utterly

ἐξ-ολοθρεύω *and mid* destroy utterly

ἐξ-όμνῡμι deny upon oath

ἐξ-ομοιόω make like; *pass* become like

ἐξ-ομολογέω *and mid* confess, admit; agree; thank, praise

ἐξ-ονειδίζω reproach, abuse

ἐξ-ονομάζω, ἐξ-ονομαίνω call by name; speak out, utter

ἐξονομακλήδην *adv* by name

ἐξόπι(σ)θεν *adv and prep with gen* behind, backward(s); from behind

ἐξοπίσω *adv* behind; hereafter

ἐξ-οπλίζω arm *or* equip completely

ἐξοπλισίᾱ ᾱς ἡ **ἐξόπλισις** εως ἡ complete equipment; mustering under arms

ἐξ-οπτάω bake thoroughly

ἐξ-οράω ▸ ἐξεῖδον

ἐξ-οργίζω make very angry

ἐξ-ορθόω set upright

ἐξ-ορίζω banish

ἐξ-ορκίζω, ἐξ-ορκόω bind by oath; exorcize

ἐξορκιστής οῦ ὁ exorcist

ἐξόρκωσις εως ἡ binding by oath

ἐξ-ορμάω *act tr* start, get going; send out; impel; excite; *act intr and pass* set out, go away

ἐξ-ορούω leap out of

ἐξ-ορύσσω dig out *or* up

ἐξ-οστρακίζω banish by ostracism

ἐξ-οτρῡ́νω excite, urge on

ἐξ-ουδενέω, ἐξ-ουδενόω, ἐξ-ουθενέω despise, set at naught

ἐξουσίᾱ ᾱς ἡ means, fortune; right, power, permission, liberty; free will; authority, rule; magistrate, government; abundance

ἐξ-ουσιάζω + *gen* have power *or* authority over

ἐξ-οφέλλω increase exceedingly

ἐξοχή ῆς ἡ preference, prominence

ἔξοχος ον prominent; excellent

■ **ἔξοχα** *with gen* standing out among

ἐξ-υβρίζω become insolent; commit violence; revolt

ἐξυπαν-ίσταμαι rise from under

ἐξύπερθε *adv* from above

ἐξυπ-ηρετέω be altogether at one's service

ἐξ-υπνίζω rouse from sleep

ἔξυπνος ον awakened

ἐξυφ-αίνω finish weaving

ἐξυφ-ηγέομαι *mid* lead the way

ἔξω *adv and prep with gen* on the outside, outwards, outside; beyond; far from, except

ἔξωθεν *adv* from outside; outside

ἐξ-ωθέω push out; chase, drive, expel; reject

ἐξώλεια ᾱς ἡ utter ruin

ἐξώλης ες utterly ruined

ἐξωμιδοποιΐᾱ ᾱς ἡ the making of ἐξωμίδες

ἐξωμίς ίδος ἡ short sleeveless coat

ἐξ-ωνέομαι *mid* buy off, buy in advance; ransom, redeem

ἔξωρος ον untimely; inconvenient

ἐξώστης ου ὁ one who drives out

ἐξωτάτω outermost

ἐξώτερος ᾱ ον outer

ἔοικα *pf with pres sense* be *or* look like; seem, have the appearance (of); be fit, right *or* fair

ἔολπα *see* **ἔλπω**

ἔοργα *see* **ἔρδω**

ἑορτάζω keep a festival

ἑορτή ῆς ἡ festival, feast, holiday

ἑός ἑή ἑόν his, hers; his *or* her own

ἐπ-αγάλλομαι *mid* + *dat* exult in

ἐπαγγελίᾱ ᾱς ἡ announcement; promise; public denunciation

ἐπ-αγγέλλω announce, tell, proclaim, make known; promise; command; demand, ask; *mid* promise, offer; profess [a calling]; claim; command

ἐπ-άγγελμα ατος τό promise; profession, business

ἐπ-αγείρω gather together; *mid* assemble in a crowd

ἐπάγερσις εως ἡ a gathering

ἐπ-αγῑνέω ▸ **ἐπάγω**

ἐπ-αγλαΐζομαι *mid* exult in

ἐπ-άγω *act tr* lead, bring *or* drive to *or* on; add; apply; impel, cause, instigate; seduce; *act intr* march up, advance; *mid* bring *or* draw to oneself; call to help; mention, quote; procure; bring on oneself

ἐπαγωγή ῆς ἡ bringing on; advancing, attack

ἐπαγωγός όν seductive

ἐπ-αγωνίζομαι *mid* compete for a thing

ἐπ-ᾴδω sing to; lead the song; charm by singing; heal by incantations

ἐπ-αείρω ▸ **ἐπαίρω**

ἐπ-αέξω make grow *or* prosper

ἐπ-αθροίζομαι *pass* assemble in crowds

ἐπ-αιγίζω rush upon (of a wind)

ἐπ-αιδέομαι *pass* be ashamed (of)

ἐπαινέτης ου ὁ praiser, author of a panegyric

ἐπ-αινέω approve, sanction; consent (to); praise, commend; thank, congratulate; advise, persuade

ἐπ-αίνημι ▸ **ἐπαινέω**

ἔπαινος ου ὁ praise, eulogy; panegyric; reward

ἐπαινός ή όν dread

ἐπ-αίρω *act tr* lift up, set up; excite, rouse, instigate; seduce, induce; exalt, make proud; *intr* raise oneself; *pass* be excited, induced *or* impelled; rise, be roused, be proud; exult in, be proud

ἐπ-αισθάνομαι *mid* perceive, feel; learn, hear

ἐπ-αΐσσω rush *or* dart upon, assault; *mid* rush at

ἐπάϊστος ον heard of, known

ἐπ-αισχῡ́νομαι *pass* be ashamed of

ἐπ-αιτέω demand in addition; beg

ἐπ-αιτιάομαι *mid* state as a cause; bring a charge against; accuse

ἐπ-αίτιος ον guilty; blamed for

ἐπ-ᾱΐω hear, listen to; perceive, understand; be expert (in)

ἐπ-ακολουθέω follow, accompany, join; be attached (to); yield; understand

ἐπ-ακροάομαι *mid* hearken *or* listen to

ἐπακτήρ ῆρος ὁ hunter

ἐπάκτιος (ᾱ) ον on the shore

ἐπακτός ή όν imported, foreign, alien

ἐπακτρίς ίδος ἡ boat, light vessel, canoe

ἐπ-αλαλάζω raise the war-cry

ἐπ-αλάομαι *pass* wander about

ἐπ-αλαστέω be troubled at

ἐπ-αλείφω smear over

ἐπ-αλέξω defend, assist + *dat*; keep off

ἐπ-αληθεύω verify

ἐπαλλαγή ῆς ἡ mutual union; exchange

ἐπ-αλλάσσω exchange, interchange

ἐπ-άλληλος ον mutual

ἔπαλξις εως ἡ parapet; defence

ἐπ-αμάομαι *mid* heap up together

ἐπ-αμείβω change; exchange

ἐπαμμένος ▸ **ἐφημμένος** *see* **ἐφάπτω**

ἐπαμοιβαδίς *adv* alternately, interchangeably

ἐπαμύντωρ ορος ὁ defender, helper

ἐπ-αμῡ́νω + *dat* defend, help

ἐπ-αμφοτερίζω doubt, hesitate; play a double game

ἐπᾱ́ν, ἐπήν ▸ ἐπειδάν

ἐπανα-βαίνω go up; mount (on horseback)

ἐπανα-βιβάζω cause to mount on

ἐπαναβληδόν *adv* thrown over

ἐπ-αναγκάζω force, compel

ἐπάναγκες *adv* necessarily, on compulsion

ἐπαν-άγω *act tr* lead *or* bring up; put to sea; excite; lead *or* bring back; *act intr* return; *pass* put to sea; set sail against; be carried to

ἐπαναγωγή ῆς ἡ sailing out, attack

ἐπαν-αίρω *and mid* raise one against another

ἐπανα-λαμβάνω resume, repeat

ἐπανα-μένω stay on

ἐπανα-μιμνῄσκω remind one again

ἐπανα-παύομαι rest upon; rely on

ἐπανα-πλέω, ἐπανα-πλώω sail out against; sail back; overflow

ἐπανάσεισις εως ἡ brandishing

ἐπανάστασις εως ἡ rising up, rebellion

ἐπανα-στρέφω turn *or* wheel round

ἐπανα-τείνω hold up to

ἐπανα-τέλλω rise

ἐπανα-τίθημι put upon

ἐπανα-φέρω bring back; refer to; report; return

ἐπανα-χωρέω retreat

ἐπαναχώρησις εως ἡ retreat

ἐπάν-ειμι go up; return, go back; go home

ἐπαν-ειπεῖν *aor infin* proclaim in addition; offer by public proclamation

ἐπαν-έρομαι, ἐπαν-είρομαι *mid* ▸ ἐπανερωτάω

ἐπαν-έρχομαι ▸ ἐπάνειμι

ἐπαν-ερωτάω question again

ἐπαν-ήκω come back again

ἐπ-ανθέω bloom; appear on the surface

ἐπαν-ῑ́ημι let loose; abandon

ἐπαν-ισόω make equal

ἐπαν-ίσταμαι *mid* stand upon; rise, stand up; revolt

ἐπάνοδος ου ἡ return, rising up

ἐπαν-ορθόω *and mid* set up, set upright; re-establish; amend, improve, correct

ἐπανόρθωμα ατος τό **ἐπανόρθωσις** εως ἡ a correcting, improving

ἐπάντης ες steep, rugged

ἐπ-αντλέω draw [water]; pour over

ἐπάνω *adv* above; formerly; superior to

ἐπάνωθεν *adv* from above; inland

ἐπάξιος ᾱ ον worthy, deserving; suitable

ἐπ-αξιόω think worthy, right *or* suitable

ἐπαοιδή ▸ ἐπῳδή

ἐπ-απειλέω threaten besides

ἐπαρᾱ́ ᾶς ἡ curse

ἐπ-αράομαι *mid* call down curses upon

ἐπ-αραρίσκω fasten to; fit on; *intr* fit tightly *or* exactly

ἐπ-αράσσω dash in(to) pieces

ἐπάρᾱτος ον accursed

ἐπάργυρος ον overlaid with silver, silver-mounted

ἐπ-αρήγω + *dat* help, assist

ἐπάρκεια ᾱς ἡ **ἐπάρκεσις** εως ἡ help, aid, assistance

ἐπ-αρκέω suffice; remain valid; help, aid, assist; supply, furnish; hinder, prevent

ἐπαρκούντως *adv* sufficiently

ἐπάρουρος ον attached to the soil (as a serf)

ἐπ-αρτάομαι *pass* impend

ἐπαρτής ές ready, equipped

ἐπ-αρτύω, ἐπ-αρτῡ́νω fix to

ἐπαρχίᾱ ᾱς ἡ government of a province

ἔπαρχος ου ὁ commander, governor, prefect

ἐπ-άρχω + *gen* rule, govern; *mid* begin a libation

ἐπαρωγός οῦ ὁ helper

ἐπ-ασκέω work carefully at, practise

ἐπασσύτερος ᾱ ον crowded, one after another

ἐπ-ᾴσσω ▸ **ἐπαΐσσω**

ἐπ-αυδάω *and mid* call upon

ἐπ-αυλίζομαι *mid and pass* be in camp near; pass the night near

ἔπαυλις εως ἡ dwelling, quarters, fold

ἔπαυλος ου ὁ fold, stable; dwelling

ἐπ-αυξάνω, ἐπ-αύξω increase, enlarge, augment

ἐπαύρεσις εως ἡ enjoyment, fruit

ἐπαύριον *adv* tomorrow

ἐπ-αυρίσκω touch; reach; enjoy, taste, share; *mid* obtain; involve oneself in; enjoy, reap

ἐπ-αυχέω exult in, boast of

ἐπ-αΰω + *dat* shout over

ἐπ-αφρίζω foam up

ἐπαφρόδῑτος ον lovely, charming

ἐπ-αφύσσω pour over in addition

ἐπαχθής ές onerous; troublesome, grievous

ἐπεάν ▸ **ἐπήν**

ἐπεγ-γελάω + *dat* laugh at, mock at

ἐπ-εγείρω arouse, awaken; excite; *pass* be roused; awake

ἐπέδρη ης ἡ ▸ **ἐφέδρα**

ἐπεί *conj* when, after, since; as soon as; as often as; because, seeing that; although; since really

ἐπείγω press, urge, pursue, drive, hasten, press on with; *pass* hurry; long for

ἐπειδάν, ἐπειδή *conj* ▸ **ἐπεί**

ἐπειδήπερ, ἐπεὶ ἦ *conj* since really

ἐπ-εικάζω conjecture

ἔπ-ειμι[1] be on *or* at, be fixed upon; be existing, at hand *or* forthcoming; be added; live after, be left; be in charge of + *dat*

ἔπ-ειμι[2] go *or* come to *or* upon; go through; approach, advance against, attack; befall, enter one's mind; impend

ἐπ-ειπεῖν *aor infin* say besides, add

ἐπείπερ *conj* since really

ἐπ-είρομαι ▸ **ἐπέρομαι**

ἐπ-ειρύω ▸ **ἐπερύω**

ἐπ-ειρωτάω, ἐπ-ειρωτέω ▸ **ἐπερωτάω**

ἐπεισαγωγή ῆς ἡ introduction, bringing in in addition; entrance

ἐπεισαγώγιμος ον **ἐπείσακτος** ον brought in from abroad

ἐπεισ-βαίνω go into (on)

ἐπεισ-βάλλω invade again

ἐπείσ-ειμι, ἐπεισ-έρχομαι enter besides, likewise *or* after; come in *or* on; appear

ἐπεισόδιον ου τό dialogue scene in tragedy

ἐπείσοδος ου ἡ entrance

ἐπεισ-πῑ́πτω + *dat* fall in on; invade besides

ἐπεισ-πλέω sail in *or* on besides; sail in against, attack

ἐπεισ-φέρω bring in besides; *mid* bring in for oneself; *pass* intervene

ἐπεισ-φρέω let in after

ἔπειτα *adv* thereupon, thereafter, then, from then on; further; therefore, nevertheless

ἐπείτε ▸ **ἐπεί τε** since, because

ἔπειτεν ▸ **ἔπειτα**

ἐπεκ-βαίνω disembark

ἐπεκ-βοηθέω come out to aid

ἐπεκ-διδάσκω teach thoroughly in addition

ἐπεκδι-ηγέομαι ▸ **ἐπεκδιδάσκω**

ἐπεκδρομή ῆς ἡ excursion, expedition

ἐπέκεινα *adv* over there, beyond

ἐπ-εκθέω rush out against

ἐπεκ-πλέω sail out against

ἐπέκπλους ου ὁ sailing out against

ἐπεκ-τρέχω + *dat* rush *or* sally out to attack

ἐπ-ελαύνω drive upon *or* over; lay (metal) beaten out into plates over (a surface); lead on; *intr* come, march *or* drive up; approach

ἐπ-ελπίζω lead to hope

ἐπεμ-βαίνω step on *or* in; stand upon; tread down, insult

ἐπεμ-βάλλω put on besides; add; offer; flow in besides

ἐπεμβάτης ου ὁ horseman

ἐπεμ-πίπτω + *dat* fall upon

ἐπ-εναρίζω kill on top of (another)

ἐπεν-δῡ́νω, ἐπεν-δύομαι put on besides

ἐπενδύτης ου ὁ upper garment

ἐπ-ενήνοθα *pf* have grown upon

ἐπεν-θρῴσκω + *dat* leap *or* rush upon

ἐπεν-τανύω, ἐπεν-τείνω stretch upon; *pass* lean upon

ἐπεν-τέλλω command besides

ἐπεν-τῡ́νω, ἐπεντύω prepare, equip; *pass* be ready

ἐπεξάγω lead out against; lengthen a front line; *intr* march out

ἐπεξαγωγή ῆς ἡ lengthening of a line of battle

ἐπέξ-ειμι ▸ ἐπεξέρχομαι

ἐπεξ-ελαύνω drive on against

ἐπεξ-εργάζομαι do besides; slay once more

ἐπεξ-έρχομαι go out against, advance against; march out, sally forth, attack; punish, proceed against, pursue; go on, wander through; go through, inspect; execute

ἐπεξέτασις εως ἡ repeated inspection

ἐπεξ-ευρίσκω invent besides

ἐπεξῆς ▸ ἐφεξῆς

ἐπεξόδια ων τά sacrifice at a departure

ἐπέξοδος ου ἡ a march out against

ἐπ-έοικα *pf* be like; be likely; be convenient, fitting *or* reasonable

ἐπ-εργάζομαι *mid* cultivate besides, encroach upon

ἐπεργασίᾱ ᾱς ἡ unlawful cultivation of sacred land

ἐπ-ερείδω urge on; apply vast strength to

ἐπ-ερέφω roof [a building]

ἐπ-έρομαι *mid* **▸ ἐπερωτάω**

ἐπ-ερύω draw *or* pull on *or* up; *mid* draw on oneself

ἐπ-έρχομαι go *or* come up, towards, forward *or* on; approach, attack; occur, befall, come into one's mind; go over; visit; go through, examine; execute; be at hand, impend

ἐπ-ερωτάω question, ask; inquire of; consult

ἐπερώτημα ατος τό **ἐπερώτησις** εως ἡ question, inquiry; demand

ἐπεσβολίᾱ ᾱς ἡ hasty speech

ἐπεσβόλος ον talking idly

ἐπ-εσθίω eat besides

ἐπέτε(ι)ος (ᾱ) ον lasting the whole year; yearly

ἐπέτης ου ὁ attendant, servant

ἐπετήσιος ον **▸ ἐπέτειος**

ἐπ-ευθῡ́νω direct

ἐπ-ευφημέω applaud; demand aloud; shout agreement

ἐπ-εύχομαι *mid* pray to; invoke; wish; call down [a curse] on; boast, exult, triumph

ἐπ-έχω *act tr* have *or* hold upon; place upon; hold out, present, offer; have opposite oneself; keep shut; hold fast, retain, hinder; delay, retard; reach to, extend; have in one's power; *act intr* be intent upon, turn one's mind to; stop, stay, wait; desist, hold back; *mid* aim at; put (to the lips); offer; delay

ἐπήβολος ον + *gen* partaking of, master of

ἐπηγκενίς ίδος ἡ plank (of a ship)

ἐπ-ηγορεύω, ἐπ-ηγορέω + *dat* reproach, criticize

ἐπηετανός (ή) όν lasting; abundant, plentiful

ἐπήκοος ον listening to; audible; within hearing

ἐπ-ηλυγάζομαι *mid* overshadow; hide oneself

ἔπηλυς (*gen* υδος) **ἐπηλύτης** (*gen* ου) ὁ/ἡ one coming, immigrant, foreigner

ἐπημοιβός όν in turn, changing

ἐπ-ημύω drop *or* sink at

ἐπήν ▸ **ἐπάν**

ἐπ-ηπύω shout to, applaud

ἐπήρατος ον lovely, charming

ἐπ-ηρεάζω + *dat* revile, abuse, insult; threaten

ἐπήρεια ᾱς ἡ insult, malice

ἐπήρετμος ον rowing; furnished with oars

ἐπηρεφής ές hanging over, covering; steep

ἐπητής (*gen* οῦ) considerate, kind

ἐπ-ήτριμος ον close, in crowds

ἐπητύς ύος ἡ kindness

ἐπ-ηχέω re-echo

ἐπί *adv* on, at *or* to it; afterwards, then; on the contrary, besides; *prep with acc* extending over, towards, up to; against; until; during; in quest of; *with numbers* about, nearly; *with gen* on, upon, at, by, near, with; towards; in the presence of; during, in the time of; over; with regard to, concerning; on the grounds of; *with dat* on, in, at, near, beside; upon, after; towards, against; during, in the time of; immediately after; in addition to; by reason of, on the grounds of, for the purpose of, for the sake of, with respect to; in honour of, on the condition of; in the power *or* under the rule of

ἔπι ▸ **ἔπεστι** it is there *or* at hand

ἐπ-ιάλλω send to; lay on; cause

ἐπιάλμενος *see* **ἐφάλλομαι**

ἐπι-ανδάνω ▸ **ἐφανδάνω**

ἐπ-ιάχω shout to; shout aloud

ἐπίβαθρον ου τό passenger's fare

ἐπι-βαίνω set foot on, tread *or* walk upon; go up, mount, ascend; go over, cross, arrive at; set on, attack, fall upon; *tr* cause to mount; bring, put *or* send upon; make arrive at

ἐπι-βάλλω *act tr* throw, cast *or* lay upon; put on; *act intr* go towards; fall upon, attack; think of; fall to, be due; *mid* put on oneself; take upon oneself; + *gen* desire (earnestly), covet

ἐπι-βαρέω burden

ἐπίβασις εως ἡ attack; approach

ἐπι-βάσκω lead into

ἐπι-βατεύω be a sailor *or* passenger; tread upon; mount; lean upon

ἐπιβάτης ου ὁ horseman; sailor; naval soldier, marine; passenger

ἐπιβατός ή όν accessible

ἐπιβήτωρ ορος ὁ one who mounts; male animal, boar, bull

ἐπι-βιβάζω cause to ascend

ἐπι-βιόω live through; survive; live to see

ἐπι-βλέπω look at *or* upon, regard (with envy)

ἐπίβλημα ατος τό tapestry, hangings; patch

ἐπιβλής ῆτος ὁ bar, bolt

ἐπι-βοάω *and mid* cry out to; call to aid, invoke; decry

ἐπιβοήθεια ᾱς ἡ succour, coming to help

ἐπι-βοηθέω + *dat* come to help

ἐπιβόημα ατος τό a call to

ἐπιβόητος ον cried out against, ill spoken of

ἐπιβολή ῆς ἡ a throwing *or* putting on; attack; attempt, project; cover; layer; penalty

ἐπιβουκόλος ὁ cowherd; herdsman

ἐπιβουλευτής οῦ ὁ one who plots against + *gen*

ἐπι-βουλεύω + *dat* plot *or* plan against [someone]; lay snares; lie in wait for; have a mind to, intend, aim at

ἐπιβουλή ῆς ἡ plot, plan against (someone); treachery, deceit; lying in wait, laying snares

ἐπίβουλος ον plotting against, insidious

ἐπι-βρέμω roar out

ἐπι-βρῑ́θω weigh down

ἐπιβρόντητος ον stunned

ἐπιβώτωρ ορος ὁ shepherd

ἐπίγαιος ▸ **ἐπίγειος**

ἐπι-γαμβρεύω marry one's brother's widow

ἐπιγαμίᾱ ᾱς ἡ intermarriage

ἐπίγαμος ον marriageable

ἐπι-γδουπέω shout out *or* in applause

ἐπίγειος ον on the earth, earthly

ἐπι-γελάω laugh at *or* about approvingly

ἐπι-γίγνομαι *mid* be born, come *or* live after; follow, elapse; approach, come, happen; fall upon, attack

ἐπι-γιγνώσκω recognize, know exactly, observe; discover, become conscious of; contrive; decide

ἐπι-γνάμπτω bend; make [someone] alter his intentions

ἐπιγνώμων ον deciding upon; arbiter; overseer

ἐπίγνωσις εως ἡ knowledge

ἐπίγονος η ον born after

ἐπιγουνίς ίδος ἡ thigh

ἐπιγράβδην *adv* scratching

ἐπίγραμμα ατος τό **ἐπιγραφή** ῆς ἡ inscription, epigram

ἐπι-γράφω scratch [the surface], graze; write upon, inscribe; order by letter; enter in a register; *mid* paint on for oneself

ἐπίγρῡπος ον with a hooked beak, hook-nosed

ἐπίδᾱμος ον ▸ **ἐπιδήμιος**

ἐπι-δαψιλεύομαι *mid* give abundantly in addition

ἐπιδεής ές needy, in want of

ἐπίδειγμα ατος τό specimen, example, pattern

ἐπιδείκνῡμι, ἐπιδεικνύω show forth, exhibit, show as a specimen; represent; demonstrate, prove; *mid* show oneself, make oneself seen *or* heard

ἐπιδεικτικός ή όν showy, for display

ἐπίδειξις εως ἡ a showing, exhibition, display; review; specimen, pattern; panegyric; proof

ἐπιδέκατος η ον one in ten; the tenth part; one and one tenth

ἐπι-δέκομαι ▸ **ἐπιδέχομαι**

ἐπιδέξιος ον to the right

ἐπίδεξις εως ἡ ▸ **ἐπίδειξις**

ἐπι-δέρκομαι look at

ἐπιδευής ές ▸ **ἐπιδεής**

ἐπι-δεύομαι ▸ **ἐπιδέομαι** *see* **ἐπιδέω**

ἐπι-δέχομαι *mid* receive *or* admit in addition

ἐπι-δέω[1] bind on; bandage

ἐπι-δέω[2] want, lack; *pass* + *gen* be in want of, need; fall short of, be inferior (to)

ἐπίδηλος ον manifest, plain, conspicuous, known

ἐπι-δημέω, ἐπι-δημεύω be at home; return home; be a stranger in a place

ἐπιδήμιος ον living at home, native; spread among the people; living as a stranger

ἐπιδημιουργός οῦ ὁ controller of magistrates; magistrates sent annually by Doric states to their colonies

ἐπίδημος ον ▸ **ἐπιδήμιος**

ἐπιδια-βαίνω cross over in addition *or* one after the other

ἐπιδια-γῑνώσκω consider anew

ἐπιδι-αιρέω distribute; *mid* share among themselves

ἐπιδια-κρῑ́νω decide finally

ἐπιδια-τάσσομαι command in addition

ἐπιδια-φέρομαι go across after

ἐπι-διδάσκω teach in addition

ἐπι-δίδωμι *act tr* give besides; give with; deliver, yield; *act intr* increase, improve, grow; *mid* add; present

ἐπι-δίζημαι *mid* seek *or* inquire for besides

ἐπι-δῑνέω swing round; *pass* move in a circle; *mid* reflect upon

ἐπιδι-ορθόω set fully in order

ἐπιδιφριάς άδος ἡ chariot rail

ἐπιδίφριος ον on the chariot seat

ἐπι-διώκω pursue further

ἐπίδοξος ον causing expectation; to be expected, likely

ἐπίδοσις εως ἡ addition, contribution; increase, progress

ἐπιδοχή ῆς ἡ reception in addition

ἐπίδρομος ον to be taken by storm, assailable

ἐπι-δύω go down *or* set upon

ἐπιείκεια ᾱς ἡ propriety, decency; equity, fairness; clemency

ἐπιείκελος ον + *dat* like

ἐπιεικής ές fitting, suitable; fair, decent; moderate, kind; proper, fit; likely

■ **ἐπιεικῶς** properly, justly; moderately

ἐπιεικτός ή όν yielding; conquered

ἐπι-έλπομαι *mid* hope for

ἐπι-έννῡμι put on over

ἐπιζάφελος ον vehement, furious

ἐπι-ζάω ▸ **ἐπιβιόω**

ἐπι-ζεύγνῡμι, ἐπι-ζευγνύω fasten *or* join to

ἐπιζεφύριος ον towards the west

ἐπι-ζέω boil *or* flash up; inflame

ἐπιζήμιος ον hurtful

ἐπι-ζημιόω punish

ἐπι-ζητέω seek for; long *or* wish for, crave, covet

ἐπι-ζώννῡμι gird on

ἐπι-ζώω ▸ **ἐπιζάω**

ἐπιήρανος ον **ἐπίηρος** ον pleasing, pleasant

ἐπιθαλασσίδιος ον **ἐπιθαλάσσιος** (ᾱ) ον lying *or* living on the coast

ἐπιθανάτιος ον condemned to death

ἐπι-θαρσῡ́νω encourage

ἐπι-θειάζω invoke the gods; conjure (the gods)

ἐπιθειασμός οῦ ὁ appeal to the gods

ἐπι-θεραπεύω be compliant *or* courteous; be intent on

ἐπίθεσις εως ἡ a laying upon; attack

ἐπι-θεσπίζω pronounce oracles

ἐπιθετικός ή όν ready to attack

ἐπίθετος ον added; not natural, affected, studied

ἐπι-θέω run at *or* after

ἐπίθημα ατος τό cover, lid

ἐπι-θορυβέω make a noise at; applaud

ἐπι-θρῴσκω leap upon

ἐπι-θῡμέω + *gen* desire, long for, wish, covet

ἐπιθῡμητής οῦ ὁ one who desires *or* longs for [something]; lover, adherent

ἐπιθῡμητικός ή όν desiring

ἐπιθῡμίᾱ ᾱς ἡ desire, longing, wish, lust

ἐπιθῡμίᾱμα ατος τό incense

ἐπ-ῑθῡ́νω direct against; guide straight

ἐπι-θύω sacrifice after

ἐπ-ῑθύω rush at

ἐπι-θωῦσσω ring to; shout to

ἐπιίστωρ (*gen* ορος) + *gen* acquainted with; accomplice in [a thing]

ἐπικαθ-αιρέω pull down besides

ἐπικάθ-ημαι sit upon; weigh upon; besiege

ἐπικαθ-ίζω set upon; sit upon

ἐπικαθ-ίσταμαι *mid* put down for oneself

ἐπικαίριος ον opportune, suitable, convenient; necessary; considerable, important, chief

ἐπίκαιρος ον convenient, suitable, proper, opportune

ἐπι-καίω kindle *or* burn at

ἐπι-καλέω summon, call in; invoke; give a surname *or* nickname; accuse, reproach + *dat*; *mid* call to oneself, call to aid; challenge

ἐπικάλυμμα ατος τό covering cloak

ἐπι-καλύπτω cover up, hide

ἐπικαμπή ῆς ἡ bend, curve, projection

ἐπι-κάμπτω bend; wheel round

ἐπικάρσιος ον head foremost; sideways, crosswise, at an angle

ἐπικατα-βαίνω go down against

ἐπικατ-άγομαι *pass* come to land afterwards

ἐπικατα-δαρθάνω fall asleep afterwards

ἐπικατα-κλύζω overflow besides

ἐπικατα-κοιμάομαι *pass* lie down to sleep on

ἐπικατα-λαμβάνω overtake, catch up

ἐπικατα-μένω stay still longer

ἐπικατάρᾱτος ον accursed

ἐπικατα-ρριπτέω throw down after

ἐπικατα-σφάζω, ἐπικατα-σφάττω kill upon *or* at

ἐπικατα-ψεύδομαι *mid* tell lies in addition

ἐπικάτ-ειμι go down into

ἐπίκαυτος ον burnt at the end

ἐπί-κειμαι *mid* be laid *or* lie upon, in, at *or* near; entreat; press upon, attack; impend; be imposed

ἐπι-κείρω cut, mow off *or* down; baffle

ἐπι-κελαδέω shout at; shout in applause

ἐπικέλευσις εως ἡ exhortation, cheering on

ἐπι-κελεύω *and mid* exhort, cheer on again

ἐπι-κέλλω drive to the shore; run ashore

ἐπι-κέλομαι *mid* call upon *or* to

ἐπι-κεράννῡμι mix in; mix after

ἐπικερδίᾱ ᾱς ἡ profit in trade

ἐπι-κερτομέω mock; tease

ἐπι-κεύθω hide from

ἐπικηρῡκείᾱ ᾱς ἡ negotiation through heralds

ἐπι-κηρῡκεύομαι *mid* send a message by a herald; treat, transact

ἐπι-κηρύσσω proclaim publicly

ἐπι-κίδνημι spread over; *mid* be extended over, be spread over

ἐπικίνδῡνος ον dangerous; in danger

ἐπι-κίρνημι ▸ **ἐπικεράννυμι**

ἐπι-κλάω break, bend, move; dispirit

ἐπι-κλείω praise the more

ἐπίκλημα ατος τό reproach, accusation

ἐπίκληρος ου ἡ daughter and heiress

ἐπίκλησις εως ἡ surname; name

ἐπίκλητος ον called, assembled; called to help

ἐπι-κλῑ́νω bend towards; lay upon; *intr* recline, turn

ἐπίκλοπος ον thievish; wily, cunning

ἐπι-κλύζω overflow

ἐπίκλυσις εως ἡ flood, overflow

ἐπι-κλύω listen to

ἐπι-κλώθω (of the Fates spinning the thread of destiny) spin to; assign, allot

ἐπίκοινος ον common

ἐπι-κοινόω communicate

ἐπι-κοινωνέω have in common with

ἐπι-κομπέω boast
ἐπι-κόπτω slay
ἐπι-κοσμέω adorn; celebrate
ἐπι-κουρέω + *dat* help, assist, serve as a mercenary; keep off from
ἐπικούρημα ατος τό protection
ἐπικουρίᾱ ᾱς ἡ help, auxiliary forces
ἐπικουρικός ή όν helping, auxiliary
ἐπίκουρος ον helping, assisting
ἐπι-κουφίζω relieve; lift up
ἐπι-κραίνω, ἐπι-κραιαίνω accomplish, fulfil
ἐπικράτεια ᾱς ἡ mastery, supremacy; realm
ἐπι-κρατέω prevail over, conquer, overcome; obtain, achieve; rule, govern
ἐπικρατής ές superior, victorious, violent
ἐπικράτησις εως ἡ overcoming, overwhelming
ἐπι-κρεμάννῡμι, ἐπι-κρέμαμαι *pass* hang over, threaten
ἐπι-κρῑ́νω decide
ἐπίκριον ου τό yard-arm of a ship
ἐπι-κρύπτω hide, conceal; *mid* hide oneself
ἐπι-κτάομαι *mid* gain besides; win; enlarge
ἐπι-κτείνω kill besides *or* again
ἐπίκτησις εως ἡ new gain
ἐπίκτητος ον gained besides, newly acquired
ἐπικῡδής ές glorious, splendid; important
ἐπι-κυΐσκομαι become doubly pregnant
ἐπι-κυλινδέω roll (down) upon
ἐπι-κύπτω stoop down over
ἐπι-κῡρόω confirm, ratify; determine
ἐπι-κύρω + *dat* fall in with; meet
ἐπι-κωκύω lament over
ἐπι-κωμῳδέω mock, satirize in comedy
ἐπι-λαγχάνω succeed [someone else in an office on a vacancy]; have allotted to one; fall to one's lot
ἐπι-λαμβάνω take *or* seize besides; lay hold of, catch, oppress, attack; retain; prevent; fall in with; live to see; reach; *mid* seize, hold fast; keep to; attack; blame; object to; fall in with; get possession of
ἐπίλαμπτος ον ▸ **ἐπίληπτος**
ἐπι-λάμπω shine again; dawn
ἐπι-λανθάνομαι *mid usu* + *gen* forget; forget wilfully
ἐπι-λεαίνω smooth over; make plausible
ἐπι-λέγω say at *or* besides, add; name; select, pick out; *mid* collect, choose for oneself; read; think over; fear
ἐπι-λείβω pour upon
ἐπι-λείπω *act tr* leave behind; omit; *act intr* fail, be gone *or* wanting; give out; be dried up; *pass* be left
ἐπι-λείχω lick
ἐπίλειψις εως ἡ failure
ἐπίλεκτος ον chosen
ἐπι-λεύσσω look towards *or* at; see before [oneself]
ἐπίληθος ον causing to forget
ἐπι-λήθω ▸ **ἐπιλανθάνομαι**
ἐπιληΐς ίδος ἡ captured
ἐπι-ληκέω beat time to (dancers)
ἐπίληπτος ον caught (in)
ἐπιλησμονή ῆς ἡ forgetfulness
ἐπιλήσμων ον forgetful
ἐπιλίγδην *adv* grazing
ἐπ-ιλλίζω wink at
ἐπι-λογίζομαι *mid and pass* reflect (upon), consider
ἐπίλογος ου ὁ consideration; conclusion
ἐπίλοιπος ον still left; future
ἐπι-λῡπέω annoy *or* grieve besides
ἐπι-λῡ́ω loose; decide; refute; *mid* release; protect

ε

ἐπι-λωβεύω mock at

ἐπι-μαίνομαι *pass and mid + dat* be madly in love with

ἐπι-μαίομαι *mid* touch, feel; seize; strive after, seek to obtain

ἐπι-μανθάνω learn besides *or* after

ἐπι-μαρτυρέω bear witness (to)

ἐπιμαρτυρίᾱ ᾱς ἡ calling to witness

ἐπι-μαρτῡ́ρομαι *mid* call to witness; call on earnestly, implore

ἐπιμάρτυρος ου ὁ witness

ἐπι-μάσσομαι *fut from* **ἐπιμαίομαι**

ἐπίμαστος ον dirty, squalid

ἐπι-μαχέω protect in war

ἐπιμαχίᾱ ᾱς ἡ defensive alliance

ἐπίμαχος ον easily attacked, assailable

ἐπι-μειδ(ι)άω smile at

ἐπιμέλεια ᾱς ἡ care, diligence, attention; training, practice; direction, management

ἐπι-μελέομαι (*also* ἐπι-μέλομαι) *pass + gen* take care of, pay attention to; manage, superintend; take pains over

ἐπιμελής ές caring for, careful, zealous; causing care; object of care

ἐπιμελητής οῦ ὁ provider, guardian; manager, superintendent, inspector, curator; financial officer (at Athens and in Egypt)

ἐπι-μέλομαι ▸ **ἐπιμελέομαι**

ἐπι-μέμονα *pf* strive after

ἐπι-μέμφομαι *mid* find fault (with); blame, grumble at, complain

ἐπι-μένω stay on; adhere to; wait, await; expect

ἐπιμετα-πέμπομαι *mid* send for after

ἐπι-μετρέω measure out to

ἐπι-μήδομαι *mid* devise against

ἐπι-μήνιος ον monthly

ἐπι-μηνίω be angry

ἐπι-μηχανάομαι *mid* devise against; devise besides

ἐπιμήχανος ον contriving

ἐπι-μῑ́γνῡμι, ἐπι-μείγνῡμι *and mid* mix in *or* with; converse; meet

ἐπι-μιμνῄσκομαι *pass + gen* remember, recall to mind; mention

ἐπι-μίμνω ▸ **ἐπιμένω**

ἐπι-μίξ *adv* confusedly, pell-mell

ἐπιμιξίᾱ ᾱς ἡ mixing with (others), dealings

ἐπι-μίσγω ▸ **ἐπιμίγνυμι**

ἐπιμονή ῆς ἡ delay

ἐπι-μύζω murmur at

ἐπίνειον ου τό anchorage, dock, port; arsenal

ἐπι-νέμω allot, distribute; lead to pasture; *mid* graze; devastate

ἐπι-νεύω nod at *or* to; assent; grant

ἐπινέφελος ον clouded

ἐπινεφρίδιος ον on the kidneys

ἐπι-νέω[1] (of the Fates spinning the thread of destiny) spin to

ἐπι-νέω[2] load with; heap *or* pile up

ἐπινῑ́κειος ον of victory, triumphal

ἐπινῑ́κιος ον belonging to victory

ἐπι-νίσσομαι *+ gen* go *or* flow over, overflow

ἐπι-νοέω think of; contrive, devise; observe, perceive

ἐπίνοια ᾱς ἡ thought, intention, project; thinking; afterthought

ἐπινύμφειος ον bridal

ἐπι-νωμάω allot, distribute

ἐπίξῡνος ον ▸ **ἐπίκοινος**

ἐπι-ορκέω swear falsely, forswear oneself

ἐπιορκίᾱ ᾱς ἡ perjury, false swearing

ἐπίορκος ον perjured, forsworn ■ **τό ἐπίορκον** false oath

ἐπι-όσσομαι look at

ἐπίουρος ου ὁ guard; chief

ἐπιοῦσα ης ἡ the coming day

ἐπιούσιος ον sufficient for the day, daily

ἐπίπᾱν *adv* on the whole, generally

ἐπιπαρα-νέω heap up besides

ἐπιπαρα-σκευάζομαι *mid* provide oneself with besides

ἐπιπάρ-ειμι[1] be present *or* near

ἐπιπάρ-ειμι[2] come on too; advance against; march on the heights parallel with [someone below]

ἐπι-πάσσω sprinkle upon

ἐπίπεδος ον level, flat

ἐπι-πείθομαι *pass* + *dat* obey; be persuaded

ἐπι-πέλομαι *mid* + *dat* come near, approach

ἐπι-πέμπω send besides *or* after; send to

ἐπίπεμψις εως ἡ a sending to

ἐπι-πέτομαι *mid* fly to

ἐπι-πίλναμαι approach

ἐπι-πῑ́νω drink besides

ἐπι-πῑ́πτω + *dat* fall upon *or* into; attack; befall; put to shore

ἔπιπλα ων τά movables, goods and chattels; furniture

ἐπι-πλάζομαι *pass* be driven *or* wander over

ἐπίπλεος ᾱ ον full

ἐπίπλευσις εως ἡ a sailing against, naval attack

ἐπι-πλέω sail upon *or* with; sail against

ἐπι-πληρόω man [a ship] afresh

ἐπι-πλήσσω strike at; blame, reprove, reproach

ἐπίπλοα ▸ ἔπιπλα

ἐπίπλοος[1] ου ὁ the membrane enclosing the entrails

ἐπίπλοος[2] ου ὁ sailing against *or* upon, attack of a fleet, naval expedition

ἐπι-πλώω ▸ ἐπιπλέω

ἐπι-πνέω, ἐπι-πνείω breathe *or* blow upon; blow at *or* after

ἐπιπόδιος ᾱ ον upon the feet

ἐπι-ποθέω long *or* yearn for

ἐπιπόθησις εως ἡ **ἐπιποθίᾱ** ᾱς ἡ longing for

ἐπιπόθητος ον longed for

ἐπιποιμήν ένος ὁ/ἡ shepherd(ess)

ἐπι-πολάζω be on the surface (of); get to the top, prevail

ἐπιπόλαιος ον on the surface, superficial

ἐπιπολή ῆς ἡ surface, top

ἐπίπολος ου ὁ servant

ἐπιπονέω persevere in work

ἐπίπονος ον painful, laborious, painful toil; (of omens) portending toil

ἐπι-πορεύομαι *pass* march *or* travel to *or* against

ἐπι-πρέπω be prominent at, be conspicuous; fit, suit

ἐπιπρο-ϊάλλω send out *or* place before one

ἐπιπρο-ῑ́ημι send forth towards; send out; steer towards

ἐπίπροσθεν *adv* before, near; in the way

ἐπι-πταίρω sneeze at (a good omen); be gracious to

ἐπι-πωλέομαι *mid* go about, inspect; reconnoitre

ἐπιπώλησις εως ἡ inspection

ἐπι-ρράπτω sew on

ἐπι-ρρᾱ́σσω ▸ ἐπιρρήσσω

ἐπι-ρρέζω sacrifice on *or* at

ἐπι-ρρέπω bend towards; sink down

ἐπι-ρρέω flow on the surface (of); stream to

ἐπι-ρρήσσω dash against; push forward violently; *intr* burst forth

ἐπι-ρρῑπτέω, ἐπι-ρρῑ́πτω throw upon

ἐπίρροθος[1] ον reviling, scolding

ἐπίρροθος[2] ον coming to the rescue; protector; giving help against

ε

ἐπίρρυτος ον watered

ἐπι-ρρώνῡμι strengthen, encourage; *pass* recover strength, take heart

ἐπι-ρρώομαι *mid* be active; flow down

ἐπίσαγμα ατος τό load, burden

ἐπι-σάσσω heap *or* load on; saddle

ἐπι-σείω shake at *or* against

ἐπι-σεύω put in motion against, incite; *pass* be stirred; hurry *or* hasten towards; rush at, attack

ἐπι-σημαίνω put a mark on; announce; give a sign of approval; appear as a sign *or* omen; *mid* mark with a sign for oneself

ἐπίσημον ου τό mark, device; symbol, emblem

ἐπι-σῑμόω cause to turn sideways

ἐπι-σῑτίζομαι *mid* provide oneself with food; forage

ἐπισῑτισμός οῦ ὁ supplying with provisions

ἐπι-σκέπτομαι *mid* ▸ ἐπισκοπέω

ἐπι-σκευάζω prepare, equip, get ready; restore; pack on; *mid* prepare for oneself

ἐπισκευή ῆς ἡ repair, restoration; raising up

ἐπίσκεψις εως ἡ inspection; inquiry

ἐπίσκηνος ον before the tent, openly

ἐπι-σκηνόω live in; be immanent *or* inherent

ἐπι-σκήπτω impose on, enjoin; implore, entreat; press; wish [someone something]; accuse; *mid* refuse; indict, summon; (Attic legal term) denounce (so as to bring a prosecution for perjury)

ἐπι-σκιάζω overshadow; hide

ἐπίσκιος ον shading; overshadowed

ἐπι-σκοπέω look upon *or* at; regard, review, inspect, visit, examine, consider; pay attention to, take care of

ἐπισκοπή ῆς ἡ visitation, inspection; office of an overseer *or* bishop

ἐπίσκοπος[1] ου ὁ overseer, guardian; bishop

ἐπίσκοπος[2] ον hitting the mark; convenient

■ **ἐπισκοπά** successfully, with good aim

ἐπι-σκοτέω + *dat* darken, overshadow

ἐπι-σκύζομαι *mid* grow furious over [something]

ἐπι-σκυθίζω ply with drink in the Scythian manner (i.e. with unmixed wine)

ἐπισκύνιον ου τό skin of the brows

ἐπι-σκώπτω laugh *or* mock at; jest

ἐπισμυγερῶς *adv* shamefully, miserably; to one's cost

ἐπισπαστήρ ῆρος ὁ handle of the door

ἐπισπαστός ή όν drawn upon oneself; (of a noose) tightly-drawn

ἐπι-σπάω draw after (one), draw along; drag on; pull to; seize; gain; *mid* draw to oneself, induce, seduce; obtain; become as if uncircumcised

ἐπι-σπείρω sow upon

ἐπίσπεισις εως ἡ pouring out on, libation

ἐπι-σπένδω pour upon, offer a libation

ἐπι-σπέρχω incite; rage furiously

ἐπι-σπεύδω urge, hasten; hurry on

ἐπισπονδαί ων αἱ new treaty

ἐπι-σσείω etc. *see* ἐπισείω

ἐπίσσωτρον ου τό metal hoop of a wheel

ἐπισταδόν *adv* one after another, successively

ἐπίσταθμος ου ὁ commandant of a place; at the door

ἐπίσταμαι *pass* understand, know, have insight (in), be skilled *or* experienced (in); be able; think, believe

ἐπιστασίᾱ ᾱς ἡ **ἐπίστασις** εως ἡ stopping, checking, halt; assembly; inspection; attention

ἐπι-στατέω + *gen or dat* be put in charge of be prefect *or* overseer; command, preside over

ἐπιστάτης ου ὁ one who is present; one who stands upon something; the man behind; commander, overseer, prefect; master; (at Athens) the president of the council and assembly

ἐπι-στείβω + *acc* tread on

ἐπι-στέλλω send to, send a message; command

ἐπι-στενάζω, ἐπι-στενάχω, ἐπι-στένω groan over, lament at

ἐπιστεφής ές filled to the brim (with wine)

ἐπι-στέφω offer; *mid* fill to the brim

ἐπιστήμη ης ἡ knowledge, intelligence, insight; skill; science, art

ἐπιστήμων ον prudent, intelligent, skilful; learned

ἐπι-στηρίζομαι lean upon

ἐπίστιον ου τό dock for ships; slip *or* shed for ships

ἐπίστιος ▸ **ἐφέστιος**

ἐπιστολεύς έως ὁ vice-admiral; letter carrier, courier

ἐπιστολή ῆς ἡ message, order; letter

ἐπιστολιᾱφόρος ου ὁ bearer of dispatches

ἐπιστολιμαῖος ον existing only in letters

ἐπι-στομίζω curb, bridle; stop [the voice]

ἐπι-στοναχέω roar at

ἐπιστρατείᾱ ᾱς ἡ **ἐπιστράτευσις** εως ἡ expedition against

ἐπι-στρατεύω *and mid* + *dat* march against

ἐπιστρεφής ές intense; attentive, careful; anxious

ἐπι-στρέφω *act* turn to, direct to; turn round *or* back; force back; correct; *act intr, mid and pass* turn oneself around, back *or* forward(s); visit; care for

ἐπιστροφάδην *adv* round about

ἐπιστροφή ῆς ἡ a turning to; warning; punishment; care, regard; a turning back, wheeling round, return; change

ἐπίστροφος ον conversant with

ἐπι-στρωφάω visit, frequent

ἐπισυν-άγω gather together

ἐπισυναγωγή ῆς ἡ assembly; being gathered together

ἐπισυν-τρέχω run together to

ἐπισύστασις εως ἡ a riotous meeting

ἐπι-σφάζω, ἐπι-σφάττω slaughter *or* kill over

ἐπισφαλής ές unsteady; dangerous

ἐπι-σφραγίζομαι *mid* put a seal *or* mark upon

ἐπισφύριον ου τό clasp over the ankle (to fasten the greaves there)

ἐπισχερώ *adv* in single file, one after another

ἐπισχεσίᾱ ᾱς ἡ pretext

ἐπίσχεσις εως ἡ stopping, checking; moderation, reluctance

ἐπ-ισχύω make strong; be insistent

ἐπ-ίσχω ▸ **ἐπέχω**

ἐπι-σωρεύω heap up

ἐπίταγμα ατος τό **ἐπιταγή** ῆς ἡ order, command

ἐπίτακτοι ων οἱ reserve, rear-guard

ἐπι-ταλαιπωρέω labour still more

ἐπίταξις εως ἡ ▸ **ἐπίταγμα**

ἐπι-ταράσσω trouble yet more

ἐπιτάρροθος ου ὁ/ἡ helper, assistant

ἐπι-τάσσω *and mid* arrange at; place behind; put in command; command, order, impose + *dat*

ἐπιτάφιος ον funeral

ἐπι-ταχῡ́νω hasten on *or* forward

ἐπι-τείνω stretch upon *or* over; strain, urge, heighten, increase; excite

ἐπι-τειχίζω build a fortress, fortify

ἐπιτείχισις εως ἡ **ἐπιτειχισμός** οῦ ὁ the building of a fortress; fort

ἐπιτείχισμα ατος τό fortification

ἐπι-τελέω finish, complete, accomplish, perform; sacrifice; pay; *mid* take upon oneself; end

ἐπιτελής ές accomplished, complete

ἐπι-τέλλω *and mid + dat of person* command; *pass* rise (of the stars)

ἐπι-τέμνω make a cut into, cut off

ἐπίτεξ εκος ἡ about to bring forth

ἐπι-τέρπομαι *pass + dat* delight in

ἐπι-τεχνάομαι *mid* contrive (for a purpose *or* to meet an emergency)

ἐπιτέχνησις εως ἡ contrivance, additional improvement

ἐπιτήδειος (ᾱ) ον fit, convenient, useful, serviceable; necessary
■ **τὰ ἐπιτήδεια** necessaries, provisions
■ **ὁ ἐπιτήδειος** relation, friend

ἐπιτηδές (*or* ἐπίτηδες) *adv* for the purpose, purposely; sufficiently

ἐπιτήδευμα ατος τό **ἐπιτήδευσις** εως ἡ pursuit, business, practice; study; habits, manner of life

ἐπι-τηδεύω do on purpose, pursue, practise; invent

ἐπι-τήκω *tr* melt upon; pour when melted over

ἐπι-τηρέω watch for, wait attentively

ἐπι-τίθημι *act tr* put *or* lay upon; impose on, cause; grant; add; close by putting before; *act intr and mid* put on oneself *or* for oneself; engage oneself in, undertake; + *dat* attack, make an attempt upon

ἐπι-τῑμάω honour, value; pronounce judgement; punish, fine; blame, reprove

ἐπιτί́μησις εως ἡ blame, reproach

ἐπιτῑμήτωρ ορος ὁ avenger; protector

ἐπιτῑμίᾱ ᾱς ἡ enjoyment of civil rights; punishment, reproach

ἐπίτῑμος ον enjoying civil rights

ἐπιτλῆναι *aor infin* bear patiently

ἐπιτολή ῆς ἡ [of a star] rising

ἐπι-τολμάω endure (to), stand firm

ἐπίτονος ου ὁ stretched rope; back stay (of a mast)

ἐπι-τοξάζομαι shoot at

ἐπι-τραπέω commit, entrust

ἐπι-τρέπω *act tr* turn to *or* towards; give over, entrust, put into one's hands; leave; admit, allow, permit; ordain; *act intr* turn to; entrust oneself to; yield, succumb; *mid* turn oneself to, incline to; entrust oneself to

ἐπι-τρέφω feed, bring up; *pass* (of posterity) grow (up) after; grow up

ἐπι-τρέχω run at, upon, after *or* over; attack, oppress, overrun

ἐπι-τρῑ́βω rub on the surface; weaken, afflict, destroy

ἐπίτριπτος ον crafty, cunning

ἐπιτροπαῖος (ᾱ) ον tutelar, delegated

ἐπι-τροπεύω be guardian, tutor, trustee *or* governor

ἐπιτροπή ῆς ἡ entrusting, charge, trust; decision, arbitration; guardianship

ἐπίτροπος ου ὁ trustee, guardian, governor

ἐπιτροχάδην *adv* fluently, trippingly

ἐπι-τυγχάνω + *gen or dat* meet with, fall in with; reach, attain, obtain, succeed
■ **ὁ ἐπιτυχών** the first person one meets, the man in the street

ἐπιτύμβιος ον belonging to a tomb, at *or* over a tomb

ἐπι-φαίνομαι *pass* **ἐπι-φαίνω** appear, become conspicuous; show oneself

ἐπιφάνεια ᾱς ἡ appearance, manifestation

ἐπιφανής ές conspicuous, manifest; excellent, famous, illustrious

ἐπίφαντος ον conspicuous, still living

ἐπι-φαύσκω shine out

ἐπι-φέρω bring, carry *or* put upon *or* up; cause, bring about; add, increase; throw *or* lay upon, impose, inflict; impute, reproach; *mid* bring with oneself; *pass* rush on, attack, rebuke; follow, chase

ἐπι-φημίζω *mid* foretell (bad) omens

ἐπιφήμισμα ατος τό word of (bad) omen

ἐπι-φθέγγομαι *mid* call out at; sound a charge

ἐπι-φθονέω + *dat* envy, bear a grudge against; hate

ἐπίφθονος ον envious, jealous, hostile; envied, hated

ἐπι-φλέγω burn; consume

ἐπι-φοιτάω, ἐπι-φοιτέω go *or* come repeatedly to, visit frequently; invade; come after

ἐπιφορᾱ́ ᾱς ἡ addition to pay

ἐπι-φορέω ▸ ἐπιφέρω

ἐπιφόρημα ατος τό dessert

ἐπίφορος ον carrying towards; favourable

ἐπι-φράζομαι *mid* think of, reflect on, consider; contrive; discover

ἐπι-φρονέω be prudent

ἐπιφροσύνη ης ἡ thoughtfulness, presence of mind

ἐπίφρων ον thoughtful, prudent

ἐπι-φῡ́ομαι *mid* + *dat* grow upon *or* at, cling to

ἐπι-φωνέω call out to

ἐπι-φώσκω draw towards dawn

ἐπι-χαίρω + *dat* rejoice at

ἐπίχαλκος ον covered with brass *or* copper

ἐπίχαρις ι pleasing, agreeable, engaging

ἐπίχαρτος ον delightful

ἐπι-χειμάζω pass the winter at

ἐπίχειρα ων τά wages; earned money

ἐπι-χειρέω + *dat* put one's hand to; attack; undertake, attempt, try, venture, manage

ἐπιχείρημα ατος τό **ἐπιχείρησις** εως ἡ undertaking, beginning, attempt, project; attack

ἐπιχειρητής οῦ ὁ enterprising man of action

ἐπι-χέω pour *or* shed over, upon *or* at; *mid and pass* flood in

ἐπιχθόνιος ον earthy

ἐπίχολος ον producing bile

ἐπι-χορηγέω supply besides, procure in addition

ἐπιχορηγίᾱ ᾱς ἡ supply, additional help

ἐπι-χράομαι *mid* + *dat* make use of; converse with

ἐπι-χράω, ἐπι-χραύω + *dat* rush upon, attack

ἐπι-χρῑ́ω anoint, besmear; *mid* anoint oneself

ἐπίχρῡσος ον overlaid with gold

ἐπι-χωρέω come towards *or* against, advance; yield, concede

ἐπι-χωριάζω visit often

ἐπιχώριος ον native, indigenous, in the fashion of the country

ἐπι-ψαύω touch on the surface

ἐπι-ψηλαφάω grope for

ἐπι-ψηφίζω put to the vote; *mid* vote, decree, confirm by vote

ἐπιωγή ῆς ἡ shelter, anchorage, landing-place

ἐπ-οικέω go *or* live as a settler *or* colonist; dwell in; be a neighbour

ἐπ-οικοδομέω build up, repair; build upon

ἔποικος ου ὁ settler, colonist; foreigner; inhabitant; (near) neighbour

ἐπ-οικτείρω, ἐπ-οικτίζω have compassion with

ἐπ-οίχομαι *mid* go *or* come towards, approach; attack; go over, through *or* along; review, inspect; work at

ε

ἐπ-οκέλλω *tr and intr* run ashore; be wrecked

ἕπομαι† *mid* + *dat* follow; accompany, escort; pursue

ἐπ-όμνῡμι, ἐπ-ομνύω swear upon *or* by

ἐπομφάλιος ον upon the navel

ἐπονείδιστος ον shameful, to be reproached

ἐπ-ονομάζω give a name *or* surname; call by name

ἐπ-οπῑ́ζομαι *mid* regard with awe

ἐποποιΐᾱ ᾱς ἡ epic poetry

ἐποποιός οῦ ὁ epic poet

ἐπ-οπτάω roast upon

ἐπ-οπτεύω look on *or* at; inspect, watch over

ἐπ-όπτης ου ὁ watcher, guardian; witness

ἐπ-ορέγω hand to; *mid and pass* stretch oneself towards; desire still more

ἐπ-ορθρεύομαι *mid* rise early

ἐπ-όρνῡμι arouse, stir up, excite; send to; *pass* rise, rush on

ἐπ-ορούω + *dat* rush at, fall upon

ἐπ-ορχέομαι *mid* dance to the tune of + *gen*

ἔπος εος τό word; speech, tale, saying; promise; oracle; maxim; advice, order; legend, report; song, epic poem; thing, story, something

■ **ὡς ἔπος εἰπεῖν** as the saying is; almost, practically

ἐπ-οτρῡ́νω incite, stir up, rouse

ἐπουράνιος ον heavenly

ἔπουρος ον blowing favourably

ἐπ-οφείλω owe besides *or* still

ἐπ-οχέομαι + *dat* ride upon

ἐπ-οχετεύω bring water by a channel to a place

ἔποχος ον riding *or* mounted upon; firm in the saddle

ἔποψ οπος ὁ hoopoe

ἐπόψιμος ον that can be looked on *or* seen

ἐπόψιος ᾱ ον visible, manifest; all-seeing

ἔποψις εως ἡ view; range of vision, sight

ἑπτά seven

ἑπταβόειος ον **ἑπτάβοιος** ον of seven bulls' hides

ἑπταετής (*or* ἑπταέτης) ές seven years old, for seven years

ἑπτακαίδεκα seventeen

ἑπτακαιδέκατος η ον seventeenth

ἑπτάκις *adv* seven times

ἑπτακισμῡ́ριοι αι α seventy thousand

ἑπτακισχῑ́λιοι αι α seven thousand

ἑπτακόσιοι αι α seven hundred

ἑπτάλογχος ον of seven lances; under seven leaders

ἑπτάμηνος ον of seven months

ἑπτάπηχυς υ seven cubits long

ἑπταπόδης (*gen* ου) seven feet long

ἑπτάπυλος ον seven-gated

ἑπτάτονος ον seven-toned

ἕπταχα *adv* in seven parts

ἑπτέτης ες ▸ **ἑπταέτης**

ἕπω be busy *or* engaged with; go; come

ἐπῳδή ῆς ἡ incantation, magic song; spell, charm

ἐπῳδός όν acting as a charm; enchanter, helper

■ **ἡ ἐπῳδός** concluding stanza, epode

ἐπωμίς ίδος ἡ upper part of the shoulder; arm and shoulder

ἐπώμοτος ον on oath; sworn witness

ἐπωνυμίᾱ ᾱς ἡ surname, name

ἐπώνυμος ον **ἐπωνύμιος** ον named after, surnamed; giving one's name to

ἐπωτίδες ων αἱ beams projecting like oars on each side of a ship's bows, cat-heads; battering beams of a ship

ἐπ-ωφελέω aid, help

ἐπωφέλημα ατος τό help

ἐπώχατο *from* **ἐπέχω** they were shut

ἔρᾱζε *adv* to the earth

ἔραμαι ▸ **ἐράω**

ἐραννός ή όν lovely (of places)

ἐρανιστής οῦ ὁ contributor to an ἔρανος

ἔρανος ου ὁ meal to which everyone contributed a share, picnic; contribution; kindness

ἐρασιχρήματος ον loving money, covetous

ἐράσμιος ον **ἐραστός** ή όν lovely, charming, pleasant, amiable; welcome

ἐραστής οῦ ὁ lover, friend

ἐρατεινός ή όν ▸ **ἐράσμιος**

ἐρατίζω lust for

ἐρᾱτύω ▸ **ἐρητύω**

ἐράω *and pass* + *gen* love passionately, fall in love (with); desire, long for

ἐργάζομαι *mid* work, be busy; do, perform, accomplish, effect, cause; earn; carry on a trade; do to, commit upon

ἐργάθω ▸ **εἴργω**

ἐργαλεῖον ου τό tool, instrument

ἐργασείω have a mind to do

ἐργασίᾱ ᾱς ἡ work, business, occupation; husbandry; trade; effect; working at; workmanship; gain, profit

ἐργαστήριον ου τό workshop, factory

ἐργαστικός ή όν laborious, industrious

ἐργάτης ου ὁ worker, workman

ἐργατικός ή όν ▸ **ἐργαστικός**

ἐργάτις ιδος ἡ *fem of* **ἐργάτης**

ἔργμα ατος τό ▸ **ἔργον**

ἕργμα ατος τό confinement, prison

ἐργο-λαβέω contract for the carrying out of work

ἔργον ου τό work, deed, action, enterprise; fact, reality; business, occupation, employment, labour; husbandry; trade; war, combat; great *or* hard work; product of labour, building, cornfield; thing, matter, piece; circumstance

ἔργω ▸ **εἴργω**

ἐργώδης ες troublesome, difficult

ἔρδω (*also* ἕρδω) do, make, act; offer, sacrifice

ἐρεβεννός ή όν dark, gloomy

ἐρέβινθος ου ὁ chick-pea

ἔρεβος ους τό the dark nether world

ἐρεείνω *and mid* ask

ἐρεθίζω, ἐρέθω provoke, irritate, tease, excite

ἐρείδω ἐρείσω ἤρεισα *act tr* prop, support; press, urge, push; *act intr* lean against; rush on; *pass and mid* + *dat* prop *or* support oneself, lean upon; be fixed in

ἐρείκω tear, break, crush; pierce; burst

ἐρείπια ων τά ruins

ἐρείπω *act tr* pull down, dash down; *intr and pass* fall down in ruins

ἔρεισμα ατος τό prop, support

ἐρεμνός ή όν dark, gloomy

ἐρέπτομαι *mid* feed on

ἐρέσσω *aor* ἤρεσσα row; move quickly, ply

ἐρέτης ου ὁ rower

ἐρετμόν οῦ τό oar

ἐρεύγομαι[1] spit out, vomit; splash up, surge; break out

ἐρεύγομαι[2] roar

ἐρευθέδανον ου τό (a plant) madder

ἐρεύθω make red

ἔρευνα ης ἡ inquiry

ἐρευνάω search after, inquire (into), examine

ἐρέφω cover, roof in; crown

ἐρέχθω rend; dash, shatter

ἐρέω[1] *fut* I shall say

ἐρέω[2], **ἐρέομαι** *mid* **εἴρομαι** ask, inquire, question

ἐρημίᾱ ᾱς ἡ solitude, desert, loneliness; helplessness; absence, want

ἐρῆμος (*or* ἔρημος) (η) ον lonely, solitary, desert, desolate, waste; helpless, needy, destitute
■ **ἡ ἐρήμη (δίκη)** trial in which one party does not appear (thus letting the judgement go by default)

ἐρημόω make solitary, desolate, devastate, evacuate; deprive, bereave; abandon

ἐρήμωσις εως ἡ desolation; devastation

ἐρητύω keep back, check, hinder, restrain

ἐριαύχην (*gen* ενος) with a high-arching neck

ἐριβρεμέτης (*gen* ου) loud-thundering (of Zeus)

ἐριβῶλαξ (*gen* ακος) **ἐρίβωλος** ον with large clods, very fertile

ἐρίγδουπος ον thundering, loud-roaring

ἐριδαίνω ▸ ἐρίζω

ἐριδμαίνω provoke, irritate

ἐρίδουπος ον ▸ **ἐρίγδουπος**

ἐρίζω quarrel, contend, rival; be a match for, be equal to

ἐρίηρος ον dear, loving, beloved

ἐρῑθείᾱ ᾱς ἡ canvassing for public office, intringuing

ἐριθηλής ές luxurious, fertile

ἔρῑθος ὁ/ἡ day labourer; reaper

ἐρικῡδής ές glorious, famous

ἐρίμῡκος ον loud-bellowing

ἐρῑνεός οῦ ὁ wild fig-tree

Ἐρῑνῦς ύος ἡ Erinus (an avenging Fury) revenge, punishment; curse; destruction

ἔριον ου τό wool

ἐριούνης ου ὁ **ἐριούνιος** ου ὁ helper; luck-bringer (of Hermes)

ἐριουργέω work in wool

ἔρις ιδος ἡ quarrel, strife, discord, animosity; jealousy; combat; zeal, contention

ἐρισθενής ές very mighty

ἔρισμα ατος τό cause of a quarrel

ἐριστάφυλος ον with large clusters

ἐριστός ή όν be disputed

ἐρίτῑμος ον most honoured, highly prized

ἐρίφειος ον of a kid

ἔριφος ου ὁ/ἡ **ἐρίφιον** ου τό goat, kid

ἑρκεῖος (*or* ἕρκειος) ον belonging to a yard *or* enclosure; house-protecting

ἑρκίον ου τό **ἕρκος** εος τό fence, enclosure, hedge, wall; farmyard; defence, protection; snare, net

ἑρκτή ῆς ἡ ▸ **εἱρκτή**

ἕρμα[1] ατος τό prop, support, defence; reef, rock; hill; foundation, cause

ἕρμα[2] ατος τό earring; foundation, cause

ἕρμαιον ου τό godsend, windfall

ἑρμηνείᾱ ᾱς ἡ speech; interpretation

ἑρμηνεύς έως ου **ἑρμηνευτής** οῦ ὁ herald; interpreter, expounder

ἑρμηνεύω expound, interpret, translate, explain

ἑρμῑ́ς ῖνος ὁ bed-post

ἑρμογλυφεῖον ου τό sculptor's workshop

ἔρνος εος τό shoot, scion, child

ἐρξίης ου ὁ worker

ἔρομαι *mid* ask, inquire

ἑρπετόν οῦ τό creeping animal, reptile; living being

ἕρπω, ἑρπύζω creep, crawl; go; come

ἔρρω ἐρρήσω ἤρρησα walk slowly, go away; perish, be lost

ἐρρωμένος η ον strong, stout; vigorous

ἔρρωσο *aor impv from* **ῥώννυμι** *written at the end of a letter* farewell

ἔρση ης ἡ (*also* ἕρση) dew, dewdrop; new-born *or* late-born lamb

ἐρσήεις εσσα εν dewy; fresh

ἔρσην (*gen* ενος) ▸ **ἄρρην**

ἐρύγμηλος ον loud-bellowing

ἐρυθαίνω make red; *pass* become red, blush

ἐρύθημα ατος τό redness; inflammation

ἐρυθραίνομαι, ἐρυθριάω blush

ἐρυθρός ᾱ́ όν red

ἐρῡ́κω, ἐρῡκανάω, ἐρῡκάνω keep back, stop, restrain, check, hinder; keep away; *mid and pass* be detained

ἔρυμα ατος τό fence, bulwark; fort; castle

ἐρυμός ή όν fortified, protected

ἐρύομαι *mid* save, rescue, protect; watch, observe; lie in wait (for), espy; keep off, check

ἐρυσάρματες ων οἱ chariot-drawing (of horses)

ἐρυσίβη ης ἡ mildew

ἐρυσίπτολις protecting the city

ἐρυστός ή όν drawn

ἐρύω draw, push; bend [a bow]; tear off *or* away, snatch from; drag, pull, trail; *mid* draw to oneself, snatch; outweigh

ἐρχατάομαι *pass* be shut up

ἔρχομαι† *mid* come, go, arrive at; march, travel, drive; flow, fly; go away, march out; be lost; come back, return; be about to do

ἐρῶ *fut from* **λέγω**

ἐρωδιός οῦ ὁ heron

ἐρωέω[1] flow, stream

ἐρωέω[2] rest, repose, cease from; stay behind; *intr* drive *or* push back

ἐρωή[1] ῆς ἡ quick motion, force, impetus

ἐρωή[2] ῆς ἡ rest

ἐρώμενος ου ὁ the beloved, loved one

ἔρως ωτος ὁ love; desire

ἐρωτάω† ask, request; inquire

ἐρώτημα ατος τό **ἐρώτησις** εως ἡ question; questioning

ἐρωτικός ή όν of love; prone to love, amorous

ἐς ▸ **εἰς**

ἐσθέω clothe

ἔσθημα ατος τό **ἐσθής** ῆτος ἡ **ἔσθησις** εως ἡ garment, dress, clothing

ἐσθίω† eat

ἐσθλός ή όν good, kind; generous, noble; brave, valiant; valuable; lucky, favourable

ἔσθος τό ▸ **ἔσθημα**

ἔσθ' ὅτε *adv* sometimes

ἔσθω ▸ **ἔδω, ἐσθίω**

ἑσμός οῦ ὁ swarm, flock; plenty

ἔσομαι *fut from* **εἰμι**

ἔσοπτρον ου τό mirror

ἑσπέρᾱ ᾱς ἡ evening; west

ἑσπέριος ᾱ ον **ἕσπερος** ον in the evening; western

ἕσπερος ου ὁ ▸ **ἑσπέρα**

ἔσπετε ▸ **εἴπετε** *see* **εἶπον**

ἑσπόμην *aor from* **ἕπομαι**

ἑσσόομαι ▸ **ἡσσάομαι**

ἔσσυμαι *see* **σεύω**

ἐσσύμενος η ον eager, hasty

ἕσσων ον ▸ **ἥσσων**

ἔστε *adv and conj* till, until; as long as; up to

ἑστίᾱ ᾱς ἡ hearth; house, home, family; altar; Hestia (goddess of the hearth)

ἑστίᾱμα ατος τό **ἑστίᾱσις** εως ἡ feast, banquet

ἑστιᾱ́τωρ ορος ὁ entertainer

ἑστιάω entertain, give a feast; *pass* be a guest, be feasted

ἑστιοῦχος ον guarding the house; with holy altars

ἑστιῶτις (*gen* ιδος) belonging to the house

ἕστωρ ορος ὁ pole-nail, peg at the end of the pole

ἐσχάρᾱ ᾱς ἡ hearth; fireplace; pan of coals; altar

ἐσχατιᾱ́ ᾶς ἡ extreme part, remotest place, end, border

ἔσχατος η ον the farthest, remotest, uttermost, extreme; latest; highest; last; worst; lowest

ἐσχατόων *fem* ωσα the farthest; lying on the edge *or* border

ἔσχον *aor from* **ἔχω**

ἔσω ▸ **εἴσω**

ἔσωθεν *adv* from within; within

ἐσώτερος ᾱ ον inner

ἑταίρᾱ ᾱς ἡ female companion *or* friend; sweetheart; courtesan, prostitute

ἑταιρείᾱ ᾱς ἡ companionship, association, brotherhood; political club

ἑταιρεῖος ᾱ ον of comrades *or* partisans

ἑταιρίᾱ ᾱς ἡ ▸ **ἑταιρεία**

ἑταιρίζω be a companion; *mid* choose as a companion

ἑταιρικός ή όν ▸ **ἑταιρεῖος**

ἑταιρίς ίδος ἡ ▸ **ἑταίρα**

ἑταῖρος ου ὁ companion, comrade, mate, friend; member of a political club

ἑταρίζω ▸ **ἑταιρίζω**

ἕταρος ου ὁ ▸ **ἑταῖρος**

ἐτεός ά όν true, real

ἑτεραλκής ές giving strength to one of two, changing, doubtful

ἑτερήμερος ον on alternate days

ἑτέρηφι *adv* with one *or* the other hand

ἑτερόγλωσσος ον speaking a foreign language

ἑτερο-διδασκαλέω teach false doctrine

ἑτερο-ζυγέω be yoked in an unequal partnership (with another)

ἑτεροῖος ᾱ ον of a different kind

ἕτερος ᾱ ον the other, one of two, another; the second; different, of another kind; at variance

ἑτέρωθεν *adv* from the other side; on the other side

ἑτέρωθι *adv* on the other side; elsewhere, to another place, sideways

ἔτης ου ὁ kinsman, clansman; friend

ἐτησίαι ων οἱ periodical winds

ἐτήσιος ον for a year; yearly

ἐτήτυμος ον true, real, genuine

ἔτι *adv* yet, as yet, yet longer, still; besides

ἑτοιμάζω ἑτοιμάσω get ready, prepare

ἑτοιμασίᾱ ᾱς ἡ readiness

ἑτοῖμος (*or* ἕτοιμος) (η) ον ready, at hand, disposable; willing, quick, active, prompt; easy; real, confirmed

ἑτοιμότης ητος ἡ readiness

ἔτος ους τό year

ἐτός *adv* without reason, for nothing

ἔτυμος ον real, true, actual

ἐτώσιος ον useless, unprofitable

εὖ (*also* ἐΰ) *adv* well, properly, rightly; luckily

εὗ ▸ **οὗ**

εὐ-αγγελίζω *and mid* bring good news

εὐαγγέλιον ου τό good news, glad tidings, the gospel; reward for good news

εὐαγγελιστής οῦ ὁ evangelist

εὐαγής ές guiltless, pure, pious; purifying; shining, conspicuous

εὔαργος ον lucky in hunting

εὐάγωγος ον easily led

εὔαδε *aor from* **ἁνδάνω**

εὐάζω cry εὖα (celebrating Bacchus)

εὐᾱής ές blowing fair; favourable

εὐαίρετος ον easy to be taken, chosen *or* known

εὐαίων (*gen* ωνος) happy; making happy

εὐᾱ́μερος ον ▸ **εὐήμερος**

εὐανδρίᾱ ᾱς ἡ plenty of good men; manly spirit

εὐάνεμος ον well aired
εὐανθής ές blooming; flowery
εὐαπήγητος ον easy to describe
εὐαπόβατος ον convenient for disembarking
εὐαποτείχιστος ον easy to blockade
εὐαρεστέω + *dat* please well
εὐάρεστος ον well-pleasing, acceptable
εὐαρίθμητος ον easy to be counted
εὐάρματος ον famous for chariots
εὐαρμοστίᾱ ᾱς ἡ harmony, evenness of temper
εὐάρμοστος ον well-adapted, harmonious, even
εὐαυγής ές bright, shining
εὐβάστακτος ον easy to be carried
εὔβατος ον accessible
εὔβοτος ον rich in pastures and cattle
εὔβοτρυς υ rich in grapes
εὐβουλίᾱ ᾱς ἡ good counsel, prudence
εὔβουλος ον well-advised, prudent
εὐγάθητος ον joyous
εὖγε ▸ **εὖ γε** well done! well said! hooray!
εὐγένεια ᾱς ἡ noble descent; generosity
εὐγένειος ον well bearded, well-maned
εὐγενής ές well-born, noble, generous
εὔγλωσσος ον eloquent
εὖγμα ατος τό boast; prayer, vow
εὔγναμπτος ον well bent
εὐγνώμων ον generous; kind; fair; sensible
εὔγνωστος ον well-known; visible
εὐ-δαιμονέω be happy *or* prosperous
εὐδαιμονίᾱ ᾱς ἡ happiness, prosperity
εὐ-δαιμονίζω consider happy
εὐδαιμονικός ή όν of happiness; happy; causing happiness
εὐδαίμων ον happy; fortunate, lucky; prosperous, wealthy
εὐδείελος ον far-seen
εὔδηλος ον quite clear
εὐδίᾱ ᾱς ἡ fair weather; calm; security
εὐδιάβατος ον easy to be crossed
εὐδικίᾱ ᾱς ἡ justice
εὔδιος ον fair, clear, calm
εὔδμητος ον well-built
εὐ-δοκέω be pleased with; consent to
εὐδοκίᾱ ᾱς ἡ satisfaction, delight; wish
εὐ-δοκιμέω be of good reputation, be famous *or* distinguished
εὐδόκιμος ον honoured, esteemed, renowned
εὐ-δοξέω ▸ **εὐδοκιμέω**
εὐδοξίᾱ ᾱς ἡ good repute, renown; approval
εὔδοξος ον ▸ **εὐδόκιμος**
εὐδρακής ές sharp-sighted
εὕδω εὑδήσω sleep; fall asleep
εὐειδής ές well-shaped
εὐέλεγκτος ον easy to refute *or* convince
εὔελπις ι hopeful
εὐεξάλειπτος ον easy to be blotted out
εὐεξέλεγκτος ον ▸ **εὐέλεγκτος**
εὐεξίᾱ ᾱς ἡ good state; well-being
εὐέπεια ᾱς ἡ kind words; eloquence
εὐεπής ές well-speaking; well-spoken
εὐεπιβούλευτος ον open to treachery *or* stratagems
εὐεπίθετος ον easy to be attacked
εὐεργεσίᾱ ᾱς ἡ acting well, kindness, good deed; good service (to the state), the title of benefactor
εὐ-εργετέω do good, show kindness; *pass* receive a kindness
εὐεργέτημα ατος τό ▸ **εὐεργεσία**
εὐεργέτης ου ὁ benefactor; well-deserving man; the honorary title of benefactor

εὐεργής ές well-made, well-wrought; well done

εὐεργός όν doing good; easy to make

εὐερκής ές well-fenced

εὔερος ον with good wool

εὐεστώ οῦς ἡ well-being, happiness

εὐετηρίᾱ ᾱς ἡ good harvest

εὐεύρετος ον easy to find

εὐέφοδος ον easily accessible

εὔζυγος ον well-benched

εὔζωνος ον (of women) well-girdled; active

εὐηγενής ές ▸ **εὐγενής**

εὐηγεσίᾱ ᾱς ἡ good government

εὐήθεια ᾱς ἡ goodness; simplicity, silliness

εὐήθης ες good natured; simple, silly

εὐηθικός ή όν ▸ **εὐηθης**

εὐήκης ες well-pointed

εὐήλατος ον easy to ride over

εὐημέρεω be happy *or* successful

εὐημερίᾱ ᾱς ἡ fine *or* happy day

εὐήμερος ον bringing a fine day

εὐήνεμος ον ▸ **εὐάνεμος**

εὐήνωρ (*gen* ορος) manly; giving manly strength

εὐήρατος ον lovely

εὐήρετμος ον rowing well; well-rowed

εὐήρης ες manageable

εὐηφενής ές wealthy

εὐθάλασσος ον prosperous by sea

εὐθαρσής ές courageous, manly

εὐθενέω *and pass* thrive, be prosperous

εὐθεράπευτος ον easy to win by kindness *or* attention

εὔθετος ον convenient

εὐθέως ▸ **εὐθύς**

εὐθηνέω ▸ **εὐθενέω**

εὐθηνιάρχης ου ὁ commissioner of the food-supply

εὔθριξ (*gen* τριχος) having beautiful hair

εὔθρονος ον with beautiful throne

εὐθύ *adv* ▸ **εὐθύς**

εὐθυ-δρομέω run *or* come straight

εὐ-θῡμέω *and mid* be of good cheer, be happy

εὐθῡμίᾱ ᾱς ἡ cheerfulness, gladness

εὔθῡμος ον well-disposed; cheerful, glad; eager

εὐθῡ́νη ης ἡ **εὔθῡνα** ης ἡ giving an account; account, vindication; chastisement; (at Athens) public examination of the conduct of officials (held on the expiration of their term of office)

εὐθῡ́νω *and mid* make *or* direct straight, guide; correct; blame; accuse, call to account; examine the conduct (of an official); punish

εὐθύς εῖα ύ straight, direct; plain, honest

■ **εὐθύς, εὐθύ, εὐθέως** *adv* forthwith, at once; without reserve; for instance; straight to *or* towards

εὐθύτης ητος ἡ straightness; justice, righteousness

εὐθύωρον *adv* ▸ **εὐθύς**

εὔιος ον shouting; rejoicing; Bacchic

εὔιππος ον with good horses; well-mounted

εὐκαθαίρετος ον easy to conquer

εὐκαιρέω have leisure

εὐκαιρίᾱ ᾱς ἡ opportunity

εὔκαιρος ον in time, seasonable, opportune

εὐκαμπής ές well-bent, curved; flexible

εὐκάρδιος ον stout-hearted

εὔκαρπος ον fruitful

εὐκατάλυτος ον easy to destroy

εὐκαταφρόνητος ον despicable

εὐκατέργαστος ον easy to work *or* digest

εὐκατηγόρητος ον easy to accuse

εὐκέατος ον easily split

εὔκερως ων well-horned

εὔκηλος ον ▶ **ἕκηλος**

εὐκλεής ές famous, glorious, noble

εὔκλεια ᾱς ἡ good repute, renown

εὐκλειής ▶ **εὐκλεής**

εὐκλῄς (*gen* ῖδος) well-closed

εὐκνήμῑς (*gen* ῑδος) with good greaves

εὔκολος ον well-disposed; easy; contented

εὐκομιδής ές well cared for

εὔκομος ▶ **ἠύκομος**

εὔκοπος ον easy, without pains

εὐκοσμίᾱ ᾱς ἡ good order; modesty, decency

εὔκοσμος ον well-ordered; well-adorned, graceful; easy to arrange

εὐκρινής ές well-ordered; distinct, clear

εὐκρότητος ον well-hammered

εὐκταῖος ᾱ ον prayed for, votive

εὐκτίμενος η ον **εὔκτιτος** ον well-built, well-made; good to live on

εὐκτός ή όν wished for, desirable

εὐλάβεια ᾱς ἡ caution, circumspection; awe, fear; piety

εὐλαβέομαι *pass* be cautious, circumspect *or* careful; fear, beware of; reverence, worship; care for

εὐλαβής ές cautious, circumspect, anxious; conscientious; devout

εὐλάζω plough

εὐλάκᾱ ἡ ploughshare

εὐλείμων ον rich in meadows

εὔλεκτρος ον fit for marriage, bridal, lovely

εὐλή ῆς ἡ maggot, worm

εὔληπτος ον easily conquered *or* taken

εὔληρα ων τά reins

εὐ-λογέω praise; give thanks; bless

εὐλογητός ή όν blessed

εὐλογίᾱ ᾱς ἡ praise, eulogy; fair-speaking; blessing; kindness, bounty

εὔλογος ον reasonable; probable

εὔλοφος ον with a fine plume *or* crest (of a helmet)

εὔλυτος ον easy to dissolve

εὐμάθεια ᾱς ἡ readiness at learning, docility

εὐμαθής ές docile; easily learned *or* understood

εὐμάρεια ᾱς ἡ (*also* εὐμαρείᾱ ᾱς ἡ) easiness; convenience; possibility; protection against; abundance; comfort; shitting

εὐμαρής ές easy; convenient

εὐμεγέθης ες very large *or* great

εὐμένεια ᾱς ἡ good will

εὐμενής ές **εὐμενέτης** (*gen* ου) well-disposed, kind; favourable; convenient

εὐμετάβολος ον changeable, fickle

εὐμετάδοτος ον liberal

εὐμεταχείριστος ον easy to manage *or* conquer

εὔμηλος ον rich in sheep

εὐμήχανος ον inventive, ingenious

εὔμιτος ον with fine threads

ἐϋμμελίης (*gen* ου) skilled in thrusting spears; armed with a good ash spear

εὔμνᾱστος ον well-remembering

εὔμορφος ον well-shaped

εὐμουσίᾱ ᾱς ἡ taste for beauty and art

εὔμουσος ον musical

εὐνάζω put to sleep; place in ambush; lull to sleep; assuage; *pass and mid* lie down; go asleep; rest; have sexual intercourse

εὐναιετάων ουσα ον **εὐναιόμενος** η ον well-inhabited *or* peopled

εὐναῖος ᾱ ον in one's bed, on one's couch; matrimonial; resting

εὐνᾱ(σ)τήριον ου τό **εὐνή** ῆς ἡ bed, couch; marriage-bed; bedroom; stone used as an anchor

ε

εὐνῆθεν *adv* out of bed

εὐνήτρια ᾱς ἡ **εὖνις**[1] ιδος ἡ wife

εὖνις[2] ι(δ)ος ὁ/ἡ + *gen* one who is bereft *or* destitute

ἐΰννητος ον well-woven

εὐνοέω be well-disposed, favourable *or* friendly

εὔνοια ᾱς ἡ good will, kindness, favour

εὐνοϊκός ή όν benevolent, friendly

εὐ-νομέομαι *pass* have good laws

εὐνομίᾱ ᾱς ἡ having good laws; order, legal constitution

εὔνοος ον (*also* εὔνους ουν) well-disposed, kind, friendly, benevolent

εὐνουχίζω castrate

εὐνοῦχος ου ὁ eunuch; chamberlain

εὐνώμᾱς (*gen* ου) quick-moving, mobile

εὔξε(ι)νος ον hospitable
■ **πόντος εὔξε(ι)νος** the Black Sea

εὔξεστος ον **εὔξοος** ον well-polihsed

εὐξυμ-, εὐξυν- *see* **εὐσυμ-, εὐσυν-**

εὔοδος ον easy to travel over *or* on

εὐοῖ *int* euoi! (ecstatic cry used in the worship of Dionysus)

εὔοικος ον convenient for dwelling in; economical

εὔολβος ον very wealthy

εὔοπλος ον well-armed

εὐόργητος ον good-tempered

εὐορκέω keep one's oath

εὔορκος ον true to one's oath; according to an oath

εὔορμος ον with good anchorage

εὐοσμίᾱ ᾱς ἡ sweet fragrance

εὐπάθεια ᾱς ἡ sensual enjoyment, luxury; comfort, ease

εὐπαθέω enjoy oneself, make merry

εὐπαιδίᾱ ᾱς ἡ having good children

εὔπαις (*gen* παιδος) having good children

εὐπάρεδρος ον persevering; constantly waiting (on)

εὐπατέρεια ᾱς ἡ daughter of a noble father

εὐπατρίδης (*gen* ου) **εὔπατρις** (*gen* ιδος) of a noble father; noble

εὐπειθής ές **εὔπειστος** ον obedient, yielding

εὔπεπλος ον with a fine robe

εὐπερίστατος ον easily ensnaring

εὐπέτεια ᾱς ἡ easiness, easiness of getting

εὐπετής ές easy, convenient, without trouble

εὐπηγής ές **εὔπηκτος** ον well put together, stout, compact

εὔπιστος ον trustworthy

εὔπλαστος ον easy to mould

εὔπλειος ον well-filled

εὐπλεκής ές **εὔπλεκτος** ον well-plaited

εὔπλοια ᾱς ἡ good sailing

εὐπλόκαμος ον **εὐπλοκαμῖς** (*gen* ῖδος) with fine locks

εὐπλυνής ές well-washed

εὐποίητος ον well made, well-wrought

εὐποιΐᾱ ᾱς ἡ beneficence

εὔπομπος ον well-conducting

εὐπορέω *aor* εὐπόρησα have abundance *or* plenty (of) + *gen*; be prosperous *or* successful; find a way, be able; *tr* supply in abundance

εὐπορίᾱ ᾱς ἡ facility, opportunity; means, supply, resources; plenty, wealth

εὔπορος ον easy to pass over; convenient, easy; ready, ingenious, inventive; wealthy, rich

εὐπρᾱγέω be well off

εὐπρᾱγίᾱ ᾱς ἡ **εὐπρᾱξίᾱ** ᾱς ἡ well-doing, success, welfare; good action

εὔπρᾱκτος ον easily done

εὐπρέπεια ᾱς ἡ comely appearance, beauty; speciousness, excuse

εὐπρεπής ές comely, good-looking, decent; distinguished, conspicuous; specious, shining

εὔπρηστος ον strong-blowing

εὐπρόσδεκτος ον acceptable

εὐπροσήγορος ον courteous

εὐπρόσοδος ον accessible; affable

εὐπροσωπέω make a good show

εὐπρόσωπος ον with a fine face; cheerful

εὐπροφάσιστος ον convincing, plausible

εὔπρυμνος ον with a fine stern

εὔπτερος ον well-winged

εὔπτυκτος ον easily folded

εὔπυργος ον with good towers

εὔπωλος ον with fine colts

εὐρακύλων ωνος ὁ northeast wind

εὐράξ *adv* sideways

εὐραφής ές well-sewn

εὕρεσις εως ἡ finding, discovery

εὑρετής οῦ ὁ inventor

εὑρετικός ή όν inventive

εὑρετός ή όν found, invented; to be found

εὕρημα ατος τό a thing found; windfall, unexpected gain; foundling; invention

εὔρῑνος ον **εὔρῑς** ῑ (*gen* ῖνος) keen-scented

εὔρῑπος ου ὁ strait, narrow sea; an unstable person

εὑρίσκω† find, find out, discover; invent, contrive; procure; meet; gain, obtain; (of merchandise) fetch *or* earn money

εὔροος ον fine-flowing

εὖρος[1] ου ὁ east wind, southeast wind

εὖρος[2] ους τό breadth, width

ἐΰρραφής ▸ **εὐραφής**

ἐΰρρεής ές **ἐΰρρείτης** (*gen* ου) ▸ **εὔροος**

εὐρυάγυιος ᾱ ον with wide streets

εὐρυεδής ές spacious

εὐρυθμίᾱ ᾱς ἡ harmony, keeping good time; proportion

εὔρυθμος ον in good time, fitting well; rhythmical; graceful

εὐρυκρείων (*gen* οντος) wide-ruling

εὐρυμέτωπος ον (of oxen) with broad foreheads

εὐρῡ́νω make wide *or* broad

εὐρύνωτος ον broad-backed

εὐρυόδειος ᾱ ον with broad ways (of the earth)

εὐρύοπα ὁ far-thundering; far-seeing

εὐρύπορος ον with broad ways (of the sea)

εὐρύπρωκτος ον wide-arsed, bugger

εὐρυπυλής ές with wide gates

εὐρυρέεθρος ον **εὐρυρέων** ουσα ον broad-flowing

εὐρύς εῖα ύ broad, wide; widespread

εὐρυσθενής ές wide-ruling

εὐρυφυής ές growing broad

εὐρύχορος ον with spacious places for dancing

εὐρυχωρίᾱ ᾱς ἡ open space, free room, open country

εὐρώδης ες ▸ **εὐρύς**

εὐρώεις εσσα εν mouldy; dark

εὐρώς ῶτος ὁ mould, dank, decay

εὔρωστος ον stout, strong

ἐΰς **ἐΰ** good, brave

εὐσέβεια ᾱς ἡ reverence, piety; filial love

εὐσεβέω be pious *or* religious

εὐσεβής ές pious, religious; reverent

εὔσελμος ον well-benched *or* -decked

εὔσημος ον of good omen; clear, manifest

εὔσκαρθμος ον swift-springing, bounding

εὐσκέπαστος ον well-covered, protected

εὐσκευέω be well equipped

ε

εὐσκίαστος ον well-shaded

εὔσκοπος keen-sighted; commanding a wide-view; shooting well

εὔσοια ᾱς ἡ welfare, happiness

εὔσπλαγχνος ον compassionate

ἐΰσσελμος ον ▸ **εὔσελμος**

ἐΰσσωτρος ον with good wheels

εὐσταθής ές steadfast, firmly built

εὐσταλής ές well-equipped; light-armed; happy, easy; decent, simple

εὐστέφανος ον well-crowned; well-walled

εὔστολος ον ▸ **εὐσταλής**

εὔστομος ον speaking good words; keeping silence

εὔστρεπτος ον **εὐστρεφής** ές **εὔστροφος** ον well-twisted

εὔστῡλος ον with fine pillars

εὐσύμβλητος ον easy to explain *or* guess

εὐσύμβολος ον sociable

εὐσύνετος ον intelligent

εὐσχημοσύνη ης ἡ good grace, decent behaviour

εὐσχήμων ον graceful, elegant; decent, becoming; specious, shining

εὐτακτέω be orderly; be obedient

εὔτακτος ον well-arranged; well-disciplined, orderly; modest

εὐταξίᾱ ᾱς ἡ good order, discipline, obedience

εὖτε *adv* at the time when, during the time when; as often as; in the case that; just as

εὐτειχής ές well-walled

εὐτέλεια ᾱς ἡ cheapness; frugality, economy

εὐτελής ές cheap; worthless, vile; frugal, plain

εὔτμητος ον well-cut

εὔτολμος ον daring, bold

εὔτονος ον sinewy, strong

εὐτραπελίᾱ ᾱς ἡ ready wit, liveliness; politeness

εὐτράπελος ον versatile, witty, clever; cunning

εὐτραφής ές well-fed, fat

εὐτρεπής ές ready, prepared

εὐτρεπίζω εὐτρεπιῶ get ready, prepare; repair

εὐτρεφής ές ▸ **εὐτραφής**

εὔτρητος ον well-pierced

εὔτριχος ον ▸ **εὔθριξ**

εὐτροφίᾱ ᾱς ἡ good diet, thriving condition; fatness

εὔτροχος ον with good wheels

εὔτυκτος ον well-made, well-wrought

εὐτυχέω be lucky, meet with success; turn out well

εὐτύχημα ατος τό piece of good luck; success

εὐτυχής ές lucky, fortunate, happy; prosperous, successful

εὐτυχίᾱ ᾱς ἡ ▸ **εὐτύχημα**

εὔυδρος ον well-watered

εὐυφής ές well-woven

εὐφαρέτρης (*gen* ου) with beautiful quiver

εὐφημέω speak words of good omen; observe solemn silence

εὔφημος ον speaking words of good omen; religiously silent; auspicious; of good sound

εὐφιλής ές well-beloved

εὔφλεκτος ον easy to set on fire

εὐφορέω bear good fruit; be productive

εὔφορος ον easy to bear *or* wear; able to endure, patient

εὐφραδής ές eloquent, considerate

εὐφραίνω εὐφρανῶ ηὔφρᾱνα cheer, gladden; *mid and pass* rejoice, be glad *or* cheerful

εὐφρονέων ουσα ον well-meaning; sensible

εὐφρόνη ης ἡ the kindly time, night *euphemism*

εὐφροσύνη ης ἡ merriment, cheerfulness; joy

εὔφρων ον cheerful, joyous; generous; cheering

εὐφυής ές well-grown, comely; gifted, naturally clever; serviceable

εὐφύλακτος ον easy to guard; safe

εὐφωνίᾱ ᾱς ἡ good *or* loud voice

εὔφωνος ον sweet-voiced, loud-voiced

εὔχαλκος ον finely wrought of brass *or* copper

εὔχαρις ι graceful, lovely, pleasing; witty; decent

εὐχαριστέω + *dat* be thankful (to); return thanks (to)

εὐχαριστίᾱ ᾱς ἡ thankfulness; thanksgiving

εὐχάρι(σ)τος ον thankful; pleasant; witty

εὔχειρ (*gen* ειρος) handy, dextrous

εὐχείρωτος ον easy to overcome

εὐχέρεια ᾱς ἡ readiness, dexterity; inclination

εὐχερής ές placid; easy, without trouble; ready, quick; reckless, hasty

εὐχετάομαι ▸ **εὔχομαι**

εὐχή ῆς ἡ prayer; vow; wish; curse

εὔχλοος ον fresh and green (of Demeter)

εὔχομαι boast; assert, profess; pray, beseech; wish, vow

εὖχος ους τό boast; glory; vow; wish

εὔχρηστος ον fit for use, serviceable

εὔχροος ον (*also* εὔχρους ουν) **εὐχροής** ές of good complexion

εὔχρῡσος ον rich in gold

εὐχωλή ῆς ἡ boast, pride; shout; object of pride; prayer; vow; wish

εὐχωλιμαῖος ᾱ ον bound by a vow

εὐψῡχέω be of good courage

εὐψῡχίᾱ ᾱς ἡ courage

εὔψῡχος ον courageous

εὕω *aor* εὗσα singe

εὐώδης ες sweet-scented, fragrant

εὐωδίᾱ ᾱς ἡ fragrance

εὔωνος ον cheap

εὐώνυμος ον of good name, of good omen; of the left hand

εὐῶπις (*gen* ιδος) fair-eyed, fair to look at

εὐωχέω treat well, feast, entertain; *pass* be entertained; make a hearty meal (of)

εὐωχίᾱ ᾱς ἡ feasting; good fare, good cheer

εὐώψ ῶπος ▸ **εὐῶπις**

ἐφ-αγιστεύω, ἐφ-αγνίζω observe holy rites; make offerings on a grave

ἐφ-αιρέω choose in addition

ἐφ-άλλομαι *mid* spring upon *or* towards

ἔφαλος ον by the sea

ἐφάμιλλος ον disputed; rivalling; equal

ἐφ-ανδάνω + *dat* please

ἐφάπαξ *adv* at once, once for all

ἐφ-άπτω fasten to, tie to; decree, cause; *mid* + *gen* touch, grasp; undertake, partake of; reach, attain

ἐφ-αρμόζω fit on, adapt, put on; add; *intr* be fit

ἐφέδρᾱ ᾱς ἡ siege

ἐφ-εδρεύω sit at *or* upon; lie in wait

ἔφεδρος ον seated upon; lying in wait; lying in reserve; fresh enemy

ἐφέζομαι *mid* sit upon, by *or* near

ἐφ-ελκύω, ἐφ-έλκω draw on, attract; drag, trail after; *mid* draw to *or* after oneself

■ **ἐφελκόμενος** *pass participle* straggler

ἐφ-έννῡμι ▸ **ἐπιέννυμι**

ἐφεξῆς ▸ **ἑξῆς**

ἐφ-έπω follow; pursue, press on, drive on; run through; strive after, manage; *mid* + *gen* follow, pursue; yield, obey

ἐφέσπερος ον western

ἐφέστιος ον at the hearth, at the fireside; inmate, domestic; suppliant; protector of the household

ἐφέται ῶν οἱ the ephetae (the court at Athens which tried cases of homicide)

ἐφετμή ῆς ἡ order, injunction

ἐφευρετής οῦ ὁ inventor

ἐφ-εψιάομαι *mid* + *dat* mock at

ἐφ-ηβάω grow to maturity

ἐφηβείᾱ ᾱς ἡ the training given to 18-year-old Athenians

ἔφηβος ου ὁ grown-up youth; at Athens, one who had reached the age of 18 and would now do his military service

ἐφ-ηγέομαι *mid* + *dat* lead to [a place]

ἐφ-ήδομαι feel (mischievous) joy

ἐφ-ήκω arrive at; be present

ἔφ-ημαι sit at, on *or* by

ἐφημερίᾱ ᾱς ἡ daily service; selection of priests on duty

ἐφημέριος ον **ἐφήμερος** ον lasting one day, during the day, for one day, ephemeral

ἐφημοσύνη ης ἡ ▸ **ἐφετμή**

ἑφθός ή όν boiled

ἐφ-ιζάνω, ἐφ-ίζω *tr* set; *intr* sit on, at *or* by

ἐφ-ῑ́ημι *act tr* send to, against *or* at; launch, let go; incite; lay upon, impose, decree; permit, abandon, yield; *act intr* abandon oneself to + *dat*; *mid* + *gen* aim at, long for, desire; command, enjoin

ἐφ-ικνέομαι *mid* reach, arrive at; hit, touch

ἐφῑ́μερος ον longed for

ἐφίππιον ου τό saddle, saddle-cloth

ἔφιππος ον mounted, on horseback

ἐφ-ίστημι *act tr* set *or* place upon, at *or* near; establish, set up, fix, appoint, order; set over; check, stop; *act intr and mid* stand on, tread on; stand near; approach, impend, be at hand; surprise; stand against; assist; be set over, be at the head, direct; set [the mind] to, attend; halt, stop

ἐφ-οδεύω *and mid* go the rounds, inspect

ἐφ-οδιάζω supply with money *or* stores for travelling; *mid* receive money for travelling

ἐφόδιον ου τό money *or* supplies for travelling, travelling allowance

■ **τὰ ἐφόδια** ways and means, maintenance

ἔφοδος[1] ον accessible

ἔφοδος[2] ου ἡ way to, approach; communication, access; attack

ἐφόλκαιον ου τό rudder

ἐφολκός ον enticing

ἐφ-ομαρτέω go along (with), accompany

ἐφ-οπλίζω equip, get ready, prepare

ἐφ-οράω look on, oversee, inspect, observe; visit; choose; live to see

ἐφορεύω be an ephor (Spartan magistrate)

ἐφ-ορμάω stir up against; *pass* be stirred up *or* roused; set upon, assail, attack

ἐφ-ορμέω lie at anchor; blockade

ἐφορμή ῆς ἡ access, attack

ἐφόρμησις εως ἡ anchorage; blockade

ἐφ-ορμίζομαι *pass* come to anchor

ἔφορμος[1] ον lying at anchor

ἔφορμος[2] ου ὁ ▸ **ἐφόρμησις**

ἔφορος ου ὁ overseer, guardian; ephor (Spartan magistrate)

ἐφ-υβρίζω act violently *or* grossly antisocially; insult; maltreat

ἔφυδρος ον watery, bringing rain

ἐφ-υμνέω sing at *or* over; sing a funeral song; wish one something; curse

ἐφύπερθεν *adv* from above, above; over along

ἐφ-υστερίζω be later

ἐχέγγυος ον trustworthy, secure; on security

ἐχέθῡμος ον under self-control

ἐχεπευκής ές sharp, piercing

ἐχέφρων ον sensible, prudent
ἐχθαίρω *aor* ἤχθηρα hate
ἐχθαρτέος ᾱ ον to be hated, hateful
ἐχθές *adv* ▸ **χθές** yesterday
ἐχθοδοπέω show enmity towards
ἐχθοδοπός ή όν hateful
ἔχθος ους τό **ἔχθρᾱ** ᾱς ἡ hatred, enmity
ἐχθρός ᾱ́ όν hated, hateful; hating, hostile
■ **ὁ ἐχθρός** enemy, adversary
ἔχθω hate
ἔχιδνα ης ἡ adder, viper
ἐχῖνος ου ὁ hedgehog
ἔχμα ατος τό hindrance, obstacle, defence against; support, prop
ἐχυρός ᾱ́ όν firm, strong, secure, safe
ἔχω† *act tr* have; hold; possess, have wealth; inhabit; rule, govern; suffer; occupy; obtain, seize; have put on; contain, compass; know, be able; cause, imply, infer; preserve; detain; protect; retain, restrain, check, hinder; direct to, aim at; *act intr* behave, be disposed; be, be in a state + *adv*; stand fast, keep one's ground, hold out, endure; reach to; *mid* have *or* hold for oneself; *mid and pass* hold oneself to, cling to, depend upon; hold fast, continue; be attached *or* fixed to; border on, be next to; concern, affect; abstain, refrain
ἕψημα ατος τό what can be boiled
ἕψησις εως ἡ boiling
ἑψητός ή όν boiled
ἑψιάομαι *mid* jest, amuse oneself
ἕψω ἑψήσω ἥψησα boil
ἔωθα ▸ **εἴωθα**
ἕωθεν *adv* at dawn
ἑωθινός ή όν early in the morning
ἑωλοκρᾱσίᾱ ᾱς ἡ dregs, remains
ἕωμεν (*or* ἑῶμεν) *aor subj* we have had our fill (of war)
ἔῳξα *aor from* **οἴγνυμι**
ἑῷος ᾱ ον in the morning, at dawn; eastern
ἑώρᾱ ᾱς ἡ suspension, string
ἕως[1] ω ἡ dawn (of day), daybreak, morning; east
ἕως[2] *conj* as long as, while; until; in order that; *adv* for some time; till when
ἕωσπερ *conj and adv* until
ἑωσφόρος ου ὁ morning-star

Ζζ

ζ, Ζ (ζῆτα) sixth letter of the alphabet
■ **ζ′** *as a numeral* = 7
ζάγκλον ου τό sickle
ζᾱής ές strong blowing, stormy
ζάθεος ᾱ ον most holy
ζάκοτος ον very angry
ζάλη ης ἡ surge, spray; storm
ζαμενής ές very violent, raging, angry
ζάπλουτος ον very rich
ζατρεφής ές well-fed
ζαφλεγής ές fiery, vigorous
ζαχρηής ές vehement, impetuous, stormy
ζάχρῡσος ον rich in gold
ζάω ζήσω *or* βιώσομαι ἐβίων live, be alive; lead a life; live on, be strong
ζείδωρος ον corn-producing
ζειρᾱ́ ᾶς ἡ long cloak
ζευγ-ηλατέω drive a team of oxen; plough

ζ

ζευγηλάτης ου ὁ driver of a team of oxen, ploughman

ζευγῑ́της ου ὁ yoked in pairs ■ **οἱ ζευγῖται** the third of Solon's four classes of citizens (so called from their being able to keep a team (ζεῦγος) of oxen)

ζεύγλη ης ἡ collar of the yoke (through which the beasts' heads were put); cross-bar of the double rudder

ζεῦγμα ατος τό band, bond; bar, impediment; bridge

ζεύγνῡμι ζεύξω ἔζευξα join *or* link together; yoke, harness, fetter; marry, unite; join by a bridge, throw a bridge over, close; calk [ships]

ζεῦγος ους τό yoke, team; carriage, vehicle; pair, couple

ζευκτήριος ᾱ ον fit for joining *or* yoking

ζεῦξις εως ἡ yoking, harnessing; joining by a bridge

ζέφυρος ου ὁ zephyr, west wind; west

ζέω *aor* ἔζεσα boil, seethe; be hot, rage

ζηλεύω ▸ **ζηλόω**

ζηλήμων ον jealous

ζῆλος ου ὁ eagerness, emulation, admiration, jealousy, envy, zeal, passion, anger; enviable happiness

ζηλοτυπέω be jealous, envy

ζηλόω rival, vie with; admire, praise; envy, be jealous; strive to win

ζήλωμα ατος τό emulation, pursuit; high fortune

ζήλωσις εως ἡ emulation

ζηλωτής οῦ ὁ rival, admirer; zealot

ζηλωτός ή όν admired; envied; enviable

ζημίᾱ ᾱς ἡ damage, loss; penalty, punishment; fine

ζημιόω damage, punish; fine; *pass* be hurt, suffer damage

ζημιώδης causing loss, ruinous

ζημίωμα ατος τό punishment, penalty, fine

ζητέω seek, seek for; inquire into, examine; endeavour, desire, demand

ζήτημα ατος τό seeking, inquiry, examination; question, problem

ζήτησις εως ἡ seeking, seeking for, searching, inquiry, investigation; problem, dispute

ζητητής οῦ ὁ inquirer, searcher

ζητητός ή όν sought for

ζιζάνιον ου τό darnel (a weed that grows in wheat)

ζόη ης ἡ ▸ **ζωή**

ζορκάς άδος ἡ ▸ **δορκάς**

ζόφος ου ὁ darkness, gloom; realm of darkness (i.e. the underworld); west

ζύγαστρον ου τό wooden chest *or* book

ζυγόδεσμον ου τό yoke-thong (the band for fastening the yoke to the pole)

ζυγόν οῦ τό **ζυγός** οῦ ὁ yoke, cross-bar; team, pair; bridge of a lyre; bank of oars; beam [of a balance], balance; row, line

ζυγωτός ή όν yoked

ζῡ́μη ης ἡ leaven; corruption

ζῡμῑ́της (*gen* ου) leavened

ζῡμόω leaven, cause to ferment

ζωάγρια ων τά reward for saving a life

ζωγραφέω paint, paint a picture of + *acc*

ζωγραφίᾱ ᾱς ἡ painting

ζωγράφος ου ὁ painter

ζωγρέω take alive, take captive; spare and leave alive; restore to life

ζωγρίᾱ ᾱς ἡ catching alive

ζῴδιον ου τό small animal; small figure, image

ζωή ῆς ἡ life; lifetime; manner *or* mode of life; subsistence; property, goods

ζῶμα ατος τό girdle, belt, jock-strap; part of the armour

ζωμός οῦ ὁ soup, sauce

ζώνη ης ἡ belt, girdle; waist, loins

ζώννῡμι ζώσω ἔζωσα gird; *mid* gird oneself (for battle *or* work)

ζωο-γονέω produce living beings; preserve alive

ζῷον ου τό (*also* ζῶον ου τό) living being, animal, creature, beast; figure, image, picture, painting, ornament

ζωο-ποιέω make alive, bring to life; preserve alive

ζῳός ή όν (*also* ζωός ή όν) alive

ζωρός όν strong, unmixed (of wine)

ζώς ζών ▸ **ζωός**

ζωστήρ ῆρος ὁ girdle, belt

ζῶστρον ου τό girdle

ζωτικός ή όν full of life, lively, animated

Hη

η, Η (ἦτα) seventh letter of the alphabet
■ **η′** *as a numeral* = 8

ἦ *adv* truly, in truth; *particle expressing interrogation* surely ...? surely ... not?

ἤ *conj* or; if, whether; than
■ **ἤ** ... **ἤ** either ... or; whether ... or

ᾗ *adv* where; whither; how, as, as far as

ἦ[1] ▸ **ἦν** *from* **εἶναι** I was

ἦ[2] ▸ **ἔφη** *from* **ἠμί** ▸ **φημί** he said

ᾖα[1] ▸ **ᾔειν** *from* **ἰέναι**

ᾖα[2] ▸ **τὰ ἤια**

ἠβαιός ᾱ́ όν small, little, tiny
■ **οὐδὲ ἠβαιόν** not in the least

ἡβάσκω reach puberty; become marriageable

ἡβάω be in the prime of youth

ἥβη ης ἡ youth, prime of youth; vigour; young men; manhood

ἡβηδόν *adv* in manhood

ἡβητικός ή όν **ἡβός** ή όν youthful

ἤγαγον *aor from* **ἄγω**

ἠγάθεος ᾱ ον most holy

ἡγεμονεύω guide, lead the way; be leader, rule, command

ἡγεμονίᾱ ᾱς ἡ leading the way, leadership, command, top position; sovereignty, supremacy

ἡγεμονικός ή όν of *or* for a leader, ready to lead *or* guide

ἡγεμόσυνα ων τά thank-offerings for safe conduct

ἡγεμών όνος ὁ/ἡ guide, leader; chief, ruler, commander; prince, governor

ἡγέομαι *mid* think, mean, believe; + *dat* lead the way, go before; lead the van; be leader, ruler *or* chief

ἠγερέθομαι be gathered together

ἡγηλάζω guide

ἡγητήρ ῆρος ὁ **ἡγήτωρ** ορος ὁ ▸ **ἡγεμών**

ἠδέ and
■ **ἠμέν** ... **ἠδέ** both ... and

ἤδη *adv* already, now; forthwith; besides, further; therefore; even; yet

ᾔδη *plpf (with impf meaning) from* **οἶδα**

ἥδομαι† *pass* rejoice, be pleased *or* glad, enjoy oneself, delight

ἡδονή ῆς ἡ joy, pleasure, delight, enjoyment; lust; comfort; profit, gain; mischievous joy

ἧδος τό ▸ **ἡδονή**

ἡδυεπής ές sweet-speaking

ἥδυμος ον sweet, refreshing

ἡδύοσμον ου τό mint

ἡδυ-παθέω live pleasantly; enjoy oneself

η

ἡδύπνοος ον sweet-breathing, auspicious

ἡδύπολις agreeable to the city

ἡδύποτος ον pleasant to drink

ἡδύς εῖα ύ sweet, pleasant, lovely, agreeable; joyous, amiable; dear; well-disposed, kind

ἥδυσμα ατος τό relish, seasoning, spice

ἠέ (*or* ἦε) ▸ **ἤ**

ἠέλιος ▸ **ἥλιος**

ἠέπερ ▸ **ἤπερ**

ἠερέθομαι float, hang waving in the air; be flighty, turn with every wind

ἠέριος ᾱ ον early in the morning

ἠερόεις εσσα εν **ἠεροειδής** ές misty, dark

ἠεροφοῖτις ιδος ἡ walking in the dark

ἠερόφωνος ον loud-voiced

ἠήρ ἠέρος ▸ **ἀήρ**

ἠθάς (*gen* άδος) accustomed to; acquainted with; usual, customary

ἠθεῖος ᾱ ον dear, beloved; trusty, honoured

ᾔθεος ου ὁ ▸ **ἠΐθεος**

ἠθμός οῦ ὁ (*also* ἠθμός οῦ ὁ) strainer, sieve

ἦθος ους τό accustomed place, seat, station, abode, stable; disposition, character, temper; custom; morality

ἤια ατος τό provisions, food; prey

ἠΐθεος ους τό youth, bachelor

ἤϊκτο *from* **ἔοικα** he was like

ἠϊόεις εσσα εν with high banks *(the meaning is doubtful)*

ἤϊος ου ὁ shooting *or* shining (of Phoebus)

ἠϊών όνος ἡ shore, beach

ἦκα *adv* softly, gently; slowly

ἤκεστος η ον untouched by the goad, unmanageable

ἥκιστα *adv* least, not at all

ἤκιστος η ον *sup adj from adv* **ἦκα** slowest, slackest

ἥκιστος η ον *sup from* **ἥσσων** least, poorest, worst

ἧκου ▸ **ἧπου**

ἥκω have come, be here; be back; have come to, possess; arrive, come to pass, occur

ἠλάκατα ων τά wool on the distaff

ἠλακάτη ης ἡ distaff, spindle

ἤλασα *aor from* **ἐλαύνω**

ἠλασκάζω, ἠλάσκω wander, stray; shun, flee from

ἤλεκτρον ου τό **ἤλεκτρος** ου ὁ/ἡ electron, alloy of gold and silver; amber

ἠλέκτωρ (*gen* ωρος) the beaming sun; fire

ἠλεός ή όν crazed, distraught; making crazed

ἦλθον *aor from* **ἔρχομαι**

ἡλιαίᾱ ᾱς ἡ law-court, jury; at Athens, the supreme court *and* the public place in which it was held

ἠλίβατος ον steep, abrupt

ἤλιθα *adv* very much, exceedingly

ἠλίθιος ᾱ ον silly; vain, idle

ἠλιθιότης ητος ἡ silliness

ἡλικίᾱ ᾱς ἡ time of life, age; prime of life, manhood; those of the same age; those fit to bear arms, comrades; age, time; stature, bodily growth

ἡλικιώτης ου ὁ of the same age; comrade

ἧλιξ ικος ▸ **ἡλικιώτης**

ἥλιος ου ὁ sun; sunlight, daylight; east; the sun-god

ἡλιοστερής ές protecting from the sun

ἡλιτόμηνος ον prematurely born

ἡλιῶτις (*gen* ιδος) belonging to the sun

ἧλος ου ὁ nail, stud

ἤλυσις εως ἡ coming; step, gait

ἧμα ατος τό something thrown, dart, javelin

ἠμαθόεις εσσα εν sandy

ἧμαι sit; be at leisure; lie in wait

ἦμαρ ατος τό ▸ **ἡμέρα**

ἡμάτιος ᾱ ον by day; daily
ἡμεῖς we
ἠμελημένως *adv* carelessly; in a state of neglect
ἠμὲν ... ἠδέ both ... and
ἡμέρᾱ ᾱς ἡ day; daylight; time; time of life; fate
ἡμερεύω pass the day, live on
ἡμερήσιος (ᾱ) ον **ἡμερινός** ή όν **ἡμέριος** ον by day, of day, daily; a day long; short-lived
ἡμερίς ίδος ἡ the cultivated vine
ἡμεροδρόμος ου ὁ day-runner, courier
ἥμερος ον tame; civilized, cultivated; gentle
ἡμεροσκόπος ου ὁ day-watcher
ἡμεροφύλαξ ακος ὁ ▸ ἡμεροσκόπος
ἡμερόω tame; cultivate; *mid* subdue
ἡμέτερος ᾱ ον our; ours
ἠμί *impf* ἦν (*1 sg*) ἦ (*3 sg*) say
ἡμίβρωτος ον half-eaten
ἡμιδαής ές half-burnt
ἡμιδᾱρεικόν οῦ τό a half-daric (Persian money)
ἡμιδεής ές half-full
ἡμίεργος ου ὁ a thing half-done
ἡμιθανής ές ▸ **ἡμιθνής**
ἡμίθεος ου ὁ demigod
ἡμιθνής (*gen* ῆτος) half-dead
ἡμικύκλιον ου τό semicircle
ἡμιμναῖον ου τό a half mina (Attic money)
ἡμιμόχθηρος ον half a villain; half-wretched
ἡμιόλιος ᾱ ον one and a half; half as much *or* as large again
ἡμιόνειος ᾱ ον **ἡμιονικός** ή όν of mules
ἡμίονος ου ὁ/ἡ mule
ἡμιπέλεκκον ου τό half-axe
ἡμίπλεθρον ου τό half-plethron (measure of distance or space)
ἡμιπλίνθιον ου τό half-brick
ἥμισυς εια υ half
ἡμιτάλαντον ου τό half-talent (as a weight)
ἡμιτέλεστος ον **ἡμιτελής** ές half-finished
ἡμίτομος ον half-cut
ἡμιωβολιαῖος ᾱ ον as large as a half-obol
ἡμιωβόλιον ου τό half-obol (Attic coin)
ἡμιώριον ου τό **ἡμίωρον** ου τό half-hour
ἦμος *conj* when, while; as soon as
ἠμύω sink, droop
ἥμων (*gen* ονος) spear-throwing
ἤν ▸ **ἐάν**
ἤνεγκα, ἤνεγκον *aor from* **φέρω**
ἠνεμόεις εσσα εν ▸ **ἀνεμόεις**
ἡνίᾱ ᾱς ἡ rein, bridle
pl (*also* τὰ ἡνία)
ἡνίκα *conj* when, at the time when
ἡνίον *see* **ἡνία**
ἡνιοποιεῖον ου τό saddler's shop
ἡνιοστρόφος ου ὁ ▸ **ἡνίοχος**
ἡνιοχείᾱ ᾱς ἡ chariot-driving; directing, management
ἡνιοχέω, ἡνιοχεύω hold the reins, drive
ἡνίοχος ου ὁ **ἡνιοχεύς** έως ὁ driver, charioteer
ἦνις (*gen* ιος) **ἤνῑς** (*gen* ῑος) yearling (of cows) *(the meaning is doubtful)*
ἠνορέη ης ἡ strength, manliness
ἦνοψ (*gen* οπος) shining
ἠνώγεα *see* **ἄνωγα**
ἠοίη ης ἡ morning
ἠοῖος ᾱ ον in the morning; eastern
ἦος ▸ **ἕως**
ἧπαρ ατος τό liver, heart
ἠπεδανός ή όν feeble, weakly
ἤπειρος ου ἡ continent, mainland; inland

ἠπειρόω convert into mainland

ἠπειρώτης ου ὁ **ἠπειρῶτις** ιδος ἡ of the mainland, continental, Asiatic

ἠπειρωτικός ή όν *adj* of the mainland, continental; Asiatic

ἧπερ *conj* where; just as

ἠπεροπεύς έως ὁ **ἠπεροπευτής** οῦ ὁ deceiver

ἠπεροπεύω deceive, cheat

ἠπιόδωρος ον kindly giving

ἤπιος ᾱ ον gentle, mild, kind, friendly; soothing

ἦπου (*or* ἦ που) *adv* certainly, doubtless

ἤπου (*or* ἤ που) *adv* or perhaps ...? (making a hesitant suggestion)

ἠπύτα ου ὁ crier; loud-calling

ἠπύω cry aloud, cry to; sound, roar

ἦρ ἦρος τό ▸ **ἔαρ**

ἦρα[1] *aor from* **αἴρω**

ἦρα[2] *acc sg* favour, kindness
▪ **ἦρα φέρειν** to do a favour

ἠρέμα *adv* softly, gently, quietly; slowly; slightly

ἠρεμαῖος ᾱ ον gentle, quiet

ἠρεμέω be *or* keep quiet *or* unchanged

ἠρεμίᾱ ᾱς ἡ stillness, rest

ἤρεμος ον ▸ **ἠρεμαῖος**

ἦρι *adv* early, in the morning

ἠριγένεια ᾱς ἡ early-born, early-rising

ἠρινός ή όν ▸ **ἐαρινός**

ἠρίον ου τό mound, tomb

ἠρόμην *aor from* **ἐρωτάω**

ἡρωϊκός ή όν heroic, of heroes

ἡρῷος ᾱ ον ▸ **ἡρωικός**
▪ **τὸ ἡρῷον** temple of a hero

ἥρως ωος ὁ hero; demigod
▪ **οἱ ἥρωες ἐπώνυμοι** the eponymous heroes at Athens after whom the tribes were named

ἧσσα ης ἡ defeat

ἡσσάομαι *pass* be less, weaker *or* inferior; be defeated *or* beaten; be subject, be under the control of; lose one's cause

ἥσσων ον less, weaker, inferior; defeated, subject, yielding
▪ **ἧσσον** *adv less*

ἡσυχάζω rest, be quiet; stop, halt; be silent; give up resistance; *tr* calm, soothe

ἡσυχαῖος ᾱ ον quiet, still, gentle; slow, cautious; peaceable; placid; untroubled, secure; secret

ἡσυχῇ *adv* ▸ **ἡσύχως**

ἡσυχίᾱ ᾱς ἡ stillness, quiet, silence; loneliness; rest, leisure; ease, contentment

ἡσύχιος ον **ἥσυχος** ον ▸ **ἡσυχαῖος**

ἦτε *adv* truly, doubtless, surely

ἤτε *conj* or, or also

ἤτοι *conj* surely, verily, indeed; now; therefore

ἦτορ τό heart, mind, soul; life, spirit, vigour

ἦτρον ου τό belly, abdomen

ἡττ- ▸ **ἡσσ-**

ἠϋγένειος ον ▸ **εὐγένειος**

ἠΰζωνος ▸ **εὔζωνος**

ἠΰκομος ον lovely-haired

ηὗρον *aor from* **εὑρίσκω**

ἠΰς ἠΰ ▸ **ἐΰς**

ἠΰτε *conj* as, just like, as if

ἡφαιστότευκτος ον made *or* wrought by Hephaestus

ἠχέω sound, ring; cause to sound, utter

ἠχή ῆς ἡ sound, noise; cries; rumour

ἠχήεις εσσα εν sounding, roaring

ἧχι *adv* where

ἦχος ου ὁ **ἦχος** τό ▸ **ἠχή**

ἠχώ οῦς ἡ sound, echo; lament; report, rumour

ἠῶθεν *adv* from morning, at dawn

ἠῶθι *adv* early in the morning

ἠών όνος ἡ ▸ **ἠϊών**

ἠῷος η ον ▸ **ἑῷος**

ἠώς ἠοῦς ἡ ▸ **ἕως**[1]

Θθ

θ, Θ (θῆτα) eighth letter of the alphabet
■ **θ′** *as a numeral* = 9

θαάσσω sit

θαιρός οῦ ὁ hinge of a door

θᾱκέω sit

θᾱ́κημα ατος τό **θᾱ́κησις** εως ἡ sitting; seat; residence

θᾶκος ου ὁ seat

θαλάμη ης ἡ ▸ **θάλαμος**

θαλαμηπόλος ον belonging to the bridal chamber; chamber-maid; eunuch of the bed-chamber
■ **ὁ θαλαμηπόλος** bridegroom
■ **ἡ θαλαμηπόλος** bridesmaid

θαλαμιή ῆς ἡ hole in the ship's side for an oar

θαλαμιός οῦ ὁ rower of the lowest bench (of a trireme) who had the lowest pay

θάλαμος ου ὁ chamber, apartment, bedroom; women's apartment; bridal chamber; store-room, treasury; palace

θάλασσα ης ἡ sea, sea-water

θαλασσεύω be at sea

θαλάσσιος ᾱ ον of the sea, maritime, seafaring

θαλασσο-κρατέω be master of the sea

θαλασσοκράτωρ ορος ὁ/ἡ master of the sea

θάλεα έων τά good things, delights

θαλέθω bloom; be swollen (up)

θαλερός ᾱ́ όν blooming, fresh, young, vigorous, lusty; copious, abundant

θαλίᾱ ᾱς ἡ bloom, happiness; good cheer, feast

θαλλός οῦ ὁ young shoot, sprouting twig; olive-branch; foliage

θάλλω θαλλήσω ἔθηλα sprout, shoot, bloom, flourish; be abundant, rich *or* swelling; grow; prosper; be esteemed

θάλος ους τό ▸ **θαλλός**

θαλπιάω be warm

θάλπος ους τό warmth, heat

θάλπω warm, heat; inflame; be *or* become warm, glow

θαλπωρή ῆς ἡ warming, comfort

θάλυς εια υ blooming
■ **θάλεια δαίς** delicious feast

θαλῦσια ων τά offering of first-fruits

θαμά *adv* often, frequently; in crowds

θαμβέω be astonished *or* amazed (at); shudder

θάμβος ους τό astonishment; horror

θαμέες ω(ν) οἱ/αἱ **θαμειός** ᾱ́ όν frequent, thick, in crowds

θαμίζω come often, frequent; be often *or* constantly engaged (with *or* in a thing)

θαμινά *adv* ▸ **θαμά**

θάμνος ου ὁ bush, shrub

θαν *often from* **θνῄσκω**

θανάσιμος ον belonging to death; deadly; mortal, dying; dead

θανατάω long for death

θανατηφόρος ον death-bringing

θανατόεις εσσα εν ▸ **θανάσιμος**

θάνατος ου ὁ death, murder, execution

θανατόω put to death, kill, slay, execute

θᾱ́ομαι ▸ **θεάομαι**

θάπτω† bury, inter

θαργηλιών ῶνος ὁ the eleventh month of the Athenian year (May to June)

θαρσαλέος ᾱ ον (*also* θαρραλέος ᾱ ον) bold, daring, courageous; insolent, presumptuous; encouraging

θαρσέω, θαρρέω be bold, daring, courageous, confident *or* presumptuous; believe confidently

θάρσησις εως ἡ confidence

θάρσος ους τό courage, boldness, confidence; daring, presumption

θάρσυνος ον confident, of good cheer

θαρσῦνω, θαρρῦνω ▸ **θρασύνω**

θᾱ́σσω sit

θᾱ́σσων *comp from* **ταχύς** swifter, quicker, faster

θᾱ́τερον ▸ **τὸ ἕτερον**

θαῦμα ατος τό wonder, marvel, wondrous thing; astonishment, admiration

θαυμάζω θαυμάσομαι be astonished *or* amazed, wonder; admire, esteem; wonder at; be curious to learn

θαυμαίνω admire, gaze upon

θαυμάσιος ᾱ ον marvellous, wonderful, wondrous, extraordinary, strange; admirable, excellent

θαυμαστός ή όν ▸ **θαυμάσιος**

θαυματοποιός οῦ ὁ juggler, conjurer

θάω suckle, feed; *mid* suck; milk

θεά ᾶς ἡ **θέαινα** ης ἡ goddess

θέᾱ ᾱς ἡ a seeing, looking at, view; spectacle, sight

θέᾱμα ατος τό sight, spectacle

θεᾱ́ομαι *mid* view, behold, observe; reflect, know; admire, gaze at

θεᾱρός οῦ ὁ ▸ **θεωρός**

θεᾱτής οῦ ὁ onlooker, spectator

θεᾱτός ή όν to be seen, visible

θεᾱτρίζω expose to ridicule

θέᾱτρον ου τό theatre, stage; spectators, audience; play

θέειον ου τό ▸ **θεῖον**

θεειόω fumigate with brimstone

θειασμός οῦ ὁ superstition

θειλόπεδον ου τό sunny place

θείνω θενῶ ἔθεινα beat, strike, hit

θεῖον ου τό brimstone

θεῖος[1] ου ὁ uncle

θεῖος[2] ᾱ ον of gods, divine; holy, sacred; godlike, superhuman, sublime, august

■ **τὸ θεῖον** deity, divine being

■ **τὰ θεῖα** divine things; religion, oracles, worship

θειότης ητος ἡ divinity, divine nature

θείω[1] ▸ **θέω** run

θείω[2] ▸ **θῶ** *from* **τίθημι**

θειώδης ες sulphurous

θέλγω charm, enchant; blind, cheat, seduce; fascinate, win

θέλημα ατος τό **θέλησις** εως ἡ a willing, will

θελκτήριος ον charming, enchanting

■ **τὸ θελκτήριον** spell, charm; delight

θέλκτρον ου τό ▸ **θελκτήριον**

θέλω ▸ **ἐθέλω**

θέμεθλα ων τά **θεμείλια** ων τά *see* **θεμέλιος**

θεμέλιος ου ὁ **θεμέλιον** ου τό foundation stone; base, bottom, foundation

θεμελιόω found; make firm

θέμις ιστος ἡ divine right, law, custom, prerogative, privilege; judicial sentence; tax

θεμιστεύω give law; give oracles

θεμι(σ)τός ή όν lawful, just

θεμόω drive, bring

θέναρ αρος τό flat of the hand

θεοβλαβής ές stricken with madness

θεογεννής ές of divine descent

θεογονίᾱ ᾱς ἡ genealogy of the gods

θεοδίδακτος ον taught by God

θεόδμητος ον god-built

θεοειδής ές **θεοείκελος** ον godlike

θεόθεν *adv* from the gods

θεολόγος ου ὁ theologian

θεόμαντις εως ὁ soothsayer

θεο-μαχέω fight against the gods

θεομαχίᾱ ᾱς ἡ battle of the gods

θεομάχος ον fighting against God

θεοπροπέω prophesy

θεοπροπίᾱ ᾱς ἡ **θεοπρόπιον** ου τό prophecy, oracle

θεοπρόπος ον prophetic; prophet, soothsayer

θεός ου ὁ/ἡ god, goddess; deity, divine being

θεοσέβεια ᾱς ἡ fear of the gods

θεοσεβής ές god-fearing, religious

θεοστυγής ές god-hating; hated by god

θεότης ητος ἡ divinity

θεουδής ές fearing god

θεοφάνια ων τά (spring festival at Delphi)

θεοφιλής ές beloved by god; blessed

θεράπαινα ης ἡ maid-servant

θεραπείᾱ ᾱς ἡ **θεράπευμα** ατος τό service, attendance, courting, deference, flattery; care, worship; fostering, nurture, medical treatment, nursing; servants, retinue

θεραπευτής οῦ ὁ ▶ **θεράπων**

θεραπευτικός ή όν courteous, obedient

θεραπευτός ή όν that may be fostered

θεραπεύω serve, attend, wait on; court, flatter, honour, win; take care of, treat carefully, tend, nurse, heal; cultivate; pay attention to

θεράπων οντος ὁ servant, attendant, waiter; companion in arms, comrade

θερείᾱ ᾱς ἡ summertime

θερίζω θεριῶ ἐθέρισα pass the summer; reap; cut off; destroy

θερινός ή όν in summer

θερισμός οῦ ὁ a reaping; harvest-time; crop

θεριστής οῦ ὁ reaper

θερμαίνω θερμανῶ ἐθέρμηνα warm, heat; burn; *pass* become warm *or* hot

θερμασίᾱ ᾱς ἡ warmth, heat

θέρμη ης ἡ warmth; fever; hot spring

θερμός ή όν warm, hot; rash

θερμότης ητος ἡ ▶ **θερμασία**

θερμουργός όν hot in acting, rash

θέρμω ▶ **θερμαίνω**

θέρομαι θέρσομαι ἐθέρην *pass* become warm *or* hot; be burnt

θέρος ους τό summer; harvest

θέσις εως ἡ setting, placing; condition, situation; proposition

θέσκελος ον marvellous

θέσμιος ον according to law

θεσμοθέτης ου ὁ law-giver; Athenian magistrate (one of the six junior archons who judged cases assigned to no special court)

θεσμός οῦ ὁ place; statute, law, rule; custom, institution (such as the Areopagus)

θεσμοφόρια ων τά a festival held by the Athenian women in honour of Demeter

θεσμοφοριάζω keep the Thesmophoria

θεσμοφόρος ον lawgiving

θεσμοφύλαξ ακος ὁ guardian of the law

θεσπέσιος (ᾱ) ον divinely sounding *or* singing; divine, august, unspeakable

θεσπιδαής ές blazing prodigiously

θεσπιέπεια *adj fem only* prophetic

θεσπίζω θεσπιῶ prophesy

θέσπις ιος ὁ/ἡ something inspired (by god) *or* divine

θέσπισμα ατος τό oracle

θέσφατος ον announced *or* decreed by god; made by god

θετός ή όν adopted

θέω run, hasten

θεωρέω look at, view, behold, observe; be a spectator; consider, contemplate, examine; perceive

θεώρημα ατος τό sight, spectacle

θεωρίᾱ ᾱς ἡ looking at, seeing, viewing; curiosity; presence at a festival; examination, contemplation, theory; festival, spectacle; sending of ambassadors to an oracle

θεωρικός ή όν belonging to a spectacle *or* festival
■ **τὰ θεωρικά** money to pay for seats in the theatre

θεωρίς ίδος ἡ sacred ship for carrying ambassadors

θεωρός οῦ ὁ spectator; ambassador sent to a festival *or* oracle

θεώτερος ᾱ ον ▸ **θειότερος**

θηγάνη ης ἡ whetstone

θήγω whet, sharpe; incite, encourage

θηέομαι ▸ **θεάομαι**

θηητήρ ῆρος ὁ ▸ **θεατής**

θηκαῖος ᾱ ον like a chest *or* coffin, suitable for a coffin

θήκη ης ἡ box, chest; tomb, coffin; sheath

θηλάζω θηλάσω *and mid* suckle; suck

θηλέω flourish

θηλή ῆς ἡ teat, nipple

θηλυδρίᾱς ου ὁ effeminate man

θῆλυς εια υ female; effeminate; delicate, gentle

θημών ῶνος ὁ heap

θήν *adv* certainly, surely

θήρ θηρός ὁ wild beast, beast of prey; monster

θήρᾱ ᾱς ἡ hunting, hunt; game

θηρᾱτέος ᾱ ον to be pursued *or* sought eagerly

θηρᾱτικός ή όν belonging *or* pertaining to hunting

θήρᾱτρον ου τό hunting equipment

θηράω *and mid* hunt, chase, pursue; catch

θήρειος ον of wild beasts

θηρευτής οῦ ὁ hunter

θηρευτικός ή όν belonging *or* pertaining to the hunt

θηρεύω ▸ **θηράω**

θηρητήρ ῆρος ὁ **θηρήτωρ** ορος ὁ ▸ **θηρευτής**

θηριο-μαχέω fight with wild beasts

θηρίον ου τό ▸ **θήρ**

θηριώδης ες full of wild beasts; beastly, brutal

θηροβολέω kill wild beasts

θής θητός ὁ labourer, serf (at Athens, a member of the fourth class in Solon's constitution)

θησαυρίζω treasure up, lay in

θησαυρός οῦ ὁ store-room, treasure-house, treasury; store, treasure, vaults of a bank

θητείᾱ ᾱς ἡ hired service

θητεύω work for hire

θίασος ου ὁ band of revellers celebrating Bacchus; procession; dance; company

θιγγάνω θίξομαι ἔθιγον + *gen* touch, handle, take hold of; reach, gain

θῑ́ς θῑνός ὁ/ἡ heap (of sand), sand; beach, shore; sand-bank, sandy desert

θλάω θλάσω ἔθλασα crush, bruise

θλῑ́βω press; rub; oppress, confine

θλῖψις (*also* θλίψις) εως ἡ oppression, affliction, distress

θνῄσκω† (*also* θνήσκω) die, perish; be killed

θνητογενής ές of mortal race

θνητοειδής ές of mortal nature

θνητός ή όν mortal; human

θοάζω hurry along; move quickly; ▸ **θάσσω**

θοινάω entertain; eat

θοίνη ης ἡ banquet, feast; enjoyment

θολερός ά όν muddy, dirty; troubled

θόλος ου ἡ round building with a conical roof; a vaulted chamber; (at Athens) the building in which the prytaneis dined

θοός[1] ή όν quick, swift

θοός[2] ή όν sharp, pointed

θοόω make pointed

θορή ῆς ἡ **θορός** οῦ ὁ seed of the male, semen

θόρνυμαι copulate

θορυβάζομαι be troubled
θορυβέω make a noise *or* uproar; applaud; murmur; trouble, disturb
θόρυβος ου ὁ noise; uproar, confusion
θούριος ᾱ ον **θοῦρος** ον (*fem* θοῦρις (*gen* ιδος)) rushing on, impetuous
θόωκος ου ὁ ▶ **θῶκος, θᾶκος**
θρᾱνῑ́της ου ὁ rower of the top bench (of a trireme)
θράσος ους τό ▶ **θάρσος**
θρᾱ́σσω θρᾱ́ξω trouble
θρασυκάρδιος ον stout-hearted
θρασυμέμνων ον enduring, bold
θρασῡ́νω θρασυνῶ *act tr* encourage; *act intr, pass and mid* take comfort; be bold
θρασύς εῖα ύ ▶ **θαρσαλέος**
θρασυ-στομέω speak overboldly *or* impudently
θρασύτης ητος ἡ boldness, audaciousness, audacity
θραύω *tr* break, shiver, crush
θρέμμα ατος τό nursling, child; (of sheep and goats) creature; breed
θρέομαι cry, lament
θρεπτήρια ων τά **θρέπτρα** ων τά food; reward for bringing up
θρεψ *likely to be from* **τρέφω**
θρηνέω wail, lament
θρῆνος ου ὁ a wailing, lamenting; dirge
θρῆνυς υος ὁ footstool
θρησκεία ᾱς ἡ worship, religious observance; religion
θρησκεύω observe religiously
θρῆσκος ον religious
θριαμβεύω triumph; lead in triumph
θρίαμβος ου ὁ hymn; procession, triumph
θριγκός οῦ ὁ cornice, projection; coping-stone; culmination
θριγκόω surround with a cornice, fence in, finish
θρῖδαξ ακος ἡ lettuce
θρίξ τριχός ἡ hair; wool, bristle
θροέω cry aloud, shriek; utter, tell, speak; frighten; *pass* be afraid
θρόμβος ου ὁ lump
θρομβώδης ες clotty, clotted
θρόνα ων τά flowers (in embroidery)
θρόνος ου ὁ seat, chair; throne
θρόος ου ὁ (*also* θροῦς οῦ ὁ) cry, shout; murmur; report
θρῡλέω babble, chatter; discuss, be always talking about
θρῡλίσσω crush, shiver, smash
θρύον ου τό rush
θρυπτικός ή όν easily broken; effeminate
θρύπτω grind, crush; *pass* be *or* become enfeebled *or* enervated; boast
θρῴσκω θοροῦμαι ἔθορον spring, leap, fly; assault
θρωσμός οῦ ὁ height; hill
θυγάτηρ τρός ἡ daughter
θυγατριδέος ου ὁ grandson (son of a daughter)
θυγατριδῆ ῆς ἡ granddaughter (daughter's daughter)
θυγάτριον ου τό little daughter
θύελλα ης ἡ whirlwind, storm
θυήεις εσσα εν fragrant
θυηλή ῆς ἡ burnt-offering
θυηπολέω perform sacrifices
θυῖα ᾱς ἡ **θυϊάς** άδος ἡ Bacchante
θύϊνος η ον made of cedar wood
θῡ́λακος ου ὁ **θῡλάκιον** ου τό bag, pouch
θῦμα ατος τό offering, sacrifice
θῡμαίνω θῡμανῶ be angry
θῡμαλγής ές heart-grieving
θῡμᾱρής ές well-pleasing, dear
θῡμηγερέων taking heart
θῡμηδής ές well-pleasing
θῡμήρης ▶ **θυμαρής**
θῡμίᾱμα ατος τό incense; stuff for embalming

θῡμιᾱτήριον ου τό censer
θῡμιάω burn as incense
θῡμοβόρος ον **θῡμοδακής** ές mortifying, distressing
θῡμοειδής ές courageous; angry, hot, wild
θῡμολέων (*gen* οντος) lion-hearted
θῡμο-μαχέω fight with all one's heart; fight desperately
θῡμοραϊστής (*gen* οῦ) life-destroying
θῡμός οῦ ὁ soul, life; will, desire; appetite; resolution; thought; mind, heart, sense; courage, spirit, passion, anger, wrath
θῡμο-φθορέω torment the soul, break the heart
θῡμοφθόρος ον life-destroying; heart-breaking
θῡμόω make angry; *pass* become angry *or* excited
θύννος ου ὁ tunny(-fish)
θῡ́νω ▸ **θύω**
θυόεις εσσα εν fragrant
θύον ου τό a fragrant wood (thyme *or* citron)
θύος εος τό incense; offering
θυόω make fragrant
θύρᾱ ᾱς ἡ fold of a door; door, gate; palace, royal court; entrance, threshold; table, board, raft
θύρᾱζε *adv* to the door; outside the door, outdoors
θύρᾱθεν, θύρηθε *adv* from outside; outside
θυραῖος ᾱ ον outside the door, outdoor(s), absent, abroad; alien, stranger
θύρᾱσι *adv* outside, out of doors; abroad
θυρεός οῦ ὁ door-stone; large shield
θύρετρα ων τά ▸ **θύρα**
θυρίς ίδος ἡ small door; window
θυρόω furnish with doors, shut, close
θύρσος ου ὁ thyrsus (wreathed staff of followers of Bacchus)
θύρωμα ατος τό door with frame, portal
θυρών ῶνος ὁ anteroom, vestibule
θυρωρός οῦ ὁ/ἡ door-keeper
θυσανόεις εσσα εν tasselled, fringed
θύσανος ου ὁ tassel, tuft
θυσανωτός ή όν ▸ **θυσανόεις**
θύσθλα ων τά sacred implements
θυσίᾱ ᾱς ἡ sacrificing; sacrifice
θυσιαστήριον ου τό altar
θύσιμος ον fit for sacrifice
θυσσανόεις εσσα εν ▸ **θυσανόεις**
θυστάς άδος ἡ sacrificial
θυτήρ ῆρος ὁ sacrificer
θῡ́ω[1] move oneself quickly, rush on *or* along; roar, rage
θύω[2] *act* burn [incense]; offer burnt-sacrifice; offer, sacrifice; slay, kill; *mid* sacrifice for oneself
θυώδης ες fragrant
θύωμα ατος τό incense
θωή ῆς ἡ penalty
θωκέω, θῶκος *see* **θακέω, θᾶκος**
θωμ- *see* **θαυμ-**
θῶμιγξ ιγγος ὁ cord, string
θωπείᾱ ᾱς ἡ flattery
θωπεύω flatter, fawn on; serve
θωρᾱκίζω θωρακίσω arm with a breastplate
θωρᾱκοποιός οῦ ὁ maker of breastplates
θωρᾱκοφόρος ον wearing a breastplate
θώρᾱξ ᾱκος ὁ breastplate, cuirass
θωρηκτής οῦ ὁ ▸ **θωρακοφόρος**
θωρήσσω arm with a breastplate; equip, arm
θώς θωός ὁ/ἡ jackal
θωῦμα etc. *see* **θαῦμα**
θωΰσσω θωΰξω cry aloud, shout
θώψ θωπός ὁ flatterer

Ιι

ι, Ι (ἰῶτα) sixth letter of the alphabet
■ **ι′** *as a numeral* = 10

ἰᾱ́ ᾱς ἡ sound, voice, cry

ἴα ἰῆς one; *see* **ἴος**

ἰά ων τά *pl from* **ἰός** arrows

ἰαίνω *aor* ἴηνα warm, heat; refresh, cheer

ἰακχάζω, ἰακχέω raise the cry to Bacchus

ἴακχος ου ὁ the cry to Bacchus

ἰάλλω ἰαλῶ ἴηλα send, throw *or* put forth; attack

ἴᾱμα ατος τό remedy, healing

ἰαμβεῖον ου τό iambic verse

ἰαμβοφάγος ου ὁ bad reciter of iambic verses

ἰᾱ́ομαι ἰάσομαι ἰᾱσάμην heal, cure

ἰάπτω move, stir; send, thrust; hit, wound, hurt

ἰᾱ́σιμος ον healable

ἴᾱσις εως ἡ a healing, cure, remedy

ἴασπις ιδος ἡ jasper

ἰαστί *adv* in Ionic fashion; in the Ionian mode of music

ἰᾱτήρ ῆρος ὁ ▸ **ἰατρός**

ἰᾱτορίᾱ ᾱς ἡ art of healing

ἰᾱτρείᾱ ᾱς ἡ ▸ **ἴασις**

ἰᾱτρεῖον ου τό infirmary

ἰᾱτρεύω be a physician, heal

ἰᾱτρικός ή όν medical

ἰᾱτρός οῦ ὁ physician, surgeon

ἰαύω pass the night, sleep

ἰαχέω, ἰάχω cry aloud, shout

ἶβις ιος ἡ ibis (Egyptian bird)

ἰγνῦᾱ ἡ hollow of the knee

ἰδ *likely to be from* **ὁράω**

ἰδέ[1] (*or* ἴδε) lo! behold!

ἰδέ[2] ▸ **ἠδέ** and

ἰδέᾱ ᾱς ἡ appearance, form; way, manner, nature; opinion, notion, idea

ἴδη ης ἡ woody mountain; wood, timber

ἰδιο-βουλέω act in accordance with one's own will

ἴδιος ᾱ ον one's own, personal, private; peculiar, strange
■ **ἰδίᾳ** *adv* separately, privately, for oneself
■ **ἴδιοι λόγοι** ordinary private conversation

ἰδιότης ητος ἡ specific character

ἰδιοτρόφος ον feeding individuals

ἰδῑ́ω sweat

ἰδιωτεύω be a private person, live in retirement; know nothing of *+ gen*

ἰδιώτης ου ὁ private person, single citizen; private soldier; bungler

ἰδιωτικός ή όν belonging to a private *or* single person; common, trivial; ignorant, uneducated

ἰδνόομαι *aor* ἰδνώθην *pass* writhe

ἰδού *aor impv from* **ὁράω** look! there!

ἰδρείᾱ ᾱς ἡ knowledge, skill

ἴδρις ι knowing, skilful, experienced

ἰδρόω sweat, perspire

ἵδρῡμα ατος τό foundation; building; statue, image

ἱδρύω make sit down; fix, settle, establish; *pass* be established, settled *or* seated; sit still; be placed *or* situated; *mid* establish, found for oneself, build, erect

ἱδρώς ῶτος ὁ sweat, perspiration

ἰδυῖα ἡ knowing, sensible

ἱέρᾱξ ᾱκος ὁ hawk, falcon

ἱεράομαι ἱερᾱ́σομαι *mid* be a priest(ess)

ἱερᾱτεία ᾱς ἡ **ἱερᾱ́τευμα** ατος τό priesthood, body of priests

ἱερᾱτεύω be a priest *or* priestess

ἱέρεια ᾱς ἡ priestess

ἱερεῖον ου τό victim; cattle to be killed

ἱερεύς έως ὁ priest

ἱερεύω sacrifice; slaughter

ἱερόθυτον ου τό offered flesh

ἱερομηνίᾱ ᾱς ἡ **ἱερομήνια** ων τά festive month; festivity

ἱερομνήμων ονος ὁ ambassador to the Amphictyons; chief magistrate

ἱεροποιός οῦ ὁ overseer of sacrifices

ἱεροπρεπής ές appropriate to a holy place, person *or* matter; holy

ἱερός ᾱ́ όν vigorous, strong; holy, sacred

■ **τὸ ἱερόν, τὰ ἱερά** victim, sacrifice, offering, dedication; holy place, temple, oracle; omen, auspices, mystery, sacred rite, worship

ἱεροσῡλέω rob a temple

ἱεροσῡλιᾱ ᾱς ἡ temple-robbery

ἱερόσῡλος ου ὁ temple-robbing, sacrilegious

ἱερουργέω perform sacred rites

ἱερουργίᾱ ᾱς ἡ worship

ἱεροφάντης ου ὁ initiating priest

ἱερόω dedicate

ἱερωσύνη ης ἡ office of a priest; priest's salary

ἱζάνω, ἵζω *act tr* cause to sit; *act intr and mid* sit down, place oneself; encamp; sink in

ἰή ῆς ἡ ▸ **ἰά**

ἰήιος ον wailing, mournful; helper (in need)

ἴημα ατος τό ▸ **ἴᾱμα**

ἵημι† *act tr* send (off), let go; utter; cast, throw, shoot; let down; *act intr* flow; *mid* be driven; hasten, hurry; + *gen* long for, desire

ἴησις etc. ▸ **ἴασις**

ἰθᾱγενής ές **ἰθαιγενής** ές of good birth, legitimate; genuine; natural

ἰθεῖα, ἰθέως *see* **εὐθύς**

ἴθμα ατος τό gait, step

ἰθύθριξ (*gen* τριχος) with straight hair

ἰθυμαχίᾱ ᾱς ἡ fair, stand-up fight

ἰθύντατα *adv* most rightly

ἰθῡ́νω ▸ **εὐθύνω**

ἰθυπτΐων (*gen* ωνος) (of a javelin) flying straight on

ἰθύς[1] εῖα ύ ▸ **εὐθύς**

ἰθύς[2] ύος ἡ direct course; undertaking; bent of mind, endeavour

ἰθύω go straight on, rush (up)on; strive after, desire

ἱκανός ή όν sufficient, enough, copious; fit, serviceable, becoming; empowered; considerable, respectable, trustworthy

ἱκανότης ητος ἡ sufficiency; ability

ἱκανόω make able *or* sufficient

ἱκᾱ́νω *and mid* ▸ **ἵκω**

ἴκελος η ον + *dat* like, similar to

ἱκέσιος ᾱ ον ▸ **ἱκετήριος**

ἱκετείᾱ ᾱς ἡ **ἱκέτευμα** ατος τό supplication

ἱκετεύω supplicate

ἱκετήριος ᾱ ον suppliant, entreating

■ **ἡ ἱκετηρίᾱ** olive branch of suppliants; entreaty

ἱκέτης ου ὁ suppliant, entreating; one protected

ἱκετήσιος ᾱ ον ▸ **ἱκετήριος**

ἱκέτις ιδος ἡ *fem of* **ἱκέτης**

ἰκμάς (*gen* άδος) moisture

ἴκμενος ον favourable (of the wind)

ἱκνέομαι *mid* ▸ **ἵκω**

ἴκρια ων τά props of a ship; deck; board; scaffold

ἱκτήρ (*gen* ῆρος) suppliant

ἱκτήριος ᾱ ον ▸ **ἱκετήριος**

ἰκτῖνος ου ὁ kite

ἵκω, ἱκᾱ́νω, ἱκνέομαι come; arrive at, reach; come upon *or* over; come as a suppliant, implore

ἰλαδόν *adv* in troops

ἱλάομαι ▸ **ἱλάσκομαι**

ἵλαος ον gracious; propitious; gentle, cheerful

ἱλαρός ά όν cheerful, merry

ἱλαρότης ητος ἡ gaiety

ἱλάσκομαι ἱλάσομαι ἱλασάμην *mid* propitiate, reconcile; appease; atone for

ἱλασμός οῦ ὁ atonement

ἱλαστήριον ου τό means of propitiation, mercy-seat

ἵλεως ων ▸ **ἵλαος**

ἴλη ης ἡ crowd, band, troop

ἵλημι, ἱλήκω be propitious

ἰλιγγιάω be *or* become giddy

ἴλιγγος ου ὁ giddiness, swoon

ἰλλάς άδος ἡ rope, band, noose

ἴλλω roll; force together, shut up; *pass* turn round

ἰλῦς ύος ἡ mud, slime

ἱμάντινος η ον of leather thongs

ἱμᾱ́ς άντος ὁ thong, strap; rein; shoe-string; door-latch; girdle of Venus

ἱμάσθλη ης ἡ whip

ἱμάσσω ἱμάσω ἵμασα whip, scourge

ἱματίζω clothe

ἱμάτιον ου τό garment; upper garment, cloak; piece of cloth

ἱματισμός οῦ ὁ clothing

ἱμείρω *and mid and pass + gen* long for, desire

ἱμερόεις εσσα εν exciting desire; lovely, charming; longing

ἵμερος ου ὁ longing, yearning; love; charm

ἱμερτός ή όν lovely, longed for

ἵνα *adv* there; where; to what place, to where; *conj* that, in order that

ἰνδάλλομαι *pass* appear; appear like, look like

ἰνίον ου τό neck, nape

ἶνις ὁ son

ἴξαλος: ~ **αἴξ** wild goat, stone buck

ἰξῦς ύος ἡ groin, waist

ἰοδνεφής ές violet

ἰοδόκος ον holding arrows; quiver

ἰοειδής ές violet-coloured

ἰόεις εσσα εν ▸ **ἰοειδής**

ἰόμωρος ον arrow-shooting; braggart *(the meaning is uncertain)*

ἴον ου τό a violet

ἰονθάς (*gen* άδος) shaggy

ἰός[1] ου ὁ arrow

ἰός[2] ου ὁ poison; rust

ἴος ἴα ἴον one, the same

ἰότης ητος ἡ will, desire

ἰού (*or* ἰοῦ) oh! woe!; hey!

ἰουδαΐζω live in the Jewish fashion

ἰουδαϊσμός οῦ ὁ Judaism

ἴουλος ου ὁ down on the cheek

ἰοχέαιρα ᾱς ἡ shooting arrows

ἰπνός οῦ ὁ oven, furnace; kitchen

ἱππαγρέτης ου ὁ leader (one of three) of Sparta horseguards

ἱππαγωγός όν transporting horses

ἱππάζομαι *mid* drive horses; drive a chariot; ride

ἱππαρμοστής οῦ ὁ ▸ **ἵππαρχος**

ἱππαρχέω + *gen* command the cavalry

ἵππαρχος ου ὁ cavalry commander

ἱππάς άδος ἡ riding-coat

ἱππασίᾱ ᾱς ἡ ▸ **ἱππεία**

ἱππάσιμος ον fit for horses; fit for riding (of a horse)

ἱππείᾱ ᾱς ἡ riding, driving; horsemanship; cavalry

ἵππειος ᾱ ον ▸ **ἱππικός**

ἱππεύς έως ὁ horseman, rider, charioteer, knight

■ **οἱ ἱππεῖς** the knights (the second class of citizen in Attica, required to possess land and a horse)

ἱππεύω ride, be a horseman

ἱππηλάσιος ον fit for riding *or* driving on

ἱππηλάτα ου ὁ horseman, knight

ἱππήλατος ον ▸ **ἱππηλάσιος**

ἱππημολγός οῦ ὁ mare-milker

ἱππικός ή όν of a horse, for riding *or* driving; for horsemen; skilled in riding
- ■ **ἡ ἱππική** horsemanship
- ■ **τὸ ἱππικόν** cavalry

ἵππιος ᾱ ον rich in horses; of horsemen

ἱππιοχαίτης (*gen* ου) shaggy with horse-hair

ἱππιοχάρμης (*gen* ου) chariot-fighter

ἱπποβότης (*gen* ου) breeding horses

ἱππόβοτος ον fed on by horses

ἱππόδαμος ον taming horses

ἱππόδασυς εια υ thick with horse-hair (of helmets)

ἱπποδέτης (*gen* ου) bridling horses

ἱπποδρομίᾱ ᾱς ἡ horse-race

ἱππόδρομος ου ὁ race-course (for chariots)

ἱπποδρόμος ου ὁ light horseman

ἱππόθεν *adv* from the horse

ἱπποκέλευθος ον driving horses

ἱπποκόμος ου ὁ groom; boy attendant on a knight in war, squire

ἱππόκομος ον of horse hair

ἱπποκορυστής οῦ ὁ charioteer, knight

ἱππο-κρατέω be superior in cavalry; *pass* be inferior in cavalry

ἱππομανής ές swarming with horses; (of an Arcadian plant) which makes horses mad

ἱππο-μαχέω fight on horseback

ἱππομαχίᾱ ᾱς ἡ fighting on horseback, a cavalry action

ἱππόνώμᾱς (*gen* ου) guiding horses

ἱπποπόλος ον breeding horses

ἵππος ου ὁ/ἡ horse, mare; chariot; charioteers
- ■ **ἡ ἵππος** cavalry

ἱπποσύνη ης ἡ horsemanship

ἱππότης ου ὁ **ἱππότα** ου ὁ man on horseback, rider; horseman, knight

ἱπποτοξότης ου ὁ mounted archer

ἱππο-τροφέω feed *or* keep horses

ἱπποτροφίᾱ ᾱς ἡ the feeding of horses

ἱπποτρόφος ον feeding *or* keeping horses

ἵππουρις ▸ **ἱππόκομος**

ἱπποφόρβιον ου τό a lot of horses out grazing; troop of horses; stable

ἵπτομαι *mid* press hard; punish

ἱ̄ράομαι etc. *see* **ἱεράομαι**

ἱ̄ρήϊον ου τό ▸ **ἱερεῖον**

ἱ̄ρήν ένος ὁ (*also* εἴρην ενος ὁ) Spartan young man who had become 21 and was now entrusted with authority over his juniors

ἶρηξ ηκος ὁ ▸ **ἱέραξ**

ἶρις ιδος ἡ rainbow

ἱ̄ρός όν *see* **ἱερός**

ἴ̄ς ἰνός ἡ sinew, nerve, muscle; strength, force

ἰσάγγελος ον like an angel

ἰσάζω make equal; balance (of someone holding scales); *mid* make oneself equal

ἰσηγορίᾱ ᾱς ἡ equal freedom of speech; equality of rights

ἴσθμιον ου τό necklace

ἰσθμός οῦ ὁ neck of land; isthmus

ἰσθμώδης ες isthmus-like

ἴσκε he said

ἴσκω make like *or* equal; think *or* consider like; suppose, think

ἰσοδίαιτος ον equal in manner of life

ἰσόθεος ον godlike

ἰσοκίνδῡνος ον equal to the danger

ἰσοκρατής ές equal in power

ἰσοκρατίᾱ ᾱς ἡ equal right of citizens, democracy

ἰσομέτρητος ον equal in measure

ἰσομέτωπος ον with equal forehead *or* front

ἰσομοιρέω have equal share *or* rights

ἰσομοιρίᾱ ᾱς ἡ equal share; partnership

ἰσόμοιρος ον **ἰσόμορος** ον having (an) equal share; enjoying the same rights

ἰσονομέομαι *mid* have equal rights

ἰσονομίᾱ ᾱς ἡ equality of rights, the equality of a Greek democracy

ἰσονομικός ή όν democratic

ἰσοπαλής ές equal in fight, well-matched

ἰσόπεδος ον level, even

ἰσοπλατής ές equal in breadth

ἰσόπλευρος ον equilateral

ἰσοπληθής ές equal in number

ἰσορροπίᾱ ᾱς ἡ equipoise, equilibrium

ἰσόρροπος ον equally balanced; equivalent; equally matched

ἴσος η ον (*also* ἶσος η ον, ἔ σος η ον) equal; the same; proportionate; equally distributed, reasonable, due, fair, impartial
- **ἡ ἴση, τὸ ἴσον, τὰ ἴσα** equality, equilibrium, equal share *or* proportion, right, equity, compensation
- **ἴσον, ἴσα** *adv* equally
- **ἴσως** *adv* perhaps, probably; fairly; *with numerals* about

ἰσοσκελής ές with equal legs, isosceles

ἰσοτέλεια ᾱς ἡ equality in taxation

ἰσοτέλεστος ον making all equal at last (of Death)

ἰσότης ητος ἡ equality

ἰσότῑμος ον equally honoured

ἰσοφαρίζω + *dat* be a match for, cope with

ἰσοφόρος ον equal in strength

ἰσοχειλής ές level with the edge

ἰσόψηφος ον having an equal vote, equal in authority; with *or* by an equal number of votes

ἰσόψῡχος ον having the same mind

ἰσόω make equal; *mid and pass* be equal

ἱστά(ν)ω ▸ἵστημι

ἵστημι† *act tr* cause to stand; set, place, establish, fix; set up, raise up; stir, begin; stop, check; balance, weigh; appoint; *act intr* stand, be placed; place oneself; rise, arise, begin; lie, be situated; stand firm, be fixed; be inactive; continue

ἱστιάω etc. ▸ἑστ-

ἱστιητόριον ου τό public inn

ἱστίον ου τό sail

ἱστοδόκη ης ἡ mast-holder (on which the mast rested when let down)

ἱστοπέδη ης ἡ hole for fixing the mast in

ἱστορέω *and mid* inquire, question, search; know by inquiry; narrate

ἱστορίᾱ ᾱς ἡ inquiry, knowledge, information; science; narration; history

ἱστός οῦ ὁ ship's mast; loom; warp; web

ἱστουργέω work at the loom, weave

ἵστωρ (*gen* ορος) knowing; judge

ἰσχαλέος ᾱ ον dry, thin

ἰσχανάω, ἰσχάνω hold back, check; cling to + *gen*

ἰσχίον ου τό socket of the hip-bone

ἰσχναίνω ἰσχνανῶ ἴσχνᾱνα make dry, withered *or* thin

ἰσχνός ή όν dry; thin; lean

ἰσχνόφωνος ον with a weak voice, stammering

ἰσχῡρίζομαι ἰσχῡριοῦμαι ἰσχῡρισάμην make oneself strong; exert oneself; insist strongly (upon); affirm; persist in

ἰσχῡρός ᾱ ον strong, mighty, powerful; firm, fortified; safe, lasting; resolute; violent

ἰσχῦς ύος ἡ strength, power, firmness, force; troops

ἰσχῦω be strong, mighty, powerful

ἴσχω ▸ **ἔχω**

ἰτέᾱ ᾱς ἡ willow; wicker shield

ἰτέϊνος η ον of willow, made of wicker

ἴτης ου ὁ bold, impetuous; insolent, impudent

ἴττω ▸ **ἴστω** *see* **οἶδα**

ἴτυς υος ἡ rim of a wheel; edge of a shield

ἰῡγή ῆς ἡ **ἰῡγμός** οῦ ὁ cry, howling, shout, yelling

ἰΰζω yell, shout, shriek

ἴφθῑμος (η) ον strong, stout, stalwart

ἶφι *adv* strongly, stoutly, mightily

ἴφιος ᾱ ον strong; fat

ἰχθυάω fish (for)

ἰχθύδιον ου τό little fish

ἰχθυοειδής ές fish-like; swarming with fish

ἰχθυοφάγος ου ὁ fish-eater

ἰχθῦς ύος ὁ fish

ἰχθυώδης ες ▸ **ἰχθυοειδής**

ἰχνεύμων ονος ὁ Pharaoh's rat, a weasel-like Egyptian animal that hunts down crocodile's eggs

ἰχνευτής οῦ ὁ (of a dog) a tracker

ἰχνεύω track, track down, find out

ἴχνος ους τό **ἴχνιον** ου τό footstep, track, trace; *pl* movement, gait

ἰχώρ ῶρος ὁ blood of the gods, ichor; lymph

ἴψ ἰπός ὁ worm that bores through horn and wood

ἰώ *int* oh! woe! (a cry of either joy or sorrow)

ἰωγή ῆς ἡ defence, shelter

ἰωή ῆς ἡ a roaring, whistling, sounding

ἰῶκα ▸ **ἰωκήν**

ἰωκή ῆς ἡ battle-din

ἰῶτα τό iota, the smallest letter, jot

ἰωχμός οῦ ὁ ▸ **ἰωκή**

Κκ

κ, Κ (κάππα) tenth letter of the alphabet ■ κ′ *as a numeral* = 10

κά ▸ **κέ** *see* **ἄν**

καβ-βάλλω ▸ **καταβάλλω**

κάγ ▸ **κατά γε**

κάγκανος ον dry

καγχάζω, καγχαλάω laugh aloud; shout

κάδ ▸ **κατὰ δέ**

καδίσκος ου ὁ balloting-urn

κάδος ου ὁ pitcher, jar, pail

καθά (καθ' ἅ) just as

καθ-αγ(ν)ίζω καθαγ(ν)ιῶ dedicate, devote, offer; burn; bury

καθαίρεσις εως ἡ a taking down, destruction

καθαιρετέος ᾱ ον to be put down

καθ-αιρέω take *or* pull down; close [the eyes of the dead]; demolish, destroy, kill; overpower; take away, carry off, seize; achieve; condemn; obtain; catch, surprise

καθαίρω καθαρῶ ἐκάθηρα clean, cleanse, purify; purge, clear; wash off

καθ-άλλομαι *mid* spring down

καθᾱμέριος ᾱ ον ▸ **καθημέριος**

καθανύω ▸ **κατανύω**

καθάπαξ *adv* once and for all, absolutely

καθάπερ *adv* just as

καθ-άπτω tie to, fasten on, attach to, take hold of; *mid* lay hold of, seize, attack, scold; call to witness

καθαρεύω keep oneself clean *or* pure

καθαρίζω καθαριῶ make clean, purify, purge

καθαριότης ητος ἡ purity, cleanliness

καθαρισμός οῦ ὁ ▸ **καθαρμός**

κάθαρμα ατος τό off-scourings, rubbish, filth; outcast

καθ-αρμόζω fit to

καθαρμός οῦ ὁ a cleansing, purifying; atonement

καθαρός ᾱ́ όν pure, clean, unsoiled; sound; undisturbed; unmixed, unalloyed, genuine; guiltless, innocent, chaste; honest; perfect

καθαρότης ητος ἡ purity

καθάρσιος ον purifying, cleansing, atoning

κάθαρσις εως ἡ ▸ **καθαρμός**

καθαρτής οῦ ὁ purifier, atoner

καθέδρᾱ ᾱς ἡ seat, chair; sitting still *or* inactive

καθέζομαι καθεδοῦμαι sit down, sit still, encamp

καθ-είργνῡμι ▸ **κατείργω**

καθεῖς ▸ **καθ' εἷς** one by one

καθεκτός ή όν to be held back

καθ-έλκω, καθ-ελκύω draw down; launch

καθεξῆς *adv* in succession, one after the other

καθεύδω καθευδήσω *impf* ἐκάθευδον sleep, be at rest

καθ-ευρίσκω find out

καθ-εψιάομαι + *gen* make fun of

καθηγεμών όνος ὁ guide

καθ-ηγέομαι *mid* lead the way, guide, show the way; do first; explain, expound

καθηγητής οῦ ὁ leader, guide; teacher

καθ-ηδυπαθέω squander in luxury

καθ-ήκω have come down; have arrived; be fitting, proper *or* sufficient

κάθ-ημαι be seated; sit in court; sit still *or* idle; stop; be encamped

καθημερινός ή όν daily

καθημέριος ᾱ ον of today

καθ-ιδρῡ́ω make sit down; set down, establish, settle; consecrate, dedicate

καθ-ιερεύω, καθ-ιερόω dedicate, vow, offer

καθ-ίζω, καθ-ιζάνω *act tr* make sit down; set down; place, establish, appoint, constitute; place in a certain condition; *act intr and mid* sit down, be settled *or* seated

καθ-ῑ́ημι *act tr* send down; let down; let return; *act intr and mid* come down; move on

καθ-ικετεύω implore

καθ-ικνέομαι *mid* come to, arrive at; touch [the heart]

καθ-ιππάζομαι *mid* ride down, overrun with horse

καθ-ίστημι *act tr* set down, put down, place; establish, appoint, constitute, ordain; place in a certain condition; *act intr (also mid)* be placed, set down, established *or* appointed; stand; appear; come to; be in a certain condition; become *or* have become; stand still, be fixed, ordained; exist; be in value; *mid* set down *or* place for oneself

καθό ▸ **καθ' ὅ** in so far as

κάθοδος ου ἡ way down *or* back

καθολικός ή όν universal

καθόλου *adv* on the whole, generally

καθ-ομολογέω grant, consent (to); confess, allow

καθ-οπλίζω arm, equip; overcome

καθοράω *and mid* look down; see from afar; behold, view, perceive, know

καθ-ορμίζω bring to anchor; *mid and pass* come into harbour

καθότι *adv* insofar as, in what manner

καθ-υβρίζω be insolent, haughty *or* wicked; insult, treat with contempt

κάθυδρος ον full of water

καθυπ-άρχω exist, fall to one's lot

καθύπερθεν *adv* from above; above, on high; before
■ **τὰ καθύπερθεν** the upper country, i.e. further inland

καθυπέρτερος ᾱ ον upper, higher, superior
■ **καθυπέρτατος** η ον highest

καθ-υπνόω *and mid* fall asleep; sleep sound

καθυφ-ΐημι *and mid* let go, abandon, betray; yield

καθώς *adv* as, how

καθώσπερ *adv* just as

καί *conj* and, also, even, though; especially
■ **καί ... καί** both ... and

καιετάεις εσσα εν rich in caverns *or* chasms

καινίζω καινιῶ make new

καινοπαθής ές never suffered before

καινο-ποιέω make new

καινός ή όν new; unheard of, strange

καινότης ητος ἡ newness

καινο-τομέω begin something new, make innovations

καινουργέω act in a new way, begin something new

καινόω make new; consecrate anew

καίνυμαι excel; surpass

καίνω κανῶ ἔκανον kill

καίπερ *conj* although

καίριος ᾱ ον happening at the right time and place, seasonable; (of part of the body) vital; deadly

καιρός οῦ ὁ proportion, due measure; right place; right time *or* season, opportunity; time, circumstances; critical moment; embarrassment; importance, influence; profit, success

καιροσέων *gen pl fem from* **καιρόεις** εσσα εν close-woven

καίτοι *adv* and yet, and indeed; however; although

καίω† kindle, set on fire, burn, waste; *pass* be set on fire, be burnt; burn

κακ-αγγελέω bring bad news

κακάγγελτος ον caused by bad news

κακανδρίᾱ ᾱς ἡ unmanliness

κάκη ης ἡ ▸ **κακία**

κακ-ηγορέω abuse, speak ill of, slander

κακίᾱ ᾱς ἡ badness, wickedness, vice, cowardice, shame; disgrace; reproach

κακίζω κακιῶ make cowardly; abuse, blame; *pass* be reproached *or* blamed; play the coward

κακκεῖαι, κακκῆαι *see* **κατακαίω**

κακκείοντες ▸ **κατακείοντες**

κακόβιος ον living wretchedly

κακογείτων (*gen* ονος) neighbour of misery, bad neighbour

κακοδαιμονάω, κακοδαιμονέω be possessed by an evil spirit

κακοδαιμονίᾱ ᾱς ἡ misfortune; possession by a demon; raving madness

κακοδαίμων ον unhappy, wretched

κακοδοξέω have a bad reputation

κακοείμων ον badly clad

κακοεργίᾱ ᾱς ἡ ▸ **κακουργία**

κακοήθεια ᾱς ἡ malignity

κακοήθης ες malicious

κακόθροος ον (*also* κακόθρους ουν) slanderous

κακοΐλιος ου ἡ unhappy Ilios (i.e. Troy)

κακολογέω abuse, slander, accurse

κακολογίᾱ ᾱς ἡ slander

κακομήχανος ον contriving evil, mischievous

κακόνοια ᾱς ἡ ill-will, enmity

κακόνομος ον with bad laws

κακόνοος ον ill-disposed, hostile

κακόξεινος ον unfortunate in guests, inhospitable

κακοξύνετος ον wise for evil

κακοπάθεια ᾱς ἡ suffering, distress

κακο-παθέω suffer evil, be distressed

κακοπινής ές exceedingly filthy, foul

κακο-ποιέω do ill; hurt, spoil

κακοποιός οῦ ὁ wrong-doer

κακόπους (*gen* ποδος) with bad feet

κακο-πρᾱγέω be unfortunate, fail in one's enterprise

κακοπρᾱγίᾱ ᾱς ἡ misadventure; failure

κακοπρᾱ́γμων ον mischievous

κακός ή όν bad, evil; useless, unfit; mean, vile, cowardly; foul, unfair, wicked, mischievous, shameful; injurious, hurtful; miserable, wretched

■ **τὸ κακόν** evil, ill, mischief, distress, suffering; damage; vice

κακοσκελής ές with bad legs

κακοστομέω use bad language about, abuse

κακοτεχνέω act maliciously

κακότεχνος ον artful, wily

κακότης ητος ἡ badness; cowardice; misfortune, distress; defeat

κακοτροπίᾱ ᾱς ἡ bad habits

κακοτυχέω be unfortunate

κακουργέω do evil, act badly; hurt, damage; ravage

κακούργημα ατος τό **κακουργίᾱ** ᾱς ἡ bad *or* wicked deed, wickedness

κακοῦργος ου ὁ someone doing evil, someone who is mischievous *or* villainous; wrong-doer, criminal, knave

κακουχέω treat badly

κακοφραδής ές devising evil, giving bad advice

κακόφρων ον ill-disposed, malignant; foolish

κακόω treat badly, maltreat, vex, hurt, destroy; make angry, exasperate

κάκτανε *see* **κατακτείνω**

κάκωσις εως ἡ ill-treatment; humiliation; suffering, distress

καλάμη ης ἡ stalk of corn; stubble

καλαμηφόρος ον carrying reeds

καλάμινος η ον of reed *or* cane

κάλαμος ου ὁ reed, cane; writing-reed

καλάσῑρις ιος ἡ long garment worn by females

καλαῦροψ οπος ἡ shepherd's staff

καλέω† call, call by name; summon, call to help; invoke, implore; summon before the court; invite; *pass* be called

■ **καλούμενος** *pple* so-called

καλήτωρ ορος ὁ crier

καλινδέομαι *pass* roll, wallow; be busy with

καλλείπω ▸ **καταλείπω**

καλλιβόᾱς (*gen* ου) beautiful sounding

καλλίβοτρυς (*gen* υος) with beautiful grapes

καλλιγύναιξ (*gen* αικος) with beautiful women

καλλιέλαιος ου ἡ cultivated olive

καλλιεπέομαι use flowery speech

καλλιερέω sacrifice with good omens, give good omens

καλλίζωνος ον with beautiful girdles

καλλίθριξ (*gen* τριχος) with beautiful hair *or* mane

καλλίκομος ον with fine hair

καλλικρήδεμνος ον with fine hair-bands

κάλλιμος ον ▸ **καλός**

καλλιπάρῃος ον with beautiful cheeks

καλλιπλόκαμος ον with beautiful locks

καλλιρέεθρος ον **καλλίρροος** ον beautifully flowing

καλλιστεῖον ου τό prize of beauty *or* valour

καλλιστεύω *and mid* be the most beautiful

καλλίσφυρος ον with beautiful ankles

καλλίφθογγος ον sounding beautifully

καλλίχορος ον with beautiful dancing-places

καλλονή ῆς ἡ **κάλλος** ους τό beauty; ornament; excellence; beautiful thing

καλλῡ́νω καλλυνῶ beautify, embellish; *mid* boast, pride oneself (up)on

καλλωπίζω make beautiful, embellish, adorn; *mid* adorn oneself; boast, pride oneself (up)on; be affected *or* coy

καλλώπισμα ατος τό **καλλωπισμός** οῦ ὁ embellishment, ornament, finery

καλοδιδάσκαλος ου ὁ/ἡ teacher of virtue

καλοκᾱγαθίᾱ ᾱς ἡ nobleness and goodness

κᾶλον ου τό wood

καλο-ποιέω do good

καλόπους ποδος ὁ shoemaker's last

καλός ή όν beautiful, fair, charming, lovely, pretty; honest, noble, good, right, virtuous; agreeable, auspicious, favourable, dear
■ **καλὸς κἀγαθός** honest man, gentleman, aristocrat
■ **τὸ καλόν** the beautiful, beauty; virtue, honesty, honour; joy, happiness

κάλος ου ὁ ▸ **κάλως**

κάλπις ιδος ἡ pitcher, urn

καλύβη ης ἡ hut, cabin

κάλυμμα ατος τό covering, veil

κάλυξ υκος ἡ husk, shell; cup; bud; *pl* earrings

καλυπτός ή όν enveloping

καλύπτρᾱ ᾱς ἡ covering, cover; veil

καλύπτω cover, envelop, conceal

καλχαίνω be agitated in mind, ponder deeply; make purple; make dark and troubled (like a stormy sea)

καλώδιον ου τό rope, cord

κάλως ω ὁ rope, cable

κάμαξ ακος ἡ pole for vines

καμάρᾱ ᾱς ἡ chamber, vault; covered carriage

καματηρός ά όν wearisome; sick

κάματος ου ὁ weariness; toil, labour; distress

καμηλάτης ου ὁ camel driver

κάμηλος ου ὁ/ἡ camel

κάμῑλος ου ὁ anchor-cable

κάμῑνος ου ἡ furnace, kiln

καμῑνώ οῦς ἡ furnace-woman

καμμονίη ης ἡ endurance, victory

κάμμορος ον unfortunate

κάμνω καμοῦμαι ἔκαμον work hard; labour, exert oneself; be weary, exhausted *or* tired; be sick *or* ill; feel trouble; *mid* work *or* till laboriously; gain by hard work

καμπή ῆς ἡ a bending, curve, turning

κάμπτω κάμψω ἔκαμψα bend, bow, turn around; make someone alter his or her sentiments

καμπύλος η ον curved, bent

κἄν ▸ **καὶ ἄν, καὶ ἐάν**

κανναῖος ου ὁ **κανανῑ́της** ου ὁ zealot

καναχέω clash, clang

καναχή ῆς ἡ ringing sound, clash, gnashing, noise

καναχίζω ▸ **καναχέω**

κάνδυς υος ὁ kaftan

κάνε(ι)ον ου τό basket; dish

κάνθαρος ου ὁ beetle

κανθήλιος ου ὁ pack-ass

κάνναβις ιος ἡ hemp; garment of hemp

καννεύσας ▸ **κατανεύσας**

κανοῦν ▸ **κάνεον**

κανών όνος ὁ rod, bar; weaving-staff; handle of the shield; rule, ruler, level; precept, law; model, standard (of excellence)

κάπετος ου ἡ ditch, trench; hole, grave

κάπη ης ἡ manger

καπηλεῖον ου τό shop; tavern

καπηλεύω be a retail-dealer, sell; adulterate, corrupt

κάπηλος ου ὁ retailer, huckster, shopkeeper; innkeeper

καπίθη ης ἡ a Persian measure

κάπνη ης ἡ chimney

καπνίζω καπνιῶ ἐκάπνισα light a fire; blacken with smoke; be black with smoke

καπνοδόκη ης ἡ smoke-hole

καπνός οῦ ὁ smoke, steam, vapour

κάπριος ον like a wild boar; *noun* ▸ **κάπρος**

κάπρος ου ὁ wild boar

κάρ¹ ▸ **κάρα** head

κάρ² καρός τό chip, hair *(meaning uncertain, but conveying something worthless)* ■ **ἐν καρὸς αἴσῃ** at a hair's worth

κάρᾱ ᾱτος τό head; person; top, summit

καρᾱδοκέω watch, expect eagerly

καρᾱδοκίᾱ ᾱς ἡ expectation

κάρᾱνος ου ὁ chief, lord

καρᾱ́τομος ον cut off from the head

καρβατίνη ης ἡ peasant's shoe

καρδίᾱ ᾱς ἡ heart, mind, soul; stomach

καρδιογνώστης ου ὁ knower of hearts

κάρδοπος ου ἡ kneading-trough

κάρη τό ▸ **κάρα**

καρκαίρω ring; quake

καρκίνος ου ὁ cancer, crab

καρπαίᾱ ᾱς ἡ a mimic dance

καρπάλιμος ον swift, quick, hasty

καρπός¹ οῦ ὁ fruit, corn, harvest, produce; profit, success

καρπός² οῦ ὁ wrist

καρπο-φορέω bear fruit

καρποφόρος ον fruit-bearing

καρπόω bear fruit; *mid* gather fruit, reap; have the enjoyment of; plunder

καρρέζω ▸ **καταρέζω**

κάρτα *adv* very, very much

καρτερέω be firm, steadfast *or* patient; endure, bear, persist in

καρτέρησις εως ἡ **καρτερίᾱ** ᾱς ἡ patience, endurance; abstinence, self-control

καρτερικός ή όν enduring, patient

καρτερόθῡμος ον stout-hearted

καρτερός ᾱ́ όν strong, firm, staunch; enduring, steadfast; mighty, valiant, courageous, brave; violent, obstinate, cruel

κάρτιστος η ον ▸ **κράτιστος**

κάρτος εος τό ▸ **κράτος**

καρτῡ́νω ▸ **κρατύνω**

κάρτυον ου τό nut

καρφαλέος ᾱ ον dry; [of sounds] hollow

κάρφη ης ἡ **κάρφος** εος τό dry stalk, hay, straw, chaff, dry stick

κάρφω κάρψω make dry *or* withered

καρχαλέος ᾱ ον rough, hoarse, dry

καρχαρόδους (*gen* όδοντος) with sharp teeth

κασίᾱ ᾱς ἡ cassia (an Arabian spice)

κασιγνήτη ης ἡ sister

κασίγνητος η ον brotherly, sisterly ■ **ὁ κασίγνητος** brother

κάσις ιος ὁ/ἡ brother, sister

κασσίτερος ου ὁ tin

κάστωρ ορος ὁ beaver

κατά *adv* downwards, down; entirely; *prep with acc* downwards, down; over; among, throughout, along; near, opposite, at; during, about; because of; in search of; in relation to,

concerning, according to, answering to; after; *with gen* from above, down from; down upon; opposite to, against
■ **κατὰ τρεῖς** three at a time
■ **κατὰ φῦλα** by tribes
■ **κατ' ἐνιαυτόν** year by year

κᾳ̑τα ▸ **καί εἶτα**

κατα-βαίνω go *or* come down, go down to the sea; (of a fighter) go into the arena; fall down; condescend; come to; enter into

κατα-βάλλω throw *or* cast down, overthrow; let fall, drop, lay down; slay, destroy; pay down, pay; bring *or* carry down, store up; throw away, reject, disparage

K

κατα-βαρέω, κατα-βαρῦνω weigh down, burden, molest

κατάβασις εως ἡ going down, way *or* march down, descent

κατα-βιβάζω cause to go down, lead *or* bring down

κατα-βιβρώσκω eat up

κατα-βιόω live through; bring life to an end

κατα-βλᾱκεύω spoil by carelessness

κατα-βλώσκω go through

κατα-βοάω + *gen* cry aloud, cry out against, complain of

καταβοή ῆς ἡ outcry against; report; accusation

καταβολή ῆς ἡ attack, payment, foundation

κατα-βραβεύω decide against

κατα-βροχθίζω swallow down

κατα-βυρσόω cover over with hides

κατάγαιος ον ▸ **κατάγειος**

καταγγελεύς έως ὁ announcer

κατ-αγγέλλω announce, proclaim

κατάγγελτος ον denounced, betrayed

κατάγειος ον underground; on the ground

καταγέλαστος ον ridiculous

κατα-γελάω laught at, mock

κατάγελως ωτος ὁ mockery, ridiculousness

κατα-γηράσκω, κατα-γηράω grow old

κατα-γιγνώσκω observe, discover, perceive; think ill of; charge with, condemn, give judgement against (someone *gen*)

κατ-αγῑνέω ▸ **κατάγω**

κάταγμα ατος τό wool drawn *or* spun out, flock of wool

κατ-άγνῡμι *act tr* break in *or* to pieces, shatter, shiver; *act intr and pass* be broken, burst

κατάγνωσις εως ἡ + *gen* thinking ill of, contempt for; condemnation

κατα-γοητεύω bewitch, enchant, cheat by trickery

κατ-αγορεύω denounce

κατα-γράφω scratch, write down

κατ-άγω lead, bring *or* carry down; lead to a place; bring down from the sea to the land; lead *or* bring back *or* home; *mid* come to land, put in; return

καταγωγή ῆς ἡ landing, putting in; harbour, quarters

καταγώγιον ου τό quarters, inn, hotel

κατ-αγωνίζομαι *mid* overpower

κατα-δαίομαι divide, rend asunder

κατα-δακρῡ́ω weep, lament

κατα-δαμάζομαι subdue completely

κατα-δαπανάω use up, spend entirely

κατα-δάπτω rend to pieces

κατα-δαρθάνω fall asleep

καταδεής ές needy
■ **καταδεέστερος** inferior, weaker, less

κατα-δείδω fear greatly

κατα-δείκνῡμι show, make known; teach

κατα-δειλιάω neglect from fear *or* cowardice; show signs of fear

κατα-δέομαι *pass* + *gen* entreat earnestly

κατα-δέρκομαι *pass* look down upon

κατα-δεύω wet

κατα-δέχομαι *mid* admit, receive back

κατα-δέω[1] bind to; fetter, imprison; tie up, close, shut up; check; convict, condemn

κατα-δέω[2] + *gen* want, lack, need

κατάδηλος ον very manifest *or* conspicuous

κατα-δημοβορέω consume public goods

κατα-διαιτάω + *gen* (of an arbiter) decide against

κατα-δίδωμι flow into

κατα-δικάζω + *gen* give judgement against, condemn; *mid* obtain judgement against someone else, gain one's lawsuit

καταδίκη ης ἡ condemnation; fine

κατα-διώκω pursue, chase

κατα-δοκέω, κατα-δοξάζω think ill of someone, suspect; think, suppose, judge

κατα-δουλόω enslave, subdue

καταδούλωσις εως ἡ enslaving, subjugation

κατα-δρέπω pluck off

καταδρομή ῆς ἡ raid, inroad; vehement attack, invective

κατα-δυναστεύω ▸ **καταδουλόω**

κατα-δῡ́νω ▸ **καταδύομαι** *mid*

κατα-δύω *act tr* submerge, dip; cause to sink; *act intr and mid* go under water, sink; enter; go down, set; creep into; hide oneself; put on [garments *or* arms]

κατ-ᾴδω annoy by singing, charm by singing; sing to; sing a spell; conjure

κατα-έννῡμι clothe, cover

κατ-αζαίνω dry up

κατα-ζεύγνῡμι yoke together, harness; bind, tie, fetter, imprison

κατα-θάπτω bury, inter

κατα-θεάομαι *mid* look down upon, behold, watch, view

κατα-θέλγω subdue by charms

κατάθεμα ατος τό curse; accursed thing

κατα-θεματίζω curse

κατα-θέω run down; make an inroad *or* raid; overrun, attack

κατα-θεωρέω ▸ **καταθεάομαι**

κατα-θνῄσκω die (away), be dying

καταθνητός ή όν mortal

κατα-θορυβέω shout down

κατα-θρῴσκω leap down *or* over

κατ-αθῡμέω lose all heart, be utterly despondent

καταθῡ́μιος ᾱ ον being in *or* upon the mind

κατα-θύω slaughter, sacrifice; dedicate

καταιβατός όν accessible; downward-leading

κατ-αιδέομαι feel *or* be ashamed; stand in awe of

κατ-αικίζω disfigure, spoil completely

κατ-αινέω agree, assent to, approve of; grant, promise

κατ-αίρω come to land; (of birds) make a swoop

κατ-αισθάνομαι *mid* perceive *or* understand fully

κατ-αισχῡ́νω disgrace, dishonour; shame, put to shame; deceive; *pass* feel ashamed

κατα-ῐ̈́σχω possess

κατ-αιτιάομαι *mid* accuse, lay to someone's charge, impute

καταῖτυξ υγος ἡ leather skull-cap

κατα-καίνω ▸ **κατακτείνω**

κατακαίριος ον deadly

κατα-καίω burn down

κατα-καλέω summon

κατα-καλύπτω envelop, cover up

κατα-καυχάομαι *mid* + *gen* boast against, exult over; treat with contempt, have no fear of

κατά-κειμαι *mid* lie down; recline at table; lie hid, still *or* sick

κατα-κείρω cut down; consume, waste; shear off, give a short haircut

κατα-κείω go to sleep

κατα-κερτομέω abuse violently

κατα-κηλέω enchant

κατα-κηρόω cover with wax

κατα-κηρύσσω proclaim by a herald

κατα-κλαίω *and mid* bewail, lament

κ

κατα-κλάω break off, break in *or* to pieces; move *or* shake someone's heart

κατα-κλείω shut up *or* in, blockade; compel, oblige

κατα-κληροδοτέω distribute by lot

κατα-κλήω ▸ **κατακλείω**

κατα-κλῑ́νω lay down; make [someone] recline (at a meal); *pass* lie down

κατάκλισις εως ἡ making to recline (at a meal), sitting (at a meal); celebration (of a marriage)

κατα-κλύζω inundate

κατακλυσμός οῦ ὁ inundation, flood

κατα-κοιμάω, κατα-κοιμίζω put to sleep; lull to sleep; let fall into oblivion; sleep through; *pass* fall asleep

κατ-ακολουθέω + *dat* follow, obey

κατα-κολπίζω run into [a bay]

κατα-κολυμβάω dive

κατακομιδή ῆς ἡ exportation

κατα-κομίζω bring down to the sea; import; *pass* arrive, come into harbour

κατ-ακοντίζω shoot down

κατα-κόπτω cut down, slay, kill; coin money; rend, tear to pieces

κατάκορος ον excessive

κατα-κοσμέω arrange, put in order; adorn

κατ-ακούω hear, hearken to, obey, be subject to

κατάρκρᾱς *adv* thoroughly

κατα-κρατέω prevail, be superior

κατα-κρεμάννῡμι hang up, hang on

κατα-κρεουργέω cut to pieces (as a butcher does meat), lacerate

κατᾱκρῆθεν *adv* from the head downwards; entirely

κατάκρῑμα ατος τό ▸ **κατάκρισις**

κατα-κρῑ́νω + *gen or acc* give judgement against, condemn

κατάκρισις εως ἡ judgement, condemnation

κατα-κρύπτω hide, conceal

κατακρυφή ῆς ἡ pretext, evasion

κατα-κτάομαι *mid* gain, possess

κατα-κτείνω kill, destroy, execute

κατα-κυλῑ́ομαι *pass* roll *or* fall down

κατα-κύπτω bend down, stoop

κατα-κῡριεύω + *gen* gain dominion over

κατα-κῡρόω ratify; *pass* be fulfilled *or* realized

κατα-κωλῡ́ω keep back, hinder (from doing)

κατα-λαλέω talk loudly; slander

καταλαλίᾱ ᾶς ἡ slander, calumny

κατάλαλος ου ὁ slanderer

κατα-λαμβάνω *act tr* seize, lay hold of, take possession of, take away, occupy; catch, overtake, surprise, discover, find out, meet; *act intr* happen, come to pass, befall; hold fast *or* back, check; bind by oath; oblige; *mid* seize for oneself, occupy, conquer; understand, apprehend

κατα-λάμπω shine upon

κατ-αλγέω suffer pain

κατα-λέγω[1] recite, count up, relate, tell, explain, mention; pick out, choose; enlist, enrol

κατα-λέγω[2] ▸ **καταλέχομαι**

κατα-λείβομαι *pass* trickle *or* drop down

κατάλειμμα ατος τό remnant, residue

κατα-λείπω leave behind, bequeath; spare one's life; forsake, abandon; lose; *pass* remain behind; be impending; *mid* leave behind for oneself, retain, reserve to oneself

κατα-λεύω stone to death

κατα-λέχομαι lie down, go to bed

κατ-αλέω grind down

κατα-λήθομαι *mid* + *gen* forget wholly

καταληπτέος ᾱ ον to be seized

κατάληψις εως ἡ seizing, catching, capture; assault

κατα-λιθόω, κατα-λιθάζω stone to death

κατα-λιμπάνω ▸ **καταλείπω**

κατα-λῑπαρέω entreat earnestly

καταλλαγή ῆς ἡ reconciliation

κατ-αλλάσσω change, exchange; reconcile; *pass* become reconciled; *mid* exchange for oneself

καταλογάδην *adv* by way of conversation, in prose

καταλογεύς έως ὁ an officer who enrols citizens

κατ-αλογέω despise

κατα-λογίζομαι *mid* count among; count up, number; consider

κατάλογος ου ὁ counting up; catalogue, list

κατάλοιπος ον remaining

καταλοφάδεια *adv* on the neck

κατάλυμα ατος τό inn

καταλύσιμος ον to be dissolved *or* repaired

κατάλυσις εως ἡ dissolving, disbanding; destruction, end, overthrow, expulsion; resting-place, inn

κατα-λύω *act tr* dissolve; destroy, end, abolish, depose, dismiss, disband; *act intr and mid* make peace, become reconciled; make halt, repose, alight, cease

κατα-λωφάω + *gen* rest *or* recover from

κατα-μανθάνω learn exactly; know well; search out; perceive; consider; understand

κατα-μαργέω be stark mad

κατα-μάρπτω catch hold of

κατα-μαρτυρέω bear witness against

κατ-αμάω mow down; *mid* pile *or* heap up

κατ-αμβλῡ́νω make blunt

κατα-μεθύσκω make drunk

κατα-μείγνῡμι ▸ **καταμίγνυμι**

κατ-αμελέω + *gen* neglect

κατάμεμπτος ον blameworthy, abhorred

κατα-μέμφομαι *mid* blame, accuse, reproach

κατάμεμψις εως ἡ blaming, finding fault

κατα-μένω stay behind, remain; remain fixed, continue

κατα-μερίζω distribute

κατα-μετρέω measure out to

κατα-μηνύω give information; + *gen* bear witness against

κατα-μιαίνω *pass* wear mourning dress; taint, defile

κατα-μῑ́γνῡμι mix up; *mid* be mixed with, intrude oneself

καταμόνᾱς *adv* alone, apart

κατ-αμύσσω scratch, tear

κατα-μῡ́ω close the eyes

καταμφι-καλύπτω envelop fully

κατ-αναγκάζω obtain by force; overpower by force, fetter

κατανάθεμα ατος τό curse

κατ-αναθεματίζω curse

κατ-ανᾱλίσκω consume, spend; waste

κατα-ναρκάω + *gen* be burdensome to

κατα-νάσσω beat down

κατα-ναυμαχέω conquer at sea

κατα-νέμω distribute; divide; *mid* divide among themselves

κατα-νεύω nod agreement; consent, grant

κατα-νέω[1] spin out

κατα-νέω[2] heap *or* pile up

κατ-ανθρακόω burn to coal

κατα-νοέω perceive, observe, watch, learn; take to heart; consider

κατ-αντάω come to; arrive at

κατάντης ες downhill, downwards ■ **κάταντα** *adv*

κατάντησιν *adv* just opposite

καταντικρύ, καταντίον, καταντιπέρᾱς *adv* just opposite; downwards

κατάνυξις εως ἡ stupefaction

κατα-νύσσω prick; aggrieve

κατ-ανύ(τ)ω finish; arrive at; alight; accomplish, fulfil, grant

κατα-ξαίνω scratch; tear to pieces; stone to death

κατάξιος ον quite worthy

κατ-αξιόω think worthy, esteem; desire

καταπακτός ή όν fastened downwards

κατα-πάλλομαι *mid* leap down

κατα-πατέω tread *or* trample down

κατάπαυμα ατος τό rest, comfort

κατάπαυσις εως ἡ stopping; deposing

κατα-παύω lay to rest, stop, finish, assuage; check, hinder; depose; *intr* rest

κατα-πεδάω fetter, hamper

κατ-απειλέω threaten

κατα-πειράζω try, put to the test

καταπειρητηρίη ης ἡ sounding line

κατα-πέμπω send down

κατάπερ *adv* ▸ **καθάπερ**

κατα-πέσσω digest; swallow, suppress

κατα-πετάννῡμι spread out over; spread *or* cover with

καταπέτασμα ατος τό curtain, veil

κατα-πέτομαι *mid* fly down

κατα-πετρόω stone to death

κατα-πεφνεῖν *aor infin* kill

κατα-πήγνῡμι *act tr* stick fast, fix; *act intr and pass* be firmly fixed, stand fast

κατα-πηδάω leap down

κατα-πίμπλημι fill full

κατα-πίνω swallow down

κατα-πίπτω fall down; subside, sink

κατα-πισσόω cover with pitch

κατα-πλάσσω besmear, plaster

καταπλαστῦς ύος ἡ plaster

κατα-πλέκω entwine; unroll, unweave; finish

κατα-πλέω sail down; put to shore; sail back

κατάπληξις εως ἡ consternation, terror

κατα-πλήσσω strike down; terrify, confound; *pass* be frightened *or* amazed

κατάπλους ου ὁ sailing down; landing; course, passage, return

κατα-πλουτίζω enrich

κατα-πλώω ▸ **καταπλέω**

κατα-πολεμέω conquer in war, overcome

κατα-πολῑτεύομαι *mid* ruin by one's policy

κατα-πονέω subdue after a hard struggle

κατα-ποντίζω, κατα-ποντέω *tr* throw into the sea; drown

καταποντιστής οῦ ὁ pirate

κατα-πορνεύω prostitute

κατα-πρᾱ́σσω effect, accomplish, achieve; *mid* achieve for oneself, obtain

κατα-πρᾱΰνω appease

καταπρηνής ές head foremost *or* downwards

κατα-πρῑ́ω saw to pieces

καταπρο-δίδωμι betray utterly

καταπρο-ῑ̈́σσομαι do with impunity

κατα-πτήσσω cower down, creep away; be timid

κατάπτυστος ον despicable

κατα-πτῡ́ω + *gen* spit upon, abhor

κατα-πτώσσω ▶ **καταπτήσσω**

κατα-πῡ́θομαι *pass* become rotten

κατ-άρᾱ ᾱς ἡ curse

κατ-αράομαι *mid* curse, utter imprecations; wish someone evil

κατ-αράσσω dash down, smash; push back

κατάρᾱτος ον cursed; abominable

κατ-αργέω make inactive *or* barren; undo, abolish, remove, release

κάταργμα ατος τό introductory *or* first offering

κατ-αργυρόω overlay with silver; bribe

κατα-ρέζω stroke, caress

κατ-αρέομαι ▶ **καταράομαι**

κατ-αριθμέω *and mid* count up *or* among

κατ-αρκέω be fully sufficient

κατ-αρνέομαι *pass* deny strongly

κατα-ρρᾳθῡμέω be careless, lose by carelessness

κατα-ρρακόω tear to rags

καταρράκτης ου ὁ **καταρρακτός** ή όν precipitous, gushing down; waterfall

κατα-ρράπτω stitch on *or* over; stitch tight

κατα-ρρέπω fall down; cause to fall

κατα-ρρέω flow down; fall down; collapse

κατα-ρρήγνῡμι *act tr* break *or* tear down; tear to *or* in pieces; *act intr and pass* fall down; burst out

κατα-ρροφέω swallow down

καταρρυής ές flowing down

κατα-ρρυπαίνω soil, dirty

κατάρρυτος ον irrigated, watered; alluvial

κατ-αρρωδέω be afraid

καταρρώξ (*gen* ῶγος) precipitous, broken

κάταρσις εως ἡ landing place

κατ-αρτάω, κατ-αρτίζω adjust well, prepare, restore, repair, equip

κατάρτισις εως ἡ **καταρτισμός** οῦ ὁ restoration, perfection

κατ-αρτῡ́ω prepare, adjust, arrange; train, master

κατ-άρχω + *gen* begin, do first; *mid* begin the rites

κατα-σβέννῡμι *act tr* quench, extinguish; *act intr and pass* be quenched

κατα-σείω shake down, throw down; beckon

κατα-σεύομαι *mid* rush down

κατα-σημαίνω mark; *mid* seal

κατα-σήπω let rot; *intr* rot away

κατα-σῑγάω remain silent

κατα-σῑτέομαι *mid* eat up

κατα-σιωπάω be silent; make silent, silence; *mid* impose silence

κατα-σκάπτω dig down, demolish

κατασκαφή ῆς ἡ demolishing, destruction; tomb

κατασκαφής ές underground

κατα-σκεδάννῡμι scatter about

κατα-σκέπτομαι *mid* ▶ **κατασκοπέω**

κατα-σκευάζω prepare, adjust, furnish, adorn; get ready; make, build, found; provide, supply, contrive; *mid* prepare oneself *or* for oneself

κατασκευή ῆς ἡ preparation, equipment, furniture; building; state, condition; baggage

κατα-σκηνάω, κατα-σκηνόω take up one's quarters; pitch a tent, encamp

κατασκήνωσις εως ἡ a encamping, rest(ing place)

κατα-σκήπτω rush down upon; be hurled down upon; assail, attack

κατασκιά(ζ)ω overshadow; bury

κατάσκιος ον overshadowed

κατα-σκοπέω inspect, view, examine; spy out, explore

κατάσκοπος ου ὁ spy, scout

κατα-σκώπτω mock

κατα-σοφίζομαι *mid* outwit, cheat

κατα-σπάω draw *or* pull down

κατα-σπείρω sow; spread out; cause

κατα-σπένδω pour out as a libation; pour upon; ▸ **σπένδω**

κατα-σπέρχω press *or* urge upon

κατα-σπουδάζομαι be earnest about

κατα-στάζω trickle down, drip

κατα-στασιάζω overthrow by a counter-faction

κατάστασις εως ἡ establishing, appointing, arrangement, presentation, equipment; state, condition; surety; constitution, nature

καταστάτης ου ὁ arranger, establisher

κατα-στεγάζω cover over

καταστέγασμα ατος τό a covering, roof

κατάστεγος ον roofed, covered

κατα-στείβω tread *or* step on

κατα-στέλλω arrange; keep down, repress

κατα-στένω sigh over

καταστεφής ές wreathed

κατάστημα ατος τό condition, state, bearing

καταστολή ῆς ἡ dress

κατα-στόρνῡμι ▸ **καταστρώννυμι**

κατ-αστράπτω flash lightning

κατα-στρατοπεδεύω *act tr* cause to encamp; *act intr and mid* encamp

κατα-στρέφω turn over, overturn, bring to an end; *mid* subdue

κατα-στρηνιάω behave wantonly towards

καταστροφή ῆς ἡ overturning, overthrowing, sudden turn, end, death, perdition; subduing

κατάστρωμα ατος τό deck [of a ship]

κατα-στρώννῡμι spread over; kill, overthrow; cover

κατα-στυγέω shudder at

κατα-σῡ́ρω drag away; plunder

κατα-σφάζω slaughter, kill

κατα-σφρᾱγίζω seal up

κατάσχεσις εως ἡ occupation, possession

κατα-σχίζω cleave asunder, break *or* burst open

κατα-σχολάζω linger, tarry

κατα-σώχω rub *or* grind to powder; pound, bruise

κατα-τάσσω arrange, draw up in order; classify; appoint

κατα-τείνω stretch out, strain, force; *intr* exert oneself; extend *or* run towards

κατα-τέμνω cut into pieces, mutilate; cut [trenches]

κατα-τήκω *act tr* cause to melt, dissolve; *act intr and pass* melt, pine away

κατα-τίθημι place *or* put down, lay down, propose [a prize]; lay in, preserve; pay; *mid* lay down for oneself, deposit, lay up in store; put away, lay aside; neglect; put an end to

κατα-τιτρώσκω wound

κατατομή ῆς ἡ a cutting into pieces, mutilation

κατα-τοξεύω shoot down

κατα-τραυματίζω injure, wound; disable, cripple (of ships)

κατα-τρέχω run down; attack, rush on against; run over, overrun

κατα-τρῖβω rub down *or* in pieces; wear away *or* out; waste, exhaust; *pass* be worn out *or* exhausted; be weary

κατα-τρῡ́χω rub down; wear out, exhaust

κατα-τρωματίζω ▶ **κατατραυματίζω**

κατα-τυγχάνω reach, obtain; be successful

κατ-αυδάω declare aloud, speak publicly

κατ-αυλέω play on the flute; *mid* listen to the flute playing

κατ-αυλίζομαι *pass* encamp, pass the night

κατα-φαίνομαι *pass* appear, become visible

καταφανής ές visible; conspicuous, manifest

κατάφαρκτος ον ▶ **κατάφρακτος**

κατα-φαρμάσσω poison, bewitch

κατα-φατίζω assure, protest

καταφερής ές sloping downwards, inclined, setting

κατα-φέρω carry *or* bring down; *pass* be driven down; be carried to

κατα-φεύγω flee down; take flight; resort to

κατάφευξις εως ἡ flight; refuge; evasion

κατά-φημι say yes, assent to

κατα-φθείρω ruin

κατα-φθίνω perish, waste away

κατα-φθίω ruin, destroy, kill; *pass* perish, waste away, be ruined *or* destroyed

καταφ-ῑ́ημι let glide down

κατα-φιλέω kiss tenderly, caress

κατα-φλέγω burn down

κατα-φοβέω frighten

κατα-φοιτάω come down constantly *or* regularly

κατα-φονεύω kill, slaughter

κατα-φορέω ▶ **καταφέρω**

κατα-φράζομαι *mid and pass* consider, ponder

κατάφρακτος ον fenced in; covered, decked

κατα-φρονέω despise, disdain, scorn; think of, suppose

καταφρόνημα ατος τό

καταφρόνησις εως ἡ contempt, disdain

καταφρονητής οῦ ὁ despiser

καταφρονητικῶς *adv* scornfully

κατα-φυγγάνω ▶ **καταφεύγω**

καταφυγή ῆς ἡ ▶ **κατάφευξις**

καταφῡλαδόν *adv* in *or* by tribes

κατα-φωράω catch in the act, discover; convict

κατα-χαίρω feel mischievous joy

κατα-χαλκόω cover with brass

κατα-χαρίζομαι *mid* do a favour; flatter; do *or* give up (something) out of courtesy

κατα-χειροτονέω + *gen* vote against

κατα-χέω pour down upon *or* over, shed; let fall; throw down; spread out; *pass* fall down; flow out; *mid* cause to be melted down

καταχθόνιος ον underground, infernal

κατα-χορδεύω mince up as if for a sausage

κατα-χορηγέω spend lavishly, squander

κατα-χόω ▶ **καταχώννῡμι**

κατα-χράω be enough, suffice; *mid* make use of, use up, consume; misuse; destroy, murder

κατα-χρῡσόω overlay with gold, gild

κατα-χώννῡμι cover with earth, inter

κατα-χωρίζω place properly

κατα-ψάω stroke

κατα-ψεύδομαι *mid* tell lies about; pretend, feign

κατα-ψευδομαρτυρέομαι *pass* be condemned by false witnesses

κατα-ψευστός ή όν invented, feigned

κατα-ψηφίζομαι *mid* + *gen* vote against

κατα-ψήχω rub down; *pass* crumble away

κατα-ψῡ́χω cool

κατέαται ▸ **κάθηνται**

κατ-έδω ▸ **κατεσθίω**

κατ-είβω let flow down, shed; *mid* flow down; elapse

κατείδωλος ον full of idols

κατ-εικάζω make (a)like; guess; *pass* be (a)like

κατ-ειλέω force together, enclose

κατ-ειλίσσω wrap around, enfold

κατ-ειλύω cover up

κάτ-ειμι go *or* come down, fall *or* flow down; come back

κατ-εῖπον *aor* speak against, accuse; speak out, tell, denounce

κατ-είργω, κατ-είργνῡμι press hard; confine; force; hinder

κατ-ειρύω ▸ **κατερύω**

κατ-ελεέω have pity

κατ-ελπίζω hope confidently

κατ-εναίρω, κατ-εναρίζω kill, destroy

κατεναντίον, κατέναντι *adv* opposite

κατένωπα, κατενώπιον *adv* + *gen* right opposite

κατεξουσιάζω + *gen* exercise authority over

κατεπ-ᾴδω use charms against

κατ-επείγω press hard, oppress; urge; hasten

κατ-εργάζομαι *mid* accomplish, achieve, effect; acquire, gain; overcome, oppress; kill

κατ-έργνῡμι, κατ-έργω ▸ **κατείργω**

κατ-ερείκω tear, rend

κατ-ερείπω demolish, destroy, cast down; *intr* fall down, perish

κατ-ερητῡ́ω, κατ-ερῡκάνω, κατ-ερῡ́κω hold back, detain, hinder

κατ-ερύω draw down; launch

κατ-έρχομαι ▸ **κάτειμι**

κατ-εσθίω, κατ-έσθω eat up, consume

κάτευγμα ατος τό vow, wish, prayer; votive offering

κατ-ευθῡ́νω make straight; direct

κατ-ευλογέω bless

κατ-ευνά(ζ)ω lull to sleep; soothe; *pass* lie down to sleep

κατ-εύχομαι *mid* wish, pray, vow, curse

κατ-ευωχέομαι feast, make merry

κατεφ-άλλομαι *mid* spring down upon

κατεφ-ισταμαι rise up against

κατ-έχω *act tr* keep down *or* back; direct to; check, restrain, withhold, delay; occupy, possess, keep; bear, suffer; *act intr* come to pass, happen, befall; dwell, sojourn; continue; stop, cease; *mid* keep for oneself, retain; stop, make a halt

κατ-ηγορέω + *gen* speak against; accuse, blame, reproach; + *acc* assert, state, signify, indicate, prove

κατηγόρημα ατος τό **κατηγορίᾱ** ᾱς ἡ accusation, reproach, charge

κατήγορος ου ὁ accuser

κατήκοος ον obedient, subject; listener, spy

κατ-ηπιάω assuage

κατ-ηρεμίζω, κατ-ηρεμέω calm, soothe

κατηρεφής ές covered; roofed; overshadowed

κατήρης ες well-supplied

κατήφεια ᾱς ἡ dejection; shame

κατηφέω be dejected *or* mute (with horror or grief)

κατηφής ές dejected, downcast

κατηφών όνος ὁ knave, reprobate

κατ-ηχέω resound; teach; inform

κατ-ιάπτω hurt, disfigure

κατῑθύ *adv + gen* opposite

κατ-ῑόομαι *pass* grow rusty

κατ-ισχναίνω make thin *or* lean

κατ-ισχῡ́ω gather strength; + *gen* have power over; prevail over

κατ-ίσχω ▸ **κατέχω**

κάτ-οιδα *pf* know exactly

κατ-οικέω *act tr* inhabit; regulate by laws; *act intr and mid* settle down; dwell

κατοίκησις εως ἡ settling (in a place), settlement, colonization; dwelling, abode

κατοικητήριον ου τό **κατοικίᾱ** ᾱς ἡ dwelling, habitation; settlement, colony (especially a military colony in Egypt)

κατ-οικίζω remove to a colony, settle; colonize, found *or* establish a colony in; *pass* be *or* become a colonist; be colonized

κατ-οικτείρω have compassion; pity

κατ-οικτίζω excite pity; ▸ **κατοικτείρω**; *mid* lament

κατ-οκνέω doubt, hesitate

κατ-ολοφῡ́ρομαι *mid* bewail, lament

κατ-όμνῡμι *and mid* confirm by oath; + *gen* accuse on oath

κατ-όνομαι *pass* criticize bitterly, abuse

κατόπιν, κατόπισθεν *adv* behind, after; afterwards

κατ-οπτεύω spy out, discover

κατ-όπτης ου ὁ spy

κάτοπτος ον visible

κάτοπτρον ου τό mirror

κατ-ορθόω *act tr* set right, make straight, manage well; mend; erect; keep sound; *act intr and mid* be successful, prosperous

κατόρθωμα ατος τό success, emendation

κατ-ορύσσω bury, inter

κατ-ορχέομαι *mid* dance in triumph over; insult, mock

κατ-ουρίζω bring into port with a fair wind, bring safe into port; bring to fulfilment; come to fulfilment

κατοχή ῆς ἡ holding fast; detention

κάτοχος ον constrained

καττάδε ▸ **κατά τάδε**

κάτω *adv* down, downwards; beneath, below; in the nether world; down to the coast

κάτωθεν *adv* from below; below

κατ-ωθέω thrust down

κατωμάδιος ον down from the shoulder

κατωμαδόν *adv* from the shoulder

κατωμοσίᾱ ᾱς ἡ accusation on oath

κατῶρυξ (*gen* υχος) imbedded in the earth, underground
■ **ἡ κατῶρυξ** pit, cavern

κατώτατος η ον nethermost

κατώτερος ᾱ ον lower

καυλός οῦ ὁ stalk, stem; shaft (of a spear); hilt (of a sword)

καῦμα ατος τό heat

καυματίζω consume by heat

καυσ *likely to be from* **καίω**

καύσιμος ον combustible

καῦσις εως ἡ a burning

καυσόομαι *pass* perish from heat; burn with intense heat

καύστειρα ης burning, hot

καύσων ωνος ὁ ▸ **καῦμα**

καυ(σ)τηριάζω brand, cauterize

καυχάομαι *mid* boast

καύχημα ατος τό **καύχησις** εως ἡ object of boasting; a boast

καχεξίᾱ ᾱς ἡ neglected state

κάχληξ ηκος ὁ pebble, gravel, shingle

κᾶω, κᾴω ▶ **καίω**

κέ(ν) ▶ **ἄν**

κεάζω split, shiver

κέαρ ατος τό ▶ **κῆρ** heart

κέγχρος ου ὁ millet; spawn of fish

κεδάννῡμι ▶ **σκεδάννυμι**

κεδνός ή όν careful; able, excellent, trusty; dear, valued; respectable

κεδρίᾱ ᾱς ἡ cedar-resin

κέδρινος ον of cedar-wood

κέδρος ου ἡ cedar tree

κεῖθεν, κεῖθι ▶ **ἐκεῖθεν, ἐκεῖθι**

κεῖμαι be laid down, lie; lie inactive, idle, still, sick, despised, dead *or* unburied; be situated; be ready, present *or* extant; be in value; be fixed *or* proposed

κειμήλιον ου τό treasure, ornament

κεῖνος η ον ▶ **ἐκεῖνος**

κεινός ή όν ▶ **κενός**

κειρίᾱ ᾱς ἡ wide strips of linen (to stretch over one's bed-frame as a support for the mattress, as opposed to the less comfortable esparto cords); bandage; grave clothes

κείρω κερῶ ἔκειρα cut off, clip, shear; hew off; eat off, consume entirely; waste, ravage; *mid* cut off one's hair

κεῖσε ▶ **ἐκεῖσε**

κείω[1] split, cleave

κείω[2] wish to lie down; wish to go to bed

κεκαδών *aor pple from* **χάζω**

κεκαφηώς υῖα ός weak, gasping forth

κέκονα *see* **καίνω**

κεκρύφαλος ου ὁ woman's hood; hair net

κελαδεινός ή όν noisy, roaring

κέλαδέω cry aloud, shout aloud

κέλαδος ου ὁ noise, tumult, sound, clap

κελάδων (*gen* οντος) ▶ **κελαδεινός**

κελαινεφής ές with dark clouds; shrouded in dark clouds (of Zeus)

κελαινός ή όν dark, gloomy, black

κελαινώπᾱς ᾱ ὁ black-faced, gloomy

κελαρύζω κελαρύξω ripple, murmur

κέλευθος ου ἡ way, road, path; gait; journey

κέλευ(σ)μα ατος τό **κελευσμοσύνη** ης ἡ order, command; call

κελευστής οῦ ὁ commander of rowers (who called out the time to them)

κελευτιάω exhort repeatedly

κελεύω exhort, command, order, bid; beseech, desire; grant, permit

κέλης ητος ὁ courser, race-horse; swift-sailing yacht

κελητίζω ride a race-horse

κελήτιον ου τό yacht

κέλλω κέλσω ἔκελσα drive on, push ashore; run ashore

κέλομαι *mid* ▶ **κελεύω** *and* **καλέω**

κέλωρ ωρος ὁ son

κεμάς άδος ἡ young deer

κέν ▶ **ἄν**

κένανδρος ον empty of men

κενεαυχής ές vainglorious, extremely boastful

κενεός ή όν ▶ **κενός**

κενεών ῶνος ὁ flank; groin

κενοδοξίᾱ ᾱς ἡ vainglory, extreme boastfulness

κενόδοξος ον vainglorious, extremely boastful

κενός ή όν empty, hollow, void; destitute, bereft; vain, idle, fruitless

κενότης ητος ἡ emptiness

κενοτάφιον ου τό empty tomb, cenotaph

κενοφωνίᾱ ᾱς ἡ empty talk

κενόω empty; unpeople; bereave, strip

κεντέω, κεντόω prick, sting, goad, stab, pierce; incite; scourge, beat, torture

κεντρηνεκής ές goaded on

κέντρον ου τό sting, prick, goad, spur; pain

κεντρόω furnish with stings; pierce

κεντυρίων ωνος ὁ centurion

κέντωρ ορος ὁ goader, driver

κέομαι ▸ **κεῖμαι**

κεραίᾱ ᾱς ἡ sail-yard; beam, pole; the apex of a letter, dot, tittle

κεραΐζω destroy, plunder, ravage; kill, exterminate; sink [a ship]

κεραίω ▸ **κεράννῡμι**

κεραμαείᾱ ᾱς ἡ pottery

κεραμεοῦς ᾶ οῦν earthen, of clay

κεραμεύς έως ὁ potter

κεραμεύω be a potter

κεραμικός ή όν **κεράμι(ν)ος** η ον ▸ **κεραμεοῦς**

κεράμιον ου τό earthenware vessel

κεραμίς ίδος *or* ῖδος ἡ tile

κέραμος[1] ου ὁ potter's earth, clay; pot, jar, earthenware; tile

κέραμος[2] ου ὁ prison, dungeon

κεράννῡμι κεράσω ἐκέρασα mix, mix up; temper, blend together

κεραοξόος ον polishing horn

κεραός ά όν horned

κέρας ᾱτος *or* ως τό horn, antlers; bow; horn for blowing *or* drinking; mountain-peak, branch of a river; wing of an army *or* fleet, flank
■ **ἐπὶ κέρως** in single file, in column

κερασός οῦ ὁ cherry (tree)

κεράστης (*gen* ου) horned

κεράτινος η ον of horn

κεράτιον ου τό fruit of the carob tree

κεραύνιος (ᾱ) ον thunderstruck

κεραυνός οῦ ὁ lightning, thunderbolt

κεραυνόω strike with the thunderbolt

κεράω ▸ **κεράννῡμι**

κερδαίνω κερδανῶ ἐκέρδᾱνα win, gain, profit, be benefited (by); spare, save trouble

κερδαλέος ᾱ ον profitable; crafty, cunning

κερδαλεόφρων ον greedy for gain

κερδίων ον more profitable

κέρδιστος η ον most profitable *or* useful; most cunning

κέρδος ους τό gain, profit, advantage, wages, pay; greediness for gain; *pl* cunning arts, tricks

κερδοσύνη ης ἡ cunning

κερκίς ίδος ἡ weaver's shuttle

κέρκουρος ου ὁ light vessel, cutter

κέρμα ατος τό small coin, change

κερτομέω mock, deride, scoff, mortify

κερτόμησις εως ἡ **κερτομίᾱ** ᾱς ἡ mockery

κερτόμιος ον **κέρτομος** ον stinging, mocking

κέσκετο ▸ **ἔκειτο** *from* **κεῖμαι**

κεστός ή όν embroidered

κευθάνω ▸ **κεύθω**

κευθμός οῦ ὁ **κευθμών** ῶνος ὁ **κεῦθος** ους τό hiding place; hole, den, dwelling; abyss, depth

κεύθω κεύσω ἔκευσα *act tr* hide, conceal, keep secret; *act intr and pass* be hidden

κεφάλαιον ου τό chief point, main thing; summary, sum, chief result; (of money) capital

κεφαλαιόω sum up, put under headings; beat on the head

κεφαλαίωμα ατος τό sum, total

κεφαλαλγής ές causing a headache

κεφαλή ῆς ἡ head; end, point; source, top; head (meaning the whole person)

κεφαλίς ίδος ἡ little head; chapter

κέω ▸ **κείω**

κῇ, κή ▸ **πῇ, πή**

κηδείᾱ ᾱς ἡ affinity, connexion by marriage

κήδειος ον dear, beloved; sepulchral

κηδεμών όνος ὁ tutor, guardian, protector; relation; chief mourner

κήδεος ον ▸ **κήδειος**

κηδεστής οῦ ὁ allied by marriage

κηδεστίᾱ ᾱς ἡ connexion by marriage

κήδευμα ατος τό affinity

κηδεύω care for, tend; bury; *tr* ally oneself in marriage

κήδιστος η ον dearest

κῆδος εος τό care, concern, mourning; burial; distress, sorrow, misery; affinity; marriage

κήδω κηδήσω grieve, distress, mortify; hurt, damage; *mid* be troubled, anxious *or* distressed; + *gen* care for, be anxious *or* distressed for

κηκῑ́ς ῖδος ἡ grease, juice, ooze

κηκίω *and pass* gush forth

κήλε(ι)ος ον blazing

κηλέω charm, fascinate, delight; beguile, seduce; soothe

κηληθμός οῦ ὁ fascination

κηλητήριον ου τό charm

κηλῑ́ς ῖδος ἡ stain; blemish; ignominious punishment

κῆλον ου τό arrow

κηλώνειον ου τό **κηλωνήϊον** ου τό pump, machine for drawing water

κημόω muzzle

κῆνσος ου ὁ capitation-tax; census, registration of taxation

κήξ κηκός ἡ sea-gull

κηπίον ου τό little garden, appendage

κῆπος ου ὁ garden, orchard

κηπουρός οῦ ὁ gardener

κῆρ κῆρος τό heart, breast

κήρ κηρός ἡ fate, death; goddess of death; doom, destruction, mischief, evil

κηρεσσιφόρητος ον driven on by the Fates

κηρίον ου τό honeycomb

κηροδέτης (*gen* ου) bound together by wax

κηρόθι *adv* heartily

κηρός οῦ ὁ wax

κήρυγμα ατος τό a herald's proclamation, order; sermon, teaching

κηρῡ́κ(ε)ιον ου τό **κηρῡκήιον** ου τό herald's staff

κηρῡκηΐη ης ἡ herald's office

κῆρυξ ῡκος ὁ herald, town crier; ambassador; preacher; (at Athens) the crier who made proclamations in the public assemblies

κηρῡ́σσω be a herald, proclaim *or* summon as a herald; order publicly; announce; praise; preach

κῆτος ους τό abyss; sea-monster

κητώεις εσσα εν (of Lacedaemon) rich in caverns

κηφήν ῆνος ὁ drone; lazy fellow

κηώδης ες **κηώεις** εσσα εν fragrant

κιβδηλεύω forge [coin etc.]

κίβδηλος ον adulterated, spurious; (of coinage) base; bastard; fraudulent

κῑβωτός οῦ ἡ **κῑβώτιον** ου τό chest, box; ark; ark of the covenant

κιγχάνω ▸ **κιχάνω**

κίδναμαι ▸ **σκεδάννυμαι**

κιθάρᾱ ᾱς ἡ **κίθαρις** ιος ἡ lyre; lyre-playing

κιθαρίζω play the lyre

κιθάρισις εως ἡ lyre-playing

κιθάρισμα ατος τό piece of music for the lyre

κιθαριστής οῦ ὁ player on the lyre

κιθαριστικός ή όν for lyre-playing; skilled in lyre-playing

κιθαριστύς ύος ἡ art of playing the lyre

κιθαρῳδέω sing to the lyre

κιθαρῳδός οῦ ὁ player on the lyre

κιθών ῶνος ὁ ▸ **χιτών**

κίκι εως τό castor-oil; castor-plant

κικλήσκω ▸ **καλέω**

κῖκυς υος ἡ strength, vigour

κίναδος εος τό fox

κίναιδος ου ὁ catamite, lewd person

κινάμωμον ου τό ▸ **κιννάμωμον**

κινδῡ́νευμα ατος τό ▸ **κίνδυνος**

κινδῡνευτής οῦ ὁ rash *or* foolhardy man

κινδῡνεύω get into danger, run a risk, be in danger; be bold *or* daring; be likely *or* possible; *pass* be exposed to danger, be hazarded

κίνδῡνος ου ὁ danger, risk, hazard, venture, experiment; law-suit; battle

κῑνέω move, set in motion, urge on, advance; shake, stir, arouse, trouble, excite; turn, change; *pass* be put in motion, be moved; march on; be shaken

κῑ́νησις εως ἡ motion; tumult, disturbance

κιννάμωμον ου τό cinnamon

κῑ́νυμαι *pass* be moved, move

κινυρός ᾱ́ όν whining, wailing

κῑόκρᾱνον ου τό capital of a column

κίρκος ου ὁ hawk

κιρνάω, κίρνημι ▸ **κεράννυμι**

κισσήρης ες ivy-clad

κισσός οῦ ὁ ivy

κισσοφόρος ον crowned with ivy

κισσύβιον ου τό bowl, cup

κίστη ης ἡ chest, box

κιττός ου ὁ ▸ **κισσός**

κιχάνω *and mid* arrive at; catch, meet, find

κίχλη ης ἡ thrush

κίχρημι lend; *mid* borrow

κίω go (away)

κῑ́ων ονος ὁ/ἡ column, pillar

κλαγγή ῆς ἡ sound; song; scream, noise

κλαγγηδόν *adv* with a noise

κλάδος ου ὁ branch; shoot; olive-branch (wound round with wool and presented by suppliants)

κλάζω κλάγξω ἔκλαγξα sound, clash, clang; scream, make a noise

κλαίω[†] weep, wail, lament, have cause to repent; bewail

κλάσις εως ἡ breaking

κλάσμα ατος τό fragment, morsel

κλαυθμός οῦ ὁ **κλαῦμα** ατος τό weeping, wailing; woe

κλαυσ *likely to be from* **κλαίω**

κλαυσίγελως ωτος ὁ smiles and tears

κλαυστός ή όν to be bewailed; mournful

κλάω[1] κλάσω ἔκλασα break off; break in pieces

κλᾱ́ω[2] **κλᾴω** ▸ **κλαίω**

κλεηδών όνος ἡ ▸ **κληδών**

κλεῖθρον ου τό bolt, bar, lock

κλεινός ή όν renowned, famous; noble

κλείς κλειδός ἡ bar, bolt; key; hook; hook *or* tongue of a clasp; collar bone

κλεισιάς άδος ἡ ▸ **κλισιάς**

κλείσιον ου τό servants' hall

κλεισίον ου τό hut, stable

κλειστός ή όν ▸ **κλητός**

κλειτός ή όν ▸ **κλεινός**

κλείω[1] ▸ **κλέω**

κλείω[2] shut, close; confine; block up

κλέμμα ατος τό theft; trick

κλέος τό report, fame, rumour; glory, good repute, honour

κλέπτης ου ὁ thief; cheat, rogue

κλεπτικός ή όν thievish

κλεπτοσύνη ης ἡ thievishness, roguery

κλέπτω[†] steal, purloin; do stealthily *or* secretly; cheat, deceive; conceal, hide

κλεψύδρᾱ ᾱς ἡ water-clock (used to time speeches in the law-courts)

κλέω make famous, praise, extol; *pass* become famous

κλήδην *adv* by name

κληδοῦχος ου ὁ/ἡ having charge *or* custody of a place; priest(ess)

κλη(η)δών όνος ἡ omen, presage; favourable cry; rumour, report; glory, repute; ▸ **κλέος**

κλῄζω praise, extol; call, name; *pass* be called

κλήθρη ης ἡ alder

κλῇθρον ου τό ▸ **κλεῖθρον**

κληΐζω ▸ **κλῄζω**

κληΐς ῗδος ἡ ▸ **κλείς**

κληϊστός ή όν ▸ **κλῃστός**

κληΐω ▸ **κλείω²**

κλῆμα ατος τό **κληματίς** ίδος ἡ shoot, branch; vine-twig; brushwood, faggots

κληρονομέω inherit, gain by inheritance

κληρονομίᾱ ᾱς ἡ inheritance, patrimony, property

κληρονόμος ον getting a share; heir(ess)

κλῆρος ου ὁ lot, drawing lots (many officials at Athens obtained their offices by lot); share, portion, inheritance; estate, piece of land; an allotment (of land assigned to citizens); the clergy (as opposed to the laity)

κληρουχέω possess [land in a foreign country] by allotment

κλρουχίᾱ ᾱς ἡ allotment of land to citizens in a foreign country

κληροῦχος ον possessing an allotment (of land in a foreign country), colonist

κληρόω appoint by lot, allot, assign; *pass* be allotted to; *mid* draw lots; obtain by lot

κλήρωσις εως ἡ a choosing by lots

κληρωτήριον ου τό a machine for allocating public duties by lot

κλῄς κλῃδος ▸ **κλείς**

κλῆσις εως ἡ calling, shouting; invitation; summons

κλῄσις εως ἡ blockading

κλητεύω summon into court

κλητός ή όν called; chosen; welcome

κλήτωρ ορος ὁ witness for a legal summons

κλῄω ▸ **κλείω²**

κλῑ́βανος ου ὁ pan, baking oven

κλίμα ατος τό (*also* κλῖμα ατος τό) (*region, district*); (*climate*)

κλῖμαξ ακος ἡ ladder, staircase; entanglement of the limbs of wrestlers

κλῑ́νη ης ἡ **κλῑνάριον** ου τό couch, bed; bier, litter

κλῑνοπετής ές bedridden

κλῑντήρ ῆρος ὁ armchair, couch, bed

κλῑ́νω κλινῶ ἔκλῑνα *act tr* incline, bend; turn; put to flight; make recline; *act intr* lean, sink, be sloping; lie down at table; *mid* lie against, recline; *pass* be bent, lean; rest, support oneself against; stoop, sink, fall down; lie down; be situated

κλισίᾱ ᾱς ἡ hut, tent, cabin; couch; bed, nuptial bed; company of guests

κλισιάς άδος ἡ *pl* folding door, gate

κλισίηθεν *adv* out of the tent

κλισίηνδε *adv* to the tent

κλισίηφι *adv* in the tent

κλίσιον ου τό ▸ **κλείσιον**

κλισμός οῦ ὁ reclining chair

κλῑτύς ύος ἡ slope, hillside

κλοιός οῦ ὁ dog-collar, pillory

κλονέω press hard, drive before oneself; agitate; *pass* flee in confusion; be chased wildly

κλόνος ου ὁ press of battle, turmoil, throng

κλοπεύς έως ὁ thief; secret wrong-doer

κλοπή ῆς ἡ theft, fraud; secret flight; trick

κλόπιος ᾱ ον thievish

κλοτοπεύω spin out time by false pretences

κλύδων ωνος ὁ wave, billow, surge; throng

κλυδωνίζομαι *pass* be tossed (about) by the waves

κλυδώνιον ου τό little wave

κλύζω wash, splash; ripple over; rinse, wash out *or* away; *pass* surge

κλύσμα ατος τό a liquid used for washing out

κλυτοεργός όν famous for work

κλυτόπωλος ον famous for horses

κλυτός ή όν heard of, famous, glorious; noble, splendid; audible, loud, noisy

κλυτοτέχνης (*gen* ου) famous artist

κλυτότοξος ον famous archer

κλύω hear, listen to; learn by hearing; perceive; know; obey; be spoken of

κλῶθες ων αἱ (female) spinners (the three Fates who spun the thread of life)

κλώθω spin

κλωμακόεις εσσα εν rocky

κλών κλωνός ὁ shoot, sprout, twig

κλωπεύω steal

κλώψ κλωπός ὁ thief, robber

κνάπτω scratch, lacerate, card

κναφεῖον ου τό fuller's shop (see next entry)

κναφεύς έως ὁ fuller (a person who cleans and thickens freshly woven cloth)

κνάφος ου ὁ instrument of torture

κνᾱ́ω scrape, grate

κνέφας ους τό darkness, dusk, twilight

κνήθομαι *pass* itch

κνήμη ης ἡ shin-bone, leg

κνημῑδοφόρος ον wearing greaves (see next entry)

κνημῑ́ς ῖδος ἡ greave (armour covering the shin); legging

κνημός οῦ ὁ (of a mountain) projecting limb, shoulder

κνησιάω itch

κνῆστις εως ἡ scraping-knife, grater

κνίζω scrape, scratch; itch; irritate, tease

κνῖσα ης ἡ **κνῑ́ση** ης ἡ steam of burnt-offerings; fat

κνῑσήεις εσσα εν steaming with burnt fat

κνυζέομαι *mid* (of a dog) whine, whimper

κνυζηθμός οῦ ὁ whining

κνύζημα ατος τό stammering

κνυζόω make dim

κνώδαλον ου τό dangerous animal, monster

κνώδων οντος ὁ sword; a projecting tooth on the blade of a hunting spear

κνώσσω sleep

κόγχη ης ἡ mussel(-shell)

κογχυλιᾱ́της ου ὁ shell-limestone

κογχύλιον ου τό muscle, cockle, shell

κοδράντης ου ὁ sum of money: a quarter of a Roman 'as'

κόθεν ▸ **πόθεν**

κόθορνος ου ὁ buskin (high boot worn by tragic actors and thus the emblem of tragedy)

κοιλαίνω κοιλανῶ ἐκοίληνα hollow out

κοιλίᾱ ᾱς ἡ hollow of the belly; belly; womb

κοῖλος η ον hollow, hollowed; lying in a valley

κοιμάω, κοιμέω lull to sleep; calm, soothe, assuage; *pass and mid* go to bed; fall asleep; rest, cease

κοίμημα ατος τό sleep
■ **κοιμήματα αὐτογέννητα** intercourse of a mother with her own child

κοίμησις εως ἡ sleeping, sleep

κοιμίζω ▸ **κοιμάω**

κοινᾱνέω ▸ **κοινωνέω**

κοινολεχής ές bedfellow

κοινο-λογέομαι *mid* consult together

κοινόπλους ον sailing together

κοινόπους (*gen* ποδος) walking together

κοινός ή όν common, public, belonging to the state; kindred; affable, popular, impartial; (of meats) profane
■ **τὸ κοινόν** community, state, republic; public affair, administration; state authorities, public treasury; guild, league
■ **κοινῇ, κοινῶς** in common, publicly

κοινότοκος ον of *or* from the same parents

κοινόω make common; communicate; make unclean, pollute, profane; *mid* have communion; consult *or* act in common; make public

κοινωνέω *usu* + *gen* have a share in, partake of

κοινωνίᾱ ᾱς ἡ communion; share; company, society; association; charity, alms

κοινωνικός ή όν communicative, generous

κοινωνός όν common; partner, fellow

κοῖος ᾱ ον ▸ **ποῖος**

κοιρανέω be master *or* lord; rule, command

κοιρανίδης ου ὁ ▸ **κοίρανος**

κοίρανος ου ὁ ruler; lord, master

κοιταῖος ᾱ ον lying in bed

κοίτη ης ἡ **κοῖτος** ου ὁ going to bed; sleep; couch, bed; marriage-bed; embryo; offspring

κοιτών ῶνος ὁ bedchamber

κόκκινος η ον scarlet

κόκκος ου ὁ kernel; scarlet berry

κόκκῡξ ῡγος ὁ

κολάζω *and mid* hold in check, tame; punish, chastise; correct

κολακείᾱ ᾱς ἡ flattery, fawning

κολακευτικός ή όν flattering, fawning

κολακεύω flatter, deceive

κολακικός ή όν ▸ **κολακευτικός**

κόλαξ ακος ὁ flatterer

κόλασις εως ἡ punishing; correction

κολαστήριον ου τό punishment, prison

κολαστής οῦ ὁ punisher, chastiser

κολαφίζω cuff; box someone's ears

κολεόν οῦ τό sheath (of a sword)

κόλλᾱ ης ἡ glue

κολλάω glue (together), cement; *pass* attach oneself to, cleave to

κολλήεις εσσα εν **κολλητός** ή όν glued together, cemented; welded

κόλλησις εως ἡ gluing together; welding

κολλούριον ου τό (*also* κολλῡ́ριον ου τό) eye-salve

κόλλοψ οπος ὁ peg *or* screw of the lyre (by which the strings were tightened)

κολλυβιστής οῦ ὁ money-changer

κολοβόω shorten

κολοιός οῦ ὁ jackdaw

κολοκύνθη ης ἡ pumpkin

κόλος ον curtailed; stump-horned, hornless

κολοσσός οῦ ὁ gigantic statue

κολοσυρτός οῦ ὁ noise, uproar; noisy rabble

κολούω curtail, shorten, lessen, abridge

κόλπος ου ὁ bosom; womb; fold of a garment; bay; hollow, depth

κολυμβάω dive

κολυμβήθρᾱ ᾱς ἡ swimming bath; pond

κολυμβητής οῦ ὁ diver, swimmer

κολῳάω croak, brawl, scold

κολώνη ης ἡ **κολωνός** οῦ ὁ hill; mound, tomb

κολωνίᾱ ᾱς ἡ colony

κολῳός οῦ ὁ screaming

κομάω, κομέω[1] let the hair grow long; have long hair; be proud *or* haughty

κομέω[2] tend, take care of

κόμη ης ἡ the hair, foliage

κομήτης ου ὁ long-haired, feathered, grassy; comet

κομιδή ῆς ἡ care, attendance; carrying of supplies, transport, stores; recovery; going *or* coming; passage; return

■ **κομιδῇ** *adv* with care, wholly, altogether, very much so, indeed

κομίζω κομιῶ ἐκόμισα take care of, tend, mind; receive hospitably; manage; carry away, convey; store up; fetch, bring back; *pass* be carried *or* conveyed; travel, take oneself to; return; *mid* shelter, entertain; get, gain, procure; keep, save, preserve; bring to, rescue, recover

κόμμι ιδος *or* εως τό gum

κομμωτικός ή όν of *or* for embellishment

κομπάζω, κομπέω boast, brag

κομπώδης ες boastful

κομψείᾱ ᾱς ἡ refinement, subtlety, affectation

κομψεύω *and mid* refine upon, quibble upon; make a display of wit

κομψός ή όν refined, well-dressed; pretty; elegant; witty, clever, exquisite; studied, affected

κοναβέω sound, clash, resound

κόναβος ου ὁ noise, clashing

κόνδυλος ου ὁ knuckle

κονίᾱ ᾱς ἡ dust; sand; cinders, ashes; lime-powder; plaster

κονιᾱτός ή όν whitewashed

κονιάω whitewash, plaster *or* whiten over

κονιορτός οῦ ὁ dust, cloud of dust

κόνις εως ἡ ▸ **κονία**

κονῑσαλος ου ὁ ▸ **κονιορτός**

κονῑω cover, fill *or* sprinkle with dust; raise dust; be in great haste

κοντός οῦ ὁ pole, punting-pole

κοπάζω grow tired *or* weary

κοπίς ίδος ἡ knife, sword; axe

κόπος ου ὁ a striking, beating; wailing; weariness, trouble, pain

κοπρίᾱ ᾱς ἡ **κόπριον** ου τό **κόπρος** ου ἡ dung, manure; filth, dirt; dung-yard, stable

κοπροφόρος ον carrying dung

κοπρόω befoul with dung

κόπτω strike, cut, fell, cut off; lay waste, damage, hurt, wound, tire out, weary; hammer, forge, coin; knock, peck; *mid* beat oneself; mourn; get coined

κόραξ ακος ὁ raven

κορᾰσιον ου τό little girl

κόρδᾱξ ᾱκος ὁ **κορδακισμός** οῦ ὁ an obscene dance in Old Comedy

κορέννῡμι κορέσω ἐκόρεσα satisfy; glut, surfeit; *pass and mid* have one's fill; grow weary of

κορέω sweep, brush

κόρη ης ἡ girl, maiden; newly-married woman; daughter; doll, puppet; eye-ball; long sleeve

κορθύ(ν)ω lift up; *pass* rise

κόρημα ατος τό brush, broom

κορμός οῦ ὁ tree trunk

κόρος[1] ου ὁ lad, youth; warrior; boy, son; one who is youthful *or* noble

κόρος[2] ου ὁ satiety, surfeit; insolence

κόρρη ης ἡ **κόρση** ης ἡ side of the forehead, temple

κορυβαντιάω be in in an ecstatic frenzy like a Corybant

κορυθᾱϊξ (*gen* ῑκος) **κορυθαίολος** ον with glancing helmet

κόρυδος ου ὁ lark

κόρυμβος ου ὁ top, peak; cluster of fruit *or* flowers

κορύνη ης ἡ club, staff

κορυνήτης ου ὁ **κορυνηφόρος** ου ὁ club-bearer

κόρυς υθος ἡ helmet

κορύσσω equip with a helmet; arm, equip, array; (of waves) make crested; *pass* rise, swell; arm oneself

κορυστής (*gen* οῦ) armed

κορυφαῖος ᾱ ον at the head; leader, chief, first man; (in Attic drama) the leader of the chorus

κορυφή ῆς ἡ top, summit; crown of the head

κορυφόω bring to a head; *pass* rise high

κορώνη[1] ης ἡ crow, raven

κορώνη[2] ης ἡ handle of a door; tip of a bow (on which the bowstring was hooked)

κορωνίς (*gen* ίδος) curved

κ

κόσκινον ου τό sieve

κοσμέω order, arrange; equip; keep in order; rule, govern; adorn, deck, embellish; honour, extol

κόσμησις εως ἡ adorning, arrangement; ornament

κοσμητής οῦ ὁ (at Athens and elsewhere) the magistrate in charge of the ephebes

κοσμητός ή όν well-arranged

κοσμήτωρ ορος ὁ arranger, ruler, commander

κοσμικός ή όν of the world, earthly

κόσμιος ᾱ ον orderly, modest; chaste, decent, obedient; regular, well-arranged

κοσμιότης ητος ἡ decency

κοσμοκράτωρ ορος ὁ ruler of the world

κόσμος ου ὁ order, arrangement; decency, good behaviour; regularity, good government, constitution; world, universe; ornament, decoration, finery; glory, honour

κόσος η ον ▸ **πόσος**

κότε, κοτέ ▸ **πότε, ποτέ**

κότερος ▸ **πότερος**

κοτέω κοτέσσομαι *and mid* bear a grudge, be angry

κοτήεις εσσα εν angry

κότος ου ὁ grudge, anger, hatred

κοτύλη ης ὁ small cup; nearly half a pint; socket of the hip bone

κοτυληδών όνος ὁ sucker of the inkfish; socket of the hip-joint

κοτυλήρυτος ον flowing abundantly

κουλεόν ▸ **κολεόν**

κουρᾱ́ ᾱς ἡ a shearing, clipping

κουρεῖον ου τό barber's shop

κουρεύς έως ὁ barber

κούρη ης ἡ ▸ **κόρη**

κούρητες ων οἱ young men

κουρίδιος ᾱ ον lawfully wedded

κουρίζω be youthful *or* vigorous

κουρίξ *adv* by the hair

κοῦρος ου ὁ ▸ **κόρος**

κουροτρόφος ον rearing *or* bringing up boys

κουφίζω κουφιῶ *act tr* make light, lift up; relieve, help, assuage; *act intr and pass* be light; rise; be relieved

κούφισις εως ἡ lightening, relief

κουφολογίᾱ ᾱς ἡ light talk

κουφόνοος ον light-minded, silly, thoughtless

κοῦφος η ον light, unloaded; nimble, dextrous; indifferent, little; soft; digestible; easy, light-minded; vain

κόφινος ου ὁ basket

κόχλος ου ὁ mussel, shell-fish (used for dyeing purple)

κράββατος ου ὁ couch, bed

κραδαίνω, κραδάω swing, brandish

κραδίᾱ ᾱς ἡ ▸ **καρδία**

κρᾱ́ζω croak; scream; bay

κραίνω, κραιαίνω accomplish, fulfil, bring to pass; rule, command

κραιπάλη ης ἡ intoxication, drinking-bout; hangover

κραιπνός ή όν rapid, swift, sweeping, rushing; rash, hot

κραναός ή όν rocky, stony

κράνεια ᾱς ἡ **κρανείη** ης ἡ cornel-tree

κρᾱνίον ου τό skull

κράνος τό helmet

κρᾶσις εως ἡ mixing, blending; temperature

κράσπεδον ου τό border, edge; fringe

κρᾶτα τό ▸ **κάρα**

κραταιγύαλος ον with strong breastplates

κραταιΐς εως ἡ force, bulk

κραταιός ᾱ́ όν strong, mighty

κραταιόω strengthen; *pass* become strong

κραταίπεδος ον with hard ground

κραταίρῑνος ον with a hard hide *or* shell

κρατερός ᾱ́ όν ▸ **καρτερός**

κρατερόφρων ον stout-hearted

κρατερῶνυξ (*gen* υχος) with strong hooves *or* claws

κρατευταί ῶν οἱ forked stand *or* frame on which a spit turns

κρατέω be strong *or* mighty, have power, be lord, rule; conquer, subdue, prevail over; obtain by force; surpass; hold fast, seize; check, hinder

κρᾱτήρ ῆρος ὁ mixing vessel, bowl, basin

κρᾱτηρίζω pour out a libation

κρατιστεύω be best, excel

κράτιστος η ον strongest, mightiest; most excellent, best; bravest; noblest

κράτος ους τό strength, might, power, force; violence; dominion, rule, superiority, ascendancy, victory

κρατῡ́νω κρατυνῶ ἐκαρτυνάμην *and mid* strengthen, fortify, secure; + *gen* rule, govern; possess

κρατύς ύος ὁ strong, mighty

κραυγάζω, κραυγανάομαι ▸ **κράζω**

κραυγή ῆς ἡ crying, screaming

κρέας ως τό flesh, meat

κρεῖον τό meat-tray, dresser

κρείσσων ον (*also* κρείττων ον) stronger, mightier, better; braver; superior, surpassing, lord, master, victor; nobler; worse, more dangerous

κρείων οντος ὁ **κρείουσα** ης ἡ lord, master, ruler; mistress

κρεμάννῡμι κρεμῶ ἐκρέμασα hang, hang up
pass **κρέμαμαι** be hung up *or* suspended; be in suspense

κρεμαστός ή όν hung up, hanging

κρέξ κρεκός ἡ corn-crake, land-rail (a bird)

κρεουργηδόν *adv* cut up in butcher's fashion

κρεοφάγος ον eating flesh, carnivorous

κρέσσων ον ▸ **κρείσσων**

κρήγυος ον agreeable, delighting

κρήδεμνον ου τό head-dress, veil; battlements; lid, cover

κρῆθεν *adv* from the head, from above

κρημνός ου ὁ steep precipice, slope, steep bank *or* edge

κρημνώδης ες precipitous, steep

κρηναῖος ᾱ ον of a spring *or* fountain

κρήνη ης ἡ spring, fountain, well

κρηπῑ́ς ῖδος ἡ shoe, boot; foundation, base; enclosing wall

κρησφύγετον ου τό place of refuge

κρητήρ ῆρος ὁ ▸ **κρατήρ**

κρῖ κρῖος τό ▸ **κρῑθή**

κρίζω *aor* ἔκρικον creak, screech

κρῑθή ῆς ἡ barley

κρῑ́θινος η ον of barley

κρίκος ου ὁ ring, circle, bracelet

κρῖμα ατος τό (*also* κρίμα ατος τό) sentence, judgement; accusation, condemnation

κρῑ́νω† separate, divide; pick out, choose, prefer, approve; judge, decide, explain, think, believe; accuse, bring to trial, examine, question; condemn; *mid* choose for oneself; *pass* be chosen, judged *or* decided; be accused, tried *or* condemned; contend, fight

κρῑοπρόσωπος ον ram-faced

κρῑός οῦ ὁ ram; battering-ram

κρίσις εως ἡ separation; discord, dispute; choosing, deciding, judgement, sentence; trial, examination, lawsuit, court of justice, punishment; issue, event, outcome

κριτήριον ου τό means for judging, test; court of justice; law-suit

κριτής οῦ ὁ judge

κριτικός ή όν able to judge

κριτός ή όν chosen, picked out

κροαίνω ▸ **κρούω**

κρόκη ης ἡ wool, thread

κροκόδειλος ου ὁ lizard; crocodile

κροκόπεπλος ον saffron-robed

κρόκος ου ὁ the crocus; saffron

κροκύς ύδος ἡ flock *or* nap on woollen cloth

κρόμ(μ)υον ου τό onion

κρόσσαι ων αἱ battlements; steps

κροταλίζω rattle; cause to rattle

κρόταλον ου τό rattle, castanet

κρόταφος ου ὁ side of the forehead, temple

κροτέω knock, strike; clap the hands; (of a smith) hammer *or* weld together

κροτητός ή όν rattling

κρότος ου ὁ a clapping, applause; rattling noise

κρουνός οῦ ὁ spring, well

κρούω knock, strike; beat; clap
■ **πρύμναν κρούεσθαι** row back stern foremost

κρύβδα, κρύβδην ▸ **κρύφα**

κρυερός ᾰ́ όν chilly; awful

κρῡμός οῦ ὁ frost; wintertime

κρυόεις εσσα εν ▸ **κρυερός**

κρύος εος τό frost, ice

κρυπτάδιος ᾱ ον ▸ **κρυπτός**

κρυπτή ῆς ἡ vault, crypt

κρυπτός ή όν hidden, covered; secret

κρύπτω hide, conceal, cover

κρυσταλλίζω shine like crystal, be as clear as crystal

κρύφα, κρυφῇ, κρυφηδόν *adv* secretly

κρυφαῖος ᾱ ον **κρύφιος** ᾱ ον ▸ **κρυπτός**

κρωβύλος ου ὁ tuft of hair; crest

κρωσσός οῦ ὁ pitcher, jar, urn

κτάομαι† *mid* gain, get for oneself, acquire
■ **κέκτημαι** *pf* possess, have

κτέαρ ατος ὁ ▸ **κτῆμα**

κτεατίζω ▸ **κτάομαι** *and* **κέκτημαι**

κτείνω† slay, kill, murder

κτείς κτενός ὁ comb

κτενίζω comb

κτενῶ *fut from* **κτείνω**

κτέρεα έων τά gifts for the dead, funeral honours

κτερίζω, κτερεΐζω pay funeral honours; bury with due honours

κτερίσματα ων τά ▸ **κτέρεα**

κτῆμα ατος τό possession, property, goods, treasure

κτηνηδόν *adv* like beasts

κτῆνος εος τό *mostly in pl* κτήνεα possession, property; cattle, sheep

κτήσιος ᾱ ον of one's property

κτῆσις εως ἡ a getting, acquiring; possession, property, goods

κτητός ή όν gained, acquired; worth getting, desirable

κτήτωρ ορος ὁ owner

κτίδεος ᾱ ον made of the skin of a marten-cat

κτίζω κτίσω ἔκτισα people, colonize; found, establish, institute; create

κτίλος ου ὁ ram

κτιλόω tame; *mid* win the affections of

κτίννῡμι, κτιννύω ▸ **κτείνω**

κτίσις εως ἡ **κτίσμα** ατος τό founding, foundation, establishing; creation; creature

κτίστης ου ὁ founder, creator

κτιστύς ύος ἡ ▸ **κτίσις**

κτυπέω crash, ring, resound; thunder

κτύπος ου ὁ crash, sound, noise, rattling clash; cries

κύαθος ου ὁ dipper *or* cup (for drawing wine out of the mixing-bowl)

κυαμευτός ή όν chosen by beans

κύαμος ου ὁ bean; vote by beans; election (at Athens in which those who drew white beans were chosen as public officers)

κυάνεος ᾱ ον dark-blue; dark

κυανόπεζα ης ἡ dark-footed

κυανόπρῳρος ον **κυανοπρῴρειος** ον with dark prow

κύανος ου ὁ azure stone, blue steel

κυανοχαίτης (*gen* ου) **κυανοχαίτα** dark-haired, dark-maned

κυανῶπις (*gen* ιδος) dark-eyed

κυβείᾱ ᾱς ἡ dice-playing; deceit, trickery

κυβεῖον ου τό casino

κυβερνάω be a helmsman; steer; direct, guide, govern

κυβέρνησις εως ἡ steering; governing

κυβερνήτης ου ὁ **κυβερνητήρ** ῆρος ὁ steersman; governor

κυβερνητικός ή όν skilled in steering *or* governing

κυβευτής ου ὁ dice-player, gambler

κυβεύω play at dice

κυβιστάω turn a somersault, turn over

κυβιστητήρ ῆρος ὁ diver, tumbler, one who pitches headlong; mountebank

κύβος ου ὁ cube

κυδάζω revile

κῡδαίνω praise, glorify, honour, adorn

κῡδάλιμος ον glorious

κῡδάνω κῡδανῶ boast ▸ **κυδαίνω**

κῡδιάνειρα ᾱς ἡ men-honouring

κῡδιάω be proud, exult

κῡ́διστος η ον most glorious, noblest

κυδοιμέω rave, rage; drive in confusion

κυδοιμός οῦ ὁ tumult, confusion, uproar, the din of battle

κῦδος εος τό glory, fame, renown; pride

κῡδρός ᾱ́ όν ▸ **κυδάλιμος**

κυέω, κυΐσκομαι *pass* be pregnant

κυκάω stir up, mix, throw into confusion; *pass* get into confusion, be panic-stricken

κυκεών ῶνος ὁ mixed drink (consisting of barley-meal, grated cheese and wine)

κυκλεύω suround, beset

κυκλέω *act tr* move round and round, wheel along; turn in a circle; *act intr and mid* form a circle round; move in a circle, turn around

κύκλιος (ᾱ) ον **κυκλόεις** εσσα εν circular

κυκλόθεν *adv* in a circle, all around

κύκλος ου ὁ circle, anything circular; ring, wheel, disk, eye, shield; town-wall; circular motion, orbit, cycle

κυκλόσε *adv* in a circle, all around

κυκλοτερής ές circular

κυκλόω make round *or* circular; turn in a circle; encircle; *mid* form into a circle, form a circle; enclose

κύκλωσις εως ἡ an encircling, enclosing

κύκνος ου ὁ swan

κυλινδέω ▸ **κυλίνδω**

κυλίνδω *aor* ἐκύλῖσα roll (on *or* along); *pass* be rolled; roll along; wallow (in the dirt as a sign of grief)

κύλιξ ικος ἡ drinking cup

κύλισμα ατος τό **κυλισμός** οῦ ὁ rolling; stirred up dirt

κυλΐω ▸ **κυλίνδω**

κυλλῆστις ιος ὁ Egyptian bread

κυλλοποδῑ́ων (*gen* ονος) crook-legged (of Hephaestus); deformed, crippled

κυλλός ή όν crooked; maimed

κῦμα ατος τό wave, billow, surge

κῡμαίνω κυμανῶ *and pass* swell *or* rise in waves

κῡματίᾱς (*gen* ου) surging; causing waves

κῡματοᾱγής ές breaking like waves

κῡματοπλήξ (*gen* ῆγος) wave-beaten

κῡματόομαι *pass* rise in waves

κῡματωγή ῆς ἡ beach, place where the waves break

κύμβαλον ου τό cymbal

κύμβαχος[1] ου ὁ crown of the helmet

κύμβαχος[2] ον head-foremost

κύμινδις ιδος ὁ night-hawk

κύμῑνον ου τό cumin

κυνάμυια ᾱς ἡ dog-fly

κυνάριον ου τό little dog

κυνέη ης ἡ (*also* κυνῆ ῆς ἡ) dog's skin leather cap

κύνεος ᾱ ον like a dog; shameless

κυνέω κυνήσομαι kiss

κυνηγέσιον ου τό chase, hunt; hunting expedition; pack of hounds; game

κυνηγετέω chase, pursue

κυνηγέτης ου ὁ **κυνηγός** οῦ ὁ/ἡ huntsman, huntress

κυνηγετικός ή όν of hunting

κυνηγίᾱ ᾱς ἡ ▸ **κυνηγέσιον**

κυνίδιον ου τό little dog

κυνικός ή όν like a dog

κυνίσκος ου ὁ little dog

κυνοκέφαλος ον dog-headed

κυνόμυια ᾱς ἡ ▸ **κυνάμυια**

κυνοραιστής οῦ ὁ dog-tick

κυνοσπάρακτος ον torn by dogs

κύντατος η ον most shameless

κύντερος ᾱ ον more shameless

κυνώπης (*gen* ου) **κυνῶπις** (*gen* ιδος) dog-eyed

κυπαρίσσινος η ον of cypress wood

κυπάρισσος ου ἡ cypress

κύπειρον ου τό **κύπειρος** ου ὁ a sweet-smelling marsh plant, perhaps galingale

κύπελλον ου τό goblet

κύπερος ου τό ▸ **κύπειρος**

κύπτω bend forward, stoop

κυρβασίᾱ ᾱς ἡ Persian bonnet, turban

κύρβις εως ὁ/ἡ movable pillar with laws inscribed on it

κυρέω hit *or* light upon, reach, meet with, arrive at; gain, obtain; happen, come to pass ▸ **τυγχάνω**

κῡριακός ή όν belonging to a lord *or* master; belonging to the Lord Christ

κῡριεύω + *gen* rule, be lord

κῡ́ριος ᾱ ον having power, ruling; valid, legal, entitled, capable; appointed, regular, authorized; principal
- **ὁ κῡ́ριος** lord, master, ruler, owner; the Lord Christ
- **ἡ κῡρίᾱ** mistress, lady
- **ἡ κῡρίᾱ ἐκκλησίᾱ** one of the assemblies held at Athens on a regular schedule
- **τὸ κῡ́ριον** legal power; statute; appointed time

κῡριότης ητος ἡ dominion; ruler

κυρίσσω κυρίξω butt, knock against

κύρμα ατος τό godsend, booty, prey

κῦρος τό power, authority; decision; ratification; validity

κῡρόω *and mid* make valid, confirm, ratify; decide; accomplish

κύρτη ης ἡ **κύρτος** ου ὁ fishing-basket

κυρτός ή όν curved, arched

κυρτόω curve, bend, arch

κῡ́ρω *and mid* ▸ **κυρέω**

κῡ́ρωσις εως ἡ ▸ **κῦρος**

κύστις εως, ιος *or* ιδος ἡ bladder

κύτος ους τό hollow, vessel, urn; skin; shield, cuirass

κῡφός ή όν bent, curved, stooping

κυψέλη ης ἡ chest, box

κύω ▸ κυέω

κύων κυνός ὁ/ἡ dog, bitch; monster; dog-star; sea-dog (a fish)

κῴ ▸ πῴ

κῴας τό fleece, sheepskin

κώδεια ᾱς ἡ head of a poppy

κῴδιον ου τό **▸ κῶας**

κώδων ωνος ὁ/ἡ bell; patrol

κώκῡμα ατος τό **κωκῡτός** οῦ ὁ a shrieking, wailing

κωκύω wail, lament; bewail

κώληψ ηπος ἡ hollow of the knee

κῶλον ου τό limb, member; foot, leg, knee; part; side, wall

κώλῡμα ατος τό hindrance, impediment, disqualification

κωλῡτής οῦ ὁ hinderer

κωλῡτικός ή όν hindering

κωλῡ́ω hinder, prevent, check, forbid

κῶμα ατος τό deep sleep, trance

κωμάζω revel, go in a festival procession, celebrate a feast; be playful

κωμάρχης ου ὁ head of a village

κωμαστής οῦ ὁ reveller

κώμη ης ἡ village

κωμήτης ου ὁ villager

κωμικός ή όν belonging to comedy, comic

κωμογραμματεύς έως ὁ clerk of a village

κωμόπολις εως ἡ village, town, borough

κῶμος ου ὁ festival procession, revel, merry-making; band of revellers; feast, banquet

κωμῳδέω ridicule

κωμῳδίᾱ ᾱς ἡ comedy

κωμῳδ(ι)οποιός οῦ ὁ comic poet

κωμῳδός οῦ ὁ comic actor *or* poet

κώνειον ου τό hemlock

κώνωψ ωπος ὁ gnat, mosquito

κωπεύς έως ὁ wood for oars

κώπη ης ἡ handle of an oar *or* sword *or* key; oar

κωπήεις εσσα εν with a handle *or* hilt

κωπήρης ες furnished with oars

κώρυκος ου ὁ leather bag

κῶς, κώς ▸ πῶς, πώς

κωτίλλω talk round, wheedle

κωφός ή όν blunt, dumb, deaf and dumb, mute, speechless; dull, weak, stupid; senseless, without meaning

κωφότης ητος ἡ deafness

λ, Λ (λάμβδα) eleventh letter of the alphabet ■ λʹ *as a numeral* = 30

λᾶας ος ὁ stone; rock; crag

λαβ aor stem *from* **λαμβάνω**

λαβή ῆς ἡ handle, hilt; (in athletics) hold

λαβραγόρης ου ὁ bold talker, braggart

λαβρεύομαι *mid* talk boldly

λάβρος ον rapid, furious, vehement, boisterous, violent

λαβύρινθος ου ὁ labyrinth, maze

λαγνεία ᾱς ἡ lust

λαγός οῦ ὁ ▸ **λαγῶς**

λαγχάνω λήξομαι ἔλαχον obtain by lot *or* fate; draw lots; be chosen by lot; receive a share; give a share

λαγῶς (*or* λαγώς) ῶ ὁ **λαγωός** οῦ ὁ hare

λάδανον ου τό ▸ **λήδανον**

λάζομαι ▸ **λαμβάνω**

λαθ aor stem *from* **λανθάνω**

λᾱ́θᾱ ης ἡ ▸ **λήθη**

λαθικηδής ές banishing care

λᾱθίπονος ον forgetful of sorrow

λάθρα, λάθρᾱ *adv* secretly, stealthily; without one's knowledge

λαθραῖος ᾱ ον secret, stealthy

λᾶϊγξ ιγγος ἡ pebble

λαῖλαψ απος ἡ storm, hurricane

λαιμός οῦ ὁ throat, gullet

λᾱΐνεος ᾱ ον **λᾱ́ϊνος** ον of stone

λαιός ᾱ́ όν left (hand)

λαισήϊον ου τό light shield

λαῖτμα ατος τό depth *or* gulf (of the sea)

λαῖφος ους τό piece of cloth, sail; ragged garment

λαιψηρός ᾱ́ όν swift, quick

λᾱκέω ▸ **ληκέω** ▸ **λάσκω**

λάκκος ου ὁ hole, pit; cistern; pond

λακπάτητος ον trodden down

λακτίζω λακτιῶ kick with the foot, trample (up)on; kick (against the goad); move in convulsions

λακτιστής (*gen* οῦ) kicking, trampling

λακωνίζω imitate *or* side with the Lacedaemonians

λακωνισμός οῦ ὁ siding with the Lacedaemonians; imitation of the Lacedaemonians

λακωνιστής (*gen* οῦ) imitating the Lacedaemonians

λαλέω talk, chatter; speak, teach, praise

λάλημα ατος τό talk, prattling

λαλιᾱ́ ᾶς ἡ talking, chat; dialect

λάλος ον talkative

λαμβάνω† take, seize, grasp, catch, capture, obtain; meet with, incur, suffer; receive, take in; choose, select; take away, steal; receive hospitably; comprehend, understand, perceive; come upon, overtake, find out, detect, convict; *mid* + *gen* keep hold of, grasp, touch; get possession of, win, gain, obtain

λαμπαδηδρομίᾱ ᾱς ἡ **λαμπαδηφορίᾱ** ᾱς ἡ torch-race (an Athenian ceremony at the festivals of Prometheus, Hephaestus, Pan and Athena)

λαμπᾰ́διον ου τό small torch

λαμπάς άδος ἡ torch; sun, light; lamp; torch-race; *adj* lighted by torches

λαμπετάω ▸ **λάμπω**

λαμπρός ᾱ́ όν bright, shining, beaming, brilliant; limpid; clear, sonorous, keen; fresh; manifest, evident; splendid, magnificent; noble

λαμπρότης ητος ἡ brilliancy, splendour; glory, honour

λαμπροφωνίᾱ ᾱς ἡ clear voice

λαμπρόφωνος ον clear-voiced

λαμπρῡ́νω make bright, polish; *mid* be *or* become clear *or* notorious

λαμπτήρ ῆρος ὁ stand for torches; torch; beacon-light

λάμπω *and mid* shine, be bright *or* brilliant

λανθάνω† escape a person's notice, be hidden, unnoticed; cause to forget; *mid* + *gen* forget

λάξ *adv* with the heel *or* foot

λαξευτός ή όν cut *or* hewn in stone

λάξις ιος ἡ allotment of land

λᾱός οῦ ὁ people, crowd, host, army; *pl* men, soldiers, fellows

λᾱοσσόος ον stirring the men

λᾱοφόρος ον ▸ **λεωφόρος**

λαπάρη ης ἡ flank, loins

λάπτω lick, lap

λάρναξ ακος ἡ receptacle; chest, urn, coffin

λάρος ου ὁ gull

λᾱρός ᾱ́ όν dainty, sweet, delicious

λαρυγγίζω λαρυγγιῶ shout at the top of one's voice

λάρυγξ υγγος ὁ throat, gullet

λάσθη ης ἡ mockery, insult

λασιαύχην (*gen* ενος) maned, with rough *or* shaggy neck

λάσιος ᾱ ον shaggy, woolly; shaggy with bushes *or* brushwood

λάσκω λακήσομαι ἐλάκησα crash, cry, ring, shriek; speak loud, shout; crack *or* burst asunder

λᾱτομέω quarry stones

λατρείᾱ ᾱς ἡ **λάτρευμα** ατος τό service, servitude, hired labour; worship

λάτρις ιος ὁ/ἡ workman for hire; servant, slave

λαυκανίη ης ἡ throat

λαύρᾱ ᾱς ἡ lane, passage, defile

λάφῡρον ου τό booty, spoil

λαφῡρο-πωλέω sell booty

λαφῡροπώλης ου ὁ seller of booty

λαφύσσω λαφύξω swallow, devour

λαχ *aor stem from* **λαγχάνω**

λαχανασιμός οῦ ὁ gathering of vegetables

λάχανον ου τό greens, vegetables

λάχεια *adj fem only* well-tilled, fertile

λάχεσις εως ἡ ▸ **λάχος**

λάχνη ης ἡ wool; woolly hair; downy beard

λαχνήεις εσσα εν woolly; hairy

λάχνος ου ὁ ▸ **λάχνη**

λάχος τό lot, share; section; fate

λάω wish

λέαινα ης ἡ lioness

λεαίνω λεανῶ ἐλέηνα polish, smooth; make agreeable; pound in a mortar

λέβης ητος ὁ kettle, cauldron; basin, urn

λεγεών ῶνος ὁ/ἡ (*also* λεγίων ωνος ὁ/ἡ) legion

λέγω[1] ▸ **λέχω** lull asleep, lay asleep; *mid* lie down to sleep

λέγω[2†] pick, gather; reckon among; tell, relate, speak, say, declare, assert, promise; call, name; order, request; recite, read; *mid* gather for oneself, count up; converse, discourse; *pass* be told, related *or* said

■ **ὁ λεγόμενος** the so-called

λεηλατέω drive away booty, plunder

λείᾱ ᾱς ἡ booty, plunder

λειαίνω ▸ **λεαίνω**

λείβω pour out; pour out a libation

λεῖμμα ατος τό ▸ **λείψανον**

λειμών ῶνος ὁ **λειμωνιάς** άδος ἡ meadow, pasture

λειμώνιος ᾱ ον of a meadow

λειμωνόθεν *adv* from a meadow

λειογένειος ον smooth-chinned

λεῖος ᾱ ον smooth, polished; level, flat; bald, beardless

λειότης ητος ἡ smoothness

λειποστρατίᾱ ᾱς ἡ **λειποστράτιον** ου τό desertion

λειπο-ψῡχέω faint, swoon; be dejected

λειποψῡχίᾱ ᾱς ἡ faint, swoon

λείπω[†] *act tr* leave, leave remaining *or* behind; abandon, desert; *act intr* be gone; fail, come short of; *mid* leave behind, bequeath; *pass and mid* be left, be left behind, remain; be inferior *or* weaker; be abandoned; be far from; want, lack

λειριόεις εσσα εν lily-like; delicate

λεϊστός ή όν ▸ **ληϊστός**

λειτουργέω perform public duties; (at Athens) bear the charges of public duties (such as manning a trireme or putting on a play); officiate, minister

λειτουργίᾱ ᾱς ἡ public service; expenditure for the state (see last entry); divine service

λείχω lick

λείψανον ου τό remnant

λεκάνη ης ἡ dish, plate, pot

λεκτικός ή όν eloquent

λεκτός ή όν picked out; said; to be spoken

λέκτρον ου τό couch, bed; bed-clothes; marriage-bed; marriage

λελιημένος η ον longing for

λελογισμένως *adv* deliberately

λέμμα ατος τό husk

λέντιον ου τό linen cloth, napkin

λέξις εως ἡ speech, mode of speech, style

λεοντέη ης ἡ (*also* λεοντῆ ῆς ἡ) lion's skin

λέπαδνον ου τό broad leather strap, yoke

λέπας τό bare rock *or* hill

λεπάς άδος ἡ limpet

λεπιδωτός ή όν scaly, scaled

λεπίς ίδος ἡ scale, shell

λέπρᾱ ᾱς ἡ leprosy

λεπρός ᾱ́ όν leprous

λεπταλέος ᾱ ον fine, delicate

λεπτόγεως ων with poor soil

λεπτός ή όν cleaned of the husks; thin, fine, slender, delicate, lean, narrow, small, weak; subtle, clever

λεπτουργέω do fine work

λέπω peel *or* bark, strip off the rind *or* husks

λέσχη ης ἡ council-hall; place where people assemble to talk and exchange news; assembly; conversation, talk

λευγαλέος ᾱ ον sad, wretched, miserable, pitiful; mischievous

λευΐτης ου ὁ Levite

λευϊτικός ή όν Levitical

λευκαίνω make white

λευκανθής ές white-blossoming, white

λευκανθίζω be white

λεύκασπις (*gen* ιδος) white-shielded

λεύκη ης ἡ white poplar; white leprosy

λεύκιππος ον with white horses

λευκοθώρᾱξ (*gen* ᾱκος) with white cuirass *or* breastplate

λευκόλινον ου τό white flax

λευκόπωλος ον ▸ **λεύκιππος**

λευκός ή όν bright, brilliant, clear; white, pale

λεύκοφρυς (*gen* υος) with white eyebrows

λευκόω whiten, paint white

λευκώλενος ον white armed

λεύκωμα ατος τό a tablet covered with gypsum (to write on), notice-board, register

λευρός ᾱ́ όν smooth, level, even

λεύσσω gaze, look (at), behold, see

λευστήρ ῆρος ὁ one who stones, executioner

λεύω stone

λεχεποίης (*gen* ου) meadowy, grassy (of the river Asopus)

λέχος ους τό couch, bed; bier; marriage-bed; marriage

λέχοσδε *adv* to bed

λέχριος ᾱ ον slanting, oblique

λέχω ▸ **λέγω**[1]

λέων οντος ὁ lion

λεωργός οῦ ὁ offender

λεώς ώ ὁ ▸ **λᾱός**

λεωσφέτερος ον one of their own people

λεωφόρος ον highway, thoroughfare

λήγω cease, leave off; abate, assuage; keep back

λήδανον ου τό gum

λῄζω ▸ **ληΐζω**

λήθη ης ἡ a forgetting, forgetfulness

λήθω ▸ **λανθάνω**

ληϊάς άδος ἡ captive

ληϊβότειρα ᾱς ἡ crop-devouring

ληΐζω *and mid* make plunder *or* spoil; rob, ravage

ληΐη ης ἡ ▸ **λεία**

λήϊον ου τό cornfield, crop

ληΐς ίδος ἡ ▸ **λεία**

ληϊστήρ ῆρος ὁ robber, plunderer

ληϊστός ή όν to be seized as booty

ληϊστύς ύος ἡ plundering, robbing

ληῖτις ιδος ἡ dispenser of booty

λήκυθος ου ἡ oil-flask

λῆμα ατος τό will, purpose; courage; arrogance, pride

λῆμμα ατος τό income; profit, gain; gratification

ληνός οῦ ὁ/ἡ wine-press; trough (for watering cattle)

ληξιαρχικόν
■ **τό ~ γραμματεῖον** the register of each Athenian deme

ληξιάρχικος ου ὁ the officer at Athens who kept order in the ἐκκλησίᾱ

λῆξις εως ἡ assigning, lot, share

ληρέω talk idly; be foolish *or* silly

λήρημα ατος τό **λῆρος** ου ὁ idle talk, nonsense, frivolousness

λησμοσύνη ης ἡ ▸ **λήθη**

ληστείᾱ ᾱς ἡ robbery, piracy, plundering

ληστεύω ▸ **ληΐζω**

ληστήριον ου τό band of robbers

ληστής οῦ ὁ robber, pirate, buccaneer

ληστικός ή όν inclined to rob; piratical

λήσω *fut from* **λανθάνω**

λῆψις εως ἡ a taking, seizing, receiving

λήψομαι *fut from* **λαμβάνω**

λιάζομαι *pass* bend sideways; withdraw, recede; fall

λίᾱν *adv* very much; too much
■ **καὶ λίᾱν** certainly, of course

λιαρός ᾱ́ όν warm, tepid; soft

λίβανος ου ὁ frankincense (tree)

λιβανωτός οῦ ὁ frankincense

λιβανωτρίς ίδος ἡ censer

λιβανωτοφόρος ον bearing frankincense

λιβάς άδος ἡ drop; water; stream

λιβερτῖνος ου ὁ freedman

λίγα *adv from* **λιγύς**

λιγαίνω cry aloud with clear voice

λίγγω sound, twang

λίγδην *adv* scrapingly

λιγνῦς ύος ἡ smoke mixed with flame

λιγυπνείων (*gen* οντος) shrill-blowing, whistling

λιγυρός ᾱ́ όν **λιγύς** εῖα ύ shrill, clear, sharp, piercing, clear-toned

λιγύφθογγος ον clear-voiced

λίζω ▸ **λίγγω**

λίην ▸ **λίαν**

λιθάζω stone

λίθαξ (*gen* ακος) **λίθεος** ον **λίθινος** ον of stone, stony, rocky

λιθίδιον ου τό small stone

λιθο-βολέω pelt with stones, stone

λιθοκόλλητος ον inlaid with precious stones

λιθόλευστος ον stoned to death

λιθολόγος ου ὁ mason

λίθος[1] ου ὁ stone, marble

λίθος[2] ου ἡ precious stone, jewel

λιθοσπαδής ές made by tearing out stones

λιθόστρωτος ον paved with stones

λιθοτομίᾱ ᾱς ἡ quarry

λιθουργός όν working in stone
■ **ὁ λιθουργός** stone-mason

λιθο-φορέω carry stones

λικμάω winnow; scatter like chaff

λικμητήρ ῆρος ὁ winnower

λίκνον ου τό winnowing-fan; basket cradle

λικνοφόρος ου ὁ the bearer of the sacred basket

λῑκριφίς *adv* sideways

λιλαίομαι long for, desire, crave

λῑμαίνω *aor* ἐλίμηνα suffer from hunger

λιμήν ένος ὁ harbour, haven, port, bay; refuge; gathering-place

λιμναῖος ᾱ ον marshy, stagnant

λίμνη ης ἡ lake, pool, pond; artificial basin; swamp; sea

λιμνώδης ες like a lake, marshy

λῑμοκτονίᾱ ᾱς ἡ killing by hunger *or* abstinence from food

λῑμός οῦ ὁ hunger; famine

λίνεος ᾱ ον **λινοῦς** ἡ οῦν of flax, linen

λινοθώρηξ (*gen* ηκος) with a linen cuirass

λίνον ου τό flax, linen; thread; fishing net *or* line; linen cloth; wick

λίνος ου ὁ song of Linos (a mythical minstrel)

λιπ *aor stem from* **λείπω**

λίπα *adv* unctuously

λῐπαρέω persist, persevere; entreat, beg earnestly

λῐπαρής ές persisting, persevering; entreating; liberal, lavishing

λῐπαρίᾱ ᾱς ἡ perseverance

λιπαροκρήδεμνος ον with bright headband

λιπαροπλόκαμος ον with shining locks

λιπαρός ᾰ́ όν oily, shining, fat, greasy; bright, brilliant; rich, blessed, copious, ample; comfortable, easy; splendid; fresh

λιπαρῶς *adv from* **λιπαρής** *and* **λιπαρός**

λιπάω be fat and sleek

λίπος εος τό fat, oil

λιποστρατίᾱ ᾱς ἡ ▸ **λειποστρατία**

λιπο-ψῡχέω faint

λιπόω ▸ **λιπάω**

λῑ́ς[1] ὁ *nom and* λῖν *acc only epic* lion

λῑ́ς[2] ▸ **λισσή** *adj fem only* smooth

λῑ́ς[3] λῑτός ὁ linen, linen cloth

λίσσομαι *mid* beg, pray, entreat, beseech, implore

λισσός ή όν smooth

λιστός ή όν be moved by prayer

λιστρεύω dig round

λίστρον ου τό shovel

λιτανεύω ▸ **λίσσομαι**

λιτή ῆς ἡ prayer, entreaty

λίτομαι ▸ **λίσσομαι**

λιτότης ητος ἡ plainness, simplicity

λίτρᾱ ᾱς ἡ pound *(a weight)*; a silver coin (of Sicily)

λίτρον ου τό carbonate of soda

λιχνείᾱ ᾱς ἡ greed

λίχνος (η) ον greedy, curious

λίψ λιβός ὁ southwest wind

λοβός οῦ ὁ lobe of the ear *or* liver

λογάδην *adv* picked out

λογάς (*gen* άδος) gathered, picked

λογίᾱ ᾱς ἡ collection (for the poor)

λογίζομαι λογιοῦμαι *mid* count, reckon, calculate; reckon among; consider, reason, reflect; conclude, infer, judge, think

λογικός ή όν rational, belonging to the reason

λόγιμος η ον considerable

λόγιος ᾱ ον eloquent; learned ▪ **τὸ λόγιον** oracle

λογισμός οῦ ὁ reckoning, computation, arithmetic; consideration, thought, reasoning, reflection; cause, conclusion, judgement; project; reason, insight

λογιστής οῦ ὁ calculator; (at Athens) an auditor (one of a board which audited the accounts of magistrates leaving office)

λογιστικός ή όν skilled in calculating; arguing, sensible

λογογράφος ου ὁ historian, annalist; professional writer of speeches

λογο-μαχέω dispute about words

λογομαχίᾱ ᾱς ἡ dispute about words

λογο-ποιέω invent stories *or* news; write speeches

λογοποιός οῦ ὁ historian, writer of fables; inventor of stories, newsmonger

λόγος ου ὁ saying, speaking, speech, mode of speaking; eloquence, discourse; conversation, talk; word, expression; assertion; principle, maxim; proverb; oracle; promise; order, command; proposal; condition, agreement; stipulation, decision; pretext; fable, news, story, report, legend; prose-writing, history, book, essay, oration; affair, incident; thought, reason, reckoning, computation, reflection, deliberation, account, consideration, opinion; cause, end; argument, demonstration; meaning, value; proportion; *New Testament* the Word

■ **λογῷ μέν (… ἐργῷ δέ)** in word (… in deed)

λόγχη ης ἡ spear-head, lance

λοέω ▸ **λούω**

λοετρόν οῦ τό ▸ **λουτρόν**

λοιβή ῆς ἡ libation, drink-offering

λοίγιος ον destructive, pernicious

λοιγός οῦ ὁ ruin, havoc, destruction, death

λοιδορέω *and mid* abuse, revile; blame

λοιδορίᾱ ᾱς ἡ abuse, reproach

λοίδορος ον abusive, reviling

λοιμός οῦ ὁ plague, pestilence

λοιμώδης ες pestilential

λοιπός ή όν remaining, surviving, future

λοισθήιος ον **λοίσθιος** (ᾱ) ον **λοῖσθος** ον left behind; last

λοξός ή όν slanting, oblique

λοπός οῦ ὁ husk, peel, bark

λουτρόν οῦ τό bath, bathing-place; ablution, baptism; libation

λουτροχόος ον pouring water for a bath

λούω wash, bathe; *mid* wash oneself

λοφιᾱ́ ᾶς ἡ mane, bristles; hill

λόφος ου ὁ neck, crest of a helmet, tuft of hair; ridge of a hill, hill

λοχᾱγέω lead a λόχος

λοχᾱγίᾱ ᾱς ἡ office of a λοχαγός

λοχᾱγός οῦ ὁ captain, leader of a λόχος

λοχάω *and mid* lie in wait (for) *or* ambush; set a trap for

λοχείᾱ ᾱς ἡ childbirth; child

λοχεῖος ᾱ ον of childbirth

λοχεύω bring forth, bear [a child]; *pass* be born

λοχηγέω ▸ **λοχᾱγέω**

λοχίζω lie in wait for; arrange men in companies; ▸ **λοχάω**

λοχῑ́της ου ὁ soldier of the same company; fellow-soldier

λόχμη ης ἡ lair, thicket

λοχμώδης ες overgrown with bushes

λόχος ου ὁ ambush; company of soldiers, band

λόω ▸ **λούω**

λύγδην *adv* with sobs

λυγίζω bend, twist; *pass* writhe

λύγξ[1] λυγκός ὁ/ἡ lynx

λύγξ[2] λυγγός ἡ hiccough

λύγος ου ἡ willow-twig

λῡγρός ᾱ́ όν sad, mournful, miserable; mischievous; cowardly

λύθρον ου τό **λύθρος** ου ὁ gore, blood; filth

λ

λυκάβᾱς αντος ὁ sun's course, year
λυκέη ης ἡ a wolf-skin
λυκηγενής ές born from light *or* Lycian-born (of Apollo)
λυκοεργής ές of Lycian workmanship
λυκοκτόνος ον wolf-slaying (of Apollo)
λύκος ου ὁ wolf
λῦμα ατος τό dirty water, filth; ruin, bane
λῡμαίνομαι λῡμανοῦμαι ἐλῡμηνάμην *mid* disgrace, outrage; maltreat; destroy, spoil; hurt
λῡμαντής οῦ ὁ **λῡμεών** ῶνος ὁ destroyer, spoiler, corrupter
λῡ́μη ης ἡ brutal outrage; maltreatment, mutilation; ruin
λῡπέω give pain to, grieve, annoy, trouble; *pass* be grieved, sad *or* mournful
λῡ́πη ης ἡ **λῡ́πημα** ατος τό sorrow, grief, pain, distress
λῡπηρός ᾱ́ όν **λῡπρός** ᾱ́ όν sad, painful, wretched, distressed
λύρᾱ ᾱς ἡ lyre
λῡσιμελής ές limb-relaxing
λύσις εως ἡ loosing, release, ransoming, deliverance; dissolution, separation; departure; divorce
λῡσιτελέω be useful, advantageous *or* profitable
λῡσιτελής ές useful, advantageous
λύσσα ης ἡ rage, fury
λυσσαίνω, λυσσάω be raving mad, rage (in battle); be angry
λυσσητήρ (*gen* ῆρος) **λυσσώδης** ες raving, raging
λυτήριος ον releasing
λύτρον ου τό ransom; atonement
λυτρόω *and mid* release on receipt of ransom
λύτρωσις εως ἡ ransoming; redemption
λυτρωτής οῦ ὁ redeemer
λυχνίᾱ ᾱς ἡ lampstand
λυχνοκαΐη ης ἡ feast of lamps
λύχνος ου ὁ light, lamp, torch
λῡ́ω loosen, untie, slacken; set free, release, redeem; dissolve, sever; destroy; abrogate, annul; atone, amend; profit; be useful; *mid* loosen for oneself; redeem, ransom, relieve, release
λωβάομαι *mid* **λωβεύω** act outrageously; insult, maltreat, disgrace; mutilate, hurt; corrupt
λώβη ης ἡ outrage, disgrace, shame; maltreatment, mutilation; ruin
λωβητήρ ῆρος ὁ slanderer; destroyer; murderer
λωβητός ή όν ill-treated, outraged, insulted; insulting
λώπη ης ἡ robe, mantle, jerkin
λωποδυτέω steal clothes
λωποδύτης ου ὁ clothes-stealer, thief, rogue
λῷστος η ον the best, dearest
λωτόεις εσσα εν rich in lotus
λωτός οῦ ὁ lotus; clover; lotus-tree and fruit; lily of the Nile
λωτοφάγος ου ὁ lotus-eater
λωφάω relax, take rest; abate; lighten
λώφησις εως ἡ cessation
λῴων ον ▸ **λωΐων**

Μμ

μ, Μ (μῦ) twelfth letter of the alphabet
■ **μ′** *as a numeral* = 40

μά *particle expressing affirmation; expressing protest*
■ **μὰ Ζῆνα** by Zeus

μάγαδις ιδος ἡ string-instrument, harp

μαγγάνευμα ατος τό ▶ **μαγεία**

μαγγανεύω use charms *or* philtres, play tricks

μαγείᾱ ᾱς ἡ magic, delusion, juggling tricks

μαγειρική ῆς ἡ cookery

μάγειρος ου ὁ cook, butcher

μαγευτική ῆς ἡ magic

μαγεύω be a magician, use the arts of magic

μαγίᾱ ᾱς ἡ ▶ **μαγεία**

μάγος ου ὁ soothsayer, astrologer, magus; enchanter, wizard

μαγοφόνια ων τά slaughter of the magi (a Persian festival)

μᾶζα (*also* μάζα) ης ἡ barley-bread

μαζός οῦ ὁ ▶ **μαστός**

μαθ *likely to be from* **μανθάνω**

μάθημα ατος τό **μάθησις** εως ἡ the act of learning; knowledge, learning, science, art, doctrine

μαθητεύω be a pupil; teach, instruct

μαθητής οῦ ὁ pupil, disciple

μαθητός ή όν to be learned

μαθήτρια ᾱς ἡ female pupil

μαῖα ᾱς ἡ good mother, foster mother, nurse

μαιμακτηριών ῶνος ὁ fifth Attic month (November)

μαιμάω be very eager (for), pant *or* quiver with eagerness; rave

μαινάς άδος ἡ maenad, bacchante; raving

μαίνω *aor* ἔμηνα make mad; *pass* μανοῦμαι ἐμάνην be mad, rave, rage, be furious *or* frenzied

μαίομαι *mid* strive, endeavour; seek

μάκαρ αρος (*fem* μάκαιρα) blessed, happy, fortunate; rich

μακαρίζω μακαριῶ call happy

μακάριος (ᾱ) ον ▶ **μάκαρ**

μακαρισμός οῦ ὁ pronouncing happy, blessing

μακαριστός ή όν to be pronounced happy, enviable; welcome

μακεδνός ή όν tall, slender

μάκελλα ης ἡ pick-axe, shovel

μάκελλον ου τό meat-market

μᾱ́κιστος η ον ▶ **μήκιστος**

μακραίων ον long-lived, lasting

μακρ-ηγορέω speak at great length

μακρημερίᾱ ᾱς ἡ season of long days

μακρόβιος ον long-lived

μακρόθεν *adv* from afar

μακροθῡμέω be long suffering; be patient

μακροθῡμίᾱ ᾱς ἡ being long-suffering, patience

μακρολογέω speak at length

μακρολογίᾱ ᾱς ἡ speaking at length

μακρός ᾱ́ όν long; tall, high, deep, far; long-lasting; tedious, prolix

μακροχρόνιος ον long-lived

μάλα *adv* much, very much, wholly, particularly, exceedingly; certainly, yes

μαλακίᾱ ᾱς ἡ softness, weakness; illness; slackness, cowardice

μαλακίζομαι *pass and mid* become weak, effeminate, lazy, cowardly *or* timid; be appeased

μαλακός ή όν soft, tender, sickly; mild, gentle; tender, delicate; effeminate, cowardly; careless, remiss; luxurious, wanton

μαλάσσω soften, appease; *pass* be softened by entreaties; be relieved

μαλερός ᾱ́ όν strong, mighty, terrible, vehement, raging; greedy

μάλη ης ἡ arm-pit

μαλθακ- *see* **μαλακ-**

μάλιστα *adv* most, most strongly; especially, mostly; most certainly; by far; *with numbers* about

μᾶλλον *adv* more, more strongly, rather, the more, yet, far; too much; by all means

μαλλός οῦ ὁ fleece

μάμμη ης ἡ grandmother; mummy

μαμωνᾶς ᾶ ὁ mammon; riches, wealth

μᾱ́ν ▸ **μήν**

μανδραγόρᾱς ου *or* ᾱ ὁ mandrake (a narcotic plant)

μανθάνω† learn, have learnt, know; ask, inquire, hear, perceive; understand

μανίᾱ ᾱς ἡ madness, frenzy; enthusiasm

μανικός ή όν **μανιώδης** ες mad, frantic, raving, revelling; ■ **μανιάς** άδος ἡ

μάννα ατος τό manna; food

μανός ή όν thin, scanty, slack

μαντείᾱ ᾱς ἡ **μαντεῖον** ου τό **μάντευμα** ατος τό gift of prophesying, divinaton, prophecy, oracle

μαντεῖος ᾱ ον ▸ **μαντικός**

μαντευτός ή όν foretold by an oracle; prescribed by an oracle

μαντεύω *and mid* prophesy, divine; presage, forebode; consult an oracle

μαντηΐη, μαντήιον ▸ **μαντεία, μαντεῖον**

μαντικός ή όν prophetic, prophesying

■ **ἡ μαντική** art of divination, prophecy

μάντις εως ὁ/ἡ soothsayer, seer, prophet

μαντοσύνη ης ὁ ▸ **μαντεία**

μάομαι ▸ **μαίομαι** rush on, hasten

μάραθον ου τό fennel

μαραίνω μαρανῶ ἐμαρᾶνα destroy, extinguish, quench; *pass* die away, disappear, decay, wither

μαρὰν ἀθά *Syriac* the Lord comes

μαργαίνω rage furiously

μαργαρῑ́της ου ὁ pearl

μάργος (η) ον raving, mad, frantic; lustful

μαρμαίρω sparkle, glisten, gleam

μαρμάρεος ᾱ ον **μαρμαρόεις** εσσα εν sparkling, glistening

μάρμαρος ον sparkling

■ **ὁ μάρμαρος** stone, rock; marble

μαρμαρυγή ῆς ἡ dazzling brightness; trembling motion

μάρναμαι ▸ **μάχομαι**

μάρπτω grasp, seize, hold, touch, reach, clasp

μάρσιπος ου ὁ bag, pouch

μαρτυρέω be a witness, bear witness; agree to, confirm; confess, praise; *pass* obtain a (good) testimony

μαρτυρίᾱ ᾱς ἡ **μαρτύριον** ου τό testimony, witness, evidence, proof; sermon

μαρτῡ́ρομαι μαρτυροῦμαι ἐμαρτῡράμην *mid* call to witness; testify, confirm by oath, protest

μάρτυρος ου ὁ/ἡ **μάρτυς** υρος ὁ/ἡ witness; martyr

μασάομαι *mid* chew

μάσασθαι *see* **ἐπιμαίομαι**

μασθός οῦ ὁ ▸ **μαστός**

μάσσω *and mid* knead, handle

μᾶσσων ον *comp* ▸ **μακρός**

μάσταξ ακος ἡ mouth, cavity of the mouth; mouthful, morsel

μαστεύω seek, search for; endeavour, strive

μαστήρ ῆρος ὁ seeker, investigator

μαστῑγέω ▸ **μαστιγόω**

μαστῑγίᾱς ου ὁ one who is frequently whipped; good-for-nothing

μαστῑγοφόρος whip-bearer, constable

μαστῑγόω, μαστίζω whip, flog

μάστιξ ῑγος ἡ **μάστις** ιος ἡ whip, scourge; plague

μαστίω ▸ **μαστιγόω**

μαστός οῦ ὁ teat; breast, woman's breast; hill, knoll

μασχαλίζω mutilate

μασχαλιστήρ ῆρος ὁ shoulder-strap

ματᾴζω act foolishly; be deceived

ματαιολογίᾱ ᾱς ἡ idle talk

ματαιολόγος ον talking idly

μάταιος (ᾱ) ον idle, foolish, vain, inefficient; unmeaning, unfounded; thoughtless, wanton, untrue, wicked

ματαιότης ητος ἡ folly, vanity

ματαιόω make foolish; bring to nothing

ματάω miss, do in vain; loiter, linger

ματεύω ▸ **μαστεύω**

μάτην *adv* in vain; groundlessly; at random

μᾱ́τηρ μᾱτρός ἡ ▸ **μήτηρ**

ματίᾱ ᾱς ἡ folly; vain attempt

μαῦρος ▸ **ἀμαυρός**

μάχαιρα ᾱς ἡ large knife; dagger; sword

μαιραιροποιεῖον ου τό knife *or* sword factory

μαχαιροποιός οῦ ὁ knife *or* sword maker

μαχαιροφόρος ον sword-bearing

μάχη ης ἡ combat, fight, battle; battle-field; single combat; quarrel

μαχήμων ον ▸ **μάχιμος**

μαχητής οῦ ὁ fighter, warrior; warlike

μαχητός ή όν conquerable

μάχιμος (η) ον warlike

μαχλοσύνη ης ἡ lust, lewdness

μάχομαι† *mid* fight, make war; resist, withstand; quarrel, dispute

μάψ, μαψιδίως *adv* rashly, thoughtlessly, at random; in vain, fruitlessly, falsely; indecorously

μάω *see* **μάομαι**

μέγαθος τό *see* **μέγεθος**

μεγάθῡμος ον high-minded, magnanimous

μεγαίρω *aor* ἐμέγηρα grudge, envy

μεγακήτης ες with huge sea-animals

μεγαλαυχέω *and mid* boast highly

μεγαλεῖος ᾱ ον magnificent, splendid; haughty

μεγαλειότης ητος ἡ magnificence, majesty

μεγαλ-ηγορέω boast

μεγαλήτωρ (*gen* ορος) high-minded, heroic; overweening

μεγαλίζομαι *pass* be proud

μεγαλοπρᾱ́γμων ον disposed to do great deeds, forming great designs

μεγαλοπρέπεια ᾱς ἡ magnificence, splendour; love of splendour

μεγαλοπρεπής ές magnificent, splendid; magnanimous, liberal, fond of pomp

μεγαλο-φρονέω be hopeful; be proud

μεγαλοφροσύνη ης ἡ greatness of mind; haughtiness

μεγαλόφρων ον high-minded; haughty

μεγαλοψῡχίᾱ magnanimity; boldness, arrogance

μεγαλῡ́νω make great *or* powerful; praise, extol; *mid* be exalted; boast

μεγαλώνυμος ον much praised; giving glory

μεγάλως, μεγαλωστί *adv from* μέγας

μεγαλωσύνη ης ἡ ▸ **μεγαλειότης**

μέγαρον ου τό chamber, hall, apartment for men *or* for women, bed-chamber; house, mansion; inner room of a temple, sanctuary

μέγας μεγάλη μέγα large, great, big, grand; spacious, long, high, wide; powerful, mighty, strong, violent; arrogant, proud; illustrious
■ **μείζων** ον *comp*
■ **μέγιστος** η ον *sup*
■ **μεγάλως, μεγαλωστί, μέγα, μεγάλα** *adv* much, very much, exceedingly

μέγεθος ους τό greatness, bulk, size; might, power, excellence; importance

μ

μεγιστᾶνες ων οἱ the chief men, grandees

μέδιμνος ου ὁ an Attic corn-measure containing 48 χοίνικες (very nearly 12 gallons)

μέδω, μεδέω think of, give heed to, attend to; devise; rule
■ **ὁ μέδων** ruler, guardian

μεθ-αιρέω catch in turn

μεθ-άλλομαι *mid* leap upon; rush after

μεθ-αρμόζω alter; correct

μέθεξις εως ἡ participation

μεθ-έπω *and mid* follow closely; obey; call upon, visit; pursue; drive on [horses] in pursuit of; manage

μεθ-ερμηνεύω translate

μέθη ης ἡ strong drink; drunkenness

μέθ-ημαι + *dat* sit among

μεθημερινός ή όν happening by day; daily

μεθημοσύνη ης ἡ carelessness, remissness

μεθήμων ον careless, lazy

μεθ-ῑ́ημι *act tr* let loose, let go; release, set free; forgive, pardon; lay in, bring to; send away; abandon; neglect; permit, allow; *act intr* cease, slacken, be careless; *mid* loose oneself from

μεθ-ιστάνω, μεθ-ίστημι *act tr* transpose, place in another way; substitute, change, remove; *act intr and pass* stand among *or* in the middle of; withdraw, retire; change one's place, go over to another party, revolt; *mid* send away, remove

μεθό ▸ **μεθ' ὅ**

μεθοδείᾱ ᾱς ἡ trick, wiliness

μέθοδος ου ἡ method of inquiry; method

μεθ-ομῑλέω + *dat* converse with

μεθόριος ᾱ ον bordering on
■ **τὰ μεθόρια** borders, frontier

μεθ-ορμάομαι *pass* rush after; follow closely

μεθ-ορμίζω *act tr* bring to another anchorage; *act intr and mid* sail to another place

μέθυ τό wine

μεθύσκω μεθύσω ἐμέθυσα make drunk; *pass* get drunk

μέθυσος η ον drunk(en)

μεθύστερος ᾱ ον later

μεθύω be drunk; be drenched

μείγνῡμι ▸ **μίγνυμι**

μειδ(ι)άω smile

μειζότερος ᾱ ον **μείζων** ον *comp from* **μέγας**

μεικτός ή όν ▸ **μικτός**

μείλᾱς ▸ **μέλας**

μείλιγμα ατος τό sedative, means of appeasing *or* soothing; propitiation

μείλινος η ον ▸ **μέλινος**

μείλιον ου τό love gift

μειλίσσω make mild, soothe, propitiate; *mid* extenuate

μειλιχίη ης ἡ mildness

μειλίχιος ᾱ ον **μείλιχος** ον mild, gentle, sweet, soft, kind, gracious, bland

μειν *aor stem from* **μένω**

μειον-εκτέω have too little, be at a disadvantage

μειόω lessen; degrade; *pass* decrease; *mid* be inferior

μειράκιον ου τό boy, lad, young man

μειρακιώδης ες youthful; boyish

μείρομαι receive as one's share
■ **ἔμμορε** *pf* he has as his share
■ **εἵμαρται** it is decreed by fate
■ **ἡ εἱμαρμένη** fate, destiny

μείς μηνός ὁ month

μείωμα ατος τό deficiency

μείων ον *comp from* **μικρός**

μελάγγαιος ον with black soil

μελαγχαίτης (*gen* ου) black-haired

μελάγχολος ον with black bile

μελάγχροος ον **μελαγχροιής** ές black-skinned, swarthy

μέλαθρον ου τό rafters of a roof; roof; house, hall

μελαίνω μελανῶ *act tr* blacken, dye black; *act intr and mid* grow black

μελάμφυλλος ον with dark foliage

μελάνδετος ον bound with black

μελανίᾱ ᾱς ἡ dark cloud, blackness

μελανόχροος ον **μελανόχρως** (*gen* οος) ▸ **μελάγχροος**

μελάνυδρος ον with black water

μελάνω ▸ **μελαίνω**

μέλᾱς αινα αν black; dark, dusky, gloomy
■ **τὸ μέλαν** black dye; ink

μέλδομαι *mid* melt

μελεδαίνω care for, tend; be anxious

μελεδών ῶνος ἡ **μελεδώνη** ης ἡ **μελέδημα** ατος τό care, sorrow

μελεδωνός οῦ ὁ/ἡ attendant, guardian, nurse

μέλει† *see* **μέλω**

μελεϊστί *adv* limb from limb

μέλεος ᾱ ον fruitless, vain; miserable, wretched

μελετάω take care of, care for; study, practise, exercise; exert oneself; project, plan; study; declaim

μελέτη ης ἡ **μελέτημα** ατος τό care, attention; study, practice, exercise; employment; pursuit; exercise of speaking; anxiety

μελετηρός ᾱ όν practising diligently

μελέτωρ ορος ὁ guardian; avenger

μέλημα ατος τό object of care, darling

μέλι ιτος τό honey

μελίγηρυς (*gen* υος) sweet-sounding

μελίη ης ἡ ash-tree, ash spear

μελιηδής ές honey-sweet

μελίκρᾱτος ον **μελίκρητος** mixed with honey

μελίνη ης ἡ millet

μέλινος η ον ashen

μέλισσα ης ἡ bee; honey

μελίσσιος ᾱ ον made by bees

μελιτόεις εσσα εν rich in honey; made of honey

μελιτόω mix with honey

μελιττουργός οῦ ὁ bee-keeper

μελίφρων ον honey-sweet; sweet to the mind, delicious

μέλλησις εως ἡ being about to do, intention; threatening, impending; delay

μελλητής οῦ ὁ delayer

μελλόγαμος ον **μελλόνυμφος** ον betrothed, about to be wedded

μέλλω† be about to, be going to, intend to; be destined to; be likely, probable *or* certain; be meaning to do; delay, hesitate, scruple
■ **μέλλων** ον *adj* future

μελοποιός οῦ ὁ lyric poet

μέλος ους τό limb; song, strain, melody

μέλπηθρον ου τό delight, amusement; sport, plaything

μέλπω *and mid* sing and dance; celebrate, praise

μέλω *and mid* be an object of care, be a care to
■ **μέλει**† **μοι** + *gen* I care for

■ **μέλομαί τινος** I take care of something

μελῳδός όν singing, melodious

μέμαα *pf from* **μάομαι** *with pres meaning*

μέμβλεται *epic pf pass from* **μέλω**

μεμβρᾱ́νᾱ ης ἡ parchment

μεμελημένως *adv* carefully

μεμετιμένος ▸ **μεθειμένος** *from* **μεθίημι**

μέμηλα *pf from* **μέλω** *with pres meaning*

μέμνημαι *pf pass from* **μιμνήσκω** remember

μέμονα *pf from* **μάομαι** *with pres meaning*

μεμπτός ή όν to be blamed, despicable; blaming

μέμφομαι blame, reproach, find fault with

μεμψιμοιρέω ▸ **μέμφομαι**

μεμψίμοιρος ον discontented, querulous

μέμψις εως ἡ blame, reproach; cause for complaint

μέν* *particle* indeed, rather, certainly ■ **μέν*** … **δέ*** on the one hand … but on the other hand

μενεαίνω long for ardently, desire; be angry

μενεδήϊος ον **μενεπτόλεμος** ον steadfast, staunch, brave

μενετός ή όν lasting, steadfast, patient

μενεχάρμης (*gen* ου) **μενέχαρμος** ον ▸ **μενεδήϊος**

μενοεικής ές plentiful; satisfying, heart-pleasing

μενοινάω, μενοινέω desire eagerly, intend, purpose

μένος ους τό desire, ardour, wish, purpose; anger; courage, spirit, vigour; power, strength; violence

μὲν οὖν* *particle* indeed, rather; yet

μενοῦνγε* *particle* yes rather

μεντᾶν ▸ **μέντοι ἄν**

μέντοι *conj* indeed, rather, certainly, of course; yet, however, nevertheless

μένω† stay, stay behind, linger; remain, continue; stand one's ground; *tr* await, expect, wait for

μερίζω μεριῶ divide into parts; attribute; *mid* divide among themselves

μέριμνα ης ἡ care, anxious thought

μεριμνάω care, be anxious *or* thoughtful

μερίμνημα ατος τό ▸ **μέριμνα**

μερίς ίδος ἡ part, portion, share; party; class, company

μερισμός οῦ ὁ dividing, distributing; separation

μεριστής οῦ ὁ divider

μέρμερος ον startling, horrible, dreadful

μερμηρίζω μερμηρίξω μεμήριξα be anxious *or* thoughtful, ponder; devise

μέρμῑς ῑθος ἡ string, cord

μέρος ους τό part, portion, share, lot; class; turn; station, rank; piece, section; party; district, place

μέροψ (*gen* οπος) mortal, endowed with speech

μεσαιπόλιος ον half-grey, i.e. middle-aged

μεσαμβρίη ▸ **μεσημβρία**

μέσαυλος ▸ **μέσσαυλος**

μεσεύω be neutral

μεσηγύ(ς) (*also* μεσσηγύ(ς)) *adv* in the middle, between; meanwhile

μεσήεις εσσα εν middling

μεσημβρίᾱ ᾱς ἡ midday; south

μεσημβρινός ή όν at noon; southern

μεσῑτεύω be a mediator

μεσόγαια ᾱς ἡ **μεσόγεια** ᾱς ἡ inland, midland

μεσόγαιος ον interior

μεσόγειοι ων οἱ inhabitants of the interior of Attica

μεσόδμη ης ἡ cross-beam, cross-plank with a hole for the mast

μεσόμφαλος ον from the centre of the earth

μεσοποτάμιος ον between two rivers

μέσος η ον middle, in the middle of; moderate, middling, indifferent; impartial, neutral
■ **τὸ μέσον** the middle, centre; space between; interval; difference; distance; middle number; moderation; impartiality, neutrality; public(ity)

μεσότοιχον ου τό partition wall

μεσο-τομέω cut through the middle

μεσουράνημα ατος τό zenith, mid-heaven

μεσόω be in the middle, be half over

μέσσατος η ον absolutely in the middle

μέσσαυλος ου ὁ **μέσσαυλον** ου τό inner court, farm, stable

μεσσηγύ ▸ **μεσηγύ**

μεσσίας ου ὁ the Messiah

μεσσοπαγής ές driven into the middle

μέσσος η ον ▸ **μέσος**

μεστός ή όν full, filled up; sated

μεστόω fill up with

μέσφα *adv* ▸ **μέχρι** till

μετά *adv* among them; besides; afterwards; *prep with acc* into the middle (of); in quest *or* pursuit of, after, behind; next to, next after; according to; *with gen* among, between; with, together with; at; according to; *with dat* among, in company with

μετα-βαίνω pass to another place, pass over *or* on

μετα-βάλλω *act tr* turn over, turn about; change, alter; exchange; *act intr, mid and pass* be changed, undergo a change; change one's mind and turn to; exchange, traffic; change one's clothes; turn oneself; take on one's back

μετάβασις εως ἡ passing over, shifting; change, revolution

μετα-βιβάζω carry over *or* away; alter

μεταβολή ῆς ἡ exchange, traffic; change; mutability

μετα-βουλεύω *and mid* alter one's plans; change one's mind

μετάγγελος ου ὁ/ἡ messenger, go-between

μεταγειτνιών ῶνος ὁ second Attic month (August to September)

μετα-γιγνώσκω change one's mind; repeal; repent of

μετάγνοια ᾱς ἡ **μετάγνωσις** εως ἡ repentance

μετα-γράφω alter something written; *mid* have something translated

μετ-άγω convey to another place; go by a different route

μετα-δαίνυμαι *mid* share a feast with (another)

μεταδήμιος ον native; at home

μετα-δίδωμι give a share of

μεταδίωκτος ον overtaken

μετα-διώκω pursue, overtake; follow close upon

μετα-δοκεῖ + *dat* change one's mind, repent

μεταδόρπιος ον during supper; after supper

μετάδοσις εως ἡ the giving a share

μεταδρομάδην *adv* running after

μεταδρομή ῆς ἡ pursuit

μετάδρομος ον pursuing; punishing

μετάθεσις εως ἡ transposition; change

μετα-θέω run after

μετα-ΐζω take one's seat beside

μετ-αίρω carry away; set out, depart

μετ-αΐσσω rush after

μετ-αιτέω demand one's share

μεταίτιος ον accessory; accomplice

μεταίχμιον ου τό space between two armies; disputed frontier

μετα-καλέω call back; call in

μετα-κῑάθω follow after; pursue; visit; march over

μετα-κῑνέω remove; *mid* depart

μετακῑνητός ή όν to be changed, to be disturbed

μετα-κίω ▸ **μετακιάθω**

μετα-κλαίω weep afterwards

μετα-κλῑ́νομαι *pass* turn to the other side

μετα-λαγχάνω get a share of

μετα-λαμβάνω get a share of, partake of; take in exchange; *mid* lay claim to, assume

μετα-λήγω + *gen* leave off

μετάληψις εως ἡ participation; changing

μεταλλαγή ῆς ἡ change

μετ-αλλάσσω exchange; alter; undergo a change

μεταλλάω question, inquire, search after

μεταλλευτής ου ὁ miner

μέταλλον ου τό pit, mine; quarry

μεταμάζιος ον between the breasts

μετα-μανθάνω learn differently; unlearn

μεταμέλεια ᾱς ἡ **μετάμελος** ου ὁ change of mind, repentance

μεταμέλει μοι + *gen of what is repented of* **μεταμέλομαι** + *pple pass* I repent

μετα-μῑ́γνῡμι, μετα-μίσγω mix among, confound

μετα-μορφόω transform

μεταμώνιος ον borne by the wind; idle, vain; useless

μετανα-γιγνώσκομαι + *gen* repent of

μετανάστασις εως ἡ migration

μετανάστης οῦ ὁ wanderer, alien

μετα-νίσσομαι pass over; go after, pursue

μεταν -ίσταμαι *mid* change one's country, emigrate

μετα-νοέω change one's mind; repent

μετάνοια ᾱς ἡ ▸ **μετάγνοια**

μεταξύ *adv and prep with gen* between; afterwards; during; meanwhile

μετα-παύομαι rest in the meantime

μεταπαυσωλή ῆς ἡ rest between

μετα-πείθω persuade to another opinion

μετα-πέμπω *and mid* send for, summon; recall

μετα-πῑ́πτω undergo a change; fall differently; be altered

μετα-ποιέω alter; *mid* lay claim to

μετα-πορεύομαι *pass* go after, avenge

μεταπρεπής ές excellent

μετα-πρέπω be conspicuous *or* excellent

μεταπύργιον ου τό wall between two towers

μετα-ρρυθμίζω transform

μετάρσιος ον lifted up; high in the air; on the high sea

μετ-αρσιόω lift up

μετα-σεύομαι *mid* rush after; rush up to

μετα-σπάω draw to the other side

μέτασσαι ων αἱ lambs of intermediate age

μετάστασις εως ἡ changing of place, removal; banishment; migration; change of government, revolution

μετα-στένω lament afterwards

μεταστοιχῑ́ *adv* in a line one after another

μετα-στρέφω *act tr* turn about *or* round; alter; *act intr and pass* change one's course, turn oneself to; + *gen* care for, regard

μετάσχεσις εως ἡ a partaking

μετασχηματίζω transform, remodel; refer *or* apply to

μετα-τάσσω arrange differently; *mid* change one's opinion

μετα-τίθημι place among; place differently; alter, change; *mid* change one's opinion, retract; be a turncoat

μετα-τρέπομαι *mid* turn oneself around; + *gen* show regard for

μετα-τροπαλίζομαι *mid intr* turn round frequently

μετ-αυδάω speak among *or* to others

μεταυτίκα *adv* immediately after, forthwith

μεταῦτις *adv* afterwards

μετα-φέρω carry to another place, transfer; change, alter; change by mistake

μετά-φημι speak among *or* to others; accost

μετα-φορέω ▸ **μεταφέρω**

μετα-φράζομαι *mid* consider after

μετάφρενον ου τό upper part of the back

μετα-φυτεύω transplant

μετα-φωνέω ▸ **μετάφημι**

μετα-χειρίζω *and mid* have in one's hands, handle, manage, treat; administer, govern; pursue, practise

μετα-χωρέω go away, migrate

μέτ-ειμι[1] be among, between *or* near
▪ **μέτεστι** + *dat of possessor & gen of thing possessed* have a claim to *or* share of

μέτ-ειμι[2] go between *or* among; go away; come up to; go after, follow, pursue, avenge; visit; strive after; practise, manage

μετ-εῖπον *see* **μετάφημι**

μετεκ-βαίνω step over into

μετεμ-βιβάζω put on board another ship

μετεν-δύω put other clothes on

μετεξέτεροι αι α some among many, certain persons

μετέπειτα *adv* afterwards, thereupon

μετ-έρχομαι ▸ **μέτειμι**[2]

μετ-εύχομαι *mid* change one's wish

μετ-έχω + *gen* have a share of, partake (of), enjoy with others

μετεωρίζω lift up, raise; excite, buoy up, encourage; *pass* rise; stay out on the high sea; be excited

μετέωρος ον lifted up, raised on high, suspended in the air, aloft; on the high sea; being in suspense, anxious, excited, elated; fluctuating, doubtful
▪ **τὸ μετέωρον** the high sea
▪ **τὰ μετέωρα** things on high, high places, heavenly bodies, phenomena of the sky

μετ-ίσχω ▸ **μετέχω**

μετοικεσίᾱ ᾱς ἡ emigration; captivity

μετ-οικέω change one's abode; be a metic *see* **μέτοικος**

μετοίκησις εως ἡ **μετοικίᾱ** ᾱς ἡ living with; change of country of residence, migration

μετ-οικίζω bring to another country, settle as colonists

μετοίκιον ου τό tax paid by a metic *see* **μέτοικος**

μέτοικος ον living with; *noun* foreigner; metic, (at Athens) a resident alien who paid a tax but had no civil rights

μετ-οίχομαι *mid* have gone through; be in pursuit of, go after

μετ-οκλάζω (of a coward crouching in ambush) squat timidly

μετ-ονομάζω call by a new name

μετόπη ης ἡ metope, stone inserted between pairs of triglyphs in the Doric order, sometimes decorated with sculpture in high relief

μετ-οπάζω give to companion

μετόπιν, μετόπισθεν *adv* behind, backwards, from behind; after(wards)

μετοπωρινός ή όν autumnal

μετόπωρον ου τό late autumn

μετουσίᾱ ᾱς ἡ **μετοχή** ῆς ἡ partaking, communion, share

μετ-οχλίζω remove out of the way by a lever *or* by force

μέτοχος ον + *gen* sharing in; partner (in)

μετρέω measure; pass over; estimate, compute

μέτρημα ατος τό a measured distance; measure, allowance

μέτρησις εως ἡ measuring

μετρητής οῦ ὁ a liquid measure = 9 gallons (40 litres)

μετρητικός ή όν of *or* for measuring

μετριάζω be moderate

μετριοπαθέω be lenient

μέτριος ᾱ ον moderate, within measure; ordinary, convenient, sufficient, tolerable; fair, just, temperate, simple, orderly, honest, modest; indifferent, little

μετριότης ητος ἡ moderation, modesty; average measure

μ

μέτρον ου τό measure, rule, standard; vessel for measuring; size, measured space; full measure; prime of life; [in poetry] metre

μετωπηδόν *adv* with front-foremost

μετώπιος ον on the forehead

μέτωπον ου τό forehead; front, front part

μέχρι *adv and prep with gen* until, as far as; within, during; as long as

μή *adv* not, that not; in order not, lest

μηδαμά, μηδαμῇ *adv* not at all; nowhere; never

μηδαμόθεν *adv* from no place

μηδαμός ή όν ▸ **μηδείς**

μηδαμοῦ *adv* nowhere; not at all

μηδαμῶς ▸ **μηδαμά**

μηδέ *conj* and not, but not; nor, not even

μηδείς μηδεμία μηδέν no-one, none, not even one; nothing

μηδέποτε *adv* never, not at any time

μηδέπω *adv* not yet

μηδέτερος ᾱ ον neither of the two

μηδετέρωσε *adv* to neither side

μηδίζω side with the Persians

μηδισμός οῦ ὁ a siding with the Persians

μήδομαι μήσομαι ἐμησάμην devise, counsel, advise; plot, contrive, decree

μῆδος[1] εος τό thought, plan, scheme, counsel

μῆδος[2] εος τό *only in pl* genitals

μηθείς ▸ **μηδείς**

μηκάομαι *mid* bleat; shriek

μηκάς (*gen* άδος) bleating

μηκέτι *adv* no more, no longer

μήκιστος η ον longest; tallest; greatest

μῆκος ους τό length; tallness; greatness

μήκοτε ▸ **μήποτε**

μηκῡ́νω μηκυνῶ lengthen, prolong, extend

μήκων ωνος ἡ poppy; head of a poppy; poppy juice

μηλέᾱ ᾱς ἡ apple tree

μήλειος ον of a sheep

μηλοβοτήρ ῆρος ὁ shepherd

μηλόβοτος ον grazed by sheep

μῆλον[1] ου τό apple; the fruit of any tree

μῆλον[2] ου τό sheep; goat

μηλοσφαγέω kill sheep

μῆλοψ (*gen* οπος) like apples; golden

μηλωτή ῆς ἡ sheepskin, fleece

μήν[1]* *particle* truly, indeed; yet, however

■ **οὐ μὴν ἀλλά** nevertheless

μήν[2] μηνός ὁ month, new moon

μήνη ης ἡ moon

μηνιθμός οῦ ὁ ▸ **μῆνις**

μήνῑμα ατος τό cause of anger

μῆνις ιος ἡ anger, wrath

μηνίω be angry with someone *dat*

μηνοειδής ές crescent-shaped

μήνῡμα ατος τό information

μηνῡτής οῦ ὁ informer, denouncer

μήνῡτρον ου τό reward for information

μηνῡ́ω make known, denounce, betray; inform, announce

μήποτε *adv* never; lest ever, in order that never

μήπου *adv* in order that nowhere

μήπω *adv* not yet

μήπως *adv* in order that in no way

μῆρα ων τά *pl from* **μῆρος**

μήρινθος ου ἡ string, cord

μηρίον ου τό **μηρός** οῦ ὁ thigh bone, thigh

μηρῡ́ομαι *mid* furl the sails

μήστωρ ωρος ὁ counsellor; causer

μήτε *conj* and not
■ **μήτε ... μήτε** neither ... nor

μήτηρ μητρός ἡ mother

μητιάω *and mid* meditate, consider; devise, contrive, invent

μητίετα ὁ adviser, counsellor

μητιόεις εσσα εν ingenious

μητίομαι ▸ **μητιάω**

μήτις τι none, no-one, nothing; in order that no-one *or* nothing

μῆτις ιος *or* ιδος (*Attic*) ἡ wisdom, counsel, cunning; device, project

μήτοι *adv* in no way; on no account

μήτρᾱ ᾱς ἡ womb

μητραλοίᾱς ᾱ ὁ a matricide

μητρόθεν *adv* from the mother's side

μητρόξενος ου ὁ bastard

μητροπάτωρ ορος ὁ one's mother's father

μητρόπολις εως ἡ mother-city, mother-country, mother-state; capital

μητρυιᾱ́ ᾶς ἡ stepmother

μητρῷος η ον **μητρώϊος** ᾱ ον of a mother, maternal
■ **τὸ μητρῷον** the temple of Cybele at Athens which was the depository of the state archives

μήτρως ωος ὁ maternal uncle

μηχανάω *and mid* make by skill, construct, devise, contrive, prepare; *mid* procure for oneself

μηχανή ῆς ἡ **μηχάνημα** ατος τό artificial implement, instrument, machine; engine of war; contrivance, artificial means, device, mode, way

μηχανητικός ή όν **μηχανικός** ή όν **μηχανόεις** εσσα εν ingenious, inventive, clever

μηχανοποιός οῦ ὁ engineer, maker of war-engines; theatrical machinist

μηχανορράφος ον crafy, cunning

μῆχος τό ▸ **μηχανή**

μιαίνω μιανῶ ἐμίᾱνα dye; stain, soil, pollute

μιαιφονέω be *or* become blood-stained; murder

μιαιφόνος ον blood-stained; defiled with blood; murderous

μιαρίᾱ ᾱς ἡ brutality; defilement, blood-guiltiness

μιαρός ᾱ́ όν stained, polluted; wicked

μίασμα ατος τό **μιασμός** οῦ ὁ stain, defilement, pollution, abomination

μιάστωρ ορος ὁ guilty wretch, defiler; avenger

μιγάζομαι *mid* ▸ **μίγνυμαι**

μιγάς (*gen* άδος) mixed, confused

μίγδα *adv* confusedly

μῖγμα ατος τό mixture

μίγνῡμι, μῑγνύω mix, mix up, mingle, bring together; *pass and mid* be mingled *or* brought together; meet with; have sex with

μῑκρολογέομαι *mid* be a pedant, examine in minute detail, tell in painful detail

μῑκρολογίᾱ ᾱς ἡ minuteness, pedantry

μῑκρολόγος ον narrow-minded, pedantic; stingy, captious

μῑκροπολῑ́της ου ὁ citizen of a small town *or* state

μῑκρός ᾱ́ όν small, little, short; petty, mean; poor, trivial; young

μῑκρότης ητος ἡ smallness, littleness
μῑκροψῡχίᾱ ᾱς ἡ meanness of spirit
μῑκρόψῡχος ον narrow-minded
μῑκτός ή όν mixed
μῖλαξ ακος ἡ yew (tree); a convulvulus
μῑ́λιον ου τό a Roman mile
μιλτηλιφής ές painted red
μιλτοπάρῃος ον (of ships which had their bows painted red) red-cheeked
μίλτος ου ἡ red chalk, red ochre, ruddle
μιλτόω paint red
μῑμέομαι *mid* imitate, copy; represent
μῑ́μημα ατος τό **μῑ́μησις** εως ἡ imitating, imitation; copy; representation, portrait
μῑμητικός ή όν imitative
μῑμητός ή όν to be imitated *or* copied
μιμνάζω stay, remain
μιμνήσκω† remind (of), put in mind (of), admonish; *pass* remember, recall to one's mind; mention; be mindful of
μίμνω ▸ **μένω**
μῖμος ου ὁ imitator, actor, player
μίν him, her, it; himself
μινύθω diminish, lessen, weaken; decrease, decay, perish
μίνυνθα *adv* a little, very little; a short time
μινυνθάδιος ον lasting a short time
μινυρίζω *and mid* whimper, whine; warble, hum
μῖξις εως ἡ mixing; sexual intercourse
μῑξοβάρβαρος ον half-barbarian, half-Greek
μῑξοπάρθενος ον half-maiden
μῑσανθρωπίᾱ ᾱς ἡ hatred of mankind
μῑσάνθρωπος ου ὁ misanthrope, hater of mankind
μισγάγκεια ᾱς ἡ a place where mountain glens and their streams meet, meeting of the glens
μίσγω ▸ **μίγνυμι**
μῑσέω hate
μῑ́σημα ατος τό ▸ **μῖσος**
μῑσητός ή όν hated; to be hated
μισθαποδοσίᾱ ᾱς ἡ payment of wages, recompense
μισθαποδότης ου ὁ one who pays wages, recompenser, rewarder
μισθαρνέω serve for pay
μισθαρνίᾱ ᾱς ἡ hired service
μίσθιος (ᾱ) ον ▸ **μισθωτός**
μισθοδοσίᾱ ᾱς ἡ payment of wages
μισθοδοτέω pay wages
μισθοδότης ου ὁ payer of wages
μισθός οῦ ὁ wages, pay, hire, rent, salary; reward; punishment
μισθοφορᾱ́ ᾱς ἡ receipt of wages; pay
μισθοφορέω receive wages; serve for hire
μισθοφορίᾱ ᾱς ἡ hired service, service as a mercenary
μισθοφόρος ον serving for hire; mercenary, hireling
μισθόω let out for hire, farm out; *pass* be hired for pay; *mid* engage on hire
μίσθωμα ατος τό stipulated pay, rent; hired house
μίσθωσις εως ἡ letting for hire; ▸ **μίσθωμα**
μισθωτός ή όν hired, to be hired; mercenary, hireling
μῑσόδημος ον hating democracy
μῑσολογίᾱ ᾱς ἡ hatred of argument
μῑσόλογος ον hating argument
μῑσοπονηρέω hate the wicked, hate wickedness
μῖσος ους τό hatred, enmity; hateful thing *or* person
μῑσοτύραννος ον tyrant-hating
μῑσόχρηστος ον hating the good
μιστύλλω cut into little pieces
μίτος ου ὁ thread; web
μίτρᾱ ᾱς ἡ girdle; head-dress

μιτρηφόρος ον wearing a μίτρᾱ

μιτώδης ες thread-like

μνᾶ ᾶς ἡ mina (sum of money) (= 100 drachmas)

μνάομαι *mid* covet, strive after; woo, court; ▶ **μιμνήσκομαι**

μνείᾱ ᾱς ἡ ▶ **μνήμη**

μνῆμα ατος τό **μνημεῖον** ου τό memorial, remembrance; monument; sepulchre

μνήμη ης ἡ memory, remembrance; faculty of memory; monument; mention, relation; renown

μνημονεύω remember; recollect; mention

μνημονικός ή όν with a good memory

μνημοσύνη ης ἡ ▶ **μνήμη**

μνημόσυνον ου τό ▶ **μνῆμα**

μνήμων ον mindful, remembering, unforgetting

μνησ *likely to be from* **μιμνήσκω**

μνησικακέω remember old wrongs, be resentful

μνηστεύω *and mid* woo, court, seek in marriage; *pass* be betrothed

μνηστήρ ῆρος ὁ wooer, suitor

μνῆστις εως ἡ ▶ **μνήμη**

μνηστός ή όν wooed, wedded

μνηστύς ύος ἡ wooing, seeking in marriage

μογέω toil, labour; suffer, be in distress

μογιλάλος ον stammering, hardly-speaking, dumb

μογερός ᾱ́ όν distressed, wretched

μόγις *adv* with toil, hardly, scarcely

μογοστόκος ον causing throes in childbirth

μόδιος ου ὁ a measure of corn

μόθος ου ὁ noise *or* throng of battle

μοῖρα ᾱς ἡ part, portion, division; portion of booty *or* of a meal; political party; share; that which is one's due, due reverence; rank; lot, destiny, fate; man's appointed doom, death

μοιρηγενής ές favourite of fortune

μοιρίδιος ᾱ ον destined, fated

μοιχάγρια ων τά fine imposed on one caught in adultery

μοιχαλίς ίδος ἡ adulteress

μοιχάω commit adultery

μοιχείᾱ ᾱς ἡ adultery

μοιχεύω commit adultery (with)

μοιχίδιος ᾱ ον begotten in adultery

μοιχός οῦ ὁ adulterer

μολ *likely to be from* **βλώσκω**

μόλιβος ου ὁ ▶ **μόλυβδος**

μόλις *adv* with difficulty, hardly

μολοβρός ου ὁ dirty fellow, beggar

μολπή ῆς ἡ song, dance, music; play, sport, amusement

μολύβδαινα ης ἡ **μολυβδίς** ίδος ἡ leaden weight (used to sink a fishing line)

μόλυβδος ου ὁ lead

μολῡ́νω μολυνῶ stain, sully

μολυσμός οῦ ὁ defilement, pollution

μομφή ῆς ἡ blame, complaint

μοναρχέω be a monarch

μοναρχίᾱ ᾱς ἡ monarchy, sovereignty; the rule of one

μόναρχος ου ὁ monarch

μονάς άδος ἡ a unit

μοναχῇ (*also* μοναχῆ) *adv* in one way only

μονή ῆς ἡ staying; abiding; tarrying; stopping place, mansion

μόνιμος ον staying; steadfast, constant; faithful

μονογενής ές only child

μονοειδής ές of one kind, uniform

μονόκροτος ον with one bench of oars

μονομαχέω fight in single combat

μονομαχίᾱ ᾱς ἡ single combat

μονόξυλος ον made of one piece of wood

μόνος η ον alone, only; forsaken, left alone

■ **μόνον** (*also* μόνως) *adv* only, merely

μονόφθαλμος ον one-eyed

μονόω leave alone; make single *or* solitary; *pass* be forsaken; be taken on one side

μόρᾱ ᾱς ἡ division of Spartain infantry (one of the six regiments in which all Spartans of military age were enrolled)

μορίᾱ ᾱς ἡ a sacred olive tree

μόριμος ον ▸ **μόρσιμος**

μόριον ου τό part; division; limb

μορμολυκεῖον ου τό bogey, bugbear, spectre, phantom

μορμολύττομαι *mid* frighten [children]

μορμῦρω roar

μορμώ οῦς ἡ **μορμών** όνος ἡ a hideous she-monster (used by nurses to frighten children), bugbear, spectre

μορόεις εσσα εν mulberry-like

μόρος ου ὁ fate, destiny; death

μόρσιμος ον destined, appointed by fate; foredoomed to die

μορύσσω soil, defile

μορφή ῆς ἡ form, shape, figure, appearance; beauty, grace

μόρφνος η ον dark-coloured (of an eagle)

μορφόω form, shape

μόρφωσις εως ἡ shaping; form, semblance

μόσσῡν ῡνος ὁ wooden tower *or* house

μόσχειος ον of a calf; of calf-skin

μοσχοποιέω make a calf

μόσχος ου ὁ shoot, sprout; descendant; calf, young bull

μουν- *see* **μον-**

μουνάξ *adv* alone, singly, in single combat

μουνόθεν *adv* ▸ **μουνάξ**

μουνόλιθος ον made of one stone

μοῦνος η ον ▸ **μόνος**

μουνοφυής ές grown in one, of single nature

μουνυχιών ῶνος ὁ the tenth month in the Attic calendar (April to May)

μουσικός ή όν of the Muses, devoted to the Muses, musical; musician; (lyric) poet; scholar, man of letters

■ **ἡ μουσική, τὰ μουσικά** art of the Muses, music, song, poetry, dancing, arts, literature, accomplishments

μουσοποιός όν poet, singer

μοχθέω toil, weary oneself, be troubled *or* distressed, suffer

μόχθημα ατος τό **μοχθηρίᾱ** ᾱς ἡ toil, hardship; wretchedness; badness, wickedness, depravity

μοχθηρός ᾱ όν miserable, wretched; bad, wicked, villainous

μοχθίζω suffer

μόχθος ου ὁ toil, hardship; distress, misery

μοχλεύω, μοχλέω move by a lever, prize up

μοχλός οῦ ὁ lever; bar; pole

μῡγαλῆ ῆς ἡ field-mouse, shrew-mouse

μῡδαλέος ᾱ ον dripping wet

μυδάω be dripping *or* wet; decay, rot

μύδρος ου ὁ red-hot metal; lump of metal

μῡελόεις εσσα εν full of marrow

μυελός οῦ ὁ marrow; brain

μυέω initiate into the mysteries; instruct

μύζω, μυζέω *aor* ἔμυξα suck in; mutter, moan

μῡθέομαι *mid* speak, say, tell; name, explain; consider

μῡθολογεύω, μῡθολογέω tell tales, myths *or* legends; converse fully

μῡθολογικός ή όν versed in legendary lore

μῦθος ου ὁ word, speech, public speech; narration, news, intelligence; conversation, talk; thought, project, plan; advice, order; report, tale, story; affair, occurrence

μῡθώδης ες legendary
■ **τὸ μύθωδες** the domain of the fable

μυῖα ᾶς ἡ fly

μῡκάομαι *mid* bellow, low, bray; roar

μῡκηθμός οῦ ὁ bellowing, lowing

μύκης ητος ὁ mushroom; end of a scabbard

μυκτήρ ῆρος ὁ nostril; nose; snout

μυκτηρίζω turn up the nose at, mock

μύλαξ ακος ὁ millstone

μύλη ης ἡ mill

μυλήφατος ον bruised, ground

μυλικός ή όν **μύλινος** η ον [λίθος] millstone

μυλοειδής ές like a millstone

μύλος ὁ ▸ **μύλη** *or* **μύλαξ**

μυλών ῶνος ὁ mill-house

μῡ́νη ης ἡ pretext

μυξωτήρ ῆρος ὁ ▸ **μυκτήρ**

μῡριάκις *adv* ten thousand times

μῡριάρχης ου ὁ **μῡρίαρχος** ου ὁ commander of ten thousand men

μυριάς άδος ἡ myriad (10,000)

μυρίζω anoint

μυρίκη ης ἡ tamarisk (a shrub thriving especially in marshy ground and near the sea)

μυρῑ́κινος η ον of the tamarisk (see last entry)

μῡ́ριοι αι α ten thousand

μῡριόκαρπος ον with countless fruit

μῡριόλεκτος ον said ten thousand times

μῡρίος ᾱ ον countless, numberless; immense, endless

μῡριοφόρος ον [ναῦς] big transport-ship

μύρμηξ ηκος ὁ ant

μῡ́ρομαι *mid* flow; melt into tears

μύρον ου τό fragrant oil, unguent, balsam

μυροπώλης ου ὁ perfume-seller

μυροπώλιον ου τό perfume shop

μυρρίνη ης ἡ (*also* μυρσίνη ης ἡ) myrtle, myrtle-twig

μύρτον ου τό myrtle-berry

μῦς μυός ὁ mouse

μυσαρός ᾱ́ όν foul, loathsome

μύσος ους τό abomination; atrocity

μυστήριον ου τό secret rite; mystery
■ **τὰ μυστήρια** the mysteries (e.g. of Demeter at Eleusis)

μύστης ου ὁ one initiated

μυστικός ή όν mystical; secret

μυχμός οῦ ὁ a groaning, sighing

μυχοίτατος η ον in the farthest corner

μυχόνδε *adv* to the far corner

μυχός οῦ ὁ inmost corner, interior, recess

μύω be shut *or* closed; cease; shut the eyes

μῡών ῶνος ὁ knot of muscles

μυωπάζω be short-sighted

μύωψ[1] (*gen* ωπος) short-sighted

μύωψ[2] ωπος ὁ gadfly; goad, spur

μῶλος ου ὁ toil; battle; battle-din

μῶλυ υος τό mōly (a magic herb)

μώλωψ ωπος ὁ stripe, mark, bruise

μῶμαι ▸ **μάομαι**

μωμάομαι *mid* **μωμεύω** blame, revile

μῶμος ου ὁ blame; disgrace, shame

μῶν ▸ **μὴ οὖν** surely it isn't?

μῶνυξ (*gen* υχος) with a single (i.e. uncloven) hoof

μωραίνω μωρανῶ ἐμώρᾱνα be silly *or* foolish; make foolish; *pass* become a fool; (of salt) lose its savour

μωρίᾱ ᾱς ἡ folly

μωρολογίᾱ ᾱς ἡ foolish speech

μωρός (*or* μῶρος) ᾱ́ όν foolish, stupid; tasteless;

Nν

ν, Ν (νῦ) thirteenth letter of the alphabet
■ *ν′ as a numeral* = 50

ναί *adv* truly, in truth, yes

νᾱϊάς άδος ἡ water-nymph, naiad

ναιετάω ▸ **ναίω**

νᾱ́ϊος ᾱ ον belonging to a ship

νᾱΐς ἴδος ἡ ▸ **ναϊάς**

ναίχι ▸ **ναί**

ναίω[1] dwell in, inhabit; settle someone in; *pass* be inhabited; settle

ναίω[2] ▸ **νάω**

νάκη ης ἡ **νάκος** ους τό fleece, goatskin

νᾶμα ατος τό fountain, stream

νᾱμέρτεια ᾱς ἡ ▸ **νημέρτεια**

νᾶνος ου ὁ dwarf

νᾱοποιός οῦ ὁ official in charge of the temple-fabric

νᾱός οῦ ὁ temple

ναπαῖος ᾱ ον of a wooded valley *or* dell

νάπη ης ἡ **νάπος** ους τό wooded vale, dell, glen

νάρδος ου ἡ nard; nard-oil

ναρθηκοφόρος ου ὁ staff-bearer, thyrsus-bearer

νάρθηξ ηκος ὁ reed, cane, rod

ναρκάω grow stiff *or* benumbed

νάρκισσος ου ὁ narcissus, daffodil

νᾱσιῶτις (*gen* ιδος) ▸ **νησιῶτις**

νᾶσος ου ἡ ▸ **νῆσος**

νάσσω *aor* ἔναξα stamp down

ναυᾱγέω be shipwrecked

ναυᾱγίᾱ ᾱς ἡ shipwreck

ναυᾱ́γιον ου τό (piece of a) wreck

ναυᾱγός όν shipwrecked

ναυαρχέω command a fleet

ναυαρχίᾱ ᾱς ἡ office of a commander of a fleet

ναύαρχος ου ὁ sea-captain, admiral

ναυβάτης ου ὁ sailor, seaman

ναυηγέω etc ▸ **ναυαγ-**

ναυκληρέω be a ship-owner; steer, govern

ναυκληρίᾱ ᾱς ἡ seafaring life, voyage

ναύκληρος ου ὁ shipowner, captain

ναυκρᾱρίᾱ ᾱς ἡ registry of the ναύκρᾱροι (see next entry)

ναύκρᾱρος ου ὁ (in early Athens) the chief official of a division (ναυκρᾱρίᾱ) of citizens for financial and administrative purposes

ναυκρατέω be master of the sea

ναυκρατής ές **ναυκράτωρ** (*gen* ορος) commanding the sea; shipowner

ναῦλον ου τό fare, passage-money

ναυλοχέω lie in a harbour, at anchor *or* in wait (for)

ναύλοχος ον affording safe anchorage

ναυμαχέω fight at sea

ναυμαχησείω long for a sea-fight

ναυμαχίᾱ ᾱς ἡ battle at sea

ναύμαχος ον suited to a sea-fight

ναυπηγέω build ships

ναυπηγήσιμος ον fit for shipbuilding

ναυπηγίᾱ ᾱς ἡ shipbuilding

ναυπηγός οῦ ὁ shipbuilder

ναῦς νεώς ἡ ship

ναῦσθλον ου τό ▸ **ναῦλον**

ναυσίκλειτος ον **ναυσίκλυτος** ον famous for ships

ναυσιπέρᾱτος ον to be crossed by ships, navigable

ναυσίπορος ον navigable

ναύσταθμον ου τό **ναύσταθμος** ου ὁ harbour, anchorage, naval station

ναυστολέω carry by sea; go by sea, voyage; travel over

ναύτης ου ὁ ▸ **ναυβάτης**

ναυτικός ή όν of *or* for a ship; naval; seafaring
■ **τὸ ναυτικόν** fleet, navy

ναυτιλίᾱ ᾱς ἡ seamanship, navigation, voyage

ναυτίλλομαι go by ship, sail

ναυτίλος ου ὁ sailor, seaman

ναυτοδίκαι ων οἱ judges in commercial lawsuits

νάω flow (over)

νεάζω be young *or* younger, grow *or* be young again

νεᾱκόνητος ον newly *or* lately whetted

νεᾱλής ές young, fresh

νεᾱνίᾱς ου ὁ young man, youth; youthful, impetuous, headstrong, hot-headed

νεᾱνιεύομαι *mid* be youthful, vigorous, hot-headed *or* boastful

νεᾱνικός ή όν youthful, fresh, vigorous; headstrong, insolent; hasty

νεᾶνις ιδος ἡ girl, maiden, young woman

νεᾱνίσκος ου ὁ ▸ **νεανίας**

νεᾱρός ᾱ́ όν youthful, fresh; ▸ **νέος**

νέατος η ον last, uttermost, extreme

νεβρίζω wear a fawnskin

νεβρός οῦ ὁ/ἡ young deer, fawn

νεηγενής ές newborn

νεήκης ες **νεηκονής** ές ▸ **νεακόνητος**

νεήλατον ου τό honey-cake

νέηλυς (*gen* υδος) newly come, a newcomer

νεηνίης etc ▸ **νεανίας**

νείαιρα, νείατος η ον ▸ **νέατος**

νεικέω, νεικείω quarrel, dispute; scold, abuse, insult

νεῖκος εος τό quarrel, dispute; scolding, blaming, reproach; cause of quarrel; dispute before a judge; battle, fight

νειόθεν *adv* from the bottom

νειόθι *adv* at the bottom

νειός ἡ new *or* fallow land

νείφω, νῑ́φω snow

νεκάς άδος ἡ heap of slain men

νεκρός ᾱ́ όν dead; *noun* dead body, corpse

νεκρόω kill, make dead

νέκρωσις εως ἡ making dead; deadness

νέκταρ αρος τό nectar (drink of the gods)

νεκτάρεος ᾱ ον like nectar; divine

νέκυια ᾱς ἡ sacrifice for the dead

νεκυομαντήϊον ου τό oracle of the dead

νέκυς (*gen* υος) ▸ **νεκρός**

νεμέθω *mid* graze

νεμεσάω be indignant, angry; find fault with, blame; *mid and pass* be indignant

νεμεσητός ή όν causing indignation; to be regarded with awe, awful

νεμεσίζομαι *mid* ▸ **νεμεσάω**

νέμεσις εως ἡ indignation, anger, resentment; vengeance, punishment; wrong; remorse; sense of honour

νέμος εος τό pasture; grove; wood

νέμω νεμῶ ἔνειμα divide; distribute, assign, allot, grant; possess, enjoy; inhabit; manage, control; consider; drive to pasture; graze; consume; *mid* distribute among themselves; occupy; control, manage; enjoy; graze, feed; consume; spread

νεοάλωτος ον newly caught

νεοαρδής ές newly watered

νεόγαμος ον newly wedded

νεογῑλός ή όν **νεογνός** όν new-born

νεοδᾱμώδης ους ὁ new citizen, one newly enfranchised (applied to helots freed in Sparta as a reward for service in war)

νεόδαρτος ον newly flayed

νεόθεν *adv* newly, lately

νεοθηλής ές fresh-sprouting

νεοίη ης ἡ youthful spirit

νεοκατάστατος ον newly settled

νεόκτιστος ον newly founded

νέομαι go; come; go away; return, flow back

νεομηνίᾱ ᾱς ἡ ▸ **νουμηνία**

νεοπενθής ές fresh-mourning, in new sorrow

νεόπλυτος ον newly washed

νεόποκος ον newly shorn

νεόπρῑστος ον newly sawn

νεόρραντος ον newly sprinkled

νεόρρυτος ον fresh flowing

νέορτος ον newly risen

νέος ᾱ ον young, youthful, early; thoughtless; new, fresh; unheard of, strange, unexpected
■ **νεώτερόν τι** revolution; news, bad things
■ **νέον** *adv* newly, anew, afresh; lately, just now

νεόσμηκτος ον newly cleaned

νεοσπάς (*gen* άδος) newly plucked

νεοσσεύω ▸ **νοσσεύω**

νεοσσιᾱ́ ᾶς ἡ nest of young birds

νεοσσός οῦ ὁ a young bird; child

νεόστροφος ον newly twisted

νεοσφαγής ές newly killed

νεότευκτος ον **νεοτευχής** ές newly made

νεότης ητος ἡ youth, youthfulness; body of young men

νεότομος ον newly cut

νεουργός ▸ **νεότευκτος**

νεούτατος ον newly wounded

νεόφυτος ον newly converted

νεοχάρακτος ον newly imprinted

νεοχμός όν ▸ **νέος**

νεοχμόω ▸ **νεωτερίζω**

νέποδες ων οἱ children

νέρθεν ▸ **ἔνερθεν**

νέρτερος ᾱ ον lower, nether; infernal

νεῦμα ατος τό nod, sign

νεῦμαι ▸ **νέομαι**

νευρᾱ́ ᾶς ἡ **νεῦρον** ου τό sinew, tendon; cord; bow-string; cord of a sling; strength, vigour

νευροσπαδής ές **νευρόσπαστος** ον drawn back, driven from the bow-string

νευσ *likely to be from* **νέω**[1]

νευστάζω nod

νεύω nod, beckon, bow the head, promise

νεφέλη ης ἡ cloud, darkness; bird-net

νεφεληγερέτης ου ὁ **νεφεληγερέτα** ὁ cloud-gatherer (of Zeus)

νέφος ους τό ▸ **νεφέλη**

νεφρῖτις ιδος ἡ disease of the kidneys

νεφρός οῦ ὁ kidney

νέω[1] νευσοῦμαι ἔνευσα swim

νέω[2] spin

νέω[3] heap up, pile up

νέω[4] ▸ **νέομαι**

νεωκόρος ου ὁ/ἡ sweeper in a temple, temple-servant

νεώρης ες new, young

νεώριον ου τό dockyard

νέωρος ᾱ ον ▸ **νεώρης**

νεώς[1] ώ ὁ ▸ **νᾱός**

νεώς[2] *gen from* **ναῦς**

νεώσοικοι ων οἱ sheds, docks (in which ships might be build, repaired, or kept)

νεωστί *adv* lately, recently

νεωτερίζω νεωτεριῶ make changes *or* innovations; revolutionize

νεωτερικός ή όν youthful

νεωτερισμός οῦ ὁ innovation, revolution

νεωτεριστής οῦ ὁ radical (person); revolutionary

νεωτεροποιΐᾱ ᾱς ἡ innovation, revolution

νεωτεροποιός όν innovating, revolutionary

νή *adv* yes, truly; *with acc* by [a god]!

νηγάτεος ᾱ ον newly made, splendid

νήγρετος ον unwaking, sleeping soundly

νήδυια ων τά bowels

νήδυμος ον sweet, refreshing

νηδῦς ύος ἡ belly; stomach; womb

νηέω ▸ **νέω**³ heap up

νήθω ▸ **νέω**² spin

νηϊάς άδος ἡ ▸ **ναϊάς**

νήϊος ᾱ ον ▸ **νάϊος**

νηῗς ίδος ἡ ▸ **ναῗς**

νῆϊς (*gen* ιδος) + *gen* not knowing, unpractised in

νηῗτης (*gen* ου) ▸ **νάϊος**

νηκερδής ές useless, without gain

νηκουστέω disobey

νηλεής ές pitiless; unpitied

νηλειτής ές *with fem* **νηλεῖτις** (*gen* ιδος) ▸ **νηλιτής**

νηλής ές ▸ **νηλεής**

νηλίπους (*gen* ποδος) barefooted

νηλῑτής ές *with fem* **νηλῖτις** (*gen* ιδος) guiltless

νῆμα ατος τό thread, yarn

νημέρτεια ᾱς ἡ truth

νημερτής ές infallible, unerring

νηνεμίᾱ ᾱς ἡ calm

νήνεμος ον breezeless, calm

νηός ὁ ▸ **νεώς**; ▸ **νηός** *or* **νεώς** *from* **ναῦς**

νηπενθής ές soothing sorrow , banishing pain

νηπιάζω be a child

νηπιαχεύω play like a child

νηπίαχος ον ▸ **νήπιος**

νηπιέη ης ἡ childishness

νήπιος ᾱ ον infant, childish, foolish, harmless; weak

νήποινος ον without recompense; unavenged

νηπύτιος ᾱ ον ▸ **νήπιος**

νήριτος ον numberless

νησίδιον ου τό **νησίον** ου τό **νησῖς** ῖδος ἡ small island

νησιώτης ου ὁ islander

νησιῶτις (*gen* ιδος) of an island; islander

νῆσος ου ἡ island; peninsula

νῆσσα ης ἡ duck

νηστείᾱ ᾱς ἡ a fasting

νηστεύω fast

νῆστις (*gen* ιδος *or* ιος) ὁ/ἡ fasting

νησύδριον ου τό ▸ **νησίδιον**

νητός ή όν heaped up

νηῦς ἡ ▸ **ναῦς**

νηυσιπέρητος ον ▸ **ναυσιπέρητος**

νηφάλιος ᾱ ον unmixed with wine; sober

νήφω drink no wine, be sober

νήχω *and mid* swim

νίζω νίψω ἔνιψα wash; wash off, clean; purge, cleanse; *mid* wash oneself

νῑκάω conquer, prevail; be superior *or* better; win in court; be victorious, carry the day; vanquish, overcome, surpass

νῑ́κη ης ἡ victory, conquest; Nike, the goddess of victory

νῑκητήριον ου τό prize of victory

νῑκητικός ή όν conducive to victory

νῑκηφόρος ον bringing victory; victorious

νῖκος τό ▸ **νίκη**

νίν ▸ **αὐτόν** ήν ό him, her, it

νιπτήρ ῆρος ὁ basin for washing

νίπτω ▸ **νίζω**

νίσσομαι, νῑ́σομαι go (away), go to [a place]; return

νιφάς άδος ἡ snow-flake; snow-storm; snowy

νιφετός ή όν falling snow, snowstorm

νιφόεις εσσα εν snow-covered

νιφοστιβής ές piled with snow

νῑ́φω ▸ **νείφω**

νοέω perceive, remark, notice, see; think, consider; devise, contrive; intend, have a mind to

νόημα ατος τό thought; purpose, design; understanding; mind

νοήμων ον sensible

νοητός ή όν intelligible

νόθος η ον illegitimate; spurious

νόμαιον ου τό custom, usage

νομάρχης ου ὁ **νόμαρχος** ου ὁ chief of a district, chief of an Egyptian province; district financial officer

νομάς άδος ὁ/ἡ roaming, roaming about for pasture; nomad

νομεύς έως ὁ herdsman; rib [of a ship]

νομεύω drive to pasture, put to graze; tend a flock

νομή ῆς ἡ pasture; field; grazing flock; division, distribution

νομίζω† hold *or* acknowledge as a custom *or* usage; be accustomed to; adopt as a custom or usage; think, believe, acknowledge, take for, consider as, believe in; be persuaded, judge; *pass* be in esteem; be customary

νομικός ή όν legal; learned in the law; scribe

νόμιμος ον customary; legal, lawful; honest, righteous

■ **τὰ νόμιμα** custom, usage, law

νόμισις εως ἡ usage, custom

νόμισμα ατος τό usage, institution; money, currency

νομοδιδάσκαλος ου ὁ teacher of the law

νομοθεσίᾱ ᾱς ἡ legislation

νομοθετέω give laws, ordain by law

νομοθέτης ου ὁ law giver (at Athens, one of a committee of jurors charged with the revision of the laws)

νομοθετικός ή όν law-giving

νομός οῦ ὁ dwelling, residence; district, sphere of command, province; region; ▸ **νομή**

νόμος ου ὁ custom, usage; law, ordinance, statute; principle, rule, maxim; tune, mode of singing, song, melody

νομοφύλαξ ακος ὁ guardian of the laws

νόος ου ὁ (*also* νοῦς νοῦ ὁ) mind, understanding, reason; thought, insight; purpose, intention; meaning, sense

νοσέω be sick

νοσηλείᾱ ᾱς ἡ **νόσημα** ατος τό ▸ **νόσος**

νοσηρός ᾱ́ όν unhealthy; sickly

νόσος ου ἡ sickness, disease, plague; insanity, madness; evil, distress; defect

νοσσεύω hatch

νοσσιᾱ́ ᾶς ἡ etc., ▸ **νεοσσιά** etc.

νοστέω return, come home; travel

νόστιμος ον belonging to a return; returning

νόστος ου ὁ return home; travel, journey

νόσφι(ν) *adv* far, remote, apart; *with gen* far from, away from; without, besides, except

νοσφίζω νοσφιῶ remove, put *or* take away; *mid* withdraw, retire; forsake, abandon; embezzle

νοσώδης ες ▸ **νοσηρός**

νοτερός ᾱ́ όν wet, moist; southern

νοτίη ης ἡ moisture, rain

νότιος (ᾱ) ον ▸ **νοτερός**

νοτίς ίδος ἡ ▸ **νοτίη**

νότος ου ὁ south *or* southwest wind; the south

νουθεσίᾱ ᾱς ἡ ▶ **νουθέτησις**

νουθετέω bring to mind, warn, admonish, reprimand

νουθέτημα ατος τό **νουθέτησις** εως ἡ admonition, warning

νουθετικός ή όν admonitory

νουμηνίᾱ ᾱς ἡ new moon, first of the month

νουνεχής ές sensible

νοῦς οῦ ὁ ▶ **νόος**

νοῦσος ου ἡ ▶ **νόσος**

νύ ▶ **νύν**

νυκτερευτής οῦ ὁ poacher

νυκτερευτικός ή όν fit for hunting by night

νυκτερεύω pass the night; watch by night

νυκτερινός ή όν nightly, by night

νυκτερίς ίδος ἡ bat

νύκτερος ον ▶ **νυκτερινός**

νυκτοθήρᾱς ου ὁ hunting by night

νυκτομαχίᾱ ᾱς ἡ night-battle

νυκτοφύλαξ ακος ὁ night-watchman

νύκτωρ *adv* by night

νυμφεῖος ᾱ ον bridal, nuptial ■ **τὸ νυμφεῖον** bridal-chamber; marriage

νύμφευμα ατος τό marriage; bride

νυμφεύω *and mid* wed, marry; be married

νύμφη ης ἡ bride; young wife; maiden; nymph

νυμφίδιος ᾱ ον **νυμφικός** ή όν bridal, nuptial

νυμφίος ου ὁ bridegroom; husband

νυμφόληπτος ον caught by nymphs, entranced

νυμφών ῶνος ὁ bridal-chamber

νῦν, νῡνί *adv* now, just now, at present; then, thereupon; therefore

νυν*, νυ* *enclitic adv* now, then; therefore

νύξ νυκτός ἡ night

νύος ου ἡ daughter-in-law

νύσσα ης ἡ turning-stone, pillar on the race course; winning post

νύσσω νύξω prick, pierce, wound; nudge

νυστάζω nod in sleep; fall asleep; slumber

νυχθήμερον ου τό a night and a day

νύχιος ᾱ ον ▶ **νυκτερινός**

νώ ▶ **νῶι**

νώδυνος ον soothing pain

νωθής ές **νωθρός** ά όν lazy, sluggish; stupid

νῶι, νώ we two

νωΐτερος ᾱ ον belonging to us two

νωλεμές, νωλεμέως *adv* incessantly; steadfastly

νωμάω distribute, share out; move to and fro, brandish, wield, ply; direct, guide, govern; consider, observe, perceive

νώνυμ(ν)ος ον without name *or* fame

νῶροψ (*gen* οπος) flashing

νωτίζω turn one's back

νῶτον ου τό **νῶτος** ου ὁ the back

νωχελίη ης ἡ laziness

Ξξ

ξ, Ξ (ξῖ) fourteenth letter of the alphabet
■ *ξ΄ as a numeral* = 60

ξαίνω ξανῶ ἔξηνα comb *or* card [wool]; scratch, beat

ξανθός ή όν yellow; red-yellow

ξειν- *see* **ξεν-**

ξενᾱγέω lead mercenary soldiers, guide strangers

ξενᾱγός οῦ ὁ leader of mercenaries

ξενηλασίᾱ ᾱς ἡ banishment of foreigners (especially by Spartans)

ξενίᾱ ᾱς ἡ hospitality; hospitable reception *or* entertainment; usurpation of civic rights by an alien

ξενίζω ξενιῶ receive hospitably; entertain; be like a foreigner; *pass* be astonished

ξενικός ή όν foreign, of a stranger; mercenary
■ **τὰ ξενικά** (at Athens) taxes paid by aliens

ξένιος (ᾱ) ον hospitable
■ **τὸ ξένιον** a guest's gift

ξένισις εως ἡ hospitable entertainment

ξενο-δοκέω, ξενο-δοχέω ▸ **ξενίζω**

ξενο-κτονέω kill guests *or* strangers

ξενο-λογέω engage mercenaries

ξενόομαι be abroad, go into banishment; be (lodged as) a guest, be entertained; ▸ **ξενίζω**

ξένος η ον foreign, strange; unacquainted with + *gen*
■ **ὁ ξένος** foreigner, stranger; mercenary; guest-friend
■ **ἡ ξένη** foreign country

ξενόστασις εως ἡ lodging for strangers

ξενοσύνη ης ἡ ▸ **ξενία**

ξενο-τροφέω maintain mercenary troops

ξερός ᾱ́ όν ▸ **ξηρός**

ξέστης ου ὁ jar (a Roman measure (nearly a pint))

ξέω *aor* ἔξεσα scrape; polish (by scraping); carve

ξηραίνω ξηρανῶ ἐξήρᾱνα parch up, dry up; *pass* become dry

ξηρός ᾱ́ όν dry, parched
■ **ἡ ξηρᾱ́** dry land

ξηρότης ητος ἡ dryness

ξιφίδιον ου τό dagger

ξιφοκτόνος ον killing with the sword

ξίφος ους τό sword

ξόανον ου τό carved image; wooden statue of a god

ξυήλη ης ἡ plane (for scraping wood); curved knife

ξυλίζομαι *mid* gather wood

ξύλινος η ον wooden

ξύλον ου τό wood, timber; piece of wood; tree, beam; stick, cudgel; shaft; spear; bench; cross; wooden collar, pillory

ξυλουργέω work wood

ξύλοχος ου ἡ thicket

ξύλωσις εως ἡ the wood-work, framework of a house

ξυμ/ξυν ▸ **συμ/συν**

ξῡνήϊος η ον public, common

ξῡνός ή όν ▸ **κοινός**

ξυρέω, ξυράω shear, shave

ξυρόν οῦ τό razor
■ **ἐπὶ ξυροῦ** on a razor's edge

ξυστόν οῦ τό shaft; spear, lance; pole

ξυστός ή όν polished

ξύω scrape, smooth, polish

Οο

ο, Ο (ὂ μικρόν) fifteenth letter of the alphabet
■ **ο′** *as a numeral* = 70

ὁ ἡ τό *def art* the; *pron* this

ὄαρ ὄαρος ἡ consort; wife

ὀαρίζω + *dat* chat with

ὀαριστής οῦ ὁ confidential friend

ὀαριστύς ύος ἡ friendly conversation, intimacy; company

ὀβελίσκος ου ὁ small spit, leg of a compass

ὀβελός οῦ ὁ spit; pointed pillar

ὀβολός οῦ ὁ obol (one sixth of a drachma)

ὀβριμοεργός (*gen* οῦ) forcible, doing deeds of violence

ὀβριμοπάτρη ης ἡ daughter of a mighty father

ὄβριμος ον strong, mighty

ὀγδόατος η ον ▸ **ὄγδοος**

ὀγδοήκοντα eighty

ὄγδοος η ον eighth

ὀγδώκοντα ▸ **ὀγδοήκοντα**

ὀγκηρός ᾱ́ όν pompous

ὄγκιον ου τό chest for iron tools

ὄγκος[1] ου ὁ barb, grapple-hook

ὄγκος[2] ου ὁ bulk, mass, heap, size, weight; trouble; dignity; importance, pride, self-importance

ὀγκόω puff, swell; *pass* be swollen *or* proud

ὀγμεύω make furrows, trace a straight line

ὄγμος ου ὁ furrow; (in reaping) swathe

ὄγχνη ης ἡ pear-tree; pear

ὁδαῖος ᾱ ον belonging to a way *or* journey
■ **τὰ ὁδαῖα** merchandise

ὀδάξ *adv* with the teeth

ὁδάω export for sale, sell

ὅδε ἥδε τόδε this, that

ὁδεύω go, travel, journey

ὁδηγέω show the way, guide

ὁδηγός οῦ ὁ guide

ὁδῑ́της ου ὁ traveller

ὀδμή ῆς ἡ scent, odour

ὁδοιπορέω ▸ **ὁδεύω**

ὁδοιπορίᾱ ᾱς ἡ journey, way

ὁδοιπόρος ου ὁ ▸ **ὁδῑ́της**

ὁδοποιέω make a road

ὁδός οῦ ἡ way, street, road, path; journey, voyage, march, expedition; departure, return; way, means, manner, occasion, method

ὀδός οῦ ὁ threshold

ὀδούς όντος ὁ tooth, tusk

ὁδοφύλαξ ακος ὁ watcher of the roads

ὁδόω lead the right way, guide; *pass* succeed

ὀδυνάω cause pain; *pass* feel pain, suffer

ὀδύνη ης ἡ pain, grief

ὀδυνηρός ᾱ́ όν painful

ὀδυνήφατος ον killing pain

ὄδυρμα ατος τό **ὀδυρμός** οῦ ὁ wailing, lamentation

ὀδῡ́ρομαι ὀδυροῦμαι ᾠδῡράμην *mid* wail, lament; bewail

ὀδύσσομαι *mid* be angry

ὀδών όντος ὁ ▸ **ὀδούς**

ὁδωτός ή όν practicable, passable

ὄζος ου ὁ branch, twig; offshoot, descendant (*perhaps* follower, servant)

ὄζω ὀζήσω ὤζησα smell (of something *gen*)

ὅθεν *adv* from where, from whom *or* which, for which reason

ὅθι *adv* where

ὀθνεῖος ᾱ ον foreign, strange

ὄθομαι give *or* pay heed to, regard, care for

ὀθόνη ης ἡ linen; linen garment; veil

ὀθόνιον ου τό linen bandage

ὁθούνεκα ▸ **ὅτου ἕνεκα** because

ὄθριξ (*gen* ὄτριχος) with the same hair

οἴ *int* woe!

οἷ *adv* to where

οἴᾱξ ᾱκος ὁ handle of the rudder; (of government) helm; (of the yoke) ring

οἴγνῡμι†, **οἴγω** open

οἶδα† ▸ **εἴδω** know

οἰδάω, οἰδέω, οἰδάνω *act tr* cause to swell; *act intr and pass* swell

οἶδμα ατος τό swelling, swell; swollen waves, sea

οἰέτης ες of the same age

ὀϊζῡρός ᾱ́ όν miserable, poor, wretched

ὀϊζῡ́ς ύος ἡ woe, misery

ὀϊζῡ́ω wail; toil; suffer

οἰήϊον ου τό ▸ **οἴαξ**

οἰηκίζω steer, manage

οἴησις εως ἡ opinion

οἶκα ▸ **ἔοικα**

οἴκαδε *adv* homewards, home

οἰκεῖος ᾱ ον belonging to a home, a household *or* a family; of the same kin, related; intimate, familiar; proper, one's own; private, personal; home (-grown), native; fit, suited

οἰκειότης ητος ἡ relationship, friendship

οἰκειόω make one's own; make [a person] one's friend; *pass* become an intimate friend (of)

οἰκείωσις εως ἡ appropriation

οἰκετείᾱ ᾱς ἡ (*also* οἰκέτεια ᾱς ἡ) the servants

οἰκέτης ου ὁ member of the household; servant, slave

οἰκεύς έως ὁ ▸ **οἰκέτης**

οἰκέω inhabit, occupy; settle; dwell, live; manage, govern; be situated; be governed; *pass* be inhabited, situated; be settled *or* governed

■ **ἡ οἰκουμένη** the civilized world

οἰκηϊο- etc ▸ **οἰκειο-**

οἴκημα ατος τό house, dwelling; storey; cage; brothel; prison; temple; workshop, store-room

οἴκησις εως ἡ inhabiting; house, dwelling

οἰκητήρ ῆρος ὁ **οἰκητής** οῦ ὁ inhabitant

οἰκητήριον ου τό dwelling-place, habitation

οἰκητός ή όν inhabited; habitable

οἰκήτωρ ορος ὁ ▸ **οἰκητήρ**

οἰκίᾱ ᾱς ἡ ▸ **οἶκος**

οἰκιακός ή όν belonging to a household

οἰκίδιον ου τό ▸ **οἰκίσκος**

οἰκίζω οἰκιῶ ᾤκισα build, establish, found; settle, colonize, people; transplant; *mid* settle oneself; dwell

οἰκίον ου τό ▸ **οἶκος**

οἴκισις εως ἡ settlement, colonization

οἰκίσκος ου ὁ small house, hut

οἰκιστήρ ῆρος ὁ **οἰκιστής** οῦ ὁ founder of a colony, settler

οἰκοδεσποτέω be master of a house

οἰκοδεσπότης ου ὁ master of a house

οἰκοδομέω build a house; build; found; build up, strengthen spiritually, embolden

οἰκοδόμησις εως ἡ **οἰκοδόμημα** ατος τό **οἰκοδομίᾱ** ᾱς ἡ **οἰκοδομή** ῆς ἡ the act of building; building, edifice, house

οἰκοδόμος ου ὁ architect

οἴκοθεν *adv* from one's house *or* home; from one's own resources, by one's own virtues; from the beginning

οἴκο(θ)ι *adv* in the house, at home

οἰκόνδε *adv* ▸ **οἴκαδε**

οἰκονομέω be a steward; manage, order

οἰκονομίᾱ ᾱς ἡ household management; economy

οἰκονομικός ή όν of a household; economical

οἰκονόμος ου ὁ householder, steward

οἰκόπεδον ου τό site of a house, building-site, house, building

οἰκοποιός όν making habitable

οἶκος ου ὁ house, habitation, dwelling; room, hall; temple; camp, nest; household; household property; family, household; home

οἰκος, οἰκότως ▸ **εἰκός**

οἰκουμένη ης ἡ *see* **οἰκέω**

οἰκουρέω keep *or* guard a house; stay at home

οἰκούρημα ατος τό **οἰκουρίᾱ** ᾱς ἡ watching over the house, staying at home; protection

οἰκούρια ων τά wages for housekeeping

οἰκουρός ᾱ́ όν keeping the house, domestic; staying at home

οἰκοφθορέομαι *pass* be ruined in one's household, squander one's substance

οἰκοφθορίᾱ ᾱς ἡ loss of fortune

οἰκτείρω, οἰκτίζω οἰκτιῶ ᾤκτισα *and mid* pity, bewail

οἰκτιρμός οῦ ὁ ▸ **οἶκτος**

οἰκτίρμων ον compassionate

οἰκτῑ́ρω ▸ **οἰκτείρω**

οἴκτιστος η ον *sup from* **οἰκτρός**

οἶκτος ου ὁ pity, compassion; lamentation, piteous wailing

οἰκτρός ᾱ́ όν pitiable, lamentable; mournful

οἰκωφελίη ης ἡ thrift in household affairs

οἶμαι ατος τό attack, rage

οἰμάω attack violently; (of an eagle) swoop *or* pounce (upon its prey)

οἴμη ης ἡ heroic tale; song, lay

οἴμοι *exclamation of pain, fright, pity, anger, grief or surprise*; woe is me!

οἶμος ου ὁ/ἡ way, road, course; strip of land

οἰμωγή ῆς ἡ lamentation, wailing

οἰμώζω οἰμώξομαι ᾤμωξα wail, lament; bewail

οἰνηρός ή όν of *or* belonging to wine; full of wine

οἰνίζομαι procure wine

οἰνοβαρής ές **οἰνοβαρείων** drunk with wine

οἰνόπεδος ον bearing wine
■ **τὸ οἰνόπεδον** vineyard

οἰνοπληθής ές abounding in wine

οἰνοποτάζω drink wine

οἰνοποτήρ ῆρος ὁ **οἰνοπότης** ου ὁ wine-drinker

οἰνοπώλιον ου τό wine-shop

οἶνος ου ὁ wine

οἰνοφλυγίᾱ ᾱς ἡ drunkenness

οἰνοχοέω, οἰνοχοεύω pour out wine

οἰνοχόη ης ἡ cup for ladling wine (from the mixing bowl into the cups)

οἰνοχόος ου ὁ cup-bearer

οἰνόχυτος ον of poured-out wine

οἶνοψ (*gen* οπος) ▸ **οἰνώψ**

οἰνών ῶνος ὁ wine-cellar

οἰνώψ (*gen* ῶπος) wine-coloured

οἰοβώτᾱς feeding alone

οἰόζωνος η ον single wanderer

οἰόθεν *adv* alone

οἴομαι *see* **οἴω**

οἰόομαι leave alone

οἰοπόλος ον lonely, solitary

οἶος η ον alone, only, solitary

οἷος ᾱ ον of what kind; such as
■ **οἷός τέ εἰμι** I am able, I can
■ **οἷον, οἷα** *adv* how, as, like (as), just as, for instance

οἰοχίτων (*gen* ωνος) dressed in a tunic only

ὄϊς (*also* οἶς) οἰός ὁ/ἡ sheep

οἴσπη ης ἡ unwashed wool

οἰστέος ᾱ ον be borne, bearable

ὀϊστεύω shoot arrows

ὀϊστός (*also* οἰστός) οῦ ὁ arrow

οἰστράω, οἰστρέω goad, sting; *intr* rage

οἴστρημα ατος τό sting

οἰστροπλήξ (*gen* ῆγος) stung to madness

οἶστρος ου ὁ gadfly; sting, pain; madness

οἰσΰϊνος η ον made of wickerwork

οἴσω *fut from* **φέρω**

οἶτος ου ὁ lot, fate, ruin, death

οἰχνέω go, come, go

οἴχομαι *mid* be gone, be absent, ruined *or* dead

οἴω, ὀΐω, οἴομαι, ὀΐομαι *pass* suppose, fear, think, believe; intend, purpose, mean

οἰωνίζομαι οἰωνιοῦμαι *mid* take omens from the flight and cries of birds, prophesy, augur

οἰωνιστής (*gen* οῦ) auguring, divining

οἰωνοθέτης ου ὁ **οἰωνοπόλος** ου ὁ augurer, soothsayer

οἰωνός οῦ ὁ bird of prey; bird of omen; omen, presage

ὀκέλλω *aor* ὤκειλα run aground

ὀκλάζω bend the knees, bend, sink down

ὀκνέω, ὀκνείω shrink from, scruple, hesitate, fear

ὀκνηρός ᾱ όν hesitating, shrinking; fearful, troublesome

ὄκνος ου ὁ hesitation, unreadiness, disinclination

ὀκριάομαι be made rough *or* jagged, be exasperated

ὀκριόεις εσσα εν rugged, jagged, awful

ὀκταήμερος ον for eight days, on the eighth day

ὀκτάκις *adv* eight times

ὀκτακισχίλιοι αι α eight thousand

ὀκτάκνημος ον with eight spokes

ὀκτακόσιοι αι α eight hundred

ὀκτώ eight

ὀκτωκαίδεκα eighteen

ὀκτωκαιδέκατος η ον eighteenth

ὀλβίζω ὀλβιῶ pronounce *or* consider happy

ὀλβιοδαίμων ον blessed by a god

ὄλβιος ᾱ ον prosperous, happy, fortunate, blessed; rich

ὄλβος ου ὁ happiness, bliss; wealth, power

ὀλέθριος (ᾱ) ον destructive; ruined, lost

ὄλεθρος ου ὁ destruction, ruin, loss; defeat; rogue, rascal, curse

ὀλέκω ▸ **ὄλλυμι**

ὀλετήρ ῆρος ὁ destroyer

ὀλιγάκις *adv* seldom

ὀλιγανθρωπίᾱ ᾱς ἡ scantiness of people

ὀλιγαρχέομαι *pass* live in an oligarchy

ὀλιγαρχίᾱ ᾱς ἡ oligarchy; government by a few

ὀλιγαρχικός ή όν oligarchic

ὀλιγαχόθεν *adv* from few parts

ὀλιγηπελέων having little power, faint

ὀλιγηπελίᾱ ᾱς ἡ weakness, faintness

ὀλιγογονίᾱ ᾱς ἡ scanty procreation, production of few at birth

ὀλιγόγονος ον producing few at birth

ὀλιγοδρανέων ▸ **ὀλιγηπελέων**

ὀλιγόπιστος ον having little faith

ὀλίγος η ον few, little; small, short, weak

■ **οἱ ὀλίγοι** the governing body in oligarchies, the few, aristocrats

■ **ὀλίγον** *adv* a little, little, a short time

ὀλιγοστός ή όν with few companions

ὀλιγοχρόνιος (ᾱ) ον of short duration

ὀλιγόψῡχος ον faint-hearted

ὀλιγωρέω + *gen* regard of small account, neglect

ὀλιωρίᾱ ᾱς ἡ regarding of small account, contempt, neglect

ὀλίγωρος ον scornful, contemptuous, neglecting

ὀλίζων ον lesser

ὀλισθάνω ὀλισθήσω ὤλίσθησα slip, slide

ὀλισθηρός ᾱ́ όν slippery

ὁλκάς άδος ἡ trading vessel

ὁλκός οῦ ὁ strap; lifting-engine, hauling-machine; furrow, track, trail

ὄλλῡμι† destroy, ruin, kill; lose; *mid* perish, die, be ruined
■ **ὄλωλα** *pf* be ruined

ὅλμος ου ὁ roller; mortar

ὀλόεις εσσα εν ▸ **ὀλοός**

ὀλοθρευτής οῦ ὁ destroyer

ὀλοθρεύω ▸ **ὄλλυμι**

ὀλοιός ▸ **ὀλοός**

ὀλοίτροχος ου ὁ (*also* ὀλοίτροχος ου ὁ) rolling stone, piece of rock

ὁλοκαυτέω bring a burnt-offering

ὁλοκαύτωμα ατος τό burnt-offering

ὁλοκληρίᾱ ᾱς ἡ soundness, entireness

ὁλόκληρος ον entire, perfect

ὀλολῡγή ῆς ἡ loud crying, wailing, lamentation

ὀλολύζω ὀλολύξομαι ὠλόλυξα cry aloud, wail; shout

ὀλοοίτροχος ▸ **ὀλοίτροχος**

ὀλοός ή όν destructive; hurtful, painful

ὀλοόφρων ον pernicious, meaning mischief

ὅλος η ον whole, complete, entire, all

ὁλοτελής ές perfect

ὀλοφυδνός ή όν wailing, lamenting

ὀλοφυρμός οῦ ὁ lamentation

ὀλοφῡ́ρομαι ὀλοφυροῦμαι ὠλοφῡράμην *mid and pass* wail, lament; feel pity *or* compassion

ὀλόφυρσις εως ἡ ▸ **ὀλοφυρμός**

ὀλοφώϊος ον malicious, destructive, pernicious

ὄλυνθος ου ὁ winter fig

ὄλῡρα ᾱς ἡ (a kind of grain) spelt *or* rye

ὀλῶ *fut from* **ὄλλυμι**

ὁμαδέω make a noise

ὅμαδος ου ὁ noise, din; crowd, throng

ὅμαιμος ον **ὁμαίμων** ον related by blood; brother; sister

ὁμαιχμίᾱ ᾱς ἡ defensive alliance, union for battle

ὅμαιχμος ου ὁ companion in arms

ὁμαλής ές **ὁμαλός** ή όν even, level; average

ὁμαλότης ητος ἡ evenness

ὁμαρτέω walk together; + *dat* walk beside, accompany, attend

ὁμαρτῇ, ὁμαρτήδην *adv* together, jointly

ὅμαυλος ον neighbouring, blending

ὄμβριος ᾱ ον of rain, rainy

ὄμβρος ου ὁ water, moisture; rain, shower of rain *or* snow

ὁμείρομαι + *gen* long for, long *or* wish (to do)

ὁμευνέτις ιδος ἡ bed-partner, consort

ὁμηγερής ές assembled together

ὁμηγυρίζομαι *mid* call together

ὁμήγυρις ιος ἡ assembly

ὁμηλικίᾱ ᾱς ἡ equality of age; ▸ **ὁμῆλιξ**

ὁμῆλιξ (*gen* ικος) of the same age; comrade

ὁμηρείᾱ ᾱς ἡ giving of a pledge

ὁμηρέω meet; agree

ὅμηρος ου ὁ **ὅμηρον** ου τό pledge, security; hostage

ὁμῑλαδόν *adv* in crowds

ὁμῑλέω + *dat* be together, associate, converse, be friends; live with; meet, encounter; negotiate, be engaged in

ὁμῑ́λημα ατος τό ▸ **ὁμιλία**

ὁμῑλητής οῦ ὁ friend; scholar

ὁμῑλίᾱ ᾱς ἡ living together, keeping company; conversation; instruction; assembly, meeting

ὅμῑλος ου ὁ crowd, throng of people, mob; troop of warriors; tumult of battle

ὁμίχλη ης ἡ (*also* ὀμίχλη ης ἡ) mist, fog; cloud

ὄμμα ατος τό eye, look; face; sight, image, spectacle

ὀμματοστερής ές eyeless

ὄμνῡμι†, **ὀμνύω** swear, affirm by oath; swear by

ὁμοβώμιος ον having one common altar

ὁμογάστριος ον born from the same mother

ὁμογενής ές kindred

ὁμόγλωσσος ον speaking the same language

ὁμόγνιος ον protecting the same race

ὁμογνωμονέω be of one mind

ὁμογνώμων ον having the same mind

ὁμοδοξέω ▸ **ὁμογνωμονέω**

ὁμόδουλος ου ὁ/ἡ fellow-slave

ὁμοεθνής ές of the same tribe

ὁμοήθης ες of the same character

ὁμόθεν *adv* from the same place *or* origin; hand to hand

ὁμοθῡμαδόν *adv* unanimously

ὁμοιάζω be like

ὁμοΐος ᾱ ον ▸ **ὁμοῖος**

ὁμοιοπαθής ές being similarly affected

ὁμοῖος (*or* ὅμοιος) ᾱ ον like, similar, resembling; the same, of the same rank; equal citizen; equal; common, mutual; a match for; agreeing, convenient

■ **οἱ ὁμοῖοι** all citizens who had equal right to hold state offices (especially at Sparta)

ὁμοιότης ητος ἡ likeness, resemblance

ὁμοιότροπος ον agreeing, similar

ὁμοιόω make (a)like, liken, compare; *pass* be *or* become (a)like

ὁμοίωμα ατος τό **ὁμοίωσις** εως ἡ likeness, image; likening; simile

ὁμοκλέω, ὁμοκλάω cry aloud; cheer on; reproach, threaten

ὁμοκλή ῆς ἡ loud cry, shout; command; menace

ὁμοκλητήρ ῆρος ἡ cheerer on, encourager

ὁμόκλῑνος ον neighbour at table, someone reclining on the same couch

ὁμολογέω agree with; grant, concede, allow, admit, confess; promise; assent (to), come to an agreement, make a treaty; *mid* come to an understanding *or* agreement

■ **ὁμολογεῖται** it is allowed, granted

ὁμολογίᾱ ᾱς ἡ **ὁμολόγημα** ατος τό agreement; confession, assent; terms, treaty; capitulation

ὁμολογουμένως *adv* by common consent, confessedly; agreeably to, conformably to

ὁμομήτριος ᾱ ον of the same mother

ὁμονοέω be of one mind

ὁμόνοια ᾱς ἡ unity, concord

ὁμοπάτριος ον of the same father

ὁμόπτολις (*gen* εως) of the same city

ὀμόργνῡμι wipe away

ὁμορέω border on

ὅμορος ον bordering on

ὁμορροθέω + *dat* agree with

ὁμός ή όν common; one and the same

■ **ὁμῶς** *adv* together; equally, alike

ὁμόσε *adv* straight on; to the same place

ὁμοσῑτέω + *dat* eat together with

ὁμόσῑτος ον eating together

ὁμόσκευος ον equipped in the same way

ὁμόσπλαγχνος ον kindred; brother

ὁμόσπονδος ον sharing in the drink-offering, companion at table

ὁμόσπορος ον kindred

ὁμοσπόρος ον married to the same wife

ὁμοστιχάω + *dat* walk beside

ὁμόστολος ον companion, similar

ὁμότεχνος ον of the same craft *or* trade

ὁμότῑμος ον equally honoured

ὁμοτράπεζος ον companion at table

ὁμότροπος ον ▸ **ὁμοιότροπος**

ὁμότροφος ον brought up together

ὁμοῦ *adv* together, at the same place; at once; near

ὀμοῦμαι *fut from* **ὄμνυμι**

ὁμουρέω *see* **ὁμορέω**

ὁμοφρονέω have the same mind

ὁμοφροσύνη ης ἡ concord

ὁμόφρων ον of one mind

ὁμοφυής ές of the same nature

ὁμόφῡλος ον of the same tribe

ὁμοφωνέω speak the same language

ὁμόφωνος ον speaking the same language

ὁμοχροίη ης ἡ skin; sameness of colour

ὁμόψηφος ον having an equal vote; of one mind

ὁμόω unite

ὀμφαλόεις εσσα εν (of a yoke) with a knot on the top; (of a shield) having a boss

ὀμφαλός οῦ ὁ navel; knob *or* boss of a shield; centre

ὄμφαξ ακος ἡ unripe grape

ὀμφή ῆς ἡ (divine) voice; speech; oracle

ὁμώνυμος ον of the same name

ὁμωρόφιος ον living under the same roof

ὅμως *adv* nevertheless, yet, all the same

ὁμῶς *adv see* **ὁμός**

ὁμωχέτης (*gen* ου) worshipped together

ὄναρ τό dream, vision

ὀνάριον ου τό little ass

ὄνᾱσις εως ἡ ▸ **ὄνησις**

ὄνειαρ ατος τό help, assistance; refreshment; food, victuals

ὀνείδειος ον reproachful

ὀνειδίζω ὀνειδιῶ ὠνείδισα reproach, upbraid, blame

ὄνειδος ους τό **ὀνείδισμα** ατος τό **ὀνειδισμός** οῦ ὁ reproach, blame; disgrace

ὀνείρειος ᾱ ον of dreams

ὄνειρον ου τό ▸ **ὄνειρος**

ὀνειροπολέω dream

ὀνειροπόλος ου ὁ interpreter of dreams

ὄνειρος ου ὁ dream, vision

ὀνεύω haul up

ὀνήσιμος ον useful

ὀνησίπολις (*gen* εως) benefitting the state

ὄνησις εως ἡ profit, help; bliss, delight

ὄνθος ου ὁ dung, dirt

ὀνικός ή όν [μῦλος] upper millstone

ὀνίνημι ὀνήσω ὤνησα benefit, help; gratify, delight; *mid and pass* have profit, advantage, delight *or* enjoyment

ὄνομα ατος τό name, word, term; title; fame, report; pretence, pretext

ὀνομάζω name, call by name; speak of; pronounce, enumerate; *pass* be called

ὄνομαι ὀνόσσομαι ὠνοσάμην blame, revile, find fault with; reject, despise

ὀνομαίνω ▸ **ὀνομάζω**

ὀνομακλήδην ▸ **ἐξονομακλήδην**

ὀνομάκλυτος ον famous

ὀνομαστί *adv* by name

ὀνομαστός ή όν to be named; named, renowned

ὄνος ου ὁ/ἡ ass; windlass, crane; upper millstone

ὀνοστός ή όν to be blamed

ὀνοφορβός οῦ ὁ ass-keeper

ὄντως *adv* really, actually, indeed

ὄνυξ υχος ὁ nail, talon, claw, hoof

ὄξος ους τό vinegar, poor wine; a sour individual

ὀξυβελής ές sharp-pointed

ὀξυδερκής ές sharp-sighted

ὀξύθηκτος ον sharp-edged

ὀξυκώκῡτος ον bewailed with shrill cries

ὀξυλαβέω be quick, seize an opportunity

ὀξῡ́νω ὀξυνῶ ὤξῡνα sharpen; provoke

ὀξυόεις εσσα εν sharp-pointed

ὀξύς εῖα ύ sharp, keen, pointed; pungent; piercing, shrill, clear; quick, swift; passionate, fiery; bold; active; clever

ὀξύτης ητος ἡ sharpness; quickness

ὀξύτονος ον sharp-sounding, piercing

ὀξύφωνος ον with clear voice

ὀξύχολος ον quick to anger

ὀπᾱδέω + *dat* follow, accompany

ὀπᾱδός οῦ ὁ/ἡ companion, attendant

ὀπάζω ὀπάσσω give as a companion *or* follower; add, attach; pursue, press hard; *mid* take as a companion

ὄπαιον ου τό hole in the roof (for smoke)

ὄπατρος ον of the same father

ὀπᾱ́ων ονος ὁ/ἡ (*also* ὀπέων) ▸ **ὀπαδός**

ὀπή ῆς ἡ hole, opening

ὅπῃ, ὅπη *adv* where; to which place; how, in what way

ὀπηδέω ▸ **ὀπᾱδέω**

ὁπηνίκα *adv* when; since

ὀπίζομαι *mid* care for, regard; honour; dread

ὄπιθεν ▸ **ὄπισθεν**

ὀπῑπεύω gaze at; observe, watch

ὄπις ιδος ἡ regard, respect, awe, veneration; punishment, vengeance

ὄπισθε(ν) *adv* behind, after, in future; *prep* with gen behind

ὀπίσθιος ᾱ ον belonging to the hind part

ὀπισθονόμος ον grazing backwards

ὀπισθοφύλακες ων οἱ rearguard

ὀπισθοφυλακέω guard the rear, command the rear

ὀπισθοφυλακίᾱ ᾱς ἡ command of the rear

ὀπίστατος η ον hindmost

ὀπίσω *adv* behind, backwards; in future; back; *prep* with gen after, behind

ὁπλέω make ready

ὁπλή ῆς ἡ hoof

ὁπλίζω prepare, equip, make ready, harness; arm; train; *mid* prepare for oneself; *pass and mid* get *or* be ready; be going

ὅπλισις εως ἡ equipment; arming

ὁπλῑταγωγός ον carrying the heavy-armed soldiers

ὁπλῑτεύω serve as heavy-armed soldier

ὁπλῑ́της ου ὁ heavy-armed (foot-) soldier, hoplite

ὁπλῑτικός ή όν belonging to a hoplite

ὅπλομαι prepare for oneself

ὁπλομαχίᾱ ᾱς ἡ art of using heavy-arms; tactics, the art of war

ὅπλον ου τό usu pl tool, implement; ship's tackle; arms, harness, armour, weapon; camp; ▸ **ὁπλῖται**

ὁπλότατος η ον youngest

ὁπλότερος ᾱ ον younger

ὁποδαπός ή όν of what country

ὁπόθεν *adv* from where

ὅποι *adv* to where, to there, where

ὁποῖος ᾱ ον of what sort, kind *or* quality

ὀπός οῦ ὁ juice of plants; juice of the fig-tree

ὁπόσε ▸ **ὅποι**

ὁπόσος η ον as many, as many as; as large as

ὁπότε, ὁπόταν *adv* when; whenever; because, since

ὁπότερος ᾱ ον which ... of the two

ὁποτέρωθεν *adv* from which of the two sides

ὁποτέρωσε *adv* to which of the two sides

ὅπου *adv* where; when; how; because, since

ὀπταλέος ᾱ ον ▸ **ὀπτός**

ὀπτάνομαι be seen

ὀπτασίᾱ ᾱς ἡ sight, appearance, vision

ὀπτάω roast; bake

ὀπτήρ ῆρος ὁ spy; eye-witness

ὀπτός ή όν roasted; baked

ὀπυίω, ὀπῡ́ω marry, wed; *pass* become a wife

ὀπωπή ῆς ἡ sight; (faculty of) sight

ὀπώρᾱ ᾱς ἡ late summer and early autumn; fruit-time; tree-fruit

ὀπωρίζω ὀπωριῶ gather fruit(s)

ὀπωρινός ή όν of early autumn

ὀπωρώνης ου ὁ fruiterer

ὅπως *adv* how, in what manner; as, when, as soon as; that, in order to

ὅρᾱμα ατος τό **ὅρᾱσις** εως ἡ sense of sight; sight; view

ὁρᾱτός ή όν visible

ὁράω † see, look; have sight; look to, take heed (of), beware (of); look at, behold, perceive, observe; see again; visit; understand; conceive; know; *pass* be seen, appear, become visible

ὀργάζω knead, soften

ὀργαίνω ὀργανῶ ὤργᾱνα make angry; be angry

ὄργανον ου τό instrument, implement, tool

ὀργάω swell with moisture, swell and ripen; be eager *or* excited; long for

ὀργή ῆς ἡ impulse; feeling, disposition, temper; passion; eagerness; anger, wrath; punishment

ὄργια ων τά secret rites *or* mysteries

ὀργίζω make angry; *pass* become angry

ὀργίλος η ον prone to anger

ὀργυιᾱ́ ᾶς ἡ **ὄργυια** ᾱς ἡ fathom (a length of 6 feet)

ὀρέγω, ὀρέγνῡμι *and mid* reach, stretch out, extend; offer, give; *mid and pass* stretch oneself out; reach at *or* to + *gen*; aim at, grasp at; long for, desire

ὀρειβάτης (*gen* ου) mountain ranging

ὀρεινός ή όν **ὄρειος** (ᾱ) ον mountainous, hilly; living on the mountains, mountaineer

ὀρεκτός ή όν stretched out

ὄρεξις εως ἡ desire, longing

ὀρέομαι hasten

ὀρεσίτροφος ον mountain-bred

ὀρεσσιβάτης (*gen* ου) ▸ **ὀρειβάτης**

ὀρέστερος ᾱ ον ▸ **ὀρεινός**

ὀρεστιάς άδος ἡ mountain nymph

ὀρεύς έως ὁ mule

ὀρεχθέω struggle, pant, quiver

ὁρέω ▸ **ὁράω**

ὀρεώκομος ου ὁ muleteer

ὄρθιος (ᾱ) ον straight up, rising upward(s), upright, uphill, straight on, in a column *or* file; shrill, loud, clear

ὀρθόκραιρος ᾱ ον with straight horns; with upright beaks (of ship)

ὀρθόκρᾱνος ον with high top

ὀρθοποδέω walk *or* go straight

ὀρθόπους (*gen* ποδος) uphill, steep

ὀρθός ή όν straight, upright, erect; straight forward, in a straight line;

unharmed, safe, prosperous; anxious, attentive, expecting; right, just, righteous, upright; true, exact, convenient, decent

ὀρθότης ητος ἡ upright posture; rightness, right sense

ὀρθοτομέω cut in a straight line; teach aright

ὀρθόω set upright, raise; erect, build; maintain; make straight; improve, repair; extol, exalt; bring to a happy end; *pass* stand *or* sit upright; succeed, prosper, flourish; be right *or* true

ὀρθρίζω rise early

ὄρθριος ᾱ ον **ὀρθρινός** ή όν early in the morning

ὄρθρος ου ὁ early morning, daybreak

ὁρίζω ὁριῶ ὥρισα divide, confine, define, limit; mark out by boundaries; *mid* mark out for oneself; assign; determine; define [a word]

ὀρΐνω ▸ ὄρνυμι

ὅριον ου τό boundary, frontier

ὁρκίζω make swear; adjure

ὅρκιον ου τό oath; pledge, surety; treaty, covenant; victim sacrificed at the making of a treaty

ὅρκιος ον sworn; guardian of oaths

ὅρκος ου ὁ oath; vow; sworn stipulation; form of oath

ὁρκόω make swear

ὁρκωμοσίᾱ ᾱς ἡ swearing

ὁρκωμοτέω take an oath

ὁρκωτής οῦ ὁ the officer who administers an oath

ὁρμαθός οῦ ὁ row, chain; (of bats) flight

ὁρμαίνω *aor* ὥρμηνα **ὁρμάω** *act tr* set in quick motion; rouse, stir up; consider, ponder, devise; *act intr, mid and pass* start, set out, proceed, depart; proceed *or* begin from; hurry *or* rush on, make an attack; be about, be eager, purpose; begin

ὁρμέω *and mid* be moved, lie at anchor; depend upon

ὁρμή ῆς ἡ assault, attack, onset; start, setting out, march; impulse, intention, eagerness

ὅρμημα ατος τό passionate desire; attack

ὁρμητήριον ου τό starting-place

ὁρμίζω bring into harbour, anchor, moor; *mid and pass* come to anchor, lie at anchor, reach the harbour

ὅρμος[1] ου ὁ chain; necklace

ὅρμος[2] ου ὁ anchorage, harbour

ὄρνεον ου τό bird

ὀρνΐθειος ον of a bird

ὀρνῑθοσκόπος ον observing the flight of birds

ὄρνις ῑθος ὁ/ἡ bird; fowl, cock, hen; bird of augury; augury, prophecy

ὄρνῡμι, ὀρνύω ὄρσω ὦρσα *act tr* stir (up), rouse, move; incite, chase; encourage, cheer on; cause, excite; *act intr and mid* stir oneself, start up, arise; be roused,excited *or* troubled; rush *or* hurry on, hasten; rise to do, begin

ὁροθεσίᾱ ᾱς ἡ fixing of boundaries

ὀροθῡ́νω *aor* ὠρόθυνα stir up, rouse

ὄρομαι watch, be on guard

ὄρος ους τό mountain, mountain range

ὀρός οῦ ὁ whey

ὅρος ου ὁ boundary, limit, frontier; landmark; standard; definition

ὀροσάγγαι ων οἱ *Persian* benefactors of the king

ὀρούω start up *or* forwards, rush on, hasten

ὀροφή ῆς ἡ roof, ceiling

ὄροφος ου ὁ reeds for thatching; roof

ὅρπηξ ηκος ὁ branch, twig

ὀρρωδέω be afraid, fear, dread, shrink from

ὀρρωδίᾱ ᾱς ἡ fear

ὀρσοθύρη ης ἡ side-door; raised door

ὀρτάζω ▸ἑορτάζω

ὀρτάλιχος ου ὁ young bird, chicken

ὀρτή ῆς ἡ ▸ἑορτή

ὄρτυξ υγος ὁ quail

ὄρυγμα ατος τό pit, hole, trench; mine, tunnel

ὄρυζα ης ἡ rice

ὀρυκτός ή όν dug (out)

ὀρυμαγδός οῦ ὁ loud noise, tumult, roaring

ὄρυς υος ὁ a Libyan animal (perhaps an antelope or a gazelle)

ὀρύσσω dig, dig up; cover with earth, bury; dig through

ὀρφανίᾱ ᾱς ἡ bereavement

ὀρφανίζω ὀρφανιῶ ὠρφάνισα make orphan, make destitute

ὀρφανός ή όν left orphan; destitute, bereft

ὀρφανιστής οῦ ὁ guardian

ὀρφναῖος ᾱ ον dark, dusky

ὄρχαμος ου ὁ leader, lord, master

ὄρχατος ου ὁ garden

ὀρχέομαι *mid* dance

ὀρχηδόν *adv* one after another, in a row

ὀρχηθμός οῦ ὁ **ὄρχημα** ατος τό **ὄρχησις** εως ἡ dance, dancing

ὀρχηστήρ ῆρος ὁ **ὀρχηστής** οῦ ὁ dancer

ὀρχήστρᾱ ᾱς ἡ place for dancing; orchestra (the area in the theatre where the chorus sang and danced)

ὀρχηστρίς ίδος ἡ dancing girl

ὀρχηστῦς ύος ἡ ▸ὄρχησις

ὄρχις εως *or* ιος ὁ testicle

ὄρχος ου ὁ row of vines

ὅς ἥ ὅ *pron relative* who, which, that; *demonstrative* this, that; he, she, it; *possessive* his, her, one's own

ὁσάκις *adv* as many times as

ὁσημέραι *adv* daily, day by day

ὁσίᾱ ᾱς ἡ divine law; holiness; sacred duty

ὅσιος (ᾱ) ον sanctioned by divine law *or* by the law of nature, sacred, approved by the gods; holy, pious; chaste, pure

ὁσιότης ητος ἡ piety, religiousness

ὁσιόω hallow; purify, set free from guilt by offerings

ὀσμή ῆς ἡ ▸**ὀδμή**

ὅσος η ον as great as, how great, as much, far, long as

ὅσπερ ἥπερ ὅπερ who *or* which indeed

ὄσπριον ου τό pulse (the edible seed of peas, beans, lentils, etc.)

ὄσσα ης ἡ rumour; voice

ὁσσάκι ▸**ὁσάκις**

ὁσσάτιος ᾱ ον ▸**ὅσος**

ὄσσε τώ *dual* the eyes

ὄσσομαι *mid* see; see in one's mind; forebode, foretell

ὀστέϊνος η ον of bone, bony

ὀστέον ου τό ▸**ὀστοῦν** bone

ὅστις ἥτις ὅτι whoever, whichever; who, which, that

ὀστρακίζω banish for ten years by fragments of pottery (on which the names of candidates for banishment were scratched), ostracize

ὀστρακισμός οῦ ὁ banishment by fragments of pottery, ostracism (see previous entry)

ὄστρακον ου τό fragment of pottery

ὀστρακοφορίᾱ ᾱς ἡ voting with fragments of pottery (see ὀστρακίζω)

ὄστρεον ου τό oyster

ὀσφραίνομαι ὀσφρήσομαι ὠσφρόμην smell, track by scent

ὄσφρησις εως ἡ (sense of) smell

ὀσφῦς ύος ἡ lower part of the back, hip

ὅταν *adv* whenever

ὅτε *adv* when; since

ὁτέ *adv* sometimes

ὅτι *conj* that; because; *with sup adj* as ... as possible

ὄτλος ου ὁ suffering, distress
ὄτοβος ου ὁ noise, din, sound
ὀτοτοῖ *int an expression of pain and grief* ah! woe!
ὀτραλέος ᾱ ον **ὀτρηρός** ᾱ́ όν nimble, quick
ὄτριχες *pl from* **ὄθριξ**
ὀτρυντῦς ύος ἡ encouragement
ὀτρῡ́νω *aor* ὤτρῡνα stir up, rouse, encourage, wake; send; *mid* hasten
οὐ, οὐκ, οὐχ, οὐχί not
οὗ[1] *adv* where
οὗ[2] *pron* of him(self), of her(self)
οὐά (*or* οὐᾶ) for shame!
οὐαί ah! woe!
οὖας ατος τό ▸ **οὖς**
οὐδαμά, οὐδαμῇ, οὐδαμῆ *adv* nowhere; in no direction; never; in no way, not at all
οὐδαμόθεν *adv* from no place
οὐδαμόθι ▸ **οὐδαμοῦ**
οὐδαμοῖ, οὐδαμόσε *adv* to no place
οὐδαμοῦ, οὐδαμῶς ▸ **οὐδαμά**
οὖδας εος τό ground, surface of the earth
οὐδέ *conj* but not; and not; nor; not even
οὐδείς οὐδεμία οὐδέν no-one, none, nobody, nothing; good-for-nothing, worthless, powerless
οὐδενόσωρος ον worth no notice
οὐδέποτε *adv* never
οὐδέπω (*or* οὐδέ πω) *adv* not yet
οὐδεπώποτε ▸ **οὐδέποτε**
οὐδέτερος ᾱ ον neither ... of the two
οὐδετέρωσε *adv* to neither of the two sides
οὐδός[1] οῦ ὁ ▸ **ὁδός**
οὐδός[2] οῦ ἡ ▸ **ὁδός**
οὐθείς, οὐθέν ▸ **οὐδείς, οὐδέν**
οὐκέτι *adv* no longer, no more, no further
οὔκουν *adv* not therefore? not then? is it not?; not therefore, so not; indeed not
οὐκοῦν *adv* therefore, accordingly; so then?
οὖλα ων τά gums
οὐλαί ῶν αἱ (bruised) barley for a sacrifice
οὐλαμός οῦ ὁ throng, tumult, band
οὖλε *int* greetings!; *literally* be healthy!
οὐλή ῆς ἡ scar
οὔλιος ᾱ ον pernicious, baleful
οὐλόθριξ (*gen* -τριχος) with curly hair
οὐλοκάρηνος ον curly-headed
οὐλόμενος η ον pernicious, destructive
οὖλος[1] η ον whole, entire; continuous, incessant
οὖλος[2] η ον woolly, fleecy, thick; matted
οὖλος[3] ▸ **οὔλιος**
οὐλόχυται ων αἱ ▸ **οὐλαί**
οὖν* *adv* indeed, really, certainly; therefore, accordingly, consequently
οὕνεκα *conj* on account of which, because; *prep with gen* for, on account of
οὔνομ- ▸ **ὄνομ-**
οὔπερ *adv* by no means
οὗπερ *adv* just where
οὔπῃ, οὔπη *adv* nowhere, in no way
οὔποθι *adv* nowhere
οὔποτε *adv* never
οὔπω, οὐπώποτε *adv* not yet, never yet
οὔπως *adv* in no way, not at all
οὐρᾱ́ ᾶς ἡ tail; rear-guard, rear
οὐρᾱγός οῦ ὁ leader of the rear-guard
οὐραῖος ᾱ ον of the tail, hindmost
οὐράνιος ᾱ ον heavenly, in *or* from heaven
οὐρανίωνες οἱ the heavenly gods
οὐρανόθεν *adv* from heaven

οὐρανόθι *adv* in heaven

οὐρανομήκης ες as high as heaven

οὐρανός οῦ ὁ heaven; firmament

οὔρειος η ον ▸**ὄρειος**

οὐρεσιβώτης (*gen* ου) feeding on the mountains

οὐρεύς ῆος ὁ mule

οὐρέω urinate, piss

οὐρίᾱ ᾱς ἡ favourable wind

οὐρίαχος ου ὁ lowest end

οὐρίζω[1] οὐριῶ carry with a favourable wind

οὐρίζω[2] ▸**ὁρίζω**

οὔριος ᾱ ον fair, prosperous

οὔρισμα ατος τό boundary line

οὖρον[1] ου τό urine

οὖρον[2] ου τό boundary; stretch; (of throwing) distance

οὖρος[1] ου ὁ favourable wind

οὖρος[2] ου ὁ watcher, guard

οὖρος[3] ου ὁ ▸**ὅρος**

οὐρός οῦ ὁ trench, channel

οὖς ὠτός τό ear; handle

οὐσίᾱ ᾱς ἡ being, essence, substance; property

οὐτά(ζ)ω οὔτησα hit, strike, wound, hurt

οὔτε *conj* and not

■ **οὔτε … οὔτε** neither … nor

οὐτιδανός ή όν worthless, of no account

οὔτις οὔτι no-one, nobody, nothing

οὔτοι *adv* indeed not

οὗτος αὕτη τοῦτο this, this one

οὕτω(ς), οὑτωσί *adv* thus, in this way *or* manner, so, only so

ὀυχί *adv* no, not

ὀφειλέτης ου ὁ debtor

ὀφείλημα ατος τό **ὀφειλή** ῆς ἡ debt

ὀφείλω† owe, be indebted; be bound, be under an obligation

■ **ὀφειλόμενος** η ον due

■ **τὸ ὀφειλόμενον** one's due

■ **ὤφελον** + *infin* I ought; if only I!

ὀφέλλω[1] ▸**ὀφείλω**

ὀφέλλω[2] increase, augment, strengthen; promote, help

ὄφελος τό profit, advantage; usefulness

ὀφθαλμίᾱ ᾱς ἡ disease of the eyes

ὀφθαλμιάω have bad eyes *or* a disease of the eyes

ὀφθαλμοδουλείᾱ ᾱς ἡ eye-service

ὀφθαλμός οῦ ὁ eye; face; the dearest, choicest, best, help, delight

ὄφις εως ὁ snake

ὀφλισκάνω ὀφλήσω ὦφλον incur a debt *or* punishment, lose one's cause, be found guilty (of); incur a charge

ὄφρα *conj* as long as, while; until; that, in order that

ὀφρύη ης ἡ ▸**ὀφρύς**

ὀφρυόεις εσσα εν hilly

ὀφρῦς ύος ὁ eyebrow; forehead; pride, dignity; edge, brow of a hill

ὄχα *adv* by far

ὄχανον ου τό handle (of a shield)

ὀχετεύω divert by a canal

ὀχετηγός όν drawing off water by a canal

ὀχετός οῦ ὁ conduit, canal, ditch

ὀχεύς έως ὁ handle, band, strap; clasp; bolt

ὀχεύω copulate with

ὀχέω bear, endure; *pass and mid* be carried *or* borne; drive, ride

ὄχημα ατος τό carriage, chariot; vessel

ὀχθέω be troubled *or* angered

ὄχθη ης ἡ **ὄχθος** ου ὁ height, hill; high bank of a river; edge

ὀχλέω move by a lever, roll; molest, trouble

ὀχληρός ᾱ́ όν troublesome

ὀχλίζω ▸**ὀχλέω**

ὀχλικός ή όν ▸ **ὀχλώδης**

ὀχλοποιέω make a riot

ὄχλος ου ὁ throng, crowd, the common people, mob; trouble, disturbance

ὀχλώδης ες like a mob, common, turbulent

ὀχμάζω grip fast, rein in

ὄχος ου ὁ receptacle, support; carriage, chariot

ὀχυρός ά όν firm, strong, tenable

ὀχυρόω *and mid* fortify

ὀχύρωμα ατος τό fort, stronghold, fortress

ὄψ ὀπός ἡ voice; speech, saying

ὀψάριον ου τό ▸ **ὄψον**

ὀψέ *adv* after a long time; late, too late; in the evening

ὀψείω + *gen* wish to see

ὀψίᾱ ᾱς ἡ evening; afternoon

ὀψίγονος ον late-born, to be born later

ὀψίζω *and pass* be (too) late

ὄψιμος ον **ὄψιος** ᾱ ον late, tardy

ὄψις εως ἡ faculty of sight, seeing, viewing; sight, appearance; view, vision; perception; eye; face

ὀψιτέλεστος ον of late fulfilment

ὄψομαι *fut from* **ὁράω**

ὄψον ου τό meat, fish, sauce; anything eaten with bread

ὀψοποιέω *and mid* dress *or* season meat

ὀψοποιΐᾱ ᾱς ἡ **ὀψοποιϊκή** ῆς ἡ cookery

ὀψοποιός οῦ ὁ cook

ὀψοφάγος ον one who eats delicacies (such as fish), epicure, gourmet

ὀψωνέω buy victuals (e.g. fish)

ὀψώνιον ου τό provisions; wages; ▸ **ὄψον**

Ππ

π, Π (πῖ) sixteenth letter of the alphabet ▪ **π′** *as a numeral* = 80

πᾶ, πά ▸ **πῆ, πή**

πᾱγᾱ́ ᾶς ἡ ▸ **πηγή**

παγετώδης ες icy, chilly

πάγη ης ἡ snare; trap

παγιδεύω entrap

παγίς ίδος ἡ ▸ **πάγη**

πάγκακος ον utterly bad, nefarious

πάγκαλος (η) ον most beautiful *or* good

πάγκαρπος ον rich in all sorts of fruit

παγκευθής ές all-concealing

πάγκλαυτος ον ever weeping, all tearful; all-lamented

πάγκοινος ον common to all

παγκοίτης (*gen* ου) giving rest to all

παγκόνῑτος ον covered all over with dust

παγκρατής ές all-powerful

παγκρατιάζω practise the παγκράτιον

παγκρατιαστής οῦ ὁ one who practises the παγκράτιον

παγκράτιον ου τό 'all-in' contest in wrestling and boxing

πάγος ου ὁ rock, peak, hill, crag; frost

παγχάλεπος ον most difficult

παγχάλκεος ον **πάγχαλκος** ον all-brazen

πάγχρηστος ον good for all things

πάγχρῑστος ον all-anointed

παγχρῡ́σεος ον all golden

πάγχυ *adv* quite, wholly

πάθη ης ἡ **πάθημα** ατος τό **πάθος** ους τό occurrence, accident; misfortune, suffering, loss; grief; passion

παιᾱ́ν ᾶνος ὁ saviour, physician; paean, choral song (of triumph), battle song

παιᾱνίζω chant the paean

παιγνιᾱ́ ᾶς ἡ play, sport

παιγνιήμων ον **παιγνιώδης** ες sportive, playful, fond of a joke

παιδαγωγέω lead, train *or* educate

παιδαγωγός οῦ ὁ trainer, tutor, master, teacher

παιδάριον ου τό little child, boy *or* girl

παιδείᾱ ᾱς ἡ education, teaching, training, correction, discipline; letters, knowledge, science

παιδεῖος ον ▸ **παιδικός**

παιδεραστέω love boys

παιδεραστής οῦ ὁ lover of boys

παιδεραστίᾱ ᾱς ἡ love of boys

παίδευμα ατος τό **παίδευσις** εως ἡ ▸ **παιδεία**

παιδευτής οῦ ὁ instructor, teacher, corrector

παιδεύω bring up, train, teach, instruct, educate; correct, discipline, chastise, punish

παιδίᾱ ᾱς ἡ ▸ **παιδεία**

παιδιᾱ́ ᾶς ἡ childish play; sport, game

παιδικός ή όν belonging to children, childish, young
■ **τὰ παιδικά** darling

παιδιόθεν *adv* from a child

παιδίον ου τό ▸ **παιδάριον**

παιδίσκη ης ἡ girl, prostitute, young female slave

παιδίσκος ου ὁ ▸ **παιδάριον**

παιδνός (ή) όν ▸ **παιδικός**

παιδοκτόνος ον child-killing

παιδοποιέω beget children

παιδοποιΐᾱ ᾱς ἡ procreating children

παιδοποιός όν begetting children

παιδοτρίβης ου ὁ training-master

παιδοτρόφος ον rearing children

παιδουργίᾱ ᾱς ἡ mother

παιδοφόνος ον ▸ **παιδοκτόνος**

παίζω παιξοῦμαι ἔπαισα sport, play, jest; invent in playful spirit

παιήων ονος ὁ ▸ **παιάν**

παιπαλόεις εσσα εν steep, rocky, cragged

παῖς παιδός ὁ/ἡ child, son, daughter, descendant; boy, girl, young man *or* woman; servant, slave

παιφάσσω quiver, move like lightning

παίω strike, smite; hit, wound; *intr* dash against

παιών ῶνος ὁ ▸ **παιάν**

παιωνίζω ▸ **παιανίζω**

παιώνιος ᾱ ον healing, saving

παιωνισμός οῦ ὁ chanting of the paean (see **παίαν**)

πᾱκτόω close fast; stop

παλάζω ▸ **πάλλω**

παλάθη ης ἡ fruit-cake

πάλαι *adv* of old, formerly, before; just past

παλαιγενής ές aged

παλαιόπλουτος ον rich from early times

παλαιός ᾱ́ όν old, aged; ancient; antiquated, obsolete

παλαιότης ητος ἡ age, antiquity

παλαιόω make old; abrogate [a law]; *pass* become obsolete

πάλαισμα ατος τό bout *or* fall (in wrestling); trick, artifice; struggle

παλαισμοσύνη ης ἡ art of wrestling

παλαιστής οῦ ὁ wrestler

παλαιστιαῖος ᾱ ον a palm long *or* broad

παλαίστρᾱ ᾱς ἡ wrestling ground, wrestling school

παλαίφατος ον ancient, legendary

παλαίω wrestle, struggle; overcome

παλάμη ης ἡ palm; hand; power, force; device, method, means

παλαμναῖος ου ὁ murderer; avenger

παλάσσω¹ παλάξω besprinkle, defile

παλάσσω² ▸ πάλλω

παλέω be disabled

πάλη ης ἡ wrestling, struggle

παλιγγενεσίᾱ ᾱς ἡ new birth; resurrection, regeneration (by baptism)

παλίγκοτος ον breaking out afresh; malignant

παλιλλογέω say again

παλίλλογος ον collected again

παλιμπετές *adv* back

παλιμπλάζομαι wander back

πάλιν *adv* back, backwards; reversely; again, once more

παλινάγρετος ον revocable

παλιναυτόμολος ου ὁ deserter for a second time

παλινόρμενος η ον **παλίνορσος** ον hastening back

παλίντιτος ον requited, avenged

παλίντονος ον elastic

παλιντριβής ές hardened, obstinate, crafty

παλινῳδίᾱ ᾱς ἡ recantation

παλιρρόθιος ον flowing back

παλίρροια ᾱς ἡ flowing back, ebb

παλίρρυτος ον flowing in requital

παλίσσυτος ον rushing back

παλίωξις εως ἡ pursuit in turn

παλλακεύομαι *mid* keep as a concubine

παλλακή ῆς ἡ **παλλακίς** ίδος ἡ concubine

πάλλω *aor* ἔπηλα swing, wield, whirl, brandish, shake; *mid* move quickly, quiver, tremble

πάλος ου ὁ lot

παλτόν οῦ τό dart, javelin

παλτός ή όν hurled

παλῡ́νω strew, scatter; besprinkle

παμβῶτις (*gen* ιδος) all-nourishing

παμμάχος ον ready *or* sufficient for every battle; fighting with all one's resources

παμμέγας αλη α **παμμεγέθης** ες enormous

παμμέλᾱς αινα αν all black

παμμήκης ες of enormous length

πάμμηνος ον through every month

παμμήτωρ ορος ἡ true mother, mother of all

πάμμορος ον utterly unhappy

πάμπαν, παμπήδην *adv* wholly, quite

παμπληθεί *adv* with the whole multitude

παμπληθής ές ▸ **πάμπολυς**

πάμπληκτος ον in which blows fall thick

παμποίκιλος ον highly variegated, of rich and varied work; (of fawnskin) all-spotted

πάμπολυς ολλη ολυ very much, very great

παμπόνηρος ον utterly bad

πάμπρωτος η ον the very first

παμφαής ές all-shining

παμφαίνω, παμφανάω shine brightly

παμφεγγής ές ▸ **παμφαής**

πάμφλεκτος ον all-blazing

παμφόρος ον all-productive

πάμψῡχος ον in full vigour

πάναγρος ον catching all

πανάθλιος ᾱ ον utterly unhappy

πάναιθος ον all-blazing

παναίολος ον all-shining, variegated

πανᾱ́μερος ον ▸ **πανήμερος**

πανάμωμος ον utterly blameless

πανάπαλος ον utterly tender *or* delicate

πανάποτμος ον utterly unhappy

πανάργυρος ον all of silver

πάναρχος ον all-ruling

παναφῆλιξ (*gen* ικος) quite without the friends of one's youth

παναώριος ον all-untimely, doomed to an untimely end

πανδαισίᾱ ᾱς ἡ complete banquet

πανδάκρῡτος ον most lamented; all in tears

πανδαμάτωρ (*gen* ορος) all-subduing

πανδημεί *adv* with the whole people *or* force

πάνδημος ον **πανδήμιος** ον of the whole people, public, universal; common

πάνδικος ον completely just

πανδοκεῖον ου τό inn

πανδοκεύς έως ὁ innkeeper

πανδοκεύω receive *or* entertain all; keep an inn

πάνδυρτος ον ever-lamenting

πανηγυρίζω celebrate *or* attend a festival

πανήγυρις εως ἡ public festival

πανῆμαρ *adv* all day long

πανημέριος ᾱ ον **πανήμερος** ον lasting the whole day, all day

πάνθηρ ηρος ὁ panther *or* leopard

πανθῡμαδόν *adv* in high wrath

πάνθυτος ον celebrated with full sacrifices

πανῑ́μερος ον burning with desire, ardent

παννύχιος ᾱ ον all night long

παννυχίς ίδος ἡ night festival, vigil

πάννυχος ον ▸ **παννύχιος**

πανοικ(ησ)ίᾳ *adv* with the whole house

πανομφαῖος ον author of all oracles

πανοπλίᾱ ᾱς ἡ full armour, panoply

πάνορμος ον always fit for landing

πανουργέω act wickedly

πανούργημα ατος τό wickedness

πανουργίᾱ ᾱς ἡ fraud, villainy, knavery

πανοῦργος ον crafty, cunning, villainous, knavish, wicked; knave, rogue, villain

πανόψιος ον visible to all

πανσαγίᾱ ᾱς ἡ ▸ **πανοπλία**

πανσέληνος ον of the full moon

πάνσοφος ον very wise

πανστρατιᾷ *adv* with the whole army

πανσυδίῃ, πανσυδί *adv* with all speed, in a hurry

πάνσυρτος ον accumulated

παντᾷ, παντᾶ ▸ **πάντῃ**

παντάπᾱσιν *adv* ▸ **πάνυ**

πάνταρχος ον all-ruling

πανταχῇ, πανταχῆ *adv* everywhere, in every direction, in every way; wholly

πανταχόθεν *adv* from all sides

πανταχοῖ, πανταχόσε *adv* in all directions

πανταχοῦ ▸ **πανταχῇ**

παντελής ές all-complete, entire

πάντῃ, πάντη *adv* ▸ **πανταχῇ**

πάντῑμος ον all-honoured

παντλήμων ον utterly unhappy

παντογήρως ων making all old

παντοδαπός ή όν ▸ **παντοῖος**

πάντοθεν ▸ **πανταχόθεν**

παντοῖος ᾱ ον of all kinds, manifold

παντοκράτωρ (*gen* ορος) almighty

παντοπόρος ον versatile, all-inventive

παντόπτης (*gen* ου) all-seeing

πάντοσε ▸ **πανταχόσε**

παντουργός όν ▸ **πανοῦργος**

πάντως, πάνυ *adv* wholly, entirely, altogether; at any rate; at least; very much; certainly, indeed

πανυπέρτατος η ον the very uppermost

πανύστατος η ον last of all

πανωλεθρίᾱ ᾱς ἡ utter ruin

πανώλεθρος ον **πανώλης** ες utterly ruined, destroyed; all-destructive

πάομαι πᾱ́σομαι ἐπᾱσάμην *mid* acquire; *pf* possess

παπαῖ *int exclamation of suffering or of surprise* woe! ah!

παππάζω call papa

πάππας ου ὁ papa

πάππος ου ὁ grandfather

παππῷος ᾱ ον of *or* from one's grandfather

παπταίνω *aor* ἐπάπτηνα look timidly *or* cautiously; peer around

πάρ ▸ **παρά**

παρά *adv* near, beside, along; *prep with acc* along; beside; towards; during; beyond, except; contrary to, against, in comparison with; *with gen* from beside; from alongside of, from; *with dat* by the side of, beside, near, in the presence of; according to

παρα-βαίνω go by the side of; go beyond, transgress; pass over, omit, neglect

παρα-βάλλω *act tr* throw beside, put before; put side by side, compare; *act intr* come near, approach; pass over; *mid* expose oneself; stake; rival; compare; omit, neglect; deceive, betray

παράβασις εως ἡ transgression, crime; parabasis (the part of a comedy in which the chorus comes forward and addresses the audience in the poet's name)

παραβάσκω be a παραβάτης

παραβάτης ου ὁ warrior standing beside the charioteer; transgressor

παραβατός ή όν to be transgressed

παρα-βιάζομαι *mid* use violence on [someone]; constrain, compel

παραβλήδην *adv* with a sidestroke *or* indirect cut; maliciously

παράβλημα ατος τό screen, cover

παρα-βλώσκω + *dat* protect

παραβλώψ (*gen* ῶπος) looking sideways

παρα-βοηθέω + *dat* come to help

παρα-βολεύομαι *mid* stake, risk

παραβολή ῆς ἡ comparison, simile; proverb, parable; venture

παράβολος ον risking, reckless; perilous

παραγγελίᾱ ᾱς ἡ announcement, proclamation; command, order; doctrine, teaching

παρ-αγγέλλω announce; pass the watchword, give the word of command; exhort, encourage; command, summon

παραγγέλμα ατος τό **παράγγελσις** εως ἡ ▸ **παραγγελία**

παρα-γίγνομαι *mid* + *dat* be present *or* at hand; arrive at, happen; assist, help

παρα-γιγνώσκω decide wrongly, err in one's judgement

παραγκάλισμα ατος τό that which is taken into the arms, darling

παρᾱ́γορος ον consoling

παραγραφή ῆς ἡ exception taken (by the defendant) to the admission of a suit, special plea; marginal note

παρα-γράφω write beside, add in writing

παρα-γυμνόω disclose, reveal

παρ-άγω lead beside, by *or* past; lead up *or* along, introduce, bring forward; make march sideways; delay, keep ⋯

in suspense; lead astray, mislead, deceive; *intr* pass by, on *or* away

παραγωγή ῆς ἡ sliding motion of the oars; variety in speech; fallacy, misleading

παρα-δαρθάνω sleep beside

παράδειγμα ατος τό pattern, model, example; warning

παραδειγματίζω expose to shame, make an example of

παρα-δείκνῡμι show, exhibit, represent, assign

παράδεισος ου ὁ park; paradise, the garden of Eden

παρα-δέχομαι *mid* take *or* receive from; take upon oneself (to do); admit

παρα-δηλόω hint

παραδιατριβή ῆς ἡ useless occupation

παρα-δίδωμι give over, consign, deliver, transmit; entrust; abandon, betray; grant, allow

παράδοξος ον unexpected; incredible, marvellous; strange, startling

παράδοσις εως ἡ a handing over, transmission, surrender; tradition

παρα-δράω + *dat* serve

παρα-δυναστεύω reign beside *or* with another

παρα-δύομαι *mid* steal *or* creep in *or* past

παρα-δωσείω be ready to deliver up

παρ-αείδω + *dat* sing to

παρ-αείρομαι *mid* hang down on one side

παρα-ζηλόω provoke to jealousy *or* anger

παραθαλασσίδιος ον **παραθαλάσσιος** ον on the seaside, beside the sea

παρα-θαρσῡ́νω encourage

παρα-θέω run beside *or* past; outrun

παρα-θεωρέω compare; overlook; despise

παραθήκη ης ἡ ▸ **παρακαταθήκη**

παραί ▸ **παρά**

παραιβάτης ▸ **παραβάτης**

παραίνεσις εως ἡ consolation, exhortation, advice, warning

παρ-αινέω + *dat of person advised, etc.* advise, exhort, counsel, warn, recommend

παραίρεσις εως ἡ taking away; lessening

παρ-αιρέω take away from; lessen; divert from; *mid* draw over to one's side; take away

παραίρημα ατος τό strip, band

παραίσιος ον of ill-omen

παρ-ᾱΐσσω rush on past

παρ-αιτέομαι *mid* beg from, obtain by entreaty, intercede, plead for; decline, reject

παραίτησις εως ἡ obtaining by prayer, earnest prayer

παραίτιος ον ▸ **αἴτιος**

παραίφασις εως ἡ exhortation, encouragement

παρ-αιωρέομαι *pass* hang down on one side

παρακαθ-έζομαι *mid* **παρακάθ-ημαι, παρακαθ-ίζομαι** sit down beside

παρακαθ-ίστημι put *or* place down beside

παρα-καίομαι *pass* be kept alight beside

παρα-καλέω call to, summon, send for, call to help; exhort, encourage, excite, invite; comfort

παρα-καλύπτω cover, veil

παρακατα-βάλλω throw down beside; put on; (as Attic law term) make a special claim [to property]

παρακαταθήκη ης ἡ deposit, trust, pledge

παρακατα-λείπω leave behind for protection

παρακατα-λέχομαι + *dat* lie down beside

παρακατα-πήγνῡμι drive in beside

παρακατα-τίθεμαι *mid* give in trust, deposit

παρακατ-έχω keep back

παρά-κειμαι lie beside; be ready, at hand

παρα-κελεύομαι *mid* + *dat* exhort, encourage; advise

παρακέλευσις εως ἡ
παρακελευσμός οῦ ὁ an exhorting, cheering on

παρακελευστός ή όν summoned; helper

παρακινδῡ́νευσις εως ἡ risk, venture

παρα-κινδῡνεύω venture, hazard, risk

παρα-κῑνέω move aside; *intr* be mad, beside oneself

παρα-κίω pass by

παρα-κληΐω shut out

παράκλησις εως ἡ calling to one's aid, summons; exhortation, imploring, comforting; encouraging

π

παρακλιδόν *adv* turning aside, swerving from the truth

παρα-κλῑ́νω turn *or* bend aside; open; *intr* slip away, escape

παρ-ακμάζω be past the prime, be faded *or* withered

παρακοή ῆς ἡ disobedience

παρακοίτης ου ὁ husband

παράκοιτις ιος ἡ wife

παρ-ακολουθέω + *dat* follow close; attach oneself to; understand

παρακομιδή ῆς ἡ a transporting, pasage

παρα-κομίζω carry along *or* across, convey; *mid* procure for oneself; *pass* sail beside *or* along

παρ-ακούω hear by the way; hear wrong, misunderstand; disobey

παρα-κρεμάννῡμι let hang down

παρα-κρῑ́νομαι *pass* be drawn up along

παρα-κρούω *and mid* strike aside; cheat, deceive, mislead

παρα-κτάομαι *mid* acquire over and above

παράκτιος ᾱ ον on *or* by the seashore

παρα-κύπτω stoop aside; take a sideways glance at; look at

παρα-λαμβάνω receive from another, succeed to [an office], take possession of; capture, seize; hear, learn; take with one, intercept; invite

παρα-λέγομαι sail along

παρα-λέγω wander in one's speech, rave

παρα-λείπω leave remaining; leave unnoticed, neglect

παράλειψις εως ἡ omission

παρα-λέχομαι *mid* + *dat* lie beside

παραλίᾱ ᾱς ἡ the sea coast; the eastern coast of Attica (between Hymettus and the sea)

παράλιος (ᾱ) ον ▸ **πάραλος**

παραλλαγή ῆς ἡ change, transfer; relief, relay

παραλλάξ *adv* alternately, in turn; in alternating rows

παρ-αλλάσσω change, alter; exchange; pervert, seduce; pass by; *intr* escape; deviate, vary; miss

παρα-λογίζομαι *mid* reckon wrong; cheat

παράλογος ον unexpected
■ **ὁ παράλογος** wrong reckoning, miscalculation; disappointment

πάραλος ον lying by the sea, maritime

παρα-λῡπέω grieve, trouble

παραλυτικός ή όν paralytic

παρα-λῡ́ω loosen from the side, detach from; relieve, release, set free, dismiss; affect with palsy, enfeeble

παρ-αμείβω change, alter; pass by; exceed, surpass; *mid* change for oneself; pass by, outrun

παρ-αμελέω + *gen* pass by and disregard, be heedless of

παρα-μένω stay beside, stand fast, hold out; survive

παραμηρίδια ων τά armour for the legs

παρα-μῑ́γνῡμι mix with

παρα-μιμνῄσκομαι *mid + gen of what is mentioned* mention by the way

παρα-μίμνω ▸ **παραμένω**

παρα-μίσγω ▸ **παραμίγνυμι**

παραμόνιμος ον **παράμονος** ον steadfast, faithful

παρα-μῡθέομαι *mid* exhort, cheer, encourage; advise; console, soothe

παραμῡθίᾱ ᾱς ἡ **παραμῡ́θιον** ου τό exhortation, persuasion; consolation, soothing

παρανα-γιγνώσκω read beside

παρα-ναιετάω dwell beside *or* near

παρα-νηνέω heap up beside

παρα-νήχομαι *mid* swim by *or* along the coast

παραν-ίσχω raise in answer

παράνοια ᾱς ἡ madness

παρα-νομέω break the law, offend

παρανόμημα ατος τό **παρανομίᾱ** ᾱς ἡ transgression, law-breaking

παρα-νομίζω judge wrong

παράνομος ον contrary to law, unlawful; lawless, unjust

παράνους ουν mad

πάραντα *adv* sideways

παρα-παίω be mad *or* crazy

παράπᾱν, τό παράπᾱν *adv* on the whole, altogether

παραπ-αφίσκω *only in aor* παρήπαφον mislead, beguile

παρα-πείθω win by persuasion, prevail upon; beguile

παρα-πέμπω send by *or* along; escort; leave unnoticed, be heedless of; convey, transport

παραπέτασμα ατος τό curtain, veil

παρα-πέτομαι *mid* fly by

παρα-πήγνῡμι fix beside *or* near; *pass* be fixed to

παρα-πικραίνω embitter

παραπικρασμός οῦ ὁ exasperation, provocation

παρα-πῑ́πτω fall in with; befall, happen, offer itself; commit a fault, err; + *gen* fall aside *or* away from

παρα-πλάζω cause to wander from the right way, mislead; *pass* go astray

παρα-πλέω sail along *or* by; sail up

παραπλήξ (*gen* ῆγος) **παράπληκτος** ον sloping; mad

παραπλήσιος (ᾱ) ον nearly like, resembling, about equal

παράπλους ου ὁ a sailing beside *or* by; coasting voyage

παρα-πλώω ▸ **παραπλέω**

παρα-πνέω blow by the side

παρα-ποιέω copy, counterfeit

παραπομπή ῆς ἡ escort; providing, supplies

παρα-πορεύομαι *pass* go beside *or* past

παραποτάμιος ᾱ ον beside a river

παρα-πρᾱ́σσω do beside, help in doing

παραπρεσβείᾱ ᾱς ἡ fraudulent embassy

παρα-πρεσβεύω *mid* act fraudulently as an ambassador

παρ-άπτομαι *pass* be grasped

παράπτωμα ατος τό trespass, sin

παρα-ρράπτω sew as a fringe along

παρα-ρρέω flow by *or* down; slip from memory; be lost *or* missing; steal in

παρα-ρρήγνῡμι break, rend; *intr* burst

παραρρητός ή όν to be persuaded

παρα-ρρίπτω throw aside; run the risk

παράρρῡμα ατος τό protecting cover

παρ-αρτάω, παρ-αρτέομαι prepare, make ready; be ready

παρασάγγης ου ὁ Persian mile (30 στάδια)

παρα-σάσσω stuff *or* cram in beside

παράσημος ον stamped falsely, counterfeit, base

παρα-σῑτέω board and lodge with; be honoured with a seat at the public table; be a parasite

παρα-σκευάζω get ready, prepare, equip, provide, procure, furnish; make, render; make willing; manage; *mid* prepare for oneself; prepare oneself, get ready *or* prepared

παρασκευαστής οῦ ὁ a provider

παρασκευαστικός ή όν skilled in providing

παρασκευή ῆς ἡ preparation, a getting ready, equipment, provision, furniture, pomp; force, power, armament; means, resources; scheme, plot, intrigue; (for the Jews) the day of Preparation (the day before the sabbath at the Passover)

π

παρα-σκηνέω, παρα-σκηνόω encamp beside

παρα-σκοπέω give a sidelong glance at

παρα-σπάω *and mid* draw aside *or* over; detach from someone else's side

παρα-σπονδέω act contrary to a treaty

παράσπονδος ον contrary to a treaty, faithless

παρασταδόν *adv* standing beside

παραστάς άδος ἡ pillar; *pl* doorposts, portico, vestibule

παρα-στατέω stand by *or* near

παραστάτης ου ὁ next man; comrade, helper

παραστάτις ιδος ἡ assistant

παρα-στείχω step by; pass into

παρα-στρατηγέω issue orders interfering with those of the general

παρα-σφάλλω push off sideways

παρα-σχίζω rip up lengthwise, slit up

παρα-τανύω spread beside

παράταξις εως ἡ an arranging; army drawn up for battle

παρα-τάσσω put beside others; draw up in order of battle; *mid* arrange one's men; stand prepared

παρα-τείνω *act tr* stretch out beside; stretch *or* draw out; protract, prolong; torture, stretch out on the rack; *act intr and pass* run along; be stretched; be tortured

παρατείχισμα ατος τό wall built beside

παρα-τεκταίνομαι *mid* transform, alter; falsify; build besides

παρα-τηρέω *and mid* watch, observe

παρατήρησις εως ἡ observation

παρα-τίθημι place beside *or* before; supply, provide; compare; declare, explain; *mid* set before oneself; be provided with; call in to help; deposit; entrust; stake, hazard

παρα-τρέπω turn aside, divert, mislead; make one alter one's mind; pervert, falsify

παρα-τρέχω run by *or* past; outrun; escape; run up to

παρα-τρέω swerve aside from fear

παρα-τρῖβω rub beside

παρα-τροπέω turn aside

παρα-τρωπάω ▸ **παρατρέπω**

παρα-τυγχάνω be present by chance, happen; offer itself
■ **ὁ παρατυχών** any chance person, the first person to come along

παρ-αυδάω speak to, console; speak lightly of

πάραυλος ον neighbouring, near

παραυτίκα ▸ **παραχρῆμα**

παρα-φαίνομαι *pass* show oneself

παρα-φέρω bear *or* carry by *or* along; bring forward, produce, serve up; mention, allege; carry away, avert, lead away, remove; *intr* differ, be over

παρα-φεύγω flee by *or* past

παρά-φημι *and mid* speak gently to; persuade

παρα-φθάνω *and mid* be beforehand, overtake

παρα-φορέω present

παράφορος ον staggering

παράφραγμα ατος τό breastwork on the top of a mound; bulwark

παρα-φρονέω be beside oneself, be deranged *or* mad

παραφρονίᾱ ᾱς ἡ **παραφροσύνη** ης ἡ madness

παραφρόνιμος ον **παράφρων** ον mad

παρα-φρυκτωρεύομαι *mid* make secret fire-signals to the enemy

παρα-φυλάσσω watch, take care

παρα-φύομαι *mid* grow at the side

παρα-χειμάζω pass the winter

παραχειμασίᾱ ᾱς ἡ spending the winter

παρα-χέω heap up beside; pour in beside

παρα-χράομαι *mid + dat* depreciate, undervalue, disregard; misuse

παραχρῆμα *adv* on the spot, instantly, at once, immediately, straight away, forthwith

παρα-χωρέω go aside, make room; concede, grant, yield

παρδαλέη ης ἡ panther's skin

πάρδαλις εως ἡ panther *or* leopard

παρεγ-γράφω interpolate

παρ-εγγυάω hand on, recommend; pass on the watchword *or* word of command; *+ dat* exhort, encourage, command

παρεγγύη ης ἡ call, exhortation; watchword

παρ-εδρεύω sit beside

πάρεδρος ον sitting beside; companion at table; assessor, assistant

παρ-έζομαι *mid* sit beside

παρειᾱ́ ᾶς ἡ cheek; cheek-piece (of a helmet)

παρείᾱς ου ὁ reddish-brown snake sacred to Asclepius

παρ-είκω yield, give way; permit, allow

■ **παρείκει** it is allowed *or* practicable

πάρ-ειμι[1] ▸ **παρέρχομαι**

πάρ-ειμι[2] be by, present *or* near; stand by, help, assist; have arrived; be extant, at hand *or* possible

■ **τὰ παρόντα** present circumstances

παρ-ειπεῖν *aor infin from* **παρα-λέγω**

παρ-ειρύω draw along the side

παρεισ-άγω introduce secretly

παρείσακτος ον introduced secretly

παρεισ-δέχομαι *mid* take in besides

παρεισ-δύομαι come in secretly, slip in

παρεισ-φέρω bring in beside; apply besides

παρέκ, παρέξ (*or* πάρεξ) *adv* outside, along, past *or* beyond *prep with acc* beyond, along the side of, without; *with gen* outside, before, except

■ **παρὲκ νόον** senselessly, foolishly

παρεκ-βαίνω digress, deviate

παρεκέσκετο *see* **παράκειμαι**

παρεκπρο-φεύγω flee away from before

παρεκτός *adv* besides

παρ-ελαύνω drive by *or* along; *intr* drive, ride, march, sail *or* run by, past *or* along

παρ-έλκω, παρ-ελκύω draw to the side; delay; *mid* draw to oneself

παρεμ-βάλλω throw up

παρεμβολή ῆς ἡ insertion, interpolation; fort; camp, barracks

παρενθήκη ης ἡ insertion, addition

παρεν-οχλέω trouble *or* annoy besides

παρέξ ▸ **παρέκ**

παρεξ-άγω lead past

παρέξ-ειμι ▸ **παρεξέρχομαι**

παρεξειρεσίᾱ ᾱς ἡ prow *or* stern of a ship

παρεξ-ελαύνω, παρεξ-ελάω drive out past; *intr* go, ride *or* drive past

παρεξ-έρχομαι *mid* go out beside; transgress, elude

παρεξ-ευρίσκω find out besides

παρεξ-ῑ́ημι let pass beside, allow to pass through

παρεπίδημος ον immigrant, stranger

παρ-έπομαι *mid* + *dat* follow close

πάρεργον ου τό subordinate *or* secondary business, appendages, addition

πάρεργος ον secondary, subordinate, by the way

παρ-έρχομαι *mid* go by, beside, past *or* beyond; pass; escape notice; neglect, slight; surpass, overreach, delude; overtake, outrun; come to, pass to; come forward, make one's appearance

πάρεσις εως ἡ forgiveness, remission

παρέστιος ον by *or* at the hearth, domestic

παρ-ευθῡ́νω control

παρ-ευνάζομαι *pass* sleep beside

παρεύρεσις εως ἡ pretext, pretence

παρ-ευρίσκω find out, invent

παρ-έχω hold in readiness; offer, furnish, supply, afford; allow, grant; cause, render; show, exhibit, represent, produce; *mid* offer, supply, produce *or* display from one's own means *or* one's own part

παρ-ηβάω grow old, be past one's prime

παρ-ηγορέω *and mid* exhort, encourage

παρηγορίᾱ ᾱς ἡ exhortation; consolation

παρήϊον ου τό **παρηΐ̄ς** ίδος ἡ ▸ **παρειά**

παρ-ήκω have come alongside, stretch along; pass, be past

πάρ-ημαι *mid* + *dat* sit by *or* beside; be present *or* near

παρηορίαι ῶν αἱ reins of the trace horse (see next entry)

παρήορος ον sprawling; reckless, senseless; *noun* a horse which draws by the side of the regular pair, a trace-horse

παρθενεύω *mid* remain a virgin

παρθενίᾱ ᾱς ἡ maidenhood

παρθένιος ᾱ ον **παρθενικός** ή όν of a maiden, maidenly; *noun* son of an unmarried woman

παρθενοπῑ́πης ου ὁ one who looks at maidens, seducer

παρθένος ου ἡ maiden, virgin, young woman

παρθενών ῶνος ὁ maiden's apartments; (at Athens) Parthenon, temple of Athena

παρ-ιαύω + *dat* sleep beside

παρ-ίζω place beside; *and mid* be seated beside

παρ-ῑ́ημι let fall at the side; let by, past *or* through; relax, yield, give way; remit, let pass, allow, permit; forgive, pardon; neglect, abandon, refuse; let in; *mid* beg to be let off; obtain leave from

παρ-ιππεύω ride along *or* over; ride up to

παρ-ισόω make like; *mid* vie with; *pass* make oneself equal to, measure oneself against

παρ-ίστημι *act tr* place by, beside, near *or* before; present, offer; bring to one's side, win over, persuade; make ready; explain, describe, prove; cause; *act intr and pass* stand beside, by *or* near; be near, at hand *or* present; help, assist; surrender, submit; come to one's mind, suggest itself; *mid* place at one's side; produce; win over, overcome, subdue

παρ-ίσχω keep ready; offer

πάρο̄δος ου ἡ way past, passage, passing by; entrance; (in the theatre) ⇢

the first entrance of the chorus, their first song

πάροιθεν *adv* before; *prep with gen* in front of, in the presence of

παρ-οικέω dwell by *or* along; be a neighbour *or* stranger; live in, sojourn

παροίκησις εως ἡ neighbourhood

παροικίᾱ ᾱς ἡ dwelling in a foreign land

παρ-οικίζομαι *pass* settle near

παρ-οικοδομέω build beside

πάροικος ον neighbouring; foreigner

παροιμίᾱ ᾱς ἡ proverb; parable

παρ-οινέω be drunken; treat with drunken violence

πάροινος ον drunk, drunken

παροίτερος η ον fore, front

παρ-οίχομαι *mid* have passed by

παροκωχή ῆς ἡ ▸ **παροχή**

παρ-ολιγωρέω neglect, disregard

παρ-ομοιάζω be like

παρόμοιος (α) ον nearly like *or* equal

παροξυντικός ή όν inciting, provoking

παρ-οξῡ́νω sharpen, incite, spur on, irritate

παροξυσμός οῦ ὁ inciting, provoking

παρ-οράω look at, notice; look past, overlook

παρ-οργίζω provoke to anger

παρ-ορμάω stir up, set in motion

παρ-ορμίζω bring to anchor beside

παρ-ορύσσω dig beside

πάρος *adv* before, formerly, in front; *prep with gen* before, rather than; *conj* ▸ **πρίν** before

παρ-οτρῡ́νω ▸ **παρορμάω**

παρουσίᾱ ᾱς ἡ presence; arrival, return; assistance; right time; the Advent

παροχετεύω divert [river etc.]

παροχή ῆς ἡ a supplying, offering

παροψίς ίδος ἡ dainty side-dish

παρρησίᾱ ᾱς ἡ freedom of speech, licence of speech; courage

παρρησιάζομαι speak freely

πάρφασις εως ἡ ▸ **παραίφασις**

παρ-ωθέω push aside, drive away, displace; put off

παρωροφίς ίδος ἡ eaves, cornice

πᾶς πᾶσα πᾶν all, whole, entire; every ■ **τὸ πᾶν, τὰ πάντα** the whole, everything; the universe

πᾱσιμέλουσα ης ἡ a care to all, known to all, world-famous

πάσσαλος ου ὁ peg

πάσσοφος ον ▸ **πάνσοφος**

πασσυδί *see* **πανσυδί**

πάσσω πάσω ἔπασα sprinkle upon; interweave, embroider

πᾱ́σσων ον *comp from* **παχύς**

παστάς άδος ἡ porch, colonnade, portico; bridal chamber; tomb

πάσχα ατος τό the paschal lamb; Passover

πάσχω† suffer, be affected by; be liable to

παταγέω *and mid* clatter, make a noise

πάταγος ου ὁ noise, clattering; chattering (of teeth)

πατάσσω beat, knock; kill

πατέομαι *aor* ἐπασάμην *mid* eat, taste, consume

πατέω tread, walk; tread on, trample on

πατήρ πατρός ὁ father; forefather, ancestor; founder

πάτος ου ὁ trodden *or* beaten way, path

πάτρᾱ ᾱς ἡ ▸ **πατρίς**

πατραλοίᾱς ᾱ ὁ **πατραλῴας** ου ὁ parricide

πατριᾱ́ ᾶς ἡ descent, lineage; people, tribe, family

πατριάρχης ου ὁ patriarch

πατρικός ή όν **πάτριος** (ᾱ) ον of one's father *or* forefathers; hereditary, customary, native, national
■ **ἡ πάτριος πολιτείᾱ** the constitution inherited from one's ancestors

πατρίς ίδος ἡ one's country, fatherland, native

πατριώτης ου ὁ fellow-countryman

πατρόθεν *adv* from the father's side

πατροκασίγνητος ου ὁ father's brother, uncle

πατροκτόνος ον parricidal

πατροπαράδοτος ον handed down from one's fathers

πατροῦχος ου ἡ sole heiress

πατροφονεύς έως ὁ **πατροφόνος** ον **πατροφόντης** (*gen* ου) ▸ **πατροκτόνος**

πατρῷος ᾱ ον **πατρώϊος** ᾱ ον ▸ **πάτριος**

πάτρως ωος *or* ω ὁ father's brother, uncle

παῦλα ης ἡ rest, repose, pause, end

παῦρος ον very little, small, short

παυστήρ ῆρος ὁ **παυστήριος** ον allaying; reliever

παυσωλή ῆς ἡ ▸ **παῦλα**

παύω cause to cease, stop, bring to an end; check, hinder; depose; *pass and mid* come to an end, leave off, cease, rest; be deposed

παφλάζω bubble, foam; splutter, bluster

πάχετος ον ▸ **παχύς**

πάχιστος η ον *see* **παχύς**

πάχνη ης ἡ hoar-frost

παχνόομαι *pass* be frozen

πάχος ους τό thickness

παχῦνω παχυνῶ thicken, fatten; make dull

παχύς εῖα ύ thick, fat, stout, great, large; rich, wealthy; stupid, dull
■ **πᾶσσων, παχῑων** *comp*
■ **πάχιστος** *sup*

παχύτης ητος ἡ ▸ **πάχος**

πεδάω bind, fetter, check, constrain; entangle

πέδη ης ἡ fetter

πεδιάς άδος ἡ level, even; plain country

πέδῑλον ου τό sandal; shoe; boot

πεδινός ή όν even, level, flat

πεδίον ου τό a plain, field, open country
■ **πεδίονδε** *adv* to the plain

πέδον ου τό ground, soil
■ **πέδονδε** *adv* to the ground, to the plain
■ **πεδόθεν** *adv* from the ground; from the bottom of the heart

πέζα ης ἡ foot; end, top

πεζέταιροι ων οἱ Macedonian foot-guards

πεζεύω go on foot; travel by land

πεζῇ *adv* on foot; by land

πεζικός ή όν ▸ **πεζός**

πεζομαχέω fight by land

πεζός ή όν on foot; by land
■ **ὁ πεζός** walker; foot-soldier, infantry

πειθαρχέω *and mid + dat* obey

πειθός ή όν persuasive

πείθω† *act tr* persuade, prevail upon, win over; appease, propitiate, win by entreaty; bribe; cause, impel; mislead, cheat; *act intr, mid and pass* be won over *or* persuaded; + *dat* believe, trust, rely on; listen to, obey, comply with, yield to

πειθώ οῦς ἡ persuasion, eloquence; the goddess of Persuasion

πείκω comb *or* card [wool]

πεῖνα ης ἡ **πείνη** ης ἡ hunger; famine

πεινάω be hungry *or* famished

πεῖρα ᾱς ἡ trial, attempt, proof; experience; enterprise; plot, design

πειράζω ▸ **πειράω**

πειραίνω *aor* ἐπείρηνα tie, fasten by a knot; finish, complete

πεῖραρ[1] ατος τό end, farthest point; outcome; tool

πεῖραρ[2] ατος τό rope, snare

πείρᾱσις εως ἡ **πειρασμός** οῦ ὁ temptation

πειρατήριον ου τό trial, ordeal

πειράω πειρά́σω ἐπείρᾱσα *mid and pass* try, attempt, undertake; make a trial (of); test, experience, examine; try one's skill; try to persuade; lead into temptation; know by experience

πειρητίζω ▸ **πειράω**

πείρινς ινθος ἡ wicker basket in a carriage

πείρω *aor* ἔπειρα pierce through, fix [meat] on spits; stud with nails; cleave, pass through

πεῖσα ης ἡ obedience

πεῖσμα ατος τό rope, cable

πεισμονή ῆς ἡ ▸ **πειθώ**

πείσομαι[1] *fut from* **πάσχω**

πείσομαι[2] *fut mid from* **πείθω**

πειστήριος ᾱ ον persuasive, winning

πειστικός ή όν ▸ **πειστήριος**

πέκω comb *or* card

πελαγίζω form a sea; cross the sea

πελάγιος ᾱ ον of *or* on the sea

πέλαγος ους τό the high sea, open sea

πελάζω πελῶ ἐπέλασα *act tr* bring near; *act intr and pass* approach, draw near, be brought near; reach to, meet

πέλανος ου ὁ offering-cake (of meal, honey and oil)

πέλας *adv* near; *prep with gen* near to ■ **ὁ πέλας** neighbour, fellow man

πελάτης ου ὁ neighbour

πελάω ▸ **πελάζω**

πέλεθρον ου τό ▸ **πλέθρον**

πέλεια ᾱς ἡ **πελειάς** άδος ἡ dove *or* pigeon

πελεκάω hew *or* shape with an axe

πελεκίζω behead

πέλεκκον ου τό axe-handle

πελεκᾶς ᾶντος ὁ woodpecker

πέλεκυς εως ὁ axe

πελεμίζω swing, shake; make tremble; *pass* be shaken, tremble; flee trembling

πελιτνός ή όν livid (colour)

πέλλα ης ἡ milk-pail

πέλομαι *see* **πέλω**

πελτάζω serve as peltast

πελταστής οῦ ὁ a light-armed soldier, peltast

πελταστικός ή όν armed with a light shield

πέλτη ης ἡ light shield; shaft, spear

πελτοφόρος ον ▸ **πελταστής**

πέλω *and mid* be in motion; go, come; behave; be; become; happen

πέλωρ τό monster

πελώριος (η) ον **πέλωρος** η ον huge, immense

πέμμα ατος τό cakes, baker's wares

πεμπάζω *and mid* count by fives, count

πεμπάς άδος ἡ a body of five

πεμπταῖος ᾱ ον in five days, on the fifth day

πέμπτος η ον the fifth

πεμπτός ή όν sent

πέμπω† send, send away *or* home, dismiss; send word; throw, shoot; escort, convoy, attend; conduct a procession; *mid* send for

πεμπώβολον ου τό five-pronged fork

πέμψις εως ἡ sending, mission, dispatch

πενέστης ου ὁ labourer; (Thessalian) serf

πένης (*gen* ητος) poor, needy; day-labourer

πενθερά́ ᾶς ἡ mother-in-law

πενθερός οῦ ὁ father-in-law

πενθέω mourn

πένθος ους τό grief, sorrow; misfortune

πενίᾱ ᾱς ἡ poverty, need

πενιχρός ᾱ όν ▶ **πένης**

πένομαι toil, work; be poor; prepare, be busy with

πεντάδραχμος ον worth five drachmas

πενταέτηρος ον five years old, lasting five years

πενταέτης ες (*also* πενταετής ές) lasting five years

πένταθλον ου τό pentathlon, contest of five sports (long-jump, discus-throwing, running, wrestling, boxing *or* javelin-throwing)

πένταθλος ου ὁ practising *or* winning the pentathlon (see previous entry)

πεντάκις *adv* five times

πεντακισμῡ́ριοι αι α fifty thousand

πεντακισχῑ́λιοι αι α five thousand

πεντακόσιοι αι α five hundred

πεντακοσιομέδιμνος ον reaping 500 μέδιμνοι; member of the first class (according to Solon's distribution of Athenian citizens)

πεντάπηχυς υ (*gen* εως) of five cubits

πενταπλάσιος ᾱ ον fivefold

πεντάπολις εως ἡ league of five cities

πεντάστομος ον with five months

πένταχα, πενταχῇ *adv* in five parts, five-fold

πενταχοῦ *adv* in five places

πέντε five

πεντεδραχμίᾱ ᾶς ἡ five drachmas

πεντεκαίδεκα fifteen

πεντεκαιδέκατος η ον fifteenth

πεντετάλαντος ον worth five talents

πεντετηρίς ίδος ἡ space of five years; festival celebrated every five years

πεντήκοντα fifty

πεντηκοντήρ ῆρος ὁ leader of fifty men (an officer in the Spartan army)

πεντηκοντόγυος ον of fifty acres

πεντηκοντόργυιος ον of fifty fathoms

πεντηκόντορος ον (of a ship) with fifty oars

πεντηκοντούτης ες lasting fifty years, fifty years old

πεντηκόσιοι αι α ▶ **πεντακόσιοι**

πεντηκοστός ή όν fiftieth
■ **ἡ πεντηκοστή** Pentecost

πεντηκοστύς ύος ἡ division of fifty men (in the Spartan army)

πεντήρης ους ἡ quinquereme

πέος εος τό penis

πεπαίνω *aor* ἐπέπᾱνα make ripe; *pass* be softened

πέπλος ου ὁ **πέπλωμα** ατος τό garment, robe, cloak, long dress; curtain

πεποίθησις εως ἡ trust

πέπων[1] ον ripe; soft, gentle; weakling

πέπων[2] ον dear; friend

περ enclitic *particle* much, very; even; however, at any rate

πέρᾱ *adv* beyond; farther; over; longer; *prep* with gen beyond, more than
■ **περαιτέρω** *comp* still farther, beyond

πέραθεν *adv* from beyond

περαίνω περανῶ ἐπέρᾱνα bring to an end, finish, complete, accomplish; *pass* be accomplished

περαῖος ᾱ ον on the other side (of)

περαιόω carry across; *pass* pass over

πέρᾱν *adv* on the other side, across, beyond *prep* with gen opposite, over against, beyond

πέρας ατος τό end, extremity, issue, goal; accomplishment; *adv* at last

πέρᾱσις εως ἡ end; passage from life

πέρατος η ον last, extreme

περᾱτός ή όν to be passed over

περάω περᾱ́σω ἐπέρᾱσα carry across; sell beyond the sea; pass though, traverse; *intr* come through, penetrate; come over, across *or* beyond, go too far

πέργαμον ου τό **πέργαμα** ων τά **περγαμός** οῦ ὁ castle, citadel

πέρδιξ ῑκος ὁ/ἡ partridge

πέρδομαι -παρδήσομαι -ἔπαρδον fart

πέρηθεν, πέρην ▸ **πέραθεν, πέραν**

πέρθω πέρσω ἔπερσα destroy, ravage; get by plunder

περί *adv* around, about; exceedingly; *prep with acc* about, around; near, by; in relation to, with regard to; *with gen* around, about; on account of, for, for the sake of; above, beyond, more than; *with dat* around, about; near, hard by; for, on account of

■ **περὶ πολλοῦ** of much importance

περι-αγγέλλω announce around, send a message around; send round orders

περι-άγνῡμι *pass* be echoed all round

περι-άγω *and mid* lead, drive *or* turn round *or* about; *intr* go round

περιαιρετός ή όν able to be taken off

περι-αιρέω take off all round; pull down; take away; *mid* take away from oneself; strip off; rob

περι-αλγέω be greatly pained at

περίαλλα *adv* exceedingly

περιαμπ-έχω put round about

περι-άπτω attach to, fasten round; apply to; kindle round about

περι-αστράπτω flash all around

περιαυχένιος ον running around the neck

περι-βαίνω go round; sound round; sit astride on; protect, defend

περι-βάλλω throw round, about *or* over; put round, embrace, surround; invest, attribute, ascribe; sail round, double; surpasss; *mid* throw round oneself, put on; aim at, take possession of; put round oneself for defence; encompass, surround, enclose

περίβλεπτος ον gazed at *or* on; notable, famous

περι-βλέπω *and mid* look round about, gaze on

περιβόητος ον notorious, famous, scandalous; surrounded by noise

περιβόλαιον ου τό **περιβολή** ῆς ἡ **περίβολος** ου ὁ walls, enclosure; circumference, circuit; curve; an aiming at; cover, garment, sheath, veil

περιβρύχιος ον surging around

περι-γίγνομαι *usu* + *gen* overcome, excel, be superior; result, proceed; survive, escape, remain

περιγλαγής ές full of milk

περι-γνάμπτω sail round, double [a headland]

περιγραπτός όν circumscribed, enclosed

περι-γράφω circumscribe; define, determine

περιδεής ές very timid *or* fearful

περι-δείδω fear very much

περίδειπνον ου τό funeral repast

περιδέξιος ον (equally) skilful with both hands

περι-δέω bind round

περι-δίδομαι *mid* + *gen* wager, stake

περι-δῑνέω whirl round; *pass* spin round

περι-δίω ▸ **περιδείδω**

περίδρομος ον running round, circular; standing detached

περι-δρύπτω scratch round

περι-δύω put off around

περι-ειλέω wrap around

περι-ειλίσσω ▸ **περιελίσσω**

περί-ειμι[1] ▸ **περιέρχομαι**

περί-ειμι[2] be around; be superior, surpass; result, ensue; remain, survive, be extant

περι-είργω enclose round, fence in, confine

περι-είρω insert *or* fix round

περιέλασις εως ἡ a driving round; way round

περι-ελαύνω drive *or* ride round; push round (of cups); press hard, distress

περι-ελίσσω wind *or* roll round; *mid* wind round oneself

περι-έλκω drag round *or* about

περι-έπω be busy about, attend to, take care of; honour, treat (well)

περι-εργάζομαι *mid* waste one's labour; be a busybody, meddle with other people's affairs

περίεργος ον wasting one's labour; over-careful, officious, forward; petty, paltry; interfering

περι-έργω ▸ **περιείργω**

περι-έρχομαι go round *or* about; rotate, revolve; take a round-about way; travel about *or* through; come round to; come in turn; elapse; enclose, surround; overreach, cheat

περιέσχατα ων τά outside; circuit

περι-έχω hold around, encompass, embrace, surround; overcome, gain the victory; comprehend, hold; *mid* hold fast by, cling to, insist on, protect; entreat earnestly; strive after

περι-ζώννῡμι gird round

περι-ηγέομαι *mid* + *dat* lead round

περιήγησις εως ἡ outline, contour

περι-ήκω have come round; have arrived at

περιήλυσις εως ἡ a coming round; revolution

περι-ημεκτέω be much aggrieved *or* disconcerted

περι-ηχέω sound all round

περίθεσις εως ἡ a putting on

περι-θέω run round

περίθῡμος ον very angry

περι-ίζομαι *mid* sit round about

περι-ίστημι *act tr* place *or* set round; bring to a certain state; alter; *act intr and mid* stand round about, encircle, surround; turn out, be changed into, devolve upon; avoid, shun

περι-ίσχω *see* **περιέχω**

περικάθαρμα ατος τό offscouring, refuse

περικάθ-ημαι *mid* **περικαθ-ίζω** sit down round about; beleaguer

περι-καίω scorch

περικαλλής ές very beautiful

περι-καλύπτω cover all round

περικατα-ρρέω fall down all round

περί-κειμαι lie round, embrace; be put round; be clothed

περι-κείρω shear all round

περικεφαλαίᾱ ᾱς ἡ helmet

περι-κήδομαι *mid* be very anxious

περίκηλος ον quite dry

περι-κλείω, περι-κλῄω, περι-κλῃΐω *and mid* shut in all round

περι-κλύζω wash all round

περικλυτός ή όν far-famed, renowned

περι-κομίζω carry round; *pass* go round

περικοπή ῆς ἡ mutilation; a portion of scripture (such as the Epistles and the Gospels)

περι-κόπτω cut off, mutilate; waste, plunder

περικρατής ές + *gen* mastering, having full command over

περι-κρύπτω conceal wholly

περι-κτείνω kill round about

περικτίτης ου ὁ **περικτίων** ονος ὁ neighbour

περι-κυκλόω, περι-κυκλέω encircle

περικύκλωσις εως ἡ encircling

περι-λαμβάνω seize around, embrace; surround; include

περι-λάμπω shine round about

περιλεσχήνευτος ον ▸ **περικλυτός**

περι-λιμνάζω surround with water

περίλοιπος ον remaining, surviving

περίλῡπος ον very sorrowful

περι-μαιμάω search thoroughly

περι-μάρναμαι fight for *or* round about

περιμάχητος ον fought for; highly prized

περι-μάχομαι *mid* fight around

περι-μένω wait, wait for

περίμετρος ον exceedingly large, immense

■ **τὸ περίμετρον** circumference

περιμήκης ες **περιμήκετος** ον very long *or* high

περι-μηχανάομαι *mid* devise cunningly

περι-ναιετάω dwell round

περιναιέτης ου ὁ neighbour

περι-νέω, περι-νηέω heap up round

περίνεως ω ὁ passenger

περίνοια ᾱς ἡ quick intelligence; over-cleverness

πέριξ *adv and prep* with gen or acc round about, all round

περίξεστος η ον polished all round

περι-ξυρέω shave all round

περίοδος ου ἡ a going round, way round, circuit, circumference; periodical return; cycle; period; circuitous way

περιοικίς (*gen* ίδος) *fem from* **περίοικος**

περι-οικοδομέω build round, enclose

περίοικος ον dwelling round about, neighbouring; free inhabitant of Laconia who enjoyed civil but not political liberty

περιοπτέος ᾱ ον to be overlooked; suffered *or* guarded against

περι-οράω look around for, wait for; overlook, neglect; suffer, allow; *mid* wait for; be anxious (about); consider anxiously

περιοργής ές very angry

περίορθρον ου τό dawn

περι-ορμέω, περι-ορμίζομαι *mid* anchor round

περι-ορύσσω dig round

περιουσίᾱ ᾱς ἡ surplus, residue; abundance, plenty; advantage; superiority

περιούσιος ον having more than enough; especial, peculiar

περιοχή ῆς ἡ contents; section (of a book)

περι-πατέω walk about; lead a life

περίπατος ου ὁ walk, a walking about; colonnade, hall

περι-πείρω pierce *or* bore through

περι-πέλομαι *mid* move round, revolve; surround

περι-πέμπω send round *or* about

περιπέτεια ᾱς ἡ sudden change of fortune (such as that on which Aristotle says that the plot of a tragedy can hinge)

περιπετής ές falling round, clasping, embracing; piercing; falling in with; changing suddenly

περι-πέτομαι *mid* fly (a)round

περιπευκής ές very sharp

περι-πήγνῡμι *pass* grow stiff round

περι-πίμπλημι fill full

περι-πίμπρημι set on fire round about

περι-πῑ́πτω + *dat* fall around, upon *or* into; incur; fall in with, meet

περι-πλανάομαι *pass* roam about

περι-πλέκω twist round about; *pass* fold oneself round, cling to

περιπλευμονίᾱ ᾱς ἡ inflammation of the lungs

περι-πλέω sail about; sail round, double

περίπλεως ων **περιπληθής** ές completely full; populous

περίπλοος ου ὁ (*also* περίπλους ου ὁ) a sailing round, circumnavigation; account of a coastal voyage

περι-πλώω ▸ **περιπλέω**

περι-ποιέω cause to remain over and above; save, preserve, protect; procure; *mid* save for oneself; acquire

περιποίησις εως ἡ keeping safe, preservation; an acquiring; possession

περιπόλαρχος ου ὁ commander of the boundary-patrol

περι-πολέω go round *or* about

περιπόλιον ου τό fort, garrison

περίπολος ου ὁ/ἡ patrol; boundary-guard; attendant

περι-ποτάομαι *mid* ▸ **περιπέτομαι**

περιπρό *adv* very much, exceedingly

περιπρο-χέομαι *pass* be poured out round

περι-πτύσσω *and mid* enfold, enwrap; surround

περιπτυχής ές enfolding; fallen round

περίπτωμα ατος τό change, incident

περι-ρραίνω sprinkle round

περιρραντήριον ου τό holy-water vessel

περι-ρρέω flow round; fall down; flow abundantly

περι-ρρήγνῡμι rend and tear off; *pass* be broken *or* torn all round

περιρρηδής ές + *dat* stumbling *or* reeling over

περιρροή ῆς ἡ a flowing round

περίρροος ον **περίρρυτος** ον surrounded with water, sea-girt

περι-σθενέω be exceedingly strong

περισκελής ές very hard, rigid; obstinate

περι-σκέπτομαι *mid* look round; consider well

περίσκεπτος ον to be seen on all sides, far-seen

περι-σκοπέω ▸ **περισκέπτομαι**

περι-σπάω draw off from around; *mid* be distracted

περι-σπερχέω become alarmed *or* excited

περισπερχής ές very hasty

περι-σσαίνω wag the tail around, fawn upon

περισσείᾱ ᾱς ἡ ▸ **περίσσευμα**

περι-σσείομαι *pass* wave *or* float about

περίσσευμα ατος τό abundance, plenty; remnant

περισσεύω be over and above; be too many for; have more than enough; grow, excel; shower upon, make to abound

περισσός ή όν above measure, more than enough; extraordinary, unusual, strange, monstrous; excellent; superfluous, excessive; useless; exaggerated; remaining, over; (of numbers) odd

■ **τὸ περισσόν** surplus, residue

περισσότης ητος ἡ (of numbers) oddness

περισταδόν *adv* standing round about

περι-σταυρόω palisade around; *mid* fortify oneself with a palisade

περι-στείχω step around

περι-στέλλω dress, manage, perform round; take care of, protect; clothe and bury [a corpse]; cover, wrap in

περι-στεναχίζομαι *mid* resound around

περι-στένω cram full all around

περιστερᾱ́ ᾶς ἡ pigeon, dove

περι-στεφανόω encircle with a crown

περιστεφής ές crowned round

περι-στέφω ▸ **περιστεφανόω**

περι-στίζω stick *or* prick all round with; place round in a row

περι-στοιχίζω *and mid* net in, surround with snares

περι-στρατοπεδεύω *and mid* encamp about, beleaguer

περι-στρέφω whirl *or* spin round; *pass* be turned around

περι-στρωφάομαι *mid* go round

περίστῡλος ον with pillars all round

περι-σῡλάω rob entirely

περισφύριον ου τό anklet

περι-σχίζω slit and tear off; *pass* be split *or* divided

περι-σῴζω save from death

περι-τάμνω ▸ **περιτέμνω**

περι-τείνω stretch all round

περι-τειχίζω wall all round, fortify; beleaguer

περιτείχισις εως ἡ **περιτείχισμα** ατος τό **περιτειχισμός** οῦ ὁ a walling around, blockade

περι-τέλλομαι *mid* come round, revolve

περι-τέμνω cut round, cut off, intercept; rob, rustle; *mid* rob; *pass* be cut off

περιτέχνησις εως ἡ cunning, guile

περι-τίθημι put *or* place round about; put on; confer upon, invest with; *mid* put round oneself

περι-τίλλω pluck round

περιτομή ῆς ἡ circumcision

περι-τρέπω *act tr* turn round about *or* upside down, destroy; *act intr and pass* go round

περι-τρέφομαι *pass* congeal round about

περι-τρέχω run round; run round about; run through, discuss

περι-τρέω, περι-τρομέομαι *mid* tremble round about

περι-τροπέω ▸ **περιτρέπω**

περιτροπή ῆς ἡ total change, revolution

περιτρόχαλος ον **περίτροχος** ον round

περι-τυγχάνω + *dat* fall in with, meet by chance, encounter, light upon

περι-υβρίζω insult outrageously, maltreat

περι-φαίνομαι *pass* be visible all round

περιφάνεια ᾱς ἡ full knowledge

περιφανής ές **περίφαντος** ον seen all round, manifest; famous, excellent

περι-φέρω carry round *or* about; move *or* drive round in a circle; carry *or* bring to; divulge; endure; *pass* move round, revolve; wander about

περι-φεύγω flee from

περι-φλεύω scorch *or* char all round

περίφοβος ον extremely terrified

περιφορᾱ́ ᾶς ἡ a carrying round; revolution, circuit

περιφορητός ή όν portable; notorious, infamous

περιφραδής ές very thoughtful, cautious

περι-φράζομαι *mid* consider carefully

περι-φρονέω despise

περι-φρουρέω guard on all sides

περίφρων ον ▸ **περιφραδής**

περι-φύομαι *mid* grow all round; + *dat* cling to

περιχαρής ές exceedingly glad

περι-χέω pour round about, over *or* upon; *pass* surround, be spread all round

περι-χρῡσόω gild all over

περι-χώομαι *mid* + *gen* be extremely angry about

περι-χωρέω go round; pass over to

περίχωρος ον surrounding, neighbouring

περίψημα ατος τό anything wiped off, an offscouring

περι-ψῑλόω make bald all round

περιώδυνος ον very painful

περι-ωθέω push *or* shove about; expel, reject

περιωπή ῆς ἡ circumspection, look-out, caution

περιώσιος ον immense

περκνός ή όν dark-coloured

πέρνημι *aor* ἐπέρασ(σ)α sell

περονάω pierce; *mid* pin on with a brooch

περόνη ης ἡ **περονίς** ίδος ἡ brooch, clasp

περπερεύομαι brag, boast

περσίζω imitate the Persians, speak Persian

περσιστί *adv* in the Persian language, in Persian

πέρυσι *adv* last year

περυσινός ή όν of last year, last year's

περφερέες ων οἱ escorters

πεσ *likely to be from* **πίπτω**

πέσημα ατος τό a falling

πεσσείᾱ ᾱς ἡ game of draughts

πεσσεύω play draughts

πεσσός οῦ ὁ game of draughts; playing piece for draughts

πέσσω πέψω ἔπεψα make soft *or* ripe; boil, cook; digest

πέταλον ου τό leaf, tablet

πετάννῡμι πετῶ ἐπέτασα spread out, unfold

πέτασος ου ὁ broad-brimmed hat

πετεεινός ή όν **πετεηνός** ή όν ▸ **πτηνός**

πέτομαι πετήσομαι ἐπτόμην *mid* fly, dart, rush; escape

πέτρᾱ ᾱς ἡ rock, crag; stone

πετραῖος ᾱ ον **πετρήεις** εσσα εν **πετρήρης** ες **πέτρινος** η ον rocky; living among the rocks

πετροβολίᾱ ᾱς ἡ a stoning

πετροβόλος ον throwing stones

πέτρος ου ὁ ▸ **πέτρα**

πετρώδης ες ▸ **πετραῖος**

πεύθομαι *mid* ▸ **πυνθάνομαι**

πευκάλιμος η ον sensible, prudent

πευκεδανός ή όν bitter, destructive

πεύκη ης ἡ pine; pine-wood torch

πευκήεις εσσα εν **πεύκινος** η ον of pine-wood

πεύσομαι *fut from* **πυνθάνομαι**

πέφῡκα *pf act intr from* **φύω**

πῇ, πῆ *adv* which way? where? how? why?

πῃ, πη *enclitic adv* somewhere, anywhere; somehow, in some way, in any way

πήγανον ου τό rue (a shrub with bitter leaves)

πηγεσίμαλλος ον thick-fleeced

πηγή ῆς ἡ spring, well, source

πήγνῡμι πήξω ἔπηξα *act tr* stick, fix, make firm, plant; harden, cause to congeal *or* freeze; *act intr and pass* be fixed, stiff *or* frozen; congeal

πηγός ή όν strong, stout

πηγυλίς (*gen* ίδος) icy

πηδάλιον ου τό rudder

πηδάω πηδήσομαι spring, leap, dart, rush, fly; throb

πήδημα ατος τό a leaping, leap

πηδόν οῦ τό blade of an oar

πηκτίς ίδος ἡ Lydian harp

πηκτός ή όν fixed in; compact

πήληξ ηκος ἡ helmet

πηλίκος η ον how great, much *or* old?

πήλινος (η) ον of clay; earthen doll

πηλός οῦ ὁ clay, loam; mud

πηλώδης ες like clay; muddy

πῆμα ατος τό a suffering; misery, harm

πημαίνω πημανῶ ἐπήμηνα make suffer, hurt, grieve, ruin, injure

πημονή ῆς ἡ ▸ **πῆμα**

πηνίκα *adv* at what precise time? at what hour?

πηνίον ου τό shuttle

πηός οῦ ὁ one related by marriage

πήρᾱ ᾱς ἡ wallet

πηρός ᾱ́ όν disabled, lame; blind

πηρόω maim, lame

πηχυαῖος ᾱ ον **πήχυιος** ᾱ ον a cubit long

πῆχυς εως ὁ fore-arm; cubit (the distance from the point of the elbow to the end of the little finger); middle of a bow; side of a lyre

πι *aor stem from* **πίνω**

πιάζω ▸ **πιέζω**

πῑαίνω πῑανῶ ἐπῑ́ᾱνα fatten

πῖαρ τό fat

πῖδαξ ακος ἡ spring, fountain

πῑδήεις εσσα εν rich in springs

πιεζέω, πιέζω press, squeeze; lay hold of, arrest; trouble

πίειρα *fem from* **πίων**

πιθανολογίᾱ ᾱς ἡ gift of persuasion

πιθανός ή όν persuading, persuasive, winning; plausible, credible, likely; obedient, true

πιθέω obey

πίθηκος ου ὁ monkey, ape

πιθηκοφαγέω eat ape's flesh

πίθος ου ὁ tub, cask; earthen vessel

πικραίνω πικρανῶ make bitter; *pass* grow angry

πικρίᾱ ᾱς ἡ bitterness; irritation, malice

πικρόγαμος ον unhappily married

πικρός ᾱ́ όν piercing, keen; sharp, bitter; harsh, cruel, severe, stern; morose; repugnant, odious, hateful

πικρότης ητος ἡ ▸ **πικρία**

πίλναμαι + *dat* approach

πῖλος ου ὁ felt; felt hat; felt covering; felt cuirass

πῑμελή ῆς ἡ fat

πιμπλάνω, πίμπλημι† fill (up); *pass* be *or* become full, be filled *or* satisfied

πίμπρημι ▸ **πρήθω**

πινάκιον ου τό **πίναξ** ακος ὁ board; trencher; plate; table; small tablet (on which the jurors wrote their verdict); map; painting; drawing

■ **πίναξ ἐκκλησιαστικός** public notice-board

πίνος ου ὁ dirt, filth

πινύσκω make prudent

πινυτή ῆς ἡ understanding, wisdom

πινυτός ή όν prudent, wise

πῑ́νω† drink

πῑ́ομαι *fut from* **πίνω**

πῑότης ητος ἡ fattiness

πιπρᾱ́σκω, πιπρήσκω sell; betray

πῑ́πτω† fall, fall down; be thrown down; fail, err, sin; rush upon, attack; sink down; be killed; turn out, happen

πῖσος εος τό *only in pl* meadow

πίσσα ης ἡ pitch

πιστευτικός ή όν deserving belief

πιστεύω + *dat* believe, trust, confide *or* put faith in; entrust something *acc* to; *pass* be believed *or* trusted

πίσος ου ὁ pea

πιστικός ή όν ▸ **πιθανός**

πίστις εως ἡ trust, faith, belief; faithfulness, honesty; credit, trust, security, assurance, pledge of faith, warrant, oath; treaty; hostage; argument, proof

πιστός ή όν faithful, trusty; sure, trustworthy, credible; believing, relying on

■ **τὸ πιστόν** ▸ **πίστις**

πιστότης ητος ἡ faithfulness

πιστόω make faithful *or* trustworthy; *pass* have confidence, trust in; pledge oneself; *mid* give one another pledges; bind someone by oaths

πίσυνος ον + *dat* trusting in

πίσυρες α four

πιτνάω, πίτνημι ▸ **πετάννυμι**

πίτνω ▸ **πίπτω**

πίτῡρα ων τά bran

πίτυς υος ἡ pine-tree

πιφαύσκω *and mid* let appear; show, make known, declare

πίων πῖον (*gen* πίονος) fat, plump; fertile; rich; wealthy; plentiful

πλᾱγᾱ́ ᾶς ἡ ▸ **πληγή**

πλάγιος ᾱ ον slanting, sideways

πλαγκτός ή όν wandering, roaming; mad, insane, distraught

πλαγκτοσύνη ης ἡ wandering

πλάζω *aor* ἔπλαγξα strike; beat back; drive away; mislead; *pass* wander, go astray; glance off

πλᾱ́θω + *dat* approach

πλαίσιον ου τό square

πλακοῦς οῦντος ὁ cake

πλανάω, πλανέω lead astray; deceive; *pass* go astray, wander; wander in mind, be at a loss

πλάνη ης ἡ **πλάνημα** ατος τό a wandering, going astray; error; perverseness

πλάνης (*gen* ητος) **πλανήτης** (*gen* ου) wandering, roaming; vagabond

πλάνησις εως ἡ ▸ **πλάνη**

πλάνος ον wandering; deceiving; vagabond

πλάξ ακός ἡ flat surface, plain; table-land, flat land

πλάσμα ατος τό image, figure, plastic work, imagery; fiction, forgery

πλάσσω πλάσω ἔπλασα form, mould, shape, fabricate; forge; *mid* invent for oneself; feign

πλάστης ου ὁ moulder, modeller; sculptor

πλαστός ή όν formed, moulded; forged, invented

πλάτανος ου ἡ **πλατάνιστος** ου ἡ plane-tree

πλατεῖα ᾱς ἡ (broad) street

πλάτη ης ἡ blade of an oar, oar; ship

πλάτος ους τό breadth

πλατῡ́νω πλατυνῶ make broad, widen

πλατύς[1] εῖα ύ flat, level; wide, broad

πλατύς[2] εῖα ύ salt, brackish

πλέγμα ατος τό plaited work; wreath, braid

πλεθριαῖος ᾱ ον of the size of a plethron (see next entry)

πλέθρον ου τό (a measure of length (100 feet)); (as a square measure) acre

πλεῖος ᾱ ον ▸ **πλέως**

πλειστάκις *adv* most times

πλεῖστος η ον *sup from* **πολύς** most, greatest

πλείων ον (*also* πλέων ον) *comp from* **πολύς** more, greater

πλεκτός ή όν plaited, twisted

πλέκω plait, twist; devise, contrive

πλεονάζω be more than enough; claim too much, presume on; (of a writer) be lengthy, tedious; exaggerate

πλεονάκις *adv* more frequently

πλεονεκτέω have more, claim more, be greedy; + *gen* be superior to, gain some advantage, overreach

πλεονέκτημα ατος τό ▸ **πλεονεξία**

πλεονέκτης (*gen* ου) **πλεονεκτικός** ή όν greedy, grasping; selfish

πλεονεξίᾱ ᾱς ἡ advantage, gain; superiority; greediness, grasping character, arrogance

πλέος ον ▸ **πλέως** *or* **πλήρης**

πλεύμων ονος ὁ ▸ **πνεύμων**

πλευρᾱ́ ᾶς ἡ rib; side; flank

πλευροκοπέω strike *or* break the ribs

πλευρόν οῦ τό ▸ **πλευρά**

πλευσ *likely to be from* **πλέω**

πλέω† sail, go by the sea; swim

πλέως ᾱ ων ▸ **πλήρης**

πληγή ῆς ἡ **πλῆγμα** ατος τό blow, stroke; wound; a drubbing; shock

πλῆθος ους τό mass, throng, crowd; the greater part, multitude; the people, mob; army; the popular assembly; size, length, magnitude

πληθῡ́νω make full, increase; *intr* ▸ **πληθύω**

πληθύω *and pass* **πλήθω** be *or* become full, abound, spread, swell

πληθώρη ης ἡ abundance; satiety

πλήκτης ου ὁ brawler, someone who strikes out

πληκτίζομαι *mid* + *dat* fight, scuffle with

πλῆκτρον ου τό plectrum; spear-point, oar *or* paddle

πλημμέλεια ᾱς ἡ mistake in music, false note; offence, fault, error

πλημμελέω strike a false note; err; offend

πλημμελής ές striking a false note; erring; offending

πλημ(μ)υρίς ίδος ἡ flood

πλήμνη ης ἡ hub of a wheel

πλήν *adv and prep with gen* more than; except; besides

πλήξιππος ον driving *or* working horses

πλήρης ες full, filled with; well-provided; satisfied, satiated; complete

πληροφορέω fill up, fulfil; assure, persuade fully

πληροφορίᾱ ᾱς ἡ fullness; full conviction

πληρόω make full, fill; man [a ship]; complete, supply; satiate; perform

πλήρωμα ατος τό **πλήρωσις** εως ἡ a filling up; manning; complement; crew, equipment; satiety, fullness; whole sum

πλησ *likely to be from* **πίμπλημι**

πλησιάζω *usu + dat* approach; converse, associate with

πλησίος ᾱ ον near, close by

■ **πλησίον** *adv + gen or dat* near, close to

■ **ὁ πλησίος** neighbour, fellow man

πλησιόχωρος ον neighbouring; neighbour

πλησίστιος ον swelling the sails

πλησμονή ῆς ἡ satiety, repletion

πλήσσω strike, smite, beat, hit; wound; strike back, drive away; frighten, trouble; *mid* beat oneself

πλινθεῖον ου τό brick-kiln, brickworks

πλινθεύω make into bricks; make bricks; build of bricks

πλινθηδόν *adv* in the shape of bricks

πλίνθινος η ον of bricks

πλινθίον ου τό small brick

πλίνθος ου ἡ brick

πλίσσομαι *mid* stride

πλοῖον ου τό ship, vessel

πλόκαμος ου ὁ **πλόκος** ου ὁ braid, lock of hair

πλόος ου ὁ (*also* πλοῦς οῦ ὁ) voyage; time *or* wind for sailing

πλούσιος ᾱ ον rich, wealthy

πλουτέω be rich

πλουτίζω πλουτιῶ enrich

πλουτοκρατίᾱ ᾱς ἡ government by the wealthy, plutocracy

πλοῦτος ου ὁ wealth, riches; treasure, plenty; the god of riches

πλοχμός οῦ ὁ ▸ **πλόκαμος**

πλυνός οῦ ὁ washing trough, tank *or* pit

Πλυντήρια ων τά washing festival; at Athens, in which the clothes of Athena's statue were washed

πλῡ́νω πλυνῶ ἔπλῡνα wash, cleanse

πλωΐζω sail on the sea

πλώϊμος ον **πλώσιμος** ον **πλωτός** ή όν navigable; sea-worthy; floating

πλώω ▸ **πλέω**

πνείω ▸ **πνέω**

πνεῦμα ατος τό wind, air; breath; life, spirit, mind; inspiration; ghost, spiritual being; Holy Spirit

πνευματικός ή όν spiritual, divine

πνεύμων ονος ὁ lungs

πνέω πνεύσομαι ἔπνευσα blow, breathe; exhale, smell; pant; *pass* be prudent *or* wise; have a (high etc.) spirit

πνῑγηρός ᾱ́ όν stifling, hot

πνῖγος ους τό stifling heat

πνῑ́γω stifle, choke, throttle; stew; *pass* be drowned

πνῑκτός ή όν stifled, strangled

πνο(ι)ή ῆς ἡ ▸ **πνεῦμα**

πόᾱ ᾱς ἡ grass, fodder; meadow; summer

ποδαβρός όν tender-footed

ποδᾱγός οῦ ὁ guide

ποδανιπτήρ ῆρος ὁ basin for washing the feet

ποδάνιπτρον ου τό water for washing the feet

ποδαπός ή όν of what country?

ποδάρκης ες swift-footed (of Achilles)

ποδεών ῶνος ὁ end, extremity

ποδηγός όν ▸ **ποδαγός**

ποδηνεκής ές reaching to the feet

ποδήνεμος ον swift as the wind (of Iris)

ποδήρης ες ▸ **ποδηνεκής**

ποδίζω tie the feet (of)

ποδώκεια ᾱς ἡ swiftness of foot

ποδώκης ες quick of foot

ποθεινός ή όν longed for, desired

πόθεν *adv* from what place? from where? why? how? where?

ποθεν *enclitic adv* from anywhere

ποθέω long for, desire; miss, regret

ποθή ῆς ἡ ▸ **πόθος**

πόθι, ποθι ▸ **ποῦ, που**

πόθος ου ὁ + *gen* desire, longing for; regret; want

ποῖ *adv* to where?

ποι *enclitic adv* to somewhere

ποίᾱ ᾱς ἡ ▸ **πόα**

ποιέω make, do, produce, bring about, cause, effect; perform, build, accomplish, execute; create, beget; compose, write, represent in poetry; be active; *mid* make for oneself; hold, reckon, esteem

ποίη ης ἡ ▸ **πόα**

ποιήεις εσσα εν grassy, rich in grass

ποίημα ατος τό work, piece of workmanship; instrument; poem, book

ποίησις εως ἡ a making, creating; poetry, poem

ποιητής οῦ ὁ maker, creator; poet

ποιητικός ή όν capable of making, productive; poetic

ποιητός ή όν made, fabricated; well-made

ποιηφαγέω eat grass

ποικιλίᾱ ᾱς ἡ being multi-coloured *or* variegated; embroidery; diversity, versatility

ποικίλλω variegate, colour; embroider; embellish, adorn; speak equivocally, mince matters

ποίκιλμα ατος τό ▸ **ποικιλία**

ποικιλομήτης (*gen* ου) full of various devices

ποικίλος η ον coloured, pied, dappled, worked in various colours; changeful, various, varying, variegated; intricate, ambiguous; cunning

ποικιλόστολος ον with variegated robe; (of a ship) with variegated prow

ποικιλῳδός όν singing riddles

ποιμαίνω ποιμανῶ be a shepherd; keep *or* feed a flock; guide, govern; tend; *pass* graze

ποιμήν ένος ὁ shepherd; ruler

ποίμνη ης ἡ flock, herd

ποιμνήϊος ᾱ ον of a flock *or* herd

ποίμνιον ου τό ▸ **ποίμνη**

ποινή ῆς ἡ ransom; requital, vengeance; penalty, punishment

ποίνιμος ον avenging, punishing

ποῖος ᾱ ον of what nature? of what kind?

ποιπνῡ́ω pant, gasp; hasten, bustle

ποιώδης ες ▸ **ποιήεις**

πόκος ου ὁ shorn-off wool, fleece, tuft of wool

πολεμαρχεῖον ου τό residence of a polemarch

πολεμαρχέω be a polemarch

πολεμαρχίᾱ ᾱς ἡ office of a polemarch

πολέμαρχος ου ὁ polemarch (at Athens, in earlier times the general-in-chief, later the third archon who presided in the court in which cases involving μέτοικοι were tried)

πολεμέω make war; wage war on

πολεμήϊος ᾱ ον ▸ **πολεμικός**

πολεμησείω wish for war

πολεμίζω ▸ **πολεμέω**

πολεμικός ή όν **πολέμιος** ᾱ ον of *or* for war, warlike, hostile
■ **οἱ πολέμιοι** enemy, adversary
■ **ἡ πολεμική** art of war
■ **τὸ πολεμικόν** signal for battle
■ **τὰ πολεμικά, τὰ πολέμια** matters of war, hostilities

πολεμιστής οῦ ὁ warrior

πολεμόνδε *adv* to the war

πολεμο-ποιέω cause war

πόλεμος ου ὁ war, fight, battle

πολεμόω make hostile; *mid* make someone an enemy; *pass* be made an enemy

πολεύω turn up [the soil] with a plough; wander about

πολιάς άδος ἡ guardian of the city (of Athena)

πολίζω found, build a city

πολιήτης ου ὁ ▸ **πολίτης**

πόλινδε *adv* to the city

πολιοκρόταφος ον with grey hair on the temples

πολιορκέω besiege, beleaguer; harass, pester

πολιορκίᾱ ᾱς ἡ siege

πολιός ά όν grey, white

πολιοῦχος ον protecting a city

πόλις εως ἡ city, town; (at Athens) the acropolis; city state; body of citizens

πόλισμα ατος τό ▸ **πόλις**

πολῑτάρχης ου ὁ ruler of the city *or* state

πολῑτείᾱ ᾱς ἡ **πολῑ́τευμα** ατος τό right of a citizen, citizenship; life of a citizen; government, administration; policy, constitution; democracy; commonwealth

πολῑτεύω be a citizen, live in a free state, have a certain form of government; administer public affairs; *act, mid and pass* govern, administer; be a politically active citizen; *pass* be governed

πολῑ́της ου ὁ citizen; fellow-citizen

πολῑτικός ή όν of *or* for a citizen; constitutional, civic, politic, public
■ **ὁ πολῑτικός** statesman
■ **ἡ πολῑτική** science of politics

πολῖτις ιδος ἡ female citizen

πολίχνη ης ἡ small town

πολλάκις *adv* many times, often

πολλαπλάσιος ᾱ ον **πολλαπλασίων** ον many times as many

πολλαχῇ, πολλαχῆ *adv* often; in many ways

πολλαχόθεν *adv* from many places

πολλαχόσε *adv* to many sides

πολλαχοῦ ▸ **πολλαχῇ**

πολλός όν ▸ **πολύς**

πολλοστός ή όν little, slight, the smallest, least

πόλος ου ὁ axis, pole; firmament; sundial

πολύαινος ον much-praised

πολυᾱ́ϊξ (*gen* ῑκος) impetuous

πολυανδρέω be populous

πολυανθής ές much-blossoming

πολυανθρωπίᾱ ᾱς ἡ multitude of people

πολυάνθρωπος ον populous

πολυάργυρος ον rich in silver

πολυᾱ́ρητος ον much prayed for, much-desired

πολυαρκής ές sufficient

πολυάρματος ον with many chariots

πολύαρνι *dat only* with many flocks

πολυαρχίᾱ ᾱς ἡ government by the many

πολυβενθής ές very deep

πολύβουλος ον rich in counsel

πολυβούτης (*gen* ου) rich in cattle

πολυγηθής ές delightful, much-cheering

πολύγλωσσος ον with many tongues; slanderous

πολυγονίᾱ ᾱς ἡ fecundity

πολυγόνος ον producing many at birth, prolific

πολυδαίδαλος ον very skilful

πολυδάκρυος ον **πολυδάκρῡτος** ον **πολύδακρυς** υ much-wept; weeping greatly

πολυδειράς (*gen* άδος) with many ridges

πολύδενδρος ον with many trees

πολύδεσμος ον with many bonds

πολυδίψιος ον very thirsty

πολύδωρος ον well-dowered

πολυειδής ές of many shapes

πολύευκτος ον much-desired

πολύζηλος ον much-beloved, much-desired; full of envy

πολύζυγος ον with many benches

πολυηγερής ές assembled in crowds

πολυήρατος ον lovely

πολυηχής ές much resounding

πολυθαρσής ές very bold

πολυθρῡ́λητος ον much spoken of, notorious

πολύθυτος ον with many sacrifices

πολυιδρείη ης ἡ extensive knowledge

πολύιδρις (*gen* ιος) rich in knowledge, knowing much

πολύιππος ον rich in horses

πολυκαγκής ές drying *or* parching exceedingly

πολυκαρπίᾱ ᾱς ἡ rich crop

πολύκαρπος ον rich in fruit

πολυκέρδεια ᾱς ἡ great cunning

πολυκερδής ές very crafty

πολύκερως ων many-horned (of beasts)

πολύκεστος ον richly embroidered

πολυκηδής ές very sorrowful

πολυκλήῑς (*gen* ῖδος) **πολυκληῗς** (*gen* ῗδος) with many oars

πολύκληρος ον with large inheritance

πολύκλητος ον called from many sides

πολύκλυστος ον much-dashing stormy; washed by many a wave

πολύκμητος ον wrought with much toil

πολύκνημος with many mountain spurs, mountainous

πολύκοινος ον common to many

πολυκοιρανίᾱ ᾱς ἡ rule by the many

πολυκτήμων ον very wealthy

πολύκωπος ον with many oars

πολυλήϊος ον with many cornfields

πολύλλιστος ον sought with many prayers

πολυλογίᾱ ᾱς ἡ much talk, loquacity

πολύλογος ον talkative, verbose

πολυμαθής ές knowing much

πολυμερῶς *adv* in many ways

πολυμηκάς (*gen* άδος) much-bleating

πολύμηλος ον rich in flocks

πολύμητις (*gen* ιος) of many counsels, much-devising

πολυμηχανίᾱ ᾱς ἡ inventiveness

πολυμήχανος ον inventive

πολύμνηστος ον much-wooed

πολύμοχθος ον with much toil

πολύμῡθος ον talkative

πολύξενος ον very hospitable; visited by many

πολύξεστος ον much polished

πολύοινος ον rich in wine

πολυοψίᾱ ᾱς ἡ abundance of meat *or* food

πολυπαίπαλος ον crafty, cunning

πολυπᾱ́μων ον wealthy

πολυπειρίᾱ ᾱς ἡ great experience

πολυπενθής ές very mournful

πολυπῖδαξ (*gen* ακος) with many springs

πολύπικρος ον very bitter *or* keen

πολύπλαγκτος ον **πολυπλάνητος** ον much-wandering

πολύπλοκος ον tangled, intricate

πολυποίκιλος ον much-variegated

πολύπονος ον laborious, painful

πολύπους (*gen* ποδος) many-footed; octopus, polypus

πολυπρᾱγμονέω be very busy; be meddlesome *or* officious; intrigue

πολυπρᾱγμοσύνη ης ἡ being busy with many things; meddling, overcuriousness; quarrelsomeness

πολυπρᾱ́γμων ον busy with things; meddling, officious, curious; quarrelsome

πολυπρόβατος ον rich in sheep

πολύπτυχος ον with many valleys

πολύπῡρος ον rich in wheat

πολύρραφος ον much-stitched

πολύρρην (*gen* ηνος) **πολύρρηνος** ον rich in flocks

πολύρρυτος ον much-flowing

πολύς πολλή πολύ much, many, frequent; large, ample, spacious, long; heavy, strong, mighty

■ **πλείων** ον (*also* πλέων ον) *comp* more, more numerous; larger, stronger

■ **πλεῖστος** η ον *sup* most, very much

■ **οἱ πολλοί** the majority, the many, the people

■ **οἱ πλείονες** the greater part, majority; the democrats

■ **οἱ πλεῖστοι** the greatest number

■ **τὸ πλέον** the greater part, advantage, profit

■ **πολύ, πολλά** *adv* much, very; often; far, by far; very much

πολυσαρκίᾱ ᾱς ἡ fleshiness

πολυσῑτίᾱ ᾱς ἡ abundance of corn

πολύσκαρθμος ον much-springing, swift

πολυσπερής ές widely spread

πολύσπλαγχνος ον very compassionate

πολυστάφυλος ον rich in grapes

πολυστεφής ές with many wreaths

πολύστονος ον much-sighing

πολύσχιστος ον much-split, many-branching

πολυτέλεια ᾱς ἡ great expense, sumptuousness

πολυτελής ές costly, expensive, sumptuous

πολυτῑ́μητος ον **πολύτῑμος** ον **πολύτῑτος** ον much valued, costly

πολύτλᾱς (*gen* αντος) **πολυτλήμων** ον much-enduring, persevering

πολύτλητος ον unfortunate, having endured much

πολυτρήρων ον with many doves

πολύτρητος ον with many holes, porous

πολυτροπίᾱ ᾱς ἡ versatility

πολύτροπος ον versatile, ingenious; crafty; manifold; much-wandering

πολυφάρμακος ον knowing many drugs

πολύφημος ον with many voices; much talked of

πολύφθορος ον full of destruction

πολύφλοισβος ον loud-roaring

πολύφορβος ον nourishing many

πολυφροσύνη ης ἡ great understanding

πολύφρων ον very wise, ingenious

πολύχαλκος ον rich in copper *or* bronze

πολύχειρ (*gen* ειρος) many-handed

πολυχειρίᾱ ᾱς ἡ plenty of hands

πολυχρόνιος ον lasting long

πολύχρῡσος ον rich in gold

πολυψηφίᾱ ᾱς ἡ number *or* diversity of votes

πολυψήφῑς (*gen* ῑδος) with many pebbles

πολυώνυμος ον with many names; famous

πολυωπός όν close-meshed

πόμα ατος τό drink

πομπαῖος ᾱ ον escorting

πομπείᾱ ᾱς ἡ jeering, ribaldry, buffoonery

πομπεύς έως ὁ ▸ **πομπός**

πομπεύω conduct, escort, attend; lead a procession; abuse with ribald jeers

πομπή ῆς ἡ a sending, an escorting, conduct, escort; a sending home; solemn procession

πόμπιμος ον ▸ **πομπαῖος** escorting, guiding; sent

πομπός οῦ ὁ/ἡ one who escorts, guide; messenger

πονέω *and mid intr* toil, work hard, be busy; be worn out, suffer, be distressed, feel pain; *tr* work at, perform zealously; gain by toil

πονηρίᾱ ᾱς ἡ badness, wickedness

πονηρός ᾱ́ όν bad, wicked, villainous; useless, ill, distressed, painful, dangerous

πόνος ου ὁ toil, drudgery, hard work, hardship; battle; distress, pain, suffering, grief, misery; result of labour, work

ποντίζω plunge into the sea

πόντιος ᾱ ον of *or* in the sea; *noun* lord of the sea

ποντόθεν *adv* from the sea

πόντονδε *adv* into the sea

πόντος ου ὁ sea, open sea
■ **ὁ Πόντος** the Black Sea

πόποι *int exclamation of surprise, anger or pain* ah! strange! shame!

πόρδαλις ▸ **πάρδαλις**

πορείᾱ ᾱς ἡ journey, march, way, expedition; a walking, gait; manner of life

πορεῖν *aor infin from* **πόρω** give, offer, furnish, bestow, grant
■ **πέπρωται** *pf* it has been fated *or* allotted

πορεύω bring, carry, convey, furnish; *pass* be carried; go, walk, march, travel; pass over, traverse

πορθέω destroy, waste, plunder

πορθμεῖον ου τό ferry, ford; ferry-boat; passenger's fare

πορθμεύς έως ὁ ferryman

πορθμεύω *act tr* carry *or* ferry over; *act intr and pass* be carried over

πορθμός οῦ ὁ passage; ford, strait; ferry

πορίζωποριῶ bring, conduct, convey; furnish, provide, supply; contrive, fabricate; *mid* get for oneself, procure; provide from one's own means

πόριμος ον rich in resources; inventive

πόρις ▸ **πόρτις**

πορισμός οῦ ὁ means of acquiring; means of gain

ποριστής οῦ ὁ provider, purveyor

ποριστικός ή όν able to procure

πόρκης ου ὁ ring, ferrule

πορνείᾱ ᾱς ἡ fornication; prostitution; idolatry

πορνεῖον ου τό brothel

πορνεύω *and mid* fornicate

πόρνη ης ἡ prostitute

πόρνος ου ὁ fornicator

πόρος ου ὁ passage; ford, strait, bridge, thoroughfare, way for ships; sea, river; means of achieving, resource, income, revenue

πόρπᾱξ ᾱκος ὁ handle

πόρπη ης ἡ pin, clasp, brooch

πόρρω *adv and prep with gen* forwards, onwards, further; far off, afar; before, in future; far towards; far from; far into

πόρρωθεν *adv* from far away; from long ago

πορσαίνω, πορσῦνω πορσυνῶ make ready, provide, procure; offer, present, give

πόρσω ▸ πόρρω

πόρταξ ακος ἡ **πόρτις** ιος ἡ heifer, calf

πορφύρᾱ ᾱς ἡ purple, purple-fish; purple cloth

πορφύρεος ᾱ ον (*also* πορφυροῦς ἡ οῦν) purple, purple-coloured; dark-red, bloody; bright, shining

πορφυρεύς έως ὁ fisher for purple-fish; purple-dyer

πορφυρόπωλις ιδος ἡ dealer in purple

πορφῦρω gleam darkly, heave, be agitated

ποσάκις *adv* how often?

πόσε *adv* where ... to?

πόσις[1] ιος *or* εως ἡ a drinking; drink; drinking bout

πόσις[2] εως ὁ husband

πόσος η ον how much? how great?

ποσσῆμαρ *adv* how many days?

ποσσίκροτος ον beaten by the feet

πόστος η ον which of a number?

ποταίνιος ᾱ ον new, fresh; unheard of

ποτάμιος ᾱ ον of *or* on a river

ποταμόνδε *adv* into the river

ποταμός οῦ ὁ river, stream; canal

ποταμοφόρητος ον carried away by a river

ποτάομαι *pass* fly, flit

ποταπός ή όν ▸ **ποδαπός**

πότε *adv* when?

ποτε enclitic *adv* at any time, once; sometimes

ποτέομαι ▸ πέτομαι

πότερος ᾱ ον which of the two?; either of the two
■ **πότερον** ... **ἤ** (whether) ... or

ποτέρωθι *adv* on which of two sides?

ποτέρως *adv* in which of two ways?

ποτέρωσε *adv* to which of two sides?

ποτή ῆς ἡ a flying, flight

ποτήριον ου τό drinking-cup

ποτής ῆτος ἡ drink

ποτητός ή όν winged
■ **τὸ ποτητόν** bird

ποτί ▸ πρός

ποτιβάλλω ▸ προσβάλλω

ποτίζω give to drink; water

πότιμος ον fit to drink; sweet

πότμος ου ὁ lot, destiny, fate; misfortune; death

πότν(ι)α ᾱς ἡ mistress; revered, august, noble

ποτόν οῦ τό drink, beverage; liquid, water

πότος ου ὁ a drinking; drinking bout

ποτός ή όν for drinking

ποττώς ▸ ποτὶ τώς, πρὸς τούς

ποῦ *adv* where? in what manner?

που enclitic *adv* anywhere; at any time; I suppose, perhaps

πουλυβότειρα ᾱς ἡ nourishing many

πουλύπους ▸ πολύπους

πουλύς ύ ▸ **πολύς**

πούς ποδός ὁ foot, hoof, talon; lower corner of a sail, tightening rope, sheet; gait, course; race; (unit of distance) foot

πρᾶγμα ατος τό **πρᾶξις** εως ἡ a doing, deed, transaction; action; fact, occurrence, matter, circumstance; business, task, enterprise; affair, object; condition; difficulty, annoyance, intrigue; reality; public *or* private affairs, state affairs, public business, government, politics; matter of consequence; effect, issue, success, profit

πρᾱγματείᾱ ᾱς ἡ employment, business; pursuit, diligent study, diligence; written work, history

πρᾱγματεύομαι *mid and pass* be busy, pursue a business; take in ⋯

hand, carry on; execute, accomplish, work out

πρᾶγος εος τό ▸ **πρᾶγμα**

πραιτώριον ου τό the praetorium, hall of the praetor *or* governor; encampment of the imperial bodyguard

πρᾱκτικός ή όν fit for action *or* business; active, busy, able, energetic

πρᾱ́κτωρ ορος ὁ doer, worker; tradesman; an official who executes a judgement for debt (especially public debt), bailiff; tax-collector; avenger

πρᾱνής ές bent forward, head-foremost; down-hill, steep

πρᾶξις εως ἡ ▸ **πρᾶγμα**

πρᾶος πρᾱεῖα πρᾶον soft, mild; gentle, kind, even-tempered

πρᾱότης ητος ἡ meekness, mildness, gentleness, patience

πραπίς ίδος ἡ midriff, diaphragm; understanding, mind, heart

πρασιᾱ́ ᾶς ἡ bed in a garden, garden-plot

πρᾱ́σιμος ον for sale

πρᾶσις εως ἡ sale

πράσον ου τό leek

πρᾱ́σσω† *act tr* pass through; effect, achieve, do, work; win, gain; manage, practise, adminster, transact; demand, exact [money]; *act intr* be in a certain state *or* condition; fare; *mid* do *or* exact for oneself, earn [money]

πρᾱτός ή όν for sale

πρᾱΰνω πρᾱυνῶ ἐπρᾱ́ῡνα soften, soothe

πρᾱϋπάθεια ᾱς ἡ **πρᾱΰτης** ητος ἡ ▸ **πραότης**

πρᾱΰς εῖα ύ ▸ **πρᾶος**

πρέμνον ου τό bottom of the trunk of a tree, trunk, stump

πρεπόντως *adv* in a fit manner, decently, beseemingly

πρέπω be conspicuous, distinguished *or* seen; be manifest; resemble

■ **πρέπει** + *dat* it is fitting for, it suits *or* becomes

πρεπώδης ες decent, proper, becoming

πρέσβα ης ἡ aged, august

πρεσβείᾱ ᾱς ἡ embassy; primogeniture, rank, dignity

πρεσβεῖον ου τό privilege; gift of honour

πρέσβευσις εως ἡ ▸ **πρεσβεία**

πρεσβευτής οῦ ὁ ambassador

πρεσβεύω be older *or* the eldest; take precedence, be superior, rule over; be an ambassador; send ambassadors; honour, revere, worship; mediate as an amabassador; *mid* send ambassadors; be an ambassador

πρεσβυγένεια ᾱς ἡ being first-born

πρεσβυγενής ές first-born

πρέσβυς έως ὁ old man, elder; someone revered *or* honoured

■ **οἱ πρεσβύτεροι** elders, chiefs, ancestors

■ **οἱ πρέσβεις** ambassadors

πρεσβυτέριον ου τό council of elders

πρεσβῦ́της ου ὁ ▸ **πρέσβυς**

πρεσβῦτις ιδος ἡ old woman

πρῆγμα etc *see* **πρᾶγμα**

πρήθω *aor* ἔπρησα blow out; swell out; kindle, burn

πρηκτήρ ▸ **πράκτωρ**

πρηνής ▸ **πρανής**

πρῆξις ▸ **πρᾶξις**

πρῆσις ▸ **πρᾶσις**

πρήσσω ▸ **πράσσω**

πρηστήρ ῆρος ὁ flash of lightning

πρητήριον ου τό trading-place

πρηϋ- ▸ **πρᾱϋ-**

πρίασθαι infin of aor ἐπριάμην *from* **ὠνέομαι** buy, purchase

πρίζω ▸ **πρίω**

πρίν *adv* before, formerly, first, sooner; *conj* before

■ **ὁ πρίν** ancient, former, of old

πρῑστός ή όν sawn

πρῑ́ω saw, saw up *or* asunder; seize with the teeth, hold fast

πρῑ́ων ονος ὁ saw

πρό *adv and prep with gen* before, in front; beforehand, sooner; outside; in defence of, in favour of, for; instead of, in lieu of; in comparison with

προάγγελσις εως ἡ early summons

προ-αγορεύω tell beforehand, prophesy, forewarn; publish, proclaim publicly; ordain in advance, order, command

προ-άγω lead on *or* forward; carry forward, bring on; induce, persuade; promote, advance; go on, advance, proceed, lead the way

προάγων ωνος ὁ preliminary contest; introduction

προ-αγωνίζομαι *mid* fight before

προ-αδικέω be the first to do wrong

προ-αιδέομαι *pass + dat* be indebted *or* under obligation to [someone] for a favour

προαίρεσις εως ἡ free choice; purpose; plan, mode; party, sect

προαιρετός ή όν deliberately chosen

προ-αιρέω bring forward; prefer; *mid* choose for oneself, prefer; intend, purpose

προ-αισθάνομαι *mid* perceive before, know beforehand

προ-αιτιάομαι *mid* accuse beforehand

προ-ακούω hear before

προαλής ές abrupt

προ-αμαρτάνω sin before

προ-αμῡ́νομαι *mid* defend oneself beforehand

προανα-βαίνω go up before

προαν-άγομαι *mid* put to sea before

προ-αναισιμόω, προ-ανᾱλίσκω spend *or* use up before

προαναχώρησις εως ἡ a going away before

προ-απαντάω meet before

προαπ-έρχομαι depart first

προαπο-θνῄσκω die before

προαπ-όλλῡμι destroy before; *pass* perish before

προαπο-πέμπω, προαπο-στέλλω send away first *or* before

προαπο-τρέπομαι *mid* leave off before

προαπο-φαίνομαι *mid* show first, declare before

προαπο-χωρέω go away before

προ-αρπάζω snatch up first

προάστ(ε)ιον ου τό suburb, environs

προαύλιον ου τό vestibule

προαφ-ικνέομαι *mid* arrive first *or* before

προαφ-ίσταμαι *mid* revolt before; leave off before

προ-βαίνω step forward, advance, make progress, go on; elapse; grow older; go before, be superior (to)

προ-βάλλω throw before, down *or* away; put forward, propose, oppose; stake, pledge, venture; *mid* put before oneself, hold before oneself as a defence; use a pretence, allege; throw away, abandon; propose for election; surpass

πρόβασις εως ἡ cattle

προβατικός ή όν of *or* for sheep

προβάτιον ου τό little sheep

πρόβατον ου τό cattle; flock, sheep

προ-βιβάζω bring forward; lead on; incite beforehand

προ-βλέπομαι *mid* provide for

πρόβλημα ατος τό projection, cape; guard, defence, shelter, bulwark; armour, spear; excuse, pretext; problem

προβλής (*gen* ῆτος) projecting; headland

πρόβλητος ον thrown away

προ-βλώσκω come forth (from), go out of

προ-βοάω shout before, cry out

προ-βοηθέω come to help before

προβόλαιος ου ὁ spear

προβολή ῆς ἡ **πρόβολος** ου ὁ ▸ **πρόβλημα** a putting forward [of a weapon for defence]; defence, attack; preliminary impeachment (a legal process in which the plaintiff appealed to the ἐκκλησία to support his suit before bringing it into court)

προβοσκός οῦ ὁ assistant herdsman

προβούλευμα ατος τό preliminary decree *see* **προβολή**

προ-βουλεύω consult, consider before; frame a preliminary decree *see* **προβολή**; provide for; *mid* consider first

πρόβουλος ου ὁ a commissioner to examine measures before they were proposed to the people

προγενής ές born before, old, ancient, aged

προ-γίγνομαι *mid* be born before; happen before; come forward, appear

προ-γιγνώσκω know *or* learn beforehand; decide beforehand

πρόγνωσις εως ἡ foreknowledge

πρόγονος ον born before, elder; ancestor, forefather

προ-γράφω write before; write in public

προ-δαῆναι *infin* know before

προ-δείδω fear beforehand

προ-δείκνῡμι show by way of example, point out; point before one; publish beforehand

προ-δειμαίνω fear beforehand

προδέκτωρ ορος ὁ presignifier, foreshower

πρόδηλος ον manifest beforehand, known to all

προ-δηλόω show future things

προδια-βαίνω go across before

προδια-βάλλω slander beforehand

προδια-γιγνώσκω consider before

προδια-φθείρω destroy *or* ruin beforehand

προ-διδάσκω teach beforehand

προ-δίδωμι give *or* pay in advance; give up, betray, forsake, abandon; *intr* desert, turn traitor; fail

προδι-ηγέομαι *mid* relate beforehand

πρόδικος ου ὁ advocate, guardian (of a young king at Sparta)

προ-διώκω pursue further

προ-δοκεῖ
■ **προ-δέδοκται** *pf* it was resolved beforehand

προδοκή ῆς ἡ place where one lies in wait, lurking-place

πρόδομος ον in front of the house

προδοσίᾱ ᾱς ἡ treachery

προδότης ου ὁ traitor; runaway

προδοτικός ή όν traitorous

πρόδοτος ον betrayed, abandoned

προδρομή ῆς ἡ a running forward

πρόδρομος ον running before, forerunner; scout, vanguard; skirmisher

προεδρίᾱ ᾱς ἡ presidency, precedence; the privilege of the front seats (at games, plays and public assemblies, bestowed on distinguished foreigners and citizens)

πρόεδρος ου ὁ president
■ **οἱ πρόεδροι** (at Athens) the presiding officers of the βουλή *or* ἐκκλησία

προ-εέργω obstruct by stepping in the way

προ-εθίζω accustom beforehand

πρό-ειμι[1] ▸ **προέρχομαι**

πρό-ειμι[2] be before

προ-εἰπόν *see* **προαγορεύω**

προεισ-άγω bring in before

προεισορφᾱ́ ᾶς ἡ advance payment of property tax

προεκ-θέω run out before

προεκ-κομίζω carry out before

προεκ-λέγω collect [money] in advance

προεκφόβησις εως ἡ an intimidating in advance

προ-ελαύνω *act intr and pass* ride forward, advance

προ-ελπίζω hope before

προεμ-βάλλω make an inroad, attack before

προεν-άρχομαι begin before

προ-εννέπω pronounce aloud

προενοίκησις εως ἡ a dwelling in before

προεξ-αγγέλλω announce beforehand

προεξ-άγω bring out first

προεξ-ᾱΐσσω, προεξ-ᾴσσω rush out before

προεξαν-ίστημι *act intr and mid* rise before others *or* too soon; start first

προεξέδρᾱ ᾱς ἡ chair of state

προέξ-ειμι, προεξ-έρχομαι go out before

προεξ-ορμάω start before

προεπ-αγγέλλω *and mid* promise before

προεπ-αινέω praise before

προεπανα-σείω menace before

προεπι-χειρέω attack first

προ-εργάζομαι *mid* do *or* work before; earn before

προ-ερέσσω row forward

προ-ερύω draw on *or* forward

προ-έρχομαι go forth, on *or* forward; advance; appear in public; pass; proceed, start; go first

προετικός ἡ όν prodigal, lavish

προ-ετοιμάζω prepare

προ-ευαγγελίζομαι *mid* bring glad tidings beforehand

προ-έχω *act tr* hold before; have before; know beforehand; have in preference to; *act intr* project, jut out; be before, be the first, superior, eminent; *mid* hold out before oneself, hold out as a pretext; offer

■ **οὐ προέχει** it is not better

προηγεμών όνος ὁ guide

προ-ηγέομαι *mid* go before *or* forward, lead the way; be the leader

προηγητής οῦ ὁ ▸ **προηγεμών**

προ-ηγορέω speak for others

προήκης ες pointed in front

προ-ήκω have advanced; be the first *or* superior

προθέλυμνος ον having several layers; from the root

πρόθεσις εως ἡ exhibition; purpose, design

προθέσμιος ᾱ ον appointed, fixed before

■ **ἡ προθεσμίᾱ** term, period, limitation

προ-θέω[1] run forward

προ-θέω[2] ▸ **προτίθημι**

προ-θνῄσκω die before

προ-θρῴσκω leap forward

προ-θῡμέομαι *pass* be willing, ready, eager *or* zealous; desire, endeavour

προθῡμίᾱ ᾱς ἡ willingness, readiness; zeal, wish, desire; good will

πρόθῡμος ον ready, willing; eager, earnest, zealous; well-disposed

πρόθυρον ου τό front door; space in front of a door; porch, entry

προ-θύω *and mid*

προ-ϊάλλω, προ-ϊάπτω send forth, dismiss

προ-ΐζομαι *mid* take the first seat

προ-ΐημι send before, on *or* forward; dismiss, let go; forsake, abandon, throw away; deliver over; allow; *mid* utter, pronounce; devote oneself (to); offer, present; entrust; allow, suffer; abandon, throw away, neglect

προΐκτης ου ὁ beggar

προΐξ προικός ἡ (*also* προίξ) gift, present, dowry

■ **προῖκα** *adv* freely, without return

προ-ΐστημι *act tr* place before *or* in front; *act intr and pass* place oneself before, stand before; be opposed to; protect, guard; approach, entreat; be at the head (of), be set over, be the chief, manage, govern; place before oneself; prefer

προ-ΐσχω ▶ **προέχω**

πρόκα *adv* at once, suddenly

προκάθ-ημαι *mid* sit before; protect, defend

προκαθ-ίζω *and mid* sit down before, in front *or* in public

προκαθ-ίστημι *and mid pf* be placed before

προκαθ-οράω view beforehand

προ-καίω burn before

προ-καλέω, προ-καλίζω call forth; *mid* challenge; summon, incite, invite; offer, propose; cause, effect

προ-καλινδέομαι ▶ **προκυλίνδομαι**

προκάλυμμα ατος τό curtain, covering; screen; pretext

προ-καλύπτω hang before as covering; *mid* veil *or* screen oneself; pretend

προ-κάμνω toil before; grow weary beforehand; work for another

προκατ-αγγέλλω announce beforehand

προκατα-γιγνώκσω accuse *or* condemn beforehand

προκατα-καίω burn before

προκατα-λαμβάνω seize *or* occupy beforehand, anticipate; prevent

προκατα-λέγω describe beforehand

προκατα-λύω break up *or* annul before

προκατ-αρτίζω make ready before

προκατ-άρχομαι *mid* begin first

προκατα-φεύγω escape before

προκατ-έχω occupy *or* take possession of before

προκατ-ηγορέω accuse beforehand

προκατηγορίᾱ ᾱς ἡ previous accusation

πρό-κειμαι *mid* lie before; be placed before (someone); (of a child) lie exposed; jut out; be set before *or* in front of; be proposed

προ-κήδομαι *mid* + *gen* take care of

προ-κηραίνω be anxious

προ-κηρύσσω proclaim publicly

προ-κινδῡνεύω run the first risk; fight as a champion; defend

προ-κῑνέω move forward

προ-κλαίω weep beforehand *or* aloud

πρόκλησις εως ἡ challenge; summons, proposal

προ-κλῑ́νω lean forward

πρόκλυτος ον far-famed; heard formerly, of olden times

προ-κομίζω bring forward

προκοπή ῆς ἡ progress, growth

προ-κόπτω *act tr* promote; *act intr and pass* advance, thrive

πρόκριμα ατος τό preference

προ-κρῑ́νω choose before, prefer; judge, decide; *pass* be preferred *or* thought superior

πρόκροσσος (η) ον ranged in rows

προ-κυλίνδομαι, προ-κυλινδέομαι *mid* be rolled forward; prostrate oneself

προκύπτω stoop and bend forward, peep out

προ-λαμβάνω take (away) beforehand, before *or* first; obtain first, anticipate; claim before, prefer; apprehend, surprise

προ-λέγω foretell, prophesy; tell publicly, proclaim; choose before

προ-λείπω leave, forsake; omit; *intr* cease, disappear

προ-λεσχηνεύομαι *mid* discuss orally before (with someone *dat*)

προ-λεύσσω see at a distance, foresee

προ-λοχίζω ambush, lay an ambush before

προ-μανθάνω learn before; continue learning

προμαντείᾱ ᾱς ἡ precedence in consulting an oracle

πρόμαντις εως ὁ/ἡ prophetic; prophet, priest

προ-μαρτύρομαι *mid* witness beforehand

προ-μαχέω, προ-μαχίζω *and mid* **προ-μάχομαι** fight in front *or* as a champion

προμαχεών ῶνος ὁ rampart; bulwark

πρόμαχος ον fighting before *or* in front; fighting for

προ-μελετάω practise beforehand

προ-μεριμνάω be careful before, take thought before

προμετωπίδιον ου τό skin of the forehead; front-piece (for horses)

προμήθεια ᾱς ἡ foresight; care

προμηθέομαι *pass* consider *or* take care (of) beforehand

προμηθής ές cautious, caring

προμηθίᾱ ᾱς ἡ ▸ **προμήθεια**

προ-μηνύω inform beforehand

προ-μῑ́γνυμαι *pass* have intercourse with beforehand

προ-μνάομαι *mid* woo for another; try to obtain, solicit

προμνηστῖνοι αι α one by one, one after the other

προμνήστρια ᾱς ἡ **προμνηστίς** ίδος ἡ match-maker

προ-μολεῖν *aor infin from* **προβλώσκω**

πρόμος ου ὁ foremost, leader, prince; champion

πρόνᾱος ον ▸ **προνήϊος**

προ-ναυμαχέω + *gen* fight at sea for *or* in defence of

προ-νέμομαι *mid* gain ground

προνήϊος ᾱ ον before a temple

■ **ὁ προνήϊος** vestibule *or* hall of a temple, through which one went to the ναός

προ-νηστεύω fast beforehand

προ-νῑκάω conquer beforehand

προ-νοέω *and pass* perceive beforehand, presage; consider, care *or* think beforehand; provide

προνοητικός ή όν provident, cautious

πρόνοια ᾱς ἡ foresight, forethought; providence; purpose, intention; care

προνομή ῆς ἡ a foraging; an elephant's trunk

πρόνοος ον (*also* πρόνους ουν) cautious, prudent

πρόξ προκός ἡ roe deer, fawn

πρόξεινος ου ὁ ▸ **πρόξενος**

προ-ξενέω be a public guest; be a protector *or* patron; negotiate, manage, procure; recommend

προξενίᾱ ᾱς ἡ being a πρόξενος (see next entry)

πρόξενος ου ὁ/ἡ agent of a foreign state (who enjoyed his privileges on the condition of entertaining and assisting the ambassadors and citizens of the state which he represented), consul, resident; public guest *or* host; patron

προξυγ-γίγνομαι *mid* meet with beforehand

πρόοδος ου ἡ going before, advance

πρό-οιδα *pf* know before

προ-οιμιάζομαι *mid* make a preamble

προ-οίμιον ου τό prelude, preamble, preface, introduction; hymn

προ-όμνῡμι swear before

προ-ομολογέω agree beforehand

πρόοπτος ον seen from afar, manifest

προ-οράω look forward; see before *or* from afar; foresee; provide for, consider beforehand; take care, be cautious

προ-ορίζω determine beforehand

π

προ-ορμάω *and pass* start forward *or* in advance

προ-ορμίζω moor in front

προ-οφείλω owe from a former time; *pass* be in arrears

πρόοψις εως ἡ a previous seeing

πρόπαππος ου ὁ great-grandfather

προπαρα-βάλλομαι *mid* put in rows beforehand

προπαρα-σκευάζω make ready beforehand

προπαρ-έχω offer before; *mid* provide oneself before

προπάροιθεν *adv and prep with gen* in front of, before, forward(s); along

πρόπᾱς ᾶσα αν all, altogether

προ-πάσχω suffer before

προπάτωρ ορος ὁ forefather, ancestor

πρόπειρα ᾱς ἡ previous trial

προ-πέμπω send before, in advance, on *or* forth; afford, offer; send away, dismiss; conduct, escort; pursue

προπέτεια ᾱς ἡ rashness, impetuosity

προπετής ές falling forward(s), prostrate; ready; rash, prone, hasty

προ-πηλακίζω cover with mud; maltreat, abuse, reproach

προπηλακισμός οῦ ὁ insulting treatment

προ-πῑ́νω drink to someone *dat*; give *or* trifle away

προ-πῑ́πτω, προ-πίτνω fall forward; rush forward; prostrate oneself

προ-πλέω sail before

πρόπλοος ον (*also* πρόπλους ουν) sailing before

προ-ποδίζω step forward

προ-ποιέω do beforehand; prepare

προ-πολεμέω + *gen* fight for

πρόπολος ου ὁ/ἡ servant in a temple, priest, priestess

προπομπός οῦ ὁ/ἡ escorting, carrying (especially in a procession); escort, attendant

προ-πονέω work beforehand; work *or* toil for; *mid* suffer on

πρόπονος ου ὁ previous toil

προ-πορεύομαι *pass* go forward

προπρηνής ές bent forward; lying on one's face

προπρο-κυλίνδομαι roll on and on *or* to and fro

προπύλαιον ου τό **πρόπυλον** ου τό entry, porch, vestibule

■ **τὰ προπύλαια** the gateway of Egyptian and Greek temples

προ-πυνθάνομαι learn *or* hear before

προ-ρέω flow forward

πρόρρησις εως ἡ previous announcement; order

πρόρρητος ον foretold, ordered

πρόρριζος ον by the roots; utterly, root and branch

πρός *adv* besides, over and above; *prep with acc* towards, to, upon; against, in answer to; in regard to; according to; in proportion to; in relation to; *with gen* from, from forth, from the side of; on the side of, against, towards; on the part of, in presence of, before; according to; suiting; by [a god]!; *with a passive verb* ▶ **ὑπό**; *with dat* at, on, near, hard by, in the presence of; in addition to, besides

προσάββατον ου τό eve of the Sabbath

προσ-αγορεύω address, accost, greet; call by name; speak, utter

προσ-άγω *act tr* bring on; lead on, induce; add, supply, introduce; *act intr* advance, approach; *mid* attach to oneself, win over; induce

προσαγωγή ῆς ἡ a bringing on; admission, access; solemn procession

προσαγωγός όν attractive

προσ-ᾴδω sing to; agree, consent

προσ-αιρέομαι *mid* choose in addition to

προσ-ᾱΐσσω rush to

προσ-αιτέω ask besides; beg of

προσ-ακούω hear besides

προσ-αλείφω smear upon

προσ-αμῡ́νω defend, come to aid

προσανα-βαίνω go up *or* mount besides

προσ-αναγκάζω force besides

προσαν-αιρέομαι *mid* undertake besides

προσ-αναισιμόω, προσ-ανᾱλίσκω spend *or* consume besides

προσανα-πληρόω fill up *or* replenish besides; fill up by addition

προσανα-τίθεμαι *mid* take on oneself in addition; consult with; unbosom oneself

προσάν-ειμι go up to

προσαν-ειπεῖν *aor infin* announce besides

προσαν-έχω approach

προσάντης ες up-hill, steep; arduous, adverse, hostile

προσαπ-αγγέλλω report besides

προσ-απειλέω threaten besides

προσαπο-βάλλω lose besides

προσαπο-γράφω denounce besides

προσαπο-δείκνῡμι prove besides

προσαπ-όλλῡμι, προσαπ-ολλύω *act tr* destroy *or* kill besides; *act intr and mid* perish besides

προσαπο-στέλλω send off besides

προσ-άπτω *act tr* attach *or* fasten to; add, attribute, grant; *act intr* be added; *mid* touch, lay hold of

προσ-αραρίσκω join, fit to

προσ-αρκέω + *dat* lend aid (to), assist

προσ-αρμόζω attach, fit to

προσ-αρτάω fasten, join to

προ-σάσσω store up in advance

προσ-αυδάω accost, call by name

προσ-αύω burn partly

προσαφ-ικνέομαι *mid* arrive besides

προσαφ-ίστημι cause to revolt besides

προσ-βαίνω go towards, up *or* to; come near, step on; attack

προσ-βάλλω *act tr* throw to *or* upon; apply to, affix; add, assign; thrust, hit, shine upon; offer, present; *act intr and mid* throw oneself upon; approach, attack; come to land; strike against; contribute

πρόσβασις εως ἡ access, ascent

προσβατός ή όν accessible

προσ-βιάζομαι *pass* be pressed towards

προσ-βιβάζω bring *or* convey to

προσ-βλέπω look at *or* on

προσ-βοάομαι *mid* call to oneself, call in

προσ-βοηθέω come to aid

προσβολή ῆς ἡ a throwing upon; a falling upon, attack, assault; landing; landing-place (for ships)

προσ-βωθέω ▸ **προσβοηθέω**

προσ-γελάω smile upon

προσ-γίγνομαι *mid* + *dat* come to; attach oneself to; be present; arrive; happen to

προσ-γράφω add in writing

προσ-δανείζω lend in addition

πρόσδεγμα ατος τό reception

προσ-δεῖ + *gen* there is still need of

προσ-δέομαι *pass* + *gen* need besides; ask besides

προσ-δέρκομαι *pass* look at; look around

προσ-δέχομαι *mid* receive, accept; admit; wait for, expect; suppose

προσ-δέω[1] tie to

προσ-δέω[2] *see* **προσδεῖ** *also* **προσδέομαι**

π

προσ-δηλέομαι *mid* ruin besides

προσδια-λέγομαι *pass* converse with besides

προσδια-φθείρω destroy besides

προσ-δίδωμι give besides

προσ-δοκάω ▸ **προσδέχομαι**

προσ-δοκέω seem besides, be thought besides

προσδοκίᾱ ᾱς ἡ expectation, anticipation

προσδόκιμος ον expected

προσ-εάω let approach

προσ-εγγίζω approach

προσεγ-γράφω inscribe besides

προσεδρείᾱ ᾱς ἡ blockade, siege

προσ-εδρεύω + *dat* sit near; adhere, be in regular attendance, keep to

πρόσεδρος ον enclosing

προσ-εικάζω make like, liken

προσείκελος η ον resembling

προσ-ειλέω press against

πρόσ-ειμι[1] ▸ **προσέρχομαι**

πρόσ-ειμι[2] be near, by *or* at; be added *or* attached; be there, belong to

προ-σείω hold out and shake; hold out [fear, etc.] as a bugbear

προσεκ-βάλλω expel besides

προσεκτικός ή όν attentive

προσ-ελαύνω drive *or* ride towards

προσεμ-βαίνω trample upon

προσεμ-πικραίνομαι *pass* be angry all the more

προσεμφερής ές resembling

προσ-εννέπω accost, greet

προσεξ-αιρέομαι *mid* select for oneself besides

προσ-έοικα *pf with pres meaning* resemble, be like; be fitting *or* seemly

προσεπεξ-ευρίσκω invent besides

προσεπι-κτάομαι *mid* acquire besides

προσεπι-λαμβάνομαι join in

προσεπι-στέλλω command besides

προσ-εργάζομαι *mid* effect *or* acquire besides; make *or* earn in addition

προσ-ερεύγομαι *mid* belch *or* vomit at *or* against; (of waves) break foaming against

προσ-έρπω creep on, approach

προσ-έρχομαι *mid* go *or* come up, to *or* forward; approach; mount; visit; advance, attack; (of money) come in

προσ-ερωτάω question besides

προσ-εταιρίζομαι *mid* take as a comrade

προσεταιριστός ή όν taken as a comrade, belonging to the same ἑταιρεία *or* club

προσέτι *adv* besides

προσ-ευρίσκω find besides

προσευχή ῆς ἡ prayer; place of prayer, chapel

προσ-εύχομαι *mid* pray to *or* for

προσεχής ές adjoining, close to

προσ-έχω hold to, bring to, direct to; bring to land; devote oneself to, be attached to; have besides; *mid* attach oneself to, cling to; be implicated in

■ **προσέχω τὸν νοῦν** + *dat* turn one's mind *or* attention to; attend, give heed

προσ-ζημιόω punish into the bargain

προσ-ηγορέω accost, greet; console

προσηγορίᾱ ᾱς ἡ addressing; a naming, title

προσήγορος ον addressing, accosting; imploring; accosted

προσ-ήκω have arrived, be near; reach to; concern, affect

■ **προσήκει** + *dat* it belongs to *or* concerns; it befits *or* is proper (for)

προσήκων ουσα ον belonging to; befitting, proper; related, akin

προσ-ηλόω nail to

προσήλυτος ου ὁ a newcomer, stranger, proselyte

πρόσ-ημαι *usu + dat* sit close to, lie near

προ-σημαίνω announce before, order

προσηνής ές kind, gentle; suitable

προσ-θᾱκέω sit beside

πρόσθεν *adv and prep with gen* in front of, before, to the front, forwards, further; in defence of; formerly, of old
■ **ὁ πρόσθεν** the front-rank man
■ **τὸ πρόσθεν, τὰ πρόσθεν** the front, vanguard, place in front

πρόσθεσις εως ἡ an adding; a putting on

προσ-θέω run to

προσθήκη ης ἡ addition, supplement, appendix; assistance

προσ-θιγγάνω *+ gen* touch

πρόσθιος ᾱ ον the foremost

προσ-ιζάνω, προσ-ίζω sit on, by *or* near

προσ-ῑ́ημι admit; *mid* allow to approach; admit, allow, approve, accept

προσίκελος ον ▸ **προσείκελος**

προσ-ιππεύω ride up to

προσ-ίστημι *act tr* place near; *act intr and mid* stand near *or* beside; arrive at; enter one's mind

προσ-ίσχω ▸ **προσέχω**

προσκαθ-έζομαι, προσκάθ-ημαι, προσκαθ-ίζω sit near *or* beside; besiege; keep to

πρόσκαιρος ον transitory

προσ-καλέω call to *or* on, summon; *mid* call to help; call into court

προσ-καρτερέω persevere still longer; adhere to

προσκατα-λείπω leave behind; lose besides

προσκατ-ηγορέω accuse besides

πρόσ-κειμαι *+ dat* lie near *or* upon; be joined with, involved in, added *or* imposed; belong to; be attached *or* devoted to; press close *or* hard

προ-σκέπτομαι *mid* ▸ **προσκοπέω**

προσκεφάλαιον ου τό pillow, cushion

προσκηδής ές affectionate; allied to

προσ-κηρῡκεύομαι *mid* send a herald to

προσ-κληρόομαι *pass* be associated with, keep company with

πρόσκλησις εως ἡ citation, summons

προσ-κλῑ́νω lean against; *pass* attach oneself to

πρόσκλισις εως ἡ inclination, predilection *+ dat*

προσ-κνάομαι *mid* rub oneself against

προσ-κολλάω glue to; *pass* cleave to

προσ-κομίζω carry, convey to

πρόσκομμα ατος τό stumble; offence, fault; scandal

προ-σκοπέω *and mid* see *or* consider beforehand; provide against

προσκοπή[1] ῆς ἡ a spying beforehand

προσκοπή[2] ῆς ἡ ▸ **πρόσκομμα**

προσ-κόπτω stumble; take offence

προσ-κρούω *+ dat* strike against; offend; take offence

προσ-κτάομαι *mid* gain *or* acquire besides

προσ-κυλῑ́ω roll to

προσ-κυνέω prostrate oneself before; worship

προσκυνητής οῦ ὁ worshipper

προσ-κυρέω, προσ-κύρω befall, meet with

πρόσκωπος ον rowing; rower

προσ-λαλέω speak to

προσ-λαμβάνω *and mid* take hold of; take with one *or* to oneself; receive besides *or* in addition; win besides

προσ-λεύσσω look at *or* on

προσ-λέχομαι *mid* lie near

πρόσληψις εως ἡ reception

προσ-λογίζομαι *mid* reckon in addition to

προσ-μάσσω knead (one thing) to *or* with (another)

προσ-μάχομαι *mid* + *dat* attack

προσ-μένω abide, remain; wait for

προσμετα-πέμπομαι *mid* send for besides

προσ-μῑ́γνῡμι, προσ-μῑγνύω (*also* προσ-μείγνῡμι) mix to; join to; *intr* unite oneself to; approach, arrive at, land; meet in battle

πρόσμῑξις εως ἡ approach, assault

προσ-μίσγω ▸ **προσμίγνυμι**

προσ-μισθόομαι hire besides

προσ-ναυπηγέω build still more ships

προσ-νέμω *and mid* attribute; devote, assign

προσ-νέω swim towards

προσ-νίσσομαι *mid* go to, come near

προσ-νωμάω move to

πρόσοδος ου ἡ an approaching, advance, attack; public appearance; solemn procession; path; income, revenue; return, profit

πρόσ-οιδα *pf* know besides

προσ-οικέω dwell by *or* near

προσ-οικοδομέω build in addition

πρόσοικος ον dwelling near to; neighbour

προσ-ολοφῡ́ρομαι *mid* + *dat* complain to

προσ-ομῑλέω + *dat* converse with; busy oneself with

προσ-όμνῡμι swear in addition

προσ-ομολογέω concede, grant *or* agree to besides; surrender

προσόμουρος ον + *dat* neighbouring

προσ-οράω *and mid* look at, behold

προσ-ορέγομαι *pass* entreat earnestly + *dat of person entreated*

προσ-ορμίζω anchor near; *pass and mid* put to shore

προσόρμισις εως ἡ a landing

πρόσο(υ)ρος ον adjoining; neighbour

προσ-ουδίζω dash to the earth

προσ-οφείλω, προσ-οφλισκάνω owe besides; incur *or* deserve besides

προσ-οχθίζω + *dat* be indignant with

προσόψιος ον visible

πρόσοψις εως ἡ sight; view; appearance

προσ-παίζω + *dat* make fun of, play *or* jest with

προσπαρα-καλέω call in besides

προσπαρα-σκευάζω prepare besides

προσπαρ-έχω furnish besides

προσ-πασσαλεύω nail to

προσ-πάσχω suffer besides

πρόσπεινος ον very hungry

προσ-πελάζω *act tr* bring near (to); *act intr and pass* approach

προσ-πέμπω send to

προσπερι-βάλλω put around besides; *mid* seek to obtain still more

προσ-περονάω fasten by means of a pin, fix to

προσ-πέτομαι *mid* fly, rush to

προσ-πεύθομαι *mid* ▸ **προσπυνθάνομαι**

προσ-πήγνῡμι fix to

προσ-πίλναμαι *mid* ▸ **προσπελάζω**

προσ-πῑ́πτω + *dat* fall against *or* upon; run up to; attack, assault; attach oneself to; fall in with, encounter; happen, occur; + *acc* fall down before one, supplicate

προσ-πίτνω ▸ **προσπίπτω**

προσ-πλάζω strike against

προσ-πλάσσω form *or* mould upon

προσ-πλέω + *dat* sail against

προσ-πληρόω fill up, complete; man besides

προσπλωτός ή όν navigable

προσ-πλώω ▸ **προσπλέω**

προσ-ποιέω add to; *mid* add to oneself; take to oneself, pretend, lay claim to; appropriate, arrogate; pretend, allege

προσποίησις εως ἡ acquisition, addition; claim, pretence

προσ-πολεμέω make war against

προσ-πολεμόομαι *mid* make an enemy of [someone]

προσ-πολέω attend, serve + *dat*; *pass* be escorted by a train of attendants

πρόσπολος ον serving; servant, attendant

προσ-πορεύομαι *pass* go near

προσ-πορίζω procure besides

προσ-πταίω strike against; stumble; fail, suffer defeat *or* loss

προσ-πτύσσω *mid* fold oneself close to, cling close round; entreat, solicit; embrace, treat kindly, greet

προσ-πυνθάνομαι *mid* inquire besides

προσ-ρέω flow up to

προσ-ρήγνῡμι dash against

πρόσρησις εως ἡ an addressing; a naming

πρόσσοθεν *adv* forwards

προσ-σταυρόω ▸ **προσταυρόω**

προσ-στείχω step towards

προσ-στέλλω fit to
■ **προσεσταλμένος** tight; plain, modest

προσσυμ-βάλλομαι *mid* contribute to besides

πρόσσω ▸ **πόρρω**

πρόσταγμα ατος τό **πρόσταξις** εως ἡ command, order

προσ-ταλαιπωρέω + *dat* persevere *or* persist still longer in

προστασίᾱ ᾱς ἡ a leading, governing, presidency; administration

προσ-τάσσω place to *or* beside; assign, appoint, ascribe; array; + *dat* order, ordain, enjoin

προστατείᾱ ᾱς ἡ ▸ **προστασία**

προ-στατεύω, προ-στατέω + *gen* be at the head (of), govern; manage; (of time) be close at hand

προστατήριος ᾱ ον protecting

προστάτης ου ὁ front-rank man; protector, defender, patron; leader, chief, ruler, head; suppliant

προστάτις ιδος ἡ protectress

προ-σταυρόω construct a palisade in front of *or* along

προσ-τειχίζω include within a wall

προ-στείχω go forward, advance

προσ-τελέω pay *or* spend besides

προ-στέλλω send forward; *pass* go forward

προστερνίδιον ου τό breastplate (for horses)

προσ-τήκομαι *pass* + *dat* stick fast to

προσ-τίθημι put to, upon *or* in front; enjoin, command, impose; attribute, impute; deliver; procure; apply to; add; join to; *mid* associate oneself, join; agree to; take to oneself; add for oneself

προσ-τρέπω *and mid* supplicate

προσ-τρέχω run to

προστρόπαιος ον suppliant

προστροπή ῆς ἡ entreaty, prayer

πρόστροπος ον ▸ **προστρόπαιος**

προσ-τυγχάνω obtain one's share of + *gen*; meet with by chance + *dat*

προστῷον ου τό portico

προσσυγ-γίγνομαι ▸ **προξυγγίγνομαι**

προσυμ-μίσγω intermix first

προσυν-οικέω live together before

προσφάγιον ου τό additional food; something to eat

πρόσφατος ον freshly-slain; fresh, new

προσφερής ές + *dat* resembling; serviceable

προσ-φέρω bring *or* carry to, upon *or* near; set before one; offer, furnish, provide; add, increase; apply to; *mid and pass* approach, come near; converse; rush against, attack; deal with, treat; behave oneself; take to oneself, eat; give besides

πρόσ-φημι *and mid* speak to

προσ-φθέγγομαι *mid* speak to, address

πρόσφθεγκτος ον addressed

πρόσφθεγμα ατος τό address, salutation

προσφιλής ές dear, beloved; pleasing; kind, friendly

προσ-φοιτάω go regularly to

προσφορᾱ́ ᾶς ἡ gift, present, offering; addition, increase

προσ-φορέω ▸ **προσφέρω**

πρόσφορος ον useful, suitable, expedient

προσφυής ές growing upon; natural; fitted

προσ-φύω *intr and mid* grow upon; cling to

προσ-φωνέω call in; address, greet

προσφώνημα ατος τό address, salutation

πρόσχημα ατος τό outward, show, ornament; pretence, screen, pretext

προσ-χόω heap up besides; choke up with earth, throw earth against; form by a dam

προσ-χράομαι *mid* + *dat* employ besides, use

προσ-χρῄζω, προσ-χρηΐζω require *or* desire besides

πρόσχυσις εως ἡ a sprinkling

προσ-χωρέω approach; be like; accede, consent, agree to; yield, surrender

πρόσχωρος ον adjoining, neighbouring

πρόσχωσις εως ἡ a heaping up, mound

προσ-ψαύω + *dat* touch

πρόσω ▸ **πόρρω**

πρόσωθεν *adv* from afar

προσωπο-ληπτέω be a respecter of persons

προσωπολήπτης ου ὁ respecter of persons

προσωποληψίᾱ ᾱς ἡ respect of persons

πρόσωπον ου τό face, countenance, mien; look, appearance, figure; mask (worn by actors); person

προσ-ωφελέω + *acc or dat* help, assist

προσ-ωφέλησις εως ἡ assistance, help

προ-ταλαιπωρέω suffer beforehand

προταμιεῖον ου τό ante-room of a store-room

προ-τάμνω ▸ **προτέμνω**

προ-ταρβέω fear beforehand

προ-ταρῑχεύω salt beforehand

προ-τάσσω place in front; determine beforehand

προ-τείνω stretch out *or* forward, put forward; offer, expose; pretend, promise, feign; *mid* claim, demand; pretend

προτείχισμα ατος τό outwork

προ-τελέω pay in advance

προτεραῖος ᾱ ον of *or* on the day before

προτερέω be before, in front *or* beforehand; take the lead, gain an advantage

πρότερος ᾱ ον before, forward, in front; sooner, earlier; former, older; higher, superior

■ **πρότερον** *adv* formerly, before, sooner

■ **προτέρω** *adv* further, forwards

προ-τεύχω make *or* do beforehand

προτί ▸ **πρός**

προ-τίθημι place before, prefer; set out, propose, expose, put forth, ···

present; fix; permit, allow; impose, lay to one's charge; exhibit, show, publish, ordain; bring under discussion; *mid* put before oneself; put forward on one's own part; pretend; purpose; put out publicly, proclaim, announce; prefer, offer

προ-τῑμάω *and mid* honour (something/someone *acc*) more than *or* above (something/someone *gen*), prefer, distinguish; *pass* be preferred in honour

προτί̄μησις εως ἡ preference

προτι-μῡθέομαι *mid* speak to

προ-τῑμωρέω help beforehand; *mid* revenge oneself before

προτι-όσσομαι look at; presage

προ-τίω ▶ **προτιμάω**

πρότμησις εως ἡ waist

προ-τολμάω venture before

πρότονος ου ὁ rope of the stay-sail

προτρεπτικός ή όν persuasive, admonishing

προ-τρέπω turn *or* urge forward; impel, exhort, persuade, compel; *mid* turn oneself to, devote oneself to; turn in headlong flight; exhort

προ-τρέχω run forward; outrun

πρότριτα *adv* three days before, for three successive days

προτροπάδην *adv* turned forward(s), headlong

προ-τύπτω burst forward

προὐννέπω ▶ **προ-εννέπω**

προὐξεφ-ί̄εμαι command beforehand

προ-υπάρχω be beforehand, begin with; exist before

προὖπτος ον ▶ **πρόοπτος**

προυσελέω maltreat, insult

προ-φαίνω show forth, bring to light, display; predict, foreshadow, promise; *pass* appear from afar, come to light; appear before

πρόφαντος ον foreshown, foretold

προ-φασίζομαι *mid* use as a pretence, allege, prevaricate

πρόφασις εως ἡ pretence, pretext, evasion, excuse; cause, motive; suggestion

προφερής ές preferred, excellent; older

προ-φέρω bring to, before *or* forward; produce; declare, proclaim; present, propose; throw (reproaches) in someone's teeth; *intr* surpass, exceed, be beforehand

προ-φεύγω flee forward(s); escape

προφητεί̄ᾱ ᾱς ἡ prophecy; the gift of expounding scripture, of speaking and of preaching

προφητεύω be a prophet *or* interpreter of oracles; prophesy

προφήτης ου ὁ prophet, interpreter of oracles, seer, foreteller

προφητικός ή όν prophetic

προφῆτις ιδος ἡ prophetess

προ-φθάνω outrun, anticipate, be beforehand

προ-φράζω foretell; say openly

πρόφρασσα *fem from* **πρόφρων**

πρόφρων ον kindly; willing; hearty; earnest

προφυλακή ῆς ἡ guard in front, outpost

προφυλακίς ίδος ἡ (a) look-out (ship)

προφύλαξ ακος ὁ advanced guard

προ-φυλάσσω keep guard before *or* in front; be on guard; *mid* guard oneself, ward off

προ-φυτεύω beget, plant before

προ-φύω *intr* be born before

προ-φωνέω proclaim publicly

προ-χειρίζομαι *mid* take into one's hand, choose, appoint, decree; make ready; *pass* be arranged *or* ready before

πρόχειρος ον at hand, ready; easily procured; common; cheap

προ-χειροτονέω choose *or* elect before

προ-χέω pour forth *or* out; *pass* be poured out; stream forth

πρόχνυ *adv* kneeling; precipitously

προχοή ῆς ἡ a pouring out; mouth of a river

πρόχοος ου ὁ (*also* πρόχους ου ὁ) pitcher, jug

προ-χρίω smear before

πρόχυσις εως ἡ a pouring *or* spreading out; deposit (of mud, silt, etc.) by a river

προ-χωρέω go forward, advance; make progress, succeed

προ-ωθέω thrust *or* push forward

προωλής ές ruined beforehand

πρυλέες έων οἱ foot-soldiers, champions

πρύμνα ης ἡ (*also* πρύμνη ης ἡ) stern, poop

πρύμνηθεν *adv* from the stern

πρυμνήσια ων τά ropes from a ship's stern

πρυμνός ή όν hindmost, endmost

πρυμνώρεια ᾱς ἡ foot of a mountain

πρυτανείᾱ ᾱς ἡ prytany, presidency (at Athens, a period of 35 or 36 days per year during which the πρυτάνεις of each tribe presided in the βουλή and ἐκκλησία); office of prytanis; chief command of the day

πρυτανεῖον ου τό town-hall, hall of the πρυτάνεις (see previous entry)

πρυτανικόν οῦ τό the work-place of the fifty πρυτάνεις, i.e. the tholos

πρύτανις εως ὁ prytanis, president (see πρυτανεία)

πρῴ ▸ **πρωί**

πρῳαίτερος, πρῳαίτατος *see* **πρώιος**

πρώην *adv* lately, just now; the day before yesterday

πρωθήβης (*gen* ου) *with fem* **πρωθήβη** in the first bloom of youth

πρωί, πρῴ *adv* early in the day; too early

πρωιζά ▸ **πρῴην**

πρώιμος ον **πρωινός** ή όν **πρώιος** ᾱ ον **πρῷος** ᾱ ον early, early in the day

πρωκτός οῦ ὁ arse

πρών πρῶνος ὁ headland; height

πρῷρα ᾱς ἡ fore-part of a ship, prow

πρῴρᾱθεν *adv* from the front

πρῳρεύς έως ὁ look-out man in a ship

πρωτεῖον ου τό first prize; first rank

πρωτεύω be the first, have precedence

πρώτιστος η ον first of all

πρωτόγονος ον first-born; high-born

πρωτοκαθεδρίᾱ ᾱς ἡ **πρωτοκλισίᾱ** ᾱς ἡ first seat

πρωτοπαγής ές newly built

πρωτόπλοος ον (*also* πρωτόπλους ουν) sailing for the first time; sailing first *or* foremost

πρῶτος η ον first, foremost, earliest, highest, noblest

■ **τὰ πρῶτα** the first prize *or* rank, highest degree, chief part

πρωτοστάτης ου ὁ front-rank man; file-leader; chief

πρωτοτόκια ων τά birthright, the right of the first-born

πρωτοτόκος ον giving birth for the first time

πρωτότοκος ον first-born

πταίρω ▸ **πτάρνυμαι**

πταῖσμα ατος τό stumble, false step; accident, failure, defeat

πταίω stumble (against); fail, make a mistake, undergo a mishap

πτᾱνός ή όν ▸ **πτηνός**

πταρμός οῦ ὁ sneezing

πτάρνυμαι *aor* ἔπταρον sneeze

πτελέᾱ ᾱς ἡ elm(-tree)

πτερίς ίδος ἡ fern

πτέρνα ης ἡ heel; ham

πτερόεις εσσα εν feathered, winged

πτερόν οῦ τό feather, wing; soaring, flight; augury, omen; anything like wings

πτερόω furnish with feathers *or* wings, feather

πτερύγιον ου τό little wing; pinnacle

πτέρυξ υγος ἡ ▸ **πτερόν**

πτερωτός ή όν ▸ **πτερόεις**

πτηνός ή όν feathered, winged; fledged; fleeing, swift; coy, bashful

πτήσσω *intr* crouch, cower; be frightened, tremble; flee; *tr* frighten, alarm, terrify

πτίλον ου τό feather; wing

πτίσσω ἔπτισα winnow [grain]; pound (in a mortar)

πτο(ι)έω ▸ **πτήσσω**

πτόησις εως ἡ **πτοίησις** εως ἡ fear; passion

πτολ- ▸ **πολ-**

πτολιπόρθιος ου ὁ **πτολίπορθος** ου ὁ destroyer of cities

πτόρθος ου ὁ shoot, branch

πτύγμα ατος τό a folding, fold

πτυκτός ή όν folded

πτύξ πτυχός ἡ fold; layer, plate (of metal *or* leather, used to form a shield); cleft; dell

πτύον ου τό winnowing shovel *or* fan

πτῦρω frighten, scare

πτύσμα ατος τό spittle

πτύσσω fold, fold up; *mid* be folded *or* doubled up

πτυχή ῆς ἡ ▸ **πτύξ**

πτῦω spit (out)

πτωκάς άδος ἡ ▸ **πτώξ**

πτῶμα ατος τό fall, ruin, disaster; corpse

πτώξ (*gen* πτωκός) cowering ■ **ὁ/ἡ πτώξ** hare

πτῶσις εως ἡ ▸ **πτῶμα**

πτωσκάζω, πτώσσω ▸ **πτήσσω**

πτωχείᾱ ᾱς ἡ begging, beggary

πτωχεύω be a beggar, be poor; get by begging

πτωχός ή όν beggarly, beggar

πῡγαργος ου ὁ white-rump (a kind of antelope)

πῡγή ῆς ἡ rump, buttocks

πυγμαῖος ᾱ ον of the size of a fist; pigmy

πυγμαχέω ▸ **πυκτεύω**

πυγμαχίη ης ἡ boxing

πυγμάχος ου ὁ ▸ **πύκτης**

πυγμή ῆς ἡ fist; a boxing

πυγούσιος ᾱ ον one cubit long (see next entry)

πυγών όνος ἡ elbow, cubit (the distance from the elbows to the first joint of the fingers)

πύελος ου ἡ bathing-tub; trough, sarcophagus

πυθ *aor stem from* **πυνθάνομαι**

πυθμήν ένος ὁ bottom, stand, base, foundation, root

πῡθω πύσω ἔπῡσα cause to rot; *pass* rot, decay

πῡθων ωνος ὁ ventriloquist

πύκα *adv* thickly; frequently; wisely

πυκάζω make thick *or* close; press together, shut up; cover thick, shelter; *intr* enwrap oneself

πυκιμήδης ες sensible, cautious

πυκινός ή όν ▸ **πυκνός**

πυκνί *dat from* **πνύξ**

πυκνόπτερος ον thick-feathered

πυκνός ή όν thick, close, compact, well-guarded; crowded; frequent; strong, well-made, great, mighty; careful, cautious, discreet

πυκνόστικτος ον thick-spotted

πυκνότης ητος ἡ thickness, closeness, compactness; sagacity, shrewdness

πυκνόω make thick, condense

πυκτεύω be a boxer

πύκτης ου ὁ boxer

πυκτικός ή όν skilled in boxing

πυλαγόρᾱς ου ὁ **πυλάγορος** ου ὁ delegate sent to the Amphictyonic council at Pylae

πυλ-αγορέω be a πυλαγόρας

πυλάρτης ου ὁ gate-keeper

πυλαωρός οῦ ὁ ▸ **πυλωρός**

πύλη ης ἡ gate, door, entrance, inlet; mountain-pass

πυλίς ίδος ἡ little gate

πύλος ου ὁ gateway

πυλουρός οῦ ὁ ▸ **πυλωρός**

πυλόω enclose with gates

πυλών ῶνος ὁ gateway, gate-house

πυλωρός οῦ ὁ/ἡ gatekeeper, guard

πύματος η ον uttermost, last

πυνθάνομαι† *mid* inquire, ask; hear, learn; understand, know

πύξ *adv* with the fist

πύξινος η ον of boxwood

πῦρ πυρός τό fire; lightning; fire-sign; fever; blaze

πυρᾱ́ ᾶς ἡ place where fire is kindled, funeral pyre, burial place

πυράγρᾱ ᾱς ἡ pair of fire tongs

πυρ-ακτέω make red-hot

πῡραμίς ίδος ἡ pyramid

πυργηδόν *adv* in masses

πυργο-μαχέω assail a tower

πύργος ου ὁ tower, towered wall; castle, fortress, bulwark; division *or* column of soldiers

πυργόω *mid* fence with towers; raise on high

πυργώδης ες like a tower

πύργωμα ατος τό ▸ **πύργος**

πυρεῖα ων τά contrivance to light a fire

πυρέσσω have a fever

πυρετός ή όν fever

πυρή ῆς ἡ ▸ **πυρά**

πῡρήν ῆνος ὁ stone of a fruit

πῡρηφόρος ον ▸ **πυροφόρος**

πυρίᾱ ᾱς ἡ vapour-bath

πυριήκης ες pointed in the fire

πυρίκαυστος ον burnt in the fire

πῡ́ρινος η ον of wheat

πύρινος η ον fiery

πυριφλεγής ές blazing with fire

πυρκαϊᾱ́ ᾶς ἡ funeral pyre; conflagration; stump of an olive tree

πύρνον ου τό wheaten bread

πῡρός οῦ ὁ wheat

πῡροφόρος ον wheat-bearing

πυρόω burn, waste with fire

πύρπνοος ον (*also* πύρπνους ουν) fire-breathing

πυρ-πολέω keep up a fire; waste with fire

πυρράζω (of the sky) be fiery-red

πυρρίχη ης ἡ war-dance

πυρρός ᾱ́ όν fire-coloured, red

πυρσεύω make fire signs

πυρσός[1] οῦ ὁ fire-brand; beacon

πυρσός[2] ή όν ▸ **πυρρός**

πυρφόρος ον fire-bearing, torch-bearing

πύρωσις εως ἡ fire, conflagration

πύστις εως ἡ an inquiring, asking; question, trial; report

πω enclitic *adv* yet, up to this time

πώγων ωνος ὁ beard

πωλέομαι *mid* wander about, go *or* come frequently

πωλέω† sell

πωλικός ή όν drawn by (young) horses

πωλο-δαμνέω break young horses

πῶλος ου ὁ foal; young animal, young girl, maiden, young man

πῶμα¹ ατος τό cover, lid

πῶμα² ατος τό drink, potion

πώποτε *adv* ever yet

πώρινος η ον made of tufa-stone

πῶρος ου ὁ tufa-stone

πωρόω petrify, harden

πώρωσις εως ἡ petrification, callousness, hardness of heart

πῶς *adv* how? in what way *or* manner?

πως enclitic *adv* in any way, somehow

πωτάομαι ▸ **πέτομαι**

πῶυ εος τό flock of sheep;

Ρρ

ρ, Ρ (ῥῶ) seventeenth letter of the alphabet ■ ρʹ *as a numeral* = 100

ῥά, ῥ' ▸ **ἄρα**

ῥαββ(ε)ί *Hebr* o master, o Rabbi

ῥαββουνί *Hebr* ▸ **ῥαββί**

ῥαβδίζω cudgel, flog

ῥαβδο-νομέω be an umpire

ῥάβδος ου ἡ rod, stick, wand, staff

ῥαβδοῦχος ου ὁ staff-bearer; umpire; lictor

ῥάβδωσις εως ἡ moulding (in architecture); fluting (of columns)

ῥαδινάκη ης ἡ petroleum

ῥαδινός ή όν slender, tender; swift

ῥᾴδιος ᾱ ον easy; ready, willing, compliant; heedless, reckless

ῥᾳδιούργημα ατος τό **ῥᾳδιουργίᾱ** ᾱς ἡ recklessness; laziness, indolence; wickedness, roguery

ῥαθαμίγξ ίγγος ἡ drop; grain

ῥαθαπῡγίζω give [someone] a slap on the buttocks

ῥᾳθῡμέω be idle *or* reckless

ῥᾳθῡμίᾱ ᾱς ἡ thoughtlessness, carelessness; laziness; easiness; recreation, amusement

ῥᾴθῡμος ον light-minded, careless; lazy; pleasure-seeking

ῥᾳΐζω grow easier, recover

ῥαίνω ῥανῶ ἔρρᾱνα sprinkle, besprinkle

ῥαιστήρ ῆρος ὁ/ἡ hammer

ῥαίω smash, shiver, shatter; *pass* be shattered; burst; be maltreated

ῥακά *Hebr* worthless fellow

ῥάκος ους τό rag, tatter; patch

ῥαντίζω sprinkle; cleanse, purify

ῥαντισμός οῦ ὁ a sprinkling, purification

ῥαπίζω cudgel, whip, slap in the face

ῥάπισμα ατος τό slap on the cheek

ῥαπτός ή όν sewed, stitched

ῥάπτω sew, stitch (together); contrive, plot

ῥᾳστώνη ης ἡ easiness, facility; readiness, cessation; relief, rest, ease; laziness

ῥαφανῑδόω thrust a radish up the arse

ῥαφανί̄ς ῖδος ἡ radish

ῥαφή ῆς ἡ seam

ῥαφίς ίδος ἡ needle

ῥᾱχίᾱ ᾱς ἡ surf, surge, breakers; coast

ῥαχίζω cut through the spine, cut in two

ῥάχις εως ἡ back; backbone

ῥαψῳδέω recite poems

ῥαψῳδός οῦ ὁ rhapsode, reciter of poems; singing, reciting

ῥέγκω (*also* ῥέγχω) snore, snort

ῥέδη ης ἡ wagon

ῥέεθρον ου τό ▸ **ῥεῖθρον**

ῥέζω ῥέξω ἔρρεξα do, act, work, make, effect, accomplish; sacrifice

ῥέθος εος τό limb; face

ῥεῖα *adv* easily, lightly

ῥεῖθρον ου τό river, stream; bed of a river

ῥέπω incline downwards; preponderate, prevail; incline towards

ῥεῦμα ατος τό flow, stream, river, flood; discharge; volcanic eruption

ῥέω ῥυήσομαι *and pass* flow, stream, run, gush; fall *or* drop off, melt away

ῥῆγμα ατος τό a breaking, fracture; downfall

ῥηγμῑ́ν ῖνος ἡ ▸ **ῥαχία**

ῥήγνῡμι† break, break in pieces, rend, smash; let break loose

ῥῆγος εος τό carpet, blanket, coverlet

ῥηῐ̈́διος ᾱ ον ▸ **ῥᾴδιος**

ῥηκτός ή όν to be broken *or* rent

ῥῆμα ατος τό word, saying, phrase; verb; thing

ῥηξηνορίη ης ἡ a breaking through ranks of warriors

ῥηξήνωρ (*gen* ορος) breaking through the ranks of warriors

ῥῆσις εως ἡ a saying, speaking, mode of speech; ▸ **ῥῆμα**

ῥήσσω ῥήξω ἔρρηξα tear, rend, break; beat with the feet, dance

ῥητήρ ῆρος ὁ ▸ **ῥήτωρ**

ῥητορεύω be a public speaker

ῥητορικός ή όν oratorical, rhetorical

ῥητός ή όν said, spoken; settled, determined, concerted; to be told

ῥήτρᾱ ᾱς ἡ speech; agreement, treaty; maxim, law, statute

ῥήτωρ ορος ὁ orator, public speaker; statesman; politician; rhetorician; a public speaker in the ἐκκλησία at Athens

ῥῑγεδανός ή όν causing shudders

ῥῑγέω shudder with cold, be chill; shudder at, shrink from

ῥῑ́γιον, ῥῑ́γιστος *see* **ῥῖγος**

ῥῖγος ους τό frost, cold
■ **ῥῑ́γιον** *comp adv* more frostily; more horribly
■ **ῥῑ́γιστος** *sup adj*

ῥῑγόω be cold, shiver

ῥίζα ης ἡ root; stem, origin; family

ῥιζόω let strike root; plant; *pass* be firmly rooted

ῥίμφα *adv* lightly, swiftly

ῥιμφάρματος ον with a swift chariot

ῥῑ́νη ης ἡ (tool) file

ῥῑνόν οῦ τό **ῥῑνός** οῦ ἡ skin, hide, leather; shield

ῥῑνοτόρος ον piercing shields

ῥίον ου τό peak, promontory

ῥῑπή ῆς ἡ throw, flight, swing; rushing motion; impetus

ῥῑπίζω fan [a flame]; *pass* be blown about

ῥῖπος εος τό reed mat, wicker hurdle

ῥῑπτάζω throw to and fro

ῥῑ́πτω, ῥῑπτέω ῥίψω ἔρριψα throw, cast *or* hurl down, out, away, forth, *or* to and fro

ῥῑ́ς ῥῑνός ἡ nose; *pl* nostrils

ῥῑ́ψ ῥῑπός ἡ wicker-work, mat

ῥῑψοκίνδυνος ον foolhardy

ῥοδανός ή όν waving, flickering

ῥοδοδάκτυλος ον rosy-fingered (of Dawn)

ῥοδόεις εσσα εν of roses, rose-coloured

ῥόδον ου τό rose

ῥοή ῆς ἡ ▸ **ῥόος**

ῥοθέω roar, rush, buzz, murmur

ῥόθιος ον roaring, rushing
■ **τὸ ῥόθιον** surf

ῥόθος ου ὁ a roaring *or* rushing noise

ῥοιᾱ́ ᾶς ἡ pomegranate tree

ῥοιβδέω swallow down

ῥοῖβδος ου ὁ a roaring, hissing, whizzing

ῥοιζέω whistle, whizz

ῥοιζηδόν *adv* with a rushing noise

ῥοῖζος ου ὁ ▸ **ῥοῖβδος**

ῥομφαίᾱ ᾱς ἡ large sword

ῥόος ου ὁ stream, current; flood, wave

ῥόπαλον ου τό club, stick, cudgel, mace; knocker of a door

ῥοπή ῆς ἡ inclination downwards, turn of the scale; turning-point, crisis, decision, result; weight, momentum, push, impetus

ῥόπτρον ου τό ▸ **ῥόπαλον**

ῥοῦς οῦ ὁ ▸ **ῥόος**

ῥοφέω sip greedily; swallow down

ῥοχθέω roar

ῥοώδης ες flowing, surging

ῥύᾱξ ᾱκος ὁ stream that bursts forth; stream of lava

ῥυδόν *adv* in streams; abundantly

ῥυθμίζω ῥυθμιῶ bring into proportion; order, arrange; govern, educate, train

ῥυθμός οῦ ὁ measure, rhythm; proportion, harmony, symmetry; form, shape

ῥῦμα ατος τό string of a bow; bow-shot; protection, deliverance

ῥῦμη ης ἡ swing, impetus; attack, force; street

ῥῡμός οῦ ὁ pole of a carriage

ῥύομαι *mid* save, deliver, protect, redeem; cure, heal; shield, cover; check, hold back

ῥύπα ων τά *pl of* ὁ **ῥύπος**

ῥυπαίνω, ῥυπαρεύω sully

ῥυπαρίᾱ ᾱς ἡ dirt; sordidness

ῥυπαρός ᾱ́ όν dirty

ῥυπάω, ῥυπόω be dirty

ῥύπος ου ὁ dirt, filth

ῥῦσιον ου τό booty, prey; pledge, reprisal, amends

ῥῡσίπολις εως ὁ/ἡ saving the city

ῥύσις εως ἡ stream, river, course

ῥῡσός ή όν wrinkled

ῥυστάζω drag to and fro, maltreat

ῥυστακτύς ύος ἡ dragging about, ill-treatment

ῥῡτήρ[1] ῆρος ὁ one who draws a bow, archer; rope, thong; rein

ῥῡτήρ[2] ῆρος ὁ saver, defender

ῥυτίς ίδος ἡ wrinkle

ῥυτόν οῦ τό drinking-cup (running to a point with a small hole through which the wine ran)

ῥῡτός ή όν dragged along

ῥυτός ή όν flowing

ῥωγαλέος ᾱ ον rent, ragged

ῥωμαΐζω speak Latin

ῥωμαλέος ᾱ ον strong, mighty

ῥώμη ης ἡ strength, force, might; army; energy

ῥώννῡμι ῥώσω ἔρρωσα strengthen, confirm; *pass* exert oneself; be resolved (to do)

■ **ἐρρῶσθαι** *pf infin* be strong *or* vigorous

■ **ἔρρωσο** farewell

ῥώξ ῥωγός ἡ chink, fissure, narrow passage

ῥώομαι *mid* move swiftly, rush on; dance

ῥωπήιον ου τό ▸ **ῥώψ**

ῥωχμός οῦ ὁ ▸ **ῥώξ**

ῥώψ ῥωπός ἡ shrub, bush, underwood

Σσ

σ (ς), Σ (σίγμα) eighteenth letter of the alphabet
■ *σ′ as a numeral* = 200

σαβαχθανί *Hebr* thou hast forsaken me

σαβαώθ *Hebr* hosts, armies

σαββατισμός οῦ ὁ the keeping of the Sabbath

σάββατον ου τό Sabbath (i.e. Rest); *pl* week

σάγαρις εως ἡ double axe, battle axe

σαγηνεύω catch in a net

σαγήνη ης ἡ dragnet

σαθρός ᾱ́ όν rotten, decayed, unsound, sick, perishable

σαίνω *aor* ἔσηνα wag the tail; fawn (upon), wheedle, caress; shake

σαίρω *aor* ἔσηρα sweep clean

σακέσπαλος ον brandishing a shield

σακεσφόρος ον shield-bearing

σακ(κ)ίον ου τό small bag

σακκέω strain, filter

σάκ(κ)ος ου ὁ bag, sack; sack-cloth; mourning-dress

σάκος εος τό large shield

σαλεύω *act tr* swing, shake; incite; *act intr and pass*; totter, move to and fro, be tempest-tossed, roll

σάλος ου ὁ tottering, rolling, surging; surge *or* rolling swell of the sea; disquiet

σαλπιγκτής οῦ ὁ ▸ **σαλπικτής**

σάλπιγξ ιγγος ἡ trumpet; trumpet-signal

σαλπίζω *aor* ἐσάλπιγξα sound the trumpet, give a trumpet signal

σαλπι(γ)κτής οῦ ὁ **σαλπιστής** οῦ ὁ trumpeter

σάνδαλον ου τό **σανδάλιον** ου τό sandal

σανδαράκινος η ον orange-coloured

σανίδιον ου τό catalogue

σανίς ίδος ἡ board, plank; wooden framework; writing tablet; fold of a door; pole; pillory
■ **αἱ σανίδες** (at Athens and elsewhere) tablets on which were written public notices

σάος ▸ **σῶς**

σαόφρων ον ▸ **σώφρων**

σαόω ▸ **σῴζω**

σαπρός ᾱ́ όν rotten, decayed; putrid; worthless

σαργάνη ης ἡ plait, braid; basket

σαρδάνιος ᾱ ον scornful, sarcastic

σάρδιον ου τό **σάρδιος** ου ὁ the Sardian stone, carnelian

σαρδόνυξ υχος ὁ sardonyx

σαρκίζω strip off the flesh

σαρκικός ή όν **σάρκινος** η ον of flesh, fleshy; carnal, sensual

σαρκοφάγος ον eating flesh; limestone coffin

σαρκώδης ες fleshy

σάρξ σαρκός ἡ flesh, piece of flesh; body

σαρόω sweep clean

σατᾶν ὁ *Hebr* **σατανᾶς** ᾶ ὁ satan, devil

σάτον ου τό a measure of corn

σατραπείᾱ ᾱς ἡ satrapy, the office *or* province of a satrap (see σατράπης)

σατραπεύω be a satrap (see next entry)

σατράπης ου ὁ Persian governor, satrap

σάττω fill, stuff, cram; load; equip

σαύρᾱ ᾶς ἡ **σαῦρος** ου ὁ lizard

σαρωτήρ ῆρος ὁ butt-end (of a spear)

σάφα, σαφέως *see* **σαφής**

σαφ(ην)ής ές clear, plain, manifest; distinct; true, certain, real

σαφηνίζω σαφηνιῶ make clear *or* plain; announce

σάω strain, sift

σβέννῡμι σβέσω ἔσβεσα *act tr* quench, put out, quell; *act intr and pass* be quenched, go out, die

σβεστήριος ᾱ ον serving to quench [fire]

σεαυτόν ήν (*also* σαυτόν ήν) *acc sg pron* yourself

σεβάζομαι *mid* ▸ **σέβω**

σέβας τό awe, reverence, worship, respect; astonishment; wonder; majesty; pride, glory

σέβασμα ατος τό object of awe *or* worship

σεβαστός ή όν venerable, awful, august

σέβω *and pass* feel awe, fear, shame *or* respect; honour, revere, worship; wonder

σέθεν *alternative gen of* **σύ**

σειρᾱ́ ᾶς ἡ rope, string, chain

σειραῖος ᾱ ον **σειρηφόρος** ον fastened by a rope *or* trace; (of a horse) which draws by the trace only (being harnessed by the side of the yoke-horses)

σειρός οῦ ὁ ▸ **σιρός**

σεισάχθεια ᾱς ἡ a shaking off of burdens (the name for the disburdening ordinance of Solon, by which all debts were lowered)

σεισμός οῦ ὁ earthquake

σείω shake, brandish; *mid and pass* be shaken, move to and fro
■ **σείει** there is an earthquake

σέλας αος τό brightness, light, beam; fire, flame

σεληναῖος ᾱ ον moon-lit

σελήνη ης ἡ moon, moonshine

σεληνιάζομαι be moonstruck, i.e. epileptic

σέλῑνον ου τό parsley

σέλμα ατος τό rowing bench; deck

σεμίδᾱλις εως ἡ finest wheat flour

σεμνολόγος ου ὁ one who speaks solemnly

σεμνόμαντις εως ὁ reverend seer

σεμνός ή όν august, sacred, solemn, dignified, holy; majestic, noble, stately; grave, honest; haughty, arrogant; pompous

σεμνότης ητος ἡ solemnity, dignity, majesty; pomposity

σεμνόω, σεμνῦ́νω σεμνυνῶ dignify; make solemn, pompous *or* stately; magnify, amplify; *mid* boast, be proud

σεύω put in quick motion, set on; drive *or* chase away; throw, hurl, shake; *mid and pass* rush, run, start, dart *or* spout forth; strive (for), desire

σηκάζω pen, coop up

σηκοκόρος ου ὁ herdsman

σηκός οῦ ὁ pen, fold, enclosure, stable; sacred precinct, shrine; trunk of an old olive-tree

σῆμα ατος τό sign, mark, token; omen; trace; signal, word of command; image, seal, written character, device, emblem; mound, tomb

σημαίνω σημανῶ ἐσήμηνα signify, mark, seal; give a sign *or* signal, command, rule; show a sign, point out, announce, prove; *mid* mark for oneself, note down; infer, conclude

σημαντρίς ίδος ἡ (clay) used for sealing (like our wax)

σήμαντρον ου τό seal

σημάντωρ ορος ὁ leader, commander; messenger

σημεῖον ου τό ▸ **σῆμα**

σημειόω mark (by milestones); *mid* interpret as a sign

σήμερον *adv* today

σηπεδών όνος ἡ putrefaction

σήπω *act tr* make rotten; *act intr and pass* rot, decay

σῆραγξ αγγος ἡ cleft, hollow, cave

σηρικός ή όν silken

σής σεός *or* σητός ὁ moth

σησάμινος η ον made of sesame

σήσαμον ου τό sesame

σητόβρωτος ον moth-eaten

σθεναρός ᾱ́ όν strong, mighty

σθένος ους τό strength, might; courage; power, force; army

σθενόω strengthen

σθένω be strong *or* mighty; rule, have power; be able

σιᾱγών όνος ἡ jaw-bone

σίαλον ου τό spittle

σίαλος ου ὁ fat; fat hog

σῖγα *adv* silently; secretly

σῑγάζω silence

σῑγαλόεις εσσα εν shining, glittering

σῑγάω be silent, keep silence; conceal

σῑγή ῆς ἡ silence, stillness, quiet

σῑγηλός ή όν silent, still, mute

σίγλος ου ὁ shekel (Hebrew weight and coin, = 4 Attic drachmas)

σ

σιγῦ́ν(ν)ης ου ὁ spear, javelin

σιδηρείᾱ ᾱς ἡ working in iron

σιδήρε(ι)ος ᾱ ον of iron *or* steel; hard, unfeeling

σιδήριον ου τό iron tool *or* weapon

σιδηροβρώς (*gen* ῶτος) eating iron, whetting

σιδηρόδετος ον iron-bound

σιδηροκμής (*gen* ῆτος) slain by the sword

σίδηρος ου ὁ iron, steel; iron tool, sword, knife, sickle, axe; ironmonger's shop

σιδηροῦς ᾶ οῦν ▸ **σιδήρεος**

σιδηρο-φορέω *and mid* carry arms, go armed

σιδηρόω overlay *or* cover with iron

σίζω hiss

σῑκᾱ́ριος ου ὁ assassin

σίκερα ατος τό strong drink

σίκυος ου ὁ cucumber

σιλλικύπριον ου τό wonder-tree (*ricinus*)

σίλφιον ου τό silphium, laserwort, a plant whose juice was used in food and medicine

σιμικίνθιον ου τό apron

σῑμός ή όν flat-nosed, flat; up-hill

σιναμωρέω damage, waste

σίνᾱπι εως τό mustard

σινδών όνος ἡ fine linen; linen cloth, a muslin garment

σῑνέομαι ▸ **σίνομαι**

σινιάζω sift, winnow

σῑ́νομαι σῑνήσομαι ἐσῑνάμην damage, hurt; rob, plunder, ravage

σίνος εος τό damage, harm; mischief

σίντης (*gen* ου) robbing, rapacious, ravenous

σιός οῦ ὁ ▸ **θεός**

σῑρός οῦ ὁ pit (for keeping corn in)

σισύρᾱ ᾱς ἡ **σίσυρνα** ης ἡ rough *or* furred coat

σῖτα ων τά *pl from* **σῖτος**

σῑταγωγός όν transporting grain

σῑτευτός ή όν fatted

σῑτεύω, σῑτέω feed, fatten; *pass* be fed, eat, feed on

σῑτηγός ▸ **σιταγωγος**

σῑτηρέσιον ου τό food, provisions; soldiers' provision-money

σῑ́τησις εως ἡ a feeding; public maintenance (in the Prytanaeum)

σῑτίζω ▸ **σιτεύω**

σῑτίον ου τό ▸ **σῖτος**

σῑτιστός ▸ **σιτευτός**

σῑτοδείᾱ ᾱς ἡ want of food, dearth

σῑτο-δοτέω deal out grain; *pass* be furnished with grain

σῖτολόγος ου ὁ collector of grain, keeper of the public granary

σῖτομέτριον ου τό provisions, a measured portion of grain

σῖτονόμος ον dealing out food

σῖτοποιός όν preparing food; baker, baking-woman

σῖτοπομπίᾱ ᾶς ἡ transport of grain

σῖτοπώλης ου ὁ grain merchant

σῖτος ου ὁ wheat, grain; flour, bread; food, provisions

σῖτοφάγος ον eating bread

σῖτοφόρος ον conveying provisions

σῖτοφύλακες ων οἱ grain inspectors (Athenian officials who registered imports of grain and saw that the grain-measures were correct)

σῖτώνης ου ὁ public buyer of grain

σιφλόω maim; hurt

σιωπάω ▸ **σιγάω**

σιωπή ης ἡ ▸ **σιγή**

σκάζω limp

σκαιός ᾱ́ όν left, on the left hand *or* side; western; awkward, clumsy, silly; unlucky

σκαιοσύνη ης ἡ **σκαιότης** ητος ἡ awkwardness, stupidity; coarseness

σκαίρω skip, finish

σκάλλω dig, hoe

σκαλμός οῦ ὁ the pin *or* thole of an oar (to which the Greek oar was fastened by a thong)

σκανδαλίζω give offence to, scandalize; *pass* take offence

σκάνδαλον ου τό offence, scandal

σκαπτός ή όν dug

σκάπτω dig, hoe

σκάφη ης ἡ **σκάφος** ους τό hollow vessel, trough, tub; ship, boat, canoe

σκαφίς ίδος ἡ tub, bowl

σκεδάννῡμι σκεδῶ ἐσκέδασα scatter, disperse, spread abroad; *pass and mid* be scattered, be spread about

σκέδασις εως ἡ a scattering

σκέλλω σκελῶ ἔσκηλα *act tr* dry up, parch; *act intr and pass* be parched

σκέλος ους τό leg

σκέμμα ατος τό ▸ **σκέψις**

σκεπάζω ▸ **σκεπάω**

σκέπαρνον ου τό carpenter's axe

σκέπας αος τό ▸ **σκέπη**

σκέπασμα ατος τό a covering, shelter

σκεπάω cover; shelter, ward off, provide shelter against

σκέπη ης ἡ covering; shelter, protection

σκέπτομαι *mid* ▸ **σκοπέω**

σκευαγωγέω secure one's goods

σκευάζω prepare, make ready, make; provide, equip; dress up

σκευή ῆς ἡ **σκεῦος** ους τό dress, attire; ornament; equipment; disguise; vessel, implement, tool; *pl* utensils, tools, baggage, equipment, furniture

σκευο-φορέω carry baggage

σκευοφόρος ον carrying baggage; *noun* porter, luggage-boy

σκευωρέομαι *mid* look after the luggage; contrive cunningly

σκέψις εως ἡ a examining, observation, consideration

σκηνάω, σκηνέω, σκηνόω live in a tent; dwell, live, be encamped; *mid* dwell; build for oneself

σκηνή ῆς ἡ **σκήνημα** ατος τό tent, hut, house; tabernacle, temple; stage, theatre; the wall at the back of the stage with a central door for entrances and exits by the actors; banquet

σκηνίδιον ου τό small tent

σκηνοπηγίᾱ ᾶς ἡ feast of tents *or* tabernacles

σκηνοποιός οῦ ὁ tent-maker

σκῆνος τό ▸ **σκηνή**

σκηνοφύλαξ ακος ὁ guard of tents

σκηνόω ▸ **σκηνάω**

σκήνωμα ατος τό ▸ **σκηνή**

σκηπάνιον ου τό ▸ **σκῆπτρον**

σκηπτός οῦ ὁ thunderbolt; storm, gale

σκηπτοῦχος ον bearing a staff *or* sceptre

σκῆπτρον ου τό stick, staff; sceptre

σκήπτω *act tr* prop; hurl, let fall upon; *act intr* fall upon *or* down; *mid and pass* support oneself; pretend, allege as an excuse

σκηρίπτομαι *mid* support oneself, lean against

σκῆψις εως ἡ pretence, excuse, reason

σκιᾱ́ ᾶς ἡ shadow, shade, darkness; outline; ghost, phantom, spectre

σκιᾱγραφίᾱ ᾱς ἡ scene-painting; phantom

σκιάζω σκιῶ overshadow; cover, veil

σκιᾱ-μαχέω fight in the shade; fight with a shadow, fight in vain

σκιᾱ-τροφέω *act tr* rear in the shade *or* at home, bring up tenderly; shun heat and labour; *act intr and pass* be reared in the shade *or* effeminately

σκιάω ▸ **σκιάζω**

σκίδνημι ▸ **σκεδάννῡμι**

σκιερός ᾱ́ όν shady, shaded

σκίμπους ποδος ὁ couch, low bed

σκιοειδής ές shadowy

σκιόεις εσσα εν ▸ **σκιερός**

σκῑ́πων ωνος ὁ staff

σκιρτάω bound, leap

σκληροκαρδίᾱ ᾱς ἡ hardness of heart

σκληρός ᾱ́ όν dry, hard, harsh, rough, inflexible; stiff, tough; stern, stubborn; cruel, unyielding

σκληρότης ητος ἡ hardness, stubbornness

σκληροτράχηλος ον stiff-necked

σκληρῡ́νω σκληρυνῶ harden

σκολιόν οῦ τό (*also* σκόλιον ου τό) drinking song

σκολιός ᾱ́ όν crooked, bent, slanting; tortuous, unjust

σκόλοψ οπος ὁ stake; thorn

σκόπελος ου ὁ rock, crag, promontory, look-out place

σκοπέω *and mid* look at, about *or* out; behold, survey, view; consider, regard, observe; spy out; examine, inquire (into); pay regard to, heed

σκοπή ῆς ἡ **σκοπιᾱ́** ᾶς ἡ spying, looking out, watch; watch tower, look-out

σκοπιάζω *and mid* keep watch, spy out, discover

σκοπός οῦ ὁ spy; guardian, watcher; mark, aim, object, scope

σκόροδον ου τό garlic

σκορπίζω scatter

σκορπίος ου ὁ scorpion

σκοταῖος ᾱ ον **σκοτεινός** ή όν dark, shady; in the dark; blind; secret

σκοτίᾱ ᾱς ἡ ▸ **σκότος**

σκοτίζω make dark

σκότιος (ᾱ) ον ▸ **σκοταῖος**

σκοτομήνιος ον dark and moonless

σκότος ου ὁ *or* εος τό darkness, gloom; night; blindness; swoon; nether world; place of concealment; derangement of mind; unclearness

σκοτόω make dark

σκοτώδης ες dark

σκύβαλον ου τό dirt, filth

σκυδμαίνω, σκύζομαι + *dat* be angry (with)

σκυθρωπάζω look angry *or* sullen

σκυθρωπός όν angry-looking, sullen

σκύλαξ ακος ὁ/ἡ young dog, whelp

σκῡ́λευμα ατος τό ▸ **σκῦλον**

σκῡλεύω strip [a slain enemy] (of his arms); strip [the arms] off an enemy

σκύλλω *aor* ἔσκῡλα rend, mangle; annoy

σκῦλον (*or* σκύλον) ου τό spoils; booty, prey

σκύμνος ου ὁ young animal, whelp

σκυτάλη ης ἡ stick, staff; Spartan letter-staff, Spartan dispatch, message

σκυταλίς ίδος ἡ small staff

σκύταλον ου τό ▸ **σκυτάλη**

σκῡτεύς έως ὁ shoemaker, saddler

σκῡτεύω be a shoemaker

σκῡ́τινος η ον of leather

σκῦτος ους τό leather, hide

σκῡτοτομεῖον ον τό shoemaker's shop

σκῡτοτόμος ου ὁ ▸ **σκυτεύς**

σκύφος ου ὁ cup, beaker

σκωληκόβρωτος ον worm-eaten

σκώληξ ηκος ὁ worm

σκῶλος ου ὁ pointed stake

σκῶμμα ατος τό jest, joke

σκώπτω σκώψομαι jest; jeer at, mock

σκώψ ωπός ὁ owl

σμαράγδινος η ον of emerald

σμάραγδος ου ἡ emerald

σμαραγέω sound hollow, resound; crash

σμάω rub *or* wipe off; *mid* wipe off; wipe oneself with soap *or* unguent

σμερδαλέος ᾱ ον **σμερδνός** ή όν terrible, awful

σμῆνος ους τό swarm of bees, bee-hive; crowd

σμήχω wipe off

σμικρός ᾱ́ όν ▸ **μικρός**

σμυγερός ᾱ́ όν with pain, painful

σμύρνᾱ ης ἡ myrrh

σμυρνίζω season with myrrh

σμῡ́χω burn, make smoulder

σμῶδιξ ιγγος ἡ weal, bloody stripe

σοέομαι, σοῦμαι ▸ **σεύομαι**

σολοικίζω σολοικιῶ speak incorrectly, commit a solecism

σόλοικος ον speaking incorrectly; boorish

σόλος ου ὁ mass *or* lump of iron (used in throwing)

σόος ▸ **σῶς**

σορός οῦ ἡ urn, cinerary urn; coffin

σός σή σόν *adj 2 sg possessive* your

σουδᾱ́ριον ου τό handkerchief

σοφίᾱ ᾱς ἡ cleverness, skill; prudence; craft; knowledge; wisdom; philosophy

σοφίζω make wise, instruct, teach; *mid* devise, contrive shrewdly

σόφισμα ατος τό device, cunning contrivance, craft, trick, artifice, deceit

σοφιστής οῦ ὁ crafty man, artist, master; prudent man, philosopher; teacher of wisdom *or* eloquence etc.; sophist, sham philosopher

σοφιστικός ή όν sophistic, like *or* of a sophist

σοφός ή όν clever, skilful; prudent; cunning; learned; wise

σόω ▸ **σῴζω**

σπαδίζω σπαδίξω draw off

σπάθη ης ἡ a flat blade used by weavers on the upright loom for striking the threads home so as to make the web close; broad sword

σπάκα ▸ **κύνα**

σπανίζω σπανιῶ *and pass + gen* be in want (of)

σπάνιος ᾱ ον needy; scarce, scanty; rare

σπανιότης ητος ἡ **σπάνις** εως ἡ need, scarcity

σπανιστός ή όν ▸ **σπάνιος**

σπανοσῑτίᾱ ᾱς ἡ lack of food

σπάραγμα ατος τό piece torn off; torn body

σπαραγμός οῦ ὁ tearing, rending, mangling; convulsion

σπαράσσω *and mid* tear, rend in pieces

σπάργανον ου τό swaddling-cloth

σπαργανόω wrap in swaddling-clothes

σπαργάω teem, be full, be ripe; swell with passion

σπάρτον ου τό rope, cable

σπαρτός ή όν scattered, sown

σπάσμα ατος τό **σπασμός** οῦ ὁ convulsion

σπαταλάω live luxuriously

σπάω σπάσω ἔσπασα draw, pull, drag; tear, rend; drain

σπεῖος ους τό ▸ **σπέος**

σπεῖρα ᾱς ἡ anything wound *or* coiled; coil, net; body of soldiers

σπειρίον ου τό light garment

σπεῖρον ου τό wrapper, garment, shroud; sail

σπείρω σπερῶ ἔσπειρα sow, engender; scatter, spread; *pass* be scattered

σπεκουλᾱ́τωρ ορος ὁ guard; executioner, one of the body-guard

σπένδω σπείσω ἔσπεισα pour out a drink-offering; *mid* make a treaty *or* truce, conclude a peace; stipulate by treaty

σπέος σπείους τό cave, grotto

σπέρμα ατος τό seed; race, family; descent, origin; issue, offspring

σπερμολόγος ου ὁ picking up seeds, one who picks up scraps of knowledge, a babbler

σπέρχω *act tr* drive *or* press on; *act intr and pass* hasten, hurry; be hasty and angry

σπεύδω ▸ **σπουδάζω**

σπήλαιον ου τό cave

σπιδής ές far-stretched, wide

σπιθαμή ῆς ἡ a span (the space one can span with the thumb and little finger)

σπιλάς άδος ἡ crag, rock

σπίλος ου ὁ stain, blemish

σπιλόω stain, contaminate

σπινθήρ ῆρος ὁ spark

σπλαγχνίζομαι *pass* have compassion *or* pity

σπλάγχνον ου τό innards; heart, inner nature

σπλήν ηνός ὁ spleen

σπογγίζω wipe with a sponge

σπόγγος ου ὁ sponge

σποδιᾱ́ ᾶς ἡ **σποδός** οῦ ὁ ashes; heap of ashes; dust

σπολάς άδος ἡ leather bodkin; jerkin

σπονδαρχίαι ῶν αἱ right of beginning a libation

σπονδή ῆς ἡ drink offering, libation; *pl* treaty of peace, truce

σπορᾱ́ ᾶς ἡ ▸ **σπόρος**

σποράδην *adv from* **σποράς**

σποράς (*gen* άδος) scattered, detached

σπορητός οῦ ὁ ▸ **σπόρος**

σπόριμος ον sown, to be sown; fit for sowing

σπόρος ου ὁ a sowing; seed; birth, descent; produce, crop, offspring

σπουδάζω σπουδάσομαι *intr* make haste, be zealous, busy *or* earnest; *tr* do hastily *or* earnestly, pursue zealously

σπουδαιολογέομαι *mid* speak on serious objects

σπουδαῖος ᾱ ον active, zealous; busy, serious; honest, good, grave; excellent, esteemed; serviceable, weighty

σπουδή ῆς ἡ haste, speed; zeal, earnestness, seriousness, regard, pains, trouble, rivalry

σπυρίς ίδος ἡ basket

σταγών όνος ἡ drop

σταδιο-δρομέω run a race, run in the stadium

σταδιοδρόμος ου ὁ runner (in a race)

στάδιον ου τό stade (a distance of 606 ¾ English feet); race course (that at Olympia being a stade long)

στάδιος ᾱ ον standing fast
■ **ἡ σταδίη** close fight

στάζω στάξω ἔσταξα *tr and intr* drop, drip, distil

σταθμάω *and mid* measure out, calculate; estimate, judge

στάθμη ης ἡ carpenter's line *or* rule; chalk line

σταθμός οῦ ὁ standing place; stable, fold, dwelling, quarters; resting place, station, stage, day's march; standing post, door-post; balance, weight

σταῖς σταιτός τό wheat dough

σταίτινος η ον of dough

στάλαγμα ατος τό drop

σταμῖς ῖνος ὁ pillar, rib of a ship

στάμνος ου ὁ/ἡ jar, pot

στασιάζω rise in rebellion, revolt, quarrel, dispute; be divided into factions

στασιασμός οῦ ὁ ▸ **στάσις**

στασιαστής οῦ ὁ ▸ **στασιώτης**

στασιαστικός ή όν ▸ **στασιώδης**

στάσιμος ον standing, stationary

στάσις εως ἡ a standing; position, station, condition; standing place; a rising, revolt, sedition, party-strife; discord, quarrel; party, faction

στασιώδης ες seditious; divided into factions

στασιώτης ου ὁ partisan; insurgent

στασιωτικός ή όν ▸ **στασιώδης**

στατήρ ῆρος ὁ stater, a gold *or* silver coin

στατός ή όν standing, placed

σταυρός οῦ ὁ upright stake; the Cross (as the instrument of Crucifixion)

σταυρόω fence round with a palisade; crucify

σταύρωμα ατος τό **σταύρωσις** εως ἡ palisade; stockade

σταφυλή ῆς ἡ bunch of grapes

στάχυς υος ὁ ear of corn

στέαρ ατος ὁ fat, tallow

στεγάζω ▸ **στέγω**

στεγανός ή όν covering, water-tight; closely covered, roofed

στέγαρχος ου ὁ master of the house

στέγασμα ατος τό **στέγη** ης ἡ covering, roof; ceiling; shelter, house, dwelling

στεγνός ή όν covering, sheltering; covered

στέγος τό ▸ **στέγη**

στέγω cover, shelter; protect, keep off; contain, hold; conceal, hide, keep secret; bear, endure, hold out

στείβω tread; tread on; tread under foot

στειλ *aor stem from* **στέλλω**

στειλειή ῆς ἡ **στειλειόν** οῦ τό handle

στεινο- *see* **στενο-**

στειπτός ή όν trodden on, close-pressed

στεῖρα ᾱς ἡ stem

στεῖρος ᾱ ον barren

στείχω walk, step, go, march; approach; go away

στέλεχος ους τό stump, trunk

στέλλω† *act tr* arrange; make ready, equip; furnish, fit out, clothe, adorn; send, despatch; *act intr and pass* equip oneself, make oneself ready; start, set off, depart; go, come, travel; *mid* put on [one's clothes]; send for, fetch; shrink from (a thing), avoid

στέμμα ατος τό wreath, chaplet
▪ **τὰ στέμματα** wreaths of wool wound round the suppliant's olive-branch

στέναγμα ατος τό **στεναγμός** οῦ ὁ ▸ **στόνος**

στενάζω ▸ **στένω**

στενακτός ή όν to be mourned; mournful

στεναχίζω *and mid* **στενάχω** *and mid* ▸ **στένω**

στενόπορος ον with a narrow pass *or* outlet
▪ **τὰ στενόπορα** narrows

στενός ή όν narrow, strait, scanty
▪ **τὸ στενόν, τὰ στενά** strait, narrows

στενότης ητος ἡ narrowness, straitness

σ

στενοχωρέομαι *pass* be crowded together, be confined

στενοχωρίᾱ ᾱς ἡ narrowness of space, a confined space; distress, anguish

στενόω make narrow; *pass* be compressed; be crammed *or* full

στένω sigh, moan, groan; sound, ring; *tr* bemoan, bewail, lament

στενωπός όν narrow
■ **ὁ στενωπός** narrow passage, strait

στέργημα ατος τό love-charm

στέργω love, like, be fond of; be pleased with; be content *or* satisfied; entreat

στερεός ᾰ́ όν stiff, stark, solid; strong; stubborn, constant; cruel, unrelenting

στερεόφρων ον stubborn

στερεόω make firm *or* strong

στερέω deprive, bereave (of something *gen*); *pass* + *gen* be deprived (of), lose

στερέωμα ατος τό firmness; foundation, framework; firmament

στέρησις εως ἡ privation, loss

στερίσκω ▸ **στερέω**

στέριφος η ον ▸ **στερεός** *also* **στεῖρος**

στερκτός ή όν beloved, to be loved

στέρνον ου τό breast; heart

στερνοῦχος ον (of a plain) far-stretching

στέρομαι *pass* + *gen* be deprived of, lack; suffer loss

στεροπή ῆς ἡ flash of lightning; glare

στεροπηγερέτα ου ὁ sender of lightning

στέροψ (*gen* οπος) flashing, dazzling

στερρός ᾰ́ όν ▸ **στερεός**

στεῦμαι make gestures; take on as if, show signs as if; promise, threaten

στεφάνη ης ἡ ▸ **στέφανος**

στεφανηφορέω wear a wreath

στεφανηφόρος ον **στεφανῑ́της** (*gen* ου) wearing a wreath, crowned, wreathed; having a wreath as a prize

στέφανος ου ὁ crown, wreath; circle, ring; crown of victory, prize, reward

στεφανόω encircle, surround, put round as a crown; crown, wreathe, adorn; distinguish, reward; *mid* crown oneself

στεφάνωμα ατος τό **στέφος** τό ▸ **στέφανος**

στέφω ▸ **στεφανόω**

στῆθος ους τό breast; heart, feelings; understanding

στήκω stand

στήλη ης ἡ pillar, post; boundary-post; gravestone; upright stone (inscribed with record of victories, dedications, treaties, decrees etc.)

στηλῑ́της (*gen* ου) inscribed on a pillar as infamous

στήμων ονος ὁ warp in the loom; thread

στηριγμός οῦ ὁ prop, support; firmness, steadfastness

στηρῑ́ζω *act tr* set fast, prop, confirm; *act intr* rise up; *mid and pass* be firmly fixed, have a firm footing

στιβαρός ᾰ́ όν compact, sturdy, stout

στιβάς άδος ἡ bed of straw, rushes *or* leaves; mattress

στιβέω traverse, search through

στῑ́βη ης ἡ rime, hoar-forst

στίβος ου ὁ path, footstep, track, trail

στῑ́βω ▸ **στείβω**

στιγεύς έως ὁ tattooer

στίγμα ατος τό prick, point; tattoo, blemish, stain

στιγματίᾱς ου ὁ one who has been branded *or* tattooed

στιγμή ῆς ἡ ▸ **στίγμα**

στίζω prick, sting; tattoo; brand

στικτός ή όν spotted

στίλβω shine, glitter

στιλπνός ή όν glittering

στίξ στιχός ἡ ▸ **στίχος**

στῖφος ους τό dense crowd, column of warriors

στιχάομαι *mid* march in rows

στίχος ου ὁ row, line; battle-array; line of writing *or* verse

στλεγγίς ίδος ἡ scraper; tiara

στοᾱ́ ᾶς ἡ colonnade, portico (at Athens, the name στοᾱ́ was given to various public buildings)

στοιβάς άδος ἡ ▸ **στιβάς**

στοιχεῖον ου τό first principle, element, primary matter; elements of knowledge; letter of the alphabet

στοιχέω ▸ **στιχάομαι**

στοῖχος ου ὁ ▸ **στίχος**

στολάς άδος ἡ ▸ **σπολάς**

στολή ῆς ἡ dress, garment, clothing; equipment; state-dress

στόλος ου ὁ equipment, sending, expedition, journey; army, fleet, armament; troop, people; ship's beak

στόμα ατος τό mouth; tongue, speech, language, words; face; outlet; chasm, cleft; top, point, edge; front

στόμαχος ου ὁ throat; stomach; mouth

στόμιον ου τό mouth, opening; bridle-bit

στομόω stop the mouth; harden, train

στόμωσις εως ἡ hardening; sharp speech

στοναχέω ▸ **στένω**

στοναχή ῆς ἡ ▸ **στόνος**

στοναχίζω ▸ **στεναχίζω**

στονόεις εσσα εν causing groans *or* sighs; moaning; mournful

στόνος ου ὁ sighing, groaning, lamentation

στόρνῡμι στορῶ ἐστόρεσα spread out, stretch out; cover with blankets; spread smooth, level; calm; strew over

στοχάζομαι *mid + gen* aim at, shoot at, look at; hit the mark; guess (at), conjecture

στοχασμός οῦ ὁ guess

στοχαστικός ή όν sagacious

στόχος ου ὁ aim, guess

στράπτω lighten, produce lightning

στρατάομαι *pass* be encamped

στρατάρχης ου ὁ general

στρατείᾱ ᾱς ἡ expedition, campaign; army; military service

στράτευμα ατος τό expedition; army; camp; soldiers

στρατεύω *and mid* serve as a soldier; take the field, march, fight

στρατηγέω be a general; command, lead, manage

στρατήγημα ατος τό stratagem, strategy

στρατηγίᾱ ᾱς ἡ command, strategy; (at Athens) the office of στρατηγός, a sort of minister for war

στρατηγιάω wish to be a general

στρατηγικός ή όν fit to be a general, appropriate for a general, skilled in command

στρατήγιον ου τό general's tent

στρατηγίς ίδος ἡ of a general

στρατηγός οῦ ὁ general (at Athens, the title of 10 officers elected each year to command the army and navy), leader, commander of an army; admiral; governor; consul; one of the chief magistrates of a Roman colony

στρατηλασίη ης ἡ ▸ **στρατεία**

στρατηλατέω ▸ **στρατηγέω**

στρατηλάτης ου ὁ ▸ **στρατηγός**

στρατιᾱ́ ᾶς ἡ army, force; band, company; campaign

στράτιος ᾱ ον military, warlike

στρατιώτης ου ὁ soldier, warrior, mercenary

στρατιωτικός ή όν of *or* for soldiers; suitable for military service

■ **τὸ στρατιωτικόν** the pay of the forces; the soldiery

στρατιῶτις ιδος ἡ troop-ship

στρατο-λογέω levy an army

στρατόομαι *pass* ▸ **στρατάομαι**

στρατοπεδάρχης ου ὁ commander of the imperial guard

στρατοπεδείᾱ ᾱς ἡ **στρατοπέδευσις** εως ἡ encamping; station; encamped army

στρατοπεδεύομαι *mid* encamp; lie at anchor

στρατόπεδον ου τό encampment, camp; army; fleet

στρατός οῦ ὁ an encamped army, army, body of soldiers; people

στρεβλόω twist, distort; sprain, wrench; rack, torture

στρέμμα ατος τό sprain

στρεπτός ή όν twisted, plaited; pliant, flexible
■ **ὁ στρεπτός** neck-chain; (of pastry) a twist *or* roll

στρεπτοφόρος ον wearing a necklace

στρεύγομαι *pass* be exhausted

στρεφε-δῑνέομαι *pass* be whirled *or* giddy

στρέφω *act tr* twist, turn, bend; turn about, wheel round, alter, twist back, sprain; *act intr and pass* be twisted, twist oneself, turn oneself (round about *or* to and fro); turn back, flee; roam about; attach oneself (to); be changed; evade

στρηνιάω στρηνιάσω be wanton

στρῆνος ου ὁ insolence, arrogance

στρογγύλος η ον round(ed)
■ **στρογγύλη ναῦς** merchant ship

στρόμβος ου ὁ top, whirlwind

στρουθίον ου τό **στρουθός** οῦ ὁ sparrow; ostrich

στροφάλιγξ ιγγος ἡ whirl, eddy

στροφάς (*gen* άδος) turning round, revolving

στρόφιγξ ιγγος ὁ pivot, hinge

στροφο-δῑνέομαι *pass* ▸ **στρεφοδινέομαι**

στρόφος ου ὁ rope, cord, band

στρυφνός ή όν sour; harsh, austere

στρῶμα ατος τό ▸ **στρωμνή**

στρωματόδεσμον ου τό sack for packing beds in

στρωμνή ῆς ἡ couch, bed; mattress; bedding

στρώννῡμι ▸ **στόρνυμι**

στρωτός ή όν spread

στρωφάω turn, spin; *pass* roam about; stay, dwell

στυγερός ▸ **στυγνός**

στυγέω hate, abhor, detest; fear; make hateful

στυγητός ή όν abominated

στύγιος ᾱ ον Stygian

στυγνάζω be sad *or* gloomy

στυγνός ή όν hated, abominated; horrible, terrible; gloomy, morose, sad; mournful, miserable

στῦλος ου ὁ pillar, prop

στυππεῖον ου τό the coarse fibre of flax *or* hemp, tow

στυπτηρίᾱ ᾱς ἡ alum

στυράκιον ου τό **στύραξ**[1] ακος ὁ end of a spear-shaft

στύραξ[2] ακος ὁ/ἡ storax tree

στυφελίζω στυφελίξω thrust, push; shake; drive; beat; maltreat

στυφελός (ή) όν close, dense, solid, rough, harsh

σύ σοῦ *pron 2 sg* you

συβόσῑον ου τό **συβόσειον** ου τό herd of swine

συβώτης ου ὁ (*also* συβότης ου ὁ) swineherd

συγγένεια ᾱς ἡ relationship; kinsfold, family

συγγενής ές born with, congenital, inborn; connected by birth, related; kinsman; resembling, natural

συγγενίς (*gen* ίδος) *fem from* **συγγενής**

συγ-γηράσκω + *dat* grow old together (with)

συγ-γίγνομαι *mid*+ *dat* come together, meet; converse with; come to assist; live with

συγ-γιγνώσκω + *dat* concur in opinion *or* agree (with); consent; acknowledge, concede, yield; know with; excuse, pardon, forgive; *mid* grant, allow, yield

σύγγνοια ᾱς ἡ **συγγνώμη** ης ἡ **συγγνωμοσύνη** ης ἡ pardon, forgiveness, excuse; permission

συγγνώμων ον forgiving, indulgent, allowing; pardonable

σύγγονος ον ▸ **συγγενής**

σύγγραμμα ατος τό written paper, essay; a prose work, written speech

συγγραφεύς έως ὁ writer, author; historian; prose-writer; writer of laws and statutes

συγγραφή ῆς ἡ a writing down; ▸ **σύγγραμμα**

συγγραφικῶς *adv* exactly

συγ-γράφω write *or* note down; describe, compose; write history; draw up a contract *or* resolution

συγ-γυμνάζομαι *pass* train oneself together

συγκαθ-αιρέω pull down *or* overthrow together

συγκαθ-αρμόζω inter together, bury together

συγκαθ-έζομαι *pass* **συγκάθ-ημαι** sit with

συγκαθ-ίζω *and mid* make to sit together; place together

συγκαθ-ῑ́ημι let down; *intr* stoop, condescend

συγκαθ-ίστημι establish together *or* with

συγ-κακοπαθέω, συγ-κακουχέομαι *pass* + *dat* suffer together with

συγ-καλέω call together; *mid* call to oneself

συγ-καλύπτω cover, veil completely

συγ-κάμνω + *dat* work, labour *or* suffer together *or* with

συγ-κάμπτω bend together, bend the knee

συγκατα-βαίνω go down together

συγκατ-άγω join in bringing back

συγκατα-διώκω pursue together

συγκατα-δουλόω *and mid* subdue together

συγκατα-ζεύγνῡμι entangle, yoke together, join in marriage

συγκατα-θάπτω bury jointly

συγκατάθεσις εως ἡ agreement

συγκατ-αίθω burn together

συγκάταινος ον + *dat* agreeing with

συγκατα-καίω, συγκατα-κᾱ́ω burn at once

συγκατά-κειμαι *mid* lie down with

συγκατα-κλείω, συγκατα-κληίω shut in together

συγκατα-κτάομαι *mid* acquire together

συγκατα-κτείνω slay together

συγκατα-λαμβάνω seize *or* capture together

συγκατα-λείπω leave behind together

συγκατα-λύω overthrow jointly

συγκατα-νέμομαι *mid* possess in company

συγκατα-πρᾱ́ττω *and mid* effect together

συγκατα-σκεδάννῡμι pour over at the same time

συγκατα-σκευάζω make ready *or* prepare together

συγκατα-στρέφομαι *mid* help in subduing

συγκατα-τίθεμαι *mid* deposit together at the same time; consent to

συγκατα-ψηφίζομαι *mid* condemn together; *pass* be reckoned along with

συγκατ-εργάζομαι *mid* accomplish together; help in procuring; assist

συγκατ-έρχομαι return together

συγκατ-εύχομαι *mid* pray for together

συγκατ-ηγορέω accuse together

συγκατ-οικέω dwell together

συγκατ-οικίζω colonize jointly; help in restoring

σύγ-κειμαι lie with, be together; be composed; be agreed (upon)
■ **σύγκειται** it has been *or* is agreed upon

συγ-κελεύω join in ordering

συγ-κεντέω stab down *or* to the ground

συγ-κεράννῡμι mix *or* blend together

συγ-κεφαλαιόω sum up

συγ-κινδῡνεύω be partners in danger

συγ-κῑνέω stir up together

σύγκλεισις εως ἡ a shutting up, closing up

σ

συγ-κλείω, συγ-κλῄω, συγ-κληίω *act tr* shut up, enclose, compress; encompass, surround; close, shut; *act intr and mid* be joined, concentrated, united *or* shut in

συγκληρονόμος ου ὁ + *gen* co-heir with

σύγκληρος ον assigned by the same lot; bordering, neighbouring

συγ-κληρόω assign by the same lot

σύγκλητος ον called together
■ **ἡ συγκλήτη ἐκκλησίᾱ** (at Athens) an assembly specially summoned by the στρατηγός (as opposed to the ordinary meetings)

συγ-κλῑ́νομαι *pass* + *dat* lie with

συγ-κλονέω confound utterly

σύγκλυς (*gen* υδος) washed together
■ **ἄνθρωποι σύγκλυδες** mob, rabble

συγ-κοιμάομαι *pass* + *dat* lie *or* sleep with

συγ-κοινόομαι *mid* give a share, communicate, impart

συγ-κοινωνέω get a share

συγκοινωνός όν partaking

συγκομιδή ῆς ἡ bringing together, gathering in; concourse

συγ-κομίζω bring together, gather in, collect; bury together; *mid* gather in for oneself; procure for oneself

συγ-κόπτω beat together; knock to pieces; beat soundly

σύγκρᾱσις εως ἡ a mixing together, blending

συγ-κρῑ́νω put together; compare; judge

συγ-κροτέω beat, strike *or* hammer together; drill, train well

συγ-κρούω strike together; set at variance, make enemies; *intr* collide

συγ-κρύπτω help in hiding; conceal completely

συγ-κτάομαι *mid* acquire jointly, help to acquire

συγ-κτίζω found together

συγκτίστης ου ὁ fellow-founder

συγ-κυβεύω + *dat* play at dice with

συγ-κύπτω bend forward *or* stoop and put heads together; draw nearer; conspire; be bowed down *or* bent double

συγ-κυρέω *and mid* encounter, meet; happen, come to pass

συγκυρίᾱ ᾱς ἡ coincidence, chance

συγ-χαίρω + *dat* rejoice with

συγ-χέω pour together, mix by pouring, mingle; confound, trouble, disturb; frustrate, spoil, break up

συγχορευτής οῦ ὁ partner in a dance

συγ-χόω cover over with earth; demolish

συγ-χράομαι *mid* + *dat* make joint use of, have dealings with

συγ-χύννω ▸ **συγχέω**

σύγχυσις εως ἡ a mixing, confounding; disturbing; overthrow, revolt

συγ-χώννῡμι ▸ **συγχόω**

συγ-χωρέω go together; agree, accede, assent to; give way, yield, acquiesce in, concede

■ **συγχωρεῖ** it is allowed *or* possible, it is agreed

σύειος ᾱ ον of swine

συ-ζάω + *dat* live with *or* together

συ-ζεύγνῡμι yoke together, couple, unite

συ-ζητέω + *dat* debate with

συζήτησις εως ἡ joint inquiry, discussion

συζητητής οῦ ὁ disputer

συζυγίᾱ ᾱς ἡ union; pair

σύζυγος ον yoked together; consort, mate

συ-ζωοποιέω quicken at the same time

σῡκάμῑνος ου ἡ **σῡκομορέᾱ** ᾱς ἡ mulberry-tree

σῡκῆ ῆς ἡ **σῡκέη** ης ἡ fig tree

σῦκον ου τό fig

σῡκο-φαντέω accuse falsely, slander; extort by false accusations

σῡκοφάντης ου ὁ false accuser, slanderer, informer, extorter (the basic meaning of the word may be 'fig-shower', i.e. someone who brings figs to light by shaking the tree where they are hidden by the thick foliage)

σῡκοφαντίᾱ ᾱς ἡ false accusation, slander, laying information

σῡλ-αγωγέω carry off as booty, lead captive

σῡλάω, σῡλεύω take away; strip off, despoil, pillage, plunder

σῡλη ης ἡ *usu pl* ▸ **σῦλον**

συλλαβή ῆς ἡ syllable

συλ-λαλέω talk with

συλ-λαμβάνω *mid* put *or* bring together; collect; comprehend; take away, carry away; lay hold of, seize, arrest; receive; perceive, understand; take part (in), assist, help

συλ-λέγω collect, gather, call together, levy [an army]; *pass* assemble, meet; *mid* collect for oneself

συλλήβδην *adv* taken together, in short

συλλήπτρια ᾱς ἡ **συλλήπτωρ** ορος ὁ partner, assistant

σύλληψις εως ἡ a seizing, comprehension

συλλογεύς έως ὁ (at Athens) an official who called in confiscated property

συλλογή ῆς ἡ a gathering, collecting, assembly, concourse; a levying of soldiers

συλ-λογίζομαι *mid* reckon, consider, think, reflect; infer, conclude

συλλογισμός οῦ ὁ reckoning, conclusion, inference

σύλλογος ου ὁ ▸ **συλλογή**

συλλοχῑ́της ου ὁ soldier of the same company

συλ-λῡπέομαι *pass* feel compassion

συλ-λύω help in loosing

σῦλον ου τό *usu pl* seizure of a cargo; privateering

σῦμα ατος τό ▸ **θῦμα**

συμ-βαίνω go *or* come together, meet; agree, make an agreement, make friends (with); suit, fit, correspond, be like; coincide, happen, fall out, come to pass, turn out, result, succeed

■ **συμβαίνει** it happens, it is possible

συμ-βάλλω *and mid* throw together, bring together, unite, mix, join closely; engage in, begin; set together, incite; compare, compute, guess; interpret, understand; come together, meet, join, encounter, fight; *mid* agree, make a treaty; contribute, furnish, be useful; put forth, produce, offer; judge, consider

συμ-βασείω wish to make a treaty

συμ-βασιλεύω reign jointly

σύμβασις εως ἡ treaty, agreement

συμβατήριος ον **συμβατικός** ή όν tending to agreement, conciliatory

συμ-βιάζω oppress all together, force all together

συμ-βιβάζω bring *or* put together; reconcile; compare, contrast; guess; perceive; prove; teach

συμ-βιόω + *dat* live with

συμ-βοάω cry aloud *or* shout together with; call to

συμβοήθεια ᾱς ἡ joint aid

συμ-βοηθέω render joint aid

συμβόλαιος ᾱ ον stipulated
■ **τὸ συμβόλαιον** bargain; contract; debenture; debt, money lent; symptom, token; sexual intercourse

συμβολή ῆς ἡ a meeting; encountering, engagement, battle; joint, end, joining; contribution

σύμβολον ου τό (in commerce) treaty; mark, sign, token, signal, symbol; ticket (such as those given to jurors at Athens, on presenting which they were given their fee); confession of faith, creed

συμ-βουλεύω advise, counsel; propose; *mid* take counself with, deliberate, consult

συμβουλή ῆς ἡ **συμβουλίᾱ** ᾱς ἡ **συμβούλιον** ου τό advice, counsel, consultation; senate, council

συμ-βούλομαι *pass* wish too, agree

σύμβουλος ου ὁ/ἡ adviser, counsellor

συμμαθητής οῦ ὁ school-fellow, fellow learner

συμ-μανθάνω learn together; *aor* be used to

συμ-μάρπτω grasp together

συμ-μαρτυρέω *and mid* bear witness with, corroborate

σύμμαρτυς υρος ὁ fellow-witness

συμ-μαχέω fight jointly, be allied in war; help

συμμαχίᾱ ᾱς ἡ alliance in war; allies; assistance

συμμαχικός ή όν of *or* for alliance
■ **τὸ συμμαχικόν** auxiliaries, allied forces; treaty of alliance; funds of an alliance

συμμαχίς (*gen* ίδος) *fem from* **σύμμαχος** *noun* allied state; body of allies

συμ-μάχομαι *mid* ▸ **συμμαχέω**

σύμμαχος ον allied, fighting jointly; ally; assistant, helper

συμ-μένω stay together; abide, continue

συμ-μερίζομαι *mid* **συμμετ-έχω, συμμετ-ίσχω** + *dat* receive a share along with

συμμέτοχος ον partaking in jointly

συμ-μετρέω *and mid* measure, compute, measure out; *pass* be commensurate, correspond

συμμέτρησις εως ἡ measuring by comparison, computation

συμμετρίᾱ ᾱς ἡ proportion, symmetry

σύμμετρος ον measured with, commensurate with, in due proportion, symmetrical, fitting, fitted

συμ-μητιάομαι *mid* take counsel with

συμμιγής ές ▸ **σύμμικτος**
■ **σύμμιγα** *adv* + *dat* along with

συμ-μῑ́γνῡμι *act tr* mix with, mingle with; unite; communicate with; *act intr and pass* be mingled, blended *or* united; have sexual intercourse; converse with; encounter, engage in battle, come to blows; befall

σύμμῑκτος ον intermingled, promiscuous, miscellaneous; (of troops) irregular

συμμῑμητής οῦ ὁ fellow-imitator

σύμμῑξις εως ἡ a mixing together; sexual intercourse

συμ-μίσγω ▸ **συμμίγνυμι**

συμμορίᾱ ᾱς ἡ class of taxpayers (at Athens after 377 BC, the 1200 wealthiest were divided into 20 ⋯

συμμορίαι or companies: each was called on in turn to discharge extraordinary expenses); division of the fleet

συμμορίτης ου ὁ a member of a συμμορία (see previous entry)

σύμμορος ον paying taxes along with

συμ-μορφίζω form alike

σύμμορφος ον of the same shape as

συμ-μορφόω ▶ **συμμορφίζω**

συμ-παθέω feel with, sympathize

συμπαθής ές compassionate

συμ-παίζω + *dat* play with

συμ-παίω beat *or* strike together *or* against one another

συμπαρα-γίγνομαι *mid* arrive at the same time, be present, assist

συμπαρα-θέω run along with

συμπαρα-καλέω call upon, invite, comfort *or* exhort at the same time; ask for at the same time

συμπαρα-κομίζω conduct (together)

συμπαρα-λαμβάνω take along with

συμπαρα-μένω + *dat* stay along with

συμπαρα-σκευάζω join in preparing, make ready *or* provide jointly

συμπαραστάτης ου ὁ helper

συμπαρα-τάσσομαι *mid* + *dat* be drawn up in battle-array with, fight along with

συμπάρ-ειμι[1] go along at the same time

συμπάρ-ειμι[2] be present with *or* at the same time

συμπαρ-έχω assist in causing *or* procuring

συμπαρ-ίσταμαι *mid* stand beside one at the same time

σύμπᾱς ᾱσα αν all together, all at once; the whole, in total

συμ-πάσχω suffer with, sympathize

συμ-πείθω join in persuading

συμ-πέμπω send along with; help in conducting

συμ-περαίνω *and mid* finish along with; achieve entirely

συμπερι-λαμβάνω include together with

συμπερι-πατέω + *dat* walk to and fro with

συμ-πήγνῡμι fasten; congeal

σύμπηκτος ον compact

συμ-πιέζω press together

συμ-πίνω drink with

συμ-πίπτω fall down; fall in with, meet with; come to blows; coincide; happen, come to pass; fall into

συμ-πλαταγέω clap together

συμ-πλέκω plait together; *pass* be plaited *or* entangled; come to close quarters

συμ-πλέω sail together

σύμπλεως ων completely full

συμ-πληθύω, συμ-πληρόω fill *or* man completely; complete

σύμπλοος ου ὁ/ἡ (*also* σύμπλους ου ὁ/ἡ) fellow-passenger, comrade

συμ-πνέω be of the same mind

συμ-πνῑ́γω choke up

συμ-ποδίζω fetter (the feet); entangle

συμ-πολεμέω + *dat* make war along with

συμ-πολιορκέω besiege jointly

συμπολῑτείᾱ ᾱς ἡ federal union of several states with interchange of civic rights, confederacy

συμ-πολῑτεύω *and mid* live in the same state, be a fellow-citizen

συμ-πονέω partake in work *or* misery

συμ-πορεύομαι *pass* + *dat* go *or* travel together (with)

συμ-πορίζω help in procuring

συμποσίαρχος ου ὁ president of a drinking party

συμπόσιον ου τό symposium, drinking-party

συμπότης ου ὁ fellow drinker, boon-companion

συμπρᾱ́κτωρ ορος ὁ helper, assistant

συμ-πρᾱ́σσω help in doing, assist; *mid* join in avenging

συμ-πρεσβεύω *and mid* be a fellow ambassador

σύμπρεσβυς εως ὁ fellow ambassador

συμπρεσβύτερος ου ὁ fellow elder

συμ-πρίασθαι *aor infin from* **συνωνέομαι**

συμπρο-θῡμέομαι *pass* have equal zeal *or* eagerness

συμπρο-πέμπω join in escorting

συμ-πτύσσω fold together

σύμπτωμα ατος τό chance; accident, misfortune

συμφερόντως *adv* profitably

συμφερτός ή όν united

συμ-φέρω *act tr* bring together, collect; contribute; bear jointly; *act intr* + *dat* be useful, profitable, advantageous *or* expedient (for); agree with; assist, be serviceable; *pass* come together; agree together, assent to; converse with; encounter; happen, come to pass
■ **συμφέρει** + *dat* it is profitable

συμ-φεύγω flee along with; be a fellow exile

σύμ-φημι assent, say yes, approve; promise

συμ-φιλέω join in loving

συμ-φιλονῑκέω + *dat* take sides with

συμ-φοβέω join in frightening

συμ-φοιτάω go regularly to together

συμφοιτητής οῦ ὁ schoolfellow

συμφορᾱ́ ᾶς ἡ event, chance, good luck; misfortune, disaster, calamity; defeat; success, result

συμφορεύς έως ὁ aide-de-camp (a Lacedaemonian officer)

συμ-φορέω ▸ **συμφέρω**

σύμφορος ον useful, profitable, favourable; convenient

συμφράδμων ον counsellor

συμ-φράζομαι take counsel with; consider

συμ-φράσσω press together

σύμφρουρος ον protecting

συμφυγάς άδος ὁ fellow exile

συμφύλαξ ακος ὁ fellow-watchman *or* -guard

συμ-φυλάσσω keep guard together

συμφῡλέτης ου ὁ someone from the same tribe

συμ-φῡ́ρω knead *or* mix together

συμ-φυτεύω plant along with *or* together; contrive together

σύμφυτος ον grown together, innate, natural; inborn, cognate

συμ-φῡ́ω *act tr* let grow together; *act intr and pass* grow together *or* into one

συμ-φωνέω harmonize in sound, be in unison; make an agreement

συμφώνησις εως ἡ **συμφωνίᾱ** ᾱς ἡ harmony; music

σύμφωνος ον harmonious, agreeing in sound; concordant

συμ-ψάω sweep away

συμ-ψηφίζω reckon together, count up; *mid* vote with

σύμψῡχος ον unanimous

σύν, ξύν *adv* together, at once; *prep with dat* with, in company with, together with, in connexion with; in accordance with; furnished with, by means of; under the command of

συνάγγελος ου ὁ fellow-messenger

συν-αγείρω gather together, assemble, collect

συν-άγνῡμι break in *or* to pieces, shiver

συν-αγορεύω agree to, join in recommending

συν-άγω lead *or* bring together, collect, assemble; summon, admit; contract, draw together; *pass* be assembled; be admitted

συναγωγεύς έως ὁ uniter; recruiter

συναγωγή ῆς ἡ a collecting, gathering, uniting; place of meeting, synagogue

συν-αγωνίζομαι *mid* + *mid* contend along with; assist, help

συναγωνιστής οῦ ὁ fellow-combatant; helper

συνάδελφος ον having a brother *or* sister

συν-αδικέω join in doing wrong

συν-ᾴδω accord with

συν-αείρω[1] ▸ **συναίρω**

συν-αείρω[2] raise up together; yoke together

συν-αθλέω ▸ **συναγωνίζομαι**

συν-αθροίζω gather together

σύναιμος ον related by blood

συν-αινέω join in approving; assent, agree

συν-αίνυμαι take up

συν-αιρέω seize together, bring together, bring into a small compass; seize wholly; snatch away, destroy; help in taking

συν-αίρω *and mid* raise *or* lift up together; *mid* undertake jointly

συναίτιος (ᾱ) ον accessory, accomplice

συναιχμάλωτος ου ὁ fellow captive

συν-αιωρέομαι + *dat* be held in suspense with

συν-ακολουθέω + *dat* follow along with

συν-ακούω hear at the same time

συν-αλγέω suffer pain with; feel pity

συν-ᾱλίζω bring together, collect; *pass* come together

συναλλαγή ῆς ἡ change, interchange; commerce, dealings, conversation; reconciliation, intervention; lot, vicissitude

συν-αλλάσσω *act tr* cause to associate with; reconcile, settle; *act intr* have dealings with; *pass* be united *or* reconciled, have sexual intercourse with

συναμφότερος ᾱ ον both together; both in the same manner

συνανα-βαίνω go up along with

συν-αναγκάζω compel at the same time

συναν-αιρέω destroy at the same time; destroy altogether

συνανά-κειμαι recline at table with

συν-ανᾱλίσκω spend *or* waste along with

συνανα-μῑ́γνυμαι *pass* associate with

συνανα-παύομαι *mid* refresh oneself together with

συνανα-πείθω join in persuading

συνανα-πρᾱ́σσω join in exacting [payment]

συνανα-χωρέω go back together

συναν-ίστημι *act tr* help in restoring; *act intr and mid* rise together

συν-αντάω *and mid* + *dat* meet with; happen to, befall

συνάντησις εως ἡ a meeting

συν-αντιάζω ▸ **συναντάω**

συναντι-λαμβάνομαι *mid* lay hold of along with, help

συν-άντομαι ▸ **συναντάω**

συν-ᾱορέω be joined to

συν-ᾱ́ορος ον united, linked with; consort

συναπ-άγω + *dat* lead away with

συνάπᾱς ᾱσα αν ▸ **σύμπας**

συνάπ-ειμι go away with

συναπο-βαίνω + *dat* disembark along with

συναπο-θνῄσκω + *dat* die together with

συναπο-λαμβάνω receive at the same time

συναπ-όλλῡμι destroy, lose together; *mid* perish together

συναπο-νεύω bend away according to

συναπο-πέμπω, συναπο-στέλλω send away together

συν-άπτω *and mid tr* tie *or* join together, unite; *intr* join, attach oneself (to), partake in; border on; take counsel together; come to blows

συν-αράσσω strike together, dash to pieces

συν-αρέσκει *impers* + *dat* it pleases also

συν-αρμόζω *and mid* fit together, join; agree together

συν-αρμολογέομαι be joined exactly

συν-αρμόττω ▸ **συναρμόζω**

συν-αρπάζω seize abruptly; snatch *or* carry away

συν-αρτάω knit *or* join together; *pass pf* be caught by

συν-άρχω rule jointly with, be a colleague

συν-ασπιδόω keep the shields close together

συνασπιστής οῦ ὁ fellow soldier

συν-αυδάω agree to

σύναυλος ον dwelling together

συν-αυξάνω, συν-αύξω let grow *or* increase together; *pass* grow larger together

συναφ-αιρέω *and mid* assist in delivering

συναφ-ίστημι *act tr* cause to revolt together; *act intr and mid* revolt along with

συν-άχθομαι *pass* + *dat* mourn with

συν-δαΐζω kill together with the rest, kill also

συν-δακρῡ́ω weep with

συν-δειπνέω + *dat* dine together (with)

σύνδειπνον ου τό banquet

σύνδειπνος ον dining together

σύνδεσμος ου ὁ band, union; fetter; (in grammar) conjunction

συνδεσμώτης ου ὁ fellow prisoner

σύνδετος ον bound together

συν-δέω bind together, fetter; join, unite

συνδια-βάλλω slander *or* accuse jointly; cross over together

συνδια-βιβάζω carry over with

συνδια-γιγνώσκω decide jointly

συνδι-αιτάομαι *pass* live together

συνδια-κινδῡνεύω incur danger jointly

συνδια-λύω break up *or* abolish jointly

συνδια-περαίνω help in finishing

συνδια-πολεμέω join in making war to the end

συνδια-πρᾱ́σσω effect together; *mid* help in negotiating

συνδια-σκέπτομαι *mid* **συνδια-σκοπέω** examine together with

συνδια-σῴζω help in preserving

συνδια-ταλαιπωρέω endure hardship with *or* together

συνδια-τελέω continue with to the end

συνδια-τρίβω + *dat* pass one's time with

συνδια-φέρω *and mid* bear with to the end

συνδια-χειρίζω manage jointly

συνδιέξ-ειμι go through along with

συν-δικάζω assist in judging

συν-δικέω + *dat* act as an advocate to

σύνδικος ον helping in court; advocate; attorney; assistant

■ **οἱ σύνδικοι** (at Athens) public advocates appointed to represent the state

συν-διώκω help in pursuing

συνδοκεῖ *impers* + *dat* it seems good also

συν-δοκιμάζω examine together

συν-δοξάζω join in approving of *or* in glorifying

συνδούλη ης ἡ **σύνδουλος** ου ὁ/ἡ fellow slave

συν-δράω do together

συνδρομή ῆς ἡ concourse

σύνδρομος ον running together, concurrent

σύνδυο two and two, two together, in pairs

σύνεγγυς *adv* very near together

συνεδρίᾱ ᾱς ἡ **συνέδριον** ου τό a sitting together *or* in council; a body of men assembled in council, council-board; senate; council-chamber, senate-house; the Jewish Sanhedrin

σύνεδρος ον sitting together; sitting in council

■ **οἱ σύνεδροι** select commissioners

συν-εθέλω have the same wish, consent

συν-εθίζω accustom; *pass* be used to

συνείδησις εως ἡ joint knowlege; self-consciousness; conscience

συν-ειλέω press *or* bind together

σύν-ειμι[1] ▶ **συνέρχομαι**

σύν-ειμι[2] be *or* live together, be joined, united *or* associated; have dealings (with); assist

συν-είργω shut in together; enclose *or* bind together; unite

συν-είρω string together; unite; speak on and on

συνεισ-άγω bring in with

συνεισ-βάλλω invade together

συνεισ-έρχομαι go in together

συνεισ-πῑ́πτω fall into along with; invade together

συνεισ-πλέω sail into together

συνεισ-φέρω join in contributing

συνεκ-βαίνω go out together

συνεκ-βάλλω cast out together

συνεκ-βιβάζω help in bringing out

συνέκδημος ου ὁ travelling companion

συνεκ-δίδωμι help in portioning out

συνεκ-δύομαι *mid* take off [clothes] together

συνεκ-κομίζω help in burying; help someone *dat* in bearing

συνεκ-κόπτω help in cutting off

συνεκλεκτός ή όν + *dat* chosen along with

συνεκ-πέμπω assist in sending out *or* escorting

συνεκ-πῑ́νω drink off together

συνεκ-πῑ́πτω fall out together; be thrown out together

συνεκ-πλέω, συνεκ-πλώω sail out together

συνεκ-πορίζω help in procuring *or* supplying

συνεκ-πρᾱ́σσομαι *mid* help in avenging

συνεκ-σῴζω help in preserving

συνεκ-τρέφω bring up jointly

συν-ελαύνω drive *or* bring together; clench [the teeth]; *intr* meet (in a quarrel)

συν-ελευθερόω help in freeing

συνεμ-βάλλω join in making an attack

συνέμπορος ου ὁ fellow-traveller, companion

συνεξ-αιρέω help in destroying *or* capturing

συνεξ-ακούω hear altogether *or* at the same time

συνεξ-αμαρτάνω + *dat* make a mistake, err, sin *or* commit a fault along with

συνεξ-απατάω deceive *or* cheat along with

συνέξ-ειμι ▶ **συνεξέρχομαι** go out together

συνεξ-ορμάω help to urge on

συνεοχμός οῦ ὁ joining, join
συνεπ-άγω help in leading against *or* in inciting
συνεπ-αινέω join in praising; approve, recommend
συνέπαινος ον approving
συνεπ-αιτιάομαι *mid* accuse together
συνεπ-ακολουθέω follow along with
συνεπ-αμῡ́νω help in warding off
συνεπαν-ίσταμαι *mid* join in a revolt
συνέπ-ειμι join in attacking
συνεπ-ελαφρῡ́νω help in relieving
συνεπ-εύχομαι *mid* join in a prayer *or* vow
συνεπι-βουλεύω plot against jointly
συνεπι-λαμβάνω *and mid* support, assist
συνεπι-μαρτυρέω + *dat* bear witness along with
συνεπι-μελέομαι *pass* + *gen* join in taking care of
συνεπι-σκέπτομαι *mid* **συνεπι-σκοπέω** examine along with
συνεπι-σπάομαι *mid* draw to oneself; win for oneself
συνεπι-σπεύδω join in hastening
συν-επίσταμαι *pass* know along with
συνεπι-στρατεύω + *dat* make war together with
συνεπ-ισχύω help in assisting
συνεπι-τελέω join in accomplishing
συνεπι-τίθεμαι *mid* + *dat* join in attacking
συνεπι-τρίβω destroy together
συν-έπομαι *mid* + *dat* follow close upon
συνεπ-όμνῡμι swear at the same time
συν-εργάζομαι *mid* work together
συνεργάτης ου ὁ ▸ **σύνεργος**
συν-εργέω + *dat* help in work
σύνεργος ον (*or* συνεργός όν) helping in work, co-operating
συν-έργω ▸ **συνείργω**
συν-έρδω work together
συν-ερείδω fasten, bind *or* press together
συνέρῑθος ου ὁ/ ἡ fellow-worker
συν-έρχομαι *mid* go together *or* with; meet; make an appointment *or* an agreement; encounter, meet in battle; have sexual intercourse (with); (of money) come in, be gathered
συν-εσθίω + *dat* eat together with
σύνεσις εως ἡ a joining; understanding, intelligence
συν-εστιάομαι *pass* feast together
συνέστιος ου ἡ sharing one's hearth, guest; (of Zeus) guardian of the hearth
συνεστώ οῦς ἡ living together
συνέταιρος ου ὁ companion, friend
συνετός ή όν intelligent, sensible, sagacious; intelligible
συν-ευδαιμονέω share in happiness (with)
συν-ευδοκέω + *dat* be pleased with, agree to, consent (to)
συν-εύδω, συν-ευνάζομαι *pass* sleep with, lie with
συνευνέτης ου ὁ bed-fellow, consort, concubine
σύνευνος ου ὁ/ἡ bed-fellow
συν-ευπάσχω be benefitted together
συν-ευπορέω join in providing *or* assisting
συν-εύχομαι *mid* pray together
συν-ευωχέομαι *pass* + *dat* feast together (with)
συνεφ-άπτομαι *mid* + *gen* lay hold of together
συνεφ-έλκω draw after along with
συνεφ-έπομαι *mid* + *dat* follow together

συνεφ-ίστημι *act intr and mid* superintend together; rise together with

συνέχεια ᾱς ἡ perseverance

συνεχής ές holding together, continuous, unbroken; contiguous, adjacent; frequent, unceasing

συν-έχθω hate along with

συν-έχω *act tr* hold *or* keep together; contain, comprise; constrain, compress, oppress; *act intr and pass* be joined *or* united; be affected by

συν-ηγορέω be an advocate

συνήγορος ον advocate, interceder; agreeing with

■ **οἱ συνήγοροι** (at Athens) 10 public advocates appointed annually to represent the state *or* private advocates who were not allowed to take a fee

συν-ήδομαι *pass* + *dat* rejoice with; congratulate

συνήθεια ᾱς ἡ acquaintance, intimacy; habit, usage

συνήθης ες familiar, intimate; of like mind and habits; customary, habitual

συν-ήκω come together

συν-ηλικιώτης ου ὁ of equal age

συν-ημερεύω = *dat* pass the day with

συνημοσύνη ης ἡ agreement, solemn promise

συνήορος ον ▸ **συνάορος**

συν-ηρετέω + *dat* be a friend to

συνηρεφής ές thickly covered

σύνθᾱκος ον + *dat* sitting with

συν-θάπτω help to bury

συν-θεάομαι *mid* view *or* examine together

συνθεσίη ης ἡ ▸ **συνθήκη**

σύνθεσις εως ἡ composition, combination

σύνθετος ον put together, composite, combined, complex; settled; agreed upon

συν-θέω run along with; succeed

συνθήκη ης ἡ ▸ **σύνθεσις** agreement, treaty, covenant, peace; commandment, order

σύνθημα ατος τό ▸ **συνθήκη** pre-ordained signal, token; password

συνθηρᾱτής οῦ ὁ (*also* συνθηρευτής οῦ ὁ) fellow-hunter

συν-θηράω, συν-θηρεύω hunt *or* catch together

σύνθηρος ου ὁ ▸ **συνθηρατής**

συν-θλάω crush, shatter

συν-θλῑ́βω press together

συν-θνῄσκω + *dat* die with

συν-θρύπτω break in *or* to pieces

συν-θύω sacrifice with

συν-ΐζω sit together, hold a sitting

συν-ῑ́ημι seat *or* bring together; perceive, hear; understand, know exactly; *mid* come to an agreement; perceive

συνίππαρχος ου ὁ joint commander of horse

συν-ιστάνω, συν-ίστημι *act tr* place, bring *or* set together; unite; bring together in dispute *or* battle; introduce *or* recommend to; compose, create, found, cause; prove, show; *mid* put together, produce *or* create for oneself; *act intr and mid* come *or* stand together; league together, conspire; encounter, meet in battle, be engaged *or* implicated in; be composed; begin; be combined; stand fast; continue, live, exist; stand still, make a halt

συνίστωρ ορος ὁ/ἡ knowing together with; witness

συν-ίσχω ▸ **συνέχω**

συν-ναίω dwell together

συν-νάσσω cram together

συνναυβάτης ου ὁ **συνναύτης** ου ὁ shipmate

συν-ναυμαχέω + *dat* fight at sea along with

συν-ναυστολέω go in the same ships

συν-νεύω nod assent

συν-νέω, συν-νηέω heap up together

συν-νῑκάω join in victory

συν-νοέω *and mid* consider, reflect (on)

σύννοια ᾱς ἡ meditation, deep thought; anxious thought, anxiety

σύννομος ον feeding together, gregarious; companion, friend, consort, mate

σύννους ουν meditating, thoughtful

συν-οδεύω travel along with

συνοδίᾱ ᾱς ἡ company of travellers

συνοδοιπόρος ου ὁ fellow-traveller

σύνοδος ου ἡ assembly, meeting, company; council; encounter, attack, battle

σύν-οιδα *pf* know together with; know thoroughly; be conscious

συν-οικέω + *dat* dwell *or* live together; live together in wedlock; *tr* colonize somewhere *acc* together with

συνοίκημα ατος τό a dwelling together; housemate

συνοίκησις εως ἡ **συνοικίᾱ** ᾱς ἡ cohabitation; marriage; house let out to tenants

συνοίκια ων τά festival in memory of Theseus' uniting of all of Attica under Athens

συν-οικίζω cause to live together, join in one state, concentrate; people, colonize; give in marriage

συνοίκισις εως ἡ **συνοικισμός** οῦ ὁ union into one city state (in Attica traditionally brought about by Theseus)

συν-οικοδομέω build together; build jointly

σύνοικος ον dwelling *or* living together; housemate, companion

συν-ολολύζω scream *or* shout together

συν-ομῑλέω + *dat* converse with

συν-όμνῡμι swear along with *or* together; join in a confederacy *or* a conspiracy

συν-ομολογέω *and mid* agree with *or* to; concede, promise; make a treaty with

συν-ομορέω + *dat* border on

συν-οράω see together *or* at once

συν-οργίζομαι *pass* + *dat* grow angry along with

συν-ορῑ́νω stir up, excite; *pass* rush on against each other

συν-ορμίζω bring to anchor together

σύνο(υ)ρος ον bordering on

συνουσίᾱ ᾱς ἡ a being *or* living together, connexion, association; society, party; conversation; banquet

συνουσιαστής οῦ ὁ companion, friend, disciple

συν-οφρυόομαι *mid* frown, have one's brow knitted

συνοχή ῆς ἡ connexion, meeting; contraction; anguish, distress

σύνοψις εως ἡ survey, general view

σύνταγμα ατος τό **σύνταξις** εως ἡ a putting together in order; order, arrangement; array of battle; body of troops, contingent; contribution, tax, rate, pay, pension

σύνταξις εως ἡ arranging; syntax; financial contribution to an alliance

συν-ταράσσω stir up together; disturb utterly, trouble, disquiet, confound, distress; *pass* be thrown into confusion

συν-τάσσω put together in order; put in array; arrange, organize, systematize; command, ordain; assign; *pass* collect one's thoughts; *mid* put in order for oneself; draw up in a line

συν-ταχῡ́νω *tr and intr* hasten

συν-τείνω stretch, strain, exert; direct earnestly to; *act intr* tend towards

συν-τεκμαίρομαι *mid* infer from, conjecture, estimate

συν-τεκνοποιέω + *dat* have children with

συν-τεκταίνομαι *mid* help in building *or* making

συντέλεια ᾱς ἡ joint payment *or* contribution; union of taxpayers; completion, end

συν-τελέω accomplish *or* complete together, bring quite to an end; pay joint taxes, contribute; belong to a certain class

συντελής ές paying joint taxes; tributary to

συν-τέμνω cut down; cut short, abridge, curtail; take a short cut; rush on to

συν-τήκω *act tr* melt together; *act intr and pass* melt away, fade, disappear

συν-τηρέω help in preserving, watching *or* protecting

συν-τίθημι put *or* place together, compose, construct; contrive, devise; unite, comprehend, sum up; *mid* put together for oneself; perceive, observe, hear; agree on, concert, make a treaty *or* covenant; set in order

συν-τῑμάω honour along with

συν-τιτρώσκω wound in many places

σύντομος ον cut short, abridged, shortened, concise, brief

σύντονος ον stretched, strained tight, intense; earnest; vehement

συντράπεζος ου ὁ companion at table, messmate

σύντρεις τρια three together, by threes

συν-τρέφω bring up together

συν-τρέχω run together *or* along with; come together, assemble; rush together, encounter; agree; meet

συν-τρῑ́βω rub together; crush, shiver; wear away, undo

σύντριμμα ατος τό destruction

σύντροφος ον brought up together; foster brother; living with; familiar, common; natural

συν-τυγχάνω meet with, fall in with + *dat*; happen, come to pass; chance
■ **ὁ συντυχών** anyone, the man in the street

συντυχίᾱ ᾱς ἡ incident, occurrence, chance; accident; happy event

συνυπο-κρῑ́νομαι simulate along with (others)

συνυπ-ουργέω + *dat* join in assisting

συν-υφαίνω contrive together

συν-ωδῑ́νω be in travail *or* labour together

συνῳδός όν ▸ **σύμφωνος**

συν-ωθέω thrust together

συνωμοσίᾱ ᾱς ἡ conspiracy; political club

συνωμότης ου ὁ fellow conspirator

συνώμοτος ον leagued by oath, confirmed by oath

συν-ωνέομαι *mid* buy up, hire

συνωρίς ίδος ἡ pair of horses; pair

συν-ωφελέω join in helping, be of use

σῡριγμός ου ὁ whistling, hissing

σῦριγξ ιγγος ἡ shepherd's pipe; spear-case; the hole in the nave of a wheel; pore *or* bronchial passage of the lungs

σῡρίζω play the pipe; whistle, hiss

συρμαιᾱ ᾱς ἡ purging oil; radish

συρμαΐζω purge

συρ-ράπτω sew *or* stitch together

συρ-ράσσω + *dat* dash together, fight with

συρ-ρέω flow together; come together

συρ-ρήγνῡμι *act tr* break in pieces; *act intr* rush *or* run together; clash together, break down, fall in *or* to pieces; *pass* be broken

συρφετός οῦ ὁ rubbish, sweepings, litter; mob, rabble

σῡ́ρω συρῶ ἔσῡρα drag, draw, trail along

σῦς συός ὁ/ἡ pig, sow; wild boar

συ-σκευάζω pack up; make ready, prepare; contrive; *mid* pack up, get ready for marching off; prepare, equip, contrive for oneself; win over

συ-σκευωρέομαι *mid* help in devising

συ-σκηνέω, συ-σκηνόω + *dat* live in the same tent with; mess together

συσκηνίᾱ ᾱς ἡ a dining *or* messing together

σῦσκηνος ου ὁ comrade, tent-mate

συ-σκιάζω overshadow *or* cover thickly; *intr* be thickly shaded

σύσκιος ον shady

συ-σκοπέω observe jointly

συ-σκοτάζει it grows dark

συ-σπαράσσω dishevel *or* distort utterly, tear in pieces

συ-σπάω draw together

συ-σπειράω press together; form in close order

συ-σπεύδω, συ-σπουδάζω join in hastening, be busy along with

σύσσημος ον concerted

συσ-σῑτέω + *dat* mess together with

συσσῑ́τιον ου τό common meal; mess-room, dining room

σύσσῑτος ου ὁ messmate

συσ-σῴζω help to save

σ

σύσσωμος ον united in one body

συσταδόν *adv* in close combat, hand to hand

συ-στασιάζω join in sedition, be factious

συστασιαστής οῦ ὁ **συστασιώτης** ου ὁ partisan; fellow rioter

σύστασις εως ἡ association, arrangement; a standing together, union, meeting; hardness, rigour; riot; conspiracy; close combat, conflict; sternness, sullenness

συστατικός ή όν introductory ▪ **συστατική ἐπιστολή** letter of introduction

συ-σταυρόω crucify along with

συ-στέλλω draw together, contract; abridge, condense, lessen, shorten; put together; wrap; humble; *pass* restrict oneself

συ-στενάζω + *dat* sigh (with)

σύστημα ατος τό composition; organized government, constitution

συ-στοιχέω + *dat* correspond to

συστρατείᾱ ᾱς ἡ joint campaign

συ-στρατεύω *and mid* + *dat* serve along with, join in an expedition

συστράτηγος ου ὁ joint commander

συστρατιώτης ου ὁ fellow soldier

συ-στρατοπεδεύομαι *mid* + *dat* encamp along with

συ-στρέφω twist up into a ball, gather together; combine, contract, compress; *pass* form one body *or* crowd; conspire; club together

συστροφή ῆς ἡ body of men, crowd; a sudden storm

συ-σχηματίζομαι *mid* accommodate oneself to

συφε(ι)ός οῦ ὁ pig-sty

συφορβός οῦ ὁ swineherd

συχνός ή όν frequent; numerous, copious; long; far

σφαγεύς έως ὁ murderer, butcher; sword, sacrificial knife

σφαγή ῆς ἡ slaughter, butchery; sacrifice; murder; wound; throat

σφαγιάζω ▸ **σφάττω**

σφάγιον ου τό victim; sacrifice

σφάγιος ᾱ ον killing, slaughtering

σφαδάζω struggle in convulsions

σφάζω ▸ **σφάττω**

σφαῖρα ᾱς ἡ ball; globe

σφαιρηδόν *adv* like a ball

σφαιροειδής ές ball-like, spherical

σφακελίζω become gangrenous

σφάκελος ου ὁ gangrene

σφαλερός ᾱ́ όν slippery, smooth; precarious, fallacious, delusive; perilous; tottering, reeling, staggering

σφάλλω σφαλῶ ἔσφηλα make fall *or* stumble; destroy, ruin, undo; baffle, disconcert; *pass and mid* totter, stagger, reel, fall, perish; be defeated, disappointed *or* baffled; be unsuccessful; fail; be deceived; go wrong, transgress

σφάλμα ατος τό stumble, fall, false step; failure, disaster, defeat; error, fault; blunder

σφαραγέομαι *mid* burst with a noise; crackle, hiss

σφάττω slaughter, kill, slay; sacrifice

σφεδανός ή όν vehement, eager, furious

σφεῖς σφεα they

σφέλας τό footstool

σφενδονάω sling, use the sling

σφενδόνη ης ἡ sling; hoop of a ring; stone (used with a sling)

σφενδονήτης ου ὁ slinger

σφενδονητική ῆς ἡ art of slinging

σφετερίζομαι appropriate, make one's own, usurp

σφέτερος ᾱ ον their (own)

σφηκόω make like a wasp, pinch in at the waist; bind tightly

σφήξ σφηκός ὁ wasp

σφοδρός ᾱ́ όν vehement, violent; impetuous, eager, zealous; mighty
■ **σφόδρα, σφοδρῶς** *adv* very much, vehemently

σφοδρότης ητος ἡ impetuosity

σφονδύλιος ου ὁ vertebra; vertebral column

σφρᾱγίζω σφρᾱγιῶ seal up, shut up; confirm; mark, sign

σφρᾱγῑ́ς ῖδος ἡ seal; signet-ring; sign, token; authorization

σφρᾱ́γισμα ατος τό seal

σφρηγίς ▸ **σφραγίς**

σφῦρα ᾱς ἡ hammer

σφῡρήλατος ον beaten out with the hammer

σφυρίς ίδος ἡ little basket, nose-bag

σφυρόν οῦ τό ankle

σφωέ (*gen and dat* σφωίν) *dual* both of them

σφῶϊ (*also* σφώ) (*gen and dat* σφῶϊν *or* σφῷν) *dual* both of you

σφωΐτερος ᾱ ον belonging to you two

σχ *often some part of* **ἔχω** *or a compound*

σχάζω slit; cut open (a vein)

σχεδίᾱ ᾱς ἡ raft, float; boat; pontoon-bridge

σχεδίην *adv* near, in close combat

σχεδόθεν *adv* from near, from close at hand

σχεδόν *adv* near, close; nearly, almost, pretty well, all but

σχέσις εως ἡ ▸ **σχῆμα**

σχετλιάζω complain of hardship, complain angrily

σχετλιασμός οῦ ὁ indignation, passionate complaint

σχέτλιος ᾱ ον bold; insolent; wicked; cruel, savage; unflinching, shocking, horrid; miserable, wretched; strange, astonishing

σχῆμα ατος τό bearing, mien, behaviour; figure, form, shape, outward appearance; constitution, nature; dress; manner, fashion; stateliness, dignity

σχηματίζω σχηματιῶ form, fashion, shape, dress; adorn; *mid* pretend

σχημάτιον ου τό figure in dancing

σχήσω *fut from* **ἔχω**

σχίζα ης ἡ cleft piece of wood, splinter

σχίζω split, cleave, separate

σχῖνος ου ἡ mastich tree

σχίσις εως ἡ division; by-road

σχίσμα ατος τό division, schism

σχιστός ή όν parted, divided

σχοινίον ου τό rope, cord

σχοῖνος ου ὁ rush, reed; place where rushes grow, rush-bed; rope, cord, cable; measuring-line

σχοινοτενής ές straight

σχολάζω be at leisure, have spare time; have leisure *or* time for; devote oneself to; linger, delay

σχολαῖος ᾱ ον at leisure; tardy

σχολαιότης ητος ἡ slowness

σχολή ῆς ἡ leisure, spare time, rest, ease; peace; an activity in which leisure is employed, disputation, discussion; school; delay, slowness; idleness
■ **σχολῇ** *adv* at leisure, slowly; hardly, scarcely, not at all

σῴζω† save, keep safe, preserve, protect, spare, bring back safe and sound; observe, keep secret; remember; *mid* keep *or* save for oneself

σωκέω have strength, be in a condition to (do)

σῶκος ον strong (of Hermes)

σωλήν ῆνος ὁ pipe

σῶμα ατος τό body; dead body, corpse; person, individual; slave; life, existence; sensual pleasures

σωμ-ασκέω train one's body

σωμασκίᾱ ᾱς ἡ bodily exercise

σωματικός ή όν **σωματοειδής** ές bodily, material

σῶος α ον ▸ **σῶς**

σωρεύω heap up; heap with

σωρός οῦ ὁ heap

σῶς σῶν safe and sound, healthy, entire; sure

σῶστρα ων τά reward for saving one's life *or* bringing back lost cattle *or* runaway slaves

σωτήρ ῆρος ὁ **σώτειρα** ᾱς ἡ saviour, preserver, deliverer

σωτηρίᾱ ᾱς ἡ saving, deliverance, means of preserving; safe existence; well-being, ease

σωτήριος ᾱ ον saving, delivering; saved
■ **τὰ σωτήρια** thank-offering for preservation; ▸ **σωτηρία**

σωφρονέω be sensible, reasonable, discreet *or* moderate

σωφρονίζω σωφρονιῶ bring to reason, make wise; admonish; correct, chastise

σωφρονισμός οῦ ὁ teaching of morality; self-control

σωφρονιστής οῦ ὁ chastiser, censor

σωφροσύνη ης ἡ sobriety, prudence, moderation, discretion; self-control; chastity, decent behaviour

σώφρων ον sensible, discreet, prudent; moderate, temperate, sober; modest

σώω ▸ **σῴζω**

Τ τ

τ, Τ (ταῦ) nineteenth letter of the alphabet
■ **τʹ** *as a numeral* = 300

ταβέρνη ης ἡ inn

τᾱγείᾱ ᾱς ἡ command, rule

τᾱγεύω command, rule

τάγμα ατος τό body of soldiers, division; command

τᾱγός οῦ ὁ commander, ruler; chief of a confederacy

ταινίᾱ ᾱς ἡ head-band

ταινιόω adorn with a head-band (as a conqueror)

τακτικός ή όν fit for ordering *or* arranging *or* tactics

τακτός ή όν ordered, arranged, fixed

τᾱ́κω ▸ **τήκω**

ταλαεργός όν enduring labour

ταλαιπωρέω suffer hardship *or* distress, do hard work, toil, drudge

ταλαιπωρίᾱ ᾱς ἡ hardship, hard work, distress; affliction, suffering

ταλαίπωρος ον suffering, wretched, miserable

ταλαίφρων ον **ταλαικάρδιος** ον wretched; bold, daring

ταλαντιαῖος ᾱ ον worth a talent; weighing a talent

τάλαντον ου τό talent (a weight and a sum of money, the value of the latter being 6,000 drachmas); *pl* pair of scales

ταλαπείριος ον suffering much, severely tried by fate

ταλαπενθής ές enduring pain, miserable

τάλαρος ου ὁ basket

τάλᾱς τάλαινα τάλαν enduring, patient, suffering, wretched

ταλασίᾱ ᾱς ἡ wool-spinning

ταλασιουργέω spin wool

ταλασίφρων ον ▸ **ταλαίφρων**

ταλαύρῑνος ον with a shield of tough bull's hide

ταλάφρων ον ▸ **ταλαίφρων**

τᾶλις ιδος ἡ maiden

ταμεῖον ου τό ▸ **ταμιεῖον**

ταμεσίχρως (*gen* οος) cutting the skin

ταμίᾱ ᾱς ἡ housekeeper, housewife

ταμίᾱς ου ὁ housekeeper, dispenser, steward; treasurer; controller (of the sacred treasure on the acropolis of Athens)

ταμιεῖον ου τό storehouse; treasury; chamber; the Roman *aerarium*

ταμιεύω *and mid* be a housekeeper, steward, treasurer, paymaster *or* manager; manage

τάμνω ▸ **τέμνω**

τάν, τᾶν *only in the following phrase*
■ **ὦ τάν** my good friend!

ταναήκης ες with a long point *or* edge

ταναός (ή) όν stretched, long

ταναύπους (*gen* ποδος) stretching the feet, long-striding

τανηλεγής ές bringing long woe

ταντάλόω swing, hurl down

τανύγλωσσος ον long-tongued, chattering

τανυγλώχῑς (*gen* ῑνος) with long point

τανυήκης ες ▸ **ταναήκης**

τανῦν ▸ **τὰ νῦν**

τανύπεπλος ον with long robe

τανύπους ▸ **ταναύπους**

τανυπτέρυξ (*gen* υγος) **ταναυσίπτερος** ον with outstretched wing

τανυστύς ύος ἡ a stretching, stringing

τανύφλοιος ον with thin bark, of tall *or* slender growth

τανύφυλλος ον with long leaves

τανύω ▸ **τείνω**

ταξιαρχέω be a taxiarch (see next entry)

ταξιάρχης ου ὁ **ταξίαρχος** ου ὁ taxiarch, commander of a division; captain

τάξις εως ἡ an arranging, putting in order, disposition; order, arrangement; class, post, rank, office, duty; military arrangement, line of soldiers, battle-array, order of battle; body of troops, division of an army, band, company

ταπεινός ή όν low, level; small, narrow; trifling, insignificant, poor; humble, lowly; humiliated, downcast, mean

ταπεινότης ητος ἡ lowness (of stature); lowliness, weakness; baseness, abasement; dejection, humiliation; humility

ταπεινοφροσύνη ης ἡ humility, meekness

ταπεινόφρων ον humble

ταπεινόω lower, make low; humble, bring down

ταπείνωσις εως ἡ ▸ **ταπεινότης**

τάπης ητος ὁ **ταπίς** ίδος ἡ carpet

ταράσσω stir up, disturb, trouble, confound; rouse, alarm, agitate, raise up

■ **τέτρηχα** *pf* be in uproar *or* confusion

ταραχή ῆς ἡ **τάραχος** ου ὁ disorder, confusion, tumult, noise, uproar, sedition

ταραχώδης ες confused, troubled, disordered; fickle, angry; trouble

ταρβαλέος ᾱ ον frightened

ταρβέω be afraid *or* alarmed

τάρβος ους τό **ταρβοσύνη** ης ἡ fear, fright, awe

ταρῑ́χευσις εως ἡ (of mummies) an embalming; (of fish) salting

ταρῑχευτής οῦ ὁ embalmer

ταρῑχεύω preserve by smoking *or* salting; embalm

ταρῑχήϊαι ῶν αἱ places for salting fish

τάρῑχος ου ὁ *or* ους τό salted meat; mummy

ταρσός οῦ ὁ (*also* ταρρός οῦ ὁ) frame of wicker-work; crate; mat of reeds; blade *or* flat of the oar; the flat of the foot

ταρταρόω hurl into Tartarus

τάρφος εος τό thicket

ταρφύς εῖα ύ thick, frequent, numerous

ταρχῡ́ω bury, inter

τάσσω arrange, put in order; draw up in a line *or* in order of battle; post, station, appoint; assign to a class; order, command, give instructions; fix, settle; *mid* order, arrange for oneself; agree upon among oneselves; bind oneself to paying by instalments

ταύρειος (ᾱ) ον of oxen *or* cows; of bull's hide

ταυρηδόν *adv* like a bull, staringly, savagely

ταυρο-κτονέω kill bulls

ταυροκτόνος ον bull-slaying

ταυροπόλος (η) ον hunting bulls *or* worshipped at Tauris (of Artemis)

ταῦρος ου ὁ bull, ox

ταυροσφάγος ον bull-slaughtering

ταύτῃ *adv* on this side, here; hither; in this way *or* manner

τάφε, ταφεῖν *see* **τέθηπα**

ταφεύς έως ὁ burier

ταφή ῆς ἡ ▸ **τάφος**[1]

ταφήιος η ον of *or* for a burial

τάφος[1] ου ὁ burial; grave, tomb; funeral feast

τάφος[2] τό astonishment

ταφρείᾱ ᾱς ἡ the making of a ditch

ταφρεύω make a ditch

τάφρος ου ἡ ditch, trench

τάχα *adv* quickly, soon; perhaps

ταχινός ή όν quick, swift

τάχιστος η ον *sup from* **ταχύς** swiftest, quickest, fastest

τάχος ους τό quickness, swiftness, speed

ταχυάλωτος ον captured quickly

ταχυ-ναυτέω sail fast

ταχῡ́νω hasten, make quick, be quick

ταχύπωλος ον with swift horses

ταχύρρωστος ον swift-moving

ταχύς εῖα ύ swift, quick, fast

ταχέως, ταχύ *adv* quickly, soon; at once

ταχυτής ῆτος ἡ ▸ **τάχος**

ταώς (*or* ταῶς) ώ *or* ῶ ὁ peacock

τε* *enclitic particle* and

■ **τε*** (...) **καί** both ... and

τέγγω wet, moisten; shed; *pass* be poured (forth), be softened

τέγεος ον roofed

τέγος ους τό roof; chamber, room

τέθηπα *pf aor* ἔταφον be amazed *or* astonished; wonder at

τεθριπποβάτης ου ὁ driving a four-horse chariot

τέθριππον ου τό a four-horse chariot

τεθριππο-τροφέω keep a team of four horses

τεθριπποτρόφος ον keeping a team of four horses

τεΐν ▸ **σοί** *dat from* **σύ**

τείνω τενῶ ἔτεινα *act tr* stretch, strain, extend, draw straight; stretch out, lay prostrate, lengthen; *act intr* tend to, aim at, strive; extend to; refer *or* belong to; *pass* be stretched tight; rush, run with full speed; be spread; *mid* stretch oneself *or* for oneself

τεῖος *adv* ▸ **τέως**

τεῖρος εος τό *only in pl* constellation

τείρω rub hard; rub away, wear out; distress

τεισ *likely to be from* **τίνω**

τειχεσιπλήτης ου ὁ stormer of walls

τειχέω, τειχίζω τειχιῶ build a wall *or* fort; fortify, wall in; build

τειχήρης ες besieged

τειχιόεις εσσα εν walled

τειχίον ου τό wall

τείχισις εως ἡ the building of a wall; fortress

τείχισμα ατος τό ▸ **τεῖχος**

τειχισμός οῦ ὁ ▸ **τείχισις**

τειχο-μαχέω attack the walls, besiege

τειχομαχίᾱ ᾱς ἡ attack of walls, siege

τειχοποιός οῦ ὁ officer of the board of works (whose job it was to repair the city walls)

τεῖχος ους τό wall; fortification, fortress, castle

τειχοσκοπίᾱ ᾱς ἡ looking from the walls (the name given to an episode in the third book of Homer's *Iliad*)

τειχοφύλαξ ακος ὁ guard of the walls

τειχύδριον ου τό small fortified place

τείως ▸ **τέως**

τεκ *aor stem from* **τίκτω**

τεκμαίρομαι τεκμαροῦμαι ἐτεκμηράμην *mid* know from certain signs, infer, conclude, judge; decree, ordain, appoint, show by a sign

τέκμαρ[1] τό end, goal, mark, boundary; just cause

τέκμαρ[2] τό **τεκμήριον** ου τό sign, token, mark; proof, demonstration

τεκμηριόω prove positively

τέκμωρ τό ▸ **τέκμαρ**[1] *and* **τέκμαρ**[2]

τεκνίον ου τό little child

τεκνο-γονέω bear children

τεκνογονίᾱ ᾱς ἡ childbearing

τεκνόεις εσσα εν having children

τεκνολέτειρα ᾱς ἡ bereft of children

τέκνον ου τό child

τεκνο-ποιέομαι *mid* beget children

τεκνοποιίᾱ ᾱς ἡ the begetting *or* bearing of children

τεκνο-τροφέω bring up children

τεκνόω *and mid* beget *or* bear children

τέκνωσις εως ἡ ▸ **τεκνοποιία**

τέκος εος τό ▸ **τέκνον**

τεκταίνομαι τεκτανοῦμαι ἐτεκτηνάμην *mid* make, build, frame, construct; contrive, devise

τεκτονικός ή όν belonging to the art of building; practised *or* skilled in building; *noun* carpenter, builder

τεκτοσύνη ης ἡ carpentry

τέκτων ονος ὁ carpenter, joiner, builder; master workman; metal-worker, sculptor

τελαμών ῶνος ὁ strap for supporting something; baldrick, shoulder-belt; surgeon's bandage

τελέθω be there; come forth ; become

τέλειος (ᾱ) ον complete, finished, fulfilled, accomplished; perfect, entire, full-grown, full in number; spotless; definite, fixed; accomplishing, able to do

τελειότης ητος ἡ perfection, full growth

τελειόω make perfect *or* successful

τελείω ▸ **τελέω**

τελείωσις εως ἡ completion; perfection

τελειωτής οῦ ὁ finisher

τελεόμηνος ον with full complement of months

τέλεος ▸ **τέλειος**

τελεσφορέω bring to ripeness; bear perfect offspring

τελεσφόρος ον bringing to an end, accomplishing; brought to an end, complete, fulfilled

τελετή ῆς ἡ initiation, celebration; *pl* mysteries

τελευταῖος ᾱ ον last, highest, extreme

τελευτάω complete, accomplish, finish, fulfil; *intr* end, come to an end, die, be fulfilled
■ **τελευτῶν** *pple* at last

τελευτή ῆς ἡ end, death; issue, event; success; finishing, completion

τελέω τελῶ ἐτέλεσα *act intr* end, bring to an end, complete, finish, perform, execute, fulfil; pay one's dues *or* taxes, spend money; consecrate, initiate (in the mysteries); *act intr and pass* be fulfilled, come to an end, turn out

T

τελήεις εσσα εν perfect, complete; promising success, of sure augury

τέλλω *aor* ἔτειλα *act tr* accomplish; *act intr and pass* rise, arise

τέλμα ατος τό pool, pond, marsh, swamp; mud for building with, mortar

τέλος ους τό end, issue; death; term, fulfilment, accomplishment; complete state, result, event; tax, duty, toll; cost, expense; present, offering; initiation, celebration, mysteries; body of soldiers, division, squadron; *also pl* highest *or* ideal station, full power, magistrate, government
■ **οἱ ἐν τέλει** the men in power

τέλοσδε *adv* towards the end

τέλσον ου τό boundary

τελώνης ου ὁ tax-collector

τελώνιον ου τό custom-house

τεμάχιον ου τό **τέμαχος** ους τό slice, morsel

τεμένιος ᾱ ον belonging to sacred land

τέμενος εος τό piece of land cut off for a certain purpose, king's estate; sacred land, temple-precinct

τέμνω† cut; use the knife; cut up, slaughter, sacrifice; wound; carve; cut off *or* down, sever; lay waste; fell trees; cut *or* draw a line

τέμω ▸ **τέμνω**

τέναγος ους τό shallow water; swamp

τένων οντος ὁ sinew, tendon

τέξομαι *fut from* **τίκτω**

τέρας α(τ)ος τό sign, omen, prodigy; wonder, monster

τερα(το)σκόπος ου ὁ soothsayer, diviner

τερατώδης ες marvellous, prodigious, portentous

τερεβίνθινος η ον of the turpentine tree

τερέβινθος ου ἡ the turpentine tree

τέρετρον ου τό borer, gimlet

τέρην εινα εν (*gen* ενος) smooth, soft, delicate

τέρμα ατος τό end, boundary; goal, mark

τερμιόεις εσσα εν tasselled; long-bordered; that reaches from head to foot

τέρμιος ᾱ ον last, extreme

τερπικέραυνος ον delighting in thunder (of Zens)

τερπνός ή όν delightful, pleasant

τέρπω refresh; cheer, delight, please

τερπωλή ῆς ἡ ▸ **τέρψις**

τερσαίνω, τέρσω wipe up, dry up; *pass* become dry

τερψίμβροτος ον making glad the heart of man

τέρψις εως ἡ enjoyment, delight

τεσσαράβοιος ον worth four oxen

τεσσαράκοντα forty

τεσσαρακονταετής ές forty years old

τεσσαρακοστός ή όν fortieth

τέσσαρες α four
■ **τέσσαρες καὶ δέκα** fourteen

τεσσερακοντόργυιος ον of forty fathoms

τέσσερες ▸ **τέσσαρες**

ταγών taking, seizing

τεταρταῖος ᾱ ον on the fourth day

τεταρτημόριον ου τό the fourth part

τέταρτος η ον fourth
■ **τέταρτος καὶ δέκατος** η ον fourteenth

τετίημαι *pf* be grieved
■ **τετιηώς** υῖα ός grieved

τετμεῖν *aor infin* arrive at, overtake

τετράγυος ον as large as four acres

τετραγωνοπρόσωπος ον square-faced

τετράγωνος ον with four angles, square; perfect, complete

τετράδιον ου τό guard consisting of four soldiers

τετραετής ές four years old

τετραθέλυμνος ον (of a shield) of four layers

τετραίνω bore through, perforate

τετράκις *adv* four times

τετρακισμῡ́ριοι αι α forty thousand

τετρακισχῑ́λιοι αι α four thousand

τετρακόσιοι αι α four hundred

τετράκυκλος ον four-wheeled

τετράμετρος ον consisting of four double feet (in iambic *or* trochaic verse)

τετράμηνος ον lasting four months

τετραμοιρίᾱ ᾱς ἡ fourfold pay

τετρᾱ́ορος ον drawn by four horses

τετραπάλαστος ον four handbreadths long

τετράπηχυς υ of four cubits (i.e. six feet long *or* high)

τετραπλάσιος ᾱ ον **τετραπλοῦς** ῆ οῦν fourfold

τετράπολις (*gen* εως) of four cities

τετράπους πουν four-footed

τετραρχέω be a tetrarch (a ruler under the protection of Rome of lower grade than king)

τετράρχης ου ὁ a tetrarch (see previous entry)

τετράς άδος ἡ the number four; fourth day

τετραφάληρος ον **τετράφαλος** ον with four crests *or* plumes

τετράφῡλος ον divided into four tribes

τέτραχα, τετραχῇ, τετραχθά *adv* fourfold, in four parts

τετρώροφος ον with four storeys

τέττα dear father

τέττιξ ῑγος ὁ grass-hopper; gold ornament worn in the hair

τεῦ ▸ **τοῦ** ▸ **τίνος**

τεύ ▸ **τού** ▸ **τινός**

τεύξομαι *fut from* **τυγχάνω**

τεῦχος ους τό tool, implement, utensil; armour, arms; ship's equipment; vessel, urn

τεύχω make, build, construct, work, form; cause, create

τέφρᾱ ᾱς ἡ ashes

τεφρόω reduce to ashes

τεχνάζω, τεχνάω *and mid* devise, work, make by art; execute skilfully; use tricks, devise cunningly

τέχνασμα ατος τό work of art; artifice, trick

τέχνη ης ἡ art, skill, craft, trade, science; artifice, cunning, trick; work of art

τεχνήεις εσσα εν made by art, ingenious

τέχνημα ατος τό work of art; tool; artifice, trick; cunning person

τεχνικός ή όν artistic, skilful

τεχνῑ́της ου ὁ artist, craftsman, expert; workman, master; deceiver

τέως *adv* so long, meanwhile; hitherto, till now; up till this time; for a time

τῆ *adv* there! take!

τῇ *adv* here, there, thither; in this way; where; how, as

τῇδε *adv* here, there; in this way; therefore

τήθη ης ἡ grandmother

τηθίς ίδος ἡ aunt

τῆθος τό oyster

τηκεδών όνος ἡ consumption

τήκω *act tr* melt; cause to pine, consume; *act intr and pass* melt; pine away; vanish; decay

τηλαυγής ές far-shining

τῆλε ▸ **τηλοῦ**

τηλεδαπός ή όν coming from afar, foreign, distant

τηλεθάω bloom, flourish

τηλεκλειτός ή όν **τελεκλυτός** ή όν far-famed

τηλέπορος ον far, distant

τηλεφανής ές seen *or* heard from afar

τηλίκος η ον **τηλικόσδε** ήδε όνδε **τηλικοῦτος** αύτη οῦτο(ν) so great; so much; so old *or* young

τηλόθεν *adv* from afar

τηλόθι ▸ **τηλοῦ**

τηλόσε *adv* to a distance

τηλοῦ *adv* far away, at a distance

τηλύγετος η ον youthful, late-born; spoiled child, darling child, only child

τηλωπός όν seen *or* heard from afar, far off

τημελέω take care of, tend

τήμερον *adv* today

τῆμος *adv* at that time, then; thereupon

τηνίκα, τηνικάδε, τηνικαῦτα ▸ **τῆμος**

τῆος ▸ **τέως**

τῇπερ *adv* in which way

τηρέω watch, observe, take care of, guard; keep, preserve; keep in prison

τήρησις εως ἡ a watching, guarding, preserving; prison

τητάω deprive; *pass* be in want

τῆτες *adv* this year, of *or* in this year

τηΰσιος ᾱ ον useless, vain

τιᾰ́ρᾱ ᾱς ἡ **τιήρης** εω ὁ tiara, turban

τιᾱροειδής ές like a tiara

τιέω *see* **τετίημαι**

τίη *adv* why?

τιθαιβώσσω (of bees) make a nest, make honey

τιθασεύω tame, make tractable

τιθασός ή όν tamed, tame

τίθημι† put, place, set, lay; inter; ordain, establish, order, fix; reckon, count; estimate, esteem, consider; suppose; make, cause, create, effect, appoint; *mid* take up one's quarters, bivouac; lay down one's arms, surrender

■ **ὅπλα τίθεσθαι** put on arms, fight

τιθηνέομαι tend, nurse, foster

τιθήνη ης ἡ nurse

τίκτω† bring forth, bear, beget

τίλλω τιλῶ ἔτῑλα pluck *or* pull out, tear; *mid* tear one's hair in sorrow for (someone)

τίλων ωνος ὁ a kind of fish

τῑμᾱ́ορος ▸ **τιμωρός**

τῑμάω estimate; judge, condemn; esteem, honour, respect, revere, value, cherish, love; reward, honour with; estimate the amount of punishment

τῑμή ῆς ἡ estimate, valuation, census; price, worth; penalty, punishment, damages, fine, reward; honour, esteem, distinction; place of honour, dignity, magistracy, privilege

τῑμήεις εσσα εν ▸ **τίμιος**

τί̄μημα ατος τό valuation, estimate; census, estimate of property (for taxation); property; penalty, fine

τί̄μιος ᾰ ον valued, esteemed, honoured; costly, precious

τῑμιότης ητος ἡ worth, value, preciousness

τῑμωρέω *and mid* avenge, revenge; help, succour; punish, chastise

τῑμωρητήρ ῆρος ὁ helper, avenger

τῑμώρημα ατος τό **τῑμωρίᾱ** ᾱς ἡ vengeance, punishment; help, aid, succour

τῑμωρός όν avenging, helping

τινάσσω *and mid* shake

τί̄νυμαι *mid* ▸ **τίνομαι**

τίνω (*or* τί̄νω) τείσω *or* τί̄σω ἔτεισα pay; pay a penalty *or* debt; reward; atone; *mid* avenge, punish, make suffer, take vengeance

τίπτε (*or* τί ποτε) *adv* why then?

τίς τί (*gen* τίνος) who? which? what? ■ **τί** why?

τις τι (*gen* τινος) *enclitic* anyone, someone, a certain; anything, something; many a one, each, everyone; *pl* several

τίσις εως ἡ payment; penalty, punishment, atonement, retribution, reward; vengeance

τιταίνω *aor* ἐτίτηνα stretch, spread out, extend, draw, strain; *mid* stretch oneself *or* for oneself, exert oneself

τίτθη ης ἡ nurse

τιτθός οῦ ὁ teat, nipple

τίτλος ου ὁ title, superscription

τιτός ή όν requited

τιτράω, τίτρημι ▸ **τετραίνω**

τιτρώσκω† pierce; wound, hurt; damage, cripple, do (someone) mischief

τιτύσκομαι make ready, prepare; aim at; intend, design

τίω ▸ **τιμάω**

τλᾱ́μων ον **τλήμων** ον enduring, persevering, steadfast, bold; suffering, wretched

τλῆναι *infin* suffer, endure, bear; dare, risk

τλητός ή όν suffering, patient; pliant; endurable

τμήγω cut, hew; *pass* be severed *or* dispersed

τμήδην *adv* by cutting *or* scratching

τμῆμα ατος τό **τμῆσις** εως ἡ cut, incision; section, piece

τμητός ή όν cut, hewn

τόθι *adv* there

τοι ▸ **σοι** *enclitic as adv* let me tell you; certainly; then, consequently

τοί ▸ **οἱ, οἵ**

τοιγάρ, τοιγαροῦν, τοιγάρτοι *adv* so then, therefore, accordingly; therefore indeed

τοίνυν *adv* yet, so then, therefore; further, moreover

τοῖος ᾱ ον **τοιόσδε** ᾱ́δε όνδε **τοιοῦτος** αύτη οῦτο(ν) of such kind *or* quality, just such

τοιουτότροπος ον of such kind

τοῖχος ου ὁ wall of a house; side of a ship

τοιχωρυχέω be a housebreaker, burglar

τοιχωρύχος ου ὁ housebreaker, burglar, thief

τοκάς άδος ἡ having just given birth, with cubs

τοκεύς έως ὁ begetter, parent; *pl* parents

τόκος ου ὁ a bringing forth, birth; offspring, child, son; descent; (of money) interest

τόλμα ης ἡ courage, boldness, daring; a bold *or* daring act

τολμάω bear, endure, undergo; take heart, dare

τολμήεις εσσα εν **τολμηρός** ᾱ́ όν enduring, steadfast; bold; daring

τόλμημα ατος τό adventure, enterprise

τολμητής οῦ ὁ bold *or* foolhardy man

τολμητός ή όν ventured, to be ventured

τολυπεύω achieve, accomplish; endure

τομάω be in need of cutting

τομή ῆς ἡ a cutting, hewing; cut, stroke; stump of a tree, end of a beam

τομός ή όν cutting, sharp

τόνος ου ὁ rope, cord; chord; a stretching, tension; tone, note; metre

τοξάζομαι *mid* ▶ **τοξεύω**

τόξαρχος ου ὁ lord of the bow, archer; captain of the archers

τόξευμα ατος τό missile, arrow, bolt; body of archers; bowshot

τοξευτής οῦ ὁ ▶ **τοξότης**

τοξευτός ή όν struck by an arrow

τοξεύω shoot with the bow, strike with an arrow; aim at; hit

τοξικός ή όν belonging to archery, of *or* for the bow; skilled in the use of the bow

τόξον ου τό bow; missile, arrow; archery
■ **τὰ τόξα** bow and arrows

τοξοσύνη ης ἡ archery

τοξότης ου ὁ bowman, archer; (at Athens) policeman (the police force consisted of Scythian archers)

τοξοφόρος ον bearing a bow; archer

τοπάζιον ου τό topaz

τοπάζω guess, divine

τόπαρχος ου ὁ ruling over [a place]

τόπος ου ὁ place, spot; passage in a book; region, district; space, locality; position, rank, opportunity

τορεύω work in relief, engrave

τορέω bore through

τόρμος ου ὁ hole

τορνεύω turn on a lathe

τόρνος ου ὁ compasses

τορνόω make round

τορός ᾱ́ όν piercing, shrill; clear, distinct, sharp

τοσάκις ▶ **τοσσάκι**

τόσος η ον **τοσόσδε** ηδε ονδε **τοσοῦτος** αύτη οῦτο(ν) so great, so wide, so long, so much, so little, so strong

τοσσάκι *adv* so often

τόσσος η ον ▶ **τόσος**

τότε *adv* then, at that time; formerly; just then

τοτέ *adv* at times, now and then

τοτηνίκα *adv* then

τοτοτοῖ woe!

τοὔνεκα *adv* therefore

τόφρα *adv* so long, till then, meanwhile

τραγέλαφος ου ὁ goat-stag, antelope

τραγήματα ων τά dessert, dried fruits

τραγικός ή όν tragic; majestic, pompous

τράγος ου ὁ he-goat, billy-goat

τραγοσκελής ές goat-footed

τραγῳδέω act a tragedy; declaim in tragic style

τραγῳδίᾱ ᾱς ἡ tragedy

τραγῳδικός ή όν belonging to tragic drama

τραγῳδοποιός οῦ ὁ tragic poet

τραγῳδός οῦ ὁ tragic poet *or* actor

τρᾱνής ές clear, distinct

τράπεζα ης ἡ table; dining-table; dinner, meal; money-changer's table, bank

τραπεζεύς (*gen* έως) belonging to a table, fed from a master's table

τραπεζίτης ου ὁ money-changer, banker

τραπέω tread grapes

τραυλίζω lisp, stammer

τραυλός ή όν lisping, stammering

τραῦμα ατος τό wound, hurt; loss, defeat

τραυματίᾱς ου ὁ wounded man

τραυματίζω wound

τραφερός ᾱ́ όν well-fed, fat; (of land) dry

τραχηλίζω lay bare, expose to view, lay open

τράχηλος ου ὁ neck, throat

τρᾱχῡ́νω make rough *or* rugged

τρᾱχύς εῖα ύ rough, rugged; harsh, angry

τρᾱχύτης ητος ἡ roughness, ruggedness; hardness

τρεῖς τρία three

τρέμω tremble, quiver

τρέπω† *act tr* turn, turn round, away *or* about; divert, alter, change, direct; turn to flight; hinder, prevent; *act intr, mid and pass* turn oneself; be changed

τρέφω† *act tr* make solid, congeal, curdle; feed, nourish, rear, bring up, nurse, tend; *act intr* become solid, grow up; *pass* be fed; grow (up); live; be brought up

τρέχω† run

τρέω *aor* ἔτρεσα tremble, quiver; fear; flee (from)

τρῆμα ατος τό hole, aperture

τρήρων (*gen* ωνος) timid, shy

τρητός ή όν bored through

τρηχύς εῖα ύ ▸ **τραχύς**

τρίαινα ης ἡ trident

τριᾱκάς άδος ἡ the number thirty

τριᾱκονθήμερος ον of thirty days

τριᾱ́κοντα thirty

τριᾱκονταετής ές **τριᾱκονταέτις** (*gen* ιδος) *fem* lasting thirty years

τριᾱκονταρχίᾱ ᾱς ἡ rule of thirty men

τριᾱκοντήμερος ον ▸ **τριακονθήμερος**

τριᾱκόντορος ου ἡ ship with thirty oars

τριᾱκοντούτης ες **τριᾱκοντοῦτις** (*gen* ιδος) *fem* ▸ **τριακονταέτης**

τριᾱκόσιοι αι α three hundred

τριᾱκοστός ή όν thirtieth

τριάς άδος ἡ the number three, triad

τριβή ῆς ἡ a rubbing, wearing away, spending; a practising, practice, skill; delay, evasion; pastime

τρίβολος ον three-pointed; thistle

τρίβος ου ὁ/ἡ path, road; ▸ **τριβή**

τρῑ́βω rub, thrash, grind, pound, bruise; wear away, spend, consume; damage, weaken, waste; delay, tarry; *pass* be busied with

τρίβων ωνος ὁ worn cloak; *adj* practised, versed, skilled, crafty

τρίγληνος ον with three pearls (of earrings)

τριγλώχῑς (*gen* ῑνος) three-forked

τριγονίᾱ ᾱς ἡ third generation

τρίγωνον ου τό triangle

τρίδουλος ου ὁ three times a slave, a slave through three generations

τριέλικτος ον wound three times

τριετηρίς ίδος ἡ triennial festival

τριέτης ες (*or* τριετής ές) triennial

τριετίᾱ ᾱς ἡ space of three years

τρίζω chirp, twitter, squeak, crack

τριηκ- *see* **τριακ-**

τριηραρχέω be captain of a trireme; fit out a trireme (for the state)

τριηραρχίᾱ ᾱς ἡ the fitting out of a trireme (for the state)

τριηραρχικός ή όν belonging to a trierarch

τριήραρχος ου ὁ trierarch; commander of a trireme; one who has to fit out a trireme (for the state)

τριηραύλης ου ὁ flute-player of a trireme (giving the time to the rowers)

τριήρης ους ἡ trireme, ship with three banks of oars

τριηρῖτης ου ὁ serving on board a trireme

τριηροποιός όν building triremes

τρικάρηνος ον **τρίκρᾱνος** ον three-headed

τρίκλῑνος ου ὁ dining-room

τρίλλιστος ον prayed for three times

τρίμετρος ον consisting of three double feet (in iambic, trochaic *or* anapaestic verse)

τρίμηνος ον lasting three months

τρῖμμα ατος τό a practised rogue

τριμοιρίᾱ ᾱς ἡ triple pay

τριξός ▸ **τρισσός**

τρίοδος ου ἡ the meeting of three roads

τριπάλαιστος ον three hands broad *or* long

τρίπηχυς υ three cubits long *or* tall

τρίπλαξ (*gen* ακος) threefold

τριπλάσιος ᾱ ον three times as great *or* as much

τρίπλεθρος ον three plethra long

τριπλοῦς ῆ οῦν threefold, triple

τριπόλιστος ον **τρίπολος** ον ploughed three times; much talked of

τρίπος ου ὁ **τρίπους** ποδος ὁ tripod; three-footed

τρίπτυχος ον of three layers; threefold

τρίς *adv* three times

τρισάθλιος ᾱ ον three times unhappy

τρισάσμενος η ον three times pleased

τρισκαίδεκα thirteen

τρισκαιδεκαστάσιος ον of thirteen times the value

τρισκαιδέκατος η ον thirteenth

τρίσμακαρ (*gen* αρος) three times blessed

τρισμῡ́ριοι αι α thirty thousand

τρίσπονδος ον poured out three times

τρισσός ή όν threefold

τρίστεγος ον with three storeys ■ **τὸ τρίστεγον** the third storey

τρίστοιχος ον in three rows

τρισχῑ́λιοι α three thousand

τριταγωνιστέω act the third part in a play

τριταγωνιστής οῦ ὁ player who acts the third part, a third-rate actor

τριταῖος ᾱ ον in three days; on the third day

τρίτατος η ον ▸ **τρίτος**

τριτημόριος ᾱ ον + *gen* forming a third part of

τρίτος η ον third

τριττύς ύος ἡ the number three; the sacrifice of three animals (a boar, goat and ram); (at Athens) a third of the φυλή

τριφάσιος ᾱ ον threefold, three

τρίφυλλον ου τό trefoil, clover

τρίφῡλος ον consisting of three tribes

τρίχα *adv* in three parts

τριχᾱ́ϊκες ων οἱ in three tribes

τριχῇ, τριχῆ, τριχθά ▸ **τρίχα**

τρίχῐνος η ον of hair

τριχοίνικος ον holding three χοίνικες

τριχοῦ *adv* in three places

τρίχωμα ατος τό growth of hair

τρῖψις εως ἡ a rubbing, touching; resistance to wear, durability

τριώβολον ου τό three-obol piece

τριώροφος ον of three storeys *or* floors

τρομέω *and mid* tremble, quiver; fear

τρόμος ου ὁ a trembling; fear

τροπαῖον (*or* τρόπαιον) ου τό sign of victory, trophy

τροπαῖος (*or* τρόπαιος) ᾱ ον giving victory, causing flight

τροπέω turn

τροπή ῆς ἡ a turning, turn; solstice; flight; defeat; victory; change

τρόπις εως *or* ιος ἡ ship's keel

τρόπος ου ὁ turn, direction; manner, way, fashion, custom, mode of life; character, temper

τροπός οῦ ὁ leather thong for oars

τροπο-φορέω bear with

τροπωτήρ ῆρος ὁ ▶ **τροπός**

τροφεῖα ων τά pay for bringing up, wages of a nurse; food, sustenance

τροφεύς έως ὁ ▶ **τροφός**

τροφέω ▶ **τρέφω**

τροφή ῆς ἡ food, nourishment; maintenance; rearing, nursing; means *or* mode of living; offspring, brood

τρόφιμος ον nourished, brought up; foster-child

τρόφις ι **τροφόεις** εσσα εν well-fed

τροφός οῦ ὁ/ἡ feeder, nurse

τροφο-φορέω bring (someone) nourishment, maintain, sustain

τροχάζω run along

τροχηλάτης ου ὁ charioteer

τροχήλατος ον moved on wheels

τροχιᾱ́ ᾶς ἡ wheel-track, rut; the round of a wheel

τροχίλος ου ὁ plover

τροχοειδής ές circular

τροχός οῦ ὁ wheel, potter's wheel, disk; wheel of torture

τρόχος ου ὁ course, revolution

τρύβλιον ου τό cup, bowl

τρυγάω gather in (the fruit *or* crop)

τρύγητος ου ὁ vintage, harvest

τρῡγών όνος ἡ turtle-dove

τρῡ́ζω coo; mutter

τρῡμαλιᾱ́ ᾶς ἡ hole *or* eye of a needle

τρύξ υγός ἡ must (new wine not yet fermented); dregs, refuse

τρῡ́πανον ου τό borer, auger, gimlet

τρῡπάω bore, pierce through

τρῡ́πημα ατος τό hole

τρῡσᾱ́νωρ (*gen* ορος) harassing men

τρῡτάνη ης ἡ balance, pair of scales

τρυφάλεια ᾱς ἡ helmet

τρυφάω live delicately *or* in luxury, be effeminate *or* licentious, revel; be insolent *or* haughty

τρυφερός ᾱ́ όν delicate, effeminate, luxurious

τρυφή ῆς ἡ delicacy, luxury; pride, insolence

τρύφος εος τό piece, morsel, fragment

τρῡχόω, τρῡ́χω wear out, consume, waste; distress, afflict

τρῡ́ω wear out, exhaust

τρωγλοδύτης ου ὁ dwelling in caves, troglodyte

τρώγω τρώξομαι gnaw, chew, eat

τρώκτης ου ὁ greedy knave, cheat

τρωμ- ▶ **τραυμ-**

τρωπάω change; *mid* turn oneself

τρωσ *likely to be from* **τιτρώσκω**

τρωτός ή όν vulnerable

τρωχάω run

τρώω ▶ **τιτρώσκω**

τύ ▶ **σύ**

τυγχάνω† hit [a mark]; hit upon; fall in with, meet; reach, gain, get, gain one's end; *intr* happen, be at a place; come to pass, fall out, occur by chance

τύκος ου ὁ hammer, pick; battle-axe

τυκτός ή όν made, well-made, wrought by art, artificial; made ready

τύλος ου ὁ **τύλη** ης ἡ a swelling, hard swelling, callus; nail, peg

τυλόω knob with iron; make callous

τύμβευμα ατος τό ▶ **τύμβος**

τυμβεύω bury; *intr* be buried

τυμβήρης ες buried; tomb-like

τύμβος ου ὁ mound; tomb, grave

τυμβο-χοέω throw up a mound over a grave

τυμβοχόη ης ἡ throwing up a mound

τυμβόχωστος ον thrown up into a mound, high-heaped

τυμπανίζω beat a drum

τυμπανίστρια ᾱς ἡ a woman who beats a drum

τύμπανον ου τό drum

τῦνη ▸ **σύ**

τυπή ῆς ἡ ▸ **τύπος**

τυπικός ή όν conforming to type

τύπος ου ὁ stroke, blow; impress, stamp, mark; figure, image, statue; outline, sketch, model, type; system, character

τυπόω stamp, form, model

τύπτω strike, beat, smite, hit; wound; *mid* mourn for

τύπωμα ατος τό figure; vessel, urn

τυραννεύω, τυραννέω be a tyrant *or* absolute ruler; *pass* be ruled with absolute power

τυραννικός ή όν befitting a τύραννος, princely; tyrannical

τυραννίς ίδος ἡ absolute power, monarchy, despotic rule, royalty

τύραννος ου ὁ absolute monarch, sovereign, lord, master; tyrant; *adj* princely, imperious, despotic

τυρβάζομαι *mid* be concerned; be in disorder

τύρβη ης ἡ crowd, disorder

τῡρός οῦ ὁ cheese

τύρσις εως *or* ιος ἡ tower, castle

τυτθός όν small, young

τυτθόν *adv* a little

τυφλός ή όν blind; dull; unseen, dim, invisible, secret

τυφλόω blind, make blind *or* dull

τῦφος ου ὁ smoke, mist; conceit, vanity

τῡφόω make dull *or* foolish

τῡ́φω raise smoke, smoke; smoke out, burn slowly; *pass* smoke, smoulder

τῡφώς ῶ ὁ **τῡφῶν** ῶνος ὁ hurricane

τῡφωνικός ή όν like a whirlwind

τυχ *aor stem from* **τυγχάνω**

τύχη ης ἡ chance; fortune, luck; accident

τῷ *adv* therefore, then, in this case

τωθάζω τωθάσομαι ἐτώθασα scoff at

τώς *adv* so, thus

τωὐτό ▸ **ταὐτό** ▸ **τὸ αὐτό** the same

Υ υ

υ, Υ (ὖ ψιλόν) twentieth letter of the alphabet ■ **υ′** *as a numeral* = 400

ὕαινα ης ἡ hyena

ὑακίνθινος η ον dark-blue

ὑάκινθος ου ὁ/ἡ hyacinth; sapphire

ὑάλινος η ον of glass

ὕαλος ου ὁ glass; crystal

ὑββάλλω ▸ **ὑποβάλλω**

ὑβρίζω ὑβριῶ be *or* become uncontrolled, insolent, licentious *or* extravagant; outrage, insult, affront, maltreat

ὕβρις εως ἡ **ὕβρισμα** ατος τό overweening behaviour, wantonness, insolence, licentiousness; violence, outrage, insult; assault and battery

ὑβριστής οῦ ὁ insolent, wanton, licentious *or* wicked man

ὑβριστικός ή όν given to outrageous behaviour *or* insolence; luxurious, wicked, violent

ὑγιαίνω ὑγιανῶ ὑγίᾱνα be *or* become sound *or* healthy; be sound of mind; be wholesome

ὑγίεια ᾱς ἡ health, soundness (of body)

ὑγιεινός ή όν **ὑγιηρός** ᾱ́ όν **ὑγιής** ές healthy, sound; wholesome; sound in mind, true, genuine

ὑγρός ᾱ́ όν wet, moist, liquid, flowing; pliant, supple; languid, languishing

ὑγρότης ητος ἡ wetness, moisture; suppleness

ὑδατοτρεφής ές growing in *or* by the water

ὑδατώδης ες watery

ὕδρᾱ ᾱς ἡ water-serpent, hydra

ὑδραίνω ὑδρανῶ ὕδρηνα wet; wash

ὑδρείᾱ ᾱς ἡ fetching water

ὑδρεύω draw *or* fetch water

ὑδρήϊον ου τό ▸ **ὑδρία**

ὑδρηλός ή όν watered, moist

ὑδρίᾱ ᾱς ἡ water-pot, pitcher; urn

ὑδρο-ποτέω drink water

ὑδροπότης ου ὁ water-drinker

ὕδρος ου ὁ ▸ **ὕδρα**

ὑδρο-φορέω carry water

ὑδοφόρος ον carrying water; water-carrier

ὑδρωπικός ή όν dropsical

ὕδωρ ατος τό water, rain, sweat; water of the water-clock (κλεψύδρᾱ)

ὕελος ου ὁ ▸ **ὕαλος**

ὑέτιος ᾱ ον bringing rain

ὑετός οῦ ὁ rain

ὕθλος ου ὁ nonsense, fun, buffoonery

ὑΐδιον ου τό little pig

ὑϊδοῦς οῦ ὁ grandson

ὑϊκός ή όν swinish

υἱοθεσίᾱ ᾱς ἡ adoption as a son

υἱός οῦ ὁ son, grandson

υἱωνός οῦ ὁ grandson

ὑλαγμός οῦ ὁ barking

ὑλᾱ́εις εσσα εν ▸ **ὑλήεις**

ὑλακόμωρος ον always barking

ὑλακτέω, ὑλάω *and mid* bark, howl; bark at

ὕλη ης ἡ wood, forest, woodland; timber; fuel; brushwood; matter, stuff, raw material; ballast; stock, plenty

ὑλήεις εσσα εν wooded

ὑλοτόμος ου ὁ woodcutter

ὑλώδης ες woody

ὑμεῖς *pron 2 pl* you

ὑμέναιος ου ὁ wedding-song; wedding; Hymen, the god of marriage

ὑμέτερος ᾱ ον *2 pl* your, yours

ὑμνέω sing; praise; keep talking about

ὕμνος ου ὁ song, hymn; melody

ὑμός ή όν ▸ **ὑμέτερος**

ὑπαγκάλισμα ατος τό that which is clasped in the arms; beloved one, wife

ὑπ-άγω *act tr* lead *or* bring under; yoke; summon before a court; draw from under; seduce, deceive; *act intr* withdraw, retire slowly *or* secretly; advance, go on slowly; *mid* bring under one's power; draw to oneself

ὑπαγωγή ῆς ἡ a leading down; retreat

ὑπ-αείδω accompany with the voice

ὑπαί ▸ **ὑπό**

ὑπ-αιδέομαι *pass* feel awe *or* respect

ὕπαιθα *adv* out under; escaping to one side

ὑπαίθρειος ον **ὑπαίθριος** ον **ὕπαιθρος** ον in the open air

ὑπ-αίθω set on fire

ὑπ-αινίσσομαι hint, intimate

ὑπ-ᾱΐσσω dart from under; rush on

ὑπ-αισχῡ́νομαι *pass* feel somewhat ashamed

ὑπαίτιος ον accused, guilty, responsible

ὑπακοή ῆς ἡ obedience

ὑπ-ακούω listen, hearken; answer; obey, submit to; appear in court

ὑπ-αλείφω anoint, besmear

ὑπ-αλεύομαι *mid* **ὑπ-αλύσκω** avoid, escape

ὑπάλυξις εως ἡ an escaping

U

ὑπ-ανᾱλίσκω spend gradually

ὑπανα-χωρέω withdraw by degrees

ὕπανδρος ον subject to a man, married

ὑπαν-ίσταμαι *mid* rise, stand up

ὑπ-αντάω *usu* + *dat* go to meet, meet; reply *or* object to

ὑπάντησις εως ἡ a going to meet

ὑπ-αντιάζω ▸ **ὑπαντάω**

ὑπ-απειλέω + *dat* threaten indirectly

ὑπάπ-ειμι go away secretly

ὕπαρ τό reality, a waking vision; *adv* really; in a waking state

ὕπαρξις εως ἡ existence, reality; substance, property

ὑπαρχή ῆς ἡ the beginning

ὕπαρχος ου ὁ vice-commander; governor

ὑπ-άρχω begin, be the first; lie under; come into being, arise; exist, be ready *or* at hand; belong to, fall to; be possible, sufficient *or* useful
■ **ὑπάρχων** extant, present
■ **τὰ ὑπάρχοντα** property, means, present circumstances
■ **ὑπάρχει** it is possible *or* allowed

ὑπασπίδιος ον covered by a shield

ὑπασπιστής οῦ ὁ shield-bearer, armour-bearer

ὑπ-ᾴσσω ▸ **ὑπαΐσσω**

ὑπατείᾱ ᾱς ἡ consulship (Roman)

ὑπάτοπος ον somewhat absurd

ὕπατος η ον highest; last; consul

ὕπαυλος ον under cover of a house *or* tent

ὑπάφρων ον somewhat silly

ὕπεαρ ατος τό cobbler's awl

ὑπέγγυος ον responsible

ὑπ-εικάθω, ὑπ-είκω retire, withdraw, escape; yield, give way, obey, submit to

ὕπ-ειμι[1] be *or* lie under *or* underneath; lie at the bottom; be at hand

ὕπ-ειμι[2] come on secretly; withdraw gradually

ὑπείρ ▸ **ὑπέρ**

ὑπείσᾱς, ὑφείσᾱς *aor pple* having placed [men] in ambush

ὑπεισ-δύομαι *mid* steal in

ὑπέκ, ὑπέξ *adv and prep with gen* out from under *or* from beneath

ὑπεκ-δύομαι *mid* slip out of, escape, steal out

ὑπέκ-κειμαι be brought secretly into a safe place

ὑπεκ-κομίζω carry away secretly

ὑπεκ-πέμπω send away *or* escort secretly

ὑπεκπρο-θέω run out before; outrun

ὑπεκπρο-λῡ́ω unyoke [mules] and let them graze

ὑπεκπρο-ρέω flow forth from under

ὑπεκπρο-φεύγω escape secretly

ὑπεκ-σαόω save from under

ὑπεκ-τίθεμαι *mid* remove secretly; carry away safely

ὑπεκ-τρέπω turn secretly; *mid* avoid

ὑπεκ-τρέχω run away, escape; run beyond

ὑπεκ-φέρω carry away secretly; remove a little; *intr* run away; have the start

ὑπεκ-φεύγω escape secretly

ὑπεκ-χωρέω retire secretly, withdraw

ὑπ-ελαύνω ride up to

ὑπεναντίος ᾱ ον opposite; hostile; adversary

ὑπεν-δίδωμι give way a little

ὑπένερθεν *adv and prep with gen* underneath; beneath; in the nether world

ὑπεξ-άγω lead *or* carry out secretly; *intr* withdraw secretly

ὑπεξ-αιρέω *and mid* take away, remove by stealth; take out secretly

ὑπεξ-αλέομαι *mid* escape

ὑπεξαν-άγομαι *pass* put to sea secretly

ὑπεξανα-δύομαι *mid* come up from under gradually

ὑπέξ-ειμι ▸ ὑπεξέρχομαι

ὑπεξ-ειρύω draw out from under

ὑπεξ-ελαύνω drive away secretly; *intr* march away secretly

ὑπεξ-έρχομαι go away secretly *or* slowly; withdraw, emigrate

ὑπεξ-έχω withdraw secretly, escape

ὑπεξ-ίσταμαι *mid* stand up; give way (to), avoid, shun; desist

ὑπέρ *prep with gen* over; above; across; beyond; for, on behalf of, in defence of, for the sake of, because of, by reason of; in the name of; *with acc* beyond, above, exceeding

ὑπέρᾱ ᾱς ἡ an upper rope; brace of the sailyards

ὑπερ-αγαπάω love exceedingly

ὑπερᾱής ές blowing very hard

ὑπερ-αίρω *act tr* surpass, outdo; *act intr and mid* rise above

ὑπερ-αιωρέομαι *pass + gen* be suspended over, project over; lie off [a place] at sea

ὑπέρακμος ον overripe, past the bloom of youth, sexually well-developed

ὑπεράκριος ον over *or* upon the heights

ὑπερ-αλγέω be exceedingly grieved

ὑπεραλγής ές grieving exceedingly

ὑπερ-άλλομαι *mid* leap over

ὑπερανα-τείνω stretch over

ὑπεράνω *adv* above on high

ὑπεραπο-θνῄσκω *+ gen* die for

ὑπεραπο-λογέομαι *mid + gen* speak for, defend

ὑπερ-αρρωδέω, ὑπερ-ορρωδέω fear excessively

ὑπερ-αυξάνω *intr* grow excessively

ὑπερ-αυχέω be overproud

ὑπέραυχος ον overproud

ὑπερ-άχθομαι *pass* be distressed beyond measure

ὑπερ-βαίνω step over; transgress, trespass, offend; pass over, take no notice of; go beyond

ὑπερβαλλόντως *adv* exceedingly, beyond measure

ὑπερ-βάλλω throw over *or* beyond, throw farther; exceed the right measure, overflow, surpass, outdo, excel, exaggerate, overrun; go beyond, pass over, cross, traverse, double; *mid* surpass, excel, exceed; put off, delay

ὑπερβασίᾱ ᾱς ἡ transgression, trespass, offence

ὑπερβατός ή όν to be passed over, scaleable; transposed

ὑπερ-βιάζομαι *mid* overwhelm

ὑπέρβιος ον overwhelming; overweening, excessive; passionate, wanton

ὑπερβολή ῆς ἡ a passing over, passage, mountain pass, height; excess, highest degree; pre-eminence, preponderance; delay, putting off

ὑπερβρῑθής ές exceedingly heavy

ὑπερδεής ές much inferior in number *or* undaunted

ὑπερ-δείδω, ὑπερ-δειμαίνω fear exceedingly

ὑπερδέξιος ον situated above one (on the right hand)

ὑπερ-δικέω plead for

ὑπέρδικος ον most just, more than just, severe

ὑπ-ερείδω prop, support

ὑπ-ερείπω undermine, subvert; fall down

ὑπερέκεινα *adv + gen* beyond

ὑπερεκπερισσοῦ, ὑπερεκπερισσῶς *adv* more than super-abundantly

ὑπερεκ-πλήσσομαι *pass* be frightened *or* astonished excessively

ὑπερεκ-τείνω stretch beyond measure

ὑπερεκ-χύνομαι *pass* overflow

U

ὑπερεν-τυγχάνω make intercession for

ὑπερεπ-αινέω praise exceedingly

ὑπ-ερέπτω take away from below

ὑπερ-έρχομαι go beyond

ὑπερ-εσθίω eat immoderately

ὑπέρευ *adv* exceedingly well

ὑπερ-εχθαίρω hate exceedingly

ὑπερ-έχω hold over; *intr* rise above, be above, stand out; be superior *or* more powerful, excel

ὑπερ-ήδομαι *pass* rejoice exceedingly

ὑπερήμισυς υ more than half

ὑπερηνορέων (*gen* οντος) overbearing, overweening

ὑπερηφανέω be proud *or* overweening

ὑπερηφανίᾱ ᾱς ἡ arrogance, haughtiness

ὑπερήφανος ον excellent, splendid; arrogant, overweening

ὑπερθαλασσίδιος ον above the coastline

ὑπερ-θαυμάζω wonder exceedingly

ὕπερθεν *adv* from above; above; over; beyond

ὑπερ-θρῴσκω leap over

ὑπέρθῡμος ον high-spirited

ὑπερθύριον ου τό **ὑπέρθυρον** ου τό lintel

ὑπερ-ῑ́ημι throw beyond

ὑπερ-ικταίνομαι run hurriedly

ὑπερ-ίσταμαι *mid* + *gen* stand over, protect

ὑπερίστωρ (*gen* ορος) knowing only too well

ὑπερ-ίσχω ▸ ὑπερέχω

ὑπερκάθ-ημαι *mid* sit over *or* above; lie in wait

ὑπερκατα-βαίνω step down over

ὑπέρ-κειμαι *mid* lie over *or* beyond

ὑπέρκοπος ον overbearing, overstepping all bounds

ὑπερ-κτάομαι *mid* acquire over and above, acquire through one's own fault

ὑπερκῡ́δᾱς (*gen* αντος) triumphant, exceedingly famous

ὑπερλίᾱν *adv* beyond all measure

ὑπερ-λῡπέομαι *pass* be grieved beyond measure

ὑπερ-μαχέω, ὑπερ-μάχομαι + *gen* fight for

ὑπερμεγέθης ες (*also* ὑπερμεγάθης ες) exceedingly large

ὑπερ-μεθύσκομαι *pass* be excessively drunk

ὑπερμενέων (*gen* οντος) **ὑπερμενής** ές high-spirited; excessively mighty

ὑπέρμετρος ον enormous, excessive

ὑπερμήκης ες exceedingly long *or* mighty

ὑπερ-μῑσέω hate excessively

ὑπέρμορον *adv* beyond destiny

ὑπερ-νῑκάω surpass by far, be more than conqueror

ὑπερ-νοέω think still more, trouble oneself further

ὑπερνότιος ον beyond the south wind, at the extreme south

ὑπέρογκος ον of excessive size *or* bulk; overgrown; overweening, immoderate

ὑπερ-οικέω + *gen* dwell above *or* beyond

ὑπέροικος ον dwelling above *or* beyond

ὕπερον ου τό pestle, club

ὑπεροπλίᾱ ᾱς ἡ presumption, defiance

ὑπερ-οπλίζομαι *mid* conquer by force of arms, treat scornfully

ὑπέροπλος ον overweening, arrogant

ὑπερόπτης (*gen* ου) despising, disdainful

ὑπεροπτικός ή όν **ὑπέροπτος** ον haughty, overweening, proud, disdainful

ὑπερ-οράω look over, survey; overlook, disregard, slight, despise, disdain; let pass

ὑπερόριος (ᾱ) ον over the boundaries, living abroad, foreign

ὑπεροχή ῆς ἡ superiority, excess; pre-eminence, excellence

ὑπέροχος ον prominent; distinguished

ὑπεροψίᾱ ᾱς ἡ haughtiness; disdain

ὑπερ-περισσεύομαι *mid* become excessively abundant

ὑπερπερισσῶς *adv* beyond all measure

ὑπερ-πέτομαι *mid* fly over

ὑπερ-πίμπλημι overfill

ὑπερ-πῑπτω be gone by, elapse

ὑπερ-πλεονάζω be superabundant

ὑπέρπολυς πόλλη πολυ overmuch

ὑπερ-πονέω toil exceedingly; endure for (others)

ὑπερπόντιος ον beyond the sea; across the sea

ὑπέρτατος η ον uppermost, highest

ὑπερ-τείνω stretch over; extend beyond; *intr* project beyond

ὑπερτελής ές overleaping; rising *or* appearing above

ὑπερ-τέλλω rise over

ὑπερτερίᾱ ᾱς ἡ upper frame of a carriage

ὑπέρτερος ᾱ ον upper, higher; superior, better, more excellent, stronger; further, more

ὑπερ-τίθημι *and mid* commit, entrust; delay, put off

ὑπερ-τῑμάω honour exceedingly

ὑπερ-τρέχω outrun; surpass; pass over

ὑπέρυθρος ον somewhat red

ὑπερύψηλος ον exceedingly high

ὑπερ-υψόω exalt exceedingly

ὑπερ-φαίνομαι *pass* + *gen* appear above

ὑπερ-φέρω carry over; *intr* project; excel; be superior

ὑπερφίαλος ον overbearing, arrogant, excessive, overpowerful

ὑπερ-φιλέω love exceedingly

ὑπερ-φρονέω be haughty *or* overproud; despise

ὑπέρφρων ον arrogant, disdainful

ὑπερφυής ές immense, excessive, enormous, extraordinary; strange

ὑπερ-φῡομαι *mid* surpass

ὑπερ-χαίρω rejoice exceedingly

ὑπερ-χλῑω, ὑπερ-χλῑδάω be arrogant *or* proud

ὑπ-έρχομαι *mid* go *or* come under, creep into; come up, advance slowly; deceive; fawn, flatter

ὑπερῴᾱ ᾱς ἡ palate

ὑπ-ερωέω go *or* shrink back

ὑπερώιον ου τό (*also* ὑπερῷον ου τό) upper storey, upper room

■ **ὑπερωιόθεν** *adv* from the upper storey

ὑπ-ερωτάω insert a question

ὑπεύθῡνος ον liable to give account for (one's administration), responsible (for)

■ **οἱ ὑπεύθῡνοι** (at Athens) magistrates who had to submit their accounts to public auditors

ὑπ-έχω hold under, put under, hold out; lend, grant, afford, allow; take upon oneself, submit to, suffer

ὑπήκοος ον obedient, subject

ὑπ-ημῡω bend the head

ὑπήνεμος ον sheltered from the wind

ὑπήνη ης ἡ beard

ὑπηνήτης (*gen* ου) bearded

ὑπηοῖος ᾱ ον about dawn, early

ὑπηρεσίᾱ ᾱς ἡ rower's service; crew, sailors; service

ὑπηρέσιον ου τό cushion on a rower's bench

ὑπ-ηρετέω + *dat* serve, do service; aid, obey, comply with; gratify, afford

ὑπηρέτημα ατος τό service, assistance

ὑπηρέτης ου ὁ rower, sailor; servant; assistant, underling; porter; (at Athens) the servant who attended each hoplite, the assistant of the Eleven, employed in execution of state-criminals

ὑπηρετικός ή όν fit for serving, menial, attending on

ὑπ-ίλλω draw in the tail; check, restrain

ὑπ-ισχνέομαι† *mid* **ὑπ-ίσχομαι** promise; engage, betroth; assert

ὕπνος ου ὁ sleep, sleepiness

ὑπνόω, ὑπνώω *intr and pass* sleep

ὑπό *adv and prep* with acc towards and under; towards; about; about the time of, just after; behind; in the power of; with gen under; from under; by; through, by reason of, because of, in consequence of; with; with dat under; by force of, under one's power, subject to

ὑπόβαθρον ου τό prop; rocking frame of cradle

ὑπο-βαίνω go under *or* down, stand under

ὑπο-βάλλω throw *or* put under; rejoin, retort; suggest, contrive; *mid* substitute; invent, forge

ὑπο-βλέπω *and mid* look askance, scornfully, suspiciously *or* angrily; glance at

ὑποβλήδην *adv* replying interruptingly; askance

ὑπόβλητος ον **ὑποβολιμαῖος** ᾱ ον substituted, spurious, counterfeit

ὑποβρύχιος ᾱ ον **ὑπόβρυχος** ον under water

ὑπόγαιος ον **ὑπόγειος** ον underground, subterranean

ὑπο-γίγνομαι be born after

ὑπογραμματεύς έως ὁ under-secretary

ὑπο-γραμματεύω be an under-secretary

ὑπογραμμός οῦ ὁ pattern, model

ὑπογραφή ῆς ἡ signed bill of indictment; outline, sketch, design

ὑπο-γράφω write under an inscription, add to it; sign; sketch out, delineate

ὑπόγυ(ι)ος ον close at hand

ὑπο-δαίω set on fire under

ὑπο-δάμναμαι *pass* submit

ὑποδεής ές feeble, weak; inferior

ὑπόδειγμα ατος τό sign, token; model, pattern, example

ὑπο-δείδω, ὑπο-δειμαίνω fear a little, shrink from

ὑπο-δείκνῡμι show secretly; delineate; give to understand, suggest, intimate; show, prove

ὑπο-δέμω lay as a foundation

ὑποδεξίη ης ἡ hospitality

ὑποδέξιος ᾱ ον receiving, capacious, ample

ὑπόδεσις εως ἡ binding under; sandal, shoe

ὑπο-δέχομαι *mid* receive, welcome, entertain; endure, bear; become pregnant; undertake, promise, admit, allow; (of a place) come next

ὑπο-δέω bind under; put on shoes

ὑπόδημα ατος τό sandal, shoe

ὑπόδικος ον subject to trial

ὑποδμώς ῶος ὁ underservant

ὑποδοχή ῆς ἡ reception, entertainment; supposition, opinion

ὑπόδρα *adv* looking sternly, askance *or* grimly

ὑπο-δράω + *dat* wait on, serve

ὑποδρηστήρ ῆρος ὁ waiter, servant

ὑπο-δῡ́νω, ὑπο-δύομαι *mid* slip *or* slide under *or* into, dive under; put on under; put on shoes; steal into; come on, emerge from; undertake, undergo; insinuate oneself

ὑποζάκορος ου ἡ underpriestess

ὑπο-ζεύγνῡμι yoke under; *pass* take on oneself

ὑποζύγιος ον put under the yoke ■ **τὸ ὑποζύγιον** beast of burden

ὑπο-ζώννῡμι gird under, undergird

ὑπο-θερμαίνω heat a little

ὑπόθερμος ον somewhat hot; passionate

ὑπόθεσις εως ἡ foundation; supposition; question, subject of discussion; argumentation, principle, summary; design, proposal

ὑποθήκη ης ἡ **ὑποθημοσύνη** ης ἡ hint, advice, warning

ὑπο-θορυβέω begin to make a noise

ὑπο-θωπεύω flatter a little

ὑπο-θωρήσσομαι *mid* arm oneself secretly

ὑποκάθ-ημαι *mid* **ὑποκαθ-ίζομαι** *mid* sit down at; lie in ambush

ὑπο-καίω burn from below

ὑπο-κάμπτω bend under

ὑποκατα-βαίνω go down by degrees

ὑποκατα-κλῑ́νομαι *pass + dat* submit (to)

ὑποκάτω *adv* below, beneath

ὑπό-κειμαι lie under, below *or* at the bottom; be put under the eyes; be laid down, taken for granted *or* settled; be subject to; submit; be proposed; be at hand

ὑπο-κηρύσσομαι *mid* have something proclaimed

ὑπο-κῑνέω move gently; incite a little; *intr* move a little

ὑπο-κλαίω shed secret tears

ὑπο-κλέπτομαι *pass* be defrauded

ὑπο-κλῑ́νομαι *pass* lie under

ὑπο-κλονέομαι *pass* press on in wild flight

ὑπο-κνίζομαι *pass* be tickled secretly, be somewhat excited

ὑπο-κορίζομαι *mid* talk a child's language, call by endearing names; extenuate, palliate

ὑποκρητηρίδιον ου τό stand of a mixing vessel

ὑπο-κρῑ́νομαι *mid* answer; interpret; play a part, be an actor; feign, dissemble

ὑπόκρισις εως ἡ answer; hypocrisy

ὑποκριτής οῦ ὁ actor; hypocrite

ὑπο-κρύπτω hide, keep secret

ὑπόκυκλος ον running on wheels

ὑπο-κύομαι become pregnant

ὑπο-κύπτω stoop *or* bend under; submit

ὑπόκωφος ον rather deaf

ὑπο-λαμβάνω take from below; take on one's back (as the dolphin did Arion); receive, accept; take up; answer, rejoin; take up, fight with; think, suppose, conceive, understand; follow close; draw away, entice

ὑπο-λάμπω shine from beneath; shine into

ὑπο-λέγω dictate, prompt; consider, take into account

ὑπόλειμμα ατος τό remnant

ὑπο-λείπω leave remaining, leave behind; *pass* be inferior

ὑπο-λευκαίνομαι *pass* become white underneath

ὑπολήνιον ου τό tub of a wine-press, vat

ὑπόληψις εως ἡ answer, reply; objection; assumption

ὑπολίζων ον somewhat smaller *or* fewer

ὑπο-λιμπάνω ▸ ὑπολείπω

ὑπο-λογίζομαι *mid* take into account

ὑπόλογος ου ὁ a taking into account; *adj* taken into account

ὑπόλοιπος ον left remaining *or* behind

ὑπολόχᾱγος ου ὁ under-captain

ὑπο-λῡ́ω loosen from below; untie; slacken gradually; *mid* untie one's shoes; free from secretly

ὑπο-μαλακίζομαι *pass* become a little cowardly, grow cowardly by degrees

ὑπόμαργος ον a little mad

ὑπομείων ον somewhat inferior, subordinate

ὑπο-μένω stay behind; abide, await; survive; endure; wait for; stand one's ground; undertake; resist

ὑπο-μῑ́γνῡμι + *dat* come near *or* approach secretly

ὑπο-μιμνήσκω remind; mention; *pass* remember, recollect

ὑπο-μνάομαι *mid* woo secretly

ὑπόμνημα ατος τό **ὑπόμνησις** εως ἡ reminding, mention, admonition; memorial, memoir

■ **τὰ ὑπομνήματα** memoranda, notes, minutes (of meetings)

ὑπ-όμνυμαι *mid* take an oath to postpone legal proceedings

ὑπομονή ῆς ἡ perseverance, patience; endurance

ὑπο-νείφω snow a little

ὑπονήϊος ον lying at the foot of the promontory Neion

ὑπο-νοέω suspect; conjecture, guess

ὑπόνοια ᾱς ἡ suspicion; conjecture, guess, opinion

ὑπονομηδόν *adv* by underground channels, by means of pipes

ὑπόνομος ου ὁ underground passage, mine

ὑπο-νοστέω go back, decrease, fall

ὑπο-πάσσω strew under

ὑπόπεμπτος ον sent secretly

ὑπο-πέμπω send secretly

ὑπο-περκάζω become dark-coloured by degrees

ὑπο-πετάννῡμι spread out under

ὑπόπετρος ον somewhat rocky

ὑπο-πιάζω, ὑπο-πιέζω oppress

ὑπο-πίμπλημι fill by degrees

ὑπο-πῑ́νω drink a little *or* moderately

ὑπο-πῑ́πτω fall down, prostrate oneself; get under

ὑποπλάκιος ᾱ ον under Mount Plakos

ὑπόπλεος ον **ὑποπλέως** ων + *gen* rather full

ὑπο-πλέω sail along under (the lee of)

ὑπο-πνέω blow gently

ὑποπόδιον ου τό footstool

ὑπο-ποιέω produce gradually; *mid* win by underhand tricks *or* intrigue

ὑπόπτερος ον winged, feathered

ὑπ-οπτεύω be suspicious, suspect; guess, suppose

ὑπ-όπτης ου ὁ suspicious

ὑπο-πτήσσω crouch *or* cower down; hide oneself from fear; be shy *or* abashed

ὕποπτος ον suspected, critical; suspicious, fearing

ὑπ-όρνῡμι *act tr* sitr up, rouse gradually; *act intr and mid* rise

ὑπο-ρρήγνυμαι *pass* break *or* open from beneath

ὑπόρρηνος ον suckling a lamb

ὑπ-ορύσσω dig under, undermine

ὑπο-σημαίνω order by a signal

ὑπο-σκελίζω trip [someone] up, upset

ὑπο-σπανίζομαι + *gen* be stinted of

ὑπο-σπάω draw away from under

ὑπόσπονδος ον under a truce, by way of a treaty

ὑπο-σ(σ)είω shake below, set in motion below

ὑποστάθμη ης ἡ sediment, excrement

ὑπόστασις εως ἡ foundation; substance, matter, reality, real nature; confidence

ὑπο-σταχύομαι *mid* grow up, thrive

ὑπόστεγος ον under a roof; entering a house

ὑπο-στέλλω draw *or* take down; keep back; *mid* shrink back from, conceal, dissemble

ὑπο-στένω, ὑπο-στενάζω, ὑπο-στεναχίζω sigh *or* moan; ring

ὑποστολή ῆς ἡ shrinking back, evasion

ὑπο-στόρνῡμι spread out under

ὑπο-στρατηγέω be an under-captain

ὑποστράτηγος ου ὁ subordinate commander

ὑπο-στρέφω *act tr* turn round about *or* back; *act intr and pass* wheel round, turn and flee; return; take care of; evade, elude

ὑποστροφή ῆς ἡ a turning round; retreat; return; flight

ὑπο-στρώννῡμι ▸ **ὑποστόρνυμι**

ὑπόσχεσις εως ἡ **ὑποσχεσίη** ης ἡ promise

ὑποταγή ῆς ἡ subordination, submission

ὑπο-τανύω spread out under

ὑπο-ταράσσω trouble a little, perplex

ὑπο-ταρβέω fear

ὑποταρτάριος ον under Tartarus (of the Titans)

ὑπο-τάττω place *or* arrange under; subject; *pass* + *dat* obey

ὑπο-τείνω stretch under; hold out, suggest hopes; cause; strain, sharpen, heighten

ὑπο-τειχίζω build a cross-wall

ὑποτείχισις εως ἡ **ὑποτείχισμα** ατος τό cross-wall

ὑπο-τελέω pay off, discharge a payment; pay tribute

ὑποτελής ές tributary

ὑπο-τέμνω *and mid* cut away below; cut off, intercept; thwart

ὑπο-τίθημι put *or* place under; delay, keep in suspense; substitute; pawn, mortgage; suppose, suggest, admonish, promise; *mid* lay down as a principle *or* rule; propose to oneself; intend, purpose; suggest, advise

ὑπο-τοπέω (*also* ὑπο-τοπεύω) *and mid* suspect

ὑπο-τρέμω tremble a little

ὑπο-τρέχω run (in) under; sail by *or* past; ingratiate oneself with

ὑπο-τρέω, ὑπο-τρομέω tremble a little; shrink back

ὑπότρομος ον trembling with fear

ὑπότροπος ον returning

ὑπο-τύπτω strike *or* push down; dip down

ὑποτύπωσις εως ἡ outline; model

ὕπουλος ον festering under the scar; rotten underneath; illusory

ὑπουράνιος ον under heaven

ὑπ-ουργέω serve, be helpful; perform, afford

ὑπούργημα ατος τό **ὑπουργίᾱ** ᾱς ἡ service rendered

ὑπουργός όν serviceable, helpful

ὑπο-φαίνω *act tr* show from under, bring to light, show a little; *act intr and pass* come into sight, be seen a little

ὑπόφαυσις εως ἡ an opening for light, a narrow opening

ὑπο-φείδομαι *mid* spare a little, be moderate *or* restrained

ὑπο-φέρω carry away, save, rescue; carry downwards; hold out, proffer; pretend; endure, suffer; *pass* sail downstream; be seduced *or* misled

ὑπο-φεύγω escape secretly

ὑποφήτης ου ὁ interpreter, prophet

ὑπο-φθάνω *and mid* be beforehand

ὑπο-φθέγγομαι *mid* (of a ventriloquist) speak in an undertone

ὑπο-φθονέω feel secret envy

ὑπόφθονος ον with secret envy

ὑποφορά ᾶς ἡ pretence, objection, putting forward by way of excuse

ὑπο-χάζομαι give way gradually

ὑπόχειρ (*gen* χειρος) **ὑποχείριος** ον under the hand, at hand; under one's power, subject

ὑπο-χέω pour, strew *or* spread under; administer to

ὑπ-οχλέομαι be rolled under

ὕποχος ον subject, dependent, subdued

ὑπόχρεως ων (*gen* ω) in debt

ὑπο-χρῑ́ω smear under, upon *or* a little

ὑπο-χωρέω withdraw, retire, recoil; go on steadily

ὑπόψαμμος ον sandy

ὑποψίᾱ ᾱς ἡ suspicion, jealousy

ὑπόψιος ον suspected, despised

ὑπτιάζω bend back

ὕπτιος ᾱ ον bent back; on one's back; turned up, inverted; level, flat

ὑπωμοσίᾱ ᾱς ἡ oath taken to delay proceedings at law

ὑπώπια ων τά face

ὑπ-ωπιάζω give a black eye to; annoy greatly, bruise, mortify

ὑπώρεια ᾱς ἡ foot *or* slope of a mountain

ὑπωρόφιος (ᾱ) ον under the roof

ὗς ὑός ὁ/ἡ sow, pig

ὑσμῑ́νη ης ἡ battle, combat

ὕσσωπος ου ἡ hyssop (probably the caper plant)

ὕστατος η ον last, utmost, extreme

ὑστέρᾱ ᾱς ἡ womb

ὑστεραῖος ᾱ ον following, later, next

ὑστερέω be behind, late *or* later; come too late; miss, fail; be in want of; come short of, be inferior; delay, be wanting; *pass* be in way

ὑστέρημα ατος τό **ὑστέρησις** εως ἡ deficiency, need, want

ὑστερίζω ▸ **ὑστερέω**

ὕστερος ᾱ ον the latter; coming after, following, later; younger; too late; inferior, weaker
■ **ὕστερον** *adv* afterwards, later, in future

ὑστεροφθόρος ον destroying after

ὕστριξ ιχος ὁ/ἡ porcupine

ὑφαίνω ὑφανῶ ὕφηνα weave; contrive, devise

ὑφ-αιρέω take away from under; draw away, seduce; withhold; *mid* purloin, abstract; make away with

ὕφαλος ον submarine

ὑφάντης ου ὁ weaver

ὑφαντικός ή όν skilled in weaving

ὑφαντός ή όν woven

ὑφ-άπτω set on fire from underneath

ὑφ-αρπάζω take away in an underhand manner, rob

ὕφασμα ατος τό texture, web

ὑφάω ▸ **ὑφαίνω**

ὑφειμένως *adv* dejectedly, in a subdued tone *or* manner

ὑφ-έλκω draw away under

ὑφ-έρπω creep on secretly

ὑφ-ηγέομαι *mid + dat* lead the way (for), guide; advance slowly

ὑφήγησις εως ἡ a leading, guiding

ὑφηγητήρ ῆρος ὁ **ὑφηγητής** οῦ ὁ guide

ὑφηνίοχος ου ὁ charioteer

ὑφ-ῑ́ημι *act tr* send down; put under; lower; admit, submit; *act intr and mid* yield, abate, slacken; become despondent; creep *or* steal in

ὑφ-ίστημι *act tr* place under; place secretly; *act intr and mid* stand under; post oneself secretly; stand one's ground; resist; take upon oneself, engage in; promise

ὑφ-οράω *and mid* look askance at, view with suspicion

ὑφορβός οῦ ὁ swineherd

ὑφ-ορμίζομαι *mid* come to anchor secretly

ὕφυδρος ον under water

ὑψαγόρᾱς (*gen* ου) boasting

ὑψερεφής ές with a high roof

ὑψηλός ή όν high, lofty, steep; proud, stately

ὑψηλοφρονέω be high-minded

ὑψηρεφής ές ▸ **ὑψερεφής**

ὑψηχής ές neighing with raised head, loud-neighing

ὕψι *adv* high, on high
■ **ὕψιστος** η ον highest

ὑψίβατος ον set on high

ὑψιβρεμέτης (*gen* ου) high-thundering

ὑψίζυγος ον ruling on high, high-throned (of Zeus)

ὑψικάρηνος ον high-topped

ὑψικέρως ων with high horns

ὑψίκομος ον with high foliage

ὑψίκομπος ον boastful

ὑψιπετήεις εσσα εν **ὑψιπέτης** (*gen* ου) flying on high

ὑψιπέτηλος ον with high foliage; high-reared, lofty

ὑψίπολις ι eminent in one's city

ὑψίπους (*gen* ποδος) walking on high, high-reared, lofty

ὑψίπυλος ον with high gates

ὑψίπυργος ον with lofty towers

ὕψιστος η ον *see* **ὕψι**

ὑψόθεν *adv* from on high; on high

ὑψόθι *adv* on high

ὑψόροφος ον ▸ **ὑψερεφής**

ὕψος ους τό height, top; summit, crown; sublimity, grandeur

ὑψόσε *adv* upwards

ὑψοῦ ▸ **ὕψι**

ὑψόω life high, raise

ὕψωμα ατος τό height, elevation

ὕω water, wet; send rain; rain; *pass* be rained on; rain
■ **ὕει** it is raining

φ, Φ (φῖ) twenty-first letter of the alphabet
■ **φʹ** *as a numeral* = 500

φαάντατος η ον *sup from* **φαεινός**

φαγέδαινα ης ἡ cancerous sore

φαγ *likely to be from* **ἐσθίω**

φάγος ου ὁ glutton

φαέθων ουσα ον **φαεινός** ή όν shining, beaming

φαείνω shine; illuminate; *pass* become visible

φαεννός ή όν ▸ **φαεινός**

φαεσίμβροτος ον shining on mortals

φαιδιμόεις εσσα εν **φαίδιμος** ον shining, brilliant; illustrious; famous, glorious

φαιδρός ά όν beaming, bright, joyous

φαιδρόω, φαιδρύνω cheer up, gladden

φαινόλης ου ὁ cloak

φαίνω† *act tr* bring to light, make visible, show, make clear *or* audible; display, exhibit, explain; announce, denounce, make known; promise, grant; *act intr* give light, shine; *pass* come to light, appear, shine forth; be conspicuous; make one's appearance; be denounced

φάκελος ου ὁ bundle

φακός οῦ ὁ lentil

φαλαγγηδόν *adv* in phalanxes

φαλάγγιον ου τό spider

φάλαγξ αγγος ἡ line of battle, order of battle, phalanx, body of soldiers, compact mass; round piece of wood, trunk; spider

φαλακρόομαι *pass* become bald

φαλακρός ᾱ́ όν bald

φάλαρον ου τό brazen boss; cheekpiece for a horse

φαληριάω become white with foam

φαλλός οῦ ὁ penis, phallus

φάλος ου ὁ horn (of a helmet)

φανερός (ᾱ́) όν visible, manifest, conspicuous; public; known, famous

φανερόω make visible, manifest *or* known; *pass* become known *or* famous

φανέρωσις εως ἡ manifestation

φᾱνός ή όν ▸ **φαεινός**
▪ ὁ **φᾱνός** torch of vine twigs

φαντάζομαι *pass* appear, show oneself

φαντασίᾱ ᾱς ἡ appearance; display, show; splendour; imagination

φάντασμα ατος τό appearance; apparition, phantom, vision, spectre

φανῶ *fut from* **φαίνω**

φάος ους τό light, daylight, sunlight; light of life; eye-sight; lamp, torch; life, deliverance, happiness; darling (light of my life)

φάραγξ αγγος ἡ ravine, cleft, chasm

φαρέτρᾱ ᾱς ἡ **φαρετρεών** ῶνος ὁ quiver

φαρμακείᾱ ᾱς ἡ the use of drugs *or* spells; poisoning, witchcraft; medicine

φαρμακεύς έως ὁ poisoner, sorcerer

φαρμακεύω use drugs *or* poisons; administer a drug, drug

φάρμακον ου τό drug, medicine, remedy; poison, enchanted potion; dye, colour

φαρμακοποσίᾱ ᾱς ἡ the drinking of medicine *or* poison

φαρμακός οῦ ὁ ▸ **φαρμακεύς** a scapegoat; a term of reproach

φαρμάσσω ▸ **φαρμακεύω** enchant, bewitch; temper, harden

φᾶρος (*or* φάρος) ους τό web, cloth; sheet; sail; cloak

φάρσος εος τό part, portion, division

φάρυγξ υγγος *or* υγος ἡ throat, windpipe; chasm

φάσγανον ου τό knife, sword

φάσις εως ἡ information, assertion; denunciation

φάσκω ▸ **φημί**

φάσμα ατος τό ▸ **φάντασμα**

φάσσα ης ἡ wood pigeon

φασσοφόνος ον pigeon killing

φατίζω say, speak; betroth

φάτις εως ἡ ▸ **φήμη**

φάτνη ης ἡ manger, crib

φαυλίζω φαυλιῶ depreciate, slight

φαῦλος (η) ον bad; slight, trifling; useless, mean, common, worthless; vulgar; insignificant, simple, plain, unaffected; careless, evil, malevolent

φαυλότης ητος ἡ meanness; badness

φάω shine

φέβομαι flee; shun

φέγγος ους τό light, splendour

φείδομαι *mid* + *gen* keep clear of, turn away from; spare, use sparingly

φειδώ οῦς *or* όος ἡ **φειδωλή** ῆς ἡ a sparing; thrift, parsimony

φειδωλίᾱ ᾱς ἡ thrift, economy

φειδωλός ή όν sparing, thrifty

φελλός οῦ ὁ cork

φελόνης ου ὁ ▸ **φαινόλης**

φενᾱκίζω cheat, deceive

φενᾱκισμός οῦ ὁ imposture

φένω *aor* (ἔ)πεφνον slay, murder

φέρβω feed, nourish

φέρε come on!

φερέγγυος ον giving surety *or* bail; trusty, competent

φερέοικος ον carrying one's house with one (of the Scythians); snail

φέριστος η ον **φέρτατος** η ον best, bravest, most excellent

φερνή ῆς ἡ dowry

φέρτε ▸ **φέρετε**

φ

φέρτρον ου τό **φέρετρον** ου τό bier, litter

φέρω† bear, carry, bear along; suffer, endure; fetch, bring, present; occasion, cause; pay; bring forth, produce; carry away [booty]; rob, gain, win; lead to, stretch, aim at, refer to, tend to; have in one's mouth; *pass* be carried on *or* along; move quickly, hasten, run, fly; *mid* carry away for oneself; bring with one; win, gain

■ **χαλεπῶς** *or* **βαρέως φέρειν** to bear impatiently, endure with a bad grace

φεῦ *int* ah! alas! woe! oh!

φεύγω† flee, take flight, run away; flee before [someone]; shun, shrink from, fear; be banished; be an exile; be accused *or* prosecuted

φευκτός ή όν to be avoided

φεῦξις εως ἡ ▸ **φυγή**

φή (*or* φῆ) *adv* just as

φήγινος η ον of oak

φηγός οῦ ἡ a species of oak

φήμη ης ἡ speech, talk; report, rumour; legend; saying, word; voice; prophetic voice, omen

φημι† *enclitic and mid* say, speak, tell; call by name; answer; think, believe, imagine, fancy; assert, say yes; *mid* think oneself

■ **οὔ φημι** say ... not, refuse

φημίζω speak out; spread a report

φῆμις ιος ἡ ▸ **φήμη**

φην *aor stem from* **φαίνω**

φήνη ης ἡ sea-eagle

φήρ φηρός ὁ monster

φθάνω† come *or* reach before *or* beforehand, be sooner *or* first

φθαρτός ή όν corruptible, perishable

φθέγγομαι *mid* raise one's voice, cry aloud, sound; call, speak; murmur

φθέγμα ατος τό ▸ **φθογγή**

φθείρ ρός ὁ louse

φθειρο-τραγέω eat fir-cones *or* lice

φθείρω† destroy, ruin; corrupt, spoil, waste; kill; seduce; *pass* perish, be lost *or* cast away

φθήσομαι *fut from* **φθάνω**

φθινάς (*gen* άδος) consuming, wasting, waning

φθινοπωρινός ή όν autumnal

φθινόπωρον ου τό late autumn

φθινύθω, φθίνω decay, wane, pine away, perish; *tr* consume, waste, destroy

φθῑσήνωρ (*gen* ορος) **φθῑσίμβροτος** ον man-destroying

φθίσις εως ἡ decline, perishing, waning; consumption

φθιτός ή όν decayed, dead

φθῖω ▸ **φθίνω**

φθογγή ῆς ἡ **φθόγγος** ου ὁ voice; cry, sound; speech

φθονερός ᾱ́ όν envious

φθονέω envy, be jealous, grudge, bear ill-will against (someone *dat*), refuse

φθόνησις εως ἡ **φθόνος** ου ὁ envy, grudge, jealousy, ill-will; refusal out of ill-will *or* envy

φθορᾱ́ ᾱς ἡ **φθόρος** ου ὁ corruption, decay, destruction; death; transitoriness

φιάλη ης ἡ cup, bowl, vessel, urn

φιδῑ́τιον ου τό **φειδῑ́τιον** ου τό common mess at Sparta; hall for those meals

φιλάγαθος ον loving goodness

φιλαδελφίᾱ ᾱς ἡ brotherly love

φιλάδελφος ον brotherly, sisterly

φιλαίτιος ον fond of blaming, censorious

φίλανδρος ον loving men, loving one's husband

φιλανθρωπίᾱ ᾱς ἡ love for mankind, benevolence, charity, humanity

φιλάνθρωπος ον benevolent, humane, kind

φιλαπεχθημοσύνη ης ἡ quarrelsomeness, malignity

φιλαπεχθήμων ον quarrelsome

φιλαπόδημος ον fond of travelling

φιλαργυρίᾱ ᾱς ἡ covetousness

φιλάργυρος ον fond of money, covetous

φίλαρχος ον fond of rule

φίλαυλος ον fond of the flute

φίλαυτος ον self-loving

φιλέλλην ηνος ὁ someone who is fond of the Greeks

φιλέταιρος ον loving one's comrades

φιλέω love; receive hospitably, entertain; court; kiss; be fond of; be accustomed to

φίλη ης ἡ friend, girlfriend, mistress

φιλήδονος ον fond of pleasure

φιλήκοος ον fond of hearing

φίλημα ατος τό kiss

φιλήρετμος ον loving the oar

φιλίᾱ ᾱς ἡ love, affection; friendship

φιλικός ή όν friendly, affectionate

φίλιος (ᾱ) ον of a friend, friendly; kindly

φιλιππίζω φιλιππιῶ side with Philip

φιλιππισμός οῦ ὁ siding with Philip

φίλιππος ον fond of horses

φιλίτιον ου τό friendly meal *or* the hall in which the meal was taken

φ

φιλο-γυμναστέω be fond of physical exercise

φιλογυμναστίᾱ ᾱς ἡ love for physical exercise

φιλοδέσποτος ον loving one's master

φιλο-δικέω be fond of lawsuits

φιλόδικος ον fond of lawsuits

φιλόδωρος ον fond of giving

φιλόζῳος ον fond of one's life, cowardly; fond of animals

φιλόθεος ον loving God

φιλόθηρος ον fond of hunting

φιλοικτίρμων ον **φιλοίκτιστος** ον compassionate

φίλοικτος ον piteous, moving pity

φιλο-καλέω love the beautiful

φιλόκαλος ον loving the beautiful

φιλο-κερδέω be greedy for gain

φιλοκερδής ές greedy for gain

φιλοκέρτομος ον fond of mocking

φιλοκίνδῡνος ον fond of danger, bold

φιλοκτέανος ον fond of gain, loving possessions

φιλόλογος ον fond of words *or* learning; scholar

φιλολοίδορος ον slanderous, abusive

φιλομαθής ές loving knowledge

φιλομμειδής ές sweet-smiling *or* laughter-loving (of Aphrodite)

φιλόμουσος ον fond of the Muses

φιλόμωμος ον fond of blaming

φιλονεικέω, φιλονῑκέω be fond of dispute; be ambitious *or* obstinate; quarrel

φιλονῑκίᾱ ᾱς ἡ rivalry; ambition, jealousy; obstinacy

φιλόνῑκος ον contentious, rivalling; fond of strife; obstinate

φιλοξενίᾱ ᾱς ἡ hospitality

φιλόξενος ον hospitable

φιλοπαίγμων ον fond of play, playful

φιλοπόλεμος ον fond of war, warlike

φιλόπολις (*gen* ιδος) loving one's city, patriotic

φιλο-πονέω love work, be diligent

φιλόπονος ον diligent, industrious

φιλοποσίᾱ ᾱς ἡ love of drinking

φιλοπρᾱγμοσύνη ης ἡ activity, fussiness, officiousness

φιλοπρᾱ́γμων ον busy, officious, meddlesome

φιλο-πρωτεύω strive to be the first

φιλοπτόλεμος ▸ **φιλοπόλεμος**

φίλος η ον loved, beloved, dear, pleasing; loving, friendly, fond
■ **ὁ φίλος** friend, companion; husband; lover; kinsman

φιλοσκώμμων ον fond of jesting

φιλο-σοφέω love wisdom *or* knowledge, be a philosopher, seek after knowledge; inquire into, study

φιλοσοφίᾱ ᾱς ἡ love of wisdom *or* knowledge; scientific *or* systematic study; philosophy; investigation, research

φιλόσοφος ον fond of knowledge, loving wisdom, scientific, literary, learned
■ **ὁ φιλόσοφος** philosopher

φιλόστοργος ον loving tenderly

φιλοστρατιώτης ου ὁ the soldier's friend

φιλοσώματος ον loving the body

φιλότεκνος ον fond of children

φιλο-τεχνέω love arts, practise an art

φιλότης ητος ἡ love, friendship; hospitality

φιλοτήσιος (ᾱ) ον of love *or* friendship, friendly

φιλο-τῑμέομαι *pass* love honour *or* distinction, be ambitious; take a pride in, make it one's boast; endeavour earnestly

φιλοτῑμίᾱ ᾱς ἡ love of honour *or* distinction; ambition, emulation, honour, distinction; liberality, ostentation

φιλότῑμος ον loving honour *or* distinction; ostentatious; emulous

φιλοφρονέομαι *mid and pass* be affectionate, show kindness to, be benevolent *or* well-disposed to; greet

φιλοφροσύνη ης ἡ friendliness, love, benevolence

φιλόφρων ον friendly, kindly, affectionate

φιλοχρήματος ον fond of money, covetous

φιλόχρηστος ον righteous, honest

φιλοχωρέω be fond of a certain place

φιλοψευδής ές fond of lying

φιλόψογος ον fond of blaming

φιλοψῡχέω be fond of one's life, be cowardly

φιλοψῡχίᾱ ᾱς ἡ love of life

φίλτρον ου τό love charm, spell; enticement

φιλύρᾱ ᾱς ἡ the lime *or* linden-tree

φῑμόω muzzle, gag; *pass* be silent

φῑτρός οῦ ὁ trunk of a tree

φῑτύω engender, beget

φλαυρίζω, φλαῦρος ▸ **φαυλίζω, φαῦλος**

φλαυρουργός όν working badly

φλεγέθω ▸ **φλέγω**

φλέγμα ατος τό flame, fire, heat; phlegm, a morbid humour

φλεγμαίνω *aor* ἐφλέγμᾱνα be inflamed

φλεγμονή ῆς ἡ heat, inflammation

φλέγω *act tr* set on fire; burn, scorch; inflame, torment; *act intr and pass* shine, flame, blaze, flash; be inflamed

φλέψ φλεβός ἡ vein

φλῑᾱ́ ᾶς ἡ doorpost

φλῑ́βω rub, press

φλόγεος ᾱ ον **φλογερός** ᾱ́ όν flaming, blazing

φλογίζω φλογιῶ burn up; *pass* blaze

φλογιστός ή όν burnt

φλόγωσις εως ἡ ▸ **φλεγμονή**

φλόϊνος η ον of rushes *or* reed

φλοιός οῦ ὁ smooth bark

φλοῖσβος ου ὁ roaring noise; battle-din

φλόξ φλογός ἡ fire, flame, blaze

φλόος ου ὁ (*also* φλοῦς οῦ ὁ) rush, reed

φλυᾱρέω talk nonsense, speak idly; slander

φλυᾱρίᾱ ᾱς ἡ idle talk; nonsense

φλύᾱρος ον talking idly, prattling

φλύκταινα ης ἡ blister; pustule

φοβερός ᾱ́ όν frightful, terrible; fearful, afraid

φοβέω† terrify, put to flight; *pass* be frightened, be put to flight, flee; fear, be alarmed *or* afraid; feel awe

φόβη ης ἡ hair, mane, foliage

φόβημα ατος τό terror

φοβητός ή όν **φόβητρον** ου τό frightful (thing)

φόβος ου ὁ flight; fear, fright, terror; awe

φοιβόλαμπτος ον possessed *or* inspired by Phoebus

φοῖβος η ον bright; pure; the bright *or* pure one (of Apollo)

φοινήεις εσσα εν blood-red

φοινῑ́κεος ᾱ ον **φοινῑκοῦς** ῆ οῦν purple, crimson

φοινῑκήιος ᾱ ον of the palm-tree; Phoenician

φοινῑκίς ίδος ἡ purple garment, curtain, carpet *or* flag

φοινῑκιστής οῦ ὁ wearer of purple (i.e. a Persian of the highest rank)

φοινῑκόεις εσσα εν ▸ **φοινίκεος**

φοινῑκοπάρῃος ον red-cheeked

φοῖνιξ (*gen* ῑκος) purple red, crimson
▪ **ὁ φοῖνιξ** purple dye
▪ **ὁ/ἡ φοῖνιξ** date-palm, date; phoenix (a fabulous bird); lyre

φοίνιος (ᾱ) ον **φοινός** ή όν blood red; bloody; bloodthirsty

φοινίσσω redden

φοιτάς άδος ἡ a woman roaming madly

φοιτάω go to and fro *or* up and down; hasten; roam wildly about; go regularly, frequent; (go to) visit; come in, be imported

φοίτησις εως ἡ a going to and fro

φολκός ή όν bandy-legged

φονάω be bloodthirsty

φονεύς έως ὁ/ἡ murderer

φονεύω murder, slay

φονή ῆς ἡ ▸ **φόνος**

φονικός ή όν **φόνιος** (ᾱ) ον **φονός** ή όν murderous; bloody; relating to murder *or* blood

φόνος ου ὁ murder, slaughter, massacre; dagger; deadly wound; blood shed in murder; place of murder; (in law) murder, homicide

φοξός ή όν with a pointed head

φορᾱ́ ᾶς ἡ a carrying, bearing; payment; fertility; load, burden; tax, tribute; fruit, crop; quick motion, rush, onset

φοράδην *adv* with a violent motion; carried along (in a litter)

φορβάς (*gen* άδος) nourishing

φορβή ῆς ἡ food, fodder, victuals, forage

φορεύς έως ὁ bearer

φορέω ▸ **φέρω**

φόρημα ατος τό burden; ornament

φορητός (ή) όν bearable, tolerable

φορμηδόν *adv* crosswise, like mat-work

φόρμιγξ ιγγος ἡ lyre, lute

φορμίζω play on the lyre

φορμός οῦ ὁ basket; mat; corn-measure

φόρον ου τό the forum

φόρος ου ὁ tribute (such as that paid to Athens by cities in her empire); income, revenue

φορτηγέω carry freight *or* loads

φορτηγικός ή όν carrying loads

φορτίζω load

φορτικός ή όν carrying loads; burdensome, wearisome; coarse, common, vulgar

φορτίον ου τό load, burden; freight; baggage

φορτίς ίδος ἡ ship of burden, merchantmen

φόρτος ου ὁ ▸ **φορτίον**

φορτο-φορέω carry loads

φορῡ́νω, φορύσσω stain, defile

φόως τό ▸ **φῶς**

φραγέλλιον ου τό scourge

φραγελλόω scourge

φράγμα ατος τό **φραγμός** οῦ ὁ a fencing in; fence, hedge, enclosure, wall, partition; stoppage

φραδής ές **φράδμων** ον prudent, cunning

φράζω make clear; show; pronounce, declare, tell, utter; beckon; promise; order, advise; *mid and pass* think, believe, consider; perceive, remark, notice; understand; purpose, contrive

φράσσω fence in, fortify, block up, defend, protect; *mid* fence *or* fortify for oneself

φρᾱ́τηρ ερος ὁ **φρᾱ́τωρ** ορος ὁ member of a φρᾱτρία

φρᾱτρίᾱ ᾱς ἡ tribe, clan; phratry (at Athens, a subdivision of the φῦλή)

φρέᾱρ ᾱτος τό well, water-tank

φρεᾱτίᾱ ᾱς ἡ reservoir, tank

φρεναπατάω deceive

φρεναπάτης ου ὁ soul-deceiver

φρενήρης ες sound of mind, prudent

φρενοβλαβής ές crazy, mad

φρενόθεν *adv* by a rational decision

φρενομόρως *adv* so as to destroy the mind

φρενόω make wise, inform, teach

φρήν φρενός ἡ *usu in pl* midriff; breast; soul, mind, heart; sense, understanding, reason

φρήτρη ης ἡ ▸ **φρατρία**

φρῑ́κη ης ἡ a shuddering; ruffling of the sea; awe, fear

φρῑκώδης ες awful, horrible, that causes shuddering

φριμάσσομαι *mid* (of horses) snort and leap about, neigh and prance

φρίξ φρῑκός ἡ ▸ **φρίκη**

φρῑ́σσω be ruffled; bristle; shudder, shiver, feel a chill

φροιμιάζομαι ▸ **προοιμιάζομαι**

φροίμιον ου τό ▸ **προοίμιον**

φρονέω think, be sound in mind, be wise; understand, consider, know; be minded *or* disposed; mean, intend, purpose

φρόνημα ατος τό **φρόνησις** εως ἡ mind, will; thought, insight; purpose; high spirit, pride, arrogance

φρόνιμος ον in one's senses; prudent, sensible, wise

φρόνις εως ἡ practical wisdom

φροντίζω φροντιῶ think, consider, reflect; give heed to, care about, be thoughtful

φροντίς ίδος ἡ thought, care, heed; reflection; anxiety; concern

φροντιστής οῦ ὁ thinker

φροντιστικῶς *adv* carefully

φροῦδος η ον gone away; gone, departed

φρουρᾱ́ ᾶς ἡ watch, guard; watchfulness; prison; garrison; levy, conscription

φρουραρχίᾱ ᾱς ἡ commandership in a fortress

φρούραρχος ου ὁ commander of a garrison

φρουρέω watch, keep guard, serve as a garrison; watch, guard, keep; observe, beware of

φρούρημα ατος τό watch, guard

φρουρικός ή όν belonging to a watch *or* garrison

φρούριον ου τό watchpost, fort; garrison

φρουρίς ίδος ἡ guardship

φρουρός οῦ ὁ watcher, guard

φρύαγμα ατος τό a snorting, neighing

φρυάσσω *and mid* snort, neigh

φρῡγανισμός οῦ ὁ a collecting of firewood

φρῡ́γανον ου τό dry wood, firewood

φρῡ́γω roast; parch

φρῡκτός ή όν roasted
▪ **ὁ φρῡκτός** firebrand; signal-fire, beacons

φρῡκτωρέω give signals by fire

φρῡκτώριον ου τό lighthouse

φρῡκτωρός οῦ ὁ one who watches to give signals by beacon-fires

φρῡ́νη ης ἡ toad

φυγ *aor stem from* **φεύγω**

φύγαδε *adv* to flight

φυγαδεύω chase, banish

φυγαδικός ή όν for an exile

φυγάς (*gen* άδος) fugitive, banished, exile; deserter

φυγγάνω ▸ **φεύγω**

φυγή ῆς ἡ flight, escape, banishment; place of refuge

φυγοπτόλεμος ον shunning war, cowardly

φύζα ης ἡ headlong flight; terror

φυζανικός ή όν flying, cowardly

φυή ῆς ἡ growth, stature

φῡκιόεις εσσα εν rich in seaweed

φῦκος εος τό seaweed; rouge

φυκτός ή όν to be escaped, avoidable

φυλακή ῆς ἡ a watching, keeping guard; nightwatch; watch, guard; watchfulness, caution; watchpost, life-guard, garrison; prison

φυλακίζω throw into prison

φυλακός οῦ ὁ **φυλακτήρ** ῆρος ὁ ▸ **φύλαξ**

φυλακτήριον ου τό watchpost, fort; preservation; amulet

φυλακτικός ή όν preservative; cautious

φύλαξ ακος ὁ/ἡ watcher, guard; sentinel; keeper, guardian, protector

φῡ́λαρχος ου ὁ chief of a tribe (φυλή); (at Athens) commander of cavalry provided by each tribe

φυλάσσω *act intr* watch; keep guard; serve as a garrison; be on one's guard, take heed; *act tr* watch, guard, keep, secure, preserve, protect; observe; *mid* keep guard; keep, bear in memory; take heed; shun, avoid

φῡλή ῆς ἡ tribe (ten of these were formed at Athens by Cleisthenes); people; contingent of soldiers provided by a tribe, brigade of cavalry

φυλίη ῆς ἡ wild olive tree *or* buck-thorn

φυλλάς άδος ἡ heap of leaves; foliage, leafy bushes

φύλλον ου τό leaf; *pl* foliage

φῡλοβασιλεύς έως ὁ a βασιλεύς chosen from each tribe to perform sacrifices

φῡλο-κρινέω distinguish races

φῦλον ου τό race, family; tribe, people, nation; troop; kind, sex

φῡ́λοπις ιδος ἡ din of battle; battle, strife

φῦμα ατος τό tumour, ulcer

φύξηλις (*gen* ιδος) ▸ **φυζανικός**

φύξιμος ον offering a chance of escape; able to flee
▪ **τὸ φύξιμον** place of refuge

φύξις εως ἡ ▸ **φυγή**

φῡ́ρᾱμα ατος τό dough

φῡράω φῡρᾱ́σω ἐφῡ́ρᾱσα mix up, knead

φῡ́ρω *aor* ἔφῡρσα mix, mix up, mingle, knead; confound; wet

φῦσα ης ἡ pair of bellows

φῡσάω blow, puff, snort; puff up, blow up, make swell

φῡσητήρ ῆρος ὁ blow pipe

φῡσιάω ▸ **φυσάω**

φυσικός ή όν belonging to nature; produced by nature, natural, inborn

φῡσιόω ▸ **φυσιάω**

φύσις εως ἡ birth, origin; nature, inborn quality, natural parts; temper, disposition; stature; sex; natural order; creative power; the universe; creature

φῡσίωσις εως ἡ vanity, pride

φῡταλίη ης ἡ orchard, vineyard

φυτάλμιος ον producing; from one's birth

φυτείᾱ ᾱς ἡ plantation; plant

φύτευμα ατος τό ▸ **φυτόν**

φύτευσις εως ἡ a planting

φυτεύω plant; beget; produce

φυτόν οῦ τό plant, tree; creature; child

φυτοσπόρος ου ὁ begetter, father

φυτουργός όν begetting

φῡ́ω† *act tr* produce, beget, bring forth, make to grow; get, gain; *act intr and pass* grow, spring up, come into being, be born *or* introduced; be by nature; fall to one by nature

φώκη ης ἡ seal

φωλεός οῦ ὁ hole, den (of lions and foxes)

φωνασκέω practise one's voice, learn to sing *or* declaim

φωνασκίᾱ ᾱς ἡ practice of the voice

φωνέω speak loudly, raise one's voice, sound, cry, call, speak, pronounce; address; invite, bid

φωνή ῆς ἡ voice, sound, tone, cry, speech, language, dialect, word

φωνήεις εσσα εν gifted with speech

φώνημα ατος τό ▸ **φωνή**

φώρ φωρός ὁ thief

φωράω φωρᾱ́σω detect a thief, trace, discover

φωριαμός οῦ ἡ chest, trunk

φώς φωτός ὁ man

φῶς φωτός τό ▸ **φάος**

φωστήρ ῆρος ὁ luminary, star; splendour

φωσφόρος ον bringing light; morning-star; torch-bearing

φωτεινός ή όν bright, shining

φωτίζω φωτιῶ give light, bring to light; instruct, teach

φωτισμός οῦ ὁ an enlightening, illumination

χ, Χ (χῖ) twenty-second letter of the alphabet
■ **χ′** *as a numeral* = 600

χάζω cause to retire from; bereave; *mid* give way, retire, retreat (from), desist

χαίνω yawn, gape; gasp for; utter

χαίρω rejoice, be glad, delighted *or* pleased; like, be accustomed to, delight in
■ **χαῖρε, χαίρετε** hail! welcome! farewell!
■ **χαίρειν ἐᾶν** *infin* dismiss fom one's mind

χαίτη ης ἡ long hair; mane

χάλαζα ης ἡ hail

χᾱλαργός όν swift-footed

χαλαρός ᾱ́ όν slackened, languid

χαλάω χαλάσω ἐχάλασα loosen, slacken, unstring, let fall, let loose, let go, give up; leave off, cease; become slack; gape; give way, yield; come to rest

χαλεπαίνω χαλεπανῶ ἐχαλέπηνα be severe, bad, harsh, angry *or* embittered; *pass* be treated severely

χαλεπός ή όν hard, severe, grievous, difficult, troublesome, dangerous; rough, rugged, disagreeable; bitter, harsh, cruel, angry, morose
■ **χαλεπῶς** *adv* with difficulty, hardly, scarcely; severely, harshly, angrily; ill

χαλεπότης ητος ἡ difficulty, trouble; hardship, severity, harshness

χαλέπτω oppress

χαλῑναγωγέω curb, restrain; guide with *or* as with a bridle

χαλῑνός οῦ ὁ bridle, rein

χαλῑνόω bridle [a horse]

χάλιξ ικος ὁ/ἡ gravel; mortar, cement

χαλι-φρονέω be silly

χαλιφροσύνη ης ἡ thoughtlessness

χαλίφρων ον thoughtless, silly

χάλκασπις (*gen* ιδος) with brazen shield

χαλκείᾱ ᾱς ἡ art of a smith

χαλκεῖον ου τό forge, smithy; copper vessel

χάλκειος ᾱ ον **χάλκεος** ᾱ ον **χαλκοῦς** ῆ οῦν of copper *or* bronze, brazen

χαλκεόφωνος ον with a voice of brass, i.e. strong and clear

χαλκεύς έως ὁ smith, worker in metal

χαλκευτικός ή όν skilled in metal-working

χαλκεύω forge, be a smith

χαλκεών ῶνος ὁ forge, smithy

χαλκηδών όνος ὁ chalcedony (a precious stone)

χαλκήρης ες covered *or* headed with bronze

χαλκίοικος ον with a brazen temple (of Athena)

χαλκίον ου τό copper vessel

χαλκίς ίδος ἡ nighthawk

χαλκοβαρής ές heavy with brass

χαλκοβατής ές with brazen base

χαλκοβόᾱς ου ὁ with a voice of brass

χαλκογλώχῑς (*gen* ῖνος) with point *or* barb of brass

χαλκόδετος ον brass-bound

χαλκοθώρᾱξ (*gen* ᾱκος) with a brazen breastplate

χαλκοκνήμῑς (*gen* ῑδος) with greaves of brass

χαλκοκορυστής (*gen* οῦ) armed with brass

χαλκολίβανον ου τό fine brass

χαλκοπάρῃος ον (of helmets) with cheeks *or* sides of brass

χαλκόπλευρος ον with sides of brass

χαλκόπληκτος ον forged of brass, smiting with brazen edge

χαλκόπους (*gen* ποδος) brazen-footed

χαλκόπυλος ον with gates of brass

χαλκός οῦ ὁ copper; bronze; brass; brazen vessel; copper coin; brazen arms

χαλκόστομος ον with brazen mouth

χαλκοτύπος ου ὁ copper-smith

χαλκοχίτων (*gen* ωνος) brazen-coated, clad in bronze

χάλκωμα ατος τό brazen vessel

χάλυψ υβος ὁ steel

χαμάδις, χαμᾶζε *adv* to the ground

χαμᾶθεν *adv* from the ground

χαμαί *adv* on the ground *or* earth

χαμαιευνάς (*gen* άδος) **χαμαιεύνης** (*gen* ου) sleeping on the ground

χαμαίζηλος ον low
■ **ὁ χαμαίζηλος** footstool

χαμαικοίτης (*gen* ου) ▸ **χαμαιεύνης**

χαμαῖθεν, χαμόθεν ▸ **χαμᾶθεν**

χάμψαι ῶν οἱ crocodiles

χανδάνω χείσομαι ἔχαδον hold, contain

χανδόν *adv* greedily

χάος ους τό chaos

χαρᾱ́ ᾶς ἡ joy, delight, pleasure; darling

χαράδρᾱ ᾱς ἡ rent, cleft, ravine, gully; bed of a mountain-stream; torrent

χαραδριός οῦ ὁ plover *or* curlew

χαραδρόω tear up into clefts

χαρακτήρ ῆρος ὁ stamp, mark; characteristic trait, character; token

χαράκωμα ατος τό palisaded fort, wall, palisade

χάραξ ακος ὁ/ἡ pointed stake, pole; pale; palisade, fortified camp

χαράσσω point, sharpen; scratch; notch; exasperate, irritate

χαρίεις εσσα εν graceful, lovely, charming, pleasing, pretty; elegant, accomplished, refined, witty; welcome, dear

χαριεντίζομαι χαριεντιοῦμαι *mid* jest

χαρίζομαι χαριοῦμαι *mid* show favour *or* kindness; gratify, indulge; offer willingly, give freely; offer; abandon; pardon; be pleasing, agreeable *or* acceptable

χάρις ιτος ἡ joy, pleasure; grace, loveliness; favour, kindness, good will, boon; gratitude, thanks; respect; gratification, delight; a delight
■ **χάριν** + *gen* for the sake of, on account of
■ **χάριν ἔχω** feel gratitude

χάρισμα ατος τό gift of grace, free gift, gift of God's grace

χαριτόω show favour

χάρμα ατος τό **χαρμονή** ῆς ἡ ▸ **χαρά**

χάρμη ης ἡ desire for combat, lust for battle; battle

χαρμόσυνος η ον joyful

χαροπός ή όν bright-eyed; glad-eyed

χάρτης ου ὁ leaf of paper

χαρτός ή όν delightful

χάσκω χανοῦμαι ἔχανον gape, yawn; swallow up

χάσμα ατος τό cleft, chasm

χασμάομαι *mid* yawn; gape wide, stand gaping

χατέω, χατίζω want; desire, long, wish

χαυλιόδων οντος ὁ with projecting teeth *or* tusks

χειᾱ́ ᾶς ἡ hole

χεῖλος εος τό lip; edge, brim, rim

χεῖμα ατος τό ▸ **χειμών**

χειμάδιον ου τό ▸ **χειμασία**

χειμάζω, χειμαίνω χειμανῶ *act tr* expose to a storm *or* to the winter; trouble, afflict; *act intr* be stormy; pass the winter; *pass* suffer from a storm

χειμάρροος ον (*also* χειμάρρους ουν) swollen in winter; torrent, mountain-stream

χειμασίᾱ ᾱς ἡ winter-quarters

χειμερίζω ▸ **χειμάζω**

χειμερινός ή όν **χειμέριος** (ᾱ) ον wintry; stormy

χειμών ῶνος ὁ winter; frost, cold; storm, tempest; distress, suffering

χείρ χειρός ἡ hand, fist; arm; side; close fight; nearness; deed, bravery, might, power, violence; handwriting; grappling-hook; body of men, band

χειρ-αγωγέω lead by the hand

χειραγωγός όν leading by the hand

χειρ-απτάζω handle

χειρῑδωτός όν sleeved

χείριος ᾱ ον in the power (of someone)

χειρῑ́ς ῖδος ἡ glove, sleeve; money-bag

χείριστος η ον *see* **χέρης**

χειρόγραφον ου τό manuscript note, bond

χειροδάϊκτος ον slain by the hand

χειρόδεικτος ον pointed out by the hand, manifest

χειροήθης ες accustomed to the hand, manageable

χειρόμακτρον ου τό towel, napkin

χειρο-νομέω gesticulate

χειρόομαι *mid* master, subdue; *pass* be subdued

χειροπληθής ές as large as can be held in the hand

χειρο-ποιέομαι *mid* do with one's hands

χειροποίητος ον made by hand

χειρότερος ᾱ ον ▸ **χείρων**

χειροτέχνης (*gen* ου) artisan, mechanic; artist

χειρο-τονέω stretch out one's hand; give one's vote, vote for, elect

χειροτονίᾱ ᾱς ἡ voting by show of hands, election

χειρουργέω do with the hands, execute

χειρούργημα ατος τό **χειρουργίᾱ** ᾱς ἡ manual labour; craft

χείρωμα ατος τό a mastering, subduing

χείρων *see* **χέρης**

χειρῶναξ ακτος ὁ artisan, mechanic

χειρωναξίᾱ ᾱς ἡ handicraft

χελῑδών όνος ἡ swallow

χελώνη ης ἡ tortoise; penthouse

χέραδος ους τό gravel, shingle

χερειότερος ᾱ ον **χερείων** ον ▸ **χείρων** *from* **χέρης**

χέρης (*gen* ηος *or* ειος) mean, little; weak; bad
■ **χείρων** ον *comp* less, weaker, worse, inferior
■ **χείριστος** η ον *sup* worst, lowest

χερμάδιον ου τό large stone, boulder

χερνῆτις ιδος ἡ workwoman

χέρνιβον ου τό wash(ing-)basin

χερνίπτομαι *mid* wash one's hands; sprinkle with holy water

χέρνιψ ιβος ἡ water for washing; holy water

χερόπληκτος ον struck with the hand

χερρόνησος ου ἡ **χερσόνησος** ου ἡ peninsula

χερσαῖος ᾱ ον living on dry land

χερσονησοειδής ές peninsular

χέρσος ον dry; firm; barren, destitute
■ ἡ **χέρση** mainland, continent

χεῦμα ατος τό what is poured; vessel for pouring

χέω χεῶ ἔχεα pour, pour out, shed; cause to rain *or* snow; throw up [earth]; scatter, shower; let fall; *pass* be poured out *or* thrown up, stream forth, be spread around; *mid* pour for oneself

χηλευτός ή όν plaited

χηλή ῆς ἡ hoof, talon, claw; breakwater

χηλός οῦ ὁ chest, box

χήν χηνός ὁ/ἡ goose

χηναλώπηξ εκος ὁ fox-goose (an Egyptian species living in holes)

χήνειος ᾱ ον **χήνεος** η ον of a goose

χήρᾱ ᾱς ἡ widow

χηραμός οῦ ὁ cleft, hole

χηρεύω be destitute, bereft *or* widowed

χῆρος ᾱ ον destitute, bereft ; widowed

χηρόω make destitute *or* desolate; unpeople; bereave of a husband

χηρωστής οῦ ὁ collateral relation

χήτεϊ *adv* dat *from* **χῆτος** from want *or* need of

χθαμαλός ή όν low, on the ground

χθές (*also* ἐχθές) *adv* yesterday

χθιζός ή όν of yesterday, yesterday's

χθόνιος (ᾱ) ον in, under, of *or* beneath the earth; native, indigenous; of the nether world

χθονοστιβής ές treading the earth

χθών χθονός ἡ soil, ground, earth; country

χῑλίαρχος ου ὁ **χῑλιάρχης** ου ὁ commander of a thousand men

χῑλιάς άδος ἡ the number one thousand

χῑλιαστύς ύος ὁ (at Ephesus and Samos) a division of the people

χῑλιετής ές a thousand years old

χῑ́λιοι αι α a thousand

χῑλιοστός ή όν thousandth

χῑλιοστῦ́ς ύος ἡ body of a thousand soldiers

χῑλός οῦ ὁ grass, green fodder; forage

χῑλόω feed with grass

χίμαιρα ᾱς ἡ she-goat, nanny-goat; a fire-spouting monster, with lion's head, serpent's tail and goat's body

χιονίζω snow upon

χιονόκτυπος ον beaten by snow

χιτών ῶνος ὁ undergarment, tunic; coat of mail, coat, jerkin

χιτωνίσκος ου ὁ short coat

χιών όνος ἡ snow

χλαῖνα ης ἡ cloak, mantle; carpet

χλαμυδουργίᾱ ᾱς ἡ the making of cloaks

χλαμύς ύδος ἡ upper garment, cloak; military cloak, general's cloak

χλανίδιον ου τό small cloak

χλανιδοποιίᾱ ᾱς ἡ the making of fine upper garments

χλανίς ίδος ἡ upper-garment of wool; upper-garment worn on festive occasions

χλευάζω joke, jest; mock

χλευασμός οῦ ὁ mockery, scoffing

χλῐαρός ᾱ́ όν lukewarm

χλιδάω pride oneself; be luxurious, revel

χλιδή ῆς ἡ delicacy, luxury; finery, beauty; insolence, arrogance

χλόη ης ἡ the green blade of crops or grass; young verdure

χλούνης ου ὁ wild boar

χλωρηΐς (*gen* ίδος) pale green

χλωρός ᾱ́ όν light green, yellow; pale; green, fresh, vigorous

χνοάζω get a downy *or* grey beard

χνόη ης ἡ box of a wheel; axle

χνόος ου ὁ foam, crust; the first down on the chin (of youths)

χόανος ου ὁ melting-pot, crucible

χοή ῆς ἡ a pouring; libation

χοϊκός ή όν of earth *or* clay

χοῖνιξ ικος ἡ a corn-measure; daily bread; stocks (for fastening the legs in)

χοιράς άδος ἡ like a hog *or* a hog's back, low *or* sunken (rock)

χοίρειος ᾱ ον **χοίρεος** ᾱ ον of swine

χοῖρος ου ὁ young pig, porker; cunt

χολάδες ων αἱ bowels

χολάω be bilious, angry *or* melancholy

χολή ῆς ἡ **χόλος** ου ὁ gall, bile; wrath

χολόω make angry; *pass and mid* become angry

χολωτός ή όν angry

χόνδρος ου ὁ grain, lump

χορδή ῆς ἡ gut; chord; string

χορευτής οῦ ὁ choral dancer; follower (of a god)

χορεύω *and mid* form a chorus; dance in a chorus; dance; celebrate with a choral dance

χορηγέω lead a chorus; (at the dramatic festivals in Athens) pay the expenses for a chorus

χορηγίᾱ ᾱς ἡ office of a χορηγός; equipment; means, wealth

χορηγός οῦ ὁ leader of a chorus; (at the dramatic festivals in Athens) one who defrays the costs for bringing out a chorus

χοροποιός όν arranging a chorus

χορός οῦ ὁ dancing-place; dance in a ring, choral dance; chorus, choir

χορτάζω feed, fatten

χόρτασμα ατος τό food, fodder

χόρτος ου ὁ fence, enclosure, cattle-farm; pasture; fodder, food

χοῦς χοός ὁ a liquid measure (12 κοτύλαι)

χόω throw up, heap up [earth]; dam up, fill up

χραίνω χρανῶ ἔχρᾱνα besmear, soil, pollute

χραισμέω + *dat* help, aid; defend

χραύω scratch, wound; befall

χράω[1] desire, demand

χράω[2] lend, supply; give an oracle, pronounce; *mid* borrow; consult an oracle; *pass* (of an oracle) be pronounced

χράομαι *mid* + *dat* use; be possessed of; have dealings with, converse with; have sexual intercourse with; treat, practise; + *gen* be in need of, want, yearn for

χρείᾱ ᾱς ἡ use, advantage; familiarity, dealings; service, business, office; need, necessity; want, poverty; desire

χρεῖος τό ▸ **χρέος**

χρεμετίζω neigh

χρέος ους τό debt; amends, damages; what is due; ▸ **χρεία**

χρεώ οῦς ἡ necessity; want, need

χρέως ωτος τό ▸ **χρέος**

χρεωφειλέτης ου ὁ debtor

χρή† it is necessary, it must, it is right *or* proper; it is fated; there is need

χρῄζω *usu* + *gen* want, need; desire, wish, long for; prophesy

χρηίσκομαι *mid* + *dat* need

χρῆμα ατος τό a thing, matter, business; piece, copy; fact; enterprise; amount, money; *pl* goods, money, power

χρηματίζω χρηματιῶ do business; transact state business; negotiate, debate, consult, answer; bear a name *or* title; *mid* negotiate; make money, transact business

χρηματιστής οῦ ὁ tradesman, man of business

χρηματιστικός ή όν fitted for money-making; portending gain

χρήσιμος (η) ον useful, serviceable, profitable; honest; made use of

χρῆσις εως ἡ ▸ **χρεία**

χρησμολόγος ον giving *or* interpreting oracles

χρησμός οῦ ὁ oracular response

χρησμοσύνη ης ἡ art of prophesying; want, need, poverty

χρησμῳδέω prophesy

χρησμῳδίᾱ ᾱς ἡ prophecy

χρησμῳδός όν prophesying

χρηστεύομαι *mid* be kind

χρηστηριάζομαι *mid* consult an oracle

χρηστήριος (ᾱ) ον prophetic ■ **τό χρηστήριον** oracle; victim, sacrfice

χρήστης ου ὁ creditor; debtor

χρηστολογίᾱ ᾱς ἡ flowery *or* dissembling speech

χρηστός ή όν useful, serviceable, beneficial; honest, righteous, good, brave; simple, silly

χρηστότης ητος ἡ honesty, goodness

χρῖμα ατος τό unguent, oil

χρίμπτομαι *pass* touch the surface, scratch; *pass* come near

χρῖσμα ατος τό ▸ **χρῖμα**

χρῑστός ή όν anointed; the Anointed One, Christ

χρῑ́ω besmear, anoint, colour; sting, prick

χρόᾱ ᾱς ἡ **χροίᾱ** ᾱς ἡ ▸ **χρώς**

χρόμαδος ου ὁ a gnashing

χρονίζω χρονιῶ spend time; tarry

χρόνιος (ᾱ) ον for a long time, lasting long; after a long time, late

χρόνος ου ὁ time, duration; period; term

χρονο-τριβέω ▸ **χρονίζω**

χρῡσάμπυξ (*gen* υκος) with a golden frontlet

χρῡσᾱ́ορος ον with a golden sword

χρῡσαυγής ές gold-gleaming

χρῡσεῖα ων τά gold mines

χρῡ́σεος η ον **χρῡσοῦς** ῆ οῦν golden, gilt; gold-coloured; precious; blessed, lovely

χρῡσηλάκατος ον with a golden arrow *or* spindle

χρῡσήλατος ον beaten out of gold

χρῡσήνιος ον with reins of gold

χρῡσίον ου τό ▸ **χρυσός**

χρῡσῖτις (*gen* ιδος) containing gold, like gold

χρῡσοδακτύλιος ον with gold rings

χρῡσόδετος ον bound with gold

χρῡσοειδής ές like gold

χρῡσόθρονος ον on a throne of gold

χρῡσόκομος ον golden-haired

χρῡσόλιθος ου ὁ topaz

χρῡσομίτρης (*gen* ου) with a headband of gold

χρῡσόπαστος ον embroidered with gold

χρῡσοπέδῑλος ον with sandals of gold

χρῡσόπρασος ου ὁ chrysoprase (a precious stone of golden-green colour)

χρῡσόπτερος ον with wings of gold

χρῡσόρραπις (*gen* ιδος) with a golden staff

χρῡσόρρυτος ον flowing with gold

χρῡσός οῦ ὁ gold; gold vessel; gold coin

χρῡσόστροφος twisted with gold

χρῡσο-φορέω wear gold

χρῡσοφόρος ον wearing gold

χρῡσοφύλαξ (*gen* ακος) watching gold

χρῡσοχάλῑνος ον with a golden bridle

χρῡσοχόος ου ὁ goldsmith

χρῡσόω gild

χρώζω touch; besmear, stain

χρῶμα ατος τό colour; complexion; embellishment; paint

χρώς χρωτός ὁ skin; body; flesh; complexion

χῡμός οῦ ὁ juice, flavour

χύσις εως ἡ a pouring; heap

χυτλόομαι *mid* bathe and anoint oneself

χυτός ή όν poured out; heaped up; melted

χύτρᾱ ᾱς ἡ **χυτρίς** ίδος ἡ **χύτρος** ου ὁ pot, jug

χωλεύω be lame, limp

χωλός ή όν lame, limping; maimed

χῶμα ατος τό mound; dam; tomb

χώννῡμι ▸ **χόω**

χώομαι *mid* be angry *or* indignant

χώρᾱ ᾱς ἡ space, room, place; dwelling-place; locality; station, post-station; district, region, territory, country, land; field, farm, estate; rural territory (as opposed to the town)

χωρέω give way, withdraw; go forward, start, come, go; succeed; hold, contain, have room for

χωρίζω χωριῶ part; sever, separate; *pass* be divided; be at variance; go away

χωρίον ου τό ▸ **χώρα**

χωρίς *adv and prep with gen* separately, apart, by oneself; differently, otherwise; besides; far from, without

χωρισμός οῦ ἡ separation

χωρῑ́της ου ὁ countryman, peasant

χωρῑτικός ή όν rustic, boorish

χῶρος[1] ου ὁ ▸ **χώρα**

χῶρος[2] ου ὁ northwest wind

χῶσις εως ἡ heaping up, raising a mound; filling in, blocking up by earth thrown in

Ψψ

ψ, Ψ (ψῖ) twenty-third letter of the alphabet ■ ψʹ *as a numeral* = 700

ψακάζω drizzle

ψακάς άδος ἡ drizzling rain

ψάλλω ψαλῶ ἔψηλα pull, pluck; play the lyre with the fingers; sing, praise

ψαλμός οῦ ὁ playing on the lyre; song, psalm

ψάλτης ου ὁ harpist

ψαλτήριον ου τό stringed instrument, psaltery, harp

ψάλτρια ᾱς ἡ woman lyre-player

ψάμμινος η ον sandy

ψάμμος ου ἡ sand; heap of sand; sandy desert

ψαμμώδης ες sandy

ψᾱ́ρ ψᾱρός ὁ starling

ψαύω touch; affect

ψάω touch lightly, rub; *intr* crumble away, vanish

ψέγω blame

ψεδνός ή όν thin, spare; bald

ψεκάς άδος ἡ ▸ **ψακάς**

ψέλιον ου τό bracelet, anklet

ψελιφόρος ον wearing bracelets

ψελλίζομαι *mid* stammer, speak inarticulately

ψευδάγγελος ου ὁ false messenger

ψευδάδελφος ου ὁ false brother

ψευδαπόστολος ου ὁ false apostle

ψευδενέδρᾱ ᾱς ἡ sham ambush

ψευδής ές lying, false; fictitious, sham

ψευδοδιδάσκαλος ου ὁ false teacher

ψευδοκῆρυξ ῡκος ὁ false herald

ψευδολόγος ον lying

ψευδόμαντις εως ὁ/ἡ lying prophet(ess)

ψευδο-μαρτυρέω bear false witness

ψευδομαρτυρίᾱ ᾱς ἡ false witness

ψεδυόμαρτυς υρος ὁ lying witness

ψευδοπάρθενος ου ἡ pretended virgin

ψευδοπροφήτης ου ὁ false prophet

ψευδόρκιος ον perjured

ψεῦδος ους τό lie, falsehood, untruth

ψευδο-στομέω tell lies

ψευδόφημος ον telling lies

ψευδόχρῑστος ου ὁ a false Christ

ψεύδω ψεύσω ἔψευσα cheat by lies; cheat, defraud; represent [something] as a lie; *pass* be cheated *or* deceived; be false; *mid* lie, cheat, feign; belie, falsify

ψευδώνυμος ον falsely named

ψεῦσμα ατος τό ▸ **ψεῦδος**

ψευστέω lie

ψεύστης ου ὁ liar, cheat

ψῆγμα ατος τό (gold) dust

ψηλαφάω grope one's way; feel, touch

ψήν ψηνός ὁ gall-insect

ψήρ ▸ **ψάρ**

ψηφῑδοφόρος ον entitled to vote

ψηφίζω ψηφιῶ count, reckon; put to the vote; decide; *mid* give one's vote with a pebble (which was thrown in the voting urn); vote for, resolve, decide; adjudge

ψηφῑ́ς ῖδος ἡ pebble

ψήφισμα ατος τό vote, decree, a measure passed in the ἐκκλησίᾱ at Athens; proposition

ψηφοποιός όν falsifying votes

ψηφοφορίᾱ ᾱς ἡ vote by ballot, voting

ψῆφος ου ἡ small stone, pebble; counting stone; counter; accounts; voting pebble (which was thrown in the voting urn); vote; resolution, decree, election; sentence

ψήχω rub down, curry [a horse]; stroke, pat

ψιάς άδος ἡ drop

ψιθυρίζω ψιθυριῶ whisper, mutter

ψιθυρισμός οῦ ὁ a whispering, slander

ψιθυριστής οῦ ὁ whisperer, slanderer

ψιθυρός όν whispering, slanderous

ψῑλός ή όν bare, naked; bald; stripped of; treeless; uncovered, unarmed; without heavy armour; simple, plain ■ **οἱ ψῑλοί** light troops (such as archers and slingers, as opposed to hoplites)

ψῑλόω make bare *or* bald; strip of, deprive (of)

ψιμῦθιον ου τό **ψίμῡθος** ου ὁ white lead (used to whiten the face)

ψιμῡθιόω pain with white lead

ψίττακος ου ὁ parrot

ψῑχίον ου τό crumb, morsel

ψόγος ου ὁ blame, reproach

ψολόεις εσσα εν smoky, sooty

ψοφέω make a noise; ring

ψόφος ου ὁ noise, sound; idle talk

ψύθος ους τό ▸ **ψεῦδος**

ψύλλα ης ἡ flea

ψῡχ-αγωγέω lead souls to the underworld; lead, win *or* entertain souls; delude, inveigle

ψῡχεινός ον ▸ **ψυχρός**

ψῡχή ῆς ἡ breath, spirit; life; living being, person; soul of man, heart, spirit; desire, appetite; courage; departed soul, ghost

ψῡχικός ή όν living, mental; animal, natural

ψῦχος ους τό cold, frost; winter

ψῡχρός ᾱ́ όν cool, cold, chill; unfeeling, heartless; spiritless; vain, fruitless, unreal; frigid

ψῡχρότης ητος ἡ coldness

ψῡ́χω breathe, blow; cool, refresh

ψωμίζω ψωμιῶ feed by putting little bits in the mouth

ψωμίον ου τό **ψωμός** οῦ ὁ bit, morsel

ψώρᾱ ᾱς ἡ itch, scab, scurvy, mange

ψώχω rub (into powder)

Ωω

ω, Ω (ὦ μέγα) twenty-fourth letter of the alphabet
■ **ω´** *as a numeral* = 800

ὦ o! ah!

ὤ + *voc particle expressing address* o!

ὠβά ῆς ἡ a local division of the Spartan people

ὧδε *adv* thus, so, in this manner; so very; so much; hither; here

ᾠδεῖον ου τό odeon (a public building in Athens for musical performance)

ᾠδή ῆς ἡ song, lay, poem

ὡδί ▸ **ὧδε**

ὠδῑ́ν ῖνος ἡ (*also* ὠδῑ́ς ῖνος ἡ) pains of childbirth, labour pains; birth

ὠδῑ́νω be in labour *or* travail; be in pain, suffer; toil, work painfully

ᾠδός οῦ ὁ ▸ **ἀοιδός**

ὠθέω, ὠθίζω thrust, push, force away; thrust back *or* into, push on; *mid* hurry on; push from oneself; *pass* struggle, be in dispute

ὠθισμός οῦ ὁ a thrusting, pushing, struggling; battle

ὦκα *adv from* **ὠκύς**

ὠκεανός οῦ ὁ the ocean (which surrounds the disk of the earth)

ὠκύαλος ον sailing fast

ὠκυβόλος ον quick-hitting

ὠκύμορος ον dying early; bringing early death

ὠκυπέτης (*gen* ου) swift-flying

ὠκύπορος ον swift-passing

ὠκύπους (*gen* ποδος) swift-footed

ὠκύπτερος ον swift-winged

ὠκύρ(ρ)οος ον swift-flowing

ὠκύς εῖα ύ swift, quick

ὠκυτόκος ον causing quick birth, fertilizing

ὠλένη ης ἡ elbow, lower arm

ὤλεσα *aor from* **ὄλλυμι**

ὠλεσίκαρπος ον losing its fruit

ὠλόμην *aor intr mid from* **ὄλλυμι**

ὦλλος ▸ **ὁ ἄλλος**

ὦλξ ὦλκός ἡ furrow

ὠμηστής (*gen* οῦ) eating raw flesh; savage, brutal

ὠμοβόε(ι)ος ᾱ ον **ὠμοβόϊνος** η ον of raw oxhide

ὠμογέρων οντος ὁ fresh *or* active old man

ὠμο-θετέω put raw pieces of flesh on (the altar); sacrifice

ὠμόθῡμος ον brutal

ὤμοι *int* woe is me! alas!

ὠμοκρατής ές strong-shouldered

ὦμος ου ὁ shoulder, upper arm

ὠμός ή όν raw, undressed, unripe; rude, cruel, brutal, savage

ὤμοσα *aor from* **ὄμνυμι**

ὠμότης ητος ἡ rawness; cruelty

ὠμοφάγος ον eating raw flesh

ὠμόφρων ον savage-minded

ὦν ▸ **οὖν**

ὦνα ▸ **ὦ ἄνα(ξ)**

ὠνέομαι† *mid* buy, purchase; farm public taxes *or* tolls; offer to buy

ὠνή ῆς ἡ ▸ **ὦνος**

ὠνητός ή όν bought, hired; to be bought

ὤνιος (ᾱ) ον to be bought, for sale
■ **τὰ ὤνια** market wares

ὦνος ου ὁ a buying, purchase, barter; price

ᾠόν ου τό egg

ὦρ ἡ ▸ **ὄαρ**

ὤρᾱ ᾱς ἡ ǀ *gen* care, concern, regard for

ὥρᾱ ᾱς ἡ limited time *or* period; season (of the year); fruit(s), produce; climate, weather; year; time of day; hour; moment; prime of life, youth; right time

ὡραῖος ᾱ ον **ὥριος** ᾱ ον suitable to the season, ripe; youthful, blooming, mature
■ **ἡ ὡραίᾱ** the summer season, the campaigning season; season for gathering fruit(s)
■ **τὰ ὡραῖα** fruit(s) of the season

ὠρῡ́ομαι *mid* howl, low, roar, shout

ὥς (*also* ὧς) *adv* thus, so, in this way; in this case; for instance; therefore; *with numerals* about, nearly
■ **καὶ ὥς** nevertheless
■ **οὐδὲ ὥς** not even so

ὡς *adv* as, just as; *with sup* as ... as possible; *with pple* on the grounds that, because; *conj* ▸ **ὅτι**; ▸ **ὥστε**; ▸ **ὅπως**; ▸ **ὅτε**; ▸ **ἐπειδή**

ὡς *prep with acc* to *used of motion to a person*

ὡσαννά *int* hosanna! (save now!)

ὡσαύτως *adv* in the same manner

ὡσεί *adv* as if, as though; just as; *with numerals* about

ὥσπερ *adv* just as; as soon as; as it were

ὥστε *adv* as, like as, just as; *conj* with the result that, so that, so as, on condition that, therefore

ὠτακουστέω listen anxiously *or* covertly

ὠτάριον ου τό **ὠτίον** ου τό (little) ear

ὠτειλή ῆς ἡ wound; scar

ὠτίς ίδος ἡ bustard

ὠτώεις εσσα εν with ears *or* handles

ὠφέλεια ᾱς ἡ help, assistance; profit, advantage

ὠφελέω help, aid, assist, benefit; *pass* be helped, derive profit

ὠφέλημα ατος τό ▶ **ὠφέλεια**

ὠφελήσιμος ον ▶ **ὠφέλιμος**

ὠφέλιμος ον useful, serviceable, profitable

ὠχράω turn pale

ὠχρός ᾱ́ όν pale

ὦχρος ου ὁ paleness

ὤψ ὠπός ἡ eye; face, countenance

Proper names

A

Acarnania Ἀκαρνανίᾱ ᾱς ἡ
■ **Acarnanian** Ἀκαρνανικός ή όν

Achaea Ἀχᾱΐᾱ ᾱς ἡ
■ **Achaean** Ἀχαιϊκός ή όν

Acharnae Ἀχαρναί ῶν αἱ
■ **of ~** Ἀχαρνικός ή όν
■ **man of ~** Ἀχαρνεύς έως ὁ

Achelous *river* Ἀχελῷος ου ὁ

Acheron *river* Ἀχέρων οντος ὁ

Achilles Ἀχιλλεύς έως ὁ

Actaeon Ἀκταίων ωνος ὁ

Admetus Ἄδμητος ου ὁ

Adonis Ἄδωνις ιδος ὁ

Adrastus Ἄδρᾱστος ου ὁ

Aegean Sea τὸ Αἰγαῖον (πέλαγος), ὁ Αἰγαῖος

Aegeus Αἰγεύς έως ὁ

Aegina Αἴγῑνα ης ἡ
■ **of ~** Αἰγῑναῖος α ον
■ **man of ~** Αἰγῑνήτης ου ὁ

Aegisthus Αἴγισθος ου ὁ

Aeneas Αἰνείᾱς ου ὁ

Aeschines Αἰσχίνης ου ὁ

Aeschylus Αἴσχυλος ου ὁ

Aesop Αἴσωπος ου ὁ

Agamemnon Ἀγαμέμνων ονος ὁ

Agathon Ἀγάθων ωνος ὁ

Agave Ἀγαύη ης ἡ

Agesilaus Ἀγησίλᾱος ου ὁ

Agrigentum Ἀκράγᾱς αντος ὁ
■ **of ~** Ἀκραγαντῖνος η ον

Ajax Αἴᾱς αντος ὁ

Alcestis Ἄλκηστις ιδος ἡ

Alcibiades Ἀλκιβιάδης ου ὁ

Alcmaeon Ἀλκμαίων ωνος ὁ

Alcmena Ἀλκμήνη ης ἡ

Alexander Ἀλέξανδρος ου ὁ

Alpheus *river* Ἀλφειός οῦ ὁ

Amazon Ἀμαζών όνος ἡ

Ambracia Ἀμπρακίᾱ ᾱς ἡ
■ **Ambracian** Ἀμπρακικός ή όν
■ **an Ambracian** Ἀμπρακιώτης ου ὁ
■ **Ambracian gulf** ὁ Ἀμπρακικὸς κόλπος

Amphiaraus Ἀμφιάρεως εω ὁ

Amphipolis Ἀμφίπολις εως ἡ

Amphitryon Ἀμφιτρύων ωνος ὁ

Anaxagoras Ἀναξαγόρᾱς ου ὁ

Anaximander Ἀναξίμανδρος ου ὁ

Anchises Ἀγχίσης ου ὁ

Andocides Ἀνδοκίδης ου ὁ

Andromache Ἀνδρομάχη ης ἡ

Andromeda Ἀνδρομέδᾱ ης ἡ

Andros Ἄνδρος ου ἡ
■ **of ~** Ἄνδριος α ον

Antalcidas Ἀνταλκίδᾱς ου ὁ

Antigone Ἀντιγόνη ης ἡ

Antiphon Ἀντιφῶν ῶντος ὁ

Apatouria Athenian festival in which new members were enrolled in the phratries Ἀπατούρια ων τά

Apella Dorian festival in which new members were admitted into the phratries Ἀπέλλαι ῶν αἱ

Aphrodite Ἀφροδίτη ης ἡ

Apollo Ἀπόλλων ωνος ὁ

Arcadia Ἀρκαδίᾱ ᾱς ἡ
■ **Arcadian** Ἀρκαδικός ή όν
■ **an Arcadian** Ἀρκάς άδος ὁ

Archedamus Ἀρχέδᾱμος ου ὁ

Archelaus Ἀρχέλᾱος ου ὁ

Areopagus a hill in Athens and the

council which tried homicide and some religious cases there ἡ ἐξ Ἀρείου πάγου βουλή, ἡ ἐν Ἀρείῳ πάγῳ βουλή
■ **member of** ~ Ἀρεοπαγῑ́της ου ὁ

Ares Ἄρης εως ὁ

Arginusae Ἀργινοῦσαι ων αἱ

Argo ship Ἀργώ οῦς ἡ

Argos Ἄργος ους τό
■ **Argive** Ἀργεῖος α ον
■ **Argolis** Ἀργολίς ίδος ἡ

Ariadne ʼΑριάδνη ης ἡ

Arion Ἀρῑ́ων ονος ὁ

Aristagoras Ἀρισταγόρᾱς ου ὁ

Aristides Ἀριστείδης ου ὁ

Aristogeiton Ἀριστογείτων ονος ὁ

Aristophanes Ἀριστοφάνης ους ὁ

Aristotle Ἀριστοτέλης ους ὁ

Arrephoroi two maidens who carried the robe of Athena Ἀρρηφόροι ων αἱ

Artabanus Ἀρτάβᾱνος ου ὁ

Artabazus Ἀρτάβαζος ου ὁ

Artaphernes Ἀρταφέρνης ους ὁ

Artaxerxes Ἀρταξέρξης ου ὁ

Artemis Ἄρτεμις ίδος ἡ

Artemisium Ἀρτεμίσιον ου τό

Asclepius Ἀσκλήπιος ου ὁ

Asia Ἀσίᾱ ᾱς ἡ
■ **Asian** Ἀσιανός ή όν

Asopus river Ἀσωπός οῦ ὁ

Aspasia Ἀσπασίᾱ ᾱς ἡ

Astyages Ἀστυάγης ους ὁ

Astyanax Ἀστυάναξ ακτος ὁ

Athena Ἀθήνη ης ἡ, Ἀθηναίᾱ ᾱς ἡ

Athens Ἀθῆναι ων αἱ
■ **to** ~ Ἀθήναζε
■ **at** ~ Ἀθήνησι(ν)
■ **from** ~ Ἀθήνηθεν
■ **Athenian** Ἀθηναῖος α ον

Atlas hero or mountain Ἄτλᾱς αντος ὁ

Atossa Ἄτοσσα ης ἡ

Atreus Ἀτρεύς έως ὁ

Attica Ἀττική ῆς ἡ, Ἀτθίς (γῆ) ίδος ἡ

Aulis Αὐλίς ίδος ἡ

B

Babylon Βαβυλών ῶνος ἡ
■ **Babylonian** Βαβυλώνιος ᾱ ον

Bacchus Βάκχος ου ὁ

Bellerophon Βελλεροφόντης ου ὁ

Black Sea ὁ Εὔξεινος πόντος, ὁ Πόντος

Boeotia Βοιωτίᾱ ᾱς ἡ
■ **Boeotian** Βοιώτιος ᾱ ον
■ **a Boeotian** Βοιωτός οῦ ὁ

Boreas Βορέᾱς ου ὁ

Bosphorus Βόσπορος ου ὁ

Brasidas Βρᾱσίδᾱς ου ὁ

Brauron Βραυρών ῶνος ὁ

Britain Βρεττανίᾱ ᾱς ἡ
■ **Briton** Βρεττανός οῦ ὁ

Byzantium Βυζάντιον ου τό

C

Cadmus Κάδμος ου ὁ

Calchas Κάλχᾱς αντος ὁ

Callimachus Καλλίμαχος ου ὁ

Calydon Καλυδών ῶνος ὁ

Calypso Καλυψώ οῦς ἡ

Cambyses Καμβύσης ου ὁ

Caria Καρίᾱ ᾱς ἡ
■ **Carian** Καρικός ή όν
■ **a Carian** Κάρ Καρός ὁ

Carthage Καρχηδών όνος ἡ

Carystus Κάρυστος ου ἡ

Castor Κάστωρ ορος ὁ

Cayster river Κάϋστρος ου ὁ

Cecrops Κέκροψ οπος ὁ

Centaur Κένταυρος ου ὁ

Cephissus river Κηφῑσός οῦ ὁ

Ceramicus Κεραμεικός οῦ ὁ

Cerberus Κέρβερος ου ὁ

Chaerephon Χαιρεφῶν ῶντος ὁ

Chaeronea Χαιρώνεια ας ἡ

Chalcedon Χαλκηδών όνος ἡ

Chalcidice Χαλκιδική ῆς ἡ

Chalcis Χαλκίς ίδος ἡ

Charicles Χαρικλῆς έους ὁ

Charmides Χαρμίδης ου ὁ

Charon Χάρων ωνος ὁ

Charybdis Χάρυβδις εως ἡ

Chersonese Χερσόνησος ου ἡ

Chios Χίος ου ἡ
■ **Chian** Χῖος ᾱ ον

Cimon Κίμων ωνος ὁ

Circe Κίρκη ης ἡ

Cithaeron mountain Κιθαιρών ῶνος ὁ

Cleinias Κλεινίᾱς ου ὁ

Cleisthenes Κλεισθένης ους ὁ

Cleitophon Κλειτοφῶν ῶντος ὁ

Cleomenes Κλεομένης ους ὁ

Cleon Κλέων ωνος ὁ

Clytemnestra Κλυταιμνήστρᾱ ᾱς ἡ

Cnossus Κνωσσός οῦ ἡ

Colchis Κολχίς ίδος ἡ

Conon Κόνων ωνος ὁ

Corcyra Κέρκυρα ᾱς ἡ

Corinth Κόρινθος ου ἡ
■ **Corinthian** Κορίνθιος ᾱ ον
■ **Corinthian Gulf** ὁ Κορινθιακὸς κόλπος

Creon Κρέων οντος ὁ

Crete Κρήτη ης ἡ
■ **Cretan** Κρητικός ή όν
■ **a Cretan** Κρής Κρητός ὁ

Crito Κρίτων ωνος ὁ

Croesus Κροῖσος ου ὁ

Cronos Κρόνος ου ὁ

Cyclops Κύκλωψ ωπος ὁ

Cylon Κύλων ωνος ὁ

Cyprus Κύπρος ου ἡ
■ **Cyprian** Κύπριος ᾱ ον

Cypselus Κύψελος ου ὁ

Cyrene Κῡρήνη ης ἡ

Cyrus Κῦρος ου ὁ

D

Daedalus Δαίδαλος ου ὁ

Darius Δάρειος ου ὁ

Decelea Δεκέλεια ᾱς ἡ

Delos Δῆλος ου ἡ
■ **Delian** Δήλιος ᾱ ον

Delphi Δελφοί ῶν οἱ
■ **Delphic** Δελφικός ή όν, *see also* PYTHO

Demeter Δημήτηρ Δήμητρος ἡ

Demosthenes Δημοσθένης ους ὁ

Diomedes Διομήδης ους ὁ

Dionysia the festival of Dionysus at Athens, a great drama festival Διονύσια ων τά

Dionysius Διονῦσιος ου ὁ

Dionysus Διόνῡσος ου ὁ

Dioscuri Castor and Polydeuces Διόσκοροι ων οἱ

Dodona Δωδώνη ης ἡ

Dorian Δωρικός ή όν
■ **a ~** Δωριεύς ῶς ὁ

Draco Δράκων οντος ὁ

Dryad a tree nymph Δρυάς άδος ἡ

E

Egesta Ἔγεστα ης ἡ
■ **of ~** Ἐγεσταῖος α ον

Egypt Αἴγυπτος ου ἡ
■ **Egyptian** Αἰγύπτιος ᾱ ον

Eleusis Ἐλευσῑ́ς ῖνος ἡ
■ **Eleusinian** Ἐλευσίνιος ᾱ ον
■ **the Eleusinian festivals** Ἐλευσίνια ων τά

Elis Ἦλις ιδος ἡ

Empedocles Ἐμπεδοκλῆς έους ὁ

Ephesus Ἔφεσος ου ἡ

Ephialtes Ἐφιάλτης ου ὁ

Epicurus Ἐπίκουρος ου ὁ

Epidamnus Ἐπίδαμνος ου ἡ

Epidaurus Ἐπίδαυρος ου ἡ

Epirus Ἤπειρος ου ἡ
■ **of ~** Ἠπειρωτικός ἡ όν
■ **man of ~** Ἠπειρώτης ου ὁ

Erechtheus Ἐρεχθεύς έως ὁ

Eretria Ἐρέτρια ᾱς ἡ

Eros Ἔρως ωτος ὁ

Erymanthus mountain Ἐρύμανθος ου ὁ

Erythrae Ἐρυθραί ῶν αἱ

Eteocles Ἐτεοκλῆς έους ὁ

Ethiopia Αἰθιοπίᾱ ᾱς ἡ
■ **Ethiopian** Αἰθιοπικός ἡ όν

Euboea Εὔβοια ᾱς ἡ
■ **Euboean** Εὐβοικός ἡ όν
■ **a Euboean** Εὐβοεύς ῶς ὁ

Euripides Εὐριπίδης ου ὁ

Europe Εὐρώπη ης ἡ

Eurotas river Εὐρώτᾱς ᾱ ὁ

Eurydice Εὐρυδίκη ης ἡ

Eurymedon river or general Εὐρυμέδων οντος ὁ

Euthyphro Εὐθύφρων ονος ὁ

Euxine Sea ὁ Εὔξεινος πόντος, ὁ Πόντος

F

Fury Ἐρῑνύς ύος ἡ

G

Gaia, Ge earth regarded as goddess Γῆ Γῆς ἡ

Gaul Γαλατίᾱ ᾱς ἡ
■ **Gallic** Γαλατικός ἡ όν
■ **a Gaul** Γαλάτης ου ὁ

Gela Γέλᾱ ᾱς ἡ
■ **of ~** Γελῷος α ον

Giant Γίγᾱς αντος ὁ

Glaucon Γλαύκων ωνος ὁ

Glaucus Γλαῦκος ου ὁ

Gorgias Γοργίᾱς ου ὁ

Gorgon Γοργώ οῦς ἡ

Greece Ἑλλάς άδος ἡ
■ **Greek** Ἑλληνικός ἡ όν
■ **a Greek** Ἕλλην ηνος ὁ
■ **Greek woman** Ἑλληνίς ίδος ἡ
■ **speak Greek** ἑλληνίζω
■ **in Greek fashion** Ἑλληνικῶς
■ **in the Greek language** Ἑλληνιστί

Gyges Γύγης ου ὁ

Gylippus Γύλιππος ου ὁ

H

Hades Ἅιδης ου ὁ

Halicarnassus Ἁλικαρνασσός οῦ ἡ
■ **man of ~** Ἁλικαρνασσεύς έως ὁ

Harmodius Ἁρμόδιος ου ὁ

Harpagus Ἅρπαγος ου ὁ

Hecateus Ἑκαταῖος ου ὁ

Hecate Ἑκάτη ης ἡ

Hector Ἕκτωρ ορος ὁ

Hecuba Ἑκάβη ης ἡ

Helen Ἑλένη ης ἡ

Hellespont Ἑλλήσποντος ου ὁ

Helot Εἵλως ωτος ὁ, Εἱλώτης ου ὁ

Hephaestus Ἥφαιστος ου ὁ

Hera Ἥρᾱ ᾱς ἡ

Heracles Ἡρακλῆς έους ὁ

Heraclitus Ἡράκλειτος ου ὁ

Hermes Ἑρμῆς οῦ ὁ

Hermocrates Ἑρμοκράτης ους ὁ

Herodotus Ἡρόδοτος ου ὁ

Hesiod Ἡσίοδος ου ὁ

Hipparchus Ἵππαρχος ου ὁ

Hippias Ἱππίᾱς ου ὁ

Hippocrates Ἱπποκράτης ους ὁ

Hippolytus Ἱππόλυτος ου ὁ

Homer Ὅμηρος ου ὁ

Hyperbolus Ὑπέρβολος ου ὁ

I

Icarus Ἴκαρος ου ὁ

Ida mountain Ἴδη ης ἡ
■ **of ~** Ἰδαῖος α ον

Ilissus river Ἰλῖσός οῦ ὁ

Iliad Ἰλιάς άδος ἡ

India Ἰνδίᾱ ᾱς ἡ, ἡ Ἰνδικὴ χώρᾱ
■ **Indian** Ἰνδικός ή όν
■ **an Indian** Ἰνδός οῦ ὁ

Ion Ἴων ωνος ὁ

Ionia Ἰωνίᾱ ᾱς ἡ
■ **Ionian** Ἰωνικός ή όν
■ **an Ionian** Ἴων ωνος ὁ

Iphigenia Ἰφιγένεια ᾱς ἡ

Isocrates Ἰσοκράτης ους ὁ

Italy Ἰταλίᾱ ᾱς ἡ
■ **Italian** Ἰταλικός ή όν

Ithaca Ἰθάκη ης ἡ
■ **Ithacan** Ἰθακήσιος α ον

J

Jason Ἰάσων ονος ὁ

Jocasta Ἰοκάστη ης ἡ

K

Kore Persephone Κόρη ης ἡ

L

Lacedaemon Λακεδαίμων ονος ἡ
■ **Lacedaemonian** (of people) Λακεδαιμόνιος ᾱ ον; (of things) Λακωνικός ή όν
■ **a Lacedaemonian** Λάκων ωνος ὁ
■ **Lacedaemonian woman** Λάκαινα ης ἡ

Laconia Λακωνική ῆς ἡ, *see also* SPARTA

Laches Λάχης ητος ὁ

Laertes Λᾱέρτης ου ὁ

Laius Λᾱ́ϊος ου ὁ

Lamachus Λᾱ́μαχος ου ὁ

Larissa Λᾱ́ρισα ης ἡ
■ **of ~** Λᾱρισαῖος α ον

Laurium Λαύρειον ου τό

Lemnos Λῆμνος ου ἡ
■ **Lemnian** Λήμνιος ᾱ ον

Lenaea an Athenian festival held in the winter in honour of Dionysus at which plays, especially comedies, were performed Λήναια ων τά

Leonidas Λεωνίδᾱς ου ὁ

Lesbos Λέσβος ου ἡ
■ **Lesbian** Λέσβιος α ον

Leto Λητώ οῦς ἡ

Locris Λοκρίς ίδος ἡ

Lycabettus mountain Λυκάβηττος ου ὁ

Lycia Λυκίᾱ ᾱς ἡ
■ **Lycian** Λύκιος ᾱ ον

Lycurgus Λυκοῦργος ου ὁ

Lydia Λῡδίᾱ ᾱς ἡ
■ **Lydian** Λῡ́διος ᾱ ον
■ **a Lydian** Λῡδός οῦ ὁ

Lygdamis Λύγδαμις εως ὁ

Lysander Λύσανδρος ου ὁ

Lysias Λυσίᾱς ου ὁ

M

Macedonia Μακεδονίᾱ ᾱς ἡ
■ **Macedonian** Μακεδονικός ή όν
■ **a Macedonian** Μακεδών όνος ὁ

Maeander river Μαίανδρος ου ὁ

Mantinea Μαντίνεια ᾱς ἡ

Marathon Μαραθών ῶνος ὁ

Mardonius Μαρδόνιος ου ὁ

Medea Μήδεια ᾱς ἡ

Media Μηδίᾱ ᾱς ἡ

■ **Median** Μηδικός ή όν
■ **a Mede** Μῆδος ου ὁ

Mediterranean Sea ἡ παρ' ἡμῖν θάλασσα, ἥδε ἡ θάλασσα

Megacles Μεγακλῆς έους ὁ

Megara Μέγαρα ων τά
■ **Megarian** Μεγαρικός ή όν
■ **a Megarian** Μεγαρεύς έως ὁ

Meleager Μελέαγρος ου ὁ

Melos Μῆλος ου ἡ
■ **Melian** Μήλιος ᾱ ον

Menander Μένανδρος ου ὁ

Menelaus Μενέλεως εω ὁ

Meno Μένων ωνος ὁ

Messene Μεσσήνη ης ἡ
■ **Messenian** Μεσσήνιος ᾱ ον
■ **Messenia** Μεσσηνίᾱ ᾱς ἡ

Midas Μίδᾱς ου ὁ

Miletus Μῑ́λητος ου ἡ
■ **Milesian** Μῑλήσιος ᾱ ον

Miltiades Μιλτιάδης ου ὁ

Minos Μῑ́νως ω ὁ

Minotaur Μῑνώταυρος ου ὁ

Muse Μοῦσα ης ἡ

Mycenae Μυκῆναι ων αἱ
■ **Mycenaean** Μυκηναῖος ᾱ ον

Myrmidons Μυρμιδόνες ων οἱ

Mysia Μῡσίᾱ ᾱς ἡ
■ **Mysian** Μῡ́σιος ᾱ ον
■ **a Mysian** Μῡσός οῦ ὁ

Mytilene Μυτιλήνη ης ἡ
■ **Mytilenean** Μυτιληναῖος ᾱ ον

N

Naucratis Ναύκρατις εως ἡ

Naupactus Ναύπακτος ου ἡ

Nauplia Ναυπλίᾱ ᾱς ἡ

Naxos Νάξος ου ἡ
■ **Naxian** Νάξιος ᾱ ον

Nemea Νεμέᾱ ᾱς ἡ
■ **Nemean** Νέμειος ᾱ ον

Neoptolemus Νεοπτόλεμος ου ὁ

Nestor Νέστωρ ορος ὁ

Nicias Νῑκίᾱς ου ὁ

Nile river Νεῖλος ου ὁ

Niobe Νιόβη ης ἡ

O

Odysseus Ὀδυσσεύς έως ὁ

Odyssey Ὀδυσσείᾱ ᾱς ἡ

Oedipus Οἰδίπους ποδος ὁ

Olympia Ὀλυμπίᾱ ᾱς ἡ
■ **to ~** Ὀλυμπίαζε
■ **at ~** Ὀλυμπίᾱσι
■ **Olympic** of Olympia Ὀλυμπικός ή όν, Ὀλυμπιακός ή όν
■ **Olympic games** Ὀλύμπια ων τά
■ **Olympic victor** Ὀλυμπιονῑ́κης ου ὁ
■ **Olympiad** period of four years Ὀλυμπιάς άδος ἡ

Olympus mountain Ὄλυμπος ου ὁ
■ **Olympian** of Olympus Ὀλύμπιος ον

Olynthus Ὄλυνθος ου ἡ
■ **Olynthian** Ὀλύνθιος ᾱ ον

Orestes Ὀρέστης ου ὁ

Oropus Ὠρωπός οῦ ὁ

Orpheus Ὀρφεύς έως ὁ

Ossa mountain Ὄσσᾱ ης ἡ

P

Palamedes Παλαμήδης ους ὁ

Pan Πᾱ́ν Πᾱνός ὁ

Panathenaea Athenian festival Παναθήναια ων τά

Paphos Πάφος ου ἡ
■ **Paphian** Πάφιος ᾱ ον

Paralus Athenian state vessel Πάραλος ου ἡ

Paris Πάρις ιδος ὁ

Parnassus mountain Παρνᾱσός οῦ ὁ

Parnes mountain Πάρνης ηθος ὁ

Paros Πάρος ου ἡ
■ **Parian** Πάριος ᾱ ον

Pasiphae Πᾱσιφάη ης ἡ

Patmos Πάτμος ου ἡ

Patrae Πατραί ῶν αἱ

Patroclus Πάτροκλος ου ὁ

Pausanias Παυσανίᾱς ου ὁ

Peirene fountain Πειρήνη ης ἡ

Peisistratus Πεισίστρατος ου ὁ

Peleus Πηλεύς έως ὁ

Pelion mountain Πήλιον ου τό

Peloponnese Πελοπόννησος ου ἡ
■ **Peloponnesian** Πελοποννησιακός ή όν
■ **Peloponnesians** Πελοποννήσιοι ων οἱ

Pelops Πέλοψ οπος ὁ

Penelope Πηνελόπη ης ἡ

Pentheus Πενθεύς έως ὁ

Perdiccas Περδίκκᾱς ου ὁ

Pergamum citadel of Troy Πέργαμον ου τό *or pl*

Periander Περίανδρος ου ὁ

Pericles Περικλῆς έους ὁ

Persephone Περσεφόνη ης ἡ

Perseus Περσεύς έως ὁ

Persia Περσική ῆς ἡ
■ **Persian** Περσικός ή όν
■ **a Persian** Πέρσης ου ὁ
■ **Persian woman** Περσίς ίδος ἡ

Phaeacians Φαίᾱκες ων οἱ

Phaedo Φαίδων ωνος ὁ

Phaedra Φαίδρᾱ ᾱς ἡ

Pharnabazus Φαρνάβαζος ου ὁ

Pheidias Φειδίᾱς ου ὁ

Pheidippides Φειδιππίδης ου ὁ

Philip Φίλιππος ου ὁ

Philoctetes Φιλοκτήτης ου ὁ

Phocion Φωκίων ωνος ὁ

Phocis Φωκίς ίδος ἡ

Phoenicia Φοινῑ́κη ης ἡ

Phoenix Φοῖνῑξ ῖκος ὁ

Phormio Φορμίων ωνος ὁ

Phrygia Φρυγίᾱ ᾱς ἡ
■ **Phrygian** Φρύγιος ᾱ ον
■ **a Phrygian** Φρύξ Φρυγός ὁ

Phyle Φῡλή ῆς ἡ

Pindar Πίνδαρος ου ὁ

Pindus mountain Πίνδος ου ὁ

Piraeus Πειραιεύς ῶς ὁ

Plataea Πλάταια ᾱς ἡ
■ **at ~** Πλαταιᾶσι
■ **Plataean** Πλαταιικός ή όν
■ **a Plataean** Πλαταιεύς έως ὁ

Plato Πλάτων ωνος ὁ

Plutarch Πλούταρχος ου ὁ

Pluto Πλούτων ωνος ὁ

Pnyx Πνύξ Πυκνός ἡ

Polybius Πολύβιος ου ὁ

Polybus Πόλυβος ου ὁ

Polycrates Πολυκράτης ους ὁ

Polyneices Πολυνείκης ους ὁ

Polyphemus Πολύφημος ου ὁ

Poseidon Ποσειδῶν ῶνος ὁ

Potidaea Ποτῑ́δαια ᾱς ἡ
■ **Potidaean** Ποτῑδαιατικός ή όν
■ **a Potidaean** Ποτῑδαιάτης ου ὁ

Priam Πρίαμος ου ὁ

Priene Πριήνη ης ἡ
■ **man of ~** Πριηνεύς έως ὁ

Procne Πρόκνη ης ἡ

Proconnesus Προκόννησος ου ἡ
■ **of ~** Προκοννήσιος ᾱ ον

Prodicus Πρόδικος ου ὁ

Prometheus Προμηθεύς έως ὁ

Propontis Προποντίς ίδος ἡ

Protagoras Πρωταγόρᾱς ου ὁ

Psammetichus Ψαμμήτιχος ου ὁ

Pylades Πυλάδης ου ὁ

Pylos Πύλος ου ἡ
■ **of ~** Πύλιος ᾱ ον

Pythagoras Πυθαγόρᾱς ου ὁ

Pytho Πῡθώ οῦς ἡ
■ **to ~** Πῡθώδε
■ **at ~** Πῡθοῖ
■ **Pythian** Πῡ́θιος ᾱ ον, Πῡθικός ή όν

■ **Pythian Games** Πύθια ων τά
■ **Pythia** priestess Πῡθίᾱ ᾱς ἡ, *see also* DELPHI

R

Rhadamanthus Ῥαδάμανθος ου ὁ

Rhamnus Ῥαμνοῦς οῦντος ὁ
■ **of ~** Ῥαμνούσιος ᾱ ον

Rhea Ῥέᾱ ᾱς ἡ

Rhegium Ῥήγιον ου τό

Rhesus Ῥῆσος ου ὁ

Rhodes Ῥόδος ου ἡ

Rhodian Ῥόδιος ᾱ ον

S

Salaminia Athenian state vessel Σαλαμῑνίᾱ ᾱς ἡ

Salamis Σαλαμῑ́ς ῖνος ἡ
■ **Salaminian** Σαλαμῑ́νιος ᾱ ον

Samos Σάμος ου ἡ
■ **Samian** Σάμιος ᾱ ον

Samothrace Σαμοθρᾴκη ης ἡ

Sappho Σαπφώ οῦς ἡ

Sardis Σάρδεις εων αἱ
■ **of ~** Σαρδιᾱνός ή όν

Saronic Gulf ὁ Σαρωνικὸς κόλπος

Sarpedon Σαρπηδών όνος ὁ

Scamander river Σκάμανδρος ου ὁ

Scythia Σκυθική ῆς ἡ
■ **Scythian** Σκυθικός ή όν
■ **a Scythian** Σκύθης ου ὁ
■ **Scythian woman** Σκύθαινα ης ἡ
■ **in Scythian language or fashion** Σκυθιστί

Segesta *see* EGESTA

Selinus Σελῑνοῦς οῦντος ὁ
■ **of ~** Σελῑνούντιος ᾱ ον

Semele Σεμέλη ης ἡ

Sestos Σηστος ου ἡ
■ **of ~** Σήστιος ᾱ ον

Sibyl Σίβυλλα ης ἡ

Sicily Σικελίᾱ ᾱς ἡ
■ **Sicilian** Σικελικός ή όν
■ **a (non-Greek) Sicilian** Σίκελος ου ὁ
■ **a (Greek) Sicilian** Σικηλιώτης ου ὁ

Sicyon Σικυών ῶνος ἡ
■ **Sicyonian** Σικυώνιος ᾱ ον

Sidon Σῑδών ῶνος ἡ
■ **of ~** Σῑδώνιος ᾱ ον

Sigeum Σίγειον ου τό

Silenus Σειληνός οῦ ὁ

Simonides Σιμωνίδης ου ὁ

Sitalces Σῑτάλκης ου ὁ

Socrates Σωκράτης ους ὁ

Solon Σόλων ωνος ὁ

Sophocles Σοφοκλῆς έους ὁ

Sparta Σπάρτη ης ἡ, *see also* LACEDAEMON
■ **a Spartan** citizen of Sparta Σπαρτιᾱ́της ου ὁ
■ **Spartan woman** Σπαρτιᾶτις ιδος ἡ

Sphacteria Σφακτηρίᾱ ᾱς ἡ

Sphinx Σφίγξ ιγγός ἡ

Stesichorus Στησίχορος ου ὁ

Strymon river Στρῡμών όνος ὁ

Styx river Στύξ Στυγός ἡ

Sunium cape Σούνιον ου τό

Susa Σοῦσα ων τά

Sybaris Σύβαρις εως ἡ
■ **of ~** Συβαρῑτικός ή όν
■ **man of ~** Συβαρῑ́της ου ὁ
■ **woman of ~** Συβαρῖτις ιδος ἡ

Syracuse Συρᾱκοῦσαι ων αἱ
■ **Syracusan** Συρᾱκόσιος ᾱ ον

Syria Συρίᾱ ᾱς ἡ
■ **Syrian** Σύριος α ον
■ **a Syrian** Σύρος ου ὁ
■ **in the Syrian language** Συριστί

T

Taenarus cape Ταίναρος ου ὁ

Talthybius Ταλθύβιος ου ὁ

Tanagra Τάναγρα ᾱς ἡ
■ **of ~** Ταναγρικός ή όν

Tantalus Τάνταλος ου ὁ

Tarentum Τάρᾱς αντος ὁ
■ **of ~** Ταραντῖνος η ον

Tartarus Τάρταρος ου ὁ

Taygetus mountain Τᾱΰγετον ου τό

Tecmessa Τέκμησσα ης ἡ

Tegea Τεγέᾱ ᾱς ἡ
■ **of ~** Τεγεατικός ή όν
■ **man of ~** Τεγεάτης ου ὁ

Telamon Τελαμών ῶνος ὁ

Telemachus Τηλέμαχος ου ὁ

Telephus Τήλεφος ου ὁ

Tempe Τέμπη ῶν τά

Tenedos Τένεδος ου ἡ

Tenos Τῆνος ου ἡ

Tereus Τηρεύς έως ὁ

Teucer Τεῦκρος ου ὁ

Thales Θαλῆς Θάλεω ὁ

Thasos Θάσος ου ἡ
■ **of ~** Θάσιος ᾱ ον

Thebes Θῆβαι ων αἱ
■ **to ~** Θήβαζε
■ **at ~** Θήβησι
■ **Theban** Θηβαῖος ᾱ ον

Themistocles Θεμιστοκλῆς έους ὁ

Theoclymenus Θεοκλύμενος ου ὁ

Theognis Θέογνις ιδος ὁ

Theopompus Θεόπομπος ου ὁ

Thera Θήρᾱ ᾱς ἡ

Theramenes Θηρᾱμένης ους ὁ

Thermopylae Θερμοπύλαι ων αἱ

Thersites Θερσῑ́της ου ὁ

Theseus Θησεύς έως ὁ

Thesmophoria festival Θεσμοφόρια ων τά

Thessaly Θεσσαλίᾱ ᾱς ἡ
■ **Thessalian** Θεσσαλικός ή όν
■ **a Thessalian** Θεσσαλός οῦ ὁ
■ **Thessalian woman** Θεσσαλίς ίδος ἡ

Thetis Θέτις ιδος ἡ

Thrace Θρᾴκη ης ἡ
■ **Thracian** Θρᾴκιος ᾱ ον
■ **a Thracian** Θρᾷξ Θρᾳκός ὁ
■ **Thracian woman** Θρᾷσσα ης ἡ

Thrasybulus Θρασύβουλος ου ὁ

Thucydides Θουκῡδίδης ου ὁ

Thurii Θούριοι ων οἱ
■ **people of ~** Θούριοι ων οἱ

Thyestes Θυέστης ου ὁ

Tigris river Τίγρης ητος ὁ

Timoleon Τιμολέων οντος ὁ

Timon Τίμων ωνος ὁ

Tiresias Τειρεσίᾱς ου ὁ

Tiryns Τῑ́ρυνς υνθος ἡ
■ **of ~** Τῑρύνθιος ᾱ ον

Tissaphernes Τισσαφέρνης ου ὁ

Titan Τῑτάν ᾶνος ὁ

Tmolus mountain Τμῶλος ου ὁ

Tolmides Τολμίδης ου ὁ

Trachis Τρᾱχῑ́ς ῖνος ἡ
■ **of ~** Τρᾱχῑ́νιος ᾱ ον

Triptolemus Τριπτόλεμος ου ὁ

Troezen Τροιζήν ῆνος ἡ
■ **of ~** Τροιζήνιος ᾱ ον

Troy Τροίᾱ ας ἡ
■ **Trojan** Τρωικός ή όν
■ **a Trojan** Τρώς Τρωός ὁ
■ **Trojan woman** Τρωάς άδος ἡ

Troad the area around Troy Τρωάς (γῆ) άδος ἡ

X

Xanthias Ξανθίᾱς ου ὁ

Xanthippe Ξανθίππη ης ἡ

Xanthippus Ξάνθιππος ου ὁ

Xenophanes Ξενοφάνης ους ὁ

Xenophon Ξενοφῶν ῶντος ὁ

Xerxes Ξέρξης ου ὁ

Z

Zacynthus Ζάκυνθος ου ἡ
■ **of ~** Ζακύνθιος ᾱ ον

Zeno Ζήνων ωνος ὁ

Zeus Ζεύς Διός *or* Ζηνός ὁ

Aa

a, a certain τις τι (τιν-)

abandon ἀπολείπω, καταλείπω

abbreviate συντέμνω

ability (intelligence) σύνεσις εως ἡ; (skill) δεξιότης ητος ἡ
■ **to the best of one's ~** κατὰ δύναμιν

able (clever) δεινός ἡ όν, σοφός ἡ όν, φρόνιμος ον; (having power) δυνατός ἡ όν
■ **be ~** δύναμαι + *infin*, οἷός τέ εἰμι + *infin*

aboard ἐπί + *gen*

abolish καθαιρέω, καταλύω

about (concerning) περί + *gen*; (round) περί + *acc*; *with numbers* μάλιστα, ὡς
■ **be ~ to** μέλλω + *fut infin*

above *adv* καθύπερθε(ν); *prep* ὑπέρ + *gen*

abroad: be/go ~ ἀποδημέω

absence ἀπουσία ας ἡ

absent: be ~ ἄπειμι

absolute (in power) αὐτοκράτωρ (*gen* ορος)

absolutely ἀτεχνῶς, παντάπασι, τὸ παράπαν

abstain from ἀπέχομαι + *gen*

absurd ἄτοπος ον, γελοῖος α ον

abundance εὐπορία ας ἡ, περιουσία ας ἡ

abundant ἄφθονος ον

abuse (misuse) ἀποχράομαι + *dat*; (insult) κακὰ λέγω, λοιδορέω, ὀνειδίζω

accent (pitch) τόνος ου ὁ; (way of speaking) φωνή ῆς ἡ
■ **have a foreign ~** ξενίζω

accept δέχομαι

accessible εὐπρόσοδος ον

accident τύχη ης ἡ, συμφορά ᾶς ἡ

accidentally τύχῃ; *or use* τυγχάνω + *pple*

accompany ἕπομαι + *dat*, συνακολουθέω + *dat*, συνέρχομαι + *dat*

accomplice συνεργός οῦ ὁ

accomplish πράσσω, ἐκπράσσω, ἐκτελέω, ἐργάζομαι

accord: of one's own ~ (self-moving) αὐτόματος (η) ον; (willingly) ἑκών οὖσα όν (ἑκοντ-)

according to κατά + *acc*

accordingly οὖν*

account λόγος ου ὁ
■ **give an ~** διηγέομαι
■ **on ~ of** διά + *acc*, ἕνεκα *foll gen*
■ **~-book** γραμματεῖον ου τό

accountable ὑπεύθυνος ον

accuracy ἀκρίβεια ας ἡ

accurate ἀκριβής ές

accurately ἀκριβῶς

accursed κατάρατος ον

accusation κατηγορία ας ἡ

accuse αἰτιάομαι, διαβάλλω; κατηγορέω + *gen*
■ **the ~d** ὁ φεύγων

accuser κατήγορος ου ὁ, ὁ διώκων

accustom ἐθίζω

accustomed: be ~ εἴωθα

achieve πράσσω

achievement ἔργον ου τό

acknowledge ὁμολογέω

acorn βάλανος ου ἡ

acquaintance (person) γνώριμος ου ὁ

acquire κτάομαι

acquisition (thing acquired) κτῆμα ατος τό

acquit ἀπολύω
■ **be ~ted of** σῴζομαι, φεύγω

across (through) διά + *gen*; (over) ὑπέρ + *gen*; (on the other side of) πέρα + *gen*

a

act *noun* ἔργον ου τό, πρᾶξις εως ἡ; *verb* πράσσω

action ἔργον ου τό, πρᾶξις εως ἡ

active εὔζωνος ον, δραστήριος ον; (busy) ἄσχολος ον; (eager) πρόθυμος ον

actor ὑποκριτής οῦ ὁ

adapt *tr* προσαρμόζω

add προστίθημι

addition (act of adding) προσθήκη ης ἡ
■ **in ~ to** πρός + *dat*

address *verb* προσαγορεύω

adequate ἱκανός ή όν

adjacent ὅμορος ον

adjourn ἀναβάλλομαι

adjudicate δικάζομαι

administer διοικέω

administration διοίκησις εως ἡ

admirable θαυμάσιος α ον, θαυμαστός ή όν

admiral ναύαρχος ου ὁ

admiration θαῦμα ατος τό, θάμβος ους τό

admire θαυμάζω

admit (agree) ὁμολογέω

adolescence ἥβη ης ἡ

adopt [plan etc.] αἱρέομαι; χράομαι + *dat*

adorn κοσμέω

adult *adj* τέλειος (α) ον

adulterer μοιχός οῦ ὁ

advance προχωρέω, προέρχομαι

advantage *noun* ὠφελία ας ἡ, τὸ σύμφορον
■ **gain an ~** πλεονεκτέω, ὠφελέομαι
■ **it is of ~** συμφέρει

advantageous (profitable) κερδαλέος α ον; (beneficial) πρόσφορος ον, χρήσιμος (η) ον
■ **it is ~ to** λυσιτελεῖ + *dat*

adventure τόλμημα ατος τό, πεῖρα ας ἡ

adventurous φιλοκίνδυνος ον

adverse ἐναντίος α ον

advertise κηρύσσω

advice βουλή ῆς ἡ, παραίνεσις εως ἡ

advise νουθετέω; παραινέω + *dat*, συμβουλεύω + *dat*

adviser σύμβουλος ου ὁ

advocate *noun* συνήγορος ου ὁ, σύνδικος ου ὁ

affair πρᾶγμα ατος τό
■ **the ~s of** τὰ + *gen*

afraid περίφοβος ον, περιδεής ές
■ **be ~ (of)** φοβέομαι

after μετά + *acc*
■ **~ a long time** διὰ πολλοῦ

afternoon δείλη ης ἡ

afterwards μετὰ ταῦτα, ὕστερον
■ **not long ~** οὐ διὰ πολλοῦ, ὕστερον οὐ πολλῷ

again αὖθις, πάλιν

against ἐπί + *acc*, ἐναντίον + *dat*
■ **~ one's will** ἄκων ουσα ον (ἀκοντ-)

age (period) αἰών ῶνος ὁ; (time of life) ἡλικία ας ἡ
■ **of such an ~** τηλικοῦτος αύτη οῦτο(ν)

aged (old) γεραιός ά όν

agent ὑπηρέτης ου ὁ

agile ἐλαφρός ά όν

agitate κινέω, ταράσσω

ago: long ~ πάλαι
■ **two years ~** τρίτον ἔτος τοῦτο ἐξ οὗ

agree (with) ὁμολογέω + *dat*

agreement ὁμολογία ας ἡ, σύμβασις εως ἡ
■ **make an ~ with** συμβαίνω + *dat*, συγχωρέω + *dat*

agriculture γεωργία ας ἡ

ahead πρόσθεν

aid βοήθεια ας ἡ

aim at στοχάζομαι + *gen*

air ἀήρ ἀέρος ὁ

aisle πάροδος ου ἡ

alien ἀλλότριος α ον
■ **resident ~** μέτοικος ου ὁ/ἡ

alienate ἀλλοτριόω

alive ἔμψυχος ον

all πᾶς πᾶσα πᾶν (παντ-)
■ **~ but** ὅσον οὐ
■ **~ right!** ἔστω
■ **~ who *or* that (do X)** ὅσοι αι α

allegory ὑπόνοια ας ἡ

alleviate κουφίζω

alliance συμμαχία ας ἡ
■ **defensive ~** ἐπιμαχία ᾱς ἡ

allot νέμω

allotment κλῆρος ου ὁ

allow ἐάω; ἐπιτρέπω + *dat*

allowed: it is ~ ἔξεστι(ν) + *dat*

allure δελεάζω

allusion ὑπόμνησις εως ἡ

ally *usu pl* σύμμαχος ου ὁ

almost σχεδόν, μόνον οὐ, ὅσον οὐ

alone μόνος η ον
■ **be left ~** μονόομαι

along (of movement) κατά + *acc*, παρά + *acc*

alphabet γράμματα ων τά

already ἤδη

also καί

altar βωμός οῦ ὁ

alter ἀλλοιόω

alternately ἐναλλάξ

although καίπερ + *pple*

altogether πάνυ

always ἀεί

am εἰμί

amaze ἐκπλήσσω

amazement θάμβος ους τό, κατάπληξις εως ἡ

ambassador πρεσβευτής οῦ ὁ; *pl* πρέσβεις εων οἱ

amber ἤλεκτρον ου τό

ambiguous δύσκριτος ον, ἀμφίλογος ον

ambiguously: speak ~ αἰνίσσομαι

ambition φιλοτιμία ας ἡ

ambitious φιλότιμος ον

ambush ἐνέδρα ας ἡ
■ **lie in ~** ἐνεδρεύω

amend ἐπανορθόω

amnesty ἄδεια ας ἡ

among ἐν + *dat*

amount to (of numbers) γίγνομαι

ample ἱκανός ή όν

amusing γελοῖος α ον

anarchy ἀνομία ας ἡ, ἀναρχία ας ἡ

ancestor πρόγονος ου ὁ

ancestral πάτριος (α) ον

anchor *noun* ἄγκυρα ας ἡ; *verb tr* ὁρμίζω; *verb intr* ὁρμίζομαι
■ **lie at ~** ὁρμέω

anchorage ὅρμος ου ὁ

anchovy ἀφύη ης ἡ

ancient ἀρχαῖος α ον, παλαιός ά όν

and καί
■ **~ not** οὐδέ
■ **~ so ... not** οὔκουν
■ **~ yet** καίτοι

anger *noun* ὀργή ῆς ἡ

angle γωνία ας ἡ

angry: be ~ (at) ἀγανακτέω + *dat*, δι' ὀργῆς ἔχω
■ **become ~ (at)** ὀργίζομαι + *dat*

animal ζῷον ου τό

ankle σφυρόν οῦ τό

annihilate ἀφανίζω

announce ἀγγέλλω, κηρύσσω

annoy λυπέω, ἐνοχλέω
■ **be ~ed** λυπέομαι, ἄχθομαι

annually κατὰ ἔτος

annul καταλύω

anoint χρίω, ἀλείφω

another ἄλλος η ο

answer *noun* ἀπόκρισις εως ἡ; (of oracle) χρησμός οῦ ὁ; *verb* ἀποκρίνομαι, ὑπολαμβάνω

answerable ὑπεύθυνος ον

ant μύρμηξ ηκος ὁ

antidote ἀλεξιφάρμακον ου τό

a

any τις τι (τιν-)

anywhere πού

anxiety ἐπιμέλεια ας ἡ

anxious: be ~ (for) φροντίζω + *gen*

apart from χωρίς + *gen*

apology (defence) ἀπολογία ας ἡ; (excuse) πρόφασις εως ἡ

appeal to ἀνακαλέω, μαρτύρομαι

appear φαίνομαι, δοκέω; (come on the scene) παραγίγνομαι

appearance σχῆμα ατος τό, εἶδος ους τό

appease πραΰνω; [a god] ἱλάσκομαι

appetite (desire) ἐπιθυμία ας ἡ; (for food) γαστήρ τρός ἡ

applaud ἀναθορυβέω, κροτέω

applause κρότος ου ὁ, ἔπαινος ου ὁ

apple μῆλον ου τό

appoint καθίστημι, αἱρέομαι

approach *noun* πρόσοδος ου ἡ; *verb* προσβαίνω, προσέρχομαι, προσχωρέω

approve ἐπαινέω

arch ἁψίς ῖδος ἡ

archer τοξότης ου ὁ

archery τοξική ῆς ἡ

ardent πρόθυμος ον

ardour σπουδή ῆς ἡ

argue ἀγωνίζομαι, ἀμφισβητέω

argument λόγος ου ὁ

arise (come to be) γίγνομαι; (stand *or* get up) ἀνίσταμαι

arm *noun* (part of body) βραχίων ονος ὁ; *verb* ὁπλίζω
■ **lightly ~ed** ψιλός ἡ όν

armistice σπονδαί ῶν αἱ, ἐκεχειρία ας ἡ

arms (weapons) *pl* ὅπλα ων τά

army στρατός οῦ ὁ, στρατιά ᾶς ἡ, στράτευμα ατος τό

around περί + *acc*

arouse (waken) ἐγείρω

arrange τάσσω

arrangement τάξις εως ἡ

arrest συλλαμβάνω

arrival ἄφιξις εως ἡ

arrive ἀφικνέομαι

arrogance ὕβρις εως ἡ, αὐθάδεια ας ἡ

arrogant μεγαλόφρων ον (μεγαλοφρον-), σεμνός ἡ όν

arrow τόξευμα ατος τό, οἰστός οῦ ὁ

art (skill) τέχνη ης ἡ

as (like) ὡς; (since, because) ἐπεί
■ **~ X as possible** ὡς + *sup*
■ **~ far as** μέχρι + *gen*
■ **~ great as** ὅσος η ον
■ **~ if** ὥσπερ
■ **~ many as** ὅσοι αι α
■ **~ soon as** ἐπεὶ τάχιστα

ascent ἀνάβασις εως ἡ

ascertain πυνθάνομαι, γιγνώσκω

ashamed: be ~ αἰσχύνομαι

ashes τέφρα ας ἡ

ashore: run ~ ὀκέλλω

ask [question etc.] ἐρωτάω
■ **~ for** αἰτέω

ass ὄνος ου ὁ/ἡ

assault *noun* ὕβρις εως ἡ, αἰκία ας ἡ; *verb* ὑβρίζω, αἰκίζω

assemble *tr* συλλέγω, συγκαλέω; *intr* συνέρχομαι

assembly ἐκκλησία ας ἡ

assert φάσκω
■ **~ strongly** διισχυρίζομαι

assign νέμω

assume (infer) εἰκάζω, τεκμαίρομαι

assumption ὑπόθεσις εως ἡ

astonish ἐκπλήσσω

astonishing θαυμαστός ἡ όν

astounded: be ~ θαυμάζω

astray: lead ~ παράγω

at ἐν + *dat*, ἐπί + *dat*, παρά + *dat*
■ **be ~ a loss** ἀπορέω
■ **~ first** πρῶτον
■ **~ last** τέλος
■ **~ least** γε*
■ **~ once** εὐθύς

■ ~ **some time** ποτέ
■ ~ **the hands of** πρός + *gen*, ὑπό + *gen*

atheist *adj* ἄθεος ον

Athene Ἀθήνη ης ἡ

Athenian Ἀθηναῖος α ον

Athens Ἀθῆναι ων αἱ
■ **to** ~ Ἀθήναζε
■ **in** *or* **at** ~ Ἀθήνησι(ν)
■ **from** ~ Ἀθήνηθεν

athlete ἀθλητής οῦ ὁ

attach προσάπτω

attack *noun* προσβολή ῆς ἡ; *verb* προσβάλλω + *dat*, ἐπιτίθεμαι + *dat*

attempt *noun* πεῖρα ας ἡ; *verb* ἐπιχειρέω, πειράομαι

attendant θεράπων οντος ὁ, ὑπηρέτης ου ὁ

attention: pay ~ to προσέχω (τὸν νοῦν) + *dat*

attest μαρτυρέω

Attica Ἀττική ῆς ἡ

attract ἐπισπάω

audacity τόλμα ης ἡ, θράσος ους τό

aunt τηθίς ίδος ἡ

authoritative κύριος α ον

authority (prestige) ἀξίωμα ατος τό

authorities (those in power) οἱ ἐν τέλει

autumn μετόπωρον ου τό

autumnal μετοπωρινός ή όν

available: be ~ ὑπάρχω

avenge τιμωρέω
■ ~ **oneself (on)** τιμωρέομαι

avenging τιμωρός όν

average: on ~ τὰ πολλά, ὡς ἐπὶ τὸ πολύ

avert ἀποτρέπω

avoid φεύγω

await προσδέχομαι

awake: lie ~ ἀγρυπνέω

awaken *tr* ἐγείρω; *intr* ἐγείρομαι

away: be ~ ἄπειμι

awful δεινός ή όν

awkward σκαιός ά όν

axe πέλεκυς εως ὁ

axle ἄξων ονος ὁ

Bb

baby νήπιος ου ὁ/ἡ

back[1] *noun* νῶτον ου τό
■ **on one's ~** ὕπτιος α ον
■ **at the ~** ὄπισθε(ν)

back[2] *adv* πάλιν, ὀπίσω; *in compounds* ἀνα-

back-bone ῥάχις εως ἡ

bad κακός ή όν

badge σημεῖον ου τό

baffle σφάλλω

bag ἀσκός οῦ ὁ

baggage σκεύη ῶν τά
■ **~-animal** ὑποζύγιον ου τό

bail ἐγγύη ης ἡ
■ **give ~** ἐγγυάομαι

bait δέλεαρ ατος τό

bake ὀπτάω

baker ἀρτοπώλης ου ὁ

balanced: ~ equally ἰσόρροπος ον

bald φαλακρός ά όν

bale out ἐξαντλέω

ball σφαῖρα ας ἡ

ballot-box καδίσκος ου ὁ

banish ἐκβάλλω

b

bank (of river) ὄχθη ης ἡ; (of earth) χῶμα ατος τό; (place to deposit money) τράπεζα ης ἡ

banquet ἑορτή ῆς ἡ

bar *noun* κλῇθρον ου τό

barbarian *adj* βάρβαρος ον

barber κουρεύς έως ὁ

barge ὁλκάς άδος ἡ

bark[1] *noun* (of tree) φλοιός οῦ ὁ

bark[2] (of dog) *noun* κλαγγή ῆς ἡ; *verb* ὑλακτέω

barley κριθαί ῶν αἱ

barn ἀποθήκη ης ἡ

barricade *noun* ἔρυμα ατος τό, σταύρωμα ατος τό; *verb* φράσσω, σταυρόω

barrier ἔρυμα ατος τό

base ἔδαφος ους τό

basin χερνιβεῖον ου τό

basket κανοῦν οῦ τό, ταρσός οῦ ὁ

bastard νόθος ου ὁ

bat (animal) νυκτερίς ίδος ἡ

battering-ram κριός οῦ ὁ

bath λουτρόν οῦ τό

bathe λούομαι

battle μάχη ης ἡ
■ **land ~** πεζομαχία ας ἡ
■ **sea ~** ναυμαχία ας ἡ

battlement ἔπαλξις εως ἡ

bay κόλπος ου ὁ

be εἰμί
■ **~ in a certain state** ἔχω + *adv*

beach αἰγιαλός οῦ ὁ

beacon φρυκτός οῦ ὁ

beak ῥύγχος ους τό

beam (wood) δοκός οῦ ἡ; (light) ἀκτίς ῖνος ἡ

bean κύαμος ου ὁ

bear[1] *noun* ἄρκτος ου ὁ/ἡ

bear[2] *verb* φέρω, ὑπομένω

beard πώγων ωνος ὁ

beast θήρ θηρός ὁ, θηρίον ου τό

■ **~ of burden** ὑποζύγιον ου τό

beat (strike) τύπτω, παίω; (defeat) νικάω

beautiful καλός ή όν, εὐπρεπής ές

beauty κάλλος ους τό

beaver κάστωρ ορος ὁ

because ὅτι, διότι
■ **~ of** διά + *acc*, ἕνεκα *foll gen*

become γίγνομαι

bed κλίνη ης ἡ

bee μέλισσα ης ἡ

beehive σμῆνος ους τό

beetle κάνθαρος ου ὁ

before *adv* πρότερον; *conj* πρίν; *prep* πρό + *gen*

beg [favour etc.] παραιτέομαι

beggar πτωχός οῦ ὁ

begin ἄρχομαι

beginning ἀρχή ῆς ἡ

beguile παράγω, ἀπατάω

behalf: on ~ of ὑπέρ + *gen*

behave ἔχω + *adv*, προσφέρομαι

behind ὄπισθε(ν) + *gen*

believe πιστεύω + *dat*, πείθομαι + *dat*; [in gods] νομίζω, ἡγέομαι

bell κώδων ωνος ὁ/ἡ

belong προσήκω, ὑπάρχω

below *adv* κάτω

belt ζώνη ης ἡ

bench ἕδρα ας ἡ
■ **rowing-~** σέλμα ατος τό

bend *tr* κάμπτω

benefactor εὐεργέτης ου ὁ

benefit *verb tr* ὠφελέω

bent καμπύλος η ον

beside παρά + *dat*

besiege πολιορκέω

best ἄριστος η ον, βέλτιστος η ον

bet *noun* ἐνέχυρον ου τό; *verb* παραβάλλομαι

betray προδίδωμι

better ἀμείνων ον (ἀμεινον-), βελτίων ον (βελτιον-)

between *prep* μεταξύ + *gen*; *adv* ἐν μέσῳ

beware (of) φυλάσσομαι, εὐλαβέομαι

bewitch γοητεύω, φαρμάσσω

beyond πέρα + *gen*, ὑπέρ + *gen*
■ **to ~** ὑπέρ + *acc*

big μέγας μεγάλη μέγα (μεγαλ-)

bind (tie up) δέω

bird ὄρνις ιθος ὁ/ἡ

birth γένεσις εως ἡ; (race, origin) γένος ους τό

bite δάκνω

bitter πικρός ά όν

bivouac (camp overnight) αὐλίζομαι

black μέλας αινα αν (μελαν-)

blacksmith χαλκεύς έως ὁ

blame *noun* αἰτία ας ἡ; *verb* μέμφομαι, ἐν αἰτίᾳ ἔχω
■ **to ~** αἴτιος α ον

blameworthy αἴτιος α ον

blanket χλαῖνα ης ἡ

bleach *verb* λευκόω

bless μακαρίζω

blessed μακάριος (α) ον

blind *adj* τυφλός ή όν; *verb* τυφλόω

blink μύω

blister φλύκταινα ης ἡ

block up ἐμφράσσω

blockade (besiege) πολιορκέω
■ **~ by sea** ἐφορμέω + *dat*

blood αἷμα ατος τό

blow[1] *noun* πληγή ῆς ἡ

blow[2] *verb* πνέω

blue (dark) κυάνεος α ον

blunt *adj* ἀμβλύς εῖα ύ; *verb* ἀμβλύνω

blur *verb tr* ἀμαυρόω

blush ἐρυθριάω

boar ὗς ὑός ὁ/ἡ

boast *noun* κόμπος ου ὁ; *verb* κομπάζω, ἀλαζονεύομαι

boaster ἀλαζών όνος ὁ

boat πλοῖον ου τό, σκάφος ους τό

body σῶμα ατος τό

bog ἕλος ους τό

boil *verb* ἕψω, ζέω

bold θρασύς εῖα ύ, τολμηρός ά όν

boldness τόλμα ης ἡ

bolt (e.g. on door) μοχλός οῦ ὁ

bone ὀστοῦν οῦ τό

book βίβλος ου ἡ, βιβλίον ου τό

border ὅρος ου ὁ

born: be ~ γίγνομαι, φύομαι

borrow δανείζομαι

bosom κόλπος ου ὁ

both ἀμφότεροι αι α
■ **~ ... and ...** καί … καί …, … τε* (…) καί …

bottle λήκυθος ου ἡ

bottom ἔδαφος ους τό

boundary ὅρος ου ὁ

boundless ἄπειρος ον

bow[1] *noun* (in archery) τόξον ου τό

bow[2] *noun* (of ship) πρῷρα ας ἡ

bow[3] *verb* (bend down) προσκυνέω

bowels ἔντερα ων τά

bowl κρατήρ ῆρος ὁ

box[1] *noun* κιβωτός οῦ ἡ

box[2] *verb* πυκτεύω

boxer πύκτης ου ὁ

boxing πυγμή ῆς ἡ

boy παῖς παιδός ὁ

bracelet ψέλιον ου τό

brain ἐγκέφαλος ου ὁ

bran ἄχυρα ων τά

branch κλάδος ου ὁ

brass *noun* χαλκός οῦ ὁ; *adj* χαλκοῦς ῆ οῦν

brave ἀνδρεῖος α ον

bravery ἀνδρεία ας ἡ

bread ἄρτος ου ὁ

breadth εὖρος ους τό

break *verb tr* ῥήγνυμι, καταρρήγνυμι; [oath etc.] λύω, παραβαίνω

breakfast ἄριστον ου τό
■ **have ~** ἀριστοποιέομαι

breakwater χηλή ῆς ἡ

breast (of woman) μαστός οῦ ὁ; (chest) στῆθος ους τό

breastplate θώραξ ακος ὁ

breath πνεῦμα ατος τό

breathe πνέω

bribe *noun* δῶρον ου τό; *verb* χρήμασι πείθω, διαφθείρω
■ **receive a ~** δωροδοκέω

brick πλίνθος ου ἡ

bride νύμφη ης ἡ

bridegroom νυμφίος ου ὁ

bridge γέφυρα ας ἡ

bridle ἡνία ας ἡ, χαλινός οῦ ὁ

bright λαμπρός ά όν

bring [thing] φέρω, κομίζω; [person] ἄγω
■ **~ up** [children] τρέφω

broad εὐρύς εῖα ύ

bronze *noun* χαλκός οῦ ὁ; *adj* χαλκοῦς ῆ οῦν

brooch περόνη ης ἡ

brothel πορνεῖον ου τό

brother ἀδελφός οῦ ὁ

brow ὀφρύς ύος ἡ

brown (tawny) ξανθός ή όν

brush (broom) κόρημα ατος τό

bucket ἀγγεῖον ου τό, ὑδρία ας ἡ

buckle περόνη ης ἡ

build [house] οἰκοδομέω; [ship] κατασκευάζω

building (structure) οἰκοδόμημα ατος τό; (act of ~) οἰκοδόμησις εως ἡ

bulge *noun* οἰδέω

bull ταῦρος ου ὁ

bully *noun* ὑβριστής οῦ ὁ; *verb* λυμαίνομαι, αἰκίζομαι

burden ἄχθος ους τό, βάρος ους τό

burdensome ἐπαχθής ές

burglar τοιχωρύχος ου ὁ

burial ταφή ῆς ἡ

burn *tr* καίω; *intr* καίομαι

burst καταρρήγνυμαι

bury [thing] κατορύσσω; [dead body] θάπτω

business: move *or* transact ~ χρηματίζω

busy ἄσχολος ον
■ **be ~ with** σπουδάζω περί + *acc*

butcher μάγειρος ου ὁ

buy ὠνέομαι

by (near) πρός + *dat*; *expressing agent* ὑπό + *gen*; [a god] ! νή + *acc*, ναὶ μά + *acc*
■ **no ~** [a god] ! οὐ μά + *acc*
■ **~ land** κατὰ γῆν

Cc

cabin καλύβη ης ἡ

cable κάλως ω ὁ, πεῖσμα ατος τό

cake πλακοῦς οῦντος ὁ

calculate λογίζομαι

calf μόσχος ου ὁ

call καλέω, προσκαλέω
■ **~ together** συγκαλέω
■ **~ upon** ἐπικαλέομαι
■ **~ by name** ὀνομάζω

calm *noun* (weather) γαλήνη ης ἡ; *adj* (quiet) ἥσυχος ον

camel κάμηλος ου ὁ/ἡ

camp *noun* στρατόπεδον ου τό; *verb* στρατοπεδεύομαι
■ **~ overnight** αὐλίζομαι

campaign *noun* στρατεία ας ἡ; *verb* στρατεύομαι

can (be able to) δύναμαι + *infin*, οἷός τέ εἰμι + *infin*

candidate ἀγωνιστής οῦ ὁ
■ **be a ~** ἀγωνίζομαι

canvass περιέρχομαι

cap κυνῆ ῆς ἡ

capable ἱκανός ή όν

captain λοχαγός οῦ ὁ; (of ship) ναύκληρος ου ὁ, τριήραρχος ου ὁ

captive αἰχμάλωτος ου ὁ

capture λαμβάνω, αἱρέω

captured: be ~ ἁλίσκομαι

care *noun* (anxious thought) φροντίς ίδος ἡ; (attention) ἐπιμέλεια ας ἡ
■ **take ~** φυλάσσομαι, εὐλαβέομαι, ἐπιμελέομαι

careful εὐλαβής ές, ἐπιμελής ές

carefully ἐπιμελῶς

careless ῥᾴθυμος ον, ἀμελής ές
■ **be ~** ἀμελέω

carelessness ἀμέλεια ας ἡ

cargo φορτίον ου τό

carpenter τέκτων ονος ὁ

carry[1] φέρω

carry[2]**: ~ out** [decree etc.] περαίνω

cart ἅμαξα ης ἡ

carve (sculpt) γλύφω

castle πύργος ου ὁ

cat αἴλουρος ου ὁ/ἡ

catch καταλαμβάνω

cattle κτήνη ῶν τά, βόες ῶν οἱ

caught: be ~ ἁλίσκομαι

cauldron λέβης ητος ὁ

cause αἰτία ας ἡ
■ **~ to be** καθίστημι

caution εὐλάβεια ας ἡ

cautious: be ~ εὐλαβέομαι

cautiously εὐλαβῶς

cavalry ἱππεῖς έων οἱ, ἵππος ου ἡ

cave σπήλαιον ου τό

cease (from) παύομαι + *gen or pple*, λήγω + *gen or pple*

ceaseless συνεχής ές

celebrate [a festival etc.] ἄγω

centre μέσον ου τό

certain (definite, clear) σαφής ές
■ **a ~** τις τι (τιν-)
■ **be ~** σαφῶς οἶδα

certainly πάνυ γε

chaff ἄχυρα ων τά

chain δεσμός οῦ ὁ

chair δίφρος ου ὁ, ἕδρα ας ἡ
■ **~ of state** θρόνος ου ὁ

chalk γύψος ου ἡ

challenge *noun* πρόκλησις εως ἡ; *verb* προκαλέομαι

chance τύχη ης ἡ

change *noun* μεταβολή ῆς ἡ; *verb* μεταβάλλω
■ **~ one's mind** μεταγιγνώσκω, μετανοέω

character (disposition) ἦθος ους τό

charcoal ἄνθραξ ακος ὁ

charge *noun* (accusation) αἰτία ας ἡ, ἔγκλημα ατος τό; (attack) προσβολή ῆς ἡ; *verb* (bring an accusation) ἐγκαλέω; (mount an attack) ἐπέρχομαι

chariot ἅρμα ατος τό

charioteer ἡνίοχος ου ὁ

charm χάρις ιτος ἡ

chase διώκω

chasm χάσμα ατος τό

chatter λαλέω

cheap (economical) εὐτελής ές; (worthless) φαῦλος (η) ον

cheapness εὐτέλεια ας ἡ

cheat ἐξαπατάω, φενακίζω

cheek (face) παρειά ᾶς ἡ

cheer *tr* θαρσύνω
■ **~ up** *intr* θαρσέω

C

cheese τυρός οῦ ὁ

cherry (tree) κερασός οῦ ὁ

chest[1] (breast) στῆθος ους τό, στέρνον ου τό

chest[2] (box) θήκη ης ἡ

chew τρώγω

chickpea ἐρέβινθος ου ὁ

child παῖς παιδός ὁ/ἡ, παιδίον ου τό, τέκνον ου τό

childish παιδικός ή όν

childless ἄπαις (ἀπαιδ-)

chimney κάπνη ης ἡ, ὀπή ῆς ἡ

choice αἵρεσις εως ἡ

choke ἀποπνίγω

choose αἱρέομαι, ἐκλέγω

chosen ἐξαίρετος ον

cicada τέττιξ ιγος ὁ

circle κύκλος ου ὁ

circumference περιβολή ῆς ἡ

circumnavigate περιπλέω

circumstances: in the ~ τούτων οὕτως ἐχόντων, ὡς ἐκ τῶν παρόντων

citadel ἀκρόπολις εως ἡ

citizen πολίτης ου ὁ

city πόλις εως ἡ, ἄστυ εως τό

civilize ἡμερόω

claim ἀντιποιέομαι

clap *verb* κροτέω

clash with συμπίπτω + *dat*

clay πηλός οῦ ὁ

clean *adj* καθαρός ά όν; *verb* καθαίρω

clear δῆλος η ον, σαφής ές
■ **it is ~** δῆλόν ἐστι

clerk γραμματεύς έως ὁ

clever σοφός ή όν, δεινός ή όν

cliff κρημνός οῦ ὁ

climax ἀκμή ῆς ἡ

climb ἀναβαίνω, ὑπερβαίνω

cling to ἔχομαι + *gen*, ἀντέχομαι + *gen*

cloak ἱμάτιον ου τό, χλαῖνα ης ἡ

clock: water-~ (for timing speeches in court) κλεψύδρα ας ἡ

close *verb* κλείω

cloth λίνον ου τό, ὕφασμα ατος τό

clothe ἀμφιέννυμι

clothes ἐσθής ῆτος ἡ

cloud νεφέλη ης ἡ, νέφος ους τό

clover τρίφυλλον ου τό

clown ἄγροικος ου ὁ

club[1] (weapon) ῥόπαλον ου τό

club[2] (association) ἑταιρεία ας ἡ

clue σύμβολον ου τό

clumsy σκαιός ά όν

coast παραλία ας ἡ, αἰγιαλός οῦ ὁ, ἀκτή ῆς ἡ

coax θωπεύω

cobbler σκυτοτόμος ου ὁ

cobweb ἀράχνιον ου τό

cock ἀλεκτρυών όνος ὁ

coffin σορός οῦ ἡ

coin νόμισμα ατος τό

coincide συμβαίνω, συντρέχω

cold *noun* ψῦχος ους τό; *adj* ψυχρός ά όν

collapse συμπίπτω

colleague συνεργός οῦ ὁ

collect *tr* ἀγείρω, ἀθροίζω, συλλέγω

colonist ἄποικος ου ὁ

colonize (found a colony) οἰκίζω, κατοικίζω, ἀποικίζω

colonnade στοά ᾶς ἡ

colony ἀποικία ας ἡ

colour χρῶμα ατος τό

coloured: (multi-~) ποικίλος η ον

colt πῶλος ου ὁ

column (pillar) κίων ονος ὁ; (of troops or ships) κέρας ατος *or* ως τό

combination σύστημα ατος τό, σύνθεσις εως ἡ

come ἔρχομαι
■ **~ back (from exile)** κατέρχομαι

■ ∼ **forward (to speak)** παρέρχομαι
■ ∼ **to help** βοηθέω + *dat*

comedy κωμῳδία ας ἡ

comfort (ease) εὐμάρεια ας ἡ; (consolation) παραμύθιον ου τό

command *verb* κελεύω; προστάσσω + *dat*
■ **be in** ∼ ἡγεμονεύω + *gen*, ἄρχω + *gen*; ἐφέστηκα + *dat*
■ **position of** ∼ ἀρχή ῆς ἡ, ἡγεμονία ας ἡ

commander στρατηγός οῦ ὁ, ἄρχων οντος ὁ, ἡγεμών όνος ὁ

commerce ἐμπορία ας ἡ

commercial ἐμπορικός ή όν

common κοινός ή όν

companion ἑταῖρος ου ὁ

company ὁμιλία ας ἡ

compare εἰκάζω; (balance) παραβάλλω

compasses: pair of ∼ τόρνος ου ὁ

compatible σύμφωνος ον

compatriot πατριώτης ου ὁ, πολίτης ου ὁ

compel ἀναγκάζω, βιάζω

compete ἀγωνίζομαι

competitor ἀγωνιστής οῦ ὁ, ἀνταγωνιστής οῦ ὁ

compile συγγράφω

complain ἀγανακτέω, σχετλιάζω, δεινὸν ποιέομαι

complete *adj* τέλειος (α) ον; *verb* ἐκτελέω, ἐξεργάζομαι

comrade ἑταῖρος ου ὁ

concave κοῖλος η ον

conceal κρύπτω

concede συγχωρέω

conceit ὕβρις εως ἡ, ἀλαζονεία ας ἡ

conceited σεμνός ή όν, ἀλαζών (ἀλαζον-)

concerned: as far as I am ∼ τὸ ἐπ' ἐμέ

concisely συντόμως

conclude (infer) τεκμαίρομαι

concurrent σύνδρομος ον

condemn καταγιγνώσκω + *gen*, καταδικάζω + *gen*; κατακρίνω

condense πυκνόω

condition: be in a certain ∼ ἔχω + *adv*
■ **be in a good** ∼ εὖ διάκειμαι
■ **on** ∼ **that** ἐφ' ᾧτε

confederacy (league) συνωμοσία ας ἡ; (alliance) συμμαχία ας ἡ

confess ὁμολογέω

confidence θάρσος ους τό
■ **regain** ∼ ἀναθαρσέω

confident θαρσαλέος α ον, θρασύς εῖα ύ
■ **be** ∼ θαρσέω

confirm βεβαιόω

confiscate (make public property) δημεύω

confuse (put into disorder) ταράσσω

confusion (disorder) ταραχή ῆς ἡ

congratulate μακαρίζω; συγχαίρω + *dat*

congratulation μακαρισμός οῦ ὁ

conjurer μάγος ου ὁ

conquer νικάω; κρατέω + *gen*

conscious: be ∼ **of** σύνοιδα ἐμαυτῷ

consider (think) νομίζω; (deliberate) βουλεύομαι; (examine) σκοπέω, ἐννοέω, φροντίζω

console παραμυθέομαι

conspicuous ἐπιφανής ές, περίβλεπτος ον

conspiracy συνωμοσία ας ἡ

conspirator συνωμότης ου ὁ

conspire συνόμνυμι

consternation κατάπληξις εως ἡ

constitution πολιτεία ας ἡ

consul πρόξενος ου ὁ; (Roman) ὕπατος ου ὁ

consulship (Roman) ὑπατεία ας ἡ

consult συμβουλεύομαι; [an oracle] χράομαι + *dat*

C

contempt ὀλιγωρία ας ἡ, καταφρόνησις εως ἡ
■ **treat with ~** ὀλιγωρέω + *gen*, καταφρονέω + *gen*

contend ἀγωνίζομαι

contest ἀγών ῶνος ὁ, ἅμιλλα ης ἡ

continent ἤπειρος ου ἡ

continue διατελέω + *pple*

continuous συνεχής ές

contradict ἐναντιόομαι + *dat*

contrary: ~ to παρά + *dat*
■ **on the ~** μὲν οὖν*

contrast *verb* ἀντιτίθημι

contribute εἰσφέρω, συμβάλλομαι

contribution εἰσφορά ᾶς ἡ

contrive μηχανάομαι

control *noun* κράτος ους τό; *verb* κρατέω + *gen*

controversy ἀμφισβήτησις εως ἡ

convenient σύμφορος ον, ἐπιτήδειος (α) ον

conventional νόμιμος ον

converge συντρέχω

conversation διάλογος ου ὁ

converse (with) διαλέγομαι *(+ dat)*

convict ἐλέγχω; καταγιγνώσκω + *gen*

conviction (in court) δικαίωσις εως ἡ; (certain belief) πίστις εως ἡ

convincing πιθανός ή όν

cook *noun* μάγειρος ου ὁ; *verb tr* ὀπτάω, πέσσω

cool ψυχρός ά όν

cord σπάρτον ου τό, σχοινίον ου τό

cork φελλός οῦ ὁ

corn σῖτος ου ὁ

corner (angle) γωνία ας ἡ; (nook) μυχός οῦ ὁ

cornice θριγκός οῦ ὁ

corpse νεκρός οῦ ὁ

correct (accurate) ἀκριβής ές; (true) ἀληθής ές, ὀρθός ή όν

correction ἐπανόρθωσις εως ἡ

correctness ὀρθότης ητος ὁ

corrupt *adj* (decaying, rotten) σαπρός ά όν; (bribed) δωροδόκος ον, διεφθαρμένος η ον; *verb* διαφθείρω

cost *noun* δαπάνη ης ἡ; *verb* γίγνομαι + *gen of price*

costliness πολυτέλεια ας ἡ

costly πολυτελής ές

cottage καλύβη ης ἡ

couch κλίνη ης ἡ

cough *noun* βήξ βηχός ὁ/ἡ; *verb* βήσσω

council βουλή ῆς ἡ

councillor βουλευτής οῦ ὁ

count ἀριθμέω, λογίζομαι

counterfeit *adj* παράσημος ον, κίβδηλος ον

countless ἀναρίθμητος ον; *usu pl* μυρίος α ον

country (land) χώρα ας ἡ; (native land) πατρίς ίδος ἡ

countryside ἀγροί ῶν οἱ

courage ἀνδρεία ας ἡ, ἀρετή ῆς ἡ
■ **have ~** θαρσέω, εὐθυμέω

courageous ἀνδρεῖος α ον

court (of law) δικαστήριον ου τό

courteous εὐπροσήγορος ον

cousin (male) ἀνεψιός οῦ ὁ; (female) ἀνεψιά ᾶς ἡ

cover *noun* κάλυμμα ατος τό; *verb* καλύπτω

cow βοῦς βοός ἡ

cowardice κακία ας ἡ, δειλία ας ἡ

cowardly δειλός ή όν, κακός ή όν
■ **be ~** μαλακίζομαι

cower πτήσσω

crab καρκίνος ου ὁ

craftsman τέκτων ονος ὁ

crafty δόλιος α ον

crag κρημνός οῦ ὁ

crane (bird) γέρανος ου ὁ

crate ταρσός οῦ ὁ

crawl ἕρπω

creditor χρήστης ου ὁ

crest (of hill or helmet) λόφος ου ὁ

crime ἀδίκημα ατος τό, κακουργία ας ἡ
■ **commit a ~** ἀδικέω

crippled χωλός ή όν

crisis καιρός οῦ ὁ

criticise ἐπιτιμάω, κρίνω

crooked σκολιός ά όν

crop καρπός οῦ ὁ, φορά ᾶς ἡ

cross *verb tr* [river] διαβαίνω; [mountain] ὑπερβαίνω

crosswise πλάγιος α ον

crouch πτήσσω

crow κόραξ ακος ὁ

crowd ὅμιλος ου ὁ, ὄχλος ου ὁ

crowded ἀθρόος α ον

crown (wreath) στέφανος ου ὁ
■ **royal ~** διάδημα ατος τό

crucify ἀνασταυρόω

cruel ὠμός ή όν, ἄγριος α ον

crush συντρίβω

cry (weep) δακρύω

cub βρέφος ους τό, σκύμνος ου ὁ

cuckoo κόκκυξ υγος ὁ

cucumber σίκυος ου ὁ

cup κύλιξ ικος ἡ

cupboard θήκη ης ἡ

cure *noun* ἴασις εως ἡ, ἄκος ους τό; *verb* θεραπεύω, ἀκέομαι, ἰάομαι

curl *verb tr* πλέκω

currency (coinage) νόμισμα ατος τό

curse ἀρά ᾶς ἡ

cursed ἐπάρατος ον

curtail συντέμνω

curtain παραπέτασμα ατος τό

curved καμπύλος η ον

cushion προσκεφάλαιον ου τό; (on rower's bench) ὑπηρέσιον ου τό

custom ἔθος ους τό, νόμος ου ὁ
■ **according to ~** κατὰ τὸ εἰωθός

customary εἰωθώς υῖα ός (εἰωθοτ-), νόμιμος ον

cut τέμνω, κόπτω
■ **~ off** (remove part) ἀποτέμνω; (intercept) ἀπολαμβάνω
■ **~ up** κατατέμνω

Dd

dagger μάχαιρα ας ἡ, ἐγχειρίδιον ου τό

daily καθ' ἡμέραν

dam χῶμα ατος τό

damage *noun* βλάβη ης ἡ; *verb* βλάπτω

damp ὑγρός ά ον

dance *noun* ὄρχησις εως ἡ; (choral ~) χορός οῦ ὁ; *verb* ὀρχέομαι; (in chorus) χορεύω

dancer ὀρχηστής οῦ ὁ, χορευτής οῦ ὁ

danger κίνδυνος ου ὁ
■ **be in ~ of** κινδυνεύω + *infin*

dangerous χαλεπός ή όν, ἐπικίνδυνος ον, δεινός ή όν

dappled ποικίλος η ον

dare τολμάω

daring *noun* τόλμα ης ἡ; *adj* τολμηρός ά όν, θρασύς εῖα ύ

dark σκοτεινός ή όν

darkness σκότος ου ὁ

dash *noun* ὁρμή ῆς ἡ

daughter θυγάτηρ τρός ἡ

dawn ἕως ἕω ἡ
■ **at ~** ἅμα τῇ ἕῳ, ἅμ' ἡμέρᾳ

day ἡμέρα ας ἡ
■ ~ **before** προτεραία ας ἡ
■ ~ **after** ὑστεραία ας ἡ
■ **on the same** ~ *adv* αὐθήμερον

dead: ~ **body** νεκρός οῦ ὁ

deaf κωφός ή όν

deafen ἐκκωφόω

deafness κωφότης ητος ἡ

deal out νέμω

dealer κάπηλος ου ὁ

dear φίλος η ον

death θάνατος ου ὁ

debatable ἀμφίλογος ον, ἀμφισβήτητος ον

debt χρέος ους τό, ὀφείλημα ατος τό
■ **in** ~ ὑπόχρεως ων (*gen* ω)

debtor χρηστής οῦ ὁ, ὀφειλέτης ου ὁ

decay *noun* φθορά ᾶς ἡ; *verb* σήπομαι

deceit ἀπάτη ης ἡ

deceitful δόλιος α ον

deceive ἐξαπατάω

decency εὐπρέπεια ας ἡ

decent εὐπρεπής ές, κόσμιος α ον

decide [question etc] διακρίνω; (determine, resolve) βουλεύομαι, *or use* δοκεῖ + *dat*

deck κατάστρωμα ατος τό

declamation ἐπίδειξις εως ἡ

declare φάσκω
■ ~ **war (on)** πόλεμον καταγγέλλω + *dat*; εἰς πόλεμον καθίσταμαι

decline[1] *verb tr* [offer etc.] ἐξόμνυμαι

decline[2] *verb intr* (diminish) μεταπίπτω

decorate κοσμέω

decoration κόσμος ου ὁ

decoy *noun* δέλεαρ ατος τό

decrease ἐλασσόομαι

decree [of Council at Athens] προβούλευμα ατος τό; [of Assembly] ψήφισμα ατος τό

dedicate ἀνατίθημι

deduce συλλογίζομαι

deduct ἀφαιρέω

deed ἔργον ου τό

deep βαθύς εῖα ύ

deer ἔλαφος ου ὁ/ἡ

defeat *noun* τροπή ῆς ἡ, ἧσσα ης ἡ; *verb* νικάω

defeated: be ~ ἡσσάομαι

defective ἐνδεής ές, ἐλλιπής ές

defence (fortification) ἔρυμα ατος τό; (in court) ἀπολογία ας ἡ

defend ἀμύνομαι, φυλάσσω
■ ~ **oneself in court** ἀπολογέομαι

defendant ὁ φεύγων

defender προστάτης ου ὁ

defensive: ~ **alliance** ἐπιμαχία ας ἡ

defer ἀναβάλλω

define διορίζω, διαιρέω

dejected ἄθυμος ον
■ **be** ~ ἀθυμέω

delay *noun* μονή ῆς ἡ, διατριβή ῆς ἡ; *verb tr* κωλύω; *verb intr* μένω, ἐπέχω

deliberate[1] *verb* βουλεύομαι

deliberate[2] *adj* προαιρετός ή όν

deliberately ἐκ προαιρέσεως

delicate λεπτός ή όν

delight *noun* ἡδονή ῆς ἡ, χάρις ιτος ἡ; *verb tr* ἀρέσκω + *dat*

delighted: be ~ ἥδομαι, χαίρω

demigod ἡμίθεος ου ὁ

democracy δημοκρατία ας ἡ

democratic δημοκρατικός ή όν, δημοτικός ή όν

demolish καθαιρέω

demonstration ἀπόδειξις εως ἡ

denial ἄρνησις εως ἡ

denounce μηνύω, ἐνδείκνυμι

dense πυκνός ή όν

deny ἀπαρνέομαι, οὔ φημι

depart ἀπέρχομαι

departure ἔξοδος ου ἡ

depend on ἀνάκειμαι εἰς + *acc*, ἀρτάομαι + *gen*

dependent *adj* ὑπήκοος ον

depopulate ἐρημόω
depose ἐκβάλλω
deposit *noun* παρακαταθήκη ης ἡ; *verb* κατατίθημι
depressed δύσθυμος ον
depression δυσθυμία ας ἡ
deprive ἀποστερέω, ἀφαιρέω
▪ **~ of citizen rights** ἀτιμόω
depth βάθος ους τό
descend κατέρχομαι
descendant ἔκγονος ου ὁ/ἡ
descent κατάβασις εως ἡ
describe ἐξηγέομαι
desecrate μιαίνω
desert *noun* ἔρημος (χώρα) ἡ; *verb tr* ἀπολείπω; *verb intr* αὐτομολέω
deserted ἔρημος (η) ον
deserter αὐτόμολος ου ὁ
desertion ἀπόλειψις εως ἡ
deserve ἄξιός εἰμι + *gen or infin*
designate ὀνομάζω
desirable αἱρετός ή όν
desire ἐπιθυμέω + *gen*
desist from παύομαι + *gen or pple*
desolation ἐρημία ας ἡ
despair *noun* ἀθυμία ας ἡ; *verb* ἀθυμέω, ἀθύμως ἔχω
desperate ἀνέλπιστος ον, ἄθυμος ον
despise ὀλιγωρέω + *gen*, καταφρονέω + *gen*
despondent ἄθυμος ον
dessert τραγήματα ων τά
destined εἱμαρμένος η ον, προκείμενος η ον
destiny μοῖρα ας ἡ, εἱμαρμένη ης ἡ
destroy διαφθείρω, ἀπόλλυμι, καταλύω; [city etc.] καθαιρέω
destructible διαλυτός ή όν
destruction διαφθορά ᾶς ἡ, ὄλεθρος ου ὁ
destructive ὀλέθριος (α) ον
detain ἐπέχω, κωλύω
deter ἀποτρέπω, κωλύω
deviate παρεκβαίνω
device μηχανή ῆς ἡ
devise μηχανάομαι
devout εὐσεβής ές
dew δρόσος ου ἡ
dialect γλῶσσα ης ἡ
diamond ἀδάμας αντος ὁ
dice κύβοι ων οἱ
▪ **play *or* gamble with ~** κυβεύω
die ἀποθνῄσκω, τελευτάω
diet δίαιτα ης ἡ
differ (from) διαφέρω *(+ gen)*
difference: it makes a ~ διαφέρει
different διάφορος ον, ἀλλοῖος α ον
difficult χαλεπός ή όν, δυσχερής ές
difficulties: be in ~ ἀπορέω, ἀμηχανέω
difficulty: with ~ μόλις
dig ὀρύσσω, σκάπτω
digest πέσσω
dignity τιμή ῆς ἡ, ἀξίωμα ατος τό, σεμνότης ητος ἡ
digress παρεκβαίνω
dilemma ἀπορία ας ἡ
▪ **be in a ~** ἀπορέω
din θόρυβος ου ὁ
dine δειπνέω
dining room τρίκλινος ου ὁ
dinner δεῖπνον ου τό
dip βάπτω
directions: from all ~ πανταχόθεν
▪ **in all ~** πανταχόσε
▪ **in different ~** ἄλλος … ἄλλοσε
dirt ῥύπος ου ὁ, αὐχμός οῦ ὁ
dirtiness ἀκαθαρσία ας ἡ
dirty αὐχμηρός ά όν
disadvantage βλάβη ης ἡ
disadvantageous ἀνωφελής ές, ἀνεπιτήδειος ον
disagree διίσταμαι, διαφέρομαι
disappear ἀφανίζομαι

d

disappoint σφάλλω
disarm *tr* περιαιρέομαι τὰ ὅπλα + *gen*
disarray ἀκοσμία ας ἡ, ἀταξία ας ἡ
disaster συμφορά ᾶς ἡ
disband *verb tr* διαλύω
disbelief ἀπιστία ας ἡ
disbelieve ἀπιστέω + *dat*
discard ἀφίημι
disciple μαθητής οῦ ὁ
discipline εὐταξία ας ἡ
discontent δυσχέρεια ας ἡ
discontented δυσχερής ές
■ **be ∼** δυσχεραίνω
discover (find) εὑρίσκω; (get to know) γιγνώσκω; (learn) μανθάνω
discoverer εὑρετής οῦ ὁ
discovery εὕρημα ατος τό
discreet (prudent) φρόνιμος ον, εὐλαβής ές
discriminate διακρίνω, διαγιγνώσκω
disdainful ὀλίγωρος ον
disease νόσος ου ἡ
diseased νοσώδης ες
disembark *tr* ἐκβιβάζω; *intr* ἐκβαίνω ἐκ + *gen*, ἀποβαίνω ἐκ + *gen*
disfranchise ἀτιμόω
disfranchisement ἀτιμία ας ἡ
disgrace *noun* αἰσχύνη ης ἡ; *verb* αἰσχύνω
disgraceful αἰσχρός ά όν
disguise oneself ἐπικρύπτομαι
dish λεκάνη ης ἡ
disheartened ἄθυμος ον
dishonest ἄδικος ον
dishonour *noun* ἀτιμία ας ἡ; *verb* ἀτιμάζω
dislocate διαστρέφω
dislodge ἐκκρούω
disloyal ἄπιστος ον
dismiss ἀφίημι
■ **∼ from one's thoughts** ἐάω
dismount καταβαίνω
disobedient ἀπειθής ές
disobey ἀπειθέω + *dat*
disorder ἀταξία ας ἡ
■ **in ∼** ἄτακτος ον, οὐδενὶ κόσμῳ
dispassionate ἀπαθής ές
disperse *tr* σκεδάννυμι; *intr* σκεδάννυμαι
display φαίνω, ἀποδείκνυμι
disputable ἀμφισβητήσιμος ον
dispute *noun* διαφορά ᾶς ἡ, νεῖκος ους τό; *verb* ἀμφισβητέω
disqualification κώλυμα ατος τό
dissatisfied: be ∼ with χαλεπῶς φέρω
dissolve *tr* διαλύω
dissuade ἀποτρέπω, ἀποστρέφω
distance (interval) διάστασις εως ἡ
■ **at a ∼** διὰ πολλοῦ
■ **from a ∼** πόρρωθεν
distant: be ∼ ἀπέχω
distaste ἀπέχθεια ας ἡ
distinguish διακρίνω, διαγιγνώσκω
distort διαστρέφω
distress *noun* ἀπορία ας ἡ, λύπη ης ἡ, ταλαιπωρία ας ἡ
■ **be in ∼** ἀπορέω, λυπέομαι, ταλαιπωρέω
distribute νέμω, διαδίδωμι
disturb ταράσσω
ditch τάφρος ου ἡ
dive κατακολυμβάω
diver κολυμβητής οῦ ὁ
diverge διίσταμαι
divert παρατρέπω, παροχετεύω
divide διαιρέω
divination μαντική ῆς ἡ
divine θεῖος α ον
division (act of dividing) διαίρεσις εως ἡ; (part) μέρος ους τό
divorce ἐκβάλλω, ἐκπέμπω
divulge μηνύω

dizzy: be ~ ἰλιγγιάω

do ποιέω, πράσσω

docile εὐμαθής ές, ἐπιεικής ές

dock νεώριον ου τό

doctor ἰατρός οῦ ὁ/ἡ

dog κύων κυνός ὁ/ἡ

doll κόρη ης ἡ

dolphin δελφίς ῖνος ὁ

donkey ὄνος ου ὁ/ἡ

door θύρα ας ἡ

door-keeper θυρωρός οῦ ὁ

dot στιγμή ῆς ἡ

double *adj* διπλοῦς ῆ οῦν; *verb* διπλασιάζω

doubt *noun* (disbelief) ἀπιστία ας ἡ; (suspicion) ὑποψία ας ἡ; (perplexity) ἀπορία ας ἡ; *verb* (disbelieve) ἀπιστέω + *dat*; (be suspicious) ὑποπτεύω; (be perplexed) ἀπορέω

dove πέλεια ας ἡ

down κατά + *acc*
■ **~ from** κατά + *gen*

dowry φερνή ῆς ἡ

doze καταμύω

drachma δραχμή ῆς ἡ

drag ἕλκω

dragon δράκων οντος ὁ

drain *noun* χαράδρα ας ἡ; *verb* ξηραίνω, ἀποχετεύω

draughts (game) πεσσεία ας ἡ, πεσσοί ῶν οἱ

draw[1] [bow] τοξεύω; [picture] γράφω; [sword] ἕλκω

draw[2] **up** *verb tr* τάσσω

drawn (of contest) ἰσόρροπος ον

dread δέδοικα, ὀρρωδέω

dream *noun* ἐνύπνιον ου τό, ὄνειρος ου ὁ; *verb* ὀνειροπολέω

dregs τρύξ τρυγός ἡ

drench βρέχω

drill *noun* (tool) τρύπανον ου τό; *verb* (bore) τρυπάω

drink *noun* ποτόν οῦ τό; *verb* πίνω

drinking: ~ companion συμπότης ου ὁ
■ **~ party** συμπόσιον ου τό

drip στάζω

drive ἐλαύνω
■ **~ out** ἐκβάλλω

drizzle *noun* ψακάς άδος ἡ; *verb* ψακάζω

drop *tr* καθίημι, καταβάλλω

drought αὐχμός οῦ ὁ

drown καταποντίζω

drug φάρμακον ου τό

drum τύμπανον ου τό

drunk πάροινος ον
■ **be** *or* **get ~** μεθύω, παροινέω
■ **make ~** μεθύσκω

drunkenness μέθη ης ἡ

dry *adj* ξηρός ά όν; *verb tr* ξηραίνω; *intr* ξηραίνομαι

duck νῆσσα ης ἡ

dumb ἄφωνος ον, κωφός ή όν

dung κόπρος ου ἡ

dusk δείλη ης ἡ

dust κόνις εως ἡ
■ **cloud of ~** κονιορτός οῦ ὁ

dusty αὐχμηρός ά όν

duty τὸ προσῆκον

dwarf νᾶνος ου ὁ

dye *noun* βαφή ῆς ἡ; *verb* βάπτω

Ee

each ἕκαστος η ον
■ **~ of two** ἑκάτερος α ον
■ **~ other** ἀλλήλους ας α
■ **~ time** ἑκάστοτε

eager πρόθυμος ον
■ **be ~** προθυμέομαι, σπουδάζω

eagerness προθυμία ας ἡ, σπουδή ῆς ἡ

eagle ἀετός οῦ ὁ

ear οὖς ὠτός τό
■ **~ of corn** στάχυς υος ὁ

early (early in day) *adj* ὄρθριος α ον; *adv* πρῴ

earn κτάομαι

earth γῆ γῆς ἡ

earthquake σεισμός οῦ ὁ

ease (facility) εὐπέτεια ας ἡ

east ἕως ἕω ἡ

easy ῥᾴδιος α ον, πρόχειρος ον

eat ἐσθίω

eatable ἐδώδιμος ον

eccentric ἄτοπος ον

eclipse ἔκλειψις εως ἡ

economical (frugal) φειδωλός ή όν

economy (frugality) φειδωλία ας ἡ; (management) οἰκονομία ας ἡ

edge (brim, lip) χεῖλος ους τό; (of weapon) ἀκμή ῆς ἡ; (hem, border) κράσπεδον ου τό

educate παιδεύω

education παιδεία ας ἡ

eel ἔγχελυς υος *or* εως ἡ

effeminacy ἀνανδρία ας ἡ

effeminate ἄνανδρος ον

efficient ἐνεργός όν

egg ᾠόν οῦ τό

eight ὀκτώ
■ **~ times** ὀκτάκις
■ **~ hundred** ὀκτακόσιοι αι α
■ **~ thousand** ὀκτακισχίλιοι αι α

eighteen ὀκτωκαίδεκα

eighth ὄγδοος η ον

eighty ὀγδοήκοντα

either ... or ἤ ... ἤ

elder πρεσβύτερος α ον

elect αἱρέομαι, χειροτονέω

election αἵρεσις εως ἡ, χειροτονία ας ἡ

elegance χάρις ιτος ἡ, εὐκοσμία ας ἡ

elegant χαρίεις εσσα εν (χαριεντ-), κομψός ή όν, ἀστεῖος α ον

elephant ἐλέφας αντος ὁ

eleven ἕνδεκα

elm πτελέα ας ἡ

elongated προμήκης ες

eloquence εὐέπεια ας ἡ

eloquent εὔγλωσσος ον; δεινὸς (ὴ ὸν) λέγειν

else: or ~ εἰ δὲ μή

elsewhere (at another place) ἄλλοθι; (to another place) ἄλλοσε

embalm ταριχεύω

embankment χῶμα ατος τό

embark *tr* ἐμβιβάζω; *intr* ἐμβαίνω εἰς + *acc*

embarkation εἴσβασις εως ἡ

embassy (delegation) πρεσβεία ας ἡ

embrace *verb* ἀσπάζομαι

emend ἐπανορθόω

emerald σμάραγδος ου ἡ

emigrant ἄποικος ου ὁ

emigrate ἀποικέω

eminent ἐκπρεπής ές, εὔδοξος ον

emotion πάθος ους τό
emperor βασιλεύς έως ὁ
empire ἀρχή ῆς ἡ
empress βασίλεια ας ἡ
emptiness κενότης ητος ἡ
empty κενός ή όν; (deserted) ἔρημος η ον
enchant κατακηλέω, γοητεύω
enchanter γόης ητος ὁ, μάγος ου ὁ
enclose εἴργω
encounter (meet *or* fight) ἀπαντάω + *dat*, συμβάλλω + *dat*
encourage παραμυθέομαι; παρακελεύομαι + *dat*; θαρσύνω
encouragement παρακέλευσις εως ἡ
end *noun* τέλος ους τό, τελευτή ῆς ἡ; *verb* τελευτάω
endless ἄπειρος ον, ἀπέραντος ον
endurable ἀνασχετός όν
endurance καρτερία ας ἡ
endure ὑπομένω, ὑπέχω
enemy πολέμιοι ίων οἱ; (private) ἐχθρός οῦ ὁ
energetic δραστήριος ον
enfranchised ἐπίτιμος ον
engaged: be ~ on σπουδάζω
engrave ἐγγλύφω
enjoy ἀπολαύω + *gen*; ἥδομαι + *dat*; τέρπομαι + *dat*
enlargement αὔξησις εως ἡ
enmity ἔχθρα ας ἡ
enormous ὑπερφυής ές, ὑπέρμετρος ον
enough *adj* ἱκανός ή όν; *adv* ἅλις
enquire ἐρωτάω, πυνθάνομαι
enrage παροξύνω, ἐξοργίζω
enrich πλουτίζω
enrol ἐγγράφω
enslave καταδουλόω
entangle ἐμπλέκω
enter εἰσέρχομαι
entertain ξενίζω, δέχομαι, ἑστιάομαι
enthusiasm προθυμία ας ἡ
entice ἐπάγω
enticing ἐπαγωγός όν
entirely παντελῶς
entrails ἔντερα ων τά, σπλάγχνα ων τά
entrance εἴσοδος ου ἡ, εἰσβολή ῆς ἡ
entranced νυμφόληπτος ον
entrust ἐπιτρέπω
enviable ζηλωτός ή όν
envious φθονερός ά όν
envy *noun* φθόνος ου ὁ; *verb* ζηλόω
equal ἴσος η ον
■ **on ~ terms** ἐξ ἴσου; (indecisive) ἰσόρροπος ον
equalise ἐξισόω, ὁμοιόω
equality ἰσότης ητος ἡ
equip παρασκευάζω, κατασκευάζω
■ **~ a fleet** ἐξαρτύομαι
equivalent ἀντάξιος α ον
erase ἐξαλείφω, ἀφανίζω
erratic ἀκατάστατος ον
error ἁμαρτία ας ἡ, ἁμάρτημα ατος τό
escape ἐκφεύγω, διαφεύγω
■ **~ notice** λανθάνω
escort *noun* (guide) προπομπός οῦ ὁ/ἡ, ἀγωγός οῦ ὁ; (bodyguard) δορύφοροι ων οἱ; *verb* προπέμπω
especially μάλιστα, ἄλλως τε καί
essence οὐσία ας ἡ
establish καθίστημι
established: be ~ καθίσταμαι, ὑπάρχω
estuary κόλπος ου ὁ
eternal ἀθάνατος ον, αἰώνιος (α) ον
even[1] (of numbers) ἄρτιος α ον
even[2] *adv* (still, also) καί
evening ἑσπέρα ας ἡ
■ **towards ~** πρὸς ἑσπέραν
evenly ὁμαλῶς
evenness ὁμαλότης ητος ἡ

eventually χρόνῳ, σὺν χρόνῳ

ever ποτέ

every πᾶς πᾶσα πᾶν (παντ-)
■ **~ kind of** παντοῖος α ον

everywhere πανταχοῦ

evidence (act of giving evidence) μαρτυρία ας ἡ; (proof) τεκμήριον ου τό
■ **give ~** μαρτυρέω

evident σαφής ές, δῆλος η ον

exact[1] *adj* ἀκριβής ές

exact[2]: **~ a penalty** δίκην λαμβάνω παρά *+gen*

exactness ἀκρίβεια ας ἡ

exaggerate αἴρω, μεγαλύνω

examination ἔλεγχος ου ὁ, ἐξέτασις εως ἡ

examine σκοπέω, ἐξετάζω, ἐλέγχω

example παράδειγμα ατος τό

exceed ὑπερβάλλω, ὑπερβαίνω

excel διαφέρω *+gen*

excellence ἀρετή ῆς ἡ

excellent ἄριστος η ον, σπουδαῖος α ον

except πλήν *+gen*

excess ὑπερβολή ῆς ἡ

excessively λίαν

exchange ἀνταλλάσσομαι, ἀμείβομαι

excitable ἔμπληκτος ον

excite ἐπαίρω, ἐγείρω

exclude εἴργω, ἀποκλείω

excuse πρόφασις εως ἡ
■ **make an ~** προφασίζομαι

executioner αὐθέντης ου ὁ

exempt [from tax] ἀτελής ές; [from military service] ἀστράτευτος ον

exercise *noun* μελέτη ης ἡ, ἄσκησις εως ἡ, γυμνασία ας ἡ; *verb* μελετάω, ἀσκέω, γυμνάζω

exertion προθυμία ας ἡ, ἀγωνία ας ἡ

exhaust κατατρίβω

exhausted: be ~ ἀποκάμνω

exhaustion ταλαιπωρία ας ἡ

exile *noun* (person) φυγάς άδος ὁ/ἡ; (state) φυγή ῆς ἡ; *verb tr* ἐκβάλλω

exist ὑπάρχω

existence οὐσία ας ἡ

exit ἔξοδος ου ἡ

expect προσδοκάω, προσδέχομαι
■ **as one might ~** ὡς εἰκός

expectation δόξα ης ἡ, προσδοκία ας ἡ
■ **contrary to ~** παρὰ προσδοκίαν

expedient σύμφορος ον, πρόσφορος ον

expedition στρατεία ας ἡ, στόλος ου ὁ
■ **make an ~** στρατεύομαι

expense δαπάνη ης ἡ, ἀνάλωμα ατος τό

expensive τίμιος α ον

experience *noun* ἐμπειρία ας ἡ; (thing experienced) πάθος ους τό; *verb* πάσχω

experienced ἔμπειρος ον

experiment πεῖρα ας ἡ

explain ἐξηγέομαι, φράζω

explode ἐκρήγνυμαι

explore ἐρευνάω

export *verb* ἐξάγω

exports *noun* ἐξαγώγιμα ων τά

extemporise αὐτοσχεδιάζω

extend ἐκτείνω

extinct ἐξίτηλος ον, ἄφαντος ον

extinguish ἀποσβέννυμι

extravagant δαπανηρός ά όν

extreme ἔσχατος η ον, ἄκρος α ον

eye ὀφθαλμός οῦ ὁ

eyelid βλέφαρον ου τό

eye-witness αὐτόπτης ου ὁ

Ff

fabulous μυθώδης ες
face πρόσωπον ου τό
facing ἐναντίος α ον + *dat*
fact ἔργον ου τό, πρᾶγμα ατος τό
▪ **in ~** τῷ ὄντι
faction στάσις εως ἡ
fade μαραίνομαι
fail σφάλλομαι, ἁμαρτάνω; (be deficient) ἐλλείπω
faint *verb* λιποψυχέω; *adj* (of writing etc.) ἀμυδρός ά όν
faith πίστις εως ἡ
faithful πιστός ή όν
faithless ἄπιστος ον
fall πίπτω
▪ **~ asleep** καταδαρθάνω
▪ **~ back** (yield ground) ὑποχωρέω
▪ **~ down** καταπίπτω
false ψευδής ές
fame δόξα ης ἡ, κλέος ους τό
familiar συνήθης ες
family γένος ους τό, (household) οἶκος ου ὁ
famine λιμός οῦ ὁ
famous γνώριμος ον, ἐπιφανής ές, εὐδόκιμος ον
far πόρρω, ἐπὶ πολύ; with comp πολλῷ
▪ **~ and wide** πανταχῇ
▪ **from ~ off** πόρρωθεν
farewell χαῖρε *pl* χαίρετε
▪ **bid ~** χαίρειν λέγω
farm *noun* χωρίον ου τό; *verb* γεωργέω
farmer γεωργός οῦ ὁ, αὐτουργός οῦ ὁ
farther *adv* πορρωτέρω
fast ταχύς εῖα ύ
fasten πήγνυμι, δέω
fastening σύνδεσμος ου ὁ
fasting *noun* νηστεία ας ἡ; *adj* ἄσιτος ον
fat *noun* πιμελή ῆς ἡ; *adj* παχύς εῖα ύ
fate (destiny) μοῖρα ας ἡ, εἱμαρμένη ης ἡ; (chance) τύχη ης ἡ; (what is to come) τὸ μέλλον
father πατήρ τρός ὁ
father-in-law πενθερός οῦ ὁ
fatherland πατρίς ίδος ἡ
fatten πιαίνω, παχύνω
fault αἰτία ας ἡ, ἁμαρτία ας ἡ
▪ **find ~ with** μέμφομαι, ψέγω
favour *noun* χάρις ιτος ἡ
▪ **show ~ to** χαρίζομαι + *dat*
favourable καλός ή όν, καίριος (α) ον, ἐπιτήδειος (α) ον
fawn νεβρός οῦ ὁ
fear *noun* φόβος ου ὁ; *verb* φοβέομαι
fearful (terrible) δεινός ή όν; (feeling fear) περίφοβος ον, περιδεής ές
fearless ἄφοβος ον, ἀδεής ές
feast ἑορτή ῆς ἡ
feather πτερόν οῦ τό
feed *tr* βόσκω, τρέφω
feel: ~ well εὖ ἔχω, καλῶς ἔχω
feeling αἴσθησις εως ἡ, πάθος ους τό
felt πῖλος ου ὁ
female θῆλυς θήλεια θῆλυ
fence ἕρκος ους τό, σταύρωμα ατος τό
fern πτερίς ίδος ἡ
ferry *noun* πόρος ου ὁ; *verb* πορθμεύω
ferryman πορθμεύς έως ὁ
festival ἑορτή ῆς ἡ
fetch κομίζω
fever πυρετός οῦ ὁ
few ὀλίγοι αι α
fewer ἐλάσσονες α

fickle ἀκατάστατος ον

field ἀγρός οῦ ὁ

fifteen πεντεκαίδεκα

fifth πέμπτος η ον

fifty πεντήκοντα

fig σῦκον ου τό

fight μάχομαι
▪ **~ at/by sea** ναυμαχέω

figure (shape) μορφή ῆς ἡ, σχῆμα ατος τό

file (tool) ῥίνη ης ἡ

fill πίμπλημι, πληρόω

fin πτερύγιον ου τό

finance οἰκονομία ας ἡ

find (discover) εὑρίσκω; (by enquiry) πυνθάνομαι; (by observation) γιγνώσκω; (come upon) καταλαμβάνω

finder εὑρετής οῦ ὁ

fine[1] *noun* ζημία ας ἡ, τίμημα ατος τό; *verb* ζημιόω, τιμάω

fine[2] *adj* καλός ή όν; (texture) λεπτός ή όν

finger δάκτυλος ου ὁ

finish *tr* (complete) ἐκτελέω, ἐξεργάζομαι; (make stop) παύω; *intr* παύομαι, τελευτάω

fir (tree) ἐλάτη ης ἡ, πεύκη ης ἡ

fire πῦρ πυρός τό
▪ **set on ~** ἅπτω, καίω
▪ **be on ~** καίομαι

fire-signal φρυκτός οῦ ὁ

firm βέβαιος (α) ον

firmness βεβαιότης ητος ἡ, καρτερία ας ἡ

first *adj* πρῶτος η ον; *adv* πρῶτον
▪ **be *or* arrive ~** φθάνω

fish *noun* ἰχθύς ύος ὁ; *verb* ἁλιεύω

fisherman ἁλιεύς έως ὁ

fist πυγμή ῆς ἡ

fit *verb* προσαρμόζω

fitting: it is ~ πρέπει + *dat*

five πέντε
▪ **~ times** πεντάκις
▪ **~ hundred** πεντακόσιοι αι α
▪ **~ thousand** πεντακισχίλιοι αι α

fix πήγνυμι

fixed πηκτός ή όν

flame φλόξ φλογός ἡ

flat πλατύς εῖα ύ, ὁμαλός ή όν

flatter κολακεύω, θωπεύω

flatterer κόλαξ ακος ὁ

flattery θωπεία ας ἡ, κολακεία ας ἡ

flaunt ἐπιδείκνυμι

flavour χυμός οῦ ὁ

flax λίνον ου τό

flay δέρω

flea ψύλλα ης ἡ

flee φεύγω, καταφεύγω

fleet ναυτικόν οῦ τό

flesh σάρξ σαρκός ἡ

float φέρομαι

flock πρόβατα ων τά, ποίμνη ης ἡ

flog μαστιγόω

flood *noun* ῥεῦμα ατος τό, κατακλυσμός οῦ ὁ; *verb* κατακλύζω

floor ἔδαφος ους τό, δάπεδον ου ὁ

flour ἄλευρον ου τό *usu pl*; ἄλφιτα ων τά

flourish εὐτυχέω, εὖ πράσσω; (bloom) θάλλω

flow ῥέω

flower ἄνθος ους τό

fluent εὔπορος ον

flute αὐλός οῦ ὁ

flute-player αὐλητής οῦ ὁ

fluting (of columns) ῥάβδωσις εως ἡ

fly *noun* (insect) μυῖα ας ἡ; *verb* [through the air] πέτομαι

foal πῶλος ου ὁ

foam ἀφρός οῦ ὁ

foetus βρέφος ους τό

fog ὁμίχλη ης ἡ

fold πτύσσω

follow ἕπομαι + *dat*, ἀκολουθέω + *dat*

followers (of) οἱ περί + *acc*

following: the ~ day ὑστεραία ας ἡ

food σῖτος ου ὁ

foolish μωρός ά όν, ἀνόητος ον

foolishness μωρία ας ἡ

foot πούς ποδός ὁ
■ **on ~** πεζῇ
■ **set ~ on** ἐπιβαίνω + *gen*

footsteps (tracks) ἴχνη ῶν τά

for[1] *prep* (on behalf of) ὑπέρ + *gen*
■ **~ the sake of** ἕνεκα *foll gen*
■ **~ the purpose of** εἰς + *acc*

for[2] *conj* γάρ*

forbid ἀπαγορεύω, οὐκ ἐάω

force *noun* βία ας ἡ; *verb* ἀναγκάζω
■ **by ~** βίᾳ, κατὰ κράτος
■ **in full ~** πανστρατιᾷ, πανδημεί
■ **~ one's way** βιάζομαι

ford *noun* πόρος ου ὁ; *verb* διαβαίνω

fordable διαβατός όν

forearm πῆχυς εως ὁ

forefather πρόγονος ου ὁ

forehead μέτωπον ου τό

foreign βάρβαρος ον, ξενικός (ή) όν, ἀλλότριος α ον

foreigner ξένος ου ὁ

forerunner πρόδρομος ου ὁ

foresee προοράω, προνοέω

foresight πρόνοια ας ἡ

forest ὕλη ης ἡ

forestall φθάνω, προκαταλαμβάνω

forethought πρόνοια ας ἡ

forge *noun* χαλκεῖον ου τό; *verb* [metal] χαλκεύω; [document etc.] πλάσσω; [coin] κιβδηλεύω

forged κίβδηλος ον

forgery πλάσμα ατος τό

forget ἐπιλανθάνομαι + *gen*

forgetful ἀμνήμων ον (ἀμνημον-), ἐπιλήσμων ον (ἐπιλησμον-)

forgetfulness λήθη ης ἡ

forgive συγγιγνώσκω + *gen*

forgiveness συγγνώμη ης ἡ

forgotten ἐξίτηλος ον

form (shape) μορφή ῆς ἡ, σχῆμα ατος τό

former πρότερος α ον
■ **~ ... latter** ἐκεῖνος ... οὗτος

formerly πρότερον

formless ἄμορφος ον

fort φρούριον ου τό, ἔρυμα ατος τό, τεῖχος ους τό

fortification τείχισμα ατος τό

fortify τειχίζω

fortunate εὐτυχής ές

fortune τύχη ης ἡ
■ **good ~** εὐτυχία ας ἡ
■ **bad ~** ἀτυχία ας ἡ

forty τεσσαράκοντα

foster-child θρέμμα ατος τό

found [city etc.] κτίζω, οἰκίζω

foundation (act of founding) κτίσις εως ἡ; (supports for building) ἔδαφος ους τό

founder ἀρχηγέτης ου ὁ, οἰκιστής οῦ ὁ

fountain κρήνη ης ἡ, πηγή ῆς ἡ

four τέσσαρες α
■ **~ times** τετράκις
■ **~ hundred** τετρακόσιοι αι α
■ **~ thousand** τετρακισχίλιοι αι α

fourteen τέσσαρες καὶ δέκα

fourth τέταρτος η ον

fox ἀλώπηξ εκος ἡ

fraction μέρος ους τό, μόριον ου τό

fracture *noun* κλάσις εως ἡ

fragrance εὐωδία ας ἡ, εὐοσμία ας ἡ

fragrant εὐώδης ες

frankincense λιβανωτός οῦ ὁ

frankness παρρησία ας ἡ

fraud δόλος ου ὁ, ἀπάτη ης ἡ

free *adj* ἐλεύθερος α ον
■ **set ~** λύω; [slave] ἐλευθερόω

freedom ἐλευθερία ας ἡ

freeze *tr* πήγνυμι; *intr* πήγνυμαι

frequent πυκνός ή όν, συχνός ή όν

fresh νέος α ον

f

friction τρῖψις εως ἡ

friend φίλος ου ὁ, φίλη ης ἡ

friendly φίλιος α ον, εὔνους ουν
■ **be on ~ terms with** διὰ φιλίας ἰέναι + *dat*

friendship φιλία ας ἡ

frighten φοβέω, ἐκπλήσσω

fringe κράσπεδον ου τό

frog βάτραχος ου ὁ

from (away from) ἀπό + *gen*; (out of) ἐκ + *gen*; [~ a person] παρά + *gen*
■ **~ where** ὅθεν, ὁπόθεν

front: in ~ ἐκ τοῦ ἔμπροσθε(ν)
■ **in ~ of** πρό + *gen*

frontier ὅρος ου ὁ

frost πάγος ου ὁ

frowning *adj* σκυθρωπός όν

frozen πηκτός ή όν

fruit καρπός οῦ ὁ

fugitive δραπέτης ου ὁ; ὁ φεύγων

fulfil ἐκτελέω, περαίνω
■ **~ a promise** ὑπόσχεσιν ἀποδίδωμι

fulfilment τελευτή ῆς ἡ, τέλος ους τό

full (of) πλήρης ες + *gen*; πλέως α ων + *gen*

fun παιδιά ᾶς ἡ
■ **in ~** μετὰ παιδιᾶς
■ **poke ~ at** σκώπτω

funeral ταφή ῆς ἡ, ἐκφορά ᾶς ἡ
■ **~ pyre** πυρή ῆς ἡ

furiously προπετῶς

furnace ἰπνός οῦ ὁ

furniture κατασκευή ῆς ἡ, ἔπιπλα ων τά

furrow ὁλκός οῦ ὁ, αὖλαξ ακος ἡ

further *adv* πόρρω, περαιτέρω

furthest *adj* ἔσχατος η ον

future *adj* μέλλων ουσα ον (μελλοντ-)
■ **for the ~** τὸ λοιπόν

Gg

gadfly οἶστρος ου ὁ

gain *noun* κέρδος ους τό; *verb* κερδαίνω
■ **~ advantage over** πλεονεκτέω + *gen*

gale σκηπτός οῦ ὁ

gamble (play dice) κυβεύω

games ἀγῶνες ων οἱ

gangway (of ship) ἀποβάθρα ας ἡ

garden κῆπος ου ὁ

garland στέφανος ου ὁ

garlic σκόροδον ου τό

garrison φρούριον ου τό

gate πύλη ης ἡ

gather *tr* ἀγείρω, συλλέγω; [fruit] συγκομίζομαι; [crops] δρέπω

gaze at θεάομαι; ἀποβλέπω εἰς + *acc*; προσβλέπω

general στρατηγός οῦ ὁ
■ **be *or* serve as a ~** στρατηγέω

generous ἐλευθέριος α ον

gentle πρᾶος α ον, ἤπιος α ον, μέτριος α ον

genuine γνήσιος α ον

gesticulate σχηματίζομαι

gesture σχῆμα ατος τό

get κτάομαι
■ **~ back** (recover) ἀναλαμβάνω
■ **~ up** ἀνίσταμαι

ghost φάσμα ατος τό, εἴδωλον ου τό

giant γίγας αντος ὁ

gift δῶρον ου τό

girl κόρη ης ἡ, παῖς παιδός ἡ

give δίδωμι

■ ~ **back** ἀποδίδωμι
■ ~ **in** ἐνδίδωμι
■ ~ **up** παραδίδωμι

glad ἄσμενος η ον
■ **be** ~ ἥδομαι, χαίρω

gladly ἡδέως

glass ὕαλος ου ἡ
■ **made of** ~ ὑάλινος η ον

globe σφαῖρα ας ἡ

glorious καλός ή όν, λαμπρός ά όν

glory κλέος ους τό, δόξα ης ἡ

glove χειρίς ῖδος ἡ

glue *noun* κόλλα ης ἡ; *verb* κολλάω

glued κολλητός ή όν

gnat κώνωψ ωπος ὁ

go ἔρχομαι
■ ~ **away** ἀπέρχομαι
■ ~ **down** καταβαίνω
■ ~ **out** ἐξέρχομαι
■ ~ **up** ἀνέρχομαι, ἀναβαίνω

goad *noun* κέντρον ου τό

goat αἴξ αἰγός ὁ/ἡ

god θεός οῦ ὁ

goddess θεά ᾶς ἡ, θεός οῦ ἡ

going: be ~ **to** μέλλω + *fut infin*

gold *noun* χρυσός οῦ ὁ; *adj* χρυσοῦς ἦ οῦν

good ἀγαθός ή όν
■ **do** ~ **to** εὖ ποιέω
■ ~ **luck** *or* **fortune** εὐδαιμονία ας ἡ
■ ~**-tempered** εὔκολος ον

goodwill εὔνοια ας ἡ

gorge φάραγξ αγγος ἡ

gossip *noun* λέσχη ης ἡ; *verb* ἀδολεσχέω

govern πολιτεύομαι

government οἱ ἐν τέλει

graceful χαρίεις εσσα εν (χαριεντ-)

gracious εὐμενής ές

graciously ἠπίως, εὐμενῶς

gradually κατ' ὀλίγον

granary ἀποθήκη ης ἡ

grandfather πάππος ου ὁ

grandmother τήθη ης ἡ

grapes: bunch of ~ βότρυς υος ὁ

grasp λαμβάνομαι + *gen*

grass πόα ας ἡ, χλόη ης ἡ

grasshopper τέττιξ ιγος ὁ

grateful: be ~ χάριν οἶδα, χάριν ἔχω

gratify χαρίζομαι + *dat*

gratitude χάρις ιτος ἡ

grave τάφος ου ὁ, τύμβος ου ὁ

gravel χάλιξ ικος ὁ/ἡ

graze (of animals) *tr* νομεύω; *intr* νέμομαι

great μέγας μεγάλη μέγα (μεγαλ-)

great-grandfather πρόπαππος ου ὁ

greatly πολύ, σφόδρα

Greece Ἑλλάς άδος ἡ

greed (for food) λιχνεία ας ἡ; (for gain) πλεονεξία ας ἡ, αἰσχροκέρδεια ας ἡ

greedy (for food) λίχνος (η) ον; (grasping) πλεονέκτης (*gen* ου)

Greek *adj* Ἑλληνικός ή όν
■ **speak** ~ ἑλληνίζω

Greeks Ἕλληνες ων οἱ

green χλωρός ά όν

greet ἀσπάζομαι

greeting ἀσπασμός οῦ ὁ

grey γλαυκός ή όν

grief λύπη ης ἡ; ἄλγος ους τό, πένθος ους τό

grievance ἀδικία ας ἡ

grieve λυπέομαι, ἀλγέω

grind ἀλέω, τρίβω

groan *noun* στεναγμός οῦ ὁ; *verb* στενάζω

groom ἱπποκόμος ου ὁ

grope ψηλαφάω

ground γῆ γῆς ἡ
■ **on the** ~ χαμαί
■ **to the** ~ χαμᾶζε
■ **stand one's** ~ ὑπομένω, ἀντέχω
■ **give** ~ ὑποχωρέω

groundlessly μάτην, ψευδῶς

group ὁμιλία ας ἡ

grove ἄλσος ους τό

grow *intr* αὐξάνομαι

growl ὑλακτέω

growth αὔξησις εως ἡ

grudge *noun* φθόνος ου ὁ; *verb* φθονέω
■ **bear a ~** μνησικακέω

grumble ἀγανακτέω

grunt γρύζω

guarantee *noun* ἐγγύη ης ἡ; *verb* ἐγγυάω

guard *noun* (person) φύλαξ ακος ὁ; (force) φυλακή ῆς ἡ; *verb tr* φυλάσσω
■ **be on one's ~** φυλάσσομαι
■ **keep ~** φρουρέω
■ **off one's ~** ἀφύλακτος ον

guardian ἐπίσκοπος ου ὁ

guerilla: ~ warfare πόλεμος ἄτακτος

guess *noun* στοχασμός οῦ ὁ; ὑπόνοια ας ἡ; *verb* στοχάζομαι, ὑπονοέω

guest ξένος ου ὁ
■ **~ at a drinking party** συμπότης ου ὁ

guidance ὑφήγησις εως ἡ

guide *noun* ἡγεμών όνος ὁ/ἡ; *verb tr* ἡγέομαι + *dat*

guileless ἄδολος ον

guilt αἰτία ας ἡ
■ **blood- ~** μίασμα ατος τό

guilty αἴτιος α ον

gulf κόλπος ου ὁ

gums οὖλα ων τά

gymnastics γυμναστική ῆς ἡ

Hh

habit ἔθος ους τό, τρόπος ου ὁ

hail (storm) χάλαζα ης ἡ

hair θρίξ τριχός ἡ

hairy δασύς εῖα ύ

half ἥμισυς εια υ

hall αὐλή ῆς ἡ

halve διαιρέω

hammer *noun* σφῦρα ας ἡ; *verb* κρούω

hand[1] χείρ χειρός ἡ
■ **fall into the ~s of** ὑποχείριος γίγνομαι + *dat*

hand[2]**: ~ over** (surrender) παραδίδωμι

handicraft χειρουργία ας ἡ

handle *noun* λαβή ῆς ἡ; *verb* ἅπτομαι + *gen*; διὰ χειρὸς ἔχω

hang *tr* κρεμάννυμι; *intr* κρέμαμαι
■ **~ oneself** ἀπάγχομαι

happen γίγνομαι
■ **~ to** (by chance) τυγχάνω + *pple*
■ **it ~s** συμβαίνει

happiness εὐδαιμονία ας ἡ

happy εὐδαίμων ον (εὐδαιμον-), περιχαρής ές

harass ἔγκειμαι + *dat*; ταράσσω

harbour λιμήν ένος ὁ

hard σκληρός ά όν

harden σκληρύνω

hardly μόλις

hardship πόνος ου ὁ, ταλαιπωρία ας ἡ
■ **suffer ~** ταλαιπωρέω

hare λαγώς ώ ὁ

harm *noun* βλάβη ης ἡ; *verb* βλάπτω, ἀδικέω, κακὰ ποιέω

harmless ἀσινής ές

harmonious σύμφωνος ον

harness *noun* ἱμάντες ων οἱ; *verb* ζεύγνυμι

harsh σκληρός ά όν, χαλεπός ή όν

harvest καρπός οῦ ὁ, θέρος ους τό

haste σπουδή ῆς ἡ

hat πέτασος ου ὁ

hate μισέω

hated: be ~ by ἀπεχθάνομαι + *dat*

hatred ἀπέχθεια ας ἡ, ἔχθος ους ὁ, μῖσος ους τό

haughty σεμνός ή όν

have ἔχω; *or use* ἐστί + *dat*

hawk ἱέραξ ακος ὁ

hay χόρτος ου ὁ

he οὗτος, ὅδε, ἐκεῖνος

head κεφαλή ῆς ἡ

headache: have a ~ ἀλγέω τὴν κεφαλήν

headland ἄκρα ας ἡ, ἀκρωτήριον ου τό

headlong προπετής ές

heal θεραπεύω, ἀκέομαι, ἰάομαι

health ὑγίεια ας ἡ

healthy ὑγιής ές

heap[1] χῶμα ατος τό

heap[2]**: ~ up** χόω

hear ἀκούω

heart καρδία ας ἡ

heat καῦμα ατος τό, τὸ θερμόν

heaven οὐρανός οῦ ὁ

heavy βαρύς εῖα ύ

heavy-armed: ~ soldier ὁπλίτης ου ὁ

hedge ἕρκος ους τό

hedgehog ἐχῖνος ου ὁ

heel πτέρνα ης ἡ

height ὕψος ους τό
■ **be at the ~ of** ἀκμάζω + *dat*

heir κληρονόμος ου ὁ

heiress ἐπίκληρος ου ἡ

helmet κόρυς υθος ἡ

helmsman κυβερνήτης ου ὁ

help *noun* ὠφέλεια ας ἡ, βοήθεια ας ἡ, ἐπικουρία ας ἡ; *verb* ὠφελέω; βοηθέω + *dat*; ἐπικουρέω + *dat*

helper βοηθός οῦ ὁ

helping *adj* ἐπίκουρος ον

helpless: be ~ ἀμηχανέω, ἀπορέω

helplessness ἀπορία ας ἡ

hem κράσπεδον ου τό

hemlock κώνειον ου τό

her *acc/gen/dat of* αὐτή; *possessive* αὐτῆς
■ **~ own** *reflexive possessive* ἑαυτῆς

herald κῆρυξ υκος ὁ

herb φυτόν οῦ τό

herd ἀγέλη ης ἡ

herdsman βουκόλος ου ὁ

here ἐνθάδε, αὐτοῦ
■ **to ~** δεῦρο
■ **from ~** ἐνθένδε
■ **be ~** πάρειμι

hero ἥρως ωος ὁ

heroic ἡρωικός ή όν

heron ἐρωδιός οῦ ὁ

herself *in nom intensifying* αὐτή; *reflexive* ἑαυτήν

hesitate ἀποκνέω, μέλλω

hesitation ὄκνος ου ὁ

hidden κρυπτός ή όν; *or use* λανθάνω

hide[1] *noun* (skin) δέρμα ατος τό

hide[2] *verb* κρύπτω

hideous ἄμορφος ον, δυσειδής ές

high ὑψηλός ή όν

highly: value ~ περὶ πολλοῦ ποιέομαι

hill λόφος ου ὁ, ὄρος ους τό

him *acc/gen/dat of* αὐτός

himself *in nom intensifying* αὐτος; *reflexive* ἑαυτόν

hinder κωλύω

hindrance κώλυμα ατος τό

hinge στρόφιγξ ιγγος ὁ

hint *verb* παραδηλόω, ὑπαινίσσομαι

hire (let out for ~) μισθόω; (take on ~) μισθόομαι

his *possessive* αὐτοῦ
■ **~ own** *reflexive possessive* ἑαυτοῦ

hiss *noun* συριγμός οῦ ὁ; *verb* συρίζω

historian συγγραφεύς έως ὁ, λογογράφος ου ὁ

history (written work) συγγραφή ῆς ἡ, λόγοι ων οἱ
▪ **write ~** συγγράφω

hit τύπτω, βάλλω

hive σμῆνος ους τό

hold ἔχω, κατέχω
▪ **~ out** (endure) ἀντέχω

hole τρῆμα ατος τό

holiness ὁσιότης ητος ἡ

hollow κοῖλος η ον; (empty) κενός ή όν

holy ὅσιος α ον, ἱερός ά όν

home: at ~ οἴκοι
▪ **(away) from ~** οἴκοθεν
▪ **(to) ~** οἴκαδε
▪ **be at ~** ἐπιδημέω
▪ **be away from ~** ἀποδημέω

honest δίκαιος α ον, χρηστός ή όν, ἐπιεικής ές

honey μέλι ιτος τό

honour *noun* τιμή ῆς ἡ; *verb* τιμάω, θεραπεύω

honourable καλός ή όν, ἔντιμος ον

hook ἄγκιστρον ου τό

hope *noun* ἐλπίς ίδος ἡ; *verb* ἐλπίζω

hopeful εὔελπις ι (εὐελπιδ-)

hopeless ἀνέλπιστος ον

hoplite ὁπλίτης ου ὁ

horn κέρας ατος *or* ως τό

horror ὀρρωδία ας ἡ, ἔκπληξις εως ἡ

horse ἵππος ου ὁ
▪ **on ~back** ἐφ' ἵππου

horseman ἱππεύς έως ὁ

horse-race ἱπποδρομία ας ἡ

hospitable ξένιος (α) ον

hospitality ξενία ας ἡ

hostage ὅμηρος ου ὁ

hostile ἐχθρός ά όν

hot θερμός ή όν

hotel πανδοκεῖον ου τό

hour ὥρα ας ἡ

house οἰκία ας ἡ, οἶκος ου ὁ

housekeeper ταμίας ου ὁ, οἰκονόμος ου ὁ/ἡ

housekeeping οἰκονομία ας ἡ

how *direct question* πῶς; *indirect question* ὅπως; *in exclamations* ὡς
▪ **~ big/much?** πόσος η ον
▪ **~ many?** πόσοι αι α

however *conj* μέντοι*

hull σκάφος ους τό

human ἀνθρώπειος α ον, ἀνθρώπινος η ον

humane φιλάνθρωπος ον

humble ταπεινός ή όν

humming βόμβος ου ὁ

hundred ἑκατόν

hunger πεῖνα ης ἡ, λιμός οῦ ὁ

hungry ἄσιτος ον
▪ **be ~** πεινάω

hunt *noun* θήρα ας ἡ, κυνηγέσιον ου τό; *verb* θηρεύω, κυνηγετέω

hunter θηρευτής οῦ ὁ, κυνηγέτης ου ὁ

hurry σπεύδω

hurt *noun* βλάβη ης ἡ; *verb* βλάπτω, λυμαίνομαι

hurtful βλαβερός ά όν

husband ἀνήρ ἀνδρός ὁ

husk λέμμα ατος τό

hut καλύβη ης ἡ

hymn ὕμνος ου ὁ

Ii

I ἐγώ; *emphatic* ἔγωγε

ice κρύσταλλος ου ὁ

idea διάνοια ας ἡ, νόημα ατος τό

idle ῥᾴθυμος ον, ἀργός όν
■ **be ~** ῥᾳθυμέω

if εἰ + *indic/opt*; ἐάν + *subj*
■ **~ only!** εἴθε + *opt*, εἰ γάρ + *opt*

ignorance ἄγνοια ας ἡ, ἀμαθία ας ἡ

ignorant ἀμαθής ές, ἀγνώς (ἀγνωτ-)
■ **be ~** ἀγνοέω

ill ἀσθενής ές
■ **be ~** νοσέω

illegal ἄνομος ον, παράνομος ον

ill-fated δυστυχής ές

illness νόσος ου ἡ

illogical ἄλογος ον

illusion φάντασμα ατος τό

ill-will κακόνοια ας ἡ, ἀπέχθεια ας ἡ

image εἰκών όνος ἡ, εἴδωλον ου τό

imagination φαντασία ας ἡ

imagine (conceive in mind) νοέω; (guess) εἰκάζω; (suppose) οἴομαι, ὑπολαμβάνω

imitation μίμησις εως ἡ

imitate μιμέομαι

immeasurable ἄμετρος ον

immediately εὐθύς, παραυτίκα, παραχρῆμα

immodest ἀναιδής ές, ἀναίσχυντος ον

immortal ἀθάνατος ον

immovable ἀκίνητος ον

immunity (from public duties) ἀτέλεια ας ἡ

impassable ἄπορος ον, ἀδιάβατος ον

impede ἐμποδίζω

imperceptible ἀναίσθητος ον

imperfect ἀτελής ές

impetuous προπετής ές

impiety ἀσέβεια ας ἡ

impious ἀσεβής ές
■ **be ~** ἀσεβέω

implant ἐμφύω

import εἰσκομίζω, εἰσάγω

important (noteworthy) ἀξιόλογος ον
■ **consider ~** περὶ πολλοῦ ποιέομαι

impossible ἀδύνατος ον

impregnable ἀνάλωτος ον

imprison εἵργω, καταδέω

improbable παρὰ λόγον

improve *tr/intr* προκόπτω; *intr* βελτίων γίγνομαι

improvise αὐτοσχεδιάζω

imprudent ἀλόγιστος ον

impudent θρασύς εῖα ύ, ἀναιδής ές

impulse ὁρμή ῆς ἡ

impulsive προπετής ές, νεανικός ή όν

impure ἀκάθαρτος ον

in ἐν + *dat*
■ **~ addition to** πρός + *dat*
■ **~ order to** ἵνα, ὅπως, ὡς

inaccessible δυσπρόσοδος ον

inanimate ἄψυχος ον

inappropriate ἀνεπιτήδειος ον

inaudible ἀνήκουστος ον

inborn ἔμφυτος ον

incense θυμίαμα ατος τό

incidental πάρεργος ον

incite προάγω

incline ῥέπω

income πρόσοδος ου ἡ *usu pl*

incompetent ἀδύνατος ον

incomplete ἀτελής ές, ἐλλιπής ές
inconsolable δυσπαραμύθητος ον
inconstant ἄπιστος ον, ἀστάθμητος ον
inconvenience δυσχέρεια ας ἡ
inconvenient δυσχερής ές, ἀνεπιτήδειος ον
incorruptible ἀδιάφορος ον; (by bribes) ἄδωρος ον
increase *tr* αὐξάνω; *intr* αὐξάνομαι
incredible ἄπιστος ον
incredulous ἄπιστος ον
incur ὀφλισκάνω
■ **~ charge** αἰτίαν ἔχω
incurable ἀνήκεστος ον
indeed δή
independence αὐτονομία ας ἡ, αὐτάρκεια ας ἡ
independent αὐτόνομος ον, αὐτάρκης ες
indestructible ἀδιάφθορος ον
indicate σημαίνω, δείκνυμι
indignant: be ~ δεινὸν ποιέομαι, χαλεπῶς φέρω, ἀγανακτέω
indiscreet ἀπερίσκεπτος ον
indissoluble ἄλυτος ον
indistinct ἀσαφής ές
individual ἴδιος α ον
indivisible ἀμέριστος ον
induce προτρέπω; (entice) δελεάζω
indulge in χράομαι + *dat*
inevitable ἄφυκτος ον
inexperience ἀπειρία ας ἡ
inexperienced ἄπειρος ον
inexplicable δύσφραστος ον
infantry πεζοί ῶν οἱ; *collective sg* πεζός οῦ ὁ
infer τεκμαίρομαι, εἰκάζω, συλλογίζομαι
inference συλλογισμός οῦ ὁ
inferior ἥσσων ον (ἡσσον-), χείρων ον (χειρον-)
■ **be ~ to** ἡσσάομαι + *gen*
infinite ἄπειρος ον
inflate φυσάω
inflict: ~ a penalty (on) δίκην λαμβάνω παρά + *gen*
influence *noun* δύναμις εως ἡ, ῥοπή ῆς ἡ
influential δυνατός ή όν, πιθανός ή όν
inform against μηνύω κατά + *gen*
informer μηνυτής οῦ ὁ; (in bad sense) συκοφάντης ου ὁ
infuse ἐγχέω
inhabit οἰκέω, ἐνοικέω
inhabitant ἔνοικος ου ὁ
inherit διαδέχομαι, παραλαμβάνω
inheritance κληρονομία ας ἡ
■ **receive (share of) an ~** κληρονομέω + *gen*
initiate μυέω
initiation τελετή ῆς ἡ
injure βλάπτω, ἀδικέω, κακὰ δράω
injustice ἀδικία ας ἡ
inland *adj* μεσόγαιος (α) ον
■ **go ~** ἀναβαίνω
inn (lodging) καταγώγιον ου τό, πανδοκεῖον ου τό; (wine-shop) οἰνοπώλιον ου τό
inn-keeper πανδοκεύς έως ὁ
innocent ἀναίτιος ον
innocuous ἀβλαβής ές
innovate νεωτερίζω, καινόω
innovation νεωτερισμός οῦ ὁ
innumerable ἀναρίθμητος ον
insane ἄφρων ον (ἀφρον-)
inscription ἐπίγραμμα ατος τό, ἐπιγραφή ῆς ἡ
insects ἔντομα ων τά
insert ἐπεμβάλλω
inside *prep* ἔνδον, ἔσω, ἔντος *all* + *gen*; *adv* ἔνδον, ἔσω, ἔντος
insight γνῶσις εως ἡ, φρόνησις εως ἡ
insist ἰσχυρίζομαι

insolence ὕβρις εως ἡ, ἀσέλγεια ας ἡ

insolent ὑβριστικός ή όν, ἀσελγής ές

inspect (scrutinise) ἐξετάζω

inspector κατάσκοπος ου ὁ

inspiration ἐπίνοια ας ἡ

inspire ἐμβάλλω, ἐντίθημι

instead of ἀντί *+ gen*

instinctive ἔμφυτος ον

instruct (order) κελεύω; προστάσσω + *dat*; (teach) διδάσκω

instructions: according to ~ κατὰ τὰ εἰρημένα

insufficient ἐνδεής ές

insult *noun* ὕβρις εως ἡ, αἰκία ας ἡ; *verb* ὑβρίζω, προπηλακίζω, λοιδορέω

intelligence νοῦς νοῦ ὁ, σύνεσις εως ἡ

intelligent συνετός ή όν, φρόνιμος ον

intend διανοέομαι, ἐν νῷ ἔχω; μέλλω *+ fut infin*

intense (eager) σύντονος ον; (of pain) ἰσχυρός ά όν, πικρός ά όν

intention γνώμη ης ἡ, διάνοια ας ἡ

intentionally ἑκών οὖσα όν (ἑκοντ-)

intercept ἀπολαμβάνω

interest (on money) τόκος ου ὁ

interfere πολυπραγμονέω

interior (of country) μεσόγαια ας ἡ

interlude ἐπεισόδιον ου τό

intermarriage ἐπιγαμία ας ἡ

interpolate παρεγγράφω

Interpret ἐξηγέομαι, ἑρμηνεύω, κρίνω

interpreter ἑρμηνεύς έως ὁ

interrupt (in conversation) ὑποβάλλω, ὑπολαμβάνω

interval διάστασις εως ἡ

intestines ἔντερα ων τά, σπλάγχνα ων τά

intimate οἰκεῖος α ον, συνήθης ες

into εἰς *+ acc*

intolerable ἀφόρητος ον

intricate ποικίλος η ον

introduce εἰσάγω, προσάγω

inundate κατακλύζω

invade εἰσβάλλω εἰς *+ acc*

invalid (not authoritative) ἄκυρος ον

invariable βέβαιος (α) ον, ἀκίνητος ον

invasion εἰσβολή ῆς ἡ

invent ἐξευρίσκω, μηχανάομαι

invention εὕρημα ατος τό

inventive εὔπορος ον, εὐμήχανος ον

inventor εὑρετής οῦ ὁ

invert ἀναστρέφω

investigate σκοπέω, ἐξετάζω, ἀναζητέω

investigation σκέψις εως ἡ, ζήτησις εως ἡ

invincible ἀήσσητος ον

invisible ἀφανής ές, ἄδηλος ον, ἄωρος ον

invite παρακαλέω, προσκαλέω

involuntarily ἄκων ἄκουσα ἆκον (ἀκοντ-)

inwards εἴσω

iron *noun* σίδηρος ου ὁ; *adj* σιδηροῦς ᾶ οῦν

irrational ἄλογος ον

irrefutable ἀνεξέλεγκτος ον

irregular ἀνώμαλος ον; (disordered) ἄτακτος ον

island νῆσος ου ἡ

islander νησιώτης ου ὁ

it *acc/gen/dat of* αὐτός ή ὁ

itself ἑαυτόν ήν ό

ivory ἐλέφας αντος ὁ

ivy κισσός οῦ ὁ

Jj

jackdaw κολοιός οῦ ὁ

jar πίθος ου ὁ

javelin ἀκόντιον ου τό
■ **throw ~** ἀκοντίζω

javelin-thrower ἀκοντιστής οῦ ὁ

jaw γνάθος ου ἡ

jealous φθονερός ά όν
■ **be ~** φθονέω

jealousy φθόνος ου ὁ

jeer σκώπτω

jewel λίθος ου ἡ

jewellery κόσμος ου ὁ

join *tr* συνάπτω, ζεύγνυμι; *intr* προσχωρέω + *dat*
■ **~ battle** συμβάλλω

joint (of body) ἄρθρον ου τό

joke *noun* σκῶμμα ατος τό, γελοῖον ου τό; *verb* παίζω, σκώπτω

journey *noun* ὁδός οῦ ἡ; *verb* πορεύομαι

joy χαρά ᾶς ἡ

joyful περιχαρής ές

judge *noun* (in lawcourt) κριτής οῦ ὁ; (of games) βραβεύς έως ὁ; *verb* κρίνω, δικάζω

judgement γνώμη ης ἡ

jug πρόχους ου ἡ

juice χυμός οῦ ὁ

jump πηδάω, ἅλλομαι

juryman δικαστής οῦ ὁ

just[1] *adj* δίκαιος α ον

just[2] *adv* (exactly) μάλιστα, ἀτεχνῶς
■ **~ as** ὥσπερ
■ **~ now** (recently) ἄρτι

justice δικαιοσύνη ης ἡ, τό δίκαιον

justify δικαιόω

jut out προέχω

juvenile νεανικός ή όν

juxtaposition σύνθεσις εως ἡ

Kk

keel τρόπις ιος ἡ

keep ἔχω, διατηρέω
■ **~ from** κωλύω ἀπό + *gen*
■ **~ quiet** ἡσυχάζω
■ **~ safe** σῴζομαι

kettle λέβης ητος ὁ

key κλῄς κληδός ἡ

kick λακτίζω

kidney νεφρός οῦ ὁ

kill ἀποκτείνω

killed: be ~ ἀποθνῄσκω

kiln κάμινος ου ὁ
■ **brick-~** πλινθεῖον ου τό

kind[1] *noun* γένος ους τό

kind[2] *adj* ἤπιος α ον, εὔνους ουν, εὐμενής ές

kindle ἅπτω

kindness εὔνοια ας ἡ

kindred συγγενής ές

king βασιλεύς έως ὁ

kingdom βασιλεία ας ἡ

kingfisher ἀλκυών ονος ὁ

kiss *noun* φίλημα ατος τό; *verb* φιλέω, κυνέω

kitchen ἰπνός οῦ ὁ

knead μάσσω

knee γόνυ γόνατος τό

knife μάχαιρα ας ἡ

knock (on door) κόπτω

knot ἅμμα ατος τό

know οἶδα, ἐπίσταμαι
▪ **get to ~** γιγνώσκω
▪ **~ how to** οἶδα + *infin*; ἐπίσταμαι + *infin*

knowledge ἐπιστήμη ης ἡ

known: well ~ γνώριμος ον

knuckle κόνδυλος ου ὁ

Ll

labour *noun* πόνος ου ὁ; *verb* πονέω

lack *noun* ἀπορία ας ἡ; ἔνδεια ας ἡ; *verb* ἀπορέω + *gen*; ἐνδέω + *gen*

ladder κλῖμαξ ακος ἡ

laden: be ~ with (e.g. of ship) γέμω + *gen*

ladle οἰνοχόη ης ἡ

lake λίμνη ης ἡ

lamb ἀρνίον ου τό

lame χωλός ή όν
▪ **be ~** χωλεύω

lamp λύχνος ου ὁ

land γῆ γῆς ἡ
▪ **by ~** κατὰ γῆν

language γλῶσσα ης ἡ

large μέγας μεγάλη μέγα (μεγαλ-)

lark κόρυδος ου ὁ

last[1] *adj* ὕστατος η ον, τελευταῖος α ον
▪ **at ~** τέλος

last[2] *verb* διατελέω

lasting βέβαιος (α) ον

late *adj* χρόνιος (α) ον, ὄψιος α ον; *adv* ὀψέ

later μετά, ὕστερον
▪ **not much ~** οὐ διὰ πολλοῦ

Latin: speak ~ ῥωμαΐζω

laugh γελάω
▪ **~ at** καταγελάω

laughter γέλως ωτος ὁ

launch καθέλκω

law νόμος ου ὁ

lawful ἔννομος ον, νόμιμος ον, δίκαιος α ον

lawgiver νομοθέτης ου ὁ

lawless ἄνομος ον

lawsuit δίκη ης ἡ

lay: ~ claim to ἀντιποιέομαι + *gen*
▪ **~ siege to** πολιορκέω

lazy ῥᾴθυμος ον, ἀργός όν

lead[1] (metal) μόλυβδος ου ὁ

lead[2] *verb* ἄγω, ἡγέομαι + *dat*; (of road) φέρω

leader ἡγεμών όνος ὁ/ἡ

leadership ἡγεμονία ας ἡ

leaf φύλλον ου τό, πέταλον ου τό

league συμμαχία ας ἡ, συνωμοσία ας ἡ

lean *verb* κλίνω

learn μανθάνω

learner μαθητής οῦ ὁ

least ἐλάχιστος η ον
▪ **at ~** γε*

leather *noun* σκῦτος ους τό, δέρμα ατος τό; *adj* σκύτινος η ον

leave (behind) λείπω, καταλείπω; (depart) ἀπέρχομαι

ledge (of rock) κρημνός οῦ ὁ

leek πράσον ου τό

left[1] (hand side) ἀριστερός ά όν

left[2] (remaining) λοιπός ή όν

leg σκέλος ους τό

legal νόμιμος η ον

legend μῦθος ου ὁ

legendary μυθώδης ες

legion τάγμα ατος τό

legitimate γνήσιος α ον

leisure σχολή ῆς ἡ

lend δανείζω

length μῆκος ους τό

lengthen μηκύνω

lentil φακός οῦ ὁ

lesson μάθημα ατος τό

let (allow) ἐάω; ἐπιτρέπω + *dat*
■ **~ go** (~ slip) μεθίημι, παρίημι
■ **~ go** (~ off) ἀφίημι

letter ἐπιστολή ῆς ἡ
■ **~ of alphabet** γράμμα ατος τό

level ὁμαλός ή όν

lever μοχλός οῦ ὁ

liar ψεύστης ου ὁ

libation σπονδή ῆς ἡ
■ **pour a ~** σπένδω

libel *noun* λοιδορία ας ἡ; *verb* λοιδορέω, βλασφημέω

library βιβλιοθήκη ης ἡ

lick λείχω

lid ἐπίθημα ατος τό

lie[1] (tell a ~) ψεύδομαι

lie[2] (~ down) κεῖμαι

lie[3]: **~ at anchor** ὁρμέω

life βίος ου ὁ
■ **time of ~** ἡλικία ας ἡ
■ **way of ~** δίαιτα ης ἡ

lift αἴρω

light[1] *noun* φῶς φωτός τό

light[2] *adj* κοῦφος η ον

light[3] *verb* (kindle) ἅπτω

light-armed: ~ soldier πελταστής οῦ ὁ

lighthouse φρυκτώριον ου τό

lightning ἀστραπή ῆς ἡ

like[1] *adj* ὅμοιος α ον + *dat*
■ **be ~** ἔοικα + *dat*

like[2] *verb* φιλέω, στέργω

likely: what is ~ εἰκός ότος τό
■ **it is ~ that** εἰκός ἐστι + *acc* + *infin*

likeness ὁμοιότης ητος ἡ

likewise ὡσαύτως

lily κρίνον ου τό

limb μέλος ους τό, κῶλον ου τό, ἄρθρον ου τό

limit *noun* ὅρος ου ὁ, τέλος ους τό; *noun* ὁρίζω

limpet λεπάς άδος ἡ

linen λίνον ου τό

lion λέων οντος ὁ

lioness λέαινα ης ἡ

lip χεῖλος ους τό

liquid *adj* ὑγρός ά όν

lisp τραυλίζω

list κατάλογος ου ὁ

listen to ἀκροάομαι + *gen*; ἀκούω + *gen of person*

listener ἀκροατής οῦ ὁ

little μικρός ά όν

live (be alive) ζάω; (pass one's life) διάγω; (make a living) βιοτεύω
■ **~ in** ἐνοικέω

livelihood βίος ου ὁ

liver ἧπαρ ατος τό

living ἔμψυχος ον

lizard σαύρα ας ἡ

load [ship etc.] γεμίζω

loaf ἄρτος ου ὁ

loan *noun* δάνεισμα ατος τό
■ **get a ~** δανείζομαι

lock *noun* (security device) κλῇθρον ου τό; *verb* κλείω

locust ἀκρίς ίδος ἡ

lodge καταλύω

lodger ἔνοικος ου ὁ

log ξύλον ου τό

loneliness ἐρημία ας ἡ

lonely ἔρημος η ον, μόνος η ον

long[1] μακρός ά όν

long[2]**: ~ ago** πάλαι

long[3]**: ~ for** ὀρέγομαι + *gen*; ἐπιθυμέω + *gen*

longer: no ~ οὐκέτι, μηκέτι

look βλέπω, σκοπέω
■ **~ after** ἐπιμελέομαι + *gen*
■ **~ at** προσβλέπω; ἀποβλέπω εἰς + *acc*
■ **~ down on** καθοράω
■ **~ for** ζητέω

loom ἱστός οῦ ὁ

lose ἀπόλλυμι, ἀποβάλλω

loss ζημία ας ἡ
■ **be at a ~** ἀπορέω, ἀμηχανέω

loud *use* πολύς

loudly *use* μέγα

love *noun* (affection) φιλία ας ἡ; (physical passion) ἔρως ωτος ὁ; *verb* (feel affection) φιλέω; (feel physical passion for) ἐράω + *gen*

low-lying πεδινός ή όν

loyal πιστός ή όν, βέβαιος (α) ον

loyalty βεβαιότης ητος ἡ

luck τύχη ης ἡ

lungs πλεύμονες ων οἱ

lure δελεάζω

luxurious τρυφερός ά όν

luxury τρυφή ῆς ἡ

lyre κιθάρα ας ἡ

lyre-player κιθαριστής οῦ ὁ

Mm

machine μηχανή ῆς ἡ

mad μανικός ή όν, μανιώδης ες
■ **be ~** μαίνομαι, παραφρονέω

madden ἐκπλήσσω

madness μανία ας ἡ

magic μαγευτική ῆς ἡ

magician μάγος ου ὁ

magistrate ἄρχων οντος ὁ; *pl* οἱ ἐν τέλει

magnificence μεγαλοπρέπεια ας ἡ

magnificent εὐπρεπής ές, μεγαλοπρεπής ές

maidservant θεράπαινα ης ἡ

mainland ἤπειρος ου ἡ

majority οἱ πολλοί

make ποιέω
■ **~ war** πολεμέω

male ἄρσην εν (ἀρσεν-)

man (male) ἀνήρ ἀνδρός ὁ; (human) ἄνθρωπος ου ὁ

manage πράσσω, διοικέω, μεταχειρίζω

management διοίκησις εως ἡ, οἰκονομία ας ἡ

manager ταμίας ου ὁ

mane χαίτη ης ἡ

manger φάτνη ης ἡ

manner τρόπος ου ὁ

manufacture κατεργάζομαι

manure κόπρος ου ἡ

many πολλοί αί ά
■ **~ times** πολλάκις

map πίναξ ακος ὁ

march *noun* ὁδός οῦ ἡ, πορεία ας ἡ; *verb* πορεύομαι, στρατεύω

■ **a day's ~** σταθμός οὗ ὁ
■ **~ away** ἀπελαύνω

mare ἵππος ου ἡ

marine *noun* ἐπιβάτης ου ὁ

mark *noun* σημεῖον ου τό, χαρακτήρ ῆρος ὁ; *verb* ἐπισημαίνω

market(-place) ἀγορά ᾶς ἡ

marriage γάμος ου ὁ

marry *with male subject* γαμέω; *with female subject* γαμέομαι + *dat*

marsh λίμνη ης ἡ, ἕλος ους τό

marshy λιμνώδης ες

marvellous θαυμαστός ή όν, θαυμάσιος α ον

mask πρόσωπον ου τό

mast ἱστός οῦ ὁ

master δεσπότης ου ὁ
■ **be ~ of** κρατέω + *gen*

mat φορμός οῦ ὁ

matter (affair) πρᾶγμα ατος τό
■ **it does not ~** οὐδὲν διαφέρει

mattress στρῶμα ατος τό

maze λαβύρινθος ου τό

meadow λειμών ῶνος ὁ

meal δεῖπνον ου τό

mean *verb* λέγειν βούλομαι, σημαίνω, διανοέομαι

meanwhile ἐν τούτῳ

measure *noun* μέτρον ου τό; [of corn] χοῖνιξ ικος ἡ; *verb* μετρέω

measureless ἄμετρος ον

meat κρέας έως τό

meddle πολυπραγμονέω

meddlesomeness πολυπραγμοσύνη ης ἡ

medicine (drug) φάρμακον ου τό; (medical science) ἰατρική ῆς ἡ

meet (go to ~) ἀπαντάω + *dat*; (bump into) ἐντυγχάνω + *dat*

meeting σύνοδος ου ἡ

melody μέλος ους τό

melt *tr* κατατήκω; *intr* κατατήκομαι

memorial μνημεῖον ου τό

memory μνήμη ης ἡ

mend ἐπισκευάζω

mention μνημονεύω

mercenary soldier μισθοφόρος ου ὁ

merchant ἔμπορος ου ὁ

merchant ship ὁλκάς άδος ἡ

merciful ἐλεήμων ον (ἐλεημον-)

mercy (pity) ἔλεος ους τό; (pardon) συγγνώμη ης ἡ

message ἀγγελία ας ἡ, φήμη ης ἡ

messenger ἄγγελος ου ὁ

method (system) μέθοδος ου ἡ; (manner) τρόπος ου ὁ

metre μέτρον ου τό

midday μεσημβρία ας ἡ

middle (of) μέσος η ον

might: with all one's ~ κατὰ δύναμιν

mild πρᾶος ον

milk γάλα ακτος τό

mind νοῦς νοῦ ὁ

mine[1] (for metal) *noun* μέταλλον ου τό; *verb* ὀρύσσω

mine[2] *adj possessive* ἐμός ή όν

miner μεταλλευτής οῦ ὁ

miracle θαῦμα ατος ὁ

miraculous θαυμαστός ή όν

mirror κάτοτρον ου τό

miserable ἄθλιος α ον

miserly φιλάργυρος ον

miss (not hit target) ἁμαρτάνω + *gen*, σφάλλομαι + *gen*; [opportunity etc.] παρίημι

missile βέλος ους τό

mist ὁμίχλη ης ἡ

mistake *noun* ἁμαρτία ας ἡ, ἁμάρτημα ατος τό
■ **make a ~** ἁμαρτάνω

mistress δέσποινα ης ἡ

misunderstand παρακούω

misuse ἀποχράομαι + *dat*

mix μίγνυμι, κεράννυμι

mixture κρᾶσις εως ἡ, σύγκρασις εως ἡ

mob ὄχλος ου ὁ, πλῆθος ους τό

mock σκώπτω, χλευάζω; καταγελάω + *gen*

moderate *adj* μέτριος α ον

moderation σωφροσύνη ης ἡ, μετριότης ητος ἡ

modern καινός ή όν

modest σώφρων ον (σωφρον-), μέτριος α ον

moisten βρέχω

moment (opportunity/crisis) καιρός οῦ ὁ
▪ **for the ~** πρὸς τὸ παρόν
▪ **on the spur of the ~** ἐκ τοῦ παραχρῆμα

money χρήματα ων τά
▪ **make ~** χρηματίζομαι

monkey πίθηκος ου ὁ

monster τέρας ατος τό, θηρίον ου τό

month μήν μηνός ὁ

monument μνημεῖον ου τό, μνῆμα ατος τό

moon σελήνη ης ἡ

moor [ship] ὁρμίζω

more *adj* πλείων ον (πλειον-); *adv* μᾶλλον
▪ **the ~ X, the ~ Y** ὅσῳ … τοσούτῳ
▪ **and what is ~** καὶ δὴ καί

morning ἕως ἕω ἡ

morsel ψωμός οῦ ὁ

mortal θνητός ή όν

mosquito κώνωψ ωπος ὁ

most *adj* πλεῖστος η ον
▪ **for the ~ part** ὡς ἐπὶ τὸ πολύ
▪ **~ of all** *adv* μάλιστα

mother μήτηρ τρός ἡ
▪ **~ city** μητρόπολις εως ἡ

mother-in-law πενθερά ᾶς ἡ

motion κίνησις εως ἡ

motionless ἀκίνητος ον

mould *verb* πλάσσω

moulding (in architecture) ῥάβδωσις εως ἡ

mound χῶμα ατος τό

mount *verb* ἀναβαίνω

mountain ὄρος ους τό

mourn πενθέω

mouse μῦς μυός ὁ

mouth στόμα ατος τό

move *tr* κινέω; *intr* κινέομαι

mow θερίζω

much πολύς πολλή πολύ (πολλ-)

mud βόρβορος ου ὁ

muddle *tr* ταράσσω

mule ἡμίονος ου ὁ

murder *noun* φόνος ου ὁ, σφαγή ῆς ἡ; *verb* φονεύω

murderer φονεύς έως ὁ/ἡ, αὐθέντης ου ὁ

muscle νεῦρον ου τό

Muse (goddess) Μοῦσα ης ἡ

music μουσική ῆς ἡ

must δεῖ; *or use verbal adj*

mustard σίναπι εως τό

mutilate λωβάομαι

mutiny στάσις εως ἡ

mutter γρύζω

my ἐμός ή όν *foll def article*

myrrh σμύρνα ης ἡ

myself *refl* ἐμαυτόν ήν

mythical μυθώδης ες

Nn

nail ἧλος ου ὁ; (finger/toe∼) ὄνυξ υχος ὁ

naked γυμνός ή όν

name *noun* ὄνομα ατος τό; *verb* ὀνομάζω

▪ **have a good ∼** εὖ ἀκούω

nameless ἀνώνυμος ον

narrow στενός ή όν

▪ **∼ space** στενοχωρία ας ἡ

native ἐπιχώριος ον, αὐτόχθων ον (αὐτοχθον-)

▪ **∼ land** πατρίς ίδος ἡ

naturally (by nature) φύσει; (reasonably) εἰκότως

nature φύσις εως ἡ

▪ **be by ∼** πέφυκα

naval ναυτικός ή όν

navel ὀμφαλός οῦ ὁ

navy ναυτικόν οῦ τό

near *prep* ἐγγύς + *gen*; *adv* ἐγγύς, σχεδόν, πλησίον

nearly σχεδόν, ὅσον οὐ

neat κόσμιος α ον, κομψός ή όν

necessary ἀναγκαῖος (α) ον, ἐπιτήδειος (α) ον

▪ **it is ∼** δεῖ

necessity ἀνάγκη ης ἡ

neck αὐχήν ένος ὁ, τράχηλος ου ὁ

need *noun* ἔνδεια ας ἡ; σπάνις εως ἡ; *verb* δέομαι + *gen*

needle βελόνη ης ἡ

neglect *noun* ἀμέλεια ας ἡ; *verb* ἀμελέω + *gen*

negotiate with πράσσω πρός + *acc*; χρηματίζομαι + *dat*

neigh χρεμετίζω

neighbour γείτων ονος ὁ/ἡ

neighbouring ὅμορος ον, πρόσοικος ον, πρόσχωρος ον

neither *of two* οὐδέτερος α ον, μηδέτερος α ον

▪ **∼ ... nor** οὔτε … οὔτε, μήτε … μήτε

nephew ἀδελφιδοῦς οῦ ὁ

nerves νεῦρα ων τά

nest νεοσσιά ᾶς ἡ

net δίκτυον ου τό; ἀμφίβληστρον ου τό

never οὔποτε, μήποτε, οὐδέποτε, μηδέποτε

nevertheless ὅμως

new νέος α ον, καινός ή όν

newness καινότης ητος ἡ

news τὰ ἀγγελθέντα, καινόν τι

newsmonger λογοποιός οῦ ὁ

next (following) ἐπιγιγνόμενος η ον

▪ **∼ day** ὑστεραία ας ἡ

niece ἀδελφιδῆ ῆς ἡ

night νύξ νυκτός ἡ

▪ **by ∼** νυκτός

nightingale ἀηδών όνος ἡ

nine ἐννέα

▪ **∼ times** ἐνάκις

▪ **∼ hundred** ἐνακόσιοι αι α

▪ **∼ thousand** ἐνακισχίλιοι αι α

nineteen ἐννεακαίδεκα

ninety ἐνενήκοντα

ninth ἔνατος η ον

no longer οὐκέτι, μηκέτι

nobility (of character) γενναιότης ητος ἡ; (of birth) εὐγένεια ας ἡ

noble γενναῖος α ον, εὐγενής ές

nod νεύω

▪ **∼ in assent** ἐπινεύω

▪ **∼ in dissent** ἀνανεύω

noise ψόφος ου ὁ

nonsense φλυαρία ας ἡ, λῆρος ου ὁ

▪ **talk ∼** φλυαρέω, ληρέω

noon μεσημβρία ας ἡ

no-one οὐδείς οὐδεμία οὐδέν (οὐδεν-), μηδείς μηδεμία μηδέν (μηδεν-)

noose βρόχος ου ὁ

north (wind/region) βορέας ου ὁ

nose ῥίς ῥινός ἡ

nostrils ῥῖνες ων αἱ, μυκτῆρες ων οἱ

not οὐ (οὐκ, οὐχ), μή
■ **~ at all** οὐδαμῶς, μηδαμῶς, ἥκιστά γε
■ **~ only ... but also** οὐ μόνον ... ἀλλὰ καί
■ **~ yet** οὔπω, μήπω

note[1] (in music) τόνος ου ὁ

note[2] (marginal) παραγραφή ῆς ἡ
■ **~-book** δέλτος ου ἡ

nothing οὐδέν, μηδέν

notice: escape ~ λανθάνω

notorious περιβόητος ον, πολυθρύλητος ον

nourish τρέφω

nourishment τροφή ῆς ἡ

now νῦν; (already) ἤδη

nowhere οὐδαμοῦ, μηδαμοῦ
■ **to ~** οὐδαμόσε

nudge νύσσω

null: ~ and void ἄκυρος ον

number ἀριθμός οῦ ὁ; (multitude) πλῆθος ους τό

numberless μυρίος α ον *usu pl*

nurse τροφός οῦ ὁ/ἡ

nut κάρυον ου τό

nymph νύμφη ης ἡ

Oo

oak δρῦς δρυός ἡ

oar κώπη ης ἡ

oath ὅρκος ου ὁ
■ **bind by ~** ὁρκόω

obedient ὑπήκοος ον

obey πείθομαι + *dat*

object *noun* σκοπός οῦ ὁ; *verb* ἀντιλέγω

objection ἀντιλογία ας ἡ, ἔγκλημα ατος τό

obligation ὀφείλημα ατος τό

oblique πλάγιος α ον

obliterate ἐξαλείφω, ἀφανίζω

oblong προμήκης ες

obol ὀβολός οῦ ὁ

obscene αἰσχρός ά όν, ἀπρεπής ές

obscenity ἀπρέπεια ας ἡ

obscure ἀσαφής ές, δύσκριτος ον

observe σκοπέω, θεάομαι

obstacle ἐμπόδισμα ατος τό

obstinacy αὐθάδεια ας ἡ

obstinate αὐθάδης ες

obstruct ἐμποδίζω

obstructive ἐμπόδιος ον

obtain κτάομαι
■ **~ by lot** λαγχάνω

obviously δηλονότι, σαφῶς, φανερῶς

occasion καιρός οῦ ὁ

occupy (hold) κατέχω
■ **~ oneself with** πραγματεύομαι περί + *gen*

occur (take place) γίγνομαι; (suggest itself) παρίσταμαι

odd (unusual) ἄτοπος ον; (not even) περισσός ή όν

of course πῶς γὰρ οὔ;

offence (legal) ἀδικία ας ἡ, ἀδίκημα ατος τό; (moral) ἁμαρτία ας ἡ, ἁμάρτημα ατος τό

offensive πικρός ά όν, βαρύς εῖα ύ, ἐπαχθής ές

offer παρέχω, προτείνω

offering (in temple) ἀνάθημα ατος τό

officious πολυπράγμων ον (πολυπραγμον-)

often πολλάκις
■ **as ~ as** ὁσάκις, ὁπότε

oil ἔλαιον ου τό

ointment ἀλοιφή ῆς ἡ

old (aged) γεραιός ά όν; (antique) ἀρχαῖος α ον, παλαιός ά όν
■ **~ age** γῆρας ως τό
■ **grow ~** γηράσκω
■ **so ~** τηλικοῦτος αύτη οῦτον
■ **~ man** γέρων οντος ὁ
■ **~ woman** γραῦς γραός ἡ

oligarchy ὀλιγαρχία ας ἡ, οἱ ὀλίγοι

olive (tree) ἐλάα ας ἡ
■ **~ oil** ἔλαιον ου τό

omen σημεῖον ου τό, οἰωνός οῦ ὁ

omission παράλειψις εως ἡ

omit παραλείπω, παρίημι

on ἐπί + *gen*; ἐν + *dat*
■ **~ account of** διά + *acc*
■ **~ behalf of** ὑπέρ + *gen*
■ **~ foot** πεζός ή όν
■ **~ the one had … ~ the other** μέν … δέ

once (single time) ἅπαξ; (formerly/~ upon a time) ποτέ
■ **at ~** εὐθύς

one εἷς μία ἕν (ἑν-)
■ **~ after another** ἐφεξῆς
■ **~ another** ἀλλήλους ας α
■ **~ by ~** καθ' ἕκαστον
■ **the ~ … the other** ὁ μέν … ὁ δέ
■ **~ *or* the other (of two)** ἕτερος α ον

onion κρόμμυον ου τό

only *adj* μόνος η ον; *adv* μόνον

onto εἰς + *acc*; ἐπί + *acc*

open *adj* ἀνεῳγμένος η ον; *verb tr* ἀνοίγνυμι, ἀνοίγω

openly φανερῶς

opinion γνώμη ης ἡ, δόξα ης ἡ

opponent ἐναντίος ου ὁ

opportunity καιρός οῦ ὁ

oppose ἐναντιόομαι + *dat*

opposite *adj* ἐναντίος α ον; *adv* πέραν, καταντικρύ

oppress πιέζω

oppressive βαρύς εῖα ύ

or ἤ

oracle (place *or* response) μαντεῖον ου τό, χρηστήριον ου τό; (response) χρησμός οῦ ὁ

orator ῥήτωρ ορος ὁ

order *noun* (orderly arrangement) κόσμος ου ὁ; (good discipline) εὐταξία ας ἡ; *verb* (command) κελεύω
■ **in ~** ἐφεξῆς
■ **in ~ to** ἵνα, ὅπως, ὡς

ordinary συνήθης ες, κοινός ή όν

organize διακοσμέω, διατίθημι, συσκευάζω

origin ἀρχή ῆς ἡ

orphaned ὀρφανός ή όν

ostracism ὀστρακισμός οῦ ὁ

ostracize ὀστρακίζω

ostrich στρουθός οῦ ὁ/ἡ

other ἄλλος η ο; *of two* ἕτερος α ον

otherwise (if not) εἰ δὲ μή; (in another way) ἄλλως

ought δεῖ, χρή, ὀφείλω

our ἡμέτερος α ον *foll def article*

ourselves *refl* ἡμᾶς αὐτούς άς

outbid ὑπερβάλλω

outcry καταβοή ῆς ἡ

outflank περιέχω

outline *noun* τύπος ου ὁ

outlive περιγίγνομαι

outrage *noun* ὕβρις εως ἡ, αἰκία ας ἡ

out of ἐκ (ἐξ) + *gen*

outside ἔξω + *gen*

oven ἰπνός οῦ ὁ, κάμινος ου ἡ

over ὑπέρ + *gen*

overcome (master) κρατέω + *gen*; (subdue) καταστρέφομαι; (excel) περιγίγνομαι + *gen*

overflow ὑπερβάλλω, ἐπικλύζω

overhear παρακούω

overjoyed περιχαρής ές

overlook περιοράω

overtake καταλαμβάνω

overthrow καταβάλλω, ἀναστρέφω, καθαιρέω

owe ὀφείλω

owl γλαῦξ γλαυκός ἡ

own: one's ~ οἰκεῖος α ον, ἴδιος α ον

ox βοῦς βοός ὁ

oyster ὄστρεον ου τό

Pp

pack up συσκευάζομαι

pain λύπη ης ἡ, ὀδύνη ης ἡ, πάθος ους τό
- **feel ~** ἀλγέω
- **cause ~** λυπέω

painful ἀλγεινός ή όν, λυπηρός ά όν

painless ἄλυπος ον

paint *verb* ζωγραφέω; *noun* χρώματα ων τά; (for face) ψιμύθιον ου τό

painter ζωγράφος ου ὁ

painting ζωγραφία ας ἡ

palace βασίλεια ων τά

pale ὠχρός ά όν

palisade σταυροί ῶν οἱ

palm (tree) φοῖνιξ ικος ὁ/ἡ

pan κεράμιον ου τό

panic ἔκπληξις εως ἡ, ταραχή ῆς ἡ, φόβος ου ὁ

papyrus βύβλος ου ἡ

paralysed: be ~ παραλύομαι

pardon *noun* συγγνώμη ης ἡ; *verb* συγγιγνώσκω + *dat*

parents γονεῖς έων οἱ

park παράδεισος ου ὁ

parrot ψίττακος ου ὁ

parsley σέλινον ου τό

part μέρος ους τό
- **for the most ~** ὡς ἐπὶ τὸ πολύ
- **take ~ in** μετέχω + *gen*

particular: in ~ καὶ δὴ καί

partly ... partly τὰ μέν ... τὰ δέ

partridge πέρδιξ ικος ὁ/ἡ

pass *noun* (mountain ~) εἰσβολή ῆς ἡ, στενά ῶν τά; *verb* (go past) παρέρχομαι; (of time) *tr* διάγω, διατρίβω; *intr* διέρχομαι
- **~ through** διαβαίνω
- **~ word along** παραγγέλλω

passable διαβατός όν
- **easily ~** εὔπορος ον

passage πόρος ου ὁ, διάβασις εως ἡ; (in book) χωρίον ου τό

passion πάθος ους τό

past *prep* παρά + *acc*
- **in the ~** ἐν τῷ παρελθόντι χρόνῳ

path ἀτραπός οῦ ἡ

patient: be ~ καρτερέω, ἀνέχομαι

pay *noun* μισθός οῦ ὁ; *verb* τίνω
- **give ~** μισθοδοτέω
- **receive ~** μισθοφορέω
- **~ back** ἀποδίδωμι
- **~ tax *or* tribute** φέρω, τελέω
- **~ the penalty** δίκην δίδωμι

pea πίσος ου ὁ

peace εἰρήνη ης ἡ
- **make ~** σπένδομαι, εἰρήνην ποιέομαι
- **remain at ~** εἰρήνην ἄγω

■ ~ **treaty** σπονδαί ῶν αἱ

peacock ταώς ὦ ὁ

pearl μαργαρίτης ου ὁ

pebble ψῆφος ου ἡ

pelt βάλλω

penalty δίκη ης ἡ
■ **pay the** ~ δίκην δίδωμι
■ **exact the** ~ **from** δίκην λαμβάνω παρά + *gen*

people (community) δῆμος ου ὁ; (nation) ἔθνος ους τό

perceive αἰσθάνομαι

perception αἴσθησις εως ἡ

perfect τέλειος (α) ον, ἐντελής ές

perforate τρυπάω

perfume (smell) ὀσμή ῆς ἡ, εὐοσμία ας ἡ; (substance) μύρον ου τό
■ ~**-seller** μυροπώλης ου ὁ
■ ~**-shop** μυροπώλιον ου τό

perfumed εὐώδης ες

perhaps ἴσως

perish ἀπόλλυμαι, διαφθείρομαι, ἀποθνῄσκω

perjured ἐπίορκος ον

perjury ἐπιορκία ας ἡ
■ **commit** ~ ἐπιορκέω

permanent μόνιμος ον

permit ἐάω

perplexed: be ~ ἀπορέω, ἀμηχανέω

perplexity ἀπορία ας ἡ

persecute διώκω

persevere καρτερέω + *pple*; διατελέω + *pple*

personal ἴδιος α ον, οἰκεῖος α ον

persuade πείθω

persuasion πειθώ οῦς ἡ

persuasive πιθανός ή όν

petal πέταλον ου τό

phantom φάσμα ατος τό

philosopher φιλόσοφος ου ὁ

phrase ῥῆμα ατος τό

pick [flowers etc.] δρέπω, συλλέγω
■ ~ **up** ἀναιρέομαι

pickpocket βαλαντιοτόμος ου ὁ
■ **be a** ~ βαλαντιοτομέω

picture εἰκών όνος ἡ, γραφή ῆς ἡ

piece μέρος ους τό, μόριον ου τό

pierce τρυπάω

piety εὐσέβεια ας ἡ

pig ὗς ὑός ὁ/ἡ

pillar κίων ονος ὁ/ἡ

pillow προσκεφάλαιον ου τό

pilot κυβερνήτης ου ὁ

pin περόνη ης ἡ

pine (tree) πεύκη ης ἡ, ἐλάτη ης ἡ

pious εὐσεβής ές
■ **be** ~ εὐσεβέω

pipe (musical instrument) σῦριγξ ιγγος ἡ

piracy λῃστεία ας ἡ

pirate λῃστής οῦ ὁ

pit βάραθρον ου τό, χάσμα ατος τό

pitch[1] (of voice) τόνος ου ὁ

pitch[2] (tar) πίσσα ης ἡ

pitch[3]: ~ **camp** στρατοπεδεύομαι

pitch[4]: **to such a** ~ ἐς τοσοῦτο + *gen*

pitiable ἐλεεινός όν

pity *noun* ἔλεος ους τό; *verb* οἰκτείρω + *gen*; ἐλεέω

place[1] *noun* τόπος ου ὁ, χωρίον ου τό
■ **to this** ~ δεῦρο
■ **to another** ~ ἄλλοσε
■ **take** ~ γίγνομαι

place[2] *verb* τίθημι, ἵστημι

plague νόσος ου ἡ, λοιμός οῦ ὁ

plain[1] *noun* πεδίον ου τό

plain[2] *adj* δῆλος η ον, φανερός (ά) όν
■ **it is** ~ **that I ...** δῆλός εἰμι + *pple*; φαίνομαι + *pple*

plaintiff ὁ διώκων

plait πλέκω

plan *noun* βουλή ῆς ἡ, διάνοια ας ἡ; *verb* βουλεύομαι, ἐπινοέω, διανοέομαι

plane (~ tree) πλάτανος ου ἡ

plant *noun* φυτόν οῦ τό; *verb* φυτεύω

platform βῆμα ατος τό

play *noun* (of children) παιδιά ᾶς ἡ; (on stage) δρᾶμα ατος τό; *verb* παίζω
■ **~ the lyre** κιθαρίζω

plea σκῆψις εως ἡ, πρόφασις εως ἡ

plead (as pretext or excuse) προφασίζομαι; (in defence) ἀπολογέομαι

pleader (in court) συνήγορος ου ὁ

pleasant ἡδύς εῖα ύ

please (be pleasing to) ἀρέσκω + *dat*

pleased: be ~ with ἥδομαι + *dat*

pleasure ἡδονή ῆς ἡ

plentiful ἄφθονος ον

plot *noun* ἐπιβουλή ῆς ἡ
■ **~ against** ἐπιβουλεύω + *dat*

plough *noun* ἄροτρον ου τό; *verb* ἀρόω

plunder *noun* (act of plundering) ἁρπαγή ῆς ἡ; (booty) λεία ας ἡ; *verb* πορθέω, ἁρπάζω, συλάω

poacher νυκτερευτής οῦ ὁ

pocket θυλάκιον ου τό

poem ποίησις εως ἡ, ποίημα ατος τό

poet ποιητής οῦ ὁ

poetry ποίησις εως ἡ

point[1]: beside the ~ ἔξω τοῦ λόγου
■ **to the ~** πρὸς λόγον

point[2]: ~ out ἀποδείκνυμι, δηλόω

poison φάρμακον ου τό

poisoner φαρμακεύς έως ὁ

poke κεντέω

police τοξόται ων οἱ

polished ξυστός ή όν

political πολιτικός ή όν

politician ῥήτωρ ορος ὁ

politics τὰ τῆς πόλεως πράγματα

pollute μιαίνω

polluted μιαρός ά όν

pollution μίασμα ατος τό, ἄγος ους τό

pomegranate ῥοιά ᾶς ἡ

pompous σεμνός ή όν

ponder ἐνθυμέομαι

pool λίμνη ης ἡ

poor ἄπορος ον
■ **~ man** πένης ητος ὁ

poppy μήκων ωνος ἡ

popular δημοτικός ή όν

populous πολυάνθρωπος ον

porch στοά ᾶς ἡ

position τάξις εως ἡ
■ **be in a bad ~** κακῶς διάκειμαι

possess ἔχω, κέκτημαι

possession: gain ~ of κρατέω + *gen*

possessions κτήματα ων τά, χρήματα ων τά

possible δυνατός ή όν
■ **as far as ~** κατὰ τὸ δυνατόν
■ **it is ~** ἔξεστι, πάρεστι
■ **as X as ~** ὡς + *sup*

possibly ἴσως, τάχα

postpone ἀναβάλλω

pot χύτρα ας ἡ

potter κεραμεύς έως ὁ

pour χέω

poverty πενία ας ἡ

power δύναμις εως ἡ, κράτος ους τό, ῥώμη ης ἡ
■ **in the ~ of** ἐπί + *dat*

powerful δυνατός ή όν

practice (act of practising) μελέτη ης ἡ, ἄσκησις εως ἡ, ἐπιτήδευσις εως ἡ; (habit *or* custom) ἔθος ους τό, ἐπιτήδευμα ατος τό

practise μελετάω, ἀσκέω, ἐπιτηδεύω

praise *noun* ἔπαινος ου ὁ; *verb* ἐπαινέω

pray: ~ to εὔχομαι + *dat*

prayer εὐχή ῆς ἡ

precautions: take ~ εὐλαβέομαι

precinct (sacred) τέμενος ους τό

precipice κρημνός οῦ ὁ

precipitous κρημνώδης ες

precise ἀκριβής ές

precision ἀκρίβεια ας ἡ

precursor πρόδρομος ου ὁ

prefer προαιρέομαι

pregnant ἔγκυος ον
■ **be ~** κύω

prejudge προκαταγιγνώσκω, προλαμβάνω

premature ἄωρος ον

premeditate προνοέω, προβουλεύω

preparation παρασκευή ῆς ἡ

prepare παρασκευάζω

presence παρουσία ας ἡ
■ **in the ~ of** παρά + *dat*
■ **into the ~ of** παρά +*acc*

present[1]**: be ~** πάρειμι

present[2]**: the ~** (time) τὸ νῦν
■ **for the ~** ἐν τῷ παρόντι, πρὸς τὸ παρόν
■ **at the ~ moment** τὸ παραυτίκα
■ **~ state of affairs** τὰ παρόντα

preserve σῴζομαι

press πιέζω

pressed: be hard ~ πιέζομαι, πονέω, ταλαιπωρέω

P

prestige ἀξίωμα ατος τό

pretence πρόσχημα ατος τό

pretend προσποιέομαι

pretext πρόφασις εως ἡ

prevent κωλύω

price τιμή ῆς ἡ

prick κεντέω

pride[1] (in good sense) φιλοτιμία ας ἡ; (in bad sense) ὕβρις εως ἡ

pride[2]**: ~ oneself on** ἀγάλλομαι + *dat*

priest ἱερεύς έως ὁ

priestess ἱέρεια ας ἡ

prison δεσμωτήριον ου τό

prisoner δεσμώτης ου ὁ
■ **~ of war** αἰχμάλωτος ου ὁ

private ἴδιος α ον
■ **~ citizen** (ordinary person *or* layman) ἰδιώτης ου ὁ

privately ἰδίᾳ

prize ἆθλον ου τό

probable: what is ~ εἰκός ότος τό
■ **it is ~ that** εἰκός ἐστι + *acc* + *infin*

probably κατὰ τὸ εἰκός

procession πομπή ῆς ἡ

proclaim κηρύσσω, προλέγω

proclamation κήρυγμα ατος τό

proconsul (Roman) ἀνθύπατος ου ὁ

procrastinate ἀναβάλλομαι

produce (cause) παρέχω, ποιέω

profess ἐπαγγέλλομαι

profit *noun* κέρδος ους τό, λῆμμα ατος τό; *verb intr* κερδαίνω
■ **~ by** ἀπολαύω + *gen*
■ **it ~s** συμφέρει + *dat*, λυσιτελεῖ + *dat*

profitable λυσιτελής ές, ὠφέλιμος ον

profusion ἀφθονία ας ἡ

prolong μηκύνω, ἐκτείνω

promise *noun* ὑπόσχεσις εως ἡ; *verb* ὑπισχνέομαι
■ **~ in marriage** ἐγγυάω

promontory ἀκρωτήριον ου τό, ἄκρα ας ἡ

proof (evidence) τεκμήριον ου ὁ; (test) πεῖρα ας ἡ; (demonstration) ἀπόδειξις εως ἡ

prop ἔρεισμα ατος τό

properly ἐπιεικῶς

property χρήματα ων τά, οὐσία ας ἡ

prophecy (oracle) μαντεῖον ου τό, χρηστήριον ου τό; (art of prediction) μαντεία ας ἡ, μαντική ῆς ἡ

prophesy χράω, μαντεύομαι

prophet μάντις εως ὁ, προφήτης ου ὁ

prophetic μαντικός ή όν

propitiate [a god] ἱλάσκομαι

propose προτίθημι, προφέρω
■ **~ a law** γράφω νόμον

prose: in ~ *adj* ψιλός ή όν

prosecute (at law) διώκω, κατηγορέω + *gen*

prosecution κατηγορία ας ἡ

prosecutor κατήγορος ου ὁ, ὁ διώκων

prosper (of person) εὐτυχέω; (of thing) προχωρέω

prosperity εὐπραξία ας ἡ, εὐτυχία ας ἡ, εὐδαιμονία ας ἡ

prostitute πόρνη ης ἡ

prostitution πορνεία ας ἡ

protect (guard) φυλάσσω; (save) σῴζω

protest *verb* δεινὸν ποιέομαι, σχετλιάζω

protrude ἐξίσταμαι

proud (bad sense) σεμνός ή όν, ὑπερήφανος ον
■ **I am ~ of** (good sense) ἀγάλλομαι + *dat*

prove (demonstrate) ἀποδείκνυμι, ἀποφαίνω; (turn out) ἐκβαίνω, συμβαίνω

proverb παροιμία ας ἡ, γνώμη ης ἡ
■ **in the words of the ~** τὸ λεγόμενον

provide πορίζω, παρέχω

provided that ἐφ᾽ ᾧτε + *infin*

provisions ἐπιτήδεια ων τά

provoke παροξύνω

prow πρῷρα ας ἡ

prudence σωφροσύνη ης ἡ, εὐλάβεια ας ἡ

prudent σώφρων ον (σωφρον-)

public δημόσιος α ον, κοινός ή όν
■ **be engaged in ~ life** πολιτεύομαι, τὰ δημόσια πράσσω

publicly δημοσίᾳ

pull ἕλκω, σπάω

pumpkin κολοκύνθη ης ἡ

punish κολάζω, ζημιόω

punishment ζημία ας ἡ, τιμωρία ας ἡ

pupil μαθητής οῦ ὁ

puppet κόρη ης ἡ

pure καθαρός ά όν

purification κάθαρσις εως ἡ

purify καθαίρω

purple πορφυροῦς ᾶ οῦν

purpose διάνοια ας ἡ, βουλή ῆς ἡ, γνώμη ης ἡ
■ **for the ~ of** ἐπί + *dat*
■ **for that very ~** ἐπ᾽ αὐτὸ τοῦτο
■ **on ~** ἐπιτηδές, ἐκ προνοίας
■ **to no ~** μάτην, ἄλλως

purse βαλάντιον ου τό

pursue διώκω

pursuit (study *or* occupation) ἐπιτήδευμα ατος τό

push ὠθέω

put τίθημι
■ **~ to sea** ἀνάγομαι
■ **~ in to shore** κατάγομαι
■ **~ off** (postpone) ἀναβάλλω
■ **~ on** [clothes] ἐνδύω, ἀμφιέννυμι
■ **~ up with** ἀνέχομαι

puzzling ἄπορος ον

pyre πυρά ᾶς ἡ

Qq

quality (value) ἀξία ας ἡ; (inherent property) πάθος ους τό; (distinguishing feature) ἴδιον ου τό

quarrel *noun* ἔρις ιδος ἡ; *verb* ἐρίζω + *dat*, διαφέρομαι + *dat*

quarry λιθοτομία ας ἡ

quay κρηπίς ῖδος ἡ

queen βασίλεια ας ἡ

quench κατασβέννυμι

quest ζήτησις εως ἡ

question *noun* ἐρώτημα ατος τό; *verb* ἐρωτάω

quibble *noun* σόφισμα ατος τό; *verb* σοφίζομαι

quick ταχύς εῖα ύ

quicken σπεύδω

quiet *noun* ἡσυχία ας ἡ; *adj* ἥσυχος ον
■ **keep ~** ἡσυχάζω, ἡσυχίαν ἔχω

quietly ἀτρέμα(ς), ἡσύχως

quiver[1] *verb* τρέμω

quiver[2] (for arrows) φαρέτρα ας ἡ

quote προφέρω, προβάλλομαι

Rr

rabble ὄχλος ου ὁ

race *noun* (nation) γένος ους τό, ἔθνος ους τό; (running) δρόμος ου ὁ, ἀγών ἀγῶνος ὁ; *verb* ἁμιλλάομαι, σταδιοδρομέω

radical (person) νεωτεριστής οῦ ὁ
■ **~ reform** νεωτερισμός οῦ ὁ

raft σχεδία ας ἡ

rag ῥάκος ους τό

rain *noun* ὑετός οῦ ὁ; *verb impers* (it ~s) ὕει

rainy ὄμβριος (α) ον

raise (lift) αἴρω; (make stand) ἀνίστημι

raisin ἀσταφίς ίδος ἡ

ram[1] *noun* (sheep) κριός οῦ ὁ

ram[2] *verb* (of ship) ἐμβάλλω + *dat*

random: at ~ εἰκῇ

rank τάξις εως ἡ

ransom *noun* λύτρον ου τό; *verb* λύομαι

rant δημηγορέω

rare σπάνιος α ον

rash *adj* (of person) προπετής ές

rashly ἀσκεπτῶς, προπετῶς

rather *adv* μᾶλλον
■ **~ than** μᾶλλον ἤ

ratify κυρόω

rational εὔλογος ον

rattle *noun* κρόταλον ου τό; *verb* (make to ~) κροτέω

ravage τέμνω

raven κόραξ ακος ὁ

ravine χαράδρα ας ἡ, φάραγξ αγγος ἡ

raw ὠμός ή όν

rawness ὠμότης ητος ἡ

ray ἀκτίς ῖνος ἡ

raze καθαιρέω, κατασκάπτω

razor ξυρόν οῦ τό

reach προσέρχομαι πρός + *acc*, ἀφικνέομαι πρός + *acc*

read ἀναγιγνώσκω

readiness ἑτοιμότης ητος ἡ, προθυμία ας ἡ

reading ἀνάγνωσις εως ἡ

ready ἑτοῖμος (η) ον
■ **be ~** ὑπάρχω

real ἀληθής ές

reality: in ~ ἔργῳ, ἀληθῶς

reap δρέπω, θερίζω

reaper θεριστής οῦ ὁ

reappear ἀναφαίνομαι

rear[1] *noun* (of marching column) οἱ ὄπισθε(ν)
■ **in the ~** κατὰ νώτου
■ **~-guard** οἱ ὀπισθοφύλακες

rear[2] *verb* (bring up) τρέφω

reason *noun* (cause) αἰτία ας ἡ, αἴτιον ου τό; (rational faculty) νοῦς νοῦ ὁ, λόγος ου ὁ; *verb* λογίζομαι

reasonable: it is ~ εἰκός ἐστι

reasoning λόγος ου ὁ, λογισμός οῦ ὁ

reassure θαρσύνω, παραμυθέομαι

rebel *noun* ὁ ἀποστάς, ὁ ἀφεστηκώς; *verb* ἀφίσταμαι

rebellion στάσις εως ἡ, ἐπανάστασις εως ἡ
rebound ἀναπηδάω
rebuild ἀνοικοδομέω, ἀνορθόω
rebuke ὀνειδίζω + *dat*, ἐπιτιμάω + *dat*
recall ἀνακαλέω; (from exile) κατάγω
recast ἀναπλάσσω
receive δέχομαι, λαμβάνω
recently ἄρτι, νεωστί
recess μυχός οῦ ὁ
reckon (calculate) λογίζομαι
reckless προπετής ές, ἀλόγιστος ον
reclaim ἀπαιτέω
recline κατακλίνω
recognition ἀναγνώρισις εως ἡ
recognize ἀναγνωρίζω
reconcile συναλλάσσω, διαλλάσσω
reconciliation διαλλαγή ῆς ἡ
reconnoitre κατασκοπέω
reconquer ἀνακτάομαι
reconsider ἀναλογίζομαι, ἀναπυλέω
record *noun* ἀναγραφή ῆς ἡ; *verb* ἀναγράφω, διαμνημονεύω
■ **~-office** τὸ δημόσιον
recount διεξέρχομαι
recourse: have ~ to τρέπομαι εἰς *or* πρός + *acc*, καταφεύγω εἰς *or* πρός + *acc*
recover (get back) ἀναλαμβάνω
■ **~ health** ῥαίζω, ἀναπνέω
■ **~ courage** ἀναθαρρέω
recovery ἀναπνοή ῆς ἡ
rectangular προμήκης ες
rectify ἐπανορθόω
recumbent ὕπτιος α ον
red ἐρυθρός ά όν
redistribute [land etc.] ἀναδατέομαι
reduce *tr* (lessen) ἐλασσόω
redundant περισσός ή όν
reed κάλαμος ου ὁ
reef (of rock) ἕρμα ατος τό
re-establish ἐπανορθόω
refer ἀναφέρω, ἀνάγω
refill *verb* ἀναπληρόω
refit *verb* ἐπισκευάζω
reflect (ponder) ἐνθυμέομαι, φροντίζω
reflection *noun* (in mirror) ἔμφασις εως ἡ
reform *verb* (restore) ἐπανορθόω; (innovate) νεωτερίζω
refrain from ἀπέχομαι + *gen*; ἀπέχομαι μή + *infin*
refresh ἀναψύχω
refreshment ἀναψυχή ῆς ἡ, ἀνάπαυσις εως ἡ
refuge: take ~ in καταφεύγω εἰς + *acc*
refuse οὐκ ἐθέλω, οὔ φημι, ἀρνέομαι
refutation ἔλεγχος ους τό
refute ἐξελέγχω
register *noun* ἀπογραφή ῆς ἡ; *verb* ἐγγράφω
registration ἐγγραφή ῆς ἡ
regret *noun* μετάνοια ας ἡ, μεταμέλεια ας ἡ; *verb* μετανοέω; *impers* μεταμέλει + *dat*
rehearsal διδασκαλία ας ἡ
reign *noun* ἀρχή ῆς ἡ; *verb* βασιλεύω, ἄρχω
rein ἡνία ας ἡ
reinforce (come to help) ἐπιβοηθέω + *dat*, ἐπικουρέω + *dat*
reinforcements βοήθεια ας ἡ, βοηθοί ῶν οἱ
reject ἀπωθέω, ἀποπτύω
rejoice (at) χαίρω + *dat or pple*, ἥδομαι + *dat or pple*
related (by blood) οἰκεῖος α ον, συγγενής ές
relax *tr* παρίημι, χαλάω; *intr* λωφάω
release *noun* ἀπαλλαγή ῆς ἡ; *verb* ἀπολύω, ἀπαλλάσσω, ἀφίημι
relentless ἀπαραίτητος ον
reliable πιστός ή όν, ἀξιόπιστος ον

relief ἀπαλλαγή ῆς ἡ

religion τὰ τῶν θεῶν; (piety) εὐσέβεια ας ἡ

reluctance ὄκνος ου ὁ

rely on πιστεύω + *dat*, πείθομαι + *dat*

remain μένω, καταμένω, ἐπιμένω

remaining λοιπός ή όν

remarkable διαπρεπής ές, ἀξιόλογος ον, θαυμάσιος α ον

remedy ἄκος ους τό

remember μέμνημαι + *gen*

remind ἀναμιμνῄσκω

removable ἐξαιρετός όν

removal ἀνάστασις εως ἡ

remove *tr* μεθίστημι
■ **~ from home** *intr* ἐπανίσταμαι

renew ἀνανεόομαι

rent *noun* μίσθωμα ατος τό; *verb* (let out for ~) μισθόω; (take for ~) μισθόομαι

repair ἐπισκευάζω

repay ἀποδίδωμι

repeal λύω

repeat ἐπαναλαμβάνω

repel ἀμύνομαι, ἀπωθέω

repent *impers* μεταμέλει + *dat*

repentance μεταμέλεια ας ἡ, μετάνοια ας ἡ

report *noun* φήμη ης ἡ

reply ἀποκρίνομαι, ὑπολαμβάνω

repress κατέχω

reproach *noun* ὄνειδος ους τό; *verb* ὀνειδίζω

reptile ἑρπετόν οῦ τό

repugnant ἐπαχθής ές

repulse ἀποκρούομαι

reputation δόξα ης ἡ
■ **have a good ~** καλῶς ἀκούω

request *noun* αἴτησις εως ἡ, χρεία ας ἡ; *verb* αἰτέω

rescue σῴζω
■ **come to the ~** βοηθέω + *dat*, ἐπαμύνω + *dat*

resemble ἔοικα + *dat*

resembling (like) ὅμοιος α ον + *dat*; (nearly like) παραπλήσιος (α) ον

resign *tr* παραδίδωμι; *intr* ἐξίσταμαι + *gen*

resist ἀντέχω, ἀμύνομαι, ἀνθίσταμαι + *gen*

resolute (persistent) καρτερός ά όν, ἰσχυρός ά όν

resolutely θαρραλέως

resort to τρέπομαι εἰς + *acc*

resources παρασκευή ῆς ἡ, τὰ ὑπάρχοντα

respect *noun* τιμή ῆς ἡ, αἰσχύνη ης ἡ; *verb* τιμάω, αἰσχύνομαι

respite ἀνάπαυλα ης ἡ

responsible (accountable) ὑπεύθυνος ον
■ **~ for** αἴτιος α ον + *gen*

rest[1] *noun* ἀνάπαυσις εως ἡ, παῦλα ης ἡ; *verb* (halt) ἀναπαύομαι; (keep quiet) ἡσυχάζω

rest[2]**: the ~ of** *adj* λοιπός ή όν, ὁ ἄλλος

restore (give back) ἀποδίδωμι; (rebuild) ἐπανορθόω

restrain κατέχω, ἀπέχω, κωλύω

result *noun* τέλος ους τό, τὸ γενόμενον, τὸ συμβεβηκός; *verb* ἀποβαίνω
■ **with the ~ that** ὥστε

retire (withdraw) ὑποχωρέω

retreat ἀναχωρέω
■ **~ before** ὑπεξέρχομαι

retribution νέμεσις εως ἡ

retrieve ἀναλαμβάνω

return[1] *noun* (especially from exile) κάθοδος ου ἡ; *verb intr* ἐπανέρχομαι, ἀναχωρέω
■ **~ from exile** κατέρχομαι

return[2] *verb tr* (give back) ἀποδίδωμι

reveal δηλόω, μηνύω, ἐκφαίνω

revel *noun* κῶμος ου ὁ; *verb* κωμάζω

reveller κωμαστής οῦ ὁ

r

revenge *noun* τιμωρία ας ἡ
■ **~ oneself on** τιμωρέομαι, ἀντιτιμωρέομαι

revenue πρόσοδος ου ἡ *usu pl*

revive *intr* ἀναβιόω, ἀναπνέω

revolt *noun* ἀπόστασις εως ἡ; *verb* ~ (from) ἀφίσταμαι + *gen*
■ **cause to ~** ἀφίστημι

revolution (political) νεωτερισμός οῦ ὁ
■ **make a ~** νεωτερίζω

reward *noun* (prize) δῶρον ου τό; (pay) μισθός οῦ ὁ; *verb* χάριν ἀποδίδωμι + *dat*

rhetoric ῥητορική ῆς ἡ

rhythm ῥυθμός οῦ ὁ

rib πλευρά ᾶς ἡ *usu pl*

ribbon ταινία ας ἡ

rice ὄρυζα ης ἡ

rich πλούσιος α ον

riches πλοῦτος ου ὁ

rid: get ~ of ἀπαλλάσσομαι + *gen*

riddle αἴνιγμα ατος τό

ride [horse] ἱππεύω; [chariot] ἐλαύνω; [in carriage] φέρομαι

rider ἱππότης ου ὁ

ridge λόφος ου ὁ

ridiculous γελοῖος α ον, καταγέλαστος ον

right[1] (hand side) δεξιός ά όν

right[2] (fair *or* just) δίκαιος α ον; (correct *or* genuine) ὀρθός ή όν
■ **it is ~** προσήκει, πρέπει
■ **think it ~** ἀξιόω
■ **~ time** καιρός οῦ ὁ

rigid ἄκαμπτος ον, στερεός ά όν

ring (for finger) δακτύλιος ου ὁ; σφραγίς ῖδος ἡ

rinse πλύνω

riotous ταραχώδης ες

ripe ὡραῖος α ον
■ **be ~** ἀκμάζω

rise (get up) ἀνίσταμαι; (of the sun) ἀνατέλλω; (in revolt) ἐπανίσταμαι

risk *noun* κίνδυνος ου ὁ; *verb tr* παραβάλλομαι
■ **run a ~** κινδυνεύω
■ **~ everything** διακινδυνεύω

rite τελετή ῆς ἡ

rival *adj* ἀντίπαλος ον; *verb* (compete) ἀνταγωνίζομαι; (equal) ἐξισόομαι

rivalry (mostly bad sense) φιλονικία ας ἡ

river ποταμός οῦ ὁ

road ὁδός οῦ ἡ

roar βρυχάομαι

rob ἀφαιρέομαι, ἀποστερέω

robber λῃστής οῦ ὁ

robbery κλοπή ῆς ἡ, λῃστεία ας ἡ

robe πέπλος ου ὁ

rock πέτρα ας ἡ

rocky πετρώδης ες

rod ῥάβδος ου ἡ, κανών όνος ὁ

rogue πανοῦργος ου ὁ

roll *verb tr* κυλίνδω; *intr* κυλίνδομαι

roof ὄροφος ου ὁ, τέγος ους τό

room θάλαμος ου ὁ, οἴκημα ατος τό

root ῥίζα ης ἡ

rope σχοινίον ου τό, κάλως ω ὁ

rose ῥόδον ου τό

rostrum βῆμα ατος τό

rot σήπομαι

rotten σαπρός ά όν

rotunda θόλος ου ἡ

rough (rugged) τραχύς εῖα ύ; (harsh) σκληρός ά όν

round[1] *adj* κύκλιος (α) ον

round[2] *prep* περί + *acc*

rouse ἐγείρω, παροξύνω, ἐπαίρω

row[1] *noun* (line) στίχος ου ὁ

row[2] *verb* [boat] ἐρέσσω

rower ἐρέτης ου ὁ

rowing εἰρεσία ας ἡ
■ **~-bench** σέλμα ατος τό

royal βασιλικός ή όν

rub τρίβω

■ ~ **out** ἀφανίζω, ἐξαλείφω

rubble χάλιξ ικος ὁ

rudder πηδάλιον ου τό

rude (insulting) ὑβριστικός ή όν; (boorish) ἄγροικος ον

ruin *noun* ὄλεθρος ου ὁ; *verb* ἀπόλλυμι, διαφθείρω, καθαιρέω

rule[1]: as a ~ ὡς ἐπὶ τὸ πολύ

rule[2] *noun* ἀρχή ῆς ἡ; *verb* ἄρχω + *gen*, κρατέω + *gen*; (be king) βασιλεύω

rulers οἱ ἄρχοντες, οἱ ἐν τέλει

run *verb* τρέχω

■ ~ **a risk** κινδυνεύω

■ **at a ~** δρόμῳ

runaway δραπέτης ου ὁ

runner δρομεύς έως ὁ; (in race) σταδιοδρόμος ου ὁ

running *noun* δρόμος ου ὁ

rush *noun* (hurry) ὁρμή ῆς ἡ; *verb* ὁρμάομαι, σπεύδω

Ss

sack[1] *noun* θύλακος ου ὁ

sack[2] *verb* [city] πορθέω, λῄζομαι

sacred ἱερός ά όν

■ ~ **precinct** τέμενος ους τό

sacrifice *noun* θυσία ας ἡ; *verb* θύω

sacrilege (temple robbery) ἱεροσυλία ας ἡ

■ **commit ~** ἱεροσυλέω

sacrilegious ἱερόσυλος ον

sad (of person) οἰκτρός ά όν, ἄθυμος ον

saddle ἐφίππιον ου τό

safe ἀσφαλής ές

■ **come ~ly to** σῴζομαι εἰς *or* πρός + *acc*

safety σωτηρία ας ἡ, ἀσφάλεια ας ἡ

sail *noun* ἱστίον ου τό; *verb* πλέω

sailor ναύτης ου ὁ

sake: for the ~ of ἕνεκα *foll gen*

salary μισθός οῦ ὁ

sale πρᾶσις εως ἡ

■ **for ~** ὤνιος (α) ον, πράσιμος ον

salt ἅλς ἁλός ὁ

salvation σωτηρία ας ἡ

same ὁ αὐτός ἡ αὐτή τὸ αὐτό

■ **at the ~ time (as)** ἅμα + *dat*

sample δεῖγμα ατος τό

sand ψάμμος ου ἡ

sandal πέδιλον ου τό *usu pl*

sandy ψαμμώδης ες

sane ἔμφρων ον (ἐμφρον-)

sarcasm εἰρωνεία ας ἡ

satisfactory ἐπιτήδειος (α) ον, ἱκανός ή όν

satisfied: be ~ *impers* ἀρκεῖ + *dat*

■ **be ~ with** στέργω; ἀρέσκομαι + *dat*

satisfy (please) ἀρέσκω + *dat*

sauce ὄψον ου τό

savage ἄγριος α ον

save σῴζω

saviour σωτήρ ῆρος ὁ

saw *noun* πρίων ονος ὁ; *verb* πρίω

say λέγω, φημί

saying (proverb *or* maxim) παροιμία ας ἡ

scabbard κολεός οῦ ὁ

scale (of fish etc.) λεπίς ίδος ἡ

scales τρυτάνη ης ἡ

■ **turn of the ~** ῥοπή ῆς ἡ

scapegoat φαρμακός οῦ ὁ

scar οὐλή ῆς ἡ

scarce σπάνιος α ον

scarcely μόλις

scarcity σπάνις εως ἡ, ἔνδεια ας ἡ

scarf ταινία ας ἡ

scatter *tr* διασκεδάννυμι; *intr* διασκεδάννυμαι

scattered διεσπαρμένος η ον

scent (smell, odour) ὀσμή ῆς ἡ

school διδασκαλεῖον ου τό

scoff σκώπτω

scout κατάσκοπος ου ὁ

scrape ξέω

scratch κνάω

scrutiny δοκιμασία ας ἡ

sculpt γλύφω

scythe δρέπανον ου τό

sea θάλασσα ης ἡ
■ **open ~** πέλαγος ους τό
■ **by ~** κατὰ θάλασσαν
■ **~-battle** ναυμαχία ας ἡ
■ **put out to ~** ἀνάγομαι
■ **~-coast** παραλία ας ἡ

seal[1] (ring *or* impression) σφραγίς ῖδος ἡ

seal[2] (animal) φώκη ης ἡ

seam ῥαφή ῆς ἡ

search *noun* ζήτησις εως ἡ

search for *verb* (seek) ζητέω, ἐρευνάω

season ὥρα ας ἡ

seated: be ~ κάθημαι

second δεύτερος α ον

secret *adj* (not to be divulged) ἀπόρρητος ον; (hidden) κρυπτός ή όν

secretary γραμματεύς έως ὁ

secretly λάθρᾳ, *or use* λανθάνω

secure *verb* βεβαιόω; *adj* βέβαιος (α) ον, ἀσφαλής ές

security σωτηρία ας ἡ, ἀσφάλεια ας ἡ; βεβαιότης ητος ἡ

see ὁράω

seed σπέρμα ατος τό

seek ζητέω

seem δοκέω, φαίνομαι
■ **it ~s good** δοκεῖ

seize συλλαμβάνω

self αὐτός ή ό
■ **~-control** σωφροσύνη ης ἡ
■ **~-sufficient** αὐτάρκης ες
■ **~-willed** αὐθάδης ες
■ **be ~-willed** αὐθαδίζομαι

sell πωλέω, ἀποδίδομαι

semicircle ἡμικύκλιον ου τό

send πέμπω
■ **~ for** μεταπέμπομαι

senses: be in one's ~ εὖ φρονέω

sensible φρόνιμος ον

sent *adj* πεμπτός ή όν

separate *verb tr* διαχωρίζω, διίστημι; *intr* διίσταμαι

separately χωρίς, δίχα

serious (earnest) σπουδαῖος α ον

servant οἰκέτης ου ὁ, ὑπηρέτης ου ὁ

serve [gods] θεραπεύω; (in fleet etc.) ὑπηρετέω; (as slave) δουλεύω

service ὑπηρεσία ας ἡ, θεραπεία ας ἡ

set (of sun) δύω
■ **~ (up)** ἵστημι, τίθημι
■ **~ free** λύω, ἀφίημι
■ **~ sail** αἴρω, ἀνάγομαι

setting (of sun) δυσμή ῆς ἡ

settle (arrange) καθίστημι; (manage) διοικέω; (resolve) διατίθεμαι, διακρίνομαι

seven ἑπτά
■ **~ times** ἑπτάκις
■ **~ hundred** ἑπτακόσιοι αι α
■ **~ thousand** ἑπτακισχίλιοι αι α

seventeen ἑπτακαίδεκα

seventh ἕβδομος η ον

seventy ἑβδομήκοντα

severe (harsh) τραχύς εῖα ύ, σκληρός ά όν

sew ῥάπτω

sex (gender) γένος ους τό

sexual: ~ pleasures ἀφροδίσια ων τά

shade σκιά ᾶς ἡ

shaded σκιερός ά όν
shaft (of spear) ξυστόν οῦ τό
shaggy λάσιος α ον
shake *tr* σείω
shame αἰσχύνη ης ἡ, αἰδώς οῦς ἡ
■ **feel ~** αἰσχύνομαι
shameful αἰσχρός ά όν
shameless ἀναιδής ές, ἀναίσχυντος ον
shape μορφή ῆς ἡ
shapeless ἄμορφος ον
shapely εὔμορφος ον
share *noun* μέρος ους τό; *verb* μετέχω + *gen*
■ **give a ~ of** μεταδίδωμι + *gen*
sharp ὀξύς εῖα ύ
sharpen ἀκονάω
shatter *tr* συντρίβω
shave ξυρέω
shaving κουρά ᾶς ἡ
she αὕτη, ἥδε, ἐκείνη
sheath κολεός οῦ ὁ
sheep οἶς οἰός ὁ/ἡ, πρόβατα ων τά
sheet φᾶρος ους τό
shell λεπίς ίδος ἡ
shelter καταφυγή ῆς ἡ
shepherd ποιμήν ένος ὁ
shield ἀσπίς ίδος ἡ
■ **light ~** πέλτη ης ἡ
■ **wicker ~** γέρρον ου τό
■ **~-factory** ἀσπιδοπηγεῖον ου τό
shin ἀντικνήμιον ου τό
shine ἐκλάμπω, φαίνω
shingle κάχληξ ηκος ὁ
shining λαμπρός ά όν
ship ναῦς νεώς ἡ
■ **war~** τριήρης ους ἡ
■ **merchant ~** ὁλκάς άδος ἡ
shipwrecked: be ~ ναυαγέω
shirk ἀποκνέω, ἀποτρέπομαι
shiver φρίσσω
shoe ὑπόδημα ατος τό
■ **~maker** σκυτοτόμος ου ὁ
shoot βάλλω
■ **~ arrows** τοξεύω
shop καπηλεῖον ου τό
shore αἰγιαλός οῦ ὁ
short βραχύς εῖα ύ
shoulder ὦμος ου ὁ
shout *noun* βοή ῆς ἡ; *verb* βοάω
show δηλόω, δείκνυμι, φαίνω
shrill ὀξύς εῖα ύ
shrink from ἀποκνέω + *acc or infin*
shrivel κατισχναίνω
shut κλείω
■ **~ in** ἐγκλείω, κατείργω
shuttle κερκίς ίδος ἡ
sick: be ~ νοσέω
sickle δρέπανον ου τό
side πλευρά ᾶς ἡ
sides: from all ~ πανταχόθεν
■ **on all ~** πανταχῇ, πανταχοῦ
siege πολιορκία ας ἡ
■ **lay ~ to** πολιορκέω
■ **take by ~** ἐκπολιορκέω
sieve κόσκινον ου τό
sight ὄψις εως ἡ
■ **catch ~ of** καθοράω
■ **~-seeing** θεωρία ας ἡ
sign σημεῖον ου τό; (portent) τέρας ατος τό
signal *noun* σημεῖον ου τό; *verb* σημαίνω
silence σιγή ῆς ἡ, σιωπή ῆς ἡ
■ **keep ~** σιγάω, σιωπάω
silently σιγῇ
silver *noun* ἄργυρος ου ὁ; *adj* ἀργυροῦς ᾶ οῦν
similar ὅμοιος α ον
■ **nearly ~** παραπλήσιος (α) ον
similarly ὁμοίως, ὡσαύτως
simple ἁπλοῦς ῆ οῦν
simply ἁπλῶς; (absolutely) ἀτεχνῶς
since (because) ὅτι, ἐπεί
■ **~ the time when** ἐξ οὗ

sing ᾄδω

single ἁπλοῦς ῆ οῦν

sink *tr* καταδύω; *intr* καταδύνω, καταδύομαι

sister ἀδελφή ῆς ἡ

sit καθίζω, καθέζομαι

situated κείμενος η ον

six ἕξ
■ **~ times** ἑξάκις
■ **~ hundred** ἑξακόσιοι αι α
■ **~ thousand** ἑξακισχίλιοι αι α

sixteen ἑκκαίδεκα

sixth ἕκτος η ον

sixty ἑξήκοντα

size μέγεθος ους τό

skilful (in) ἐπιστήμων ον (ἐπιστημον-) + *gen*

skill τέχνη ης ἡ

skin *noun* χροιά ᾶς ἡ; (hide) δέρμα ατος τό; (for wine) ἀσκός οῦ ὁ; *verb* ἀποδέρω

skirmish *noun* ἀκροβολισμός οῦ ὁ; *verb* ἀκροβολίζομαι

skull κρανίον ου τό

sky οὐρανός οῦ ὁ

slab (of stone) στήλη ης ἡ

slacken χαλάω, ἀνίημι

slander *noun* διαβολή ῆς ἡ; *verb* διαβάλλω

slanting πλάγιος α ον

slap ῥαπίζω

slaughter *noun* φόνος ου ὁ, σφαγή ῆς ἡ

slave δοῦλος ου ὁ

slavery δουλεία ας ἡ

sleek λιπαρός ά όν

sleep *noun* ὕπνος ου ὁ; *verb* καθεύδω
■ **go to ~** καταδαρθάνω

sleepless ἄγρυπνος ον

sleeplessness ἀγρυπνία ας ἡ

sleeve χειρίς ῖδος ἡ

slide ὀλισθάνω

slim λεπτός ή όν

slime βόρβορος ου ὁ

sling *noun* σφενδόνη ης ἡ; *verb* σφενδονάω

slinger σφενδονήτης ου ὁ

slip σφάλλομαι; (stumble) πταίω
■ **let ~** παρίημι, ἀφίημι

slow βραδύς εῖα ύ

slowly σχολῇ

small μικρός ά όν

smear ἀλείφω, χρίω

smell *noun* ὀσμή ῆς ἡ; *verb tr* ὀσφραίνομαι + *gen*; *intr* ὄζω

smile *verb* μειδιάω

smoke καπνός οῦ ὁ

smooth λεῖος α ον

snake ὄφις εως ὁ, δράκων οντος ὁ

snare *noun* ἕρκος ους τό, πάγη ης ἡ; *verb* ἐφεδρεύω

sneeze *noun* πταρμός οῦ ὁ; *verb* πταίρω

snore ῥέγκω

snort ῥέγκω

snout ῥύγχος ους τό

snow *noun* χιών όνος ἡ; *verb* νείφω

so (in such a way *or* to such an extent) οὕτω(ς); (consequently) οὖν*
■ **it is ~** οὕτως ἔχει
■ **~ great** τοσοῦτος αύτη οῦτο(ν)
■ **~ greatly** ἐς τοσοῦτο(ν)
■ **~ many** τοσοῦτοι αῦται αῦτα
■ **~ that** (in order to) ἵνα, ὅπως, ὡς; (with the result) ὥστε
■ **~ be it!** ἔστω

soak βρέχω

socket αὐλός οῦ ὁ

sod βῶλος ου ἡ

sofa κλίνη ης ἡ

soft μαλακός ή όν, ἁπαλός ή όν

soften *tr* μαλάσσω

soldier στρατιώτης ου ὁ

solemn σεμνός ή όν

solid στερεός ά όν

some τις τι (τιν-), ἔνιοι αι α
■ **~ … others** οἱ μέν … οἱ δέ
■ **~ to ~ places, others to others** ἄλλοι … ἄλλοσε

somehow πως

someone τις τινός

sometime ποτέ

sometimes ἐνίοτε

son υἱός οῦ ὁ, παῖς παιδός ὁ

song ᾠδή ῆς ἡ, ὕμνος ου ὁ

soon δι' ὀλίγου, τάχα

soothe πραΰνω

soothsayer μάντις εως ὁ, χρησμῳδός οῦ ὁ

sorry: be ~ μεταμέλομαι + *pple or gen*; impers μεταμέλει + *dat*

sorts: of all ~ παντοῖος α ον, παντοδαπός ή όν

soul ψυχή ῆς ἡ

sound *noun* φθόγγος ου ὁ; *verb* φθέγγομαι

soup ζωμός οῦ ὁ

sour ὀξύς εῖα ύ, πικρός ά όν

south μεσημβρία ας ἡ
■ **~ wind** νότος ου ὁ

sow σπείρω

space: plenty of ~ εὐρυχωρία ας ἡ
■ **lack of ~** στενοχωρία ας ἡ
■ **leave a ~** διαλείπω

spare *adj* (surplus) περισσός ή όν; *verb* φείδομαι + *gen*

sparkle στίλβω

sparrow στρουθός οῦ ὁ/ἡ

spasm σπασμός οῦ ὁ

speak λέγω
■ **~ evil of** κακὰ λέγω
■ **~ well of** εὖ λέγω
■ **~ Greek** ἑλληνίζω
■ **~ in public** δημηγορέω

speaker: public ~ ῥήτωρ ορος ὁ

spear δόρυ ατος τό, αἰχμή ῆς ἡ

special ἐξαίρετος ον

species εἶδος ους τό

specify διορίζω

specimen δεῖγμα ατος τό

speckled ποικίλος η ον

spectator θεατής οῦ ὁ

spectre φάσμα ατος τό

speculate (on) θεωρέω

speculation σκέψις εως ἡ, θεωρία ας ἡ

speech (language) φωνή ῆς ἡ, γλῶσσα ης ἡ; (oration) λόγος ου ὁ, ῥῆσις εως ἡ

speechless ἄφωνος ον

speedily ταχέως, διὰ τάχους

spend ἀναλίσκω; [time] διάγω

spider ἀράχνη ης ἡ

spike στυράκιον ου τό

spill *tr* ἐκχέω; *intr* ἐκχέομαι

spin [thread] νέω

spindle ἄτρακτος ου ὁ

spine ῥάχις εως ἡ

spirit (soul) ψυχή ῆς ἡ; (ardour) φρόνημα ατος τό, θυμός οῦ ὁ; (intention) διάνοια ας ἡ; (divine power) δαίμων ονος ὁ/ἡ

spit[1] *noun* (for roasting) ὀβελός οῦ ὁ

spit[2] *verb* πτύω

spite φθόνος ου ὁ

spiteful κακοήθης ες
■ **~ abuse** ἐπήρεια ας ἡ

splendid λαμπρός ά όν, εὐπρεπής ές

split σχίζω, διατέμνω

spoil[1] *noun* (booty) λεία ας ἡ

spoil[2] *noun* (ruin) διαφθείρω

sponge σπόγγος ου ὁ

sponsor ἐγγυητής οῦ ὁ

spread *tr* στόρνυμι

spring[1] (season) ἔαρ ῆρος τό
■ **at the start *or* return of ~** ἅμα τῷ ἦρι

spring[2] (well *or* fountain) κρήνη ης ἡ

sprinkle ἐπιπάσσω

spur[1] *noun* κέντρον ου τό

spur[2]**: ~ on** *verb* ἐποτρύνω

spurn λακτίζω, καταφρονέω + *gen*

spy *noun* κατάσκοπος ου ὁ; *verb* κατασκοπέω

square *adj* τετράγωνος ον

squash θλίβω, πιέζω

squeeze θλίβω

stable σταθμός οῦ ὁ

stag ἔλαφος ου ὁ

stage: ~(-building) σκηνή ῆς ἡ

stain *noun* μίασμα ατος τό; *verb* μιαίνω

stale σαπρός ά όν

stalk (of plant) καυλός οῦ ὁ, καλάμη ης ἡ

stammer ψελλίζομαι

stamp *noun* τύπος ου ὁ, χαρακτήρ ῆρος ὁ; *verb* [coin etc.] χαράσσω, κόπτω

stand *tr* (put in) place ἵστημι; *intr* ἵσταμαι
▪ **~ up** ἀνίσταμαι
▪ **~ by** ἐμμένω + *dat*, παρίσταμαι + *dat*
▪ **~ one's ground** ὑπομένω, ὑφίσταμαι
▪ **~ in the way of** ἐναντιόομαι + *dat*

star ἀστήρ έρος ὁ

start (set out) ἀφορμάομαι; ἄπειμι ἀπιέναι

starting-point ἀφορμή ῆς ἡ

starve *tr* λιμοκτονέω; *intr* πεινάω

state (political) πόλις εως ἡ, τὸ κοινόν
▪ **be in a certain ~** ἔχω + *adv*, διάκειμαι + *adv*

station (position) στάσις εως ἡ

stationary στάσιμος ον

statue (usu of god) ἄγαλμα ατος τό, (of human being) ἀνδριάς άντος ὁ

stay μένω

steadily βεβαίως

steady (stationary) στάσιμος ον; (steadfast) βέβαιος (α) ον

steal κλέπτω
▪ **~ away** *intr* ὑπεξέρχομαι

steel ἀδάμας αντος ὁ

steep κατάντης ες

steer κυβερνάω

step-mother μητρυιά ᾶς ἡ

stern (of ship) πρύμνη ης ἡ

steward ταμίας ου ὁ

stick *noun* ῥάβδος ου ἡ; *verb tr* κολλάω, συνάπτω; *intr* προσέχομαι + *dat*, πρόσκειμαι + *dat*

sticky γλίσχρος ον

stiff στερεός ά όν, ἄκαμπτος ον

still[1] *adj* (quiet) ἥσυχος ον

still[2] (even now) ἔτι; (nevertheless) ὅμως, μέντοι*

sting *noun* κέντρον ου τό, οἶστρος ου ὁ; *verb* δάκνω, κεντέω

stingy φειδωλός ή όν

stitch *verb* ῥάπτω

stomach γαστήρ τρός ἡ

stone *noun* λίθος ου ὁ; *adj* λίθινος ον
▪ **~-mason** λιθουργός οῦ ὁ
▪ **precious ~** λίθος ου ἡ

stop *verb tr* παύω, κωλύω; *intr* παύομαι

storm χειμών ῶνος ὁ

stormy χειμέριος (α) ον

story λόγος ου ὁ, μῦθος ου ὁ

straight εὐθύς εῖα ύ, ὀρθός ή όν

straighten ὀρθόω

strain τείνω

straits (of sea) πορθμός οῦ ὁ, στενά ῶν τά

strange δεινός ή όν, ἄτοπος ον

stranger ξένος ου ὁ

strap ἱμάς άντος ὁ

straw καλάμη ης ἡ

stream ῥεῖθρον ου τό

street ὁδός οῦ ἡ

strength ἰσχύς ύος ἡ, δύναμις εως ἡ, ῥώμη ης ἡ
▪ **have ~** ἰσχύω

strengthen βεβαιόω

stretch τείνω

strife ἔρις ιδος ἡ

strigil στλεγγίς ίδος ἡ

strike τύπτω, παίω, κρούω

string (of lyre) χορδή ῆς ἡ; (of bow) νευρά ᾶς ἡ

strip (undress) *tr* ἀποδύω; *intr* ἀποδύνω, ἀποδύομαι

strong ἰσχυρός ά όν, καρτερός ά όν

stronghold ἔρυμα ατος τό

struggle *noun* ἀγών ῶνος ὁ, ἅμιλλα ης ἡ; *verb* ἀγωνίζομαι, ἁμιλλάομαι

stubborn αὐθάδης ες; σκληρός ά όν

student μαθητής οῦ ὁ

study (learn) μανθάνω; (practise) μελετάω; (examine) ἐξετάζω

stumble πταίω, σφάλλομαι

stupefy ἐκπλήσσω

stupid ἀμαθής ές, μῶρος α ον

style (of writer) λέξις εως ἡ

subdue καταστρέφομαι

subject[1] *noun* (theme) ὑπόθεσις εως ἡ, λόγος ου ὁ; (matter) χρῆμα ατος τό

subject[2]**: ~ (to)** *adj* ὑπήκοος ον + *gen*

subjugate καταστρέφομαι

sublime ὑψηλός ή όν

substitute *verb* ὑποβάλλομαι, ἀντικαθίστημι

subtract ἀφαιρέω

subtraction ἀφαίρεσις εως ἡ

suburb προάστειον ου τό

subvert ἀναστρέφω

succeed (of people) κατορθόω, εὖ πράσσω, εὐτυχέω; (of things) προχωρέω

success εὐτυχία ας ἡ, εὐπραγία ας ἡ
■ **without ~** ἄπρακτος ον

successful εὐτυχής ές

succession διαδοχή ῆς ἡ

successor διάδοχος ου ὁ

such (of ~ a kind) τοιοῦτος αύτη οῦτο(ν)
■ **to ~ a pitch of** ἐς τοσοῦτο + *gen*

sudden αἰφνίδιος ον

suddenly ἐξαίφνης, ἄφνω

suffer πάσχω

suffice ἀρκέω

sufficient ἱκανός ή όν

suggest ὑποτίθεμαι, ὑποτείνω

suggestion ὑποθήκη ης ἡ; (advice) παραίνεσις εως ἡ

suitable ἐπιτήδειος (α) ον

suitor μνηστήρ ῆρος ὁ

sulky δύσκολος ον

sullen σκυθρωπός όν

summary κεφάλαιον ου τό

summer θέρος ους τό

summit ἄκρα ας ἡ, κορυφή ῆς ἡ

summon προσκαλέω, μεταπέμπομαι
■ **~ back from exile** κατάγω

sun ἥλιος ου ὁ

sunrise ἡλίου ἀνατολή ῆς ἡ

sunset ἡλίου δύσις εως ἡ
■ **at ~** ἅμ' ἡλίῳ καταδύντι

superficial ἐπιπόλαιος ον

superior κρείσσων ον (κρεισσον-)
■ **be ~ to** διαφέρω + *gen*

superstition δεισιδαιμονία ας ἡ

superstitious δεισιδαίμων ον (δαισιδαιμον-)

supervise ἐπιστατέω + *dat*

supper δεῖπνον ου τό
■ **have ~** δειπνέω

suppliant ἱκέτης ου ὁ
■ **be a ~** ἱκετεύω

supplication ἱκετεία ας ἡ

supplies ἐπιτήδεια ων τά
■ **get ~** ἐπισιτίζομαι

supply *verb* παρέχω, πορίζω

support[1] *noun* (prop) ἔρεισμα ατος τό

support[2] *verb* (prop up) ἐρείδω; (maintain *or* feed) τρέφω
■ **~ oneself** (make a living) βιοτεύω

suppose (assume) ὑπολαμβάνω; (think) νομίζω

suppress κατέχω
supremacy ἡγεμονία ας ἡ
sure: be ~ εὖ οἶδα
surely? ἆρ' οὐ (= ἆρα οὐ); πῶς οὐ;
surf ῥόθιον ου τό
surface ἐπιπολή ῆς ἡ
surname ἐπίκλησις εως ἡ
surpass προέχω + *gen*; ὑπερβάλλω
surplus *adj* περισσός ή όν
surrender *tr* παραδίδωμι; *intr* ἐνδίδωμι
surround περιέχω, κυκλόω
survey *verb* ἐφοράω, κατασκοπέω
survive περιγίγνομαι
suspect ὑποπτεύω, ὑπονοέω
suspend ἀρτάω, ἀνακρεμάννυμι
suspicion ὑποψία ας ἡ, ὑπόνοια ας ἡ
suspicious ὕποπτος ον
swagger ἀλαζονεύομαι
swallow[1] *noun* (bird) χελιδών όνος ἡ
swallow[2] *verb* καταπίνω
swarm ἑσμός οῦ ὁ
swear ὄμνυμι
■ **~ by** ἐπόμνυμι + *acc*
■ **~ falsely** ἐπιορκέω
sweat *noun* ἱδρώς ῶτος ὁ; *verb* ἱδρόω
sweep κορέω
sweet (pleasant) ἡδύς εῖα ύ; (to the taste) γλυκύς εῖα ύ
swell οἰδέω
swerve ἀποτρέπομαι
swift ταχύς εῖα ύ
swim νέω
swimmer κολυμβητής οῦ ὁ
swineherd συβώτης ου ὁ
sword ξίφος ους τό
■ **small ~** μάχαιρα ας ἡ
■ **~-maker** μαχαιροποιός οῦ ὁ
■ **~-factory** μαχαιροποιεῖον ου τό
sycophancy κολακεία ας ἡ
sycophant κόλαξ ακος ὁ
symbol σημεῖον ου τό, σύμβολον ου τό
sympathise with συμπάσχω + *dat*, συναλγέω + *dat*
symptom σημεῖον ου τό
system (method) μέθοδος ου ἡ; (order) κόσμος ου ὁ

Tt

table τράπεζα ης ἡ
tablet πίναξ ακος ὁ, δέλτος ου ἡ
tail κέρκος ου ἡ, οὐρά ᾶς ἡ
taint *noun* μίασμα ατος τό
take λαμβάνω, αἱρέω
■ **~ by surprise** καταλαμβάνω
■ **~ care of** ἐπιμελέομαι + *gen*
■ **~ hold of** λαμβάνομαι + *gen*
■ **~ over** παραλαμβάνω
■ **~ part in** μετέχω + *gen*
■ **~ place** γίγνομαι
talk λέγω
■ **~ about** διαλέγομαι περί + *gen*
■ **~ nonsense** φλυαρέω
talkative πολύλογος ον
tall μέγας μεγάλη μέγα (μεγαλ-)
tame *adj* ἥμερος ον; *verb* ἡμερόω
tar πίσσα ης ἡ
target σκοπός οῦ ὁ
tarnish μιαίνω
task ἔργον ου τό
taste *noun* γεῦμα ατος τό; *verb* γεύομαι + *gen*

tax φόρος ου ὁ

teach διδάσκω

teachable (person) εὐμαθής ές; (thing) διδακτός ή όν

teacher διδάσκαλος ου ὁ

teaching διδαχή ῆς ἡ

tear[1] *noun* (weeping) δάκρυον ου τό

tear[2] *noun* σχίσμα ατος τό; *verb* διασπάω

teat θηλή ῆς ἡ

tell (relate) λέγω; (order) κελεύω
■ **~ a story** μυθολογέω

temper (anger) ὀργή ῆς ἡ; (mood) τρόπος ου ὁ

temperance σωφροσύνη ης ἡ

temple νεώς ώ ὁ, ἱερόν οῦ τό

tempt πειράω, ἀναπείθω

tempting ἐπαγωγός όν

ten δέκα
■ **~ times** δεκάκις
■ **~ thousand** μύριοι αι α

tend (look after) θεραπεύω; (incline) φέρω εἰς + *acc*

tent σκηνή ῆς ἡ

tenth δέκατος η ον

tepid ὑπόθερμος ον

terms: come to ~ συμβαίνω
■ **on these ~** ἐπὶ τούτοις

terrible δεινός ή όν

terrify ἐκπλήσσω, φοβέω

terse σύντομος ον

test *noun* ἔλεγχος ου ὁ; *verb* ἐλέγχω, ἐξετάζω

testify μαρτυρέω

than ἤ

thank (be thankful) χάριν ἔχω

that[1] *pron and adj* ἐκεῖνος η ο

that[2] *conj* ὅτι, ὡς
■ **in order ~** ἵνα, ὅπως, ὡς
■ **with the result ~** ὥστε

theatre θέατρον ου τό

theft κλοπή ῆς ἡ

their *possessive* αὐτῶν
■ **~ own** *refl* ἑαυτῶν, σφέτερος α ον

them *acc/gen/dat pl of* αὐτός ή ό

themselves *refl* ἑαυτούς άς ά, σφᾶς αὐτούς άς

then (at that time) τότε, ἐνταῦθα; (next) ἔπειτα

there ἐκεῖ
■ **to ~** ἐκεῖσε
■ **from ~** ἐκεῖθεν

therefore οὖν*

they οὗτοι, οἵδε, ἐκεῖνοι

thick παχύς εῖα ύ, πυκνός ή όν; (of hair etc.) δασύς εῖα ύ

thief κλέπτης ου ὁ, λῃστής οῦ ὁ

thigh μηρός οῦ ὁ

thin λεπτός ή όν, ἰσχνός ή όν

thing χρῆμα ατος τό; (matter) πρᾶγμα ατος τό

think (regard *or* consider) νομίζω, οἴομαι, ἡγέομαι; (ponder) φροντίζω, ἐνθυμέομαι

thinness λεπτότης ητος ἡ

third τρίτος η ον

thirst δίψα ης ἡ

thirsty: be ~ διψάω

thirteen τρεῖς καὶ δέκα

thirty τριάκοντα

this *pron and adj* (the preceding) οὗτος αὕτη τοῦτο; (the following) ὅδε ἥδε τόδε

thorn ἄκανθα ης ἡ

though καίπερ + *pple*

thought (concept) διάνοια ας ἡ, νόημα ατος τό; (intellectual principle) νοῦς νοῦ ὁ; (opinion) γνώμη ης ἡ, δόξα ης ἡ; (reflection) σύννοια ας ἡ, ἐνθύμησις εως ἡ

thoughtless ἀφρόντιστος ον

thoughtlessness ἄνοια ας ἡ, ἀβουλία ας ἡ

thousand χίλιοι αι α

thread νῆμα ατος τό

threat ἀπειλή ῆς ἡ

threaten ἀπειλέω + *dat*

three τρεῖς τρία
■ **~ times** τρίς
■ **~ hundred** τριακόσιοι αι α
■ **~ thousand** τρισχίλιοι αι α

thresh ἀλοάω

throat φάρυγξ υγγος ἡ

through διά + *gen*; (by means of *or* on account of) διά + *acc*

throughout ἀνά + *acc*

throw βάλλω, ῥίπτω

thrush κίχλη ης ἡ

thunder *noun* βροντή ῆς ἡ; *verb* βροντάω

thunderbolt κεραυνός οῦ ὁ

thus οὕτως, ὧδε

tie δέω, ἅπτω

tight σύντονος ον

tile κέραμος ου ὁ
■ **~-maker** κεραμεύς έως ὁ

till *prep* μέχρι + *gen*; *conj* ἕως

time χρόνος ου ὁ
■ **after a short ~** δι' ὀλίγου
■ **at the right ~** ἐς καιρόν, ἐν καιρῷ
■ **in the ~ of** ἐπί + *gen*

timely καίριος α ον

tin κασσίτερος ου ὁ

tired: be ~ ἀποκάμνω

to (towards) πρός + *acc*; (into) εἰς + *acc*; [~ a person] ὡς + *acc*
■ **~ and fro** ἄνω κάτω

toad φρύνη ης ἡ

today σήμερον

toe δάκτυλος ου ὁ

token σημεῖον ου τό, σύμβολον ου τό

tolerable ἀνεκτός όν, φορητός (ή) όν

tolerance καρτερία ας ἡ

tolerate φέρω, ἀνέχομαι

tomb τάφος ου ὁ

tomorrow αὔριον

tongue γλῶσσα ης ἡ

too: ~ (much) λίαν
■ **~ late** ὀψέ

tooth ὀδούς όντος ὁ
■ **with the teeth** ὀδάξ

top of *adj* ἄκρος α ον

torch λαμπάς άδος ἡ

tortoise χελώνη ης ἡ

torture *noun* βάσανος ου ἡ; *verb* βασανίζω

torturer βασανιστής οῦ ὁ

totter χωλεύω

touch ἅπτομαι + *gen*

towards πρός + *acc*

tower πύργος ου ὁ

town ἄστυ εως τό

trace *noun* ἴχνος ους τό, σημεῖον ου τό; *verb* ἰχνεύω

trade *noun* ἐμπορία ας ἡ; *verb* ἐμπορεύομαι

trader ἔμπορος ου ὁ

tragedian τραγῳδός οῦ ὁ, τραγῳδοποιός οῦ ὁ

tragedy (drama) τραγῳδία ας ἡ; (disaster) συμφορά ᾶς ἡ
■ **actor in ~** τραγῳδός οῦ ὁ
■ **put on a ~** τραγῳδέω

tragic (connected with ~ drama) τραγῳδικός ή όν; (sad) ἄθλιος α ον

train (educate) παιδεύω

training μελέτη ης ἡ, ἄσκησις εως ἡ

traitor προδότης ου ὁ

trample καταπατέω, λακτίζω

transfer *tr* μεταφέρω

transgress παραβαίνω

translate μεταγράφομαι

transparent διαφανής ές

transplant μεταφυτεύω

trap *noun* πάγη ης ἡ, ἐνέδρα ας ἡ

travel *verb* ὁδοιπορέω

treachery προδοσία ας ἡ

treasure θησαυρός οῦ ὁ

treasury θησαυρός οῦ ὁ

treat χράομαι + *dat*; μεταχειρίζω
■ **~ well** εὖ ποιέω

treaty σπονδαί ὧν αἱ

tree δένδρον ου τό

tremble τρέμω, ὀρρωδέω

trench τάφρος ου ἡ

trial (attempt) πεῖρα ας ἡ; (legal) δίκη ης ἡ

■ **be on ~** φεύγω, κρίνομαι

triangle τρίγωνον ου τό

tribe φῦλον ου τό, ἔθνος ους τό

tribute (tax) φόρος ου ὁ, δασμός οῦ ὁ

trick μηχάνημα ατος τό, δόλος ου ὁ

trireme τριήρης ους ἡ

■ **commander of a ~** τριήραρχος ου ὁ

trophy τροπαῖον ου τό

trouble πρᾶγμα ατος τό

■ **cause ~ to** πράγματα παρέχω + *dat*, ἐνοχλέω + *dat*

■ **take ~ over** σπουδάζω περί + *gen*

troublesome δυσχερής ές, λυπηρός ά όν

true ἀληθής ές

trumpet σάλπιγξ ιγγος ἡ

trumpeter σαλπιγκτής οῦ ὁ

trunk (of tree) στέλεχος ους τό

trust πιστεύω + *dat*

trustworthy πιστός ή όν, ἀξιόπιστος ον

truth ἀλήθεια ας ἡ, τὸ ἀληθές

■ **in ~** τῷ ὄντι

■ **speak the ~** ἀληθεύω

try (attempt) πειράομαι; (in court) κρίνω

tub σκάφη ης ἡ

tube σῦριγξ ιγγος ἡ

tune μέλος ους τό

tunic χιτών ῶνος ὁ

tunnel ὑπόνομος ου ὁ

turban μίτρα ας ἡ

turn *noun* τροπή ῆς ἡ; *verb tr* τρέπω, στρέφω

■ **~ away** *intr* ἀποστρέφομαι

■ **~ out** (result) ἀποβαίνω

tusk ὀδούς όντος ὁ

twelve δώδεκα

twenty εἴκοσι(ν)

twice δίς

twilight κνέφας ους τό

twin *adj* δίδυμος η ον

twist *tr* πλέκω

two δύο δυοῖν

■ **~ hundred** διακόσιοι αι α

■ **~ thousand** δισχίλιοι αι α

tyranny τυραννίς ίδος ἡ

tyrant τύραννος ου ὁ

■ **be a ~** τυραννεύω

Uu

udder θηλή ῆς ἡ

ugly δυσειδής ές, αἰσχρός ά όν

ulcer ἕλκος ους τό

unable: be ~ οὐ δύναμαι + *infin*, οὐκ ἔχω + *infin*, οὐχ οἷός τέ εἰμι + *infin*

unaccustomed ἀηθής ές

unanimously μιᾷ γνώμῃ

unarmed ἄοπλος ον, γυμνός ή όν

unasked ἄκλητος ον

unbelieving ἄπιστος ον

unburied ἄταφος ον

uncaring ἀμελής ές

uncertain (of people) ἄπορος ον, ἀμήχανος ον; (of things) ἄδηλος ον

uncle θεῖος ου ὁ

■ **paternal ~** πάτρως ως ὁ

■ **maternal ~** μήτρως ως ὁ

uncommon ἀηθής ές, ἄτοπος ον

uncover ἐκκαλύπτω
uncut ἄτομος ον, ἄτμητος ον
undefended ἀφύλακτος ον
under (motion) ὑπό + *acc*; (position) ὑπό + *dat*
undergo πάσχω, ὑφίσταμαι
underground ὑπόγαιος ον
understand συνίημι, ἐπίσταμαι
undertake ἐπιχειρέω + *dat*; ὑφίσταμαι, μεταχειρίζομαι
undeserved ἀνάξιος (α) ον
undisciplined ἄτακτος ον
undoubtedly δηλονότι
undress *tr* ἀποδύω; *intr* ἀποδύομαι
uneducated ἀπαίδευτος ον
unequal ἄνισος ον
unexamined ἀνεξέταστος ον
unexpected ἀπροσδόκητος ον
unfaithful ἄπιστος ον
unfashionable ἄκομψος ον
unfasten λύω, χαλάω
unfold ἀνελίσσω
unfortified ἄφρακτος ον, ἀτείχιστος ον
unfortunate δυστυχής ές
unfriendly δυσμενής ές
ungrateful ἀχάριστος ον
ungrudging ἄφθονος ον
unguarded ἀφύλακτος ον
unharmed ἀβλαβής ές
unholy ἀνόσιος ον
unhonoured ἄτιμος ον
unimportant φαῦλος (η) ον
uninhabited ἀοίκητος ον
uninitiated ἀμύητος ον
unintentional ἀκούσιος ον
unite *tr* συνάπτω; *intr* συνέρχομαι
universal κοινός ή όν
universe: the ~ τὸ ὅλον, τό πᾶν
unjust ἄδικος ον
unknown ἄγνωστος ον
unlawful ἄνομος ον, παράνομος ον
unless εἰ μή
unlike ἀνόμοιος ον + *dat*
unlimited ἄπειρος ον, ἄμετρος ον
unlucky κακοδαίμων ον (κακοδαιμον-)
unmarried ἄγαμος ον
unmixed (of wine) ἄκρατος ον
unmoved ἀκίνητος ον
unnatural ὑπερφυής ές, ἄτοπος ον
unobserved λάθρᾳ, *or use* λανθάνω
unpleasant ἀηδής ές, δυσχερής ές
unpopular: be ~ (with) ἀπεχθάνομαι + *dat*
unprepared ἀπαράσκευος ον
unprofitable ἀνωφελής ές, ἀλυσιτελής ές
unreasonable ἄλογος ον
unreliable σφαλερός ά όν
unrestrained ἀχάλινος ον, ἀκόλαστος ον
unroll ἀνελίσσω
unscrupulous πανοῦργος ον, πονηρός ά όν
unsuccessful (of people) ἄπρακτος ον; (of things) ἀτελής ές
unsuitable ἀνεπιτήδειος ον
unsuspected ἀνύποπτος ον
until *prep* μέχρι + *gen*; *conj* ἕως (ἄν), πρίν (ἄν)
untimely ἄκαιρος ον
untrustworthy ἄπιστος ον
unusual ἀηθής ές, ἄτοπος ον
unveil ἐκκαλύπτω
unwarlike ἀπόλεμος ον
unwashed ἄλουτος ον
unwept ἄκλαυ(σ)τος ον
unwilling ἄκων ἄκουσα ἆκον (ἀκοντ-)
unwise ἄβουλος ον
unworthy ἀνάξιος (α) ον
up ἀνά + *acc*
uproar θόρυβος ου ὁ

upside down ὕπτιος α ον
▪ **turn ~** ἄνω κάτω στρέφω

urge (persuade) πείθω, ἀξιόω; (induce) προτρέπω; (incite) ἐποτρύνω; (insist) ἰσχυρίζομαι

urgently σπουδῇ

use χράομαι + *dat*

useful χρήσιμος (η) ον

useless ἄχρηστος ον, οὐτιδανός ή όν

usual εἰωθώς υῖα ός (εἰωθοτ-), συνηθής ές
▪ **as is ~** κατὰ τὸ εἰωθός

utterly παντελῶς; (of destruction) κατ' ἄκρας

vacant κενός ή όν, ἔρημος (η) ον

vacillate ὀκνέω

vain: in ~ μάτην

valid κύριος α ον, βέβαιος (α) ον

valley νάπη ης ἡ

valuable τίμιος α ον, πολυτελής ές

value *noun* τιμή ῆς ἡ, ἀξία ας ἡ; *verb* τιμάω
▪ **~ highly** περὶ πολλοῦ ποιέομαι

vanish ἀφανίζομαι

variegated ποικίλος η ον

variety ποικιλία ας ἡ

various παντοῖος α ον

vegetables λάχανα ων τά

vehicle ὄχος ου ὁ

veil *noun* προκάλυμμα ατος τό; *verb* καλύπτω

vein φλέψ φλεβός ἡ

vengeance τιμωρία ας ἡ
▪ **take ~ on** τιμωρέομαι

verbose πολύλογος ον

verbosity πολυλογία ας ἡ

versatile εὐτράπελος ον

very μάλα, σφόδρα

victim (sacrificial) ἱερεῖον ου τό

victorious: be ~ νικάω

victory νίκη ης ἡ

view θέα ας ἡ

viewing θεωρία ας ἡ

vigilance εὐλάβεια ας ἡ

vigorous εὔτονος ον

village κώμη ης ἡ

villager κωμήτης ου ὁ

villain πανοῦργος ου ὁ

vine ἄμπελος ου ὁ

vinegar ὄξος ους τό

violence βία ας ἡ

violent βίαιος (α) ον

violet ἴον ου τό

viper ἔχιδνα ης ἡ

virgin παρθένος ου ἡ

virile ἀνδρικός ή όν

virtue ἀρετή ῆς ἡ

visible φανερός (ά) όν, δῆλος η ον, ἐμφανής ές

visit φοιτάω παρά + *acc*

voice φωνή ῆς ἡ

voluntary ἑκούσιος ου ὁ

volunteer ἐθελοντής οῦ ὁ

vomit ἐξεμέω

vortex δίνη ης ἡ

vote *noun* ψῆφος ου ἡ; *verb* ψηφίζομαι

vow *noun* εὐχή ῆς ἡ

voyage πλοῦς οῦ ὁ

vulgar φαῦλος (η) ον

vulture γύψ γυπός ὁ

Ww

wage(s) μισθός οῦ ὁ
■ **get ~** μισθοφορέω

wagon ἅμαξα ης ἡ

wait μένω
■ **~ for** προσδέχομαι

wake *tr* ἐγείρω; *intr* ἐγείρομαι

walk βαδίζω

wall τεῖχος ους τό

wallet πήρα ας ἡ

wallow κυλίνδομαι

wander πλανάομαι, ἀλάομαι

wanderer ἀλήτης ου ὁ, πλανήτης ου ὁ

want (wish) βούλομαι; (be in need of) δέομαι + *gen*

war πόλεμος ου ὁ
■ **be at ~** πολεμέω
■ **declare ~** πόλεμον καταγγέλλω
■ **make ~ on** πόλεμον ἐπιφέρω + *dat*

war-cry: raise a ~ ἀναλαλάζω

war-dance πυρρίχη ης ἡ

ward off ἀμύνω, ἀρκέω

warehouse ἀποθήκη ης ἡ

warlike μάχιμος (η) ον, πολεμικός ή όν

warm *adj* θερμός ή όν; *verb* θερμαίνω

warmth καῦμα ατος τό, θέρμη ης ἡ

warn νουθετέω; παραινέω + *dat*

warship τριήρης ους ἡ

wary εὐλαβής ές

wash *tr* λούω; *intr* λούομαι

wasp σφῆξ σφηκός ὁ

waste (throw away) προίεμαι
■ **~ time** διατρίβω

watch (look at) θεάομαι, θεωρέω; (guard) φυλάσσω, τηρέω

water ὕδωρ ατος τό

water-clock (for timing speeches in court) κλεψύδρα ας ἡ

wave κῦμα ατος τό

wax κηρός οῦ ὁ

way (route) ὁδός οῦ ἡ; (manner) τρόπος ου ὁ
■ **in any ~** πως
■ **in the ~** ἐμποδών
■ **out of the ~** ἐκποδών
■ **give ~** ὑποχωρέω
■ **in every ~** πανταχῇ
■ **in this ~** ταύτῃ

we ἡμεῖς

weak ἀσθενής ές

wealth πλοῦτος ου ὁ

weapon ὅπλον ου τό *usu pl*; (missile) βέλος ους τό

wear[1] [clothes] φορέω

wear[2]**: ~ out** κατατρίβω

weasel γαλῆ ῆς ἡ

weather: good ~ εὐημερία ας ἡ

weave ὑφαίνω

weep δακρύω

weigh down βαρύνω, πιέζω

weight βάρος ους τό

welcome *verb* ἀσπάζομαι, ὑποδέχομαι

weld συγκροτέω

well[1] *noun* φρέαρ ατος τό

well[2] *adv* εὖ
■ **be ~** (of things) καλῶς ἔχω
■ **~ done!** εὖ γε

well-disposed εὔνους ουν

west ἑσπέρα ας ἡ

wet ὑγρός ά όν
■ **make ~** βρέχω

whale κῆτος ους τό

what? τί; τίνος;

■ ~ **sort of?** ποῖος α ον

whatever (of ~ kind) ὁποῖος α ον

wheat πυρός οῦ ὁ

wheel τροχός οῦ ὁ

when?[1] πότε;

when[2] *conj* ἐπεί, ὅτε

whenever ὁπότε, ὅταν, ἐπειδάν

where: ~ (at)? ποῦ;
■ ~ **to?** ποῖ;
■ ~ **from?** πόθεν;
■ ~ **on earth?** ποῦ γῆς;
■ **at the place** ~ οὗ

wherever ὅπου

whether πότερον, εἰ
■ ~ **... or** πότερον ... ἤ

which?[1] τίς τί (τιν-)
■ ~ **of two?** πότερος α ον

which[2] *rel* (the one ~) ὅς ἥ ὅ

while ἕως, *or use pple*

whip *noun* μάστιξ ιγος ἡ; *verb* μαστιγόω

whirl δίνη ης ἡ

whirlwind σκηπτός οῦ ὁ, ἄελλα ης ἡ

whisper ψιθυρίζω

white λευκός ή όν

who?[1] τίς; (τιν-)

who[2] *rel* (the one ~) ὅς ἥ ὅ

whoever ὅστις ἥτις ὅ τι

whole πᾶς πᾶσα πᾶν (παντ-), ὅλος η ον

why? τί; διὰ τί;

wickedness πονηρία ας ἡ

wickerwork πλέγμα ατος τό

wide εὐρύς εῖα ύ

widow χήρα ας ἡ

width εὖρος ους τό

wife γυνή γυναικός ἡ

wild ἄγριος α ον
■ ~ **beast** θηρίον ου τό

wilderness ἐρημία ας ἡ

willing: be ~ ἐθέλω
■ ~**(ly)** ἑκών οὖσα όν (ἑκοντ-)

willow ἰτέα ας ἡ

win (be victorious) νικάω
■ ~ **prize** φέρομαι
■ ~ **over** προσάγομαι

wind[1] *noun* ἄνεμος ου ὁ

wind[2] *verb* πλέκω

window θυρίς ίδος ἡ

wine οἶνος ου ὁ

wing (of bird) πτερόν οῦ τό; (of army) κέρας ατος *or* ως τό

wink *verb* μύω

winter χειμών ῶνος ὁ

wintry χειμερινός ή όν

wipe (off) ἀπομάσσω

wisdom σοφία ας ἡ

wise σοφός ή όν

wish *noun* βούλημα ατος τό, ἐπιθυμία ας ἡ; *verb* βούλομαι

with μέτα + *gen, or use e.g.* ἔχων, ἄγων

withdraw *intr* ἀναχωρέω, ὑποχωρέω

wither φθίνω

withered ξηρός ά όν, ἰσχνός ή όν

within ἐντός + *gen*

without ἄνευ + *gen*

withstand ἀνθίσταμαι + *dat*; ὑπομένω

witness μάρτυς υρος ὁ
■ **bear** ~ μαρτυρέω
■ **call to** ~ μαρτύρομαι

witty κομψός ή όν, ἀστεῖος α ον

wizard γόης ητος ὁ

wolf λύκος ου ὁ

woman γυνή γυναικός ἡ

wonder *noun* θαῦμα ατος τό
■ ~ **(at)** θαυμάζω

wonderful θαυμαστός ή όν, θαυμάσιος α ον

wood (log(s)) ξύλον ου τό; (forest) ὕλη ης ἡ

wooden ξύλινος η ον

woodpecker πελεκᾶς ᾶντος ὁ

wool ἔριον ου τό

word λόγος ου ὁ

work *noun* ἔργον ου τό; *verb* ἐργάζομαι

workmanship δημιουργία ας ἡ

workshop ἐργαστήριον ου τό

world (inhabited earth) οἰκουμένη ης ἡ, γῆ γῆς ἡ; (universe) κόσμος ου ὁ

worm εὐλή ῆς ἡ

worry *verb intr* φροντίζω

worse κακίων ον (κακιον-), χείρων ον (χειρον-)

worship σέβομαι

worst κάκιστος η ον, χείριστος η ον

worth *noun* ἀξία ας ἡ

worthless (of people or things) φαῦλος (η) ον; (of things) ἀχρεῖος ον

worthy (of) ἄξιος α ον + *gen*

wound (hurt) *noun* τραῦμα ατος τό; *verb* τραυματίζω

woven ὑφαντός ή όν

wrap up ἐγκαλύπτω

wreath στέφανος ου ὁ

wreathe στέφω

wreck (of ship) ναυάγιον ου τό

wrestle παλαίω

wrestler παλαιστής οῦ ὁ

wrestling: ~ ground *or* school παλαίστρα ας ἡ

write γράφω

writer συγγραφεύς έως ὁ

wrong *noun* ἀδίκημα ατος τό; *adj* κακός ή όν, ἄδικος ον
▪ **do ~ to** ἀδικέω

YyZz

yawn *verb* χάσκω

year ἐνιαυτός οῦ ὁ, ἔτος ους τό
▪ **every ~** κατ' ἐνιαυτόν
▪ **twice a ~** δὶς τοῦ ἐνιαυτοῦ

yellow ξανθός ή όν

yes ναί

yesterday χθές

yet (still) ἔτι
▪ **not ~** οὔπω, μήπω
▪ **never ~** οὐδεπώποτε, μηδεπώποτε
▪ **and ~** καίτοι

yew μῖλαξ ακος ἡ

yield *tr* παραδίδωμι; *intr* εἴκω, ἐνδίδωμι

yoke *noun* ζυγόν οῦ ὁ; *verb* ζεύγνυμι

you *sg* σύ; *pl* ὑμεῖς

young νέος α ον
▪ **~ man** νεανίας ου ὁ

your (of you sg) σός σή σόν *foll def article*; (of you pl) ὑμέτερος α ον *foll def article*

yourself *refl* σεαυτόν ήν

yourselves *refl* ὑμᾶς αὐτούς άς

youth (time of ~) ἥβη ης ἡ, ἡλικία ας ἡ

zeal σπουδή ῆς ἡ

Zeus Ζεῦς Δίος ὁ

Numerals

	Cardinals	Ordinals	Adverbs
	one, two etc.	*first, second* etc.	*once, twice* etc.
1	εἷς, μία, ἕν	πρῶτ-ος, -η, -ον	ἅπαξ
2	δύο	δεύτερος	δίς
3	τρεῖς, τρία	τρίτος	τρίς
4	τέσσαρες, τέσσαρα	τέταρτος	τετράκις
5	πέντε	πέμπτος	πεντάκις
6	ἕξ	ἕκτος	ἑξάκις
7	ἑπτά	ἕβδομος	ἑπτάκις
8	ὀκτώ	ὄγδοος	ὀκτάκις
9	ἐννέα	ἔνατος	ἐνάκις
10	δέκα	δέκατος	δεκάκις
11	ἕνδεκα	ἑνδέκατος	ἑνδεκάκις
12	δώδεκα	δωδέκατος	δωδεκάκις
13	τρεῖς καὶ δέκα	τρίτος καὶ δέκατος	τρεισκαιδεκάκις
14	τέσσαρες καὶ δέκα	τέταρτος καὶ δέκατος	τεσσαρεσκαιδεκάκις
15	πεντεκαίδεκα	πέμπτος καὶ δέκατος	πεντεκαιδεκάκις
16	ἑκκαίδεκα	ἕκτος καὶ δέκατος	ἑκκαιδεκάκις
17	ἑπτακαίδεκα	ἕβδομος καὶ δέκατος	ἑπτακαιδεκάκις
18	ὀκτωκαίδεκα	ὄγδοος καὶ δέκατος	ὀκτωκαιδεκάκις
19	ἐννεακαίδεκα	ἔνατος καὶ δέκατος	ἐννεακαιδεκάκις
20	εἴκοσι(ν)	εἰκοστός	εἰκοσάκις
23	εἴκοσι τρεῖς	εἰκοστὸς τρίτος	εἰκοσάκις τρίς
30	τριᾱ́κοντα	τριᾱκοστός	τριᾱκοντάκις
40	τεσσαράκοντα	τεσσαρακοστός	τεσσαρακοντάκις
50	πεντήκοντα	πεντηκοστός	πεντηκοντάκις
60	ἑξήκοντα	ἑξηκοστός	ἑξηκοντάκις
70	ἑβδομήκοντα	ἑβδομηκοστός	ἑβδομηκοντάκις
80	ὀγδοήκοντα	ὀγδοηκοστός	ὀγδοηκοντάκις
90	ἐνενήκοντα	ἐνενηκοστός	ἐνενηκοντάκις

	Cardinals	Ordinals	Adverbs
	one, two etc.	*first, second* etc.	*once, twice* etc.
100	ἑκατόν	ἑκατοστός	ἑκατοντάκις
200	διᾱκόσι-οι, -αι, -α	διᾱκοσιοστός	διᾱκοσιάκις
300	τριᾱκόσι-οι, -αι, -α	τριᾱκοσιοστός	τριᾱκοσιάκις
400	τετρακόσι-οι, -αι, -α	τετρακοσιοστός	τετρακοσιάκις
500	πεντακόσι-οι, -αι, -α	πεντακοσιοστός	πεντακοσιάκις
600	ἑξακόσι-οι, -αι, -α	ἑξακοσιοστός	ἑξακοσιάκις
700	ἑπτακόσι-οι, -αι, -α	ἑπτακοσιοστός	ἑπτακοσιάκις
800	ὀκτακόσι-οι, -αι, -α	ὀκτακοσιοστός	ὀκτακοσιάκις
900	ἐνακόσι-οι, -αι, -α	ἐνακοσιοστός	ἐνακοσιάκις
1,000	χῑ́λι-οι, -αι, -α	χῑλιοστός	χῑλιάκις
2,000	δισχῑ́λι-οι, -αι, -α	δισχῑλιοστός	δισχῑλιάκις
10,000	μῡ́ρι-οι, -αι, -α	μῡριοστός	μῡριάκις

Note

1 The numbers one to four decline as follows:

	εἷς *one*			δύο *two*
	m.	f.	n.	m., f. & n.
nom.	εἷς	μία	ἕν	δύο
acc.	ἕνα	μίαν	ἕν	δύο
gen.	ἑνός	μιᾶς	ἑνός	δυοῖν (a dual form)
dat.	ἑνί	μιᾷ	ἑνί	δυοῖν (a dual form)

The negatives of εἷς are οὐδείς and μηδείς (no one) and they decline in the same way, i.e. οὐδ-είς, οὐδε-μία, οὐδ-έν.

	τρεῖς *three*		τέσσαρες *four*	
	m. & f.	n.	m. & f.	n.
nom.	τρεῖς	τρία	τέσσαρες	τέσσαρα
acc.	τρεῖς	τρία	τέσσαρας	τέσσαρα
gen.	τριῶν		τεσσάρων	
dat.	τρισί(ν)		τέσσαρσι(ν)	

2 Cardinal numbers from 5 to 199 are indeclinable, except that in compound numbers (see below) εἷς, δύο, τρεῖς and τέσσαρες are declined if they occur as distinct words; hundreds and thousands decline like the plural of φίλιος. Ordinals decline in full like σοφός, except δεύτερος which declines like φίλιος.

3 In compound numbers, the smaller and the larger number can come either way around if they are linked with καί. Thus 24 can be εἴκοσι καὶ τέσσαρες or τέσσαρες καὶ εἴκοσι (as in 'four-and-twenty'). If καί is not used, the larger number comes first: εἴκοσι τέσσαρες (as in 'twenty-four').

 μῡρίοι means 'countless' or 'infinite' when accented in this way (cf. μῡ́ριοι = 10,000). It is found with this meaning in the singular (μῡρίος -ᾱ -ον).

Table of irregular verbs

Note

- compound verbs are generally given without their prefix. The most common prefix is given in brackets. Note that, in general, prose prefers the compounded forms, whereas verse uses both compound forms and forms without a prefix.
- a form beginning with a hyphen indicates that the verb is not found (or is rarely found) without a prefix in this tense or voice but that compounds of it are.
- italics indicate forms which are rarely or never found in Attic prose.
- where the word in the first column is deponent (i.e. middle in form but active in meaning) the forms given for the perfect middle/passive and aorist passive are also generally active in meaning.

Top 101 irregular verbs

See notes on previous page.

Present	Meaning	Future	Aorist
ἀγγέλλω	*I announce*	ἀγγελῶ (έω)	ἤγγειλα
ἄγω	*I lead*	ἄξω	ἤγαγον
αἰνέω (ἐπ-)	*I praise*	-αινέσω	-ῄνεσα
αἱρέω	*I take* (act.) *I choose* (mid.)	αἱρήσω	εἷλον
αἴρω	*I lift, remove*	ἀρῶ (έω)	ἦρα
αἰσθάνομαι	*I perceive*	αἰσθήσομαι	ᾐσθόμην
αἰσχῡ́νω	*I disgrace* (act.) *I am ashamed* (pass.)	αἰσχυνῶ (έω)	ᾔσχῡνα
ἀκούω	*I hear*	ἀκούσομαι	ἤκουσα
ἁλίσκομαι	*I am captured*	ἁλώσομαι	ἑάλων
ἁμαρτάνω	*I make a mistake, miss*	ἁμαρτήσομαι	ἥμαρτον
ἀνᾱλίσκω	*I spend*	ἀνᾱλώσω	ἀνήλωσα
ἄρχω	*I begin, rule*	ἄρξω	ἦρξα
ἀφικνέομαι	*I arrive*	ἀφίξομαι	ἀφῑκόμην
βαίνω	*I walk, go*	-βήσομαι	-έβην
βάλλω	*I throw*	βαλῶ (έω)	ἔβαλον
βιόω **[ζάω]**	*I live*	βιώσομαι ζήσω, ζήσομαι	ἐβίων (ἔζων, ἔζην impf.)
βούλομαι	*I want, wish*	βουλήσομαι	—

Perfect	Perfect Middle/Passive	Aorist Passive	Future Passive
ἤγγελκα	ἤγγελμαι	ἠγγέλθην	ἀγγελθήσομαι
-ἦχα	ἦγμαι	ἤχθην	ἀχθήσομαι
-ῄνεκα	-ῄνημαι	-ῃνέθην	-αινεθήσομαι
ᾕρηκα	ᾕρημαι	ᾑρέθην	αἱρεθήσομαι
ἦρκα	ἦρμαι	ἤρθην	ἀρθήσομαι
—	ᾔσθημαι (tr.)	—	—
—	—	ᾐσχύνθην	αἰσχυνοῦμαι (έο) αἰσχυνθήσομαι
ἀκήκοα	—	ἠκούσθην	ἀκουσθήσομαι
ἑάλωκα	—	—	—
ἡμάρτηκα	ἡμάρτημαι	ἡμαρτήθην	—
ἀνήλωκα	ἀνήλωμαι	ἀνηλώθην	ἀνᾱλωθήσομαι
ἦρχα	ἦργμαι	ἤρχθην	*ἀρχθήσομαι*
—	ἀφῖγμαι	—	—
βέβηκα	—	—	—
βέβληκα	βέβλημαι	ἐβλήθην	βληθήσομαι
βεβίωκα	—	—	—
—	βεβούλημαι	ἐβουλήθην	*βουληθήσομαι*

Present	Meaning	Future	Aorist
γαμέω	*I take as my wife* (act.) *I take as my husband* (mid.)	γαμῶ (έω)	ἔγημα
γελάω	*I laugh*	γελάσομαι	ἐγέλασα
γίγνομαι	*I become*	γενήσομαι	ἐγενόμην
γιγνώσκω	*I recognise*	γνώσομαι	ἔγνων
δάκνω	*I bite*	δήξομαι	ἔδακον
δεῖ	*it is necessary*	δεήσει	ἐδέησε
δείκνῡμι	*I show*	δείξω	ἔδειξα
διδάσκω	*I teach*	διδάξω	ἐδίδαξα
δίδωμι	*I give*	δώσω	ἔδωκα
δοκέω	*I seem*	δόξω	ἔδοξα
δύναμαι	*I can, am able*	δυνήσομαι	—
ἐάω	*I allow*	ἐᾱ́σω	εἴᾱσα (εἴων (αο) impf.)
ἐγείρω	*I arouse*	ἐγερῶ (έω)	ἤγειρα
ἐθέλω	*I wish*	ἐθελήσω	ἠθέλησα
εἰμί	*I am*	ἔσομαι	ἦν (impf.)
ἐλαύνω	*I drive*	ἐλῶ (άω)	ἤλασα
ἕλκω	*I drag*	-ἕλξω	εἵλκυσα
ἕπομαι	*I follow*	ἕψομαι	ἑσπόμην (εἱπόμην impf.)

Perfect	Perfect Middle/Passive	Aorist Passive	Future Passive
γεγάμηκα	γεγάμημαι	—	—
—	—	ἐγελάσθην	—
γέγονα	γεγένημαι	—	—
ἔγνωκα	ἔγνωσμαι	ἐγνώσθην	γνωσθήσομαι
—	δέδηγμαι	ἐδήχθην	δηχθήσομαι
—	—	—	—
δέδειχα	δέδειγμαι	ἐδείχθην	δειχθήσομαι
δεδίδαχα	δεδίδαγμαι	ἐδιδάχθην	διδάξομαι
δέδωκα	δέδομαι	ἐδόθην	δοθήσομαι
—	δέδογμαι	—	—
—	δεδύνημαι	ἐδυνήθην	—
εἴᾱκα	εἴᾱμαι	εἰᾱ́θην	ἐᾱ́σομαι
ἐγρήγορα (intr.)	—	ἠγέρθην	ἐγερθήσομαι
ἠθέληκα	—	—	—
—	—	—	—
-ελήλακα	ἐλήλαμαι	ἠλάθην	—
-είλκυκα	-είλκυσμαι	-ειλκύσθην	-ελκυσθήσομαι
—	—	—	—

Present	Meaning	Future	Aorist
ἔρχομαι	*I go*	εἶμι ἥξω, *ἐλεύσομαι*	ἦλθον
ἐρωτάω	*I ask*	ἐρωτήσω ἐρήσομαι	ἠρόμην ἠρώτησα
ἐσθίω	*I eat*	ἔδομαι	ἔφαγον
εὑρίσκω	*I find*	εὑρήσω	ηὗρον εὗρον
ἔχω	*I have*	ἕξω σχήσω	ἔσχον (εἶχον impf.)
ἥδομαι	*I am pleased, enjoy*	—	—
θάπτω	*I bury*	θάψω	ἔθαψα
θνῄσκω (ἀπο-)	*I die*	θανοῦμαι (έο)	ἔθανον
ἵημι	*I send, shoot*	ἥσω	ἧκα
ἵστημι	*I make stand* (tr.) *I stand* (intr.)	στήσω	ἔστησα (tr.) ἔστην (intr.)
καίω	*I burn*	καύσω	ἔκαυσα
καλέω	*I call*	καλῶ (έω)	ἐκάλεσα
κλαίω **κλᾱ́ω** (in prose)	*I weep*	κλαύσομαι κλᾱήσω	ἔκλαυσα
κλέπτω	*I steal*	κλέψω	ἔκλεψα
κρῑ́νω	*I judge*	κρινῶ (έω)	ἔκρῑνα
κτάομαι	*I obtain, gain*	κτήσομαι	ἐκτησάμην
κτείνω (ἀπο-)	*I kill*	κτενῶ (έω)	ἔκτεινα *ἔκτανον*

Perfect	Perfect Middle/Passive	Aorist Passive	Future Passive
ἐλήλυθα ἧκω	—	—	—
ἠρώτηκα	ἠρώτημαι	ἠρωτήθην	—
ἐδήδοκα	-εδήδεσμαι	ἠδέσθην	
ηὕρηκα εὕρηκα	ηὕρημαι εὕρημαι	ηὑρέθην εὑρέθην	εὑρεθήσομαι
ἔσχηκα	-έσχημαι	—	—
—	—	ἥσθην	ἡσθήσομαι
—	τέθαμμαι	ἐτάφην	ταφήσομαι
τέθνηκα	—	—	—
εἶκα	εἶμαι	εἶθην	ἑθήσομαι
ἕστηκα (intr.)	*ἕσταμαι*	ἐστάθην	σταθήσομαι
-κέκαυκα	κέκαυμαι	ἐκαύθην	-καυθήσομαι
κέκληκα	κέκλημαι	ἐκλήθην	κληθήσομαι
—	κέκλαυμαι κέκλαυσμαι	*ἐκλαύσθην*	*κλαυσθήσομαι*
κέκλοφα	κέκλεμμαι	ἐκλάπην	—
κέκρικα	κέκριμαι	ἐκρίθην	κριθήσομαι
—	κέκτημαι	ἐκτήθην	—
-έκτονα	—	—	—

Present	Meaning	Future	Aorist
λαμβάνω	*I take*	λήψομαι	ἔλαβον
λανθάνω	*I escape the notice of*	λήσω	ἔλαθον
λέγω	*I say*	ἐρῶ (έω) λέξω	εἶπον *ἔλεξα*
λείπω	*I leave*	λείψω	ἔλιπον
μανθάνω	*I learn*	μαθήσομαι	ἔμαθον
μάχομαι	*I fight*	μαχοῦμαι (έο)	ἐμαχεσάμην
μέλει	*it concerns*	μελήσει	ἐμέλησε
μέλλω	*I intend, am about (to)*	μελλήσω	ἐμέλλησα
μένω	*I stay, remain*	μενῶ (έω)	ἔμεινα
μιμνήσκω (ἀνα-)	*I remind* (act.) *I remember* (mid.)	-μνήσω	-έμνησα
νομίζω	*I think, consider*	νομιῶ (έω)	ἐνόμισα
οἴγνῡμι (ἀν-)	*I open*	-οίξω	-έῳξα
οἶδα	*I know*	εἴσομαι	ᾔδη (impf.)
ὄλλῡμι (ἀπ-)	*I destroy* (act.) *I perish* (mid.)	-ολῶ (έω)	-ώλεσα -ωλόμην (intr. mid.)
ὄμνῡμι	*I swear*	ὀμοῦμαι (έο)	ὤμοσα
ὁράω	*I see*	ὄψομαι	εἶδον (ἑώρων (αο) impf.)
ὀφείλω	*I owe*	ὀφειλήσω	ὠφείλησα ὤφελον

Perfect	Perfect Middle/Passive	Aorist Passive	Future Passive
εἴληφα	εἴλημμαι	ἐλήφθην	ληφθήσομαι
λέληθα	-λέλησμαι	—	—
εἴρηκα	εἴρημαι λέλεγμαι	ἐρρήθην ἐλέχθην	εἰρήσομαι ῥηθήσομαι λεχθήσομαι
λέλοιπα	λέλειμμαι	ἐλείφθην	λειφθήσομαι
μεμάθηκα	—	—	—
—	μεμάχημαι	—	—
μεμέληκε	—	—	—
—	—	—	—
μεμένηκα	—	—	—
—	μέμνημαι	ἐμνήσθην	μνησθήσομαι
νενόμικα	νενόμισμαι	ἐνομίσθην	νομισθήσομαι
-έῳχα	-έῳγμαι	-εῴχθην	—
—	—	—	—
-ολώλεκα (tr.) -όλωλα (intr.)	—	—	—
ὀμώμοκα	—	ὠμόθην ὠμόσθην	ὀμοσθήσομαι
ἑόρᾱκα, ἑώρᾱκα *ὄπωπα*	ἑώρᾱμαι ὦμμαι	ὤφθην	ὀφθήσομαι
ὠφείληκα	—	—	—

Present	Meaning	Future	Aorist
πάσχω	*I suffer*	πείσομαι	ἔπαθον
πείθω	*I persuade* (act.) *I obey* (mid.)	πείσω πείσομαι (mid.)	ἔπεισα (act.) *ἐπιθόμην* (mid.)
πέμπω	*I send*	πέμψω	ἔπεμψα
πίμπλημι (ἐμ-/ἐν-)	*I fill*	-πλήσω	-έπλησα
πί̄νω	*I drink*	πί̄ομαι	ἔπιον
πί̄πτω	*I fall*	πεσοῦμαι (έο)	ἔπεσον
πλέω	*I sail*	πλεύσομαι πλευσοῦμαι (έο)	ἔπλευσα
πρᾱ́σσω	*I act, do*	πρᾱ́ξω	ἔπρᾱξα
πυνθάνομαι	*I enquire, find out*	πεύσομαι	ἐπυθόμην
πωλέω **ἀποδίδομαι**	*I sell*	πωλήσω ἀποδώσομαι	*ἐπώλησα* ἀπεδόμην
ῥήγνῡμι	*I break*	-ρήξω	ἔρρηξα
στέλλω (ἀπο-, ἐπι-)	*I send*	-στελῶ (έω)	ἔστειλα
σῴζω	*I save*	σώσω	ἔσῳσα
τέμνω	*I cut*	τεμῶ (έω)	ἔτεμον
τίθημι	*I place, put*	θήσω	ἔθηκα
τίκτω	*I give birth to, beget*	τέξομαι	ἔτεκον
τιτρώσκω	*I wound*	τρώσω	ἔτρωσα

Perfect	Perfect Middle/Passive	Aorist Passive	Future Passive
πέπονθα	—	—	—
πέπεικα (tr.) πέποιθα (intr. (= *trust*))	πέπεισμαι	ἐπείσθην	πεισθήσομαι
πέπομφα	πέπεμμαι	ἐπέμφθην	πεμφθήσομαι
-πέπληκα	-πέπλησμαι	-επλήσθην	-πλησθήσομαι
πέπωκα	-πέπομαι	-επόθην	-ποθήσομαι
πέπτωκα	—	—	—
πέπλευκα	—	—	—
πέπρᾱχα (tr.) πέπρᾱγα (tr. & intr. (= *have fared*))	πέπρᾱγμαι	ἐπρᾱ́χθην	πρᾱχθήσομαι
—	πέπυσμαι	—	—
πέπρᾱκα	πέπρᾱμαι	ἐπρᾱ́θην	πεπρᾱ́σομαι
-έρρωγα (intr.)	*-έρρηγμαι*	ἐρράγην	-ραγήσομαι
-έσταλκα	ἔσταλμαι	ἐστάλην	-σταλήσομαι
σέσωκα	σέσωσμαι	ἐσώθην	σωθήσομαι
-τέτμηκα	τέτμημαι	ἐτμήθην	*τμηθήσομαι*
τέθηκα	κεῖμαι	ἐτέθην	τεθήσομαι
τέτοκα	—	—	—
—	τέτρωμαι	ἐτρώθην	τρωθήσομαι

Present	Meaning	Future	Aorist
τρέπω	*I turn* (tr.)	τρέψω	ἔτρεψα ἐτραπόμην (*I fled*)
τρέφω	*I nourish, support*	θρέψω	ἔθρεψα
τρέχω	*I run*	δραμοῦμαι (έο) -θεύσομαι	ἔδραμον
τυγχάνω	*I happen*	τεύξομαι	ἔτυχον
ὑπισχνέομαι	*I promise*	ὑποσχήσομαι	ὑπεσχόμην
φαίνω	*I reveal* (act.) *I appear, seem* (mid.)	φανῶ (έω)	ἔφηνα
φέρω	*I carry, bear*	οἴσω	ἤνεγκα ἤνεγκον
φεύγω	*I flee*	φεύξομαι	ἔφυγον
φημί	*I say*	φήσω	ἔφησα (ἔφην impf.)
φθάνω	*I anticipate*	φθήσομαι	ἔφθασα ἔφθην (like ἔστην)
φθείρω (δια-)	*I destroy, corrupt*	φθερῶ (έω)	ἔφθειρα
φοβέομαι	*I fear*	φοβήσομαι	—
φῦω	*I produce* (tr.) *I am by nature* (intr.)	φῦσω (tr.)	ἔφῡσα (tr.) ἔφῡν (intr.)
χρή	*it is necessary*	—	(ἐ)χρῆν (impf.)
ὠνέομαι	*I buy*	ὠνήσομαι	ἐπριάμην

Perfect	Perfect Middle/Passive	Aorist Passive	Future Passive
τέτροφα	τέτραμμαι	ἐτρέφθην ἐτράπην (intr.)	*τραπήσομαι*
τέτροφα	τέθραμμαι	ἐτράφην	τραφήσομαι
-δεδράμηκα	—	—	—
τετύχηκα	—	—	—
—	ὑπέσχημαι	—	—
πέφαγκα (tr.) πέφηνα (intr.)	πέφασμαι	ἐφάνθην ἐφάνην (intr.)	φανήσομαι
ἐνήνοχα	ἐνήνεγμαι	ἠνέχθην	-ενεχθήσομαι οἰσθήσομαι
πέφευγα	—	—	—
—	—	—	—
ἔφθακα	—	—	—
ἔφθαρκα -έφθορα (tr. & intr. (= *am ruined*))	ἔφθαρμαι	ἐφθάρην	-φθαρήσομαι
—	πεφόβημαι	ἐφοβήθην	—
— πέφῡκα (intr.)	—	—	—
—	—	—	—
—	ἐώνημαι (= *have bought* or *have been bought*)	ἐωνήθην	—

Map of Greece

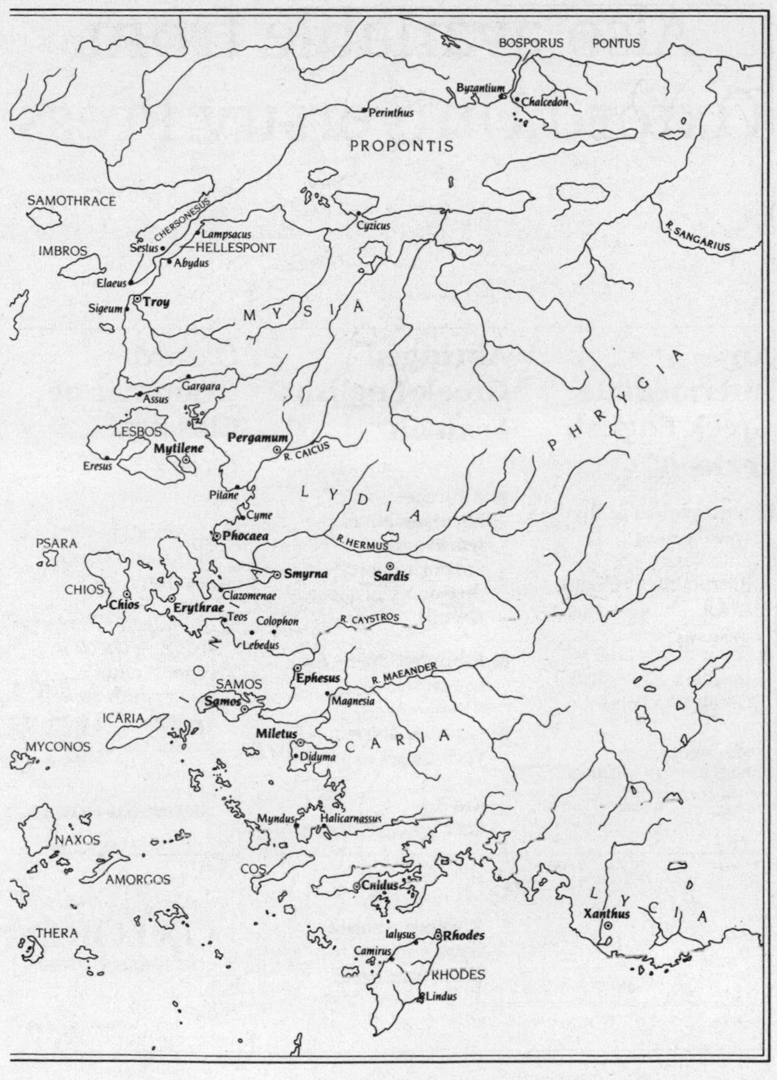
BOSPORUS
PONTUS
Byzantium
Chalcedon
Perinthus
PROPONTIS
SAMOTHRACE
CHERSONESUS
Lampsacus
Sestus
HELLESPONT
IMBROS
Abydus
Cyzicus
R. SANGARIUS
Elaeus
Troy
Sigeum
M Y S I A
P H R Y G I A
Gargara
Assus
LESBOS
Pergamum
Mytilene
R. CAICUS
Eresus
Pitane
L Y D I A
Cyme
Phocaea
R. HERMUS
PSARA
Smyrna
Sardis
CHIOS
Chios
Erythrae
Clazomenae
Teos
Colophon
R. CAYSTROS
Lebedus
Ephesus
R. MAEANDER
SAMOS
Samos
Magnesia
ICARIA
Miletus
C A R I A
MYCONOS
Didyma
Myndus
Halicarnassus
NAXOS
AMORGOS
COS
Cnidus
L Y C I A
Xanthus
THERA
Ialysus
Rhodes
Camirus
RHODES
Lindus